A Biography of World Civilizations

A Biography of World Civilizations

Volume - I

Migration of People, Ancient Egypt, Sumerian Civilization, India

Jaya S. Nagendra

GYAN

Published, 2021

Published by

Gyan Publishing House
5, Ansari Road
Daryaganj, New Delhi-110002
Phone: 011-47034999, 9811692060
www.gyanbooks.com
E-mail: books@gyanbooks.com

Printed at: Gyan Press, Delhi.

Cataloging in Publication Data—DK
Courtesy: D.K. Agencies (P) Ltd. <docinfo@dkagencies.com>

Nagendra, Jaya S., author.
A biography of world civilizations / Jaya Nagendra.
volumes cm
Includes bibliographical references and index.
Contents: volume I. Migration of people, ancient Egypt, Sumerian Civilization, India — volume II. Greece, China, Persia, Rome — volume III. Europe, The Middle East , Maya and Aztec, United States of America.
ISBN 9788121220101 (set : HB)
ISBN 9788121220347 (vol. I)

1. Civilization. I. Title.

LCC CB69.N34 2020 | DDC 909 23

Contents

Acknowledgement

I would like to express my gratitude to the greatest personalities, historical places, libraries and museums, educational documentaries, and institutions, which increased my enthusiasm to write this book, and to the friends who encouraged me to write.

Thanks to my professors and students who kindled my interest in the world civilizations in the University of Maryland. Special thanks to many authors and journals, who instilled me to see the big picture of the world and opened my mind.

Special thanks to Amit Garg, the publisher at Gyan Books in New Delhi, and to the staff in the production department including the editor for editing the manuscript, printers, and binders for all their hard work and support.

And to my husband Nagendra who patiently read the book and suggested some changes.

Image Credits

Special Thanks to Wikipedia Common: https://commons.wikimedia.org, Google Public Domain's 'fair use' Images, Archaeological Survey of India, and others as mentioned.

Introduction

The book "A Biography of the World Civilizations" is about the history of the world's major civilizations. The book has covered 11 major civilizations: Egypt, Mesopotamia (Sumer), India, China, Greece, Persia, Rome, Middle East, Europe, Aztec and Maya, and America.

By reading world history and civilizations, we understand how we are all connected originally and spread out in different paths taking different names, cultures, traditions, which has reached beyond recognition. It is about the rise and fall of civilizations and teaches us to learn lessons from past mistakes.

History is not only a tale of kings and queens, emperors and rulers, palaces and forts, swords and shields, or presidents and secretaries, it is also a story of farmers and merchants, artisans and artists, philosophers, and scientists. Hopefully, with a better knowledge of history, a clearer understanding of the world will occur.

The book also talks about how religions began, how it made a strong impression on human minds that made them to develop art, architecture, philosophy, and civilized behavior. It also shows the same religion propelling people to fight each other, and sometimes making them to follow superstitions. We find in history the development of technology, science, mathematics, astronomy that laid the foundation for future success.

Basically, this book examines the hard facts; the events that shaped this world that we are living now; beginning of science, mathematics, engineering; the social trends, and economic forces that transformed and are transforming our world. Reading all events of the world in a single book, people can understand the history comprehensively and find the roots of their own culture.

Research shows that the more educated and well informed a person or a nation is, the less violence and civil unrest among its people will prevail. In today's hyperlinked world, solving problems anywhere, solves problems everywhere. It is worth knowing as much as we could about our world because everything is connected. It instills the importance of all these places and subjects in people's mind and helps to reduce hate.

Some thoughts are impossible to understand without a sense of the historical context. As a matter of fact, geography and history are connected directly or indirectly. The deeper we go in any direction, the sooner we find how it was entangled with another, apparently in unrelated subjects. This book gives the opportunity to understand how far we have come from the hunting and gathering stage to more civilized human beings.

The task of writing a history of our world's earliest days is staggering. I am aware that historians making extravagant claims is all too common. All writers on history incline to look down towards less cultivated authors and are happily persuaded that they are better in point of style or bring new facts to light. But I find satisfaction in contributing to the labor of putting on record the story of the greatest civilizations in the world relying on dependable sources and on reliable and credible information. Innumerable historians have written on world history and I may be passed unnoticed amongst them. Nevertheless, I comfort myself with the greatness and splendor of our global history and achievements of our ancestors.

Moreover, my task of writing this book is an immensely laborious one. I had to mentally go back several thousand years and trace the history from its small beginnings up to recent times for each civilization. I eagerly wanted to finish the book as soon as possible so that I can return to 21st century! Every civilization's ramifications are so vast that any adequate treatment is hardly possible. I know most readers will take less pleasure to know the early history of civilizations other than their own, and they wish to hurry on to more modern times to read the current history. My feeling is different. I see that to know antiquity is a rewarding gratification. There is no reason to believe that knowing antiquity is unnecessary and irrelevant. In contrast, it adds dignity to the past.

I urge the readers to give attention to the kind of lives our ancestors lived, who they were, and how they acquired civilization first, and subsequently expanded their power both in politics and war.

As the adage goes, 'The study of history is the best medicine for a sick mind', in history we have a record of immeasurable types of human experience clearly presented for all to see; and in that record you can find examples and warnings; and to take best things as models, bad things to avoid.

I hope my passion for the world's past and present civilizations has not damaged truthful facts because I honestly assure the material for this book is collected from thoroughly researched and unbiased scholars.

Obviously, poverty went hand in hand with contentment all the time in history. In recent years wealth has made us greedy, and selfishness has brought us every form of physical excess. Let us not accumulate more of them.

In this book, I intend to give great attention to the world's economic, political, intellectual, literary, architectural, religious, and cultural developments that they indisputably deserve. In preparing this book, I have worked hard to provide historical events as judiciously as possible. Some glimpses of each chapter are given below.

Overview of the Contents

Migration of People: It starts with the time when humans migrated from Africa and reached different parts of the world. People inhabiting remote places, how they built cities, occupied various territories, made wars sometime for wealth, sometimes for women, and sometimes to spread civilization in barbaric regions.

It has been proved scientifically that our ancestors occupied the earth, continent by continent from the past 50,000 years, and they provide genetic evidence using several scientific methodologies like archaeological, anthropological, molecular clock technique, fossil tests, radiocarbon dating, etc. It also covers the emergence of cultural capacities, human genetic drives, growth of language, and more.

The Ancient Egypt: In this section readers will find that through exploring the ancient Egyptian ruins and tombs, we have been able to learn much about their way of life, Egypt's creation myth of Amun-Ra, Osiris, and Set; A timeline of the entire reign of the Egyptian dynastic periods from the Old Kingdom to Roman Egypt; details of Hieroglyphic writing system; details on some of important gods including Ra, Amun-Ra, Enki, Isis, and Sekhmet; details on the life of some of the most famous kings including Amenemhet I, Tutankhamun, Akhenaten, Ramesses II and III, and Ptolemy I, and Cleopatra VII; details about the pyramids and temples built; myths of the afterlife; how the water levels of the Nile caused prosperity or disaster; the daily lives of Egyptians, and more.

The Sumer - Ancient Mesopotamia: In this section readers will find Sumer's incredible history of writing systems. The script known as cuneiform, wedge-shaped signs impressed by reed stylus into clay tablets, appeared first around 3000 BCE. That was the start of writing. Sumer also known as Mesopotamia is recognized as the "cradle of civilization" mainly because of the rise of the city as we know today and the invention of writing in 4000 BCE.

Readers come to understand their Religion, Theology, Rites, and Myth. By the middle of 3000 BCE, hundreds of deities existed among Sumerians. Among them, four deities were most important: An or Anu, the sky god; Enlil, the air god; Enki, the water-god; and Ninhursag, the mother-goddess. Readers also know the Sumerian mathematics, science, calendar, medicine, and technology.

India: In this section readers will find Neolithic period's agricultural revolution; political and economic growth in ancient India; earlier Mehrgarh, Harappa and Mohenjo-Daro cultures; Mahajanapadas; great empires of Magadha, Mauryas and Guptas; southern kingdoms Cheras, Cholas, and Pandyas; later Mughal period and British rule; Social Reformers who awakened India from its miserable state; and life in India after independence.

Readers also find Ashoka the Great who ruled India around 230 BC. and his contribution to spread of Buddhism and about his inscriptions on various statutes where Social Welfare, Non-violence, Respect to Parents, Freedom of Religious Expression, and all human values he wanted are inscribed, and more.

Ancient Greece: In this section readers will find Greek's early history and from where did Greek culture come. There are many fascinating and exciting things in the world of ancient Greece, and in this book, readers are going to learn everything they will ever need to know about the history and socio-political structure of the world of ancient Greece, their philosophers, science, mathematics, Greek dramas, wars and the spread of Greek civilization.

Readers will start the amazing journey into the world of ancient Greece with a glance at the rise of Greece in the archaic era. They find out how the world changed in massive ways, and ancient Greece transmissions along with the changing times of the Hellenistic era, and more.

The Land of China: In this section readers will find the history of China's immense amount of land, more than 3,705,386 square miles ranging from over 50 degrees latitude in the north to below 20 degrees latitude in the south, from the sedimentary plains and river valleys of the east to the hostile mountains, high plateaus , and desert of Tibet and Xinjiang in the west. Kingdoms and empires have risen and fallen on this gigantic landmass. China is famous for its inventions, wisdom, games, and building projects. China is filled with ancient wisdom narrated by many philosophies starting with Confucius, Daoism/Taoism, Buddhism and Sima Quian, a Grand Historian.

China's contribution to the cultural heritage of humankind is huge and most important. China outshined any other civilizations in the world at some point of time in the past. Many of the world's greatest achievements in science, technology, philosophy, and art came from Chinese civilization. Its major inventions, which changed the world, includes paper making, Printing skills, compass, and the invention of gunpowder, and more.

Persia: In this section readers will find the history of Persia's simple beginnings among the Indo-European nomadic tribes that lived in the steppes of central Eurasia. Initially they coexisted beside several prominent Indo-European tribes. However, a tribal leader, Cyrus began a campaign of conquests around 550 BCE. In just 30 years he laid the foundations of an empire stretching its borders from India in the east, to Greece on the Mediterranean, down to Egypt and Ethiopia, and north to modern Russia. More than 30 different countries and peoples were brought together under the rule of Cyrus, who called himself the "King of the World."

Readers also learn about Prophet Zoroaster, Darius, Xerxes, Arthakhshatra (the Law of Land), flourishing of Science, and more.

Ancient Rome: In this section readers will find Rome's magnificent history, and its rise and fall. No other societies and historical periods capture our fascination as much as ancient Rome. It is a story immersed in legend, the rise and fall of monarchy, republic, and an empire filled with colorful and sometimes strange leaders and popular figures. Rome has been the source of inspiration for a many novels, movies, and television shows. Rome was a society that captures our interest even today, more than 1500 years since the fall of the great Roman Empire. Readers also find the story of the Christianization of the empire and its influence, and more.

Europe: In this section readers will find the history of Europe's dynamic past and present with an amazement. In the beginning, there was no Europe. All there was a long, graceful peninsula positioned like an image of a ship on the world's largest land mass with no name. To the west sat the ocean which no one had crossed. To the south sat two surrounded and knitted seas, scattered with islands, bays, and peninsulas of their own. To the north sat the great polar icecap, expanding and contracting through the eons like some monster. To the east sat the land-bridge to the rest of the world, waiting for all civilizations to come. Mostly it started to change from the coming of Romans. It went through many stages like wars between neighboring countries, introduction of Christianity, Renaissance, Enlightenment, and Romanticism.

Readers understand that as John Hirst said that in Europe it was not Christianity that is acknowledged but humanism from the Renaissance culture generally. Enlightenment is the dominant influence because Europe was committed to 'the universal values of the inviolable and inalienable rights of the human person' and to follow the path of 'progress and prosperity'. It also saw the destructive forces, and finally forming the European Union, and more.

The Middle East: In this section readers will find the history of the Middle East, the most ancient area of human civilization. Before Christianity, the Middle East consisted many countries with different names before it was called Middle East such as Egypt, Persia, Assyria, Canaan, Israel, Jerusalem, Judah, Samaria, Phoenicia And Philistia, Yehuda, south, center, and north of the country are called Judaea, Samaria, Galilee, Turkey, Mesopotamia (Iraq), Afghanistan, and most likely Meluha (Harappa). There are numerous references in Sumerian clay tablets about the trade transactions between Sumer and Harappa.

The readers also come to know about Middle East Before Islam, Prophet Muhammad, Muslim Ideologies, Emancipation of Slave Trade, Religion Law, Culture, and more.

Maya and Aztec: In this section readers will find the history of the Mayan civilization and how it had been hidden from the human eye until 1521 CE. Only about 500 years ago, it came to light to the outer world and was soon destroyed by Spaniards.

Readers also understand about the Background of Mesoamerica, how the first hunter-gatherers arrived in America around 21,000 BCE and the city Tenochtitlan and the Aztec builders' culture was the product of more than 22,000 years of human activity. How Maya built their remarkable jungle cities in the east of Mexico, Mayan calendars, mathematics, architects Mythology and the Destruction of Maya Civilization, and more.

United States of America: In this section readers will find how the history of America began when Captain Christopher Newport anchored his three storm-beaten ships near the estuary of Chesapeake Bay. When he sent a group of people to browse the area, they found noble forests, the ground carpeted with flowers; fair meadows, large tall trees with fresh waters; fine strawberries, four times bigger and better than in England's; oysters very large and delicate in taste; stocks of turkey nests and many eggs; and an Indian town, where the tribal Indian brought them cornbread and tobacco smoked in clay pipes with copper bowls and how they delighted of seeing richly colored birds, the fruits and berries, the fine fish, and the pleasant scenery.

Readers also find the making of America through Colonialism to Americanism, Independence, the Growth of Democracy, Segregation, Scientific Racism, Progressive Age: New Way of Thinking. Black Issues, Miracles of Age, World War II and America, United Nations, The Space Competition, The Immigration Revolution, Moon Landing, Twenty-First Century America, The Information Revolution, Technological revolution, Not-So-Bright Side of America, and more.

Readers also learn how another side of America is plagued by many social problems, such as racism, drugs, guns, divorce, and psychological disorders. Divorce is putting children's life into confusions and drug addiction of modern youth are heart-breaking. An adult growing up in America is a challenge, difficult, and dangerous process.

It is important to know that in spite of its defects, America did make considerable improvements in the national standard of living by elevating the poor to a minimum standard of living, and by opening new doors to a better life to many previously ignored people.

1

Migration of People

"To a wise man, the whole earth is open, because the true country of a virtuous soul is the entire universe."

— Democritus (460 BCE)

It has been proved scientifically that our ancestors occupied the earth, continent by continent, in the past 50,000 years providing genetic evidence using several scientific methodologies like archaeological, anthropological, molecular clock technique, fossil tests, radiocarbon dating, etc.

We started our journey as human species from our birthplace in Africa to the remote places of the earth and achieved great things. We are the culmination of over a billion years of evolutionary work of modification and meddling of our genes. Our genes carry the layers, branches, and joints that disclose the story.

Spencer Wells explains how the Y chromosome gives the definite evidence for the journey taken by early humans. Even though it is important to study the female lineage, the Y-chromosome provides the cleanest extraction of human migration history. He explains many missing links of various hypotheses and provides sufficient scientific evidence to the genetic theory. It is concluded by the collected data that all modern human genetic diversity discovered around the world was present in Africa around 60,000 years ago. The mtDNA (F) and Y-chromosome (M) provides the same dates showing that the earliest non-African genetic lineages and majority of geneticists agree that humans began to depart Africa around this time. There are some human remains found in Levant, which dates back 100,000 years. But, there may be some cases that sporadically humans migrated to Mediterranean coasts because 100,000-150,000 years ago the Levant was basically an extension of north-eastern Africa (The Levant included all countries along the eastern Mediterranean coasts) and was probably part of the original range of early Homo sapiens.

According to science the DNA, amino acids and mitochondria have no effect on a person carrying them – they are inherited baggage and markers of our ancestry. These are the markers of greatest interest to anthropologists, archeologists, and historians. It is amazing how little we know about ourselves.

Most of us can name our grandparents, some people their great-grandparents, and some their great-great-grandparents. Outside of these known facts, it is a dark and mysterious domain known as history.

Transformation of Species

From reading ancient books, we understand different types of creatures. For example, Herodotus, in the fifth-century BCE provided numerous examples of human diversity apart from writing history in his book 'Historia.' He gave first clear descriptions of human diversity, viewed through a unique classical lens. He describes the dark and mysterious Libyans, the barbaric man-eating Androphagi of the Russian north, and descriptions of people who appeared like Turkey and Mongolians. Herodotus narrates curious tales of griffins (a mythical creature with the head and wings of an eagle and the body of a lion, with pointed ears and with the eagle's legs taking the place of the forelegs) protecting precious cattle and stockpile in the mountains of Asia, and exotic descriptions of tribes in northern India who collect gold from the burrows of ants. There are mythical figures such as lion-man, monkey-man, horseman, etc. in ancient books. They are valuable glimpses of the known world at that time.

Emergence of Culture

The emergence of cultural capacities and changing physical form are related to human origins.

Physical forms changed from the state of primates to modern human-beings along with their culture. When our ancestors lived on the trees of rainforests in Africa, their physical form was like an ape with grasping hands and feet, long arms and legs, and broad chest. They gradually adapted to bipedalism. Upright walking made more contribution to the evolutionary process and cultural progress of hominids.

Cultural evolution process evolved from hunter-gatherers to complex human civilization of today by invention, diffusion, and migration:

Invention creates a new art or idea and transforms it into different parts of the world. They are adapted by others more rapidly if the inventions are useful.

In **Diffusion**, an idea or an art spreads from one person to another or one place to another place over a long distance.

Migration involves the movement of people from one place to another taking their culture with them, or adapting to the new environment and culture, sometimes leaving the old.

Culture makes humankind as a crown of creation. Culture plays an important role in the evolution of human nature, human society, and human history. Edward Taylor called culture "is a complex whole which includes knowledge, belief, art, morals, laws, customs, and any other capabilities and habits acquired by man as a member of society." It is a preliminary step for adapting to the environment. Culture is learned by teaching, observing, imitating, and transmitting from generation to generation. It is shared by other members of society for smooth communication. It gives identification to a person in a society.

To maintain a community in a unified relation, culture helped in various forms – like tools, burial customs, marriages, ways of getting food, hunting and farming, religious beliefs, social organization and so on. A cultural system is not static; it always changes according to the environment.

The Secret of Reaching Remote Locations

In this line, first there are some people of central Africa, who speak Bantu languages. They have very dark skin and live primarily in small villages at the end of the forest. Further east, there are still dark-skinned people, but they look somewhat different. They are the tallest on earth and thin Nilotic (Nile River valley) peoples of east Africa. The biggest question is how they reached such remote locations.

Spenser writes that when Geology was undertaking a revolutionary challenge in the early nineteenth century, our entire understanding of history as handed down in the ancient scriptures and bible were in question. Earlier thinkers believed in uniformitarianism that states the forces and materials found in the world today had always behaved the same way from the time immemorial. On the other hand, the catastrophists, directed by major scholars who founded Harvard University's Museum of Natural History, utterly challenged the uniformitarian thought.

Scientist Broca was an expert on Craniometrics, a method to measure smallest differences in skull morphology that would indicate inborn distinct potential in a person. He developed a detailed classification of humanity based on these minute variations. Broca's methods were published greatly in academic textbooks and they stimulated the scientific community. Soon everyone began to measure skulls and as a result numerous data about human history emerged.

Eugenics - Good Birth

Eugenics means 'good birth.' This concept existed for a long time. For example, ancient Jewish laws Talmud advised their men to sell all their assets so that they can afford to marry the daughter of a scholar with the intention that their children would be more intelligent. At the end of the nineteenth century the modern idea of eugenics really caught widely. The reasons are several: Victorian ideas of self-improvement; interest in new scientific fields such as genetics; and the wealth of developing data from physical anthropology.

The Eugenics Education Society was founded in Britain in 1907. Its specific objective was to improve the gene pool of humanity via the selective breeding of 'fit' people. The Eugenic theories that assured self-improvement through the application of scientific knowledge inspired the US and throughout Europe. Quickly 'Fitter Families' competitions were a common element in American parties, with families striving for the status and medals.

Disadvantage of Eugenic

While eugenics began as a movement devoted to social enlightenment, it was used for the forced sterilization of people held to be mentally substandard. The application of eugenic principles provided scientific justification for the systematic extermination of Jews, gypsies, homosexuals and other supposedly inferior groups by the Nazis in the 1940s.

Blood Group Discovery

Genetic variation was vital for the study of human diversity because it is the genetic change that essentially allows evolution. Until the twentieth century, the study of human diversity was limited to variation that could be observed with the naked eye.

Actually, evolution is merely a change in the genetic composition of a species over a period of time. Thus, in order to evaluate how closely related individuals are, it is important to know about their genes. If the genes are the same, then they are the same species. Physical anthropology needs a collection of varying traits known as polymorphisms (Greek for 'many forms') with a simple design of inheritance to study human diversity to categorize it.

In the 1930s an American named Bryant and an Englishman named Mourant began to test blood samples from all around the world. Next thirty years or so these two men and their colleagues examined thousands of people from hundreds of populations, both living and dead, including Egyptian mummies. In 1954 Mourant illustrated the fast expanding blood group data in the comprehensive summary of human biochemical diversity known as the Distribution of the Human Blood Groups. This was the foundation for the modern era of human genetics.

Power of Diversity

Mutation: Scientists have concluded that the most basic force is mutation and without it, polymorphism would not exist. Each of us alive today is carrying around thirty completely fresh mutations that distinguish from our parents.

Selection: The second force is known as natural selection. Selection has definitely made what we are today as sentient and cultured people. It produced the important traits of speech, bipedalism and opposable thumbs. Without natural selection, we would still be primitive ape-like species.

Genetic Drift: The third force is known as genetic drift. Scientific methods have revealed that there are twenty amino acids, which are used to make proteins. Scientists have found that often humans and animals have identical sequences, twenty or even thirty amino acids in a row. What is fascinating is that the more closely related the animals are, the more similar they are. When they measured, humans and gorillas had almost identical hemoglobin sequences, varying only in two places, while humans and horses differed by fifteen amino acids. This implies that molecules could serve as a type of molecular clock, recording the time that has passed since a common ancestor through the number of amino acid changes. Basically, we all have a history book written in our genes. Researchers have used this MOLECULAR CLOCK technique to deduce the date of the separation between humans and apes.

One Woman

Dr. Cann and her colleagues published their study on human mitochondrial diversity in 1987. They wrote their main findings clearly and succinctly: "All these mitochondrial DNA stem from one woman who is assumed to have lived about 200,000 years ago, probably in Africa." The discovery was big news and this woman became Mitochondrial Eve – the mother of us all. We all have an African great-great-grandmother who lived approximately 150,000 years ago. So, in a very short period of time, humans have spread out of Africa to populate the rest of the world.

Multi-Regionalism Vs Fossils

Anthropologists, like Carleton Coon, argued that ancient hominid or human-like species migrated out of Africa in the past couple of million years ago, established themselves in East Asia, and then evolved in their original places into modern-day humans. This hypothesis is known as multi-regionalism, and it continues in some anthropological circles even today.

Linnaeus named our species Homo sapiens (in Latin 'Wise man') because of our uniquely well-developed intellect.

Greatest Grandmother's Partner

According to researchers the female ancestor of everyone alive today lived in Africa around 150,000 years ago. Our greatest grandmother Eve represents the root of the mitochondrial family tree and unites everyone around the world in a shared maternal history. Based on the populations that have retained the clearest genetic signals from our distant grandmother, researchers started to search for the location of Eve's mate or Eve's husband or our greatest grandfather. New methods of statistical and genetic analysis were being developed almost weekly, and the intellectual climate is immaculate. Technology has opened up a field of new ways to solve old puzzles, regularly providing astonishing answers.

Greatest Grandfather is Latecomer

Researchers have found that a large number of Y polymorphisms reveal an African origin for all modern humans. They have taken a worldwide sample of men from dozens of populations on every continent, and studied using the newly discovered repository of Y polymorphisms. Accordingly, a tree diagram was constructed from the design of sequence variation. The tree diagram displayed the oldest splits in the ancestry of Y-chromosome, the root of the male family tree, which occurred in Africa, just like mtDNA for women, which also occurred in Africa.

The man (our greatest grandfather) from whom all men alive today derive their Y-chromosomes lived 59,000 years ago, more than 80,000 years after that woman (our greatest grandmother).

All African populations have greater evolutionary lineages than those found outside the continent. The genetic signal they contain is very good evidence that they are the fragments of one of the oldest human populations.

Researchers studied the language of San language (San is a language spoken in East Africa. San means Bushman) and found that they speak one of the strangest languages in the world, distinguished for its use of clicks as a part of word, like the clicking sound. No other language in the world uses click in regular word construction, and this habit has motivated linguists to study the San language for nearly 200 years since Europeans first colonized southern Africa. The languages are extremely complicated. While English has thirty-one distinguishable sounds, the San !Xu language (the '!' is !Xu sounds like a bottle opening) has 141.

It is hard to imagine how our common male and female ancestors would have looked like. It is improbable that our African ancestors were the hairy, brutish cavemen as pictured in museums. Early humans probably had quite darker skin because of the type of the environment, sunny African grassland. The dark skin provided a distinct advantage of protection from solar radiation.

60,000 years ago, our ancestors were mostly about the same height as we are today. The difference in built reflects adaptations to local environments, which can be seen in our ancestors Homo erectus and Homo ergaster too.

It is concluded by the collected data that all modern human genetic diversity discovered around the world was present in Africa around 60,000 years ago. The mtDNA (F) and Y-chromosome (M) provides the same dates showing that the earliest non-African genetic lineages and majority of geneticists agree that humans began to depart Africa around this time. There are some human remains found in Levant, which dates back 1000,000 years. But, there may be some cases that sporadically humans migrated to Mediterranean coasts because 100,000-150,000 years ago, the Levant was basically an extension of north-eastern Africa (The Levant included all of the countries along the eastern Mediterranean coasts) and was probably part of the original range of early Homo sapiens.

Navigating Far Away Places - How Humans Reached Australia 50,000 Years Ago?

The interesting thing is humans were still in Africa 60,000 years ago according to the data. Australia is 15,000 km away from east of Africa. The question is how did they reach Australia, which is 15,000 km away 50,000 years ago? How they did so early. Now Australia is the driest subcontinent on earth. More than 90 percent of the country receives less than 1,000 mm of rainfall per year. It has the planet's longer unbroken coral reef and the astounding 2,000 kilometer Great Barrier Reef. The most interesting thing about Australia is its wildlife.

The animals found in Australia are very different from anywhere else on the planet. The reason for this distinctiveness is the tremendous isolation of the place. Due to this isolation, Australia has missed the main line of mammalian evolution, with its wealth of placental species. This lack of customary mammals has produced a different path of evolution resulting in peculiar animals like the platypus and the kangaroo. Until recently, Australia had no primates – no monkeys, no apes, not even a bush baby. Humans were the only primate species on the continent.

The absence of evolutionary background in Australia indicates that humans must have colonized from somewhere else. The question is where did they come from? The journey evidently requires a considerable sea voyage. Suppose the landmass was created during the coldest part of the last ice age because of variations in sea level approximately 20,000 years ago. The answer to how and when Australia was colonized by humans is one of the important elements to solve the puzzle of how modern humans settled the entire world. If the proper answer is found, it will establish the pattern for the rest of the journey.

In South Wales, Lake Mungo is about 1,000 km west of Sydney. The water dried up over 10,000 years ago in Lake Mungo, leaving behind incredible sand and clay formations. It was found that several large species of extinct animals lived around the lakes, including the buffalo-sized Zygomaturus and a 200 kg short-faced kangaroo. All of the animals were herbivores becoming easy prey to humans.

More recent dating methods have confirmed that the human artefacts from sedimentary layers below Mungo 3 was the earliest site in the world outside Africa to be inhabited by anatomically modern humans around 60,000 years ago.

To understand how scientists estimate the date by using several scientific methods is very interesting and useful to everyone. Spencer Well describes:

> "The earliest human remains in Australia, like those elsewhere in the world, have been dated using isotopic decay methods. These methods

measure the ratio of different isotopes of an atom present in the sample. It is possible to do this because almost all atoms come in more than one 'flavor', depending on how many subatomic building blocks (particles called neutrons) they have. Through the alchemy of particle physics, the 'heavier' atoms tend to shed some of their particles over time, in the process of transforming them into the 'lighter' atoms. By knowing the rate at which this decay occurs, and measuring the ratio of the heavier to the lighter atom, it is possible to calculate how long the decay has been going on. Like the molecular clock, this atomic clock provides critical time estimations for the study of ancient human remains.

"The most widely applied form of isotopic dating is the so-called radiocarbon method, which measures the ratio of Carbon-14 (C-14) to Carbon-12 (c-12) in the sample. C-14, through a complex interaction with the atmosphere, breaks down to Nitrogen-14 (N-14). The rate of breakdown depends on the so-called half-life of C-14, which is the amount of time required for one-half of the C-14 in a sample to decay – around 5,700 years. Since the carbon is used to build organic molecules, like those found in plant and animal tissues, the method is fantastic for dating human remains. The problem is that beyond about 40,000 years ago, the estimates of C-14: C-12 ratios are not terribly accurate, since most of the C-14 has already decayed. After 5,700 years only half of the C-14 originally incorporated into the tissue when the organism was alive is still there, and after 11,400 years only a quarter is still present. By the time we get to 40,000 years only one sixty-fourth of the original C-14 is still present – less than 2 percent. This makes the sample extremely susceptible to contamination by minute quantities of modern material, which would have the effect of making the dates appear to be more recent than they actually are. For this reason, radiocarbon dating tends to be most useful for remains that are younger than around 30,000 years, and it is the method of choice for archaeological sites of the past 10,000years, where it is extremely accurate.

"Once we get beyond 40,000 years, we have to use isotopes that decay at a slower rate. Two of these are Potassium-40 (K-40) and Uranium-28, which have half-lives of 1.25 billion and 4 billion years respectively. The problem with the more stablc isotopes is that they are not usually found in the stones and bones themselves, and therefore they can be applied only to the sediments surrounding the remains – typically volcanic ash in the case of the former and lake sediments in the case of the latter."

Across Beaches

Africa is the most equatorial continent on earth and the sea level freezing temperatures are rare there. It surrounds the Old World's largest territory of rainforest, and the grasslands of the east and south support a huge variety of large mammals. The combination of rainforest and grassland in close vicinity, which is exclusive in the world, may be part of the reason that humans evolved there.

Africa was not located in the same place as it is today. Due to movement of tectonic plates, it spent most of its time between 200 and 20 million years migrating around the southern Indian Ocean, finally hitting into the Eurasian landmass around 15 million years ago. It was at this time that the great apes began to scatter all around the world. Those apes that moved east evolved into the orangutan and gibbon. The apes that remained in Africa evolved into the chimpanzee and gorilla – and eventually, 100,000 to 200,000 years ago, into anatomically modern humans. During this entire process, Africa remained in the same position geographically. But, in other continents, the climate has fluctuated dramatically.

According to paleoclimatology, the earth at 150,000 years ago was nearing the end of the Riss glaciation. The temperatures were 10 degrees colder than they are today. Around 130,000 years ago it began to warm up and tropical Africa started to get more rain as the sea level rose and moisture returned to the atmosphere. Gradual cooling began around 120,000 years ago, speeding after 70,000 years ago. This trend continued for the next 50,000 years, reaching its base around 20,000 years ago.

Humans might have assembled in these coastal grassland environments consuming food sources from the sea and the land animals living nearby.

There is indisputable evidence that early humans were capable of living away from the sea. Large dunghills, garbage dumps of shells from clams and oysters have been found in eastern Africa dating around 125,000 years ago. Human stone tools found in these dunghills show that they were living in that area and using coastal resources like rhinoceros, elephant, steak and shellfish. It appears that our distant ancestors had fairly well-developed palates even in those days of hardship.

One of the most exciting details is that they were able to exchange with coastal inhabitants thousands of kilometers away utilizing the same types of resources both in southern Africa and eastern Africa. This assumption is estimated by the similarities in tools found at the sites at the same time. It appears that humans were able to migrate over remote distances, quite rapidly, by trailing the coastline of eastern Africa.

Big Jump by Superhighway - Sandy Highway

If humans could migrate over lengthy distances within a continent, were they able to migrate to other continents using the same technologies and exploiting the same resources? The coastal route was like a prehistoric superhighway enabling a high degree of movement without requiring the complex adaptations to new environments that is required on the inland path. The resources used in Eritrea was very much the same as those in coastal Arabia, western India, south-east Asia, and – Australia. Because they moved along the sandy highway circumnavigating the continents, it allowed them the rapid migration and settlement in several continents. There was no need to cross mountain ranges or great deserts, no need to develop new toolkits or protective clothing, and no major change in food availability. The coastal route was better than the inland route. Of course, they had to cross a few open water spots that required a boat to cross. Since they were only a small group of people, probably they used a few logs bound together and crossed the water. But, there is no evidence because wood degenerates very fast. But, it is a possible inference.

It is proven that the early humans migrated to Australia as soon as they left Africa following the coastal route. In that case there should be a group of particular genetic markers along the coast, separated from the populations living in remote parts of inland. Scientists searched for a way to determine what genetic pattern of archaeological remains along the route reveal.

Tree, Root, Trunk, Branches and Markers

S. Wells has designed a mitochondrial Tree and his rational explanation for the genetic pattern development is as follows:

> "Mitochondrial DNA and Y-chromosome display deeper lineage within Africa than outside. What does this really mean? If we imagine the genetic relations among modern mitochondrial diversity as an actual tree – say a large oak – then the root and trunk, and the branches that are closest to the ground, are all found in Africans. These branches sprouted first, as the tree was growing, and they are therefore the oldest. This means that the tree started growing in Africa. As we move further up the trunk, branches start to appear that are found in non-Africans. These formed later. How far up do we have to go before we find the non-Africans? The answer is pretty high. If the tree started growing 150,000 years ago – the age of the root – then the non-African branches are much closer to the top, and do not pre-date 60,000 years. Most of human evolution has been spent in Africa, so it makes sense that there

is greater diversity there. Most of the branches on the tree were found only in Africans.

"The diversity we find around the world is divided into discrete, although related, units, and defined by markers – the descendants of an ancient mutation event. By mapping these markers on the map of the world, we can infer details of past migrations. Following the order in which the mutations occurred and estimating the date and any demographic details such as population crashes or expansion, we can gain an insight into the details of the journey. And the first piece of evidence comes from ONE MAN IN PARTICULAR, who had a rather IMPORTANT random mutation on his Y-chromosome between 31,000 and 79,000 years ago. He has been named, rather prosaically, M168 - the great …… great-grandfather of every non-African man alive today. The journeys taken by his sons and grandsons defined the subsequent course of human history."

The Y chromosome gives the definite evidence for the journeys taken by early humans. It is literally a 'journey of man.' Even though it is important to study the female lineage, the Y-chromosome provides the cleanest extraction of human migration history.

If we observe carefully at the organization of branches on the mitochondrial tree, it can be found all of the non-African mitochondrial branches originated from a particular branch of the tree trunk, suggesting that M168 man was paired with a woman named L3. Fortunately, this Eurasian woman lived around 50-60,000 years ago, suggesting that she

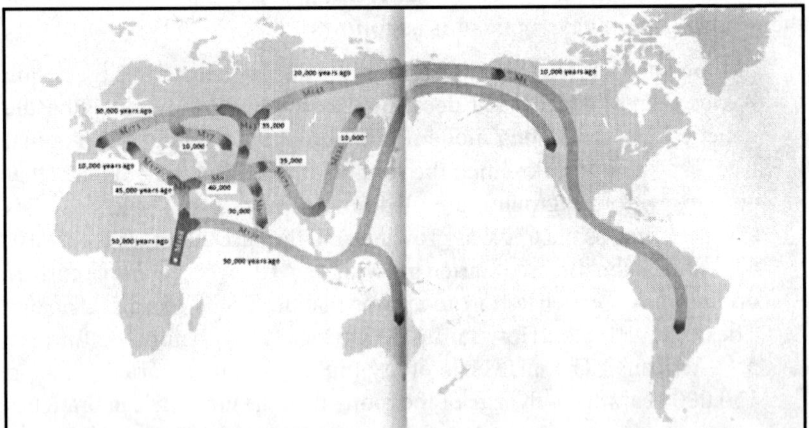

Genetic Markers Map illustrates the distribution of humans around the world

and Eurasian man could have met. Her daughters accompanied the sons of M168 man on their journey to populate the world.

In the tree metaphor, each marker defines a node on the tree, the point where a branch splits into two smaller branches.

The division of the M cluster suggests that the early migration out of Africa, which advanced along the coast of south Asia, eventually reaching south-east Asia and to Australia. Important thing to notice is that the marker M is almost absent from the Middle East, and it is not found at all in Europe. But it contains 20 percent or more of the mitochondrial types in India, and close to 100 percent of those in Australia. Scientists estimate that people who carried the M lineage never reached the interior parts of the Middle East. It appears that the M people left Africa very early and carried their distinctive genetic mark across the south of the continent down the coastal highway. The dark skin of the Australians that found in Africa suggests a direct link between Africa and Australia.

The extinct hominid species can be identified by the size and shape of their bones, tools and other artefacts also can be classified according to their style. The advancement of a worldwide form of human tools, from hammers to knives to frying pans also can be seen.

The earliest Paleolithic tools mark the early migration of modern humans to other geographic regions. That is the reason India is unusual, because there is very little evidence of the Upper Paleolithic there. There is a shortage of human remains up to the Upper Paleolithic. But, there are abundant tools from the earlier periods. The Upper Paleolithic offers no revealing signs until very late, and even then, they come in unanticipated places.

Fa Hien cave in Sri Lanka provides the earliest sign of the Upper Paleolithic in the Indian subcontinent. The earliest modern artefacts found in their dates from 31,000 years ago. Sri Lankan caves suggest that the earliest modern humans arrived in India from the south. This infers that they were living on the coast according to the theory of an early coastal migration. In Thailand also there is evidence for modern human occupation from about 37,000 years ago.

Great part of archaeological work has been made on land; probably there are missing artefacts that are hidden underwater. The sea levels have certainly fluctuated greatly over the past 100,000 years. As the continents characteristically have very thin slopes as they go down into the sea, a difference of 100 meters can make a huge difference in the amount of land exposed. For example, a decrease in sea level of this magnitude would expose as much as 200 km of land off the west coast of India. Consequently, Sri Lanka and India would have been connected by a land link; the Persian Gulf and the Gulf of Thailand would have been fertile river outlets; and Australia and New Guinea would have been two bulging boundaries of a single landmass. All things considered, the entire coastal route around the world would have been much different 50,000 years ago.

Search for the Fundamental Human Genetic Diversity

The order of genetic markers allows us to trace the journey taken by our ancestors over the past 50,000 years and exposes some fascinating relationships among people around the world. Of course, this same method can be applied for every person alive today.

Why did humans wait so long to leave Africa if all of the archaeological evidence suggests that modern humans were present there by 150,000 years ago?

Rational Aerobics

As with many notable outcomes, it depends on the right person being in the right place at the right time. That is what happened to humans also. The anthropological term 'Great Leap Forward' is to describe the drastic changes in technology at the beginning of the Upper Paleolithic period around 50-70,000 years ago. Richard Klein explains the cause for change in human behavior so significantly.

He names three noteworthy archaeological changes that happened around this time.

1. First, the wide range of tools used by humans made by more efficient stones and other materials.
2. Second, the art, which requires conceptual thought, makes its first appearance.
3. And finally, humans began to exploit food resources in a far more efficient way.

In general, these changes point to a major modification in human behavior. His reason is our DNA, which made it all possible.

Professor Richard Klein theorizes, "From this that the onset of the Upper Paleolithic marks the origin of modern language, with its rich syntax and multitude of ways to express oneself. This flowering of language skills is thought by most anthropologists to be a critical prerequisite for further social development. The development of complex social networks is almost certainly the spark that brought about the changes in Upper Paleolithic behavior." Klein believes that this happened because a change in the way in our brains were wired and was set in motion by a genetic event.

Growth of Language

Klein suggests that we can understand some ideas about what these changes may have been by looking at modern children. Child development involves the advancement from object recognition to slowly more complex understanding of the system in which objects are related to each other. The earliest phases focus on arrangement of real-world objects into more complex systems.

Children's first words, such as *mama* and *papa* are the easiest to learn, genetically programmed into human vocal anatomy in some way. They are found worldwide in all languages.

The babbling and single words continue for another year, and then around age two, a huge leap in spoken language happens. So, the outburst of linguistic complexity in a two-year-old is a result of the mastery of syntax.

He questions that if the intellectual gulf between humans and apes is crossed by a syntactic bridge, why it appears in our ancestors but not in chimps and gorillas? He answers with reason that one of the things that stop chimps from developing complex syntax is limited short-term memory. To understand the meaning of a complex sentence, we must remember the beginning when we reach the end in order to integrate them. Limited short-term memory may be the root cause of chimpanzees' minimal language skills. He also writes another reason why apes did not develop language skills is because they lived in forests whereas our ancestors gave up a life in the trees several million years ago.

From Trees to Grasslands

What forced humans to move to the grasslands from the trees in forests? Probably climate because periodical climatic changes brought destructions in African forests with low rainfall reducing their area significantly several times over the past 10 million years. Finding food became difficult that led to hunting and killing the mammals of the grasslands. Human brain developed as they learned the skills to escape from carnivores' attention that were living there.

The human population is increasingly forced through the geographic channel by pushing and pulling over thousands of years up until humans have diffused far from their original homeland.

Mainline

The Y and mtDNA data hint at two routes, one of which would have followed the coastal area to Australia around 50-60,000 years ago. What about the other, which accounts for the majority of people in the world today?

As we saw in Genetic Markers map, M168 defines a marker common to all non-African populations and unites everyone outside of Africa. Then the lineage splits into salt and pepper (M130 and M89) approximately the same age. Archeologists estimate that since the humans were in Australia between 50,000 and 60,000 years ago and the marker M130 has not been found in Africa, the age of these markers was likely at the same time.

To find the origin of these markers, ancient genetic migration around the world needs to be traced. The first stop is at the verge of a receding Mediterranean wave, just before the world dried out and trapped a few people in the Middle East around 45,000 years ago. S. Wells writes,

> "Major geographical features – seas, deserts and mountains – have always served as barriers to the dispersal of living organisms. If the rainfall drops below a certain level, desertification can happen nearly overnight. Similarly, increases in rainfall can reclaim fertile land from the sands just as suddenly. Because of this, deserts should actually be seen as ebbing and flowing ecosystems, extending their range when the climate is dry and losing it when moisture is more plentiful – like waves lapping and the edges of the other ecosystems. Paraphrasing that old saying about British weather, if you don't like the desert, simply wait a few hundred years and it will change.
>
> "The first upper Paleolithic humans may have reached the Middle East during the relatively warm and moist conditions around 50,000 years ago, when the eastern Sahara was in retreat and a gateway opened along the Red Sea. Early human populations may have moved across the strait of Bab al Mandab into southern Arabia. (A passage located between Yemen on the Arabian Peninsula, and Djibouti and Eritrea in the Horn of Africa. It connects the Red Sea to the Gulf of Aden. It is presumed that at this time, the oceans were much lower and the straits were much shallower or dry, allowing a series of emigrations along the southern coast of Asia.) During wetter periods, the Sahara would have sustained human populations. As the conditions turned drier, the Sahara would have returned to uninhabitable desert, forcing human emigration. Calvin suggests that the climatological downturn after 50,000 years may have been impetus for the migration of Upper Palaeolithic humans out of North Africa and into the Middle East."

Markers and Their Descendants and Moving Places

The descendants of M9, a man born perhaps 40,000 years ago on the plains of Iran or southern central Asia, expanded their range to the ends of the earth over the 30,000 years. People carrying M9 are Eurasian clan.

When hunters migrated eastward carrying Eurasian lineages into the interior of the continent, they encountered the most significant geographical mountain ranges of the Hindu Kush running west to east, the Himalayas running north-west to south-east and the Tien Shan running south-west to north-east. The three ranges meet in the centre, the Pamir Knot in present day Tajikistan, and each radiates off like a spoke in a wheel. The first humans to see those mountains must have been utterly wonderstruck.

Because of these mountains, Eurasian migrants would have been split into two groups: one group moved to the north of the Hindu Kush and the other to the south into the Indian subcontinent. The proof he gives for this separation is by tracing the route of the Y-chromosome. Spenser writes:

> "Those who headed north, toward central Asia, had additional mutations on their Eurasian lineage that we will trace below. The Upper Palaeolithic people who headed south had an unrelated mutation on their Y-chromosome known as M20. It is not found at appreciable frequencies outside of India – perhaps 1-2 per cent in some Middle Eastern populations. In the subcontinent, around 50 percent of men in southern India have M20. This suggests that it marks the earliest significant settlement of India, forming a uniquely Indian genetic substratum that pre-dates later migrations from the north. The ancestors of the Indian clan, who moved into southern India around 30,000 years ago, would have encountered the earlier coastal migrants still living there. From the genetic pattern, it seems likely that any admixture with them was not reciprocal: mitochondrial DNA retains strong evidence of the coastal migrants in the form of haplogroup M, while the Y-chromosome primarily shows evidence of later migrants from the north. Thinking back to the scenario we imagined for the birth of the Upper Palaeolithic in Africa, this is the pattern we would expect to see if the invaders took wives from the coastal population, but the coastal men were largely driven away, killed, or simply not given the chance to reproduce. The result would be the widespread introduction of mtDNA lineages into the Indian population, while the Coastal Y-chromosome lineages would not be nearly as common – precisely the pattern we see. Today, the frequency of the Coastal marker is only around 5 per cent in southern India, and it falls in frequency as we move northward. This pattern

suggests that the contribution from the costal populations was minimal, at least on the male side."

Eurasian people also migrated to the north of the Hindu Kush, into the middle of central Asia. Around this time another mutation happened on the Eurasian lineage known as M45. Absolute dating methods infer M45 mutation occurred approximately 35,000 years ago in central Asia. Today M45 is found only in central Asians.

The Eurasian environment was a very brutal learning place for our ancestors. Advanced problem-solving skills were critical to their survival that helped them to leap forward in their intellectual capacity to populate the world. Humans started to develop highly specialized toolkits, including bone needles to sew together animal skins into clothing that kept them warm at cold temperatures.

North-East Drive towards China

Other side of the Hindu Kush, some of these Eurasian group members migrated to the north and east and reached present day China travelling in harsh environments. This is proven by the fact that they left descendants from another Y-chromosome marker M175 that is almost completely limited to East Asia, and is entirely absent from western Asia and Europe.

M175, which arose on a Eurasian M9 chromosome, is found at the highest frequency around 30 percent in Korean populations. According to absolute dating methods, it happened roughly 35,000 years ago matching very closely with the appearance of the Upper Palaeolithic in Korea and Japan.

Independent Local Homo Sapiens Argument

Some Chinese scientists argue for an evolutionary model known as 'reginal continuity' in which east Asian erectus evolved into a local variant of Homo sapiens independently like Africa, there is absolutely no genetic evidence for this. Moreover, the genetic results show that there was not even any interbreeding between modern human immigrants to east Asia and erectus – if in fact any populations still existed 40,000 years ago that are invisible to today's archaeologists.

But in recent analysis of over 12,000 men from throughout East Asia, geneticist Li Jin and his colleagues found that every single one traces his ancestry to Africa within the past 50,000 years – because every man has our old friend M168 on his Y-chromosome. EVERYONE.

Migration to Europe

Now, the route to Asia is clear. But to Europe it required a roundabout tour. Even though Modern Europeans are direct descendants of the Middle Eastern group, they contain too many mutations. The search for the ancestors of the first Europeans is discussed here.

Neanderthals Myth

In the past anthropologists thought that modern Europeans evolved from Neanderthal ancestors or they were replaced by invading humans. But, later findings proved that Neanderthal's DNA sequence was not from modern human mtDNA and it did not belong to an ape either. It came from a hominid that shared a common ancestor with modern humans around 500,000 years ago. So it was proof that Neanderthal was not the direct ancestor of modern humans. They represented a local population of archaic hominids and later replaced by modern Homo sapiens with no visible mix. Therefore they represent a separate species. These results have been confirmed by additional genetic studies of Neanderthal remains from different parts of Europe.

Paintings from 32,000 Years Ago

The paintings discovered at Pech Merle and in several French caves demonstrate a rich artistic practice dating back around thirty thousand years, providing a unique understanding into the minds of Paleolithic Europeans.

The images painted and drawn on the walls of the Upper Paleolithic places show strong earliest evidence of conceptual and abstract thought in Europe. The amazingly detailed artwork at Chauvet cave has been dated to around 32,000 years, the oldest in France. Recently discovered drawings at Fumane cave near northern Italy dated around 35,000 years. In all these locations, the complexity of the subjects, and the skill with which they are made, denotes a sudden transition from the past. In fact, they are detailed time capsules left by early Europeans, beautifully constructed portraits of their lives, hidden away inside sealed caves until they were discovered in the nineteenth and twentieth centuries: after more than 35,000 years!!

Various kinds of tools they left along with their artwork gives a brief hint into the minds of the people who created it. How did they appear so suddenly around 35,000 years ago? The genetic marker data has the solution to solve the puzzle.

It is said that this Y-chromosome marker M173 is found at high frequency throughout Western Europe. Interestingly, the highest frequencies

Chauvet Cave Painting - 32,000 years ago

are found in the far west, in Spain and Ireland, where M173 is present in over 90 percent of men. It is the leading marker in Western Europe. The high frequency reveals two things. First, that the vast majority of western Europeans share a single male ancestor at some point in the past. And second, that something happened to cause the other lineages to be lost.

While modern humans produced tools and art with their brains, Neanderthals appear to have done it with brute force. This physically demanding lifestyle made them short-lived, about 30-50 years. Europeans expansion and Neanderthal disappearance began around 30,000 years ago.

The people who live in harsh environments like the Arctic Circle have wonderful adaptation capability. They have developed a lifestyle that allows them to survive in an environment of unimaginable harshness. The land is covered with snow and frost from September to June, and there is no edible vegetation. The people live there catching reindeer and the fish through holes in the icy rivers. For thousands of years they use the same technology for sewing their clothes from reindeer skin, living in tents constructed from hides and wooden poles, and migrating with their herds as they search for a source of nourishment.

It is difficult to imagine how humans could exist in these conditions. Still they do live and flourish in a climate that would possibly kill us. These extreme conditions are too high to allow any mental freedom. But, natural selection has favored only those intellectually capable of surviving in this icy evolutionary laboratory. There is evidence of human occupation in the Asian Arctic 20,000 years ago.

Americas

Researchers note that nobody knows when Native Americans had split from their Asian cousins and how long they were living in the Americas. An archaeological site at Clovis in New Mexico inferred carbon dating an age of 11,000 years. The samples that are emerging from the archaeological records indicate that humans had occupied the Americas around 12,000-15,000 years ago.

The problem with this scenario is that 12,000 years ago the ice age was at its most intense **level** and traversing the harshest environment was difficult as earth reached its lowest point. They propose the migration might have taken place in two stages between 6,000 and 34,000 years ago. In addition it is confirmed that Native Americans and north-east Asians shared a recent common mitochondrial ancestry.

How do these results fit with Y-chromosome data? This question was answered by Underhill who found a single nucleotide change on the Y-chromosome named M3 that was common throughout the Americas.

But the problem was that M3 was not found in Asia. Scientists from the University of Arizona reported that the ancestor of M3 was defined by a marker called 92R7, named for an undefined nucleotide change on the Y-chromosome. In combination with other nucleotide changes this pinpointed Siberia as the source population for Native Americans, confirming Wallace's results from mitochondrial DNA. This helped to trace a clear migrational route from Africa to the Middle East to the Americas, via the Eurasian steppes. A further marker known as M242 is a descendant of M45. It appears to have arisen in central Asia or southern Siberia around 20,000 years ago, and is distributed across Asia, from southern India to China to Siberia, as well as throughout the Americas. It is found at the highest frequency in Siberia, and thus it could be called a Siberian marker. It defined an evolutionary order of M45->M242->M3 that traces a migration from central Asia to the Americas within the past 20,000 years.

Spencer writes, "Interestingly, the Native American genetic data allows us to estimate how many people would have made it into the continent during these first migrations. By looking at the number of chromosomes needed to account for the present distribution of genetic lineages in the Americas, and working out how much diversity would have accumulated over the time that they have been in the continents, it is possible to account for all the mtDNA and Y-chromosomes types in Native Americans with a founding population of around ten or twenty individuals. Because some lineages would have gone extinct during the past 15,000 years, this is certainly an underestimate of the number of individuals who actually made it across. Perhaps a few dozen, or even a few hundred, actually made the trip."

After experiencing the laborious life in the freezer-like Arctic environment, the plains of North America must have seemed like the Promised Land suddenly landing on the supermarket. There was vast grassland filled with large animals. It resulted in a massive increase in population.

Because Siberians and Upper Paleolithic Europeans came from the same central Asian population, they have developed similar looking features. Moreover, early American skulls resemble more European than those of current Native Americans suggesting that their appearance has changed over time. The Mongoloid or East Asian appearance of modern Native Americans may have originated in the second wave of migration, carrying M130 from East Asia.

Something Happened That Changed Them for Ever

By 10,000 years ago all continents except Antarctica had been colonized by humans. In only 40,000 years our species had journeyed from eastern Africa to America, enduring deserts, surpassing mountains and the frozen wasteland of the far north.

Their imagination and inventiveness had placed them in good position during the journey, and they superbly well adapted to the conditions that were different from their African birthplace. When these Upper Palaeolithic nomadic people were settling into their new homes, something significant happened that changed them for ever. It could be called the Big Bang of human evolution.

When we see the densely populated villages and towns relying on farmed crops and domesticated animals, it is easy to forget that only a few hundred generations ago we were all hunters and gatherers. We think that life was always like as it now. But the deep excavation ditches in thousands of places show there was a sudden transition from hunting and gathering to settled life around 10,000 years ago.

Our ancestors began to practice agriculture by artificially clearing shrubs and bushes, and planting seeds and growing large amounts of cereals and nut-bearing trees. By specializing in plentiful species, they were able to settle in one place. According to one theory the cause for agricultural development was a sudden change in the climate around 10800 BCE to 9500 BCE. The Neolithic marked a turning point for the human species. This development is the main cause for increased population density.

Paleo-demographers who estimate the population size using archaeological and anthropological methods conclude that the entire population of the globe was around 10 million at the time agriculture originated. By the beginning of the Industrial Age, around 1750, world population had climbed to over 500 million. (Now, it is 7.7 billion.)

Disadvantages of Agriculture

Once humans adopted agriculture, they had to face famine episodes occasionally.

Another worry originating from agriculture is the increase in diseases. Hunter and gatherers were surprisingly healthy. The prolonged close contact that encourages the spread of disease occurred only after the domestication of animals in the Neolithic population. Measles is closely related to rinderpest, a disease of cattle. It is likely that domestication of livestock around 10,000 years ago introduced this disease into Neolithic populations.

Language Link

One of the most important characteristics of culture is language. There is a great deal of language variation from place to place. Language similarities had been recognized since classical times, mainly among Latin, French, Spanish and Greek. By the eighteen century scholars had begun to take a broader view, focusing on the languages of Asia, Africa and the Americas.

In 1786 Sir William Jones, then a judge in India, addressed the Royal Asiatic Society noting that Sanskrit held a close resemblance to Greek and Latin 'both in the roots of verbs and in forms of grammar, then could possibly have been produced by accident.' He concluded that 'they must have sprung from a common source.' He said that languages change over time and if there are enough deep similarities among a group of languages, then they must have had a common ancestor in the past and subsequently diverged from each other. It was his most lasting contribution since it indicated a mechanism for the origination of linguistic diversity.

The languages that Jones described were known as the Indo-European language family, based on the geographical locations of the languages.

> "Today the hypotheses that Jones advanced – that all of the Indo-European languages trace their descent from a common ancestor is widely accepted by linguists. In fact it is one of the few language families to have received universal acceptance. The implication of his model, known as the *genetic* model of language classification, is that at some point in the past there was a group of people who spoke an ancestral form of Indo-European, which later evolved into the languages we see today. He and his colleagues examined genetic data from forty two worldwide propulsions and drew a tree of their relationships based on minimizing the difference in marker frequencies between them. The tree that resulted – in effect, a genealogical tree of the populations – corresponded very well with known linguistic relationships. So, for

instance, speakers of Indo-European languages tended to group together in the genetic."

Evidence to Jones Thought

As the name suggests Indo-European languages are spoken not only in Europe, but modern Iran, Afghanistan and the Indian subcontinent all have a majority of Indo-European speakers. How did they come to speak related languages being in thousands of miles away? The first assumption is that early grassland horsemen carried their language from central Asia into India when they invaded around 1500 BCE. It is said that The Rig Veda, an early Indian religious text, records the conquest of India by mounted warriors from the north. This received justification when Mohenjo Daro and Harappa in the Indus Valley were excavated.

Other Causes

Recent research has suggested that there were perhaps other native causes for the collapse of the Harappa civilization. Perhaps a river changed its course, or social decay had set in (like the Romans 2000 years later). Whatever the causes, the invading Aryans were not necessarily the all-powerful conquerors that early archaeologists thought they were. According to this reinterpretation, Renfrew suggested two models for how the Indo-European languages could have come to India.

Renfrew's first model is that an early Neolithic migration from the Middle East carried their Proto-Indo-European (PIE) language with them. In this model, the Harappas already had Indo-European language, and thus there is no reason to conclude an Aryan invasion.

The second model gives more weight to the Rig Veda implying that there was an invasion of the Indus region by Indo-European speaking nomads from central Asia. But it was carried out by a comparatively a few people. It had no impact on the population of the subcontinent, apart from imposition of a language and culture. In both cases, the Indian genetic data shows a minor contribution from the northern steppes.

These hypotheses waited for the development of markers that were capable of distinguishing between populations from the steppe (or Aryans) and the indigenous Indian gene pool.

As discussed earlier, M20 defines the first major wave of migration into India from the Middle East, around 30,000 years ago. M20 is found at highest frequency in the south Indian populations, who speak Dravidian languages, a language family completely unrelated to Indo-European. In some southern populations, M20 reaches a frequency of over 50 percent, while it is found only sporadically outside India. Thus, M20 is an indigenous Indian marker.

Language Riddle

The discovery of a marker known as M17 is present at high frequency (40 per cent plus) from the Czech republic across to Siberia and throughout central Asia. Absolute dating methods indicate that this marker is 10-15,000 years old, and the microsatellite diversity is greatest in southern Russia and Ukraine, suggesting that it developed there. M17 is a descendant of M173, which is uniform with European origin. The origin, distribution and age of M17 strongly suggest that it was spread by the Kurgan people in their extension across the Eurasian delta. The key to solve the language puzzle is to see what it looks like in India and the Middle East.

"The answer is that M17 in India is found at high frequency in those groups speaking Indo-European languages. In the Hindi-speaking population of Delhi, for example, around 35 percent of men have this marker. Indo-European speaking groups from the south also show similarly high frequencies, while the neighboring Dravidian speakers show much lower frequencies – 10 percent or less. This strongly suggests that M17 is an Indo-European marker, and shows that there was a massive genetic influx into India from the steppes within the past 10,000 years. Taken with the archaeological data, we can say that the old hypothesis of an invasion of people – not merely their language – from the steppe appears to be true."

Fascinatingly, M17 is not found at high frequency in the Middle East, but only 5-10 per cent even in Iran who speak Farsi, a major Indo-European language. The reason is because of the inhospitable region of desert. The Iranian deserts were barriers to the movement to Indo-Europeans.

One of the first questions we might have about this group of languages is whether, like Indo-European, there is any archaeological or genetic evidence for it.

It is possible that the evolution of language does follow the same routes as the migration of humans, beginning from Africa and later diffusion to the distant corners of the globe. Still, this claim is based on circumstantial evidence – the universality of language in all human populations, extrapolation from short–term linguistic change recognized in Indo-European, and the importance of language for the development of modern human culture. Virtually all of the original signals of the human language have been lost. The diffusion of languages is a special case of cultural transmission or change.

Around 50,000 years ago, only 2,000 generations ago, all our ancestors lived in Africa.

Author Spenser Wells writes,

> "Today, we are in many ways the same Paleolithic species that left Africa only 2,000 generations ago, with the same drives and foibles. It is ironic that the final big Bang of human history, which has given us the tools to 'read' the greatest history book ever written – the one hidden in our DNA – has also created a cultural context where it is becoming increasingly difficult to carry out this work. The genetic data we have glimpsed shows unequivocally that our species has a single shared history. Each of us carrying a unique chapter, locked away inside our genome, and we owe it to ourselves and to our descendants to discover what it is. Since our ancestors came down from the trees, we have used our intellect to explore outward and extrapolate into the future. Over the past few thousand years we have changed our world – and our place in it – forever. With the development of agriculture, and the cultural chain reaction it ignited, we gained the power to choose our own evolutionary trajectory. With this power, though, came increased responsibility. One responsibility that we neglect at our peril is that of self-discovery. Once the document of our journey has been lost it will, like the footprints of our ancestors as they left Africa to colonize the globe, be gone forever."

It is clear that most European men trace their ancestry back to central Asia within the past 35,000 years. It links to a small population of Siberian hunters.

The First Historian Herodotus' 'Historia'

Historian's description that Herodotus is a father of history is not an overstatement because he wrote the first history book of the known world of his time. The comprehensive study and in-depth view of the people and events of his time has made the book unique in history. And he was a master storyteller too. The story he writes in this book is about the complex political disputes and long standing social disputes between Greek cities and Asian peoples that ended in the Greco-Persian Wars.

Herodotus was born in Halicarnassus, an ancient Greek city, and lived from 484 until 429 BCE The book starts with Croesus, the famous 600 BCE king of Lydia and Ionian Greeks of Asia. It includes mythic stories about abduction of women like Greek women by barbarians and barbarian women by Greeks. The book is mostly about war among Lydian,

Persians, and Greeks. But he is a good story teller too. He includes numerous humorous real stories, which happened really to make the book more interesting.

It is not only about the wars and invasion; it also contains all practices in Herodotus time like customs, culture, food, clothing, geography, names, temples, oracles, worships, sacrifices, funerals, real stories, and all we need to know about how everyday life was in the past. Herodotus categorically explains all types of living about Egyptians, Persians, Libyans, Greeks, Lucedonians, Indians, etc. in this book.

Even though Herodotus was a Greek historian, he honored Egypt in great length about their superb history, art, culture and their contributions to Greece. He expressed great appreciation and understanding of Egyptian history and culture and gave Egypt credit for many ideas and inventions later adopted by the Greeks. He also revealed remarkable respect for their enemy Persians. Open-minded international outlook and unbiased opinions are critical requirements for a Historian.

During his time, fanatical intolerance did not exist. The region and religious tolerance was the standard. Herodotus wrote "their Zeus is called so and so" or "their religious rite is similar to our so and so" to connect foreign practices to Greek understanding.

He wrote about each country and its people, their history, their location, their customs, and their origins and struggles, their achievements as and when the situations needed. By doing so, he provides information about the basis for their unique culture and their way of life reasonably and understandably. All through the book Herodotus exposes a lot of traditional ancient wisdom, given by numerous wise men from different tribes of that region.

We come to know that ancient people in that part of the world scrupulously depended on the oracles. They used to send messengers to Delphi to interpret their dreams or to ask whether it is proper time to start the war, or is there a chance to win the war. And also for several reasons they used to consult oracles. A priest in the Delphi temple on whom the god or goddess appears used to answer their questions and guide them accordingly. Without consulting the oracle, they never took any work. If they win the war or things happen according to the oracle, they used to build huge temples, give gifts to temples and observe elaborate festivals.

Apart from explaining the other aspects, his observation on physical nature is mind boggling. For example, he observed the people's physical structure and their behavior according to the geographical effects.

He observed and wrote that the Egyptians had thick skulls because they shaved their heads and the Persians had thin skulls because they had long hair and wore hats. Some people argue that it is a modern understanding of Vitamin D from the sun, which makes the bone thick. May be at that time Vitamin D and its effects were not known, but Herodotus' observation is remarkable. And also he explains that dreams are not messages from god, but they are concerned about our thoughts during the day. May be his mind was also studying psychological effects, not mere oracles.

Herodotus visited places, collected facts and stories from people around the countries he visited, to write this book. Many times, he did not believe the information he got and found it not so credible. In several places he writes, "I have also heard another account, which I do not at all believe," something like that. That is the honest historian's work. People in the ancient world depended on oracles. Herodotus believed them, but he doubted the dog headed man and the headless man with his face in his chest as silly.

Herodotus writes Darius was the discoverer of a greater part of Asia. Wishing to know where the Indus River met the sea, he sent a number of men to sail down the river. They started from the city of Caspatyrus, in the region called Pactyica, and sailed down the stream in an easterly direction to the sea. After a voyage of thirty months, they reached the Arabian Sea. After this voyage, Darius conquered the Indians, and made use of the sea in those parts for his further invasions.

2

Ancient Egypt

"What I hate is ignorance, smallness of imagination, the eye that sees no farther than its own lashes. All things are possible... Who you are is limited only by who you think you are."

– Egyptian Book of the Dead

Egypt is the Gift of the Nile River

To understand Egypt's history and its geographical essence, we must think about the Nile, the longest river in the world that runs across the Sahara, the largest desert in the world. Greek Historian Herodotus described Egypt as the gift of the Nile. Rainfall is very negligible in the area, so virtually all of Egypt's water comes from the Nile. The Egyptian Nile has three major sources: the longest White Nile, which lie deep within Africa in the lake region Uganda and Tanzania, and flows more than 6,400 kilometers crossing ten modern nations in the middle of changing geography; the other is Blue Nile, which joins the White Nile in Sudan. Their branches are surrounded in the Ethiopian highlands, where the summer monsoon dumps vast amounts of water. Thus, 84% of water reaches Egypt from Ethiopia.

When the climate of northeast Africa began to change in 5000 BCE, the grasslands of the east and west of the Nile River dried out and became desert. Only alternative to local herders was to migrate to a permanent water source near the Nile Valley. They settled in the valley and began to practice agriculture, but unlike seasonal rainfall in the dry regions, the area of Nile made it possible to grow the crops year-round and enabled them to settle permanently in one place. These dwellers developed a Badarian culture, after the place of el-Badari where this lifestyle was first recorded.

According to Herodotus, the founder of Egyptian state was Menes. Nile Valley is a direct water reserve, a narrow belt of green stitched in both sides by a vast and dry boundless and bare desert. The origin of ancient Egypt should be traced as much in its river and its character as in the archaeology of pyramids, rocks, and megaliths.

The river begins its course at the first waterfall caused by the interruption of hard granite stone across the narrow Nile Valley. Each rainy season, the thundering sound made by the floodwaters discharged through the confined channels over exposed rocks made the ancients believe that the flood itself was created in an underground cave beneath the waterfall. People worshipped this force of nature in the form of ram god Khnum. They measured the strength of the flood by a Nilometer, which gave an indication of the flood's strength each year.

The history of Egypt is written based on well documented texts written in hieroglyphic scripts, inscriptions on stone walls, clay tablets, wall paintings, tomb paintings, carvings, papyrus rolls, and also cuneiform texts. Ancient Egyptians were obsessed about recording their day-to-day life even keeping a small transaction of their administration from the beginning, nearly 4500 years ago.

In 1922, an English Egyptologist Howard Carter along with three companions reached a rock-cut passage excavated into the bottom of the Valley of the Kings. Carter had a reputation for his serious and scholarly approach for excavation. His companion George Herbert had weakened after a driving accident and was suffering with rheumatic pain. To escape from the cold, damp air of English winters, he was spending his time in the warmer and drier climate in Egypt. Second companion was Lady Evelyn, daughter of George Herbert, and third one was Carter's friend Arthur Callender, who had knowledge in architecture and engineering, joined the team.

Work to clear the steps started. The external hindering wall was removed to uncover the corridor, which was filled with stone pieces. With exhausting work in the heat and dust, the passage was cleared. There was another hindering wall covered with large oval seal imprints. What would this team of three see there more than three and a half thousand years later? Carter made a small hole in the plaster wall with a shovel just big enough to look through. To test toxic gases and for safety precaution, he took a candle and inserted it through the hole. Then pressing his face against the plaster wall, he gazed through the darkness inside. Moments later, after his eyes adjusted to the darkness, the details of the room began to surface. Carter stood astonished. Herbert asked, "Can you see anything?" Carter said, "Yes, yes, wonderful things. I imagine it is the greatest find ever made."

They discovered an unbroken, undamaged royal tomb from the golden age of ancient Egypt. Later Carter wrote, "Enough stuff to fill the whole upstairs Egyptian section of the British Museum." The first of four chambers alone contained treasures of unimaginable richness: three colossal golden ceremonial beds, in the shapes of marvellous creatures; golden shrines with images of gods and goddesses; painted jewellery boxes and inlaid caskets; gilded chariots and fine archery equipment; a magnificent gold throne, inlaid with silver and precious stones; vases of beautiful glowing pearls and opaque; and two life-size images of the dead king with black skin and gold garments. The royal name in hieroglyphs indicated as Tut-ankh-Amun. Carter and Tut-ankh-Amun had come face-to-face finally. They had made the greatest archaeological discovery in history.

A year later a one and a quarter ton stone was lifted from the king's tomb. Inside the tomb, there were more layers protecting the king's body with three nested coffins. Two outer coffins were made of wood, but the innermost coffin was made of solid gold. Several amulets and ritual objects were placed in each coffin. Each object was carefully removed and documented before the next layer of the coffin was examined. This process took more than eighteen months.

Divine Kingship

The framework of Egypt's dynastic rule is organized into a series of periods as following pattern:

Predynastic Period	5300-2950 BCE	
Early Dynastic Period	2950-2613 BCE	Dynasties 1-3
Old Kingdom	2613-2160 BCE	Dynasties 4-8
First Intermediate Period	2160-2055 BCE	Dynasties 9-11
Middle Kingdom	2055-1640	Dynasties 11-14
Second Intermediate Period	1640-1550 BCE	Dynasties 15-17
New Kingdom	1550-1069 BCE	Dynasties 18-20
Third Intermediate Period	1069-715 BCE	Dynasties 21-25
Late Period	715-332 BCE	Dynasties 25-31
Hellenic Period	**305-30 BCE**	Ptolemaic dynasty

The dynastic rule ended with Hellenistic queen Cleopatra in 30 BCE

The Pyramids of Giza are the important symbol of ancient Egypt. These fully formed magnificent pyramids and the sophisticated culture did not bounce into appearance without a long period of incubation. It is estimated that the origins and development of Egyptian civilization can be traced back to a remote prehistoric date, at least 2000 years before the pyramids. People living in the fertile Nile Valley and the arid grasslands developed the Egyptian culture and their unique outlook shaped by their distinct natural environment. One defining feature of early Egyptian history is its ideology of divine kingship. The belief in this system was conveyed through art, writing, ceremony, and particularly in architecture, which provides both inspiration and justification for massive royal tombs. The acquisitions of lands, forced labour, little regard for human life were the characteristics of the Pyramid Age. Kings ruled by divine right, but the rights of the subjects were neglected. The brutal exploitation of Egypt's natural and human resources was dominant in pharaonic rule.

God Incarnate

Today, the concept of nation-state looks natural and expected. Except Antarctica, the whole surface of our planet is divided into more than two hundred countries now. But it was not like that always. Before 4000 BCE, there were no such states. Instead, the identity and loyalty was based on family, community, or region. Toby Wilkinson writes that the concept of nation-state, a political territory, was created in 2950 BCE, and it was the invention of the ancient Egyptians.

In the Nile Valley, kings ruled the people from prehistoric times. At Abdju, recent excavations have uncovered graves of royal burial grounds dating back around 3800 BCE One of the earliest images of a king was painted on a beaker showing the king holding a mace in one hand and a rope tying three prisoners.

Crown and Sceptre: The artistic expression of royal rule changed rapidly. The memorial inscriptions on the palette gives pride of place to an image of the king in human form and the older palette shows the ruler as a huge lion, crushing his enemies on the battlefield.

A crown is the exemplary symbol of monarchy. Like the concept of nation-state, the crown also appears to be an ancient Egyptian invention. Egyptian kings wore two distinctive crowns indicating Lower Egypt and Upper Egypt.

Similar to other rulers, Egypt's kings also had a fascination with grand buildings to magnify their status. It emphasized one unique style of buildings as the noticeable illustration of kingship. (A portico reflecting a highly effective pattern of light and shade in Egypt's sunny climate had developed in Mesopotamia, in the middle of 4000 BCE.) Egyptians borrowed this exotic and distinctive architectural style as a symbol of royal power. The building had a whitewashed exterior known as White Wall comparable to White House as a modern superpower. The White Wall and its architectural design became the characteristic of the Egyptian monarchy.

Gods and Royal Titles: The most ancient royal title was the Horus title. It clearly identified the king as an incarnation of supreme god Horus who was worshipped in the form of falcon. The message was that if the King is a representative of a divine entity, his leadership could not be questioned. This message was inscribed on all available chances by engraving the king's seal on commodities, carved on royal monuments, showing falcon god Horus' name expressing the king as an earthly incarnation of Horus.

The second royal title was the signs of a vulture and cobra representing two goddesses. Vulture represented Upper Egypt and cobra represented Lower Egypt symbolizing two halves of the country and naming two goddesses as protectors of Egypt.

The third royal title was the double crown. Again, the double crown represented Upper Egypt and Lower Egypt and one king ruled the entire country.

Pomp and Circumstance: The ancient Egyptians were leaders of royal ceremonies.

In another palette, the king seated on an elevated throne wearing red crown and carrying the rod like a sceptre. At the other side of the altar stand fan bearers, sandal bearers and chief minister. Behind the king, men are holding big sticks as security guards. Many palettes and mace discovered offer an enticing insight into the practices of early kingships.

The most frightening examples of Egyptian's propensity are the tombs of the rulers. At one burial ground dating back to 3500 BCE, it was found an array of grave articles like a series of human long bones and skulls. The royal tombs of the first dynasty were accompanied by a chain of graves pertaining to members of the court. Some companions were all in their prime life with an average of twenty-five years or younger. Archaeologists believe that they might have been ancient examples of self-sacrifice, loyal subjects killing themselves in order to escort their masters. But recent inspection of graves gives different explanations as the bodies show the proof of death by strangulation. In early Egypt, kings had the power of life and death over their citizens and they used it to exhibit their authority. To be a simple common citizen meant suppression; to be a member of the king's inner circle meant a life of fear. As a matter of fact, not any one's life was safe and happy.

Absolute Power

The Power of Economy: Mere ideologies are not enough to reach superpower. In order to reach sustainable success for a long time, the government must implement effective economic power with valid entitlements. By the end of early Dynastic Period (3100 - 2680 BCE), the Egyptian government achieved that power by centrally monitoring the economy, financing royal building projects to an extravagant degree. How it was achieved is a story of determination, innovation, and ambition.

In ancient Egyptian ideology "maat" was personification of truth, justice, righteousness, and order. To emphasize the candid message, king Sneferu adopted a new title, netjer nefer means "the perfect god." Scholars question such interpretation.

Hieroglyphic Script

One of the greatest inventions in human history is the skill of writing. Ancient Egyptian civilization, particularly during the Old Kingdom, developed a writing system to meet the need of the royal administration to coordinate and supply large groups of workmen, maintain tax records, identify and distribute products, and record Nile floods. This encouraged the development of a scribal establishment. Maybe one or two percent of the population could read and write, but that small minority literacy provided the instrument for development and access to the power. The attraction of the transcriber profession is praised in the "Satire on the Trades."

See, there is no profession without a boss,
Except for the scribe; he is the boss.
Hence if you know writing,
It will do better for you
Than those professions I have set before you,
Each more wretched than the other.

Probably contact with Mesopotamia may have motivated ancient Egyptian writing initially, though it is unclear in which area writing first began. If someone else gave the idea of writing, then the Egyptians transformed it into something entirely original and thoroughly Egyptian. The best known method of their writing is hieroglyphs, which means "priestly writing," a name given by the ancient Greeks to the ornamental Egyptian script.

Writing life-changing powers such as transmission of knowledge, use of power and the recording of history cannot be exaggerated. Now-a-days it is practically impossible to imagine the world without writing to communicate. Probably for Egyptians it was like a revelation. It was a deliberate act of invention. The original Egyptian writing discovered from a predynastic tomb at Abdju (3100 - 2680 BCE) is inscribed on bone labels, which display the fully formed complex signs known as hieroglyphics. Archaeologists speculate whether the idea of writing originated from Egypt or Mesopotamia. If someone else gave the idea of writing, then the Egyptians transformed it into something entirely original and thoroughly Egyptian. The idea of writing may be influenced by Mesopotamia but not entirely because the hieroglyphics are so perfectly matched to the ancient Egyptian language and the individual signs perfectly reflected the Egyptian environment according to researchers. It could be imagined that an inspired genius at the court of palace contemplating on the strange signs of imported items from Mesopotamia and their encoded information, and devising a corresponding system for the Egyptian language. The best known method of their writing is hieroglyphs, which means "priestly writing," a name given by the ancient Greeks to the ornamental Egyptian script.

Egyptians rulers quickly adopted a writing system recognizing its potential. It was a valuable and marvellous innovation for the development of the economy, for competing and expanding their kingdoms, for ability to record the ownership of goods and to communicate the information to others. Commodities leaving and entering the royal treasury were labelled with the king's symbol; other consignments were labelled recording ownership and further important details such as contents, quantity, quality, and source. As an accounting tool, writing was received by Bureaucratic people with great enthusiasm. Literacy was limited to a tiny elite people in ancient Egypt. Able to read and write was the switch to the power. Egyptians recorded their sophisticated culture, kingly burials and trade with neighbouring lands displaying the features of an emerging civilization.

Hieroglyphic Alphabets.

A French scholar Jean-Francois Champollion's genius for languages enabled him to correctly translate the hieroglyphic and to unlock the secrets of ancient Egyptian history. His grammar and dictionary of the ancient Egyptian language enabled subsequent scholars to read the words of the pharaohs after an intermission of more than 2000 years. Most extraordinary finds from the tomb were hundreds of small bone labels inscribed with hieroglyphic signs.

Language

The language spoken and written in ancient Egypt is a member of the Afro-Asiatic family of languages. They also include Semitic languages such as Hebrew and Arabic, the Berber languages of North Africa and several African languages. Both Arabic and ancient Egyptian languages share a number of similar characteristics.

Art

Art was not exercised for art's sake in ancient Egypt, and also artists did not enjoy the special status. They were just craftsmen like any others. However, personal insignificance did not prevent a high degree of technical mastery, and many surviving pieces from the Old Kingdom show that they were not simply craftsmen but master sculptors. The life-sized statues of Prince Rahotpe and his wife Nofret from an early Fourth Dynasty, now in the Egyptian Museum at Cairo, project a powerful sense of nearness across a gulf of more than 4500 years.

Pyramids

First time in history, the wonderful concept of building a royal monument was credited to Imhotep, attributing ancient Egyptian wisdom and learning. Imhotep's extraordinary vision saw the development of a single-stepped tomb to six-stepped tomb, the tallest building of its time. His innovation indicates the beginning of the Pyramid Age.

Grand Designs

The first pyramids at Giza built 4500 years ago are the only surviving wonder of the ancient world standing grand and enduring. The Great Pyramid of King Khufu built by the Fourth Dynasty is the oldest and biggest. This vast Pyramid was built from 2.3 million blocks of stone, each weighing more than a ton of stone, and covering the area of thirteen acres. According to one calculation, it took approximately 20 years, requiring builders to set one block of stone in place every two minutes during a ten-hour day, working without a break. This 481 feet high pyramid was the tallest building in the world unsurpassed for 4400 years until the Eiffel Tower built in 1889 CE.

In spite of its massive size, it is engineered and aligned with breath-taking precision. No wonder there has been a range of speculation about the construction including otherworldly builders and visitors from other planets. Indeed, it is a product of something extraordinary: not extraterrestrial intelligence but a superhuman ability.

The first stage of building a pyramid is very crucial which involves laying out the plan and preparing the site. The extraordinary precision with which the Great Pyramid is aligned to the positions of the compass shows that a method involving stars must have been used. Scholars state, "Because the solar methods are not accurate enough, they might have used a pair of stars that circle the North Pole; when the two stars are in a direct vertical alignment, which can be checked with a simple plumb line, the line of sight toward them marks true north." The alignment ceremony was celebrated with great earnestness in the presence of the priest and king himself looking at the performance. After the ceremony was over, the site was cleared and levelled, and the time for construction would begin. The immensity of work seems overwhelming, but to the king's government machine, it may have appeared less daunting. They approached any large scale work dividing them into manageable units.

Working Conditions

The construction work was exhausting, merciless, hot, and dangerous. Clogging clouds of limestone dust, the blinding glare of mines surface, continuous noise of chisels, multitudes of flies; the working environment was not pleasing. Carrying the massive stone blocks from quarry to construction site was backbreaking work. About a ton weighing block had to be transported onto a wooden sledge, pulled by ropes to a track, removed from the sledge, moved into the correct position for shaping and finishing. All this labour had done at the pace of one block every two minutes for ten hours a day.

This extraordinary work was completely human achievement within the capacity of the ancient Egyptians. Scholars have calculated by experiment the amount of time and people required to accomplish this monumental job. According to their calculations four thousand men were enough to quarry, transport, and set in place more than two million stone blocks required to build the pyramid. Another four thousand workforces required to construct and maintain the vast slopes and ridges running from the main quarry site to the pyramid site. Another army of workers worked behind the screen as carpenters to make sledges to carry the stone blocks; water carriers to grease the sledges; potters to make the jars; blacksmiths to repair copper chisels; bakers, brewers, and cooks. Approximately ten thousand people were employed at a time.

The working condition of workers was very primitive: they had to sleep on bear earth along with the broken stone blocks. A narrow unit housed two teams of twenty workers. Spacious living quarters were arranged for supervisors in the back. There used to be a huge communal dining arrangement that helped to bond friendship among the workers. The hard labour to build pyramids required protein rich food. Therefore, everyday eleven cattle and thirty sheep and goats were slaughtered and dried fish was served. Also dozens of bakeries were producing ancient Egyptian staple food bread and beer. The most important and pricy dietary was grain, which was rationed, carefully administered and distributed under close supervision. Grain storage silos and granaries were kept in the royal administrative complex, containing two walls for added security.

Workers suffered injuries at work; their skeletons on the sites show the evidence of broken bones, terrible lower back stress, and painful arthritic joints. But the official record is silent about this.

The more fascinating question is 'what was the purpose for building Khufu's monuments.' What inspired such an endeavour of architecture, engineering, and absolute administrative undertaking? Why did ten thousand men work to build an artificial mountain of stone? The Egyptologists denote that it was the ideology of divine kingship - the idea was the king was a mediator between god and people, defender of order, protector of Egypt's stability and prosperity. Even the pyramid building was a form of social security which provided employment for a large section of the population.

The Great Pyramid is not only the embodiment of awesome and durable, but its uniqueness is in its unparalleled accuracy and complexity: its precise location to exact north, their extraordinary narrow channels that lead upward and outward from the burial chamber through the solid masonry, air channels pointed to the stars specifically to the Sirius (the dog star), to the constellation Orion, and two stars that rotate around the north pole. The ancient Egyptians were proficient astronomers and stars were an important part in their religion, particularly in the king's afterlife. Khufu's pyramid was a way of uniting heaven and earth for the well-being of the king forever.

The Pyramid of Giza

The Pyramids of Giza are Egyptian symbol of the fourth dynasty (2575-2450 BCE). Autobiographical inscriptions engraved on tomb walls depict their subjects including courtiers and workmen are for the service to the king. The royal servant's tombs were clustered around the king's tomb reinforcing this culture of servitude.

Fourth Dynasty

The second king's mother Hetepheres's tomb reveals the lifestyle of fourth dynasty royalty. She lived a luxury life and travelled from place to place carried on a gold-plated chair made with ebony (Ebony is hard black wood, hard enough to sink in water). The gold inlaid hieroglyphics proclaims that she is the mother of dual king; devotee of Horus; director of the king; the gracious one. Tomb included a bed with a separate shelter and two low chairs. The furniture was lightweight, easily dismantled and reassembled. Its simplicity and elegance of design, craftsmanship and luxurious materials, summarize the opulence of the Fourth Dynasty. Hetepheres's most precious properties were her jewellery boxes, one of which was designed to hold twenty silver bracelets. At this period silver was more valuable than gold because it had to be imported from distant lands. The bracelets were decorated with turquoise, lapis lazuli, and carnelian.

The two aspects of the Fourth Dynasty were Pyramid building and close association with the sun god, Ra. A sun temple designed above all to emphasize the king's unique relationship with the sun god. Sacrifices were made under the rays of the sun and offered to Ra (sun god). King Userkaf expressed his relationship with solar deity and was remembered as an offspring of Ra.

Fifth and Sixth Dynasties (2450-2175 BCE)

The private tombs of the fifth and sixth dynasties (2450-2175 BCE) are extraordinary works of art. The refinement of their painted reliefs demonstrates the skills of ancient Egyptian workmanship, skills that have been improved over generations. The officials who took the work of building pyramids seriously have space to build huge monuments and ambition to impress kings and people. The fundamental purpose of these tombs was to protect and nurture the eternal spirit of the dead person. So the tombs were presented with offerings ranging from bread, beer, furniture, jewelry, and wine. The depictions provide a wealth of information about the techniques of agriculture, craft invention, and food preparation. Egyptians believed that if the goods buried with the body were ever finished or destroyed, the scenes in the paintings would come alive and furnish the supply with their magical power. The sculptors and painters needed to depict their art according to the wish of the owner of the tomb. On some tombs the paintings of pleasures of idle rich life are recorded. In contrast, brutal punishment given to tax defaulters gives us a glimpse of the life of that time. Tax defaulters would have to walk nakedly to the whipping place and receive lashes by wooden sticks. Life was mean and miserable.

Matter of health is another story in ancient Egypt. The high rank people in society had access to the services of doctors, dentists and other medical specialists. The tombs display the elite people had vigorous good health, men were fit and masculine, and the women were youthful and graceful. By contrast, skeletons and mummified remains of common people illustrate the suffering from various painful diseases. Schistosomiasis, a parasitic disease transmitted by water nails in canals, ditches, and stagnant pools, caused blood in urine, occasionally leading to anaemia. Tuberculosis leading to deformation of the spine, and other symptoms were the result of constant hard physical work.

It is remarkable that the archives of papyrus documents in temples at Abusir attached to Neferirkare and Neferefra pyramids (2475–2455 BCE) have survived and provide us the day-to-day process of royal funerary craze in the Old Kingdom. They also reveal their obsessiveness of book keeping.

The staff of Neferirkare's temple worked on a monthly basis. First day of the month, the members of staff were required to conduct thorough inspection of the temple and its contents. The building was checked for damage, each piece of furniture and equipment was checked, arranged systematically by material, shape, and size. One sheet of papyrus lists items made from stone and flint. Regular inspection and recording was more important.

Unas's Tomb

Unas's most radical innovation was reserved for the chambers underneath the monument. He ordered a more elaborate resting place for his afterlife. His coffin was painted black to signify the earth; the ceiling of the burial chamber was studded with golden stars against a dark blue background to imitate the night sky. Around the tomb, the walls of the burial hall were lined with white alabaster (marble type white stone), grooved and painted to look like the dawn of creation. The entire building was designed as a microcosm of the universe.

The End of Innocence

The impotence of a hereditary monarchy, the dangers of climate change, the risk of uncontrolled immigration, and the aftermath of foreign links all contributed to the breaking point of Egyptian civilization. In such tumultuous period, the Egyptian's illusions about their pharaonic beliefs were shattered and their loss of confidence in the old faiths produced fertile soil for new ideas. Afterlife beliefs and burial customs changed greatly replaced by new ideas. The promise of the afterlife did not offer any consolation or security.

During this chaotic period also, Egypt accomplished a second great cultural pinnacle. During the Old Kingdom, pyramids flourished; in New Kingdom, temples and tombs flourished; and in the Middle Kingdom the golden age of literature flourished and a large number of great classics were composed. The Middle Kingdom's literary achievement shows the most complex and sophisticated ancient Egyptian society. Archaeological evidence is straightforward and impassive, but the existing writings enable us to enter into their imaginations to see the world as they saw it. It was also a time of unchallenged workmanship in jewellery and sculptures.

Civil War

Fights over the succession after the death of Pepi II in 2175 BCE triggered a crisis causing civil war. The desert colonies were abandoned, and the civilization of the pyramid builders had reached its lowest point. Less than a period of twenty years, Egypt saw seventeen kings come and go.

War between territories began and prisoners of war were captured. Nubians were compared to Nepalese Gurkhas as, "Ever since Egypt's campaigns against the sand dwellers in the early Sixth Dynasty, Nubian recruits had played an important role in Egyptian military strategy. Nubian archers were noted for their bravery and powers. The role of the Nepalese Gurkhas in the British Army is an informative parallel.

Obsession of Death and Afterlife

Ancient Egyptian civilization was obsessed with death and afterlife. Pyramids to mummies are symbols of their culture and connected to funerary customs. Their basic ambition was conquering death. Pyramids were designed as resurrection devices for kings. Mummies were designed to offer permanent homes for spirits of the dead and proper planning for the next world was believed as an important job.

Eventually, the decline of monarchy came to the end of pharaonic civilization and changed all sections of society. For the majority of common people, the change in leadership altered nothing in their lives.

Earthly success and being remembered after their death were not enough. The desires for something extraordinary like alteration or transformation or reincarnation became dominant. The ideas about what exists on the other side of death were explained, codified, written in creative and imaginative fashion. Ancient Egyptians conceived the concepts of sin, hell with dangers and demons, and final judgement before the god and the assurance of magnificent resurrection. Ultimately these ideas shaped the thoughts around the western world.

Initially, building pyramids and the luxury of resurrection was limited to kings to reach divine status. As the corrosion of monarchy began, people started to think differently about their death and resurrection. First it began inside the royal family, king Pepi's half-sister Neith got built a small pyramid that was preserved for only kings. This minor break with tradition spread out in Egyptian society. The governor Medunefer was buried surrounded by Pyramid texts in the burial chamber. Sometime later another officer decorated the walls of the burial chamber with compilation of pyramid texts. Very soon, low rank officers were decorating their wooden coffins with Pyramid Texts and new compositions. A simple division existed between the king and the citizens from the start of civilization had been demolished completely. Now every Egyptian could hope to attain divinity after death and spend time with gods.

Pyramid of Giza (2575-2450 B.C.)

Osiris - Underworld Earth God

According to a myth, the divine Osiris, who was married to his sister Isis, was the first king of Egypt. He brought his people out of barbarity and instructed them the arts of civilization. His brother Seth was jealous of him and wanted the kingship. So he killed Osiris and dispersed his body in pieces along the Nile. The mourning Isis reassembled the pieces, thus making the first mummy, and breathed life back into Osiris. In the process she became pregnant with their son Horus. When Horus developed into manhood, he defeated Seth in a bloody fight. Horus became the ruler of the living and the revived Osiris, the king of the dead. When Horus died, he became Osiris and his son the next Horus in a continuing process of life, death, resurrection, and afterlife.

When volumes of Pyramid Texts had explained the king's journey to the stars, they also explained his association with the underworld earth god Osiris. It was a new concept. Osiris was worshipped as the ruler of the underworld and he offered resurrection to the king, and later to people also. Osiris became a protector of the dead and his underworld became the favorable destination. This tendency changed the burial customs. Mummification's goal was to preserve the dead body in recognizable form by wrapping the individual limbs, fingers, and toes separately, and casting the face in linen bandages making a lifelike appearance.

The Ba (Soul) and Ka (Eternal Spirit)

As the workmanship slowly declined, tomb decorations also vanished. Experienced artists were no longer available. The mummified body was laid facing towards the east - sunrise promised the rebirth after the darkness. According to Egyptian trends, two different paths to heaven were imagined. 'The Book of Two Ways' is the Egyptian's earliest afterlife book. The soul (*ba*, second self) of the deceased person transformed as a human headed bird would fly out of the coffin and up from the tomb and enter into heaven. Again each night when the sun descended into the underworld, the mummy would return to the coffin for safety. The ba, the second self, had to be reunited with Osiris in the form of a mummified body each night.

Equivalent to *ba* was *ka* (the eternal spirit) that required the nourishment of food and drink to survive so that the dead person could travel to the underworld to the place of Osiris. The dead person had to make arrangements to that journey also.

Egyptians envisioned the place of Osiris as the divine land and its fields and landscape are lavish, it has well-watered farmlands, gardens and orchards grow abundant harvest, and a place of peace and eternity. When a person has reached the end of life, he/she can look forward to an afterlife filled with joy and happiness with satisfaction. It was a beautiful dream looking forward to die for. They thought Osiris is the presiding god and giver of eternal life.

Since the worship of Osiris began, the previous god Andjety disappeared and became a distant folk memory. Osiris cult and its mysteries spread and participating in the annual ceremonies became a lifetime goal for ancient Egyptians. Consequently, the path leading to Osiris temple became favorite memorials. Rich people installed statues of themselves and poor people made rough stone or wood slabs. Within a few generations, the terrace of the temple of Osiris and two ways leading to the temple were packed with statues intimidating the temple itself.

Osiris worship reached its peak during the Middle Kingdom and coffins were replaced by numerous types of magical objects. Those magical objects enabled them to be reborn as Osiris and travel with sun god Ra and reach a solar ship. These objects were used for afterlife function. The ivory wands engraved with figures of demons and gods were used in protective places in the house and during child-birth women wore a band to protect against evil spirits. Ironically, the reborn [person] was also vulnerable to evil spirits and wanted protection! Ancient Egyptians used innumerable magical objects for various purposes.

Here is one example of a servant statue of Middle Kingdom on which the hieroglyphic inscriptions were carved:

> "O Shabti, detailed to [serve] me … if I am summoned or if I am detailed to do any work that is to be done in the afterlife… you shall detail yourself to me every time, [whether] for maintaining the fields, irrigating the banks, or ferrying sand from east to west. You shall say, 'Look, here I am.'

Shabti was a wonderful insurance policy to life after death. Wildflowers, baskets, replicas of tiny agricultural tools were also buried with the person to remind him of his duties. (What a sad life imagination!)

Egypt was a fertile breeding ground for new ideas. In Egyptian religion, the idea of final counting of one's actions before the divine judge had a profound effect on other religions, particularly Christianity. In this concept, the unrighteous dead person is separated from the righteous one. Depending on his or her action, an individual attained divine immortal life or took second mortal birth again. The literary book, "The Instruction for King Merikara" composes:

> "When a man remains after passing away,
>
> His deeds are set alongside him…

He who reaches [the next life] without wrongdoings
Will exist there like a god."

In this system, just virtue is not enough, but one has to be free from immorality and corruption. A person can say about his many qualities and achievements, but he also should say, "I never spoke a falsehood against any living person."

Toby Wilkinson writes, "In the case of judgement before the divine court, the greatest danger was that one's own heart - seat of the intellect, fountain of emotion, and storehouse of memories - might decide to bear false witness and so tip the balance against a favourable verdict." Therefore, the Egyptians did what they thought it was right. After the rites of mummification of the body, the heart scarab (scarab is an ancient Egyptian gem cut in the form of a beetle and a potent symbol of rebirth [beetles hatch from a ball of dung, example of death and decay]) was placed over the heart inscribing instructions in Hieroglyph as to how the organ should behave when time of truth comes:

"Do not stand up against me
Do not witness against me,
Do not oppose me in the tribunal,
Do not incline against me."

Even after 4000 years, this dreadful notion of final verdict, the judgement, is still prevailing everywhere.

Tyranny

The king Mentuhotep was a founder of the First Dynasty (2950-2575 BCE) honoured as a great king, but his descendants did not enjoy the king's hard earned gains. The Twelfth Dynasty (1938-1755 BCE) ruled for 180 years with eight monarchs of a single family was considered to be a stable regime. Amenemhat I was the first king of the new dynasty. It was a golden age of the ancient Egyptian literature field. Many classic works were composed. Craftsmen created most attractive jewellery, widely extended its foreign relationship, and the Nile valley delta was reordered, well-regulated, and became an efficient country banishing the divisions of civil war.

Because the dynasty's ruler was a commoner by birth, the official records are silent about the origin of his succession. There are strong indications that the new dynasty came to power in extremely lawless time.

Amenemhat I ordered to build temples to restore the status of monarchy. Before the Twelfth Dynasty, Egyptian temples were small, irregular mud brick construction with rarely used stones at the doors and thresholds. Before, the spectacular buildings were pyramids of kings, not the temples of gods. Amenemhat I changed that custom and inaugurated monumental traditional buildings dedicated to god and goddesses to make the powerful statement of royal power. One temple measured 330 feet long by 214 feet wide with two thick walls.

Apart from building pyramids and temples, Egypt also pioneered massive state building projects, like fortresses, castles. These constructions were marvels of military architecture making deep impressions on the inhabitants living near in their mud huts. Their foreign adventures brought back thousands of slaves to work on the lands and state building projects.

As mentioned above, the budding of literature in the Twelfth Dynasty is one of the highest cultural feats of the Middle Kingdom. It is interesting to read some examples written nearly 4000 years ago.

Senusret III (1836-1818 BCE) was widely remembered as king in the dynasty. Poets and scriptwriters extolled king's virtues. Here is one example of sophistication of the literature at that time. It is the recitation on the occasion of royal visit or in front of king's statue:

"How Egypt rejoices in your strong arm:
You have safeguarded its traditions.
How the common people rejoice in your counsel:
Your power has won increase for them.
How the Two Banks rejoice in your intimidation:
You have enlarged their possessions.
How your young conscripts rejoice:
You have made them flourish.
How your revered elders rejoice:
You have made them young again."

Just one look at a usual statue of Senusret III was enough to influence a soldier to do his duty. The king used the sculpture so effectively to impress his royal power as never before. "The torso is always taut, muscular, and virile, presenting the ideal of youthful vigour beloved of Egyptian kings. But it is the face that haunts the viewer: bulging eyes under hooded lids, sunken cheeks, a brooding downturned mouth. His face is the true face of tyranny. Adding to the effect are the outsize ears, their message being that Senusret was the all-hearing monarch."

In spite of all this, it seems Egypt was facing a strong opposition within and neighbouring countries and constantly waging war.

The dynasty had begun with bang. But, the dynasty ended miserably due to lack of stable government and rebels from inside and outside of the country.

Iron Curtain

The ancient Egyptians possessed a natural superiority mindset. They thought they were the most civilized people in the world; their favourite country is protected from less fortunate neighbors by its natural borders of sea and desert. The fertile pastures of Nile Valley and delta were always a magnet for immigrants. The industry, technology and customs of immigrants have improved Egyptian civilization. The walls built by Amenemhat I created a threatening line to deter foreign aggressors. Besides, the forts enabled a regular system to guard and monitor, to intercept, to regulate the movement of peoples across the border. In spite of this iron curtain, migration increased during the Twelfth Dynasty including Palestine and Asiatic population. Under the weak rule of Amenemhat IV, the supervision may have been diminished allowing immigrants to cross the border. They built houses in their own tradition and maintained their own way of life.

Rulers of Foreign Lands

Semitic-speaking leaders of Lebanon ruled northern Egypt for more than a century (1630-1520 BCE). The loss of Memphis was a serious blow to the Thirteenth Dynasty. In addition, Egypt faced a worse situation: a combination of famine, flood, and attack. Regardless of these obstructions, the spark of Egyptian self-determination never extinguished.

Real politics is different from divine help. Nubkhepera Intef devised a solution to take control of the unruliness. It was a situation of united we stand, divided we fall. A unique document backing this alignment of power has been found at Gebtu. The king's decision on the offender was clear:

> "Have him cast out from the temple of my father, Min. Have him driven out of that temple office from son to son and generation to generation, and hurled to the ground. His provisions are to be taken away...so that his name is not remembered in this temple — as is done to one like him who rebels."

The outcome was a united and close-knit administration.

The Valley of the Kings

The Power and the Glory (Eighteenth Dynasty, 1541-1322 BCE)

The Valley of the Kings, Luxor Temple, the giants of Memnon, and the gold mask of Tutankhamun - the stunning cultural accomplishments of ancient Thebes mesmerizes Egypt's splendid opulence and artistic sponsorship on such an extravagant level. Created during the period of eight generations of the Eighteenth dynasty, these extraordinary monuments and incredible treasures are the story of a single line of family over the Nile Valley for two centuries.

Throwing out the burden of foreign domination, king Ahmose and his descendants proclaimed the new monarchy with a recharged vitality. On the stage of Thebes, the drama of divine kingship was played. Thebes town was built in Upper Egypt with the wealth created by foreign trade and victory of wars and it was transformed into the religious and royal capital of an empire. It was a 'hundred-gated city' with obelisks, temples, and giant statues overlooking the skyline in all directions. Aristocrats and bureaucrats controlled ruthlessly every aspect of people's lives and livelihoods. When the king celebrated the great rituals and ceremonies, people continued to labour in the fields.

Free from foreign rule to reach imperial power, Egypt extended its territories which reached more than two thousand miles. Foreign envoys brought exotic tributes and payments. In the south, Nubia provided Egypt mineral wealth and royal workshops with raw materials required to manufacture luxurious and sophisticated works of art.

Finally, the royal authority became disastrous. When rulers tried to push the godlike monarchy on the logical system, Egypt was turned upside down. Gradually the eighteenth dynasty faded and died paving way to another imperial order.

Order Returned

Egypt was occupied by Hykos in the north and Kushites in the south leaving only one third of the area to Egypt. Hykos had brought technological innovations to Egypt along with horses and chariots, and commenced Mediterranean commerce on grand scale. Although the administration was peaceful, King Kamose lamented on foreigners recapturing his beloved land and the glorious past. He expressed his determination: "My wish is to rescue Egypt." He fought with the enemy for a long time without any success and he succumbed to premature death. They had to wait ten long years for a new young king, Ahmose, to come to the age. With well-planned war strategies king Ahmose expelled Hykos and secured Egypt's borders.

When borders secured, trade and gold established and internal opposition suppressed, king Ahmose vision turned beyond economic and political practice to adopt ideologies also. He and his advisers realized that to secure national unity, ideas to be tailored according to the Egyptian mentality. His brilliant recommendation of family values to the royal family and ordinary mortals was to turn this family custom into a national cult. Consequently, he honoured his grandmother and mother by elevating them as national icons. He also turned his sister-wife, Ahmose-Nefertari, to the higher status.

A peculiar family relationship: "King Ahmos mother and father were full brother and sister; both of them were offspring of Tetisheri. Ahmose in turn married his full sister, Ahmose-Nefertari. When a son, future king, was born to Ahmose, Ahmose-Nefertari became a king's mother as well as king's daughter, king's sister, and king's great wife. But her brother-husband had another title planned for her. He made Ahmose-Nefertari god-Amun's wife, god's wife."!!!

Long after Ahmose and Ahmose-Nefertari were dead, their monuments had been dismantled and reused by later generations leaving their memory only in inhabitants. Royal burials attracted the attention of tomb robbers and the deceased were no longer stayed undisturbed. If the king were to enjoy the afterlife without disturbance, the solution was the type of the royal tomb had to change. As a result, two types of monuments were to be built: one tomb would be the monarch's permanent memorial to all to see; the second tomb would be built in the cliffs of western Thebes hidden away from the public. Whereabouts of king Amenhotep I tomb is a mystery so far.

Thutmosid Dynasty (1493-1390 BCE)

Without guaranteed progeny, kingship has no meaning and endangers hard-gained triumphs. Since the king Amenhotep I lacked fertility, he decided to adopt his most trusted and talented deputy Thutmose as his successor. Thutmose possessed infinite energy and determination. Under the leadership of Thutmosid Dynasty (1493-1390 BCE), Egypt extended its empire and transformed it into the most powerful and impressive civilization in the ancient world. As soon as he came to power, he declared his goal to create unrest throughout the foreign lands and conquer the rebels of the desert area. He attacked Nubia and Kerma, the capital of the Kushite kingdom with frightening speed, destroyed and burned its temples. He reached a prominent place of great spiritual significance were the religious carvings were abundant. Thutmose ordered a victory inscription to be carved over there. The following violent, bloodcurdling tone exceeds all previous records and describes the unfortunate fate of people of Kerma:

"There is not a single one of them left.
The Nubian bowmen have fallen to the slaughter,
And are laid low throughout their lands.
Their entrails drench their valleys;
Gore from their mouths pours down in torrents.
Carrion eaters swarm down up them,
And the birds carry their trophies away to another place."

At the same pitch, the inscription extols Thutmose's victory:

"He trod the earth's end in
Might and victory seeking a fight,
But he found no one
Who would stand up to him?"

Hatshepsu (1473-1458 BCE)

Women's ruling in ancient Egypt was not new. At the end of the Twelfth Dynasty, a female king, Sobekneferu briefly ruled Egypt. In late seventeenth and eighteenth dynasties, three successive generations of royal women, Tetisheri, Ahhotep, and Ahmose-Nefertari had a great role in administrative matters.

Thutmose II's sister and wife, Hatshepsu (means 'chief of noble-women') regarded herself as she is stronger than her husband. When her husband fell ill three years after becoming the king, she grabbed the throne. She pushed the boundaries of her empire further than her father. Her sovereignty was remarkable and the sheer number of buildings from rock-cut temples deep in the mountains of Sinai to stone-built shrines inside the fortresses is extraordinary. The crowning glory of her works to Ipetsu was three sets of obelisks, designed literally to point the way to the divine. On the base of one of the pairs she asked masons to carve the following text for all eternity:

"I have done this with a loving heart for my father Amun….I call to attention the people who shall live in the future, who shall consider this monument that I made for my father….It was when I was sitting in the palace that I remembered my maker. My heart directed me to make for him two obelisks of electrum [a natural alloy of gold and silver], their pinnacles touching the heavens….

"Now my mind turns this way and that, anticipating the words of the people who shall see my monument in future years and speak of what I have done.….He shall not declare what I have said to be an exaggeration.

Rather, he will say, 'How like her it is, loyal to her father!'....For I am his daughter in very truth, who glorifies him and who knows what he has ordained."

King and Country - Administration

When Thutmose III spent long periods of time on battle and crusades, he could not neglect the domestic affairs. Egypt was geographically massive having numerous local and regional traditions. The conspiracies were always hanging over the head. He realized that without a firm central government, the country could easily fall apart by internal conflict and foreign invasion. Early rulers of the New Kingdom had devised the system of government which strengthened absolute power of monarchs. The king could be a single source of power, at the same time head of state and government, commander-in-chief of the army, high priest and god's representative on earth, and the judge of policies. But, in reality, he distributed the business matters to a small handful of trusted executives.

The administration of Egypt was divided into separate departments for practical purposes. Central government administered the office of royal construction projects. The army had its own supervisor. Regional government was governed by the king's son or the supervisor of the regional appointees. Thebes was considered as a special case as it was the monarch's theological power base. Each temple had its own priesthood with economic and religious authority, first among them was the high priest of Amun, who supervised the vast landholdings and assets belonging to the temple of Ipetsut. Lastly, there was a department to manage the royal household and supplied materials. Highest of the entire royal government machine, mediator between all departments and the king was the office of vizier (Prime Minister). Basically, it was a highly effective government giving the king control over every aspect of the nation's businesses.

Temple and State

The high priest of Amun, Menkheperraseneb, held complete charge of the famous temple Amun-Ra at Ipetsut, the very important religious institute in Egypt. On his tomb, a string of titles are inscribed to demonstrate his status: superintendent of the priests of Upper and Lower Egypt; supervisor of the two thrones of the god; administrator of the advanced offices; manager of the double treasures of gold and silver; superintendent of the temple of These-khau-Amun, situated over the mysteries of two goddesses.

The cults of the previous dynasties secretive and guarded religious celebrations of divine kingship were removed and they were open to the general public. The gods had been brought out from the high walls of temples to bless the people. Earlier the people worshipped god privately in their humble homes. Now they joined together for the first time to celebrate the festivals. On festival days, the gods were borne on the shoulders of priests from temple Ipetsut through the Theban streets. Everyone on the streets could enjoy the glow of the divine presence as it passed by.

According to Egyptian concept of 'maat' (truth, justice and righteousness), the civil officer was taken oath to treat everyone impartially. In one of the temple installation, the king delivered a speech:

"These, then, are the teachings: you shall treat just the same the one known to you and the one not known to you, the one near you and the one far away."

School Rules

The country's future leaders were trained from infancy for the responsibilities they would later assume, receiving an education that was practical and professional not just academic. The future king and his friends have come into contact with Nubian and Asiatic princes, which would give them a more international outlook.

In the eighteenth dynasty, the important royal playground with garden Gurob, was a green and fertile place. Since the beginning of history, kings had built their pleasure places: plenty of birdlife made for excellent hunting, while royal women lived in the attached concubines getting busy with the making of textiles, their raw materials supplied by the fields. Royal princes and daughters were expected to learn by their mothers the skills like weaving, singing, dancing, probably reading and writing. A strict discipline was imposed when it came to the education of princes and their male companions because literacy was the key to power in ancient Egypt.

Reading and writing were first and foremost important in the school curriculum under the direction of scribes in the house of royal children. Scribe taught his students to write cursive script with pen and ink on papyrus. Gradually, students studied longer classic texts. In those days, writing skill was a widely respected profession and scribes were in great demand.

> "Look, there is no job without a controller
> Except that of the scribe: he is the controller.
> So if you are literate, it will be good for you,
> Unlike these [other] jobs I have shown you...
> Most beneficial for you is a day in the schoolroom."

"As for any scribe in any position at court,
He shall not be poor in it."

Ancient Egyptians believed the maxim "Spare the rod and spoil the child." A New Kingdom proverb stated, "A boy's ear is on his back: he hears when he is beaten." (Not now though!) The school was meant to prepare students for hard government services. The royal court had no place for corrupt intellectuals. Ambition, determination, resilience, and manly vigor were the qualities valued by the government and schools worked to prepare their pupils.

The new age of internationalism required to study foreign languages and cultures. The curriculum also included mathematics and music, even though it is not to perform, but for an ability to appreciate the singing and instrumental music. Also, the future king and his classmates would have to have a firm grasp of military strategy.

Fitness

The eighteenth dynasty rulers were brave and virile and they were expected to lead the army into battle fields and display their strength and face the enemy. In this situation, training the body was most important like the education to the mind. Energetic and physical activities were necessary to future leaders. Running, jumping, swimming, rowing, and wrestling were designed to strengthen the stamina as a weekly basis.

Consequently, the Eighteenth Dynasty secured Egypt's borders and peace with its neighbours. It was a nation of unparalleled wealth and unusual stability. It dominated Near East, established peaceful relations with other great powers, Babylonia, Assyria, and Mittani.

Golden Age

Having talent and doing excellent jobs, all Egyptian kings promoted themselves in history. Probably, in Egypt's history Amenhotep III was the only king in all dynasties who ruled the country without any military campaign for nearly forty years. In its place, he promoted all kinds of peacetime arts intensely. Amenhotep III became a king as a child while he was just two years old. He engaged in brave games in childhood and in his young age he took part in hunting wild bulls. He liked horse riding without exhaustion.

When he entered adulthood his objectives changed to construction projects. An excavation work for a pond began for his wife. It was a rowing lake measuring more than a mile long and a quarter of a mile wide (approximately 5280' X 5550'). To celebrate the opening ceremony, the king drove himself up and down in the royal pomp. From now on and rest of his rule, the country was resonating with the sounds of digging, hammering, chiseling, and building. Amenhotep III was the greatest builder in the history of ancient Egypt. Whatever and wherever he built, the king associated his name with solar deities, Ra, the son god, using descriptions of 'heir of Ra,' 'Ra's chosen one' because the king wanted to be recognized as the embodiment of solar energy in all its manifestations. He believed that the sun God's stern eyes are capable of turning rage towards Egypt's enemies defending the order; sun was maker and sustainer of life; and the bringer of fertility and productivity. Here we see the sophisticated theology being harnessed in terms of thoughts as never before.

The king beautified and decorated the buildings with fine stone sculpture. Even today more statues built by Amenhotep III survive than any previous kings. He built statutes of his mother, wife and himself up to 60 feet tall. They conveyed Amenhotep III authority and evoked a mixture of admiration and fear in every observer.

Amenhotep III supersized a giant statue, colossi sent a message also. The statue submerged in the water for several months a year and emerges again as a symbol of rebirth. A number of king's statues were carved in red granite or golden quartzite, the solar colors highlighting Amenhotep's close connection with the son god. The theory of creation and rebirth were reverberated every corner of the complex sending the message that the king was the axis of the cosmos.

Amenhotep's ambassadors travelled throughout the Near East and eastern Mediterranean and assured Egypt's existence negotiating treaties and securing positive trading agreements to maintain good relations. The hieroglyphic writing record shows that the king sent diplomatic missions to the important cities of Greek's Minoan and Mycenaean worlds. "Mycenaean trade network enabled Egypt to import precious cobalt, which was used as a dark blue dye in its glassmaking industry. Lead used to make opaque and white glass came from the Laurion peninsula of Greece."

In 1887 CE 380 baked clay documents were discovered written in cuneiform script of Mesopotamia, and in the Babylonian language of the Bronze Age revealed the complicated matters. The Amarna Letters are an archive of official correspondence found among the ruins of the "house of correspondence of the pharaoh". Amenhotep III had good diplomatic relationships with his neighbouring countries. To his subjects, he may be master of the universe, but he had to deal with six other Near East leaders and had to treat them carefully. The members of an elite group called "brother" one another. Amarna Letters show their correspondence style:

> "For me all goes well. For you may all go well… For your household, for your wives, for your sons, for your nobles, for your warriors, for your horses, for your chariots, and in your country may all go very well."
>
> "May my brother, send me unworked gold in very great quantities… and much more gold than he sent to my father. In my brother's country gold is as plentiful as dirt."

Gold was favoured currency for diplomatic exchange. A large amount of gold came from the Nubia mine where the people of the gold mining region were brutally suppressed. Without gold, Egypt was nothing.

Apart from gold, pharaoh Amenhotep III wanted to extract daughters of his fellow leaders as an ultimate prize: First, in his thirteenth year Mittanian Princess Gilukhepa arrived with plenty of gold and 317 beautiful female attendants; Second, twenty five years later to strengthen the relationship with new king he wanted another Mittanian Princess because Gilukhepa had lost her virgin bloom; Tadukhepa came with 270 woman and 30 men, and an enormous dowry including fifty-seven pounds of gold. King had married one daughter from Babylonia earlier. He again did the same trick with the Babylonian king, but he refused his demand. He complained that his first daughter is there untouched. He wrote:

> "My daughters who are married to neighbouring kings, if my messengers go there they speak with them, they send me a greeting gift. But the one with you is impoverished."

But Babylonian king showed interest in marring an Egyptian princess in exchange for his daughter. It was an insult. Amenhotep replied proudly that no daughter of Egyptian king ever married a foreigner and he did not want to break the custom. Finally, gold triumphed and king Amenhotep got his girl.

Akhenathen (1353-1336 BCE)

The most controversial and mysterious figure in ancient Egypt is the pharaoh Akhenaten (1353-1336 BCE). If his radical vision had survived, the history of ancient Egypt would have changed. Historians believe it may have changed the future of humanity also….

Amenhotep III's eldest son Prince Thutmose (named after his great grandfather) died untimely and his second son Prince Amenhotep IV declared as the king. The new king had seen his father's extravagant life and 'sed' ceremonies when he was young and it had left an everlasting impression on his mind. The amazing solar images impacted his fertile imagination. He continued his father's tradition in politics and diplomacy, took several magnificent construction projects, founded a new city in Nubia, and built a temple to Amun-Ra. During his coronation, the King of Cyprus sent a jar of "sweet oil" as a gift. A crawling letter came from a ruler of Tyre:

> "I fall at the feet of the king, my lord, seven and seven times. I am the dirt beneath the sandals of the king, my lord. My lord is the sun who comes forth over all lands day by day."

The temple Gempaaten (Gem-pa-Aten, "the Aten is found") had a big open court with a portico. Against the pillars there were twenty foot high statues of Amenhotep IV and his wife, Nefertiti, all carved with a single block of sandstone. Their unique crowns, double crown to the king and a flat crown to his queen, represented Atum, Shu, and Tefnut, the creator gods of ancient mythology in Innu. To highlight his oneness with the creator, the king ordered his sculptors to start a radical change in the way of demonstration. Every feature of the king was intentionally changed: the head was unnaturally lengthened with split eyes, long nose, noticeable chin; long muscular neck and collarbones, fat legs ended in skinny calves. In addition, on the neck, upper and lower arms, and waist of the statues, the king's names were inscribed. The fundamental purpose of this building program at Gempaaten was to provide a grand architectural setting for the celebration of royal jubilee.

In place of the traditional procession of the gods, the king and his family members were the main attraction when they travelled from palace to temple and back to palace every day. Cheering crowds greeted them standing on both sides of streets.

One year after the 'sed' festival at Gempaaten celebration, Amenhotep IV believed he was a newborn to a new life and changed his name from Amenhotep (Amun is content) to Akhenaten (Effective for the Aten). Similarly, his wife also changed her name from Nefertiti to Neferneferuaten (Beauteous are the beauties of the Aten).

New City Akhetaten (means the Horizon of the Aten)

The king Akhenaten thought if Aten were to be recognized as above all deities, there has to be a separate place truly magnifying all deities. He should have his own city. So, he located a perfect place in Middle Egypt and built a model city suited to worship Aten and to the glorification of the royal family. The king announced that it would be his resting place:

> "If I die in any town of the north, the south, the west, or the east in these millions of years, let me be brought back so that I may be buried in Akhetaten."

The One True God

Ancient kings toiled to uphold the Egyptian religion aspect, the 'maat' (truth, justice, and created order). But Akhenaten declared to live on 'maat' like the gods. Truth had no independent existence. Whatever king defined and wanted it to be, it became the truth. Traditional ceremonies like 'sed' meant to rejuvenate the king until the next one. Akhenaten's celebrations took an entirely different agenda and it was the permanent rejuvenation of the king and the entire cosmos. When Aten (Sun god Ra and also sun-disk) and king together became monarchs, the world had been taken back to the moment of creation of the universe. Akhenetan took the role of Light (sun god). Akhenaten's universe enjoyed or suffered daily re-creation, signifying the daily rebirth of the sun under the guidance of Aten, king and his queen.

For such a god which has the power of spreading the light through its rays, hidden and covered temples have no use. Worship of the Sun god Ra or Aten needed an open-air temple and big table to pile up the offerings for the god's direct consumption. The whole city of Aten was one great temple to Aten so the visible sun could be seen and worshipped anytime of the day.

A poem, 'The Great Hymn to the Aten (sun god)', written by the king himself is a masterpiece. It is inscribed on his tomb as a gesture of respect and it captures the joy of king Akhenaten:

> "You shine forth in beauty on the horizon of heaven
> O living Aten, the creator life!
> When you rise on the eastern horizon,
> You fill every land with your beauty.
>
> Beautiful, great, dazzling,
> High over every land,
> Your rays encompass the lands
> To the limit of all that you have made...
> The earth is bright when you rise on the horizon,
> And shine as Aten of the daytime.

You dispel the darkness
When you send out your rays.
The Two Lands are in festival...
All the herds are at peace in their pastures,
Trees and plants grow green,
Birds fly up from their nests...
Fish in the river leap in your presence,
Your rays are in the midst of the sea...

How manifold are your deeds,
Though hidden from sight.
Sole god, apart from whom there is no other,
You created the earth according to your desire, when you were alone.
All people, cattle, and flocks,
All upon earth that walk on legs,
All on high that fly with wings...

Your rays nurse every pasture;
When you rise, they live and prosper for you.
You made the seasons to foster everything of your making -
Winter to cool them, heat that they might taste you."

King never lost the obsession with writing and record keeping.

This hymn's richness and glorious descriptions are painted and inscribed on the walls, ceilings and floors of the royal palaces. But for ordinary people it was not accessible. Poor citizens had short and hard lives. Their bones tell the story of their living conditions, such as poor diets, high stress, and physical hardships. Some had irreparable fractures and damages to their spines by carrying heavy materials daily. Some people spent all their life kneeling and bending on mud floors working on molten metal or glass in the workshops. Due to poor diet in childhood and mimicking the mountains of food offered to Aten, people were small and prone to weakness and anaemia.

King Akhenaten and Nefertiti were present in their final public appearance during a magnificent assembly held in 1342 BCE, which was attended by foreign dignitaries. All were not impressed with this characteristic display of Egyptian superpower. King of Assyria complained, "Why should my messengers be made to stay constantly out in the sun and die in the sun?"

The End of the Line

Divine blessings did not last long for Akhenaten. His beloved daughter died at age seven, his mother died soon after, and his wife Nefertiti disappeared from the records immediately. His mother-in-law died from some unknown reason. Akhenaten died in 1336 BCE after ruling Egypt for 17 years. He was laid in the royal tomb with all kinds of things to serve him afterlife.

Akhenaten's nine year old son from his minor wife succeeded to the throne. His name: Tutankhaten "the living image of the Aten." The king changed his name and became Tutankhamun. Unfortunately, the child king Tutankhamun died in his teenage (1322 BCE) and was mummified and laid in the tomb near his father's. (He had to wait 2600 years to be discovered by an English Egyptologist Howard Carter and his team in 1922 AD!)

King Tutankhamun Tomb (1332-1323 BCE). Cairo Museum.

His child bride tried to continue the royal line, but her narrow gene pool of a brother-sister marriage had resulted in miscarriage. Two stillborn daughters were laid beside their father.

Tutankhamun's grieving widow Ankhesenamum was the last surviving successor in Akhenaten and Nefertiti. As she was not willing to marry any of her servants, she wrote a letter to the king of Hittites begging to send one of his sons to Egypt to marry her and save the kingdom: "Never shall I take a servant of mine and make him my husband!" Hittite king was surprised to see the letter and told, "Nothing like this has ever happened to me in my entire life!" Eventually he sent a prince Zannanza, but he never arrived since he had been murdered. Ankhesenamum's worst fear came true and she was forced to marry a man of her grandfather's age. Miraculously she also disappeared from the scene, no record of her anywhere. It was the end of the Eighteenth Dynasty.

Martial Law of New Kingdom (1322-1069 BCE)

The growing involvement in foreign undertakings had a profound effect on Egypt. Larger exposure to unknown peoples and cultures led to accept exotic customs and ideas from art and architecture to public and private religion. Monarchy was greatly militarized, and king appeared as a great mighty war leader at temples. The Old and Middle kingdoms recruited armies from the general public whenever it was needed to protect Egyptian interests. But for the New Kingdom, it was ill-suited because of its vast territory acquired by conquests and annexures. It required a permanent force. Therefore, at the beginning of the New Kingdom a full force of professional military organization was created for the first time in the Egyptian history.

Life of military men was not a bed of roses although it provided adventure and advancement. Training was harsh characterized by indiscriminate beatings. There were scribes for keeping records and allocating provisions, but the ration was limited. Most of the time, soldiers might not have had a proper meal in weeks. They could not leave the service because if they leave, their family members are imprisoned until they return back to service. They were registered, even circumcised for their identity. If they survived, they were allotted a plot of land by the state for cultivation.

The horse and chariot introduced from western Asia, gave Egypt a highly revolutionized military strength. The chariot was also the status symbol for the Egyptian privileged people. Like many other innovations, chariot also was brought by the foreigners to the Nile Valley. Nevertheless, Egyptians used the same technology against its inventors using chariot forces to conquer the provinces all over the Near East. It is doubtful that without the chariot, Egypt would ever have its foreign domination. For an average soldier longing for the luxury of possessing a chariot is hard work. First, he has to work from the bottom of hierarchy and work his way up through stages. The army indeed presented the opportunity to prestige and power for determined and ambitious men.

Nineteenth Dynasty (1292-1190 BCE)

PARAMESSU (RAMESSU)

King Horemheb (1319-1292 BCE) established his authority and legitimacy of his reign by creating military discipline. But one problem was that he had no heir. His solution to the problem was to identify an army man as his successor. He chose Paramessu, a son of a battalion commander, who started as a regular soldier, won the officer's commission and promotions, became a king's aide and adviser, and lastly general. Paramessu shared the same background and fundamental outlook as Horemheb. Best thing was he already had a son, and he was expecting a grandson too, a perfect ingredient to the future military dynasty. Eventually, Paramessu changed his name to Ramessu, "beloved of Amun". The stage was established for the rise of the Ramessides.

Historically Ramessu was known as Ramesses I (1292-1290 BCE). Because he was already an old man, he made a wise decision delegating most of his work to his son Seti. Within eighteen months, Ramesses died and Seti I (1290-1279) became a new king. He was young and energetic, tall and athletic with distinguished cheekbones and the characteristic curved nose of the Ramesside males. Since Horemheb's law code completely eradicated the corruption, now Seti pondered over how to restore Egypt's fortune at home and abroad. Masons started the sounds of chisels and roars to build astonishing new monuments.

Along with building monuments, his attention turned to produce eternal supply of gold. He was instructed to dig new gold mines in Egypt's eastern desert. An inscription describes the king's personal participation:

Valley of the Kings

> "His Majesty surveyed the hill country as far as the mountains, for his heart wished to see the mines from which the fine gold is brought. After his Majesty had walked uphill for many miles, he halted by the wayside to mull things over. He declared, "How irksome is a track without water! What is an expedition to do to relieve their parched throats?"

He ordered the stonecutters to leave the job in their mining sites and "dig a well in the mountains, so that it might lift up the weary and refresh the spirit of him who burns in summer." He also built a resting place in the Valley of the Kings.

Rameses II

Rameses II conquered Hittite and Kadesh forces with great talent and tactics. Afterwards his interest turned towards building several monuments. An enormous amount of stones were needed. So he demolished his predecessors Akhetaten monuments and used their stone for his own purposes.

In ancient Egyptian history, every new king built pyramids, temples, tombs, palaces more spectacular, gorgeous and luxurious in greater scale exceeding their predecessors' designs throughout the length and breadth of Egypt. Each dynasty had their own vision - structure and concept in building the monuments. Ramesses were not behind in that competition. They also built their houses of pride, 'the house of Ramesses' surrounded by huge living quarters, offices, palaces, temples, and public buildings. The encompassing cities were villages supplying fruit, vegetables, wine, and cattle. Scribes wrote wonderful literature describing the day-to-day life, atmosphere, and environment of those days: canals were filled with fish, marshes were crowded with ducks, lavish grasslands, overflowing granaries with wheat and barley. The palace covered four square miles protected by canals and sand peninsulas. Palace pillared halls were displaying the king's richness and walls were coated with different colours of tiles, depicting rivers and gardens, heraldic motifs, and prisoners of wars.

The markets and ports attracted merchants throughout the eastern Mediterranean. Since it was closer to Palestine, Egypt was a magnet for immigrants who came seeking a better life. In this background, the Bible story of Exodus has been written.

Along with exuberant descriptions of royal buildings, writers and poets also described the more intimidating side of royal projects. Hundreds of workers spent their entire life working in a large bronze-smelting factory where the highest temperature furnaces were heated by blast pipes for making armaments. "As the molten metal came out, sweating labourers poured it into molds for shields and swords. In dirty, hot, and dangerous conditions, the pharaoh's people made the weapons for the pharaoh's army. Another large area of the city was given over to stables, exercise grounds, and repair works for the king's chariot corps. The royal stud farm provided accommodation for at least 460 horses together with their trainers and grooms. The animals were exercised in a wide, pillared court, while nearby workshops produced armaments, nails and screws."

Triumph and Tragedy

Ramesses II reigned extraordinarily for sixty-years enhancing Egypt's reputation and its superpower and building the surplus number of monuments. The downside was he begot at least fifty sons and nearly fifty daughters sowing the seed for major problems for royal succession. A great fight between heirs became inevitable and finally one of his sons came to power and was called Ramesses III. He ruled three decades continuing his predecessor's work. In the meanwhile, Egypt also had a few downward

1. Nefertiti, 2. King Ramessu II, 3. Artwork at Tomb of Hatshepsut, 4. Luxor

situations: there was serious loss in military, foreign trade with Near East was weak, even though the temple's chests were filled with copper and perfumes, the granaries were empty, and workers payments were getting delayed. In such condition, the king wanted to celebrate his jubilee which erupted unrest among his subjects.

In the year 1161 BCE, the first time in history workers' strike has been recorded when workers did not get paid for 18 days. Shouting "We are hungry," they walked from their villages and attacked the funeral temples of Ramesses III and Thutmose III and staged a sit-in. They did not leave the place until their demands were met. Officials listened to worker's grievance, but they had no authority to solve the problem. The state sent delicious pastries to workers as a mockery. 'If they have no bread, let them eat cake.' The strike continued for a long time with empty promises. When jubilee time arrived, for the sake of the prestige of the nation, workers were paid on time and in full. But once the jubilee was over, the system broke down triggering the strikes again. Egypt's economic power and political stability were declining seriously.

Double-Edged Sword

For the average ancient Egyptian, only two things in life were evident: death and taxes. These two ghosts of dying and poverty haunted them from birth. Infant mortality was startlingly high; even those who endured the perils of childhood were not looking forward to a life span of more than thirty five years. Not only the poverty and poor diet contributed to short life, the unsanitary conditions of towns and villages, waterborne and infectious diseases, bilharzia, hepatitis, guinea worm, and amoebic dysentery were inevitable aspects of everyday life. "The village was full of the bleary-eyed, the one-eyed, and the blind, with inflamed and festering eyelids of all ages."

As if these health problems were not enough, the Egyptian government wanted to keep peasants in permanent poverty. Even in good years, the fields produced crops a little more than a family can survive. Because the whole land belonged to the king, farmers had to pay taxes for the freedom of farming the pharaoh's land. Egyptian rulers collected the taxes employing local agents to avoid escaping. In pre-monetary economy, the taxes were levied in the form of share of agricultural produce irrespective of plenty or famine. Defaulters were thrown in prison. Consequently, the peasant's family always trembled between utter hardship and poverty.

The hard life of a peasant is documented in a papyrus in detail from the late Twentieth Dynasty: "The text tells the story of a man named Wermai who fled from his village in Upper Egypt to the great oasis of the Western Desert to seek a better life. Instead, he found himself in even worse circumstances, subject to an uncaring and unscrupulous mayor who had the power to make his people's lives miserable. Not only did the local authorities extract taxation with all their customary ruthlessness, but they feathered their own nests by deliberately reducing the rations doled out to the already hard-pressed peasantry. As a result, people went hungry while the local bureaucrats prospered."

The most burdensome taxation levied was the corvee (unpaid work), a tax paid through labour, on demand, by every strong-bodied male in the land. Life on the corvee was hard and endless. Serious criminals were sentenced to hard labor or sent to work in the terrible conditions of gold mines.

Downward Spiral

In theory, forced labour was a part of the contract between the Egyptian people and their rulers. In return to his drudging labour, the king promised him the eternal order of the cosmos by satisfying god and Egypt's prosperity.

Every Pharaoh Instructed God with Many Demands

"Double for me the extended life span and the great reign of King Usermaatre-setepenre, the great god"; "Confer my great office on my heirs; behold, the disaffected are the abomination of your majesties!" If a king beautified the god's temples and offered more, then the gods should deliver the quid pro quo (deal) and fulfil his requests.

But the gods were no longer listening.

Cruel destiny fell on a pharaonic line. Ramesses VI, VII, and VIII - all three died within a span of eleven years. The subsequent king used less influence as state offices became corrupted.

Crime and Cover Up

The royal tombs were designed not only for resting places for kings, but also for guaranteed gateway to heaven and promise of rebirth. Therefore, it was a single most important building for every king to build a resting place for himself. This ideal holiness ideology was shattered during civil unrest, Old and Middle Kingdom pyramids were robbed and dishonoured with invulnerability. So, the New Kingdom kings built rock-cut tombs in the Valley of Kings with a hope that the mummies of Egypt's monarchs can rest in peace for all eternity. At the end of the Eighteenth Dynasty, in spite of the king's attempt to hide their tombs from vandalism, the secret of their whereabouts was leaked out and prompted to rob the rock-cut tombs. Their first target was less guarded Seventeenth Dynasty's royal tombs. As the robbers were workers and inhabitants of the village, they knew every inch of the city. So, one night in 1114 BCE, a stonemason along with his team committed a crime of the century. The record writes:

> "We opened their coffins and their mummy wrappings. We brought back the gold we found on the noble mummy of this god, together with his pectorals and other jewellery that were around his neck."

After looting all valuables in the tomb of Sobekemsaf II, robbers set fire to the coffins reducing their chests to ashes. Even though robbers were caught and got punished, the crimes repeated again and again. Corruption was now endemic in every level from priesthood to the government.

Change and Decay

After the last Ramessides Dynasty king Ramesses XI died, Egypt entered an age of overwhelming change. It was surrounded by envious powerful powers. From eleventh to fourth centuries BCE, Egypt was invaded by Libyans, Assyrians, Kushite, Babylonians, Persians and Macedonians fought over its abundant agricultural and mineral wealth. Foreign rulers and immigrants shaped ancient Egypt's culture, political organization, society and changed pharaonic civilization forever. In the meanwhile, Egypt's religion sealed itself from outside influence and turned inward-looking.

Paiankh and Harihor

Two Libyan military strong soldiers, Paiankh and Herihor were ruling Theban while last king Ramesses XI's was dying. They seized the opportunity and conquered Egypt.

The Egyptian language began to display other signs of foreign influence. Lybyan's names began to appear. Since the Middle Kingdom period, the inscriptions carved into temple walls were pure classic hieroglyphics. The spoken language differs enormously from written language indicating practically they are different languages. For the local Egyptian it was not a problem because they understood both written and spoken languages. But for Libyan scholars and priests it posed a problem. Therefore, the Libyans who were running the country then, mastered spoken language. They improved everyday grammar and simple vocabulary.

The Libyan rulers were obsessed with family trees. The recitation of long genealogies is a characteristic of oral tradition in illiterate semi nomadic societies. Even after learning written language from Egyptians, Libyans did not lose their liking of reciting a long line of their genealogies. For example, a priest had a monument carved with the names of thirteen generations of his ancestors going back three hundred years, in spite the family had been settled in the same Egyptian city and held the same office for eleven of those generations.

Libyans had no passion or interest in death and afterlife. Their hunters and gatherer ancestors were burying their dead where and when they fell without any preparation and concern. It was shocking news to Egyptians whose belief was fundamentally based on the death and afterlife. Libyans thought that Individual burials were a waste of resources. Instead, they favoured communal family tombs with trivial decoration. Sometimes their funeral materials were recycled by nearby burials. Building splendid royal funeral homes as a meeting place for mortals and divine people was completely stopped. Now they were only holes in the ground for bodies.

The once sparkling Ramesside residence was systematically torn down for its stone obelisks, statues, and building blocks to construct new buildings. Most of the time the Upper Egypt kings did not hesitate to re-inscribe the stolen monuments.

Destruction of Tombs Extravaganza by Libyans

The Theban tomb of king Merenptah's mummy placed on a silver sheet inside a silver coffin, its face covered with a mask of beaten gold within a great granite chest. Around the body stored costly treasured - inlaid bracelets and ornamental breastplates, a thick necklace of lapis lazuli beads, silver and gold bowls, and a gold mace. Even the king's fingers and toes were sheathed individually in gold leaf.

A new system arose that allowed not only kings, but others also can have the opportunity to build their tombs. A general and army leader Wendjebaendjedet's tomb did not differ from the king's tomb. The amount of gold placed around his body showed several magnificent golden cups, including one in a shape of a flower with alternating petals of gold and electrum; a heart of holy beetle on a golden chain; gold breastplate; gold statues of deities, a statue of god Ptah carved from lapis lazuli nesting in a gold shrine; and a number of gold rings.

Libyan's did not use this golden lavishness to royal tombs. Under the Libyan military regime controlled by Paiankh, state sponsored theft of valuables from the royal tombs began. He ordered his assistants to "uncover a tomb amongst tombs of the ancestors and preserve its seal until I return."

These instructions indicate the beginning of stripping royal tombs for their gold to finance the war and finance Paiankh's broader ambitions. Their first target was the Seventeenth Dynasty's Valley of the Queens, Valley of the Kings, and king's mortuary temples.

Once the work of robbing the royal tombs was completed, the next project was to find a permanent place to all royal corpses that had been so crudely removed from their resting places. They found the tomb of Amenhotep II was an ideal location. One unfortunate day around 1050 BCE, the remains of Egypt's divine kings were unceremoniously collected and pushed disorderly into one of the tomb's chambers. In this holy mess, the Thutmose IV lay with child king Siptah, Sethnakht with smallpox-ridden Ramesses V. It was a violation of everything that ancient Egypt held so holy and dearly. Most prestigious kings were bundled into an inferior storing place in the tomb of the Seventeenth Dynasty queen waiting for a permanent resting place.

All Pharaoh's beliefs on divine kingship were shattered and dissolution occurred as a broken mirror.

Oracles

Native population, the pious Egyptians still dominated especially in Thebes and Upper Egypt. During 985-960 BCE, a bitter dispute broke between the priest class 'god's servants' and the 'pure ones' over access to the temple revenues. The priests jealously protected the possession of the interior of the holy temple and it was banned to common people. The honour of offerings of food, drink, and other things were placed before the statue of Amun during the daily worship. Once the god had accepted the offer, these offerings were delivered to priests. By contrast, the pure one or common people were not allowed to the temple, they were entrusted to do secondary duties outside the temple such as carrying the statue of Amun in a procession through the streets of the city. Before, this carrying the god's statue was not so remarkable. But now, the divine oracles were dominating the minds of people with more significance. Even a small change in tilt or swing on the shoulders of the carrier had a significant effect, god's intention. The lowly porters recognized that the destiny of the entire nation rested on their shoulders and demanded a larger share of fortune. This demand brought a great conflict between priests and common people.

A Tarnished Throne

The irony is in spite of many attacks by Hykos and Libyans, the ancient Egyptian ideology of pharaonic beliefs was the final winner. So, when

Libyan dominance was established, they decided to follow the natives. As a result, the pharaonic orthodoxy returned. Menkheperra and Nesbanebdjedet II were willing to accept the supreme authority of a monarch.

Shoshenq

A charismatic and aspiring Libyan leader Shoshenq became a prominent figure. By marrying his son to king Pasebakhaennuit's eldest daughter, he established royal connections. His strategy worked and after the king's death Shoshenq occupied the throne. His accession to the throne marked the beginning of the Twenty-Second Dynasty. He centralized the power, re-established the king's political supremacy, and let Egypt to follow a traditional form of government. Now oracles were not used to govern political policy. The king was perfectly able to make decisions without the help of god Amun.

Shoshenq checked the archives and began to follow the tradition of earlier pharaohs. He ordered him to build monuments for himself to display his accomplishments by removing the New Kingdoms pharaohs' tombs in the Valley of the Kings. His conquests began to occupy neighbouring territories. In one of the places, to secure his place in the history, Shoshenq ordered a commemorative inscription to be erected inside the fortress of Magiddo. Then he led his army towards Aruna and Yehem to Gaza, the Ways of Horus, and home. Shoshenq died suddenly and all his building projects were abandoned, and his successors also displayed a hopeless poverty of aspiration. After Shoshenq, many generations started their own lavish buildings to demonstrate their achievements.

Kush

After the collapse of the New Kingdom, Kush became a dominant power in Egypt. Rulers of Kush considered themselves superior and believed they are the protectors of Egyptian sovereignty. The early Kushine rulers were faithful devotees of Amun and restored and rebuilt the damaged temple of Amun at Gebel Barkal. King Kashta "the Kushite" extended his area of authority up to Upper Egypt.

Surprisingly, Kushite king Piankhi was a pious and impartial ruler. Pious and aggressive Piankhi launched many battles with Nubians, Herakleopolis, Itj-tawy. On arriving at Herakleopolis, Piankhi threatened them with total eradication if they did not surrender within one hour. His combative language worked, and rebels surrendered. The King demonstrated his nobility by ordering his army not to kill anyone. Its granaries were loaded to the wealth at the temple of Amun. In one confrontation as a gesture of submission, Nimlot's female relatives came to beg mercy from Pinkhi's wives, daughters, and sisters as a plea, woman to woman.

Piankh's affection towards horses was extraordinary. One manuscript speaks enormously about his visit to Nimlot's palace:

> "The king's [Nimlot's] wives and daughters came to him and paid honor to him as women do. But His Majesty did not pay them any attention. [Instead] he went off to the stables, where he saw that the horses were hungry. He said… "It is more painful to me that my horses should be hungry than every [other] ill deed you have done!"

Purity of Law

As ships loaded with spoils of victory, Piankhi's army began to march towards Thebe and home. He made one fanatic decision. All four kings assembled to say goodbye to the king. Three of them were allowed to board the ship, but Nimolots were barred to enter the ship. It is not because of their weakness or any opposition, but because they were uncircumcised and had eaten fish - serious mistake in king's interpretation of religious purity of law. Moral absolutism and military strength both lived together in Kushite rule. Might and right had no place.

Piankhi systematically defeated every opponent throughout Egypt. But his love for horses and love for motherland made him return to Nubia. After his tour of conquests and victory, he decided to return to Nubia in 728 BCE On the way, Piankhi stopped at Thebes to ordain his daughter as a successor to the god's wife of Amun to ensure Kushite influence on holy city and reached Napata, the capital city. In his shining palace, without setting his foot in Egypt again, Piankhi ruled another twelve years safe and sound.

Piankhi's primary concern for going to war with Egypt was not politically motivated, but his prime objective was religious and to protect the holy places of Amun from Libyan meddling. He succeeded in his mission. It was not his concern what happened to Egypt's internal politics after him. Piankhi and his successor rejuvenated indigenous Egyptian traditions that had been neglected by Libyan rulers. The Kushites considered that it was their holy mission to restore Egypt's cultural purity.

Wheel of Fortune

Royal encouragement motivated priests and artists to look back on the pharaonic period of history and the obsession with the past influenced every part of cultural undertaking. High ranking officials adopted meaningless titles just for the sake of their antiquity. The archaic form of Old Kingdom written language was revived, and scribes composed new texts based on old phrases. It was said that an ancient Memphite Theological treatise has been copied from an ancient worm-eaten papyrus, preserved in the temple archives for more than 1000 years. But it was a product of 700 BCE, cleverly designed to look like a relic of the past written by imagining the past of cultural purity that existed in the minds of the Kushite dogmatists.

Piankhi's son Taharqo also honoured Egypt's ancient gods. In the sixth year of his rule, a natural miracle happened: "the sky rained in Nubia so that all the hills glistened, and floodwaters rose fast, day by day. The Nile reached an extraordinary height of thirty-six feet. More miraculous still were the aftereffects of such a great flood. It made all the fields good; it killed off the vermin and snakes; it warded off the depredations of locusts; and it prevented the south winds from stealing the harvest." He commissioned to document this commemorative inscription to record them for posterity, with copies carved at Gempaaten and Djanet. To celebrate this natural miracle, Taharqo invited his mother. She travelled the long journey from Napata to Egypt. For the king, it was a moment of high emotion: "I had left her as a youth of twenty years when I came with His Majesty (King Shabaqo) to Lower Egypt. And now she has come, sailing downstream, to me after years!" The deep bond between mother and son transcended the royal reserve momentarily.

Assyrian Invasion - Cow Worship

In 680 BCE, an Assyrian king Esarhaddon declared the beginning of the end of Kushite reign. He attacked Egypt in 674 BCE and was defeated by Taharqo. But Taharqo knew that the Assyrians would attack again. Three years later again Assyrian invaded Egypt successfully led by Esarhaddon himself. Taharqo had no choice but flee leaving his family at the mercy of Assyrians. Within half a day of fighting, the enemy stormed the royal palace and looted the treasures including hundreds of golden crowns on which golden cobras and serpents were decorated, eight thousand talents of silver, and fifty thousand horses. The Assyrian king boasted: "His queen, the women of his palace, Ushanahuru his heir, his other children, his possessions, horses, cattle and sheep beyond number, I carried off as booty to Assyria." To humiliate further and to celebrate his victory, Esarhaddon instructed to carve an inscription showing the crown prince shackled in rope, kneeling pitifully at his feet. Soon Assyrians renamed Egypt's towns, appointed new kings, governors, officers, port officers, officials and administrators.

Ashurbanipal, a ruthless Assyrian king, invaded third time. "His governors arrested these kings and put their hands and feet in iron cuffs and fetters... And they put to the sword the inhabitants, old and young, of the towns of Sais, Pindidi, Djanet and of all the other towns which had associated with them. They hung their corpses from stakes, flayed their skins and covered the town walls."

Public executions were held throughout the country as a warning. The Kushites were driven out to Kush. Now all of Egypt was under Assyrian's control. Assyrians ruled the country for 45 years from 702-657 BCE

Babylonian Invasion

In south Mesopotamia, Assyria's old enemy Babylonians was on the rise. Within a few months after Ashurbanipal's death, a new king came to power in Babylonia and began to capture the Egyptian territories which were lost two generations earlier. In spite of Egyptians support, Assyrians were defeated by the Babylonians in 609 BCE and Egypt was immersed into Babylonia one year later. The Babylonian king Nebuchadrezzar could not believe his luck.

Understanding the upcoming danger, Ahmose II (570-526 BCE) planned to defend the invasion. He made alliances with the Greeks because of his anti-Babylonian policy. Greeks had established colonies around the Mediterranean and Black Sea coasts. Greek wealth depended on free trade and they did not favour Babylonians because they threatened Greeks prosperity. Egypt had military interest in the Greek world because their soldiers were famous and valuable in entire regions. The pharaohs made generous donations to Greek shrines, like Delphi and married Greek princesses also.

Persia

In 559 BCE, an energetic young man Cyrus ascended to the throne of a minor, insignificant land called Persia. Soon he rebelled against his ruler and occupied his Median Empire. The Egyptian pharaohs neglected the events occurring and showed no interest. Within two decades after coming to power, Cyrus subjugated Anatolian kingdom of Lydia and then Babylonia and stretched his empire up to Hindu Kush Mountains, immediately becoming a superpower.

In the wake of this, Egyptian king Ahmose II hired more Greek soldiers, strengthening his naval forces hoping for the best. Although Cyrus' death in 530 BCE gave some relief, Ahmose cautiously ruled the country for a period of four decades. After he died in 526 BCE, **an** untrained and untested pharaoh, Psamtek III (526-525 BCE) faced a disaster. The death of a monarch is always an occasion for defenselessness when an invader is on the doorstep.

Within weeks of Cyrus's death, Persian king Cambyses attacked and captured Memphis, executed Psamtek, and effectively merged both Upper and Lower Egypt into one Persian kingdom, imposing Persian style rule. He eliminated the position of god's wife of Amun, abolished inheritance of god's wife of Amun, Ankhnesneferibra, who was serving the temple for sixty years.

Priest Wedjahorresnet

Egyptian elite people treasured their culture and traditions more than their religion. Every member of the society demonstrated his commitment to his town cult, and active participation in the local temple was a necessity to win respect in the community. When Egyptians confronted the strange gods of Persians, they decided not to fight with them, but to try to win over Persians by transforming them to follow the Egyptian way of doing things. A priest Wedjahorresnet with all his credentials managed to do that. He won the trust by sneaking inside as a king's chief physician and got access to the royal presence. He praised the Persian invasion in gleaming terms:

> "The great leader of all foreign lands, Cambyses, came to Egypt, the foreigners of all foreign lands with him. When he had assumed rule over this land throughout its length, they settled there and he became great ruler of Egypt, the great ruler of all foreign lands."

Wedjahorresnet had an extraordinary position and knowledge to guide Persian masters to Egyptianize, which would make them respectable and even turn them legitimate pharaohs. Accordingly, King Cambyses ordered to purify the temple, which was destroyed by foreigners, restored the priesthood and offers as it was before. The Persian conqueror was all ready to become a suitable pharaoh. The Egyptians lost their political independence, but they maintained their cherished cultural traditions.

Age of Invention

Instead of a great disaster, Persian invasion did some good to Egypt. The new rulers brought much needed new dynamism and energy to the government and propelled new life to its offices and infrastructures. Darius I took great interest to learn Egypt's repositories of learning, the "House of Life" housed in the major temples. He ordered, now an old and trusted

Wedjahorresnet, to restore the ruined house of life documents. Darius recognized that Egypt was not just another satrapy but had a significant ancient culture. He let local Egyptians to hold high offices. The Persians controlled the empire with a good intelligence network and tactically placed military base.

Suez Canal

To exploit Egypt's wealth, Darius' priority was to encourage marine trade between the Nile Valley and the Persian Gulf. In Upper Egypt, the land line route to Red Sea was reopened. In Lower Egypt there was no such opportunity. The solution was the greatest idea ever invented in ancient history apart from Giza pyramids. Back in king Saite's rule Nekau II (610-595 BCE), a project was initiated. After one hundred years, the necessity of the project was realized and what Nekau dreamed of, Persians delivered it. The result was building the Suez Canal of 150 feet wide that flowed about forty miles from the easternmost branch of the Nile, along the Wadi Tumilat, to the Bitter Lakes and then southward to the Gulf of Suez.

Domination of Darius

Each side of the canal, at strategic points, stood ten feet high and seven feet wide pink granite slabs with commemorative inscriptions, selected scenes and texts, which emphasized Darius accomplishments and his domination over his empire. On one side, the slab depicted the king under the protection of his Persian god Ahura Mazda with text in cuneiform; and the other side displayed a logo of Egyptian sun disk with hieroglyphic scripts. It was very uncomfortable to Egyptian's mind because Darius portrayed Egypt also as one of his conquered territories, which included Persia, Media, Babylonia, Assyria, and India. Darius exhibited, "I, a Persian, with Persians, I seized Egypt. I gave orders to dig a canal from the river that is in Egypt - the Nile is its name - to the bitter river [that is, the Red Sea] that flows from Persia." To celebrate canal's opening ceremony, Darius visited to see twenty four ships loaded with Egyptian tribute navigating to Persia. 497 BC.

Kharga Oasis

Persian's aspiration to control the desert routes across the Sahara also initiated a remarkable engineering. One of the four ports Kharga Oasis provided a connection in desert communication. The area was too dry with insufficient rainfall. To solve the problem, Persians introduced camels to Egypt, which revolutionized desert travel. Second, the Persians established an extraordinary technique to bring water trapped inside the underground to the surface throughout Kharga. This technology encouraged irrigation and enabled gardens to grow vegetables and other agricultural stuff. New towns and villages sprung with administrative buildings and temples.

An extraordinary archive has been preserved recording all developments. Individuals and institutions toiled hard to preserve valuable documents. They even preserved the receipts, household accounts, legal contracts, and everyday scribbles. The records show the inhabitants wealth was not land, but it was water. The water extracted from rock-cut aqueduct was bought and sold, rented, or even used to guarantee loans. Water was literally money.

In essence, under Darius I, Egypt was a vigorous melting pot of peoples and traditions, a place of cultural innovation, a prosperous trading centre, and a peaceful multiethnic community.

Darius's successors were less interested in Egyptian kingship and religion. As Persian's attention turned towards troublesome western parts, trade with Egypt declined, political activities relaxed, and the country was heading to difficult times.

Animal Illusion

The confused detachment of Persians drove Egyptians to reconsider their original beliefs. As a result, a surplus number of animal deities personified the local Egyptian values. Besides, gods represented age-old and permanent without any change. In spite of innumerable changes in Egypt, gods remained the same and promised ultimate salvation no matter whatever happens to life: "Change and decay in all around I see; O thou who changest not, abide with me."

A new cult of worshipping animals started. There were sacred cats at Bast, sacred dogs and gazelles at Thebes, sacred bulls at Inuit, sacred crocodiles at Shedyt, and even sacred fish at Djedet with its own temple and priest. Egypt's dead elites saw themselves lying beside a zoo of beasts, big and small.

Cow Worship

In a temple complex, hypogeum, a sacred cow worshipped as the incarnation of the goddess Isis. After its death, the cow was purified, mummified, wrapped in linen bandages, and decorated with jewelleries, and put them in the tomb. A huge stone tomb for the temple cow, which was so heavy required a team of thirty men and up to a month's wage for ten days of backbreaking work was needed to tow the cow's tomb to a place.

Pilgrims arrived at a temple city Saqqara where all mummified animals were laid, from various parts of the country searching for advice, to know the future, seeking cures for sickness hoping Osiris the baboon would mediate with god and fulfil all of their wishes. The place was crowded with fortune-tellers, interpreters of dreams, astrologers, soothsayers, and innumerable worshippers.

Herodotus writes in his book Historia that Egyptian people did not eat cows. They respected and worshiped cows and it was not permitted to sacrifice cows in religious programs since they were sacred to Goddess Isis. Soldiers from foreign countries did not like to live in Egypt because they were not allowed to eat beef over there. Herodotus writes that Egyptians were very clean, used to bathe two times a day to worship, wore clean clothes every day, observed birth days, observed ten days of mourning when someone died in the family, shaved their head, and so on.

Waiting for a Hero - Alexander

Egypt's strong confidence in its tradition worked well in happier times. But the traditions they maintained for more than 3000 years no longer worked.

When Darius III ascended the throne in 336 BCE, Alexander was securing recognition throughout Greece. The world was at a turning point.

Alexander had started his campaign and by the spring of 334 BCE he crossed Hellespont into Persia. The historical battle at the river Granikos was the beginning of the end of Darius and for Persia. Alexander was unstoppable and it was an end to Persian history.

As the Alexander's war triumph stories reached Egypt about his thirst for glory and his unbeatable army, the Egyptians started to speculate whether he could get rid of the Persians. Since they lacked native born hero, they evaluated both Darius and Alexander and finally decided Alexander looked like a lesser of two evils. Alexander was a ruthless leader. No one dared to stand in Alexander's way. They saw Alexander as a man very much like traditional pharaonic mold, a ruthless tyrant, to be respected and feared. Moreover, he was proven a winner and Egypt was looking for that kind of hero.

In 332 BCE, Alexander marched across the Egyptian border and grabbed power without any fight. The Persians simply disappeared. For

Alexander, ancient Egypt's culture and religious traditions were more fascinating. He travelled three hundred miles to visit Siwa Oasis with its famed oracle of Amun. Alexander emerges from the temple as a changed man. "He put his question to the oracle and received (or so he said) the answer that his soul desired." Thus, Macedonian ruler became the king of Egypt.

Alexander stayed in Egypt for only four months and left Egypt in April 331and never returned. He presented himself as a liberator, an enlightened ruler who respected and honoured Egypt's ancient traditions and beliefs.

Alexander wished that his body be buried within the arcade of the temple of Amun at Siwa in Egypt, but the new Leader of Macedon, Perdiccas, decided to bury him in the dynastic cemetery of the Macedonian kings at Aegina. It seemed everyone wanted Alexander's body as a jewel of legitimacy.

But Ptolemy formulated a daring plan to steal Alexander's body for political selfish reasons. As the funeral procession started from Babylon, Ptolemy's army hijacked it in Syria and diverted to Egypt. Instead of Alexander's wishes, he buried the body at Memphis, traditional capital of the pharaohs. As Alexander's superior glow spread over the seat of government, Ptolemy easily gained the right to rule Egypt. This deception caused immediate conflict between Macedon and Egypt.

When Ptolemy officially became a king, he moved Alexander's body to Alexandria and buried it again in a glass-sided coffin in a lavish new tomb. There Alexander would lie for all eternity as a founding father of new city Alexandria.

Eventually, the deadly family feuds with Alexander's surviving relatives started within twelve years of his death. First, his heir and half-brother Philip III was murdered by the order of Alexander's mother, Olympias. Then, Alexander's posthumous son, Alexander IV, was murdered by his guardian.

Alexander's successors made a threefold division of his kingdom. In the northwest, Macedon remained an independent kingdom. In the south, the Ptolemies ruled over Egypt, Cyrenaica, and Cyprus. The great central swath of territory, comprising southern Anatolia, the Near East, Mesopotamia, and Persia, had fallen to another of Alexander's generals, Seleucus, and the Seleucid Kingdom emerged as a powerful rival to the Ptolemic Empire.

Alexandria

Alexandria was a jewel in the Ptolemaic empire. Alexander himself selected the location. It was less than twenty miles from Nile River's main outlet, still unaffected by yearly floods. A twin natural harbor provided a deep-water port for shipping and loading docks. It also endowed with warehouses, shipyards, and the emporium, perfect location for a theatre and a temple to Poseidon, Greek god of the seas. The main city was built on a Hellenistic style grid system with two broad hundred-foot-wide avenues interconnecting at right angles. Each side of these boulevards stood important public offices, markets, and major temples. The Greek style tombs, law courts, gymnasiums, monuments in Egyptian and Greek styles in polished granite and shining marble displayed both Hellenistic and Greek style cultures.

1. Library of Alexandria 300 BC.

2. Papyrus documents in Library of Alexandria 300 BC

Museum

Distinguished in population, magnificence, wealth, and power, Alexandria also became the leading cultural centre of the Hellenistic world. The Museum was literally the "Shrine of the Muses" associated with nine goddesses of Art and Intelligence.

The Museum was designed based on the great schools of Plato and Aristotle, lavishly furnished, and staffed with great effort, and generously supported by the state. The Ptolemies obtained the most distinguished talent wherever it could be found. The renowned mathematician Euclid taught at the Museum; Archimedes stayed there some time and possibly invented the Archimedean Screw, an ingenious device for raising water; Scientist Eratosthenes calculated the circumference of the earth with a high degree of accuracy and disseminated his heliocentric theory, suggesting that the

Muse Name	***Domain***	***Emblem***
Calliope	Epic Poetry	Writing tablet.
Clio	History	A Scroll.
Erato	Lyric Poetry	A Musical instrument in the guitar family.
Euterpe	Song and Elegiac Poetry	A Greek instrument that's similar to a flute.
Melpomene	Tragedy	A tragic Mask.
Polyhymnia	Hymns	A Veil.
Terpsichore	Dance	S Lyre.
Thalia	Comedy	A Comedic Mask.
Urania	Astronomy	A Globe and a Compass.

earth was not the centre of the universe; and several prominent scholars like poets, historians, and physicians thrived in the Museum. It is understood that Buddhist monks were also living in Alexandria, probably who came with Alexander the Great army. This is to identify only a few of the superstars of the Alexandrian intellectual azure. There were numerous other worthy scholars; all made their contributions to the greatest intellectual institution of the classical world.

Great Library of Alexandria -Intellectual Capital of Greek World

Ptolemy I determined to promote Alexandria as a paramount intellectual centre of Greek world. He founded a scholarly academy within the palace quarter. Ptolemies picked the best brains from all over Greek empire and persuaded them to come to Alexandria promising academic freedom and a good salary from the royal treasury. The Library quickly became a powerhouse of research and teaching. The Library and Museum buildings had all facilities for scholarly community: covered walkways with resting places and seats for quiet reflections; a large dining hall; meeting places to discuss ideas in the library. It was not just any library, but the greatest collection of books in the ancient world, obtained honestly or dishonestly from the book markets in those days. Ptolemy III was so eager to obtain original editions of Greek literary classics even not hesitating to steal. He used a trick to borrow books from the libraries of Athens by depositing heavy amounts of silver talents. As soon as the books arrived, he sent a thank you note and asked them to keep the deposit and he kept the books.

During Great Library's prime time, it had half a million papyrus rolls, signifying the sum total of knowledge in every field of inquiry. "The wealth of its written holdings was matched only by its glittering array of scholarly talent, as successive directors of the library gathered about them an astonishing array of visiting academics." There were only one or two Egyptians who were entrusted to write the history of Egypt. All other academics were from Greek world: Euclid, the founder of geometry was from Platonic School in Athens; the engineer Archimedes who invented his water-lifting device; an astronomer Aristarchus of Samos who advanced the theory of solar system with sun at its centre; geographer and astronomer Eratosthenes who accurately calculated the circumference of the earth by measuring the length of the shadow cast by a stick at the same time of a day in Aswan and Alexandria; physicians immersed in the Hippocratic tradition of basic workings of the nervous, digestive, and vascular systems; and court poet Callimachus who compiled a thorough catalogue of books in the Great Library.

Light House!!

Another miracle of engineering was that on a rocky island stood a tower overlooking hundreds of feet into the sky. The tower was built from stone slabs weighing about seventy-five tons and the structure rose in three gigantic stories, by turns square, octagonal, and cylindrical. At the top of the massive statue of Zeus, a light was mounted that burned day and night. Its light magnified by mirrors was visible to long distances on the sea to direct people across Mediterranean into Egypt's thriving cities. (Sarah Parcak, an American Archaeologist and Egyptologist, identified this buried lighthouse by using satellite imaging technology.

Medicine

Medicine was always strong at Alexandria with people like Praxagoras, who was considered as one of the greatest physicians of antiquity and his student Herophilus of Chalcedon, who made dissection a regular practice. Alexandrian excellence in medicine continued to be unchallenged. The greatest physician of antiquity, Galen studied at Alexandria. His influence on later medical thinking, which continued into modern times, has been compared to that of Aristotle. Some of his ideas, especially about the spread of disease, were still alive during the mid-nineteenth century. Even after the Museum had suffered many changes and other areas of study were in decline, medicine remained strong at Alexandria. As the Roman historian Ammianus Marcellinus remarked: "When a physician wants to establish his place in the profession, all he needs to do is say he was trained at Alexandria."

No other library in ancient times came close to it in size and organization. Library at Alexandria is said to have contained from five to several hundred thousand rolls, and one roll every so often contained more than one work. Ptolemy I sent seekers to all parts of the Greek world to buy texts to fill Library's shelves, and Ptolemy III wrote "to all the world's sovereigns" to borrow texts to have them copied. Library also devoted an extraordinary amount of work to cataloguing, collating, arranging, editing, interpreting, critiquing – all the multiple qualities of working scholarship. Alexandria also remained at the precursor of intellectual life in the Mediterranean world during the Roman Empire.

Philosophy

Philosophy thrived in Alexandria, the leading type being Platonism. Neoplatonism, a synthesis of components from Platonic, Aristotelian, Pythagorean, and Stoic philosophies, passed Plato's passion for ideas into the area of mysticism.

Two Systems in One Country

The coastal area around Alexandra in Egypt might have been completely Greek, but the delta and Nile Valley were different. Greeks Ptolemaic law executed only in three cities: Alexandria, Naukratis; and Abdju, which were valuable trade centres. Thousands of immigrants from Greek world found newfoundland as a land of opportunity and made their fortunes.

Cultural and ethnic relationships between Greek cities and Egyptian rural areas were a blunder. Egyptian farmers tilled the lands as before. The ruling class had their gymnasium, defenders of Greek culture. They spoke and wrote in Greek and even after three generations in Egypt, they continued to think themselves as Greeks; they imported their own legal system from Greece and their laws existed side by side with Egyptian laws.

In towns and villages of rural areas of Egypt, local people inevitably allowed this foreign culture in their homeland. Many Egyptians embraced two names, one for official purpose and one for private matters. New temples for Greek gods mushroomed next to Egyptian gods Isis, Thoth, Baster, and Amun. Each ethnic group lived in the isolated quarters of the city. Two generations after Greek's rule, some sections of Egyptians started to express their frustration on partiality and unjust policies imposed on them and eventually they rebelled against their masters. Irritated by opposition, Ptolemy V with all his firepower suppressed the rebel and arranged public execution before his coronation festival in March 26, 196 BCE the occasion was inscribed in the country's two languages: Egyptian and Greek; and three scripts: hieroglyphics, demotic characters, and Greek known as the Rosetta Stone. At the end of Ptolemy V's death in 180 BCE, the kingdom was heading downward.

At the same time another magnificent young state was observing the happenings in Egypt with hungry eyes.

Rome and Cleopatra

When Ptolemy VI (180-145 BCE) became a king at the age of six, his mother acted as a representative on behalf of him. After family disputes between Ptolemy VI and his siblings battered the country, Romans were asked to interfere to maintain the stability.

Tyrant king Ptolemy VIII made a will promising his kingdom to Rome if he should die without a legitimate heir. He married his brother's widow who was his own sister. He murdered her son by Ptolemy VI on the day of the wedding. He punished the Jewish groups who opposed his regime and expelled many Greek intellectuals from Alexandria. He bribed Egyptian people supporting their temples and the local people turned blind eye to Ptolemy's barbaric actions.

Ptolemy married his sister-wife's younger daughter making her queen. Consequently, mother-daughter became stronger enemies. When a civil war took place in 132 BCE, Ptolemy escaped to Cyprus along with his younger wife leaving the elder one. Calculating her son would be announced as the future king, Ptolemy arranged to kidnap him. When her son was brought to Cyprus, he murdered him and sent his dead body pieces to the boy's mother on her birthday celebration. To raise the anger of local people, she put the remains of the dead body on public display. But Egyptians ignored and stayed loyal to their leader. Ptolemy's bribe was working. He returned back, regained his position, and did countless atrocities and died in 116 BCE History repeated as two royal brothers Ptolemy IX and X fought for power.

Amidst of all these disasters, Egypt's belief in the traditional gods remained. In 70 BCE, a huge new temple of Horus at Djeba where Ptolemy III had performed the foundation ceremony 167 years ago was completed and celebration was planned. The crowds who gathered to celebrate the festival hoped for a future of harmony and prosperity in their hearts.

When Cleopatra was four years old, the far away Roman senators began to plan an expedition over Egypt. In 65 BCE they proposed to annex the Nile Valley as a Roman territory, which was opposed rigorously. In 59 BCE, Julius Caesar threatened again. This time Ptolemy XII paid protection money equal to half of Egypt's annual income and made an agreement as a "friend and fellow of the Roman people." When Ptolemy XII did some ridiculous thing, the people in Alexandria revolted and sent him to exile. Ptolemy XII went to see Roman magistrate for asylum at Rhodes. He was escorted to see magistrate Marcus Porcius Cato while he was on the toilet after taking a strong dose of laxative. Once upon a time Egyptian pharaoh used to grind foreigners from their underfoot; now he was standing obediently before an insignificant man while doing barbarian bowel movement.

Back in Alexandria, the throne was given to Ptolemy's wife. After her sudden death, Ptolemy's daughter Berenike occupied the throne. As per Greek's principles, ruling the country without a husband was misfortune. Therefore, the work of finding a suitable husband began. But Berenike was stubborn and bloodthirsty. Mysteriously, the first candidate died on the route; the second one was stopped at the border by Romans; the third one was choked to death because she did not like him.

Finally, Ptolemy settled a deal to secure his throne back. He borrowed a sum of ten thousand talents - equal to Egypt's complete annual income - from a banker named Rabirius. In exchange he would be reinstated to his throne by Roman governor of Syria. On April 15, 55 BCE with an army he marched towards Alexandria, repossessed his kingdom, killed his daughter Berenike, and made Rabirius as his new finance minister.

Now, Egypt has become a province of Rome. Pledging Egypt to Rome was a great humiliation to Ptolemy.

Immediately after reoccupying his throne, Ptolemy started the age-old custom of Egypt: beautifying god's temples; building a huge new temple to the goddess Hathor; and following all ancient pharaonic traditions. To secure his dynasty, Ptolemy appointed Cleopatra as his formal replacement in 52 BCE Ironically, a few days after solar eclipse in 51 BCE, which had been predicted as a bad omen, Ptolemy died On March 7, 51 BCE Cleopatra was announced as a ruler of Egypt when she was just seventeen years old.

Cleopatra

Ptolemy XII's baby daughter Cleopatra carried the burden of Egypt's hopes and expectations on her tiny shoulders. For the next forty years after her birth, Cleopatra and chief priest Pasherenptah wrote the final chapter in the long history of Egypt.

Chief Priest Pasherenptah

High priests of Ptah had a prominent place in the country from the beginning of Egyptian history. From Generation to generation, the high priests of Ptah held priesthood jobs remaining ultra-loyal to sovereignty. By the time

Cleopatra's birth in 69 BCE, chief priest Pasherenptah had earned a great reputation. He achieved priesthood at the age of fifteen; most obediently crowned Cleopatra's father, Ptolemy XII; remained one of the most trusted members in the inner circle of the royal family.

Cleopatra was regarded as divine incarnation just like her father Ptolemy had been called as god Dionysus by Greeks, and god Osiris by Egyptians. Pasherenptah did not mind to recognizing divinity in Ptolemy as recognizing the king as a god was one of the main characteristics of pharaonic religion from the beginning.

Friendship with Romans

Some records show that when Ptolemy XII went on exile, probably he took his eleven years old daughter Cleopatra with him. If she did spend her preteen years in Rome, she might have learned valuable lessons from experience.

According to her father's will, she had to share sovereignty with her elder brother Ptolemy XIII under the protection of Rome. It was a recipe for disaster. Cleopatra ruled alone for the first eighteen months, downgrading her co-regent brother. Unfortunately, a chain of natural and political disasters followed one after another and public anger turned against Cleopatra. There was an uncommon flood causing crop failure and food shortage. Cleopatra had to take emergency measures to prevent famine. Egyptian tradition was to first pacify gods and ensure the prosperity of the country. Gods had forsaken Cleopatra at an early stage. Additionally, when she deported some criminals who had murdered the sons of the Roman governor, she became more unpopular because Egyptians feared that Roman control over them was unstoppable. As a result, Egyptians turned favour towards her brother Ptolemy XIII.

Another unpleasant event occurred in Rome. When a civil war broke in Rome between two strongest military men, Pompey and Caesar, Cleopatra sided with Pompey, an ally of Gabinius, because of her national debt. Again, local people rebelled against her and she was forced into deportation in 48 BCE Instead of begging for protection, she decided to raise an army staying with her loyal province of Palestine. By the late summer, brother and sister faced each other with their armies.

Defeated in the battle, Pompey had gone to Egypt. When Caesar arrived at Alexandria, expecting his appreciation, Ptolemy XIII killed Pompey and presented his severed head to him. Caesar was so furious to see the savage treatment of a fellow Roman general. He went straight to the palace, called

Ptolemy XIII to meet him. Taking advantage of the opportunity, Cleopatra met Caesar secretly in disguise. The historical meeting between twenty-one-year-old queen and fifty-two year old Roman general took place. Her long, curved nose and pointed chin attracted Caesar; he honoured her claim to the throne of Egypt. Disgusted with disbelief, Ptolemy XIII and his army surrounded the palace, declaring her sister Arsinoe as queen. In March 47 BCE, Roman army arrived and liberated Caesar and Cleopatra from their palace prison. Aggressive fighting began and Ptolemy was drowned in the Nile River, Cleopatra was restored to the throne with her another rival brother as her co-regent. Cleopatra and Caesar celebrated their triumph.

Cleopatra Had Won. But Egypt Had Lost

Cleopatra gave birth to a boy and she named him Ptolemy Caesar. A commemorative coin was issued to celebrate the arrival of the royal baby, decorated with the double cornucopia proclaiming the abundance and promise of the Romano-Egyptian association.

A year later another birth to priest Pasherenptah and his wife Taimhotep caused equal celebration in the country. Earlier three healthy daughters were born to them. In ancient Egypt, everyone wished male heir. It was more important to the high priest of Ptah and the hereditary holder of a highest office since eleven generations. In desperation, they turned to the native god Imhotep for a son.

Cleopatra

Imhotep was an adviser to king Netjerikhet who had lived 2670 BCE and was worshipped in Egypt as a god of wisdom, magic, and medicine. Hoping god Imhotep will bless them with a son, they prayed together "to the majesty of the god great in wonders, effective in deeds, who gives a son to him who has none: Imhotep, son of Ptah." Surprisingly, the prayer was answered. Imhotep appeared in Taimhotep's dream, promising her a son if she would arrange for his shrine to be beautified. You scratch my back, and I will scratch yours! God Imhotep's wish was fulfilled and Taimhotep delivered a baby-boy in July 15, 46 BCE

For Cleopatra, her son's birth had a deeper religious significance. To celebrate 'little Caesar' birth, she dedicated a temple to the ancient mother goddess Hathor. At Luny, she built a "birth house' to celebrate the ritual of divine procreation. She promoted the cult of Isis, one of the most popular deities of Egypt. Isis was a divine mother and protector caring for her worshippers.

When Caesar returned from campaigning in 46 BCE, Cleopatra travelled to Rome as a guest and stayed in his estate across the Tiber. The relationship between Cleopatra and Caesar was subjected to gossip when Caesar dedicated a gold statue of Cleopatra in the Roman temple of Venus. He presented an application before senators asking them to allow him to marry Cleopatra. The very act of marrying outside Italy, having children with a foreign wife, created a worst fear in Romans. The assassination of Caesar put an end to the story.

Cleopatra returned home from Rome. After one month, her brother Ptolemy XIV was easily dead elevating Cleopatra as Ptolemy XV, "the father-and-mother-loving god."

Probably gods had forsaken Egypt. Since the water in the Nile River decreased, food shortage became a huge problem and people became desperate. Crushed from hunger, they stopped looking forward to the afterlife. They turned their back to 2000 years of faith and began to fear what lay beyond the grave.

On account of murder of Caesar, Egypt had lost its protector. Cleopatra had to live with killers on one side and heirs on the other side. To make matters worse, her only survivor-sister Arsinoe was focusing on a rebel to regain Ptolemaic lands.

Cleopatra once again entangled with Rome's second hero Antony. To defeat the Parthian Empire (modern Iran), Antony required a base in the eastern Mediterranean and Egypt was the perfect place. Cleopatra desperately needed a new protector. Antony invited her to meet him at Tarsus in Anatolia.

Cleopatra with her distinct skills of presentation and propaganda turned the diplomatic meeting to a religious demonstration. She arrived by a river appearing as a goddess Isis to meet divine consort, Dionysus. Enticed by fourteen years younger queen's analogy, Antony offered his support in return for her favours. Antony and Cleopatra returned to Alexandra toward the end of the year. Nine months later, Cleopatra gave birth to twins, Alexander Helios and Cleopatra Selene, the sun, and the moon.

After the twins were born, Antony left Egypt and returned to Rome and married his rival Octavian's sister Octavia sealing a deal scorning Cleopatra. She must have realized that marrying a Roman general means a life of a single mother. In the meanwhile, the chief priest died, and his seven years old son Imhotep was appointed as a high priest. The Nile River flew with full water, agricultural production increased, and Egypt's economy returned to normal.

When Octavian refused to assist him in his campaigns, Antony once again looked at Egypt. He invited Cleopatra for a meeting at Antioch. As a bribe, Antony offered the contents of the great Library of the kings of Pergamum, two hundred thousand volumes of books, papyrus, manuscripts, etc. to the Library of Alexandria, which was destroyed during Caesar's war against Pompey. He also allocated several Roman territories around eastern Mediterranean. But it was all a delusion because the eastern lands did not belong to Antony. Fake title deeds and collection of books in return was not a legitimate exchange for troops and supplies. During the eighteenth Dynasty, Egypt was considered as a mighty bull of Asia; now, it was Rome's milking cow.

In 34 BCE, Antony won the fight over Armenia and celebrated the occasion with a great pomp. Both Antony and Cleopatra appeared before the crowd on silver thrones, in the form of Isis. He announced their children would be the rulers of Rome's eastern provinces: Alexander Helios dressed in Persian attire received Armenia, Media, and Parthia; Two year Ptolemy Philadelphus received the provinces of Phoenicia, Syria, and Cilicia.

By accepting the provinces so publicly, Cleopatra risked the anger of Roman senators and citizens.

End of the Affair

A remarkable document on papyrus records Egypt's sudden decline in the tragic years of Cleopatra's rule. Egypt's royal command granted extraordinary tax privileges to Antony's right-hand man, Publius Canidius. She gave him permission to export ten thousand bags of wheat from Egypt, which was called the breadbasket of the Roman Empire. Canidius got exemptions from all taxes on his Egyptian landholdings, along with other special privileges. The document was signed by Cleopatra, in a sense she was signing her own death warrant. Julius Caesar's nephew Octavian saw Cleopatra as a number one public enemy.

Cleopatra Wanted to Send Her Son to India

Losing in the battle of Actium, Antony and Cleopatra escaped with their lives and he fled to Libya and she to Alexandria. She dressed her ships as if she had been victorious. Antony joined her a few days later. They celebrated a huge festival. Under all this show up, Cleopatra was planning a permanent exile. Intending to send her son Cesarion to India, she had her ship ready to sail from the Nile to the Red Sea. But the native Nabataean Arabs burned her boats, and she had no escape from Alexandria. Desperately she sent a note to Octavian agreeing to surrender for the sake of her children if he liberates Egypt. Octavian did not reply.

The high priest Ptah, Imhotep died at the age of sixteen either because he was weak, or someone planned to eradicate completely Ptolemaic rule. Egypt's very soul of tradition since three hundred years of priesthood in one family came to an end. Three days later Egypt was occupied by Rome. "As Octavian's forces bore down on Alexandria by land and sea, Antony led his own army and navy through the city's gates for one last battle. Antony was defeated and, as Octavian entered the city, Cleopatra fled to her fortified treasury-cum-mausoleum in the royal quarter of Alexandria. Misinformed that his lover had already taken her own life, Antony fell on his sword. At Cleopatra's anguished insistence, his weak and almost lifeless body was lifted into her apartment, where he expired at her side. She in turn was tricked into leaving the building and promptly incarcerated in the royal palace."

It is recorded that she committed suicide by a cobra hidden in the basket. "The truth about the manner of her death no one knows."

Cleopatra died. Her memory lives on. Twenty centuries later, her life grips the western world. She is still with us. Since her death, the Nile Valley has been fought over by Romans, Arabs, Christians and Muslims.

As a successor to the extraordinary ancient tradition, Cleopatra wished her dynasty to have a future. Her son Cesarion was killed by Octavian within days of Alexandria's fall. There would be no future for the Ptolemaic Dynasty or for any dynasty of pharaohs.

"Yet alongside the last, bold assertion of divine kingship, the stones of Cleopatra's monument proclaim a deeper, more enduring truth. Next to the figure of the very last Ptolemy are carved four simple hieroglyphs: a sandal strap, a snake, a loaf of bread, and a stretch of alluvial land. The quintessence of pharaonic civilization. Together they form an epithet that had been applied to kings since time immemorial: ANKH DJET — "LIVING FOREVER."

It is a fitting inscription, not just for Cleopatra but for ancient Egypt.

Addendum

The death of Cleopatra resulted in surrendering Egypt to Rome as she had feared. The noble three thousand years old pharaonic tradition ended with her demise and Egypt was considered as the personal property of Rome, free to loot its riches. Egypt's grain was transported by ships to nourish the growing population of Rome; gold from eastern deserts filled Rome's chests; huge columns and beams of stone were sculpted to decorate buildings in Roman Empire; and most precious stone of deep purple imperial porphyry stones were transported. Egypt acted a key role in Roman commerce particularly with India, which was their favourite country. Once Egypt's strategic location linked to Arabia, Asia, Africa and Europe and contributed for its prosperity. Now, the same geographical advantages enabled its suppression by foreign rule.

New Life to Suez Canal

When Napoleon Bonaparte conducted an expedition to Egypt in 1700 AD., he wanted to annex Egypt as a French colony, and to avoid British dominance in India. Even though this expedition was purely political, the outcome was the birth of Egyptology. Napoleon took 150 scholars with him along with the army. By observing scrupulously, the Egyptian history, they published a monumental work *"Description de l'Egypte"*. That was the beginning of the scientific study of pharaonic civilization.

The first Suez Canal linking the Nile River delta and the Red Sea by Darius I was ignored, and its use was abandoned by 800 CE. Almost 1000 years it was not used causing decay in its structure. Napoleon's most important learned men were the surveyors. They determined the possibility of cutting a canal between Mediterranean and Red Sea connecting the Nile River that Darius I had built. The construction of the new Suez Canal was completed in 1869.

Beside Egypt's geopolitical significance, its acute cultural influence was also exported throughout the world, first from Egypt to Roman world.

Egyptian deep religious significance provided a fertile source for the development of Christianity. Its Virgin Mary and Child Jesus remained virtually identical to Isis and Horus.

The author Toby Wilkinson concludes, "On a subconscious level, the allure of pharaonic civilization has provided irresistibility to the Romans and their successors in the West. Beginning with Hadrian villa at Tivoli and Egyptianizing frescoes of Pompei and continuing down to the present day with art deco jewellery and the Luxor hotel in Las Vegas, ancient Egypt has continued to exert a powerful influence on western art and architecture. Individuals and popular movements have appropriated pharaonic ideas in pursuit of their particular cause. Akhenaten, to take just one example, has been co-opted as a role model by Freudian psychoanalysts, Protestant fundamentalists, fascists, Afrocentrists, new age spiritualists, and gay rights campaigners. Hollywood has been especially mesmerized by ancient Egypt's blend of exoticism and antiquity, this fascination giving rise to a succession of hugely popular films, from The Ten Commandments and Cleopatra to Raiders of the Lost Ark and The Scorpion King."

In spite of Roman rule, the emergence of Christianity, the Arab invasion, and the change of circumstances in the modern world, Egypt's ancient concepts and ideals not only survived, but also prospered. The Egyptian kings and the Nile Valley created a uniquely powerful culture which was admired from Alexander the Great to Agatha Christie. Today, the civilization of the pharaohs is alive in film, literature, architecture, design, and tourism and greatly in the imagination of the people all over the world.

The ancient Egyptians could not have wished for more!

Legacy

Many civilizations throughout the world have incorporated much of the Egyptian culture, civilization, and their way of life. The importance of Egypt to the development of Christianity is very significant and notable. Egypt was one of the initial and most fertile fields for Christian conversion and establishment of Christian institutions. Orthodox Christianity was permanently fixed in Egypt in the first purifying schools, which were established in Alexandria. The New Testament in its recognized form was first compiled in Egypt.

The Coptic knowledge is one of the bases of Egyptian national consciousness. The words 'Copt' and 'Egypt' both derive from the ancient Egyptian *Hikaptah* (House of the Spirit of Ptah) through the Greek *Aigyptos*. According to Herodotus, Egyptians were the most religious people of all people in the world.

During the early centuries of Islam, the Arabs mentioned to Egypt as *Dar al-Qibt*, the Abode of the Copts. A Roman king Nero brought Christianity to Egypt and it flourished during the first century. By the time Christianity materialized into historical recognition at the end of the third century, it was a vibrant and growing force in Egypt.

In Egypt and throughout the Roman Empire the elite could find solace in the mystery religions that mushroomed during later time, the gods like Isis, Mithra, and others. The mystery religions' attraction was their claim to expose the hidden meaning that lay behind the changing appearances of life. The educated also had Neoplatonism, which flourished in Alexandria, with its mix of philosophy, mysticism, and even magic. Through magic one could gain an illusion of being in control that was stated by one Neoplatonist philosopher who announced, "I do not come to the Gods. The Gods come to me."

Another new religion occurrence, Gnosticism (100-200 CE) offered direct experience of God through knowledge (gnosis). According to the Gnostics, 'the human self was a spark from the spiritual world caught in a material body that could be transcended.'

All those happenings left their sign on Egypt, but the religious choice that took root and covered the land for several centuries was Christianity. It too offered solace during the crisis. To the suffering it offered comfort of God's love and an assurance of ultimate justice and reward in the eternal life that had always been so important to Egyptians. But Christianity's assistance were practical as well as spiritual – a sense of affiliation in a group with a strong sense of identity, a support network in times of distress, and friends who could be trusted to put on a proper funeral when the time came.

One of the reasons for Egypt's receptiveness to Christianity was the way so many of its elements resembled the ancient religion that had dominated the imaginations of the inhabitants of the Valley of the Nile for thousands of years. The most important ancient Egyptian myth of Osiris, Isis, and Horus could be taken as a metaphor of the Holy family. Isis was compared to Mary, and similarities between Isis caring for the infant Horus and the Christian image of Mother and Child were understandable. Early Christian artists displaying the Virgin Mary and the infant Jesus were copied directly from pagan pictures of Isis and Horus.

If someone spends some time in digging similarities between Egyptian civilization and all other world civilizations, they could find innumerable resemblances in their culture, politics, philosophy, religions, medicine, names, Astronomy, architecture and so on. Without a doubt, many civilizations are influenced by Egypt and have forgotten their roots and went to oblivion as Egypt was buried under the ground for thousands of years.

3

The Sumer - Ancient Mesopotamia

> *"Ours is a world in which decline, collapse and destruction always foretells some kind of rebirth; that without sweeping away the old, the new cannot be born. And that through all the ups and downs, nothing really worthwhile is ever permanently lost, even though its creators may be long forgotten. When, perhaps sooner, perhaps later, our civilization finally lies dying in the gutter, some of us will still be looking at the stars as the ancient Mesopotamians taught us to do."*
>
> **– Kabiti-Ilani-Marduk, 800 BCE**

The script known as cuneiform, wedge-shaped signs impressed by reed stylus into clay tablets, appeared first in just before 3000 BCE. That was the start. Independent Mesopotamia disappeared from history after the subjugation of Babylon by Cyrus the Great of Persia in 539 BCE. Mesopotamia's duration was 2,500 years.

Mesopotamia's continuity is remarkable. It preserved a single civilization, using one matchless system of cuneiform writing, from beginning to end and with a single, continuously evolving literary, artistic, iconographic, mathematical, scientific, and religious tradition.

Mesopotamia was also extraordinary for its creativity. During its two and a half millennia, the cuneiform-based tradition invented or discovered almost everything we connect with civilized life. It began in a world of Neolithic villages, the farming communities with self-sufficient and self-sustaining means and ending with a world, not only of cities, empires, technology, science, law, and literary wisdom, but with a world system, a linked network of nations, with communication and trade, and fighting with each other, it spread across a large part of the globe. Such was the achievement of the writers of cuneiform.

It is surprising that the guardians of this revolutionary tradition were not from one nation or one people. In the beginning at least two communities, Semitic and non-Semitic, inhabited the land; one originally from the deserts of the west and the other from the mountains of the north. To these ethnic bases there added the genetic contribution of many invaders and conquerors, such as Gutians, Kassites, Amorites and Arameans. They all assimilated to Sumerian-Akkadian language and culture and contributed with pleasure to the further advancement of their adopted way of life.

In this manner, the civilization that was born, flourished and died in the land between the two rivers, Tigris and Euphrates, was not the achievement of any particular people, but the unique combination of ideas, styles, beliefs and behaviours.

Story of Mesopotamia

Sumer was buried under the ground for 4500 years and nobody knew its existence till recently. Until 1840 CE the knowledge about the ancient Middle East was derived from the Bible, Greek and Roman authors, and from the writings of Berosus, who wrote about Babylonian culture in 240 BCE.

The entire history of Sumer (Mesopotamia) is based on Cuneiform writings from excavated tablets, clay objects, shells, and all kinds of materials available in those days; they are in the form of records, texts, documents, myths, and poems. The writing materials utilized by ancient scribes were stone and clay tablets, bricks, stones, door sockets, bowls, vases, clay nails, cones, mortars, mace-heads, steles, plaques, and statues of stone and metal. These recorded inscriptions became a prime source of political history for modern scholars.

Assyriologists Samuel Noah Kramer has devoted twenty five years of his lifetime to study and copy the unpublished Sumerian literary texts scattered throughout museums all over the world for writing his book 'The Sumerians.' All his work is available in the University Museum, University of Pennsylvania.

Sumer (Mesopotamia) was an ancient territory in the eastern Mediterranean region related to today's Iraq, Iraq-Iran borders, Kuwait, eastern Syria, and southeast Turkey. In Greek language Mesopotamia means 'between two rivers'; meso=between, potamia=rivers. The 'two rivers' referred to be the Tigris and Euphrates. Sumer was buried under the ground for 4500 years and nobody knew its existence until recently.

Archaeological Work in Iraq

First, Abbe Beauchamp, a journalist of the Academy of Science observed the ruins in Babylonia. He employed a few native workmen, made the first archaeological excavation in Mesopotamia, and published his travel memoirs in 1790 CE.

Nippur. This excavation site was one of the largest mounds in Iraq and long strenuous work was conducted between 1889 and 1900. Archaeologists have found up to 40,000 tablets inscribed clay tablets and fragments in this mound alone dating from the 3000 BCE to Persian era. The findings contain school exercises, textbooks, mathematical tables, and literary documents.

Consequently, the East India Company in London appointed its agents in Baghdad to do some archaeological searching and exploring. In 1811, Claudius James Rich undertook the project and started examining and mapping the ruins of Babylon. Nine years later, he collected many inscribed tablets, bricks, boundary stones, and cylinders. Among them were the famous Nebuchadnezzar and Sennacherib cylinders. These collections formed the basis for the huge accumulation of Mesopotamian antiquities, which are now housed in the British Museum. Rich died in 1821 at the age of 32.

Thousands of clay documents inscribed in the cuneiform script developed by Sumerians and excavated by archaeologists in the past 120 years reveal the early history of western Asia. It was a monumental effort for archaeologists to decipher those inscriptions and discover the Sumerian people's existence by using proper dating methods.

The restoration of the Assyrian, Babylonian, and Sumerian people, long buried under the abandoned mounds is a stirring and magnificent achievement of 19th century humanism and scholarship.

This extraordinary work of archaeologists and excavators and the people responsible for the recovery and restoration of this ancient and long forgotten literature is a major contribution to humanity.

Strangely, just 200 years ago nothing was known about Sumerian culture or the very existence of Sumerian people and their language. To know more about biblical history, scholars and archaeologists started excavating in Mesopotamia looking for Assyrians because the actual name of Sumer had been erased from the mind and memory for more than two thousand years. The discovery of the Sumerians and their language was quite shocking and unexpected. This book uncovers those discoveries, written on clay tablets, about their history, social structure, religious ideas, educational practices, literary creations, values, and motivations of the civilization created in ancient Sumer.

All dating information depends entirely on archaeological, stratigraphic, and epigraphic inferences, estimations and the results of carbon-14 tests.

Archaeological excavations reveal that human settlements in Mesopotamia dating back to 10,000 BCE. The study indicates that ancient hunter-gatherer people settled in the land, domesticated animals, and turned their attention to agriculture in its fertile lands.

Dating Methods Used to Determine the Age

Dr. Kramer writes about various dating methods used to determine the age of the material excavated. For example, the radiocarbon or carbon-14 method gives the rate of decay of the radioactive carbon isotope in wood, horn, plant fibre, and bone, and it allows the time that has elapsed since the end of the material is calculated. He states that even with 200 years of discrepancy, it is not a great drawback in the case of material that is 10,000 years old.

It is important to know that the following remarkable developments occurred from hunter-gatherers to cattle breeders: to settle life in one place; transition from experimental plant cultivation to the thoughtful and calculated farming of grains and pulse plants; the building of houses and the associated gods in the temples; the burial of the dead in cemeteries; the invention of clay vessels, first by hand, then by turning the wheel; and metal productions. These stages of developments did not occur in one site only.

The date from 10,000 BCE to 9,000 BCE is classified as pre-pottery. The finds included primitive mills for grinding grain, the ruins of huts about 13 feet in diameter, and cemeteries with grave goods. The existence of copper beads is an indication of familiarity with metal, and the existence of volcanic glass (obsidian) is the indication of importing non-local materials by way of trade. The bones of sheep tell the story that they were already domesticated at the site of Baghdad.

Also, they discovered some kind of wheat and two-row barley, bones of domesticated goats, sheep, pigs, volcanic glass tools, stone vessels, clay vessels with rough painted decorations, which provide the first evidence for the production of pottery.

More on Excavation Work

The adventurous archaeological expeditions involved a tremendous amount of personal risks to specialists, to staff, to modern technical equipment, and the objectives were more than the simple search for valuable antiquities. It is estimated that the development of six generations of excavators has led to recover the artefacts more accurately. Then the discoveries were observed, measured, and photographed as precisely as possible. He writes, in the beginning the digging was unsystematic, and even though huge quantities of clay tablets, large and small objects were discovered, the locations of the finds were rarely described with any accuracy. Only after the twentieth century, excavators realized to separate the individual bricks in the walls that had previously been mistakenly thought that they were mere packed clay blocks instead of tablets. Besides, the natives also developed interest in findings and archaeologists became unwelcome making their work harder.

Excavations in Mesopotamia have been national undertakings by France, England, the United States, Germany, Iraq, Denmark, Belgium, Italy, Japan, and the former Soviet Union. Italian excavations at Tall Mardîkh have produced amazing results including several thousand cuneiform tablets dating from the 2400 BCE at Ebla. 17,000 clay cuneiform tablets and wreckages are discovered virtually intact in the order in which they had been stored on their now-crumbled shelves offering a rich source of information about Ebla.

These tablets and inscriptions have supplied invaluable information on the process of domestication, the conditions of animal husbandry, and the advances in agriculture. Their studies required the cooperation of both zoologists and paleo-botanists.

The Work of Decipherment

Later, Rich was followed by Robert Ker Porter and many others, and continued his unfinished work. Thousands of documents unearthed were written in the Akkadian language. Excavators found other trilingual documents in Persepolis and decipherment was the next task. In order to decipher the inscriptions, they had to have some idea of decipherment and the nature of the information it contained. The linguists found that the writings were not like Chaldean, Hebrew, Arabic, or Greek, and described them as long and triangular, shaped like a pyramid, and the characters did not differ from each other except in their position.

Persepolis cuneiform inscriptions proved to be a fundamental aid to the decipherers. Thomas Hyde described the characters as "Cuneiform". Unfortunately, he did not realize that those signs were meant to convey significant and meaningful speech, but he thought that they were simply meant to display as decorations and ornaments. But, two scholars, Frenchman A.H. and A.I. Silvestre de Sacy, threw some light on those cuneiform inscriptions. Frenchman A.H. Anquetil-duperron spent much of his time in India collecting manuscripts of Avesta, the sacred book of Zoroastrianism, and learning the Old Persian language. He provided some idea of Old Persian language to those who were attempting to decipher Persepolis cuneiform inscriptions. A.I. Silvestre de Sacy translated a Pahlavi inscription found in Persepolis. Eventually they were able to decipher the inscription with great commitment and dedication to their work.

These explorations and excavations lead to the decipherment of the cuneiform script and the rediscovery of the Mesopotamian civilizations. Great efforts have been made by philologists to reach conclusions about the source of the blooming civilization in southern Mesopotamia by analysing Sumerian words. These efforts are cantered on the phonetic character of Sumerian language at the beginning of 2000 BCE.

Sumer is the Birthplace of Writing in Human History

The Techniques of Writing

The long duration of prehistory ended at the turn of 4000-3000 BCE, and the threshold of the historical era is captured by the presence of writing. Names, speeches, and actions are secured in a system composed of signs representing complete words or syllables. Because clay was not suitable to draw the curved lines, a style to use straight lines achieved popularity very fast. When a writer pressed the reed harder at the beginning of a stroke on a clay tablet, it made a triangular head and the wedges were impressed into the clay. It is the Sumerians who invented this scheme and were credited for the invention of the first system of writing in the Middle East during 2234-2154 BCE.

Many scholars believe that certain clay objects and tokens found in prehistoric sections may have been used for some kind of primitive accounting. They infer, "Moreover, the extension of the writing system to include the creation of syllabograms by the use of the sound of a logogram (sign representing a word), such as *gi*, "a reed stem," used to render the verb *gi*, "to return," can only be explained in terms of the Sumerian language."

It is commonly believed that writing was invented for managing trade, for long-distance communication, and for keeping more vigilant tracking of accounts.

Clay Books - Library of Ashurbanipal

Dr. Kramer writes that in 1842 CE Paul Emile Botta "struck it rich" (archeologically speaking) at Khorsabad. The Khorsabad ruins covered the palace of the mighty king Sargon II, an 800 BCE king, who ruled Assyria (it was unknown to the excavators at that time.) The place contained several acres of Assyrian sculpture, murals, and reliefs, many of them were covered with cuneiform inscriptions. In addition to the royal palace, he found the library of King Ashurbanipal, which consisted the thousands of tablets and fragments inscribed with lexical, religious, and literary works of the ancients. By the middle of 19th century, Europe had hundreds of cuneiform inscriptions crying for decipherment, which seemed to require an enormous amount of time. But, Dr. Kramer writes that Hincks, Rawlinson, and Oppert were able to accomplish the decipherment job within a decade with perseverance and genius.

1. Sumerian Cuneiform alphabets
2. God Enki instructs his mother to create man in clay: Creation Myth, 1900-1700 BC.
3. Two cylinders telling of the construction of Ninurta 2125 BC. The poem narrates that the deity Ningirsu appeared in Gudea's dream and ordered him to build a temple.
4. Excavated clay tablets from Ashurbanipal Library. 700 BCE

With the help of the Old Persian version of Behistun inscription, Edward Hinks' first significant contribution was his success in reading correctly a number of vowels, syllables, and ideograms, and first Babylonian word pronoun 'a-na-ku' = "I". The author Dr. Kramer writes:

> "However, his major discovery, the one which proved crucial for the decipherment, did not come until 1850, and was based to some extent on the insight of Botta, who, not content with excavating alone, published in 1848 a study on the cuneiform signs that was extremely detailed. Botta did not try to read a single word, although he succeeded in getting at the meaning of several ideograms; his most fruitful contribution concerned the variants. After careful study and detailed

documentation, he showed that there were quite a number of words which, though evidently identical in reading and meaning, were written in different ways. It was this minute study of variant writings which paved the way for Hinck's paper of 1850, in which at one stroke he was able to explain the seemingly incredible fact that the Babylonian script contained hundreds of signs, as well as give the reason for existence of so many variants. The Babylonian-Assyrian script, stated Hincks, was not alphabetical, but both syllabic and ideographic, that is, the signs might represent syllables (of consonant plus vowel, vowel plus consonant, or consonant plus vowel plus consonant) which were combined in various ways to make a word, or each sign might express an entire word."

Rawlinson travelled to Behistun once again in 1847 at the risk of life and limb and made paper-pressed copies of Babylonian version. During the course of this translation work, he discovered the other all-important feature of Babylonian writing "polyphony", meaning that one and the same sign could give more than one sound or value. Now, Rawlinson could read about 150 signs without problem; he knew the reading and meaning of two hundred words of the language and was able to give a grammatical outline of it. Many other scholars like W.F. Fox Talbot, Oppert did significant work under Royal Asiatic Society in deciphering the inscriptions.

Babylonian! Assyrian! Akkadian! But the word Sumer or Sumerian was not found anywhere. Sadly, until the middle of 19th century, no one knew that Sumer or Sumerian people ever existed. In 1850 Hincks expressed some doubts concerning the usual hypothesis that it was the Semitic inhabitants of Assyria and Babylonia who had invented the cuneiform system of writing. However, in the Semitic languages the constant element is the consonant, while the vowel is variable. So, it appeared unnatural to assume that the Semites invented a syllabic system of orthography in which the vowel seemed to be as constant as the consonant. 'The distinction between soft and hard palatals and dentals is a significant feature of the Semitic languages, but the cuneiform syllabary did not seem to express this distinction adequately." Thus, Hincks began to suspect that the cuneiform system of writing was invented by non-Semitic people who paved the way to the Semites in Babylonia.

Rawlinson studied this new primitive language of the inscriptions excavated at Kuyunjik and came to the conclusion after elaborate examination that they were bilingual and considered to be "Scythian or Turanian." He concluded, "It is doubtful if any close linguistic affinities are to be traced between the primitive tongue and any available dialect of modern times. The pronominal system approaches are nearer to the Mongol and Manchu type than to any other branch of the Turanian family, but there is little or no resemblance of vocabulary."

Sumer Discovered

Jules Oppert was the one who correctly discovered and named the non-Semitic people who invented the cuneiform script. His contribution to Assyriology is outstanding. On January 17, 1869, Oppert delivered a lecture before the French Society of Numismatics and Archeology declaring that these people and their language should be called Sumerian. The reason behind this conclusion was that he had discovered an inscription which contained the title "King of Sumer and Akkad." Oppert disclosed in his lecture that the analysis of the structure of the Sumerian language led him to deduce that it had familiar similarities with Turkish, Finnish, and Hungarian languages. It was a brilliant insight into the structure of a language which was non-existent only twenty years ago at the time of his speech.

The French began their first excavation between 1877 and 1900. De Sarzec conducted eleven projects and succeeded in excavating numerous statues, chiefly of Gudea, steles (The Stele of the Vultures is one of the important sites), the Gudea cylinders, and thousands of tablets.

The second main excavation was conducted by the University of Pennsylvania, the first American expedition to conduct excavation in Mesopotamia. The excavation site was chosen at Nippur, one of the largest mounds in Iraq and long strenuous work was conducted between 1889 and 1900.

The backbreaking work and handicaps were severe and discouraging. One young archaeologist died in the field and a large member of excavators suffered serious illness. In spite of impediments, the expedition achieved magnificent and incomparable results in the inscriptional field. In the Royal Library of Ashurbanipal, they found 30,000 tablets and fragments inscribed in Sumerian language, which range over more than 2000 years from third to the last centuries of 1000 BCE.

Excavation at Lagash

Another group of German expedition unearthed inscriptions in a site at Lagash consisting a large number of administrative, economic, and lexical texts from 2500 BCE (4500 years ago). The economic texts included documents pertaining to sale deeds of houses and fields indicating that private ownership existed in Sumer. The Fara lexical texts were of extraordinary importance for the history of civilization because it disclosed the existence of Sumerian schools as far back as 2500 BCE or probably even earlier. The excavators also found a number of private and public buildings and tombs, numerous vases of stone, metal, and terra cotta, and many cylinder seals.

In 1903, the University of Chicago conducted an expedition at the site of Lugalannemundu and excavated a number of archaic tablets, remains of several temples and palaces, inscriptions and a statute bearing the name Lugaldalu that dates from about 2400 BCE.

A French expedition from 1912 to 1914 unearthed several monumental buildings, ziggurats, and cemeteries and a large number of tablets. At another site they discovered hundreds of tablets and fragments inscribed with semi pictographic signs which dated back to 2800 BCE.

The History of Mesopotamia - The Cradle of Civilization

Mesopotamia was a combination of diverse culture whose true connections were only their script, their gods, and their outlook toward women. The rights of women, the importance of literacy, and the pantheon of the gods prevailed throughout the region. Mesopotamia is known as the "cradle of civilization" mainly because of the following two occurrences in Sumer, in 4000 BCE:

1. The rise of the city as we know today.
2. And the invention of writing. Although writing was developed in Egypt, China, and some in Indus Valley, it was shaped independently in Mesopotamia. Unfortunately, the art of Indus Valley writing is totally lost.

Other important developments or inventions of Mesopotamians include domestication of animals, agriculture, irrigation, common tools, the sailboats, the chariot, weaponry, warfare, wine, beer, demarcation of time into hours, minutes, seconds, and religious rites.

In 1922 AD, an archaeologist Sir Leonard Woolley discovered the oldest known wheel in an archaeological excavation site at the site of the ancient city of Ur from Mesopotamia.

Previously Iraq was called Uruk by the ancient Sumerians and Akkadians, Erech in the Bible, and later Warka by Arabs. Many hard-working excavators published their discoveries in Royal Asiatic Society and in many other journals, but Woolley described his discoveries at Ur both for the scholar and for the layman. Through his writings, royal tombs, ziggurat, and "Flood-pit" have become household words.

Most of Southwest Asia has a dry climate today and receives less than 10 inches of rain. These arid areas are concealed in desert and often experience very high temperatures. It has not always been like that. Ancient Mesopotamia was a green land where many plants flourished because of the rich soil and sporadic rain, and the rich plant life permitted many animals to live in this area. People who lived here hunted and gathered the animals and plants. Ancient Mesopotamia and the nearby area are frequently called the Fertile Crescent or the Cradle of Civilization. The Tigris and Euphrates rivers supplied fresh water for humans, plants, and animals. The word *Mesopotamia* is Greek for 'land between rivers'.

Around 8,000 BCE., when people gradually discovered that planting a seed would make a new plant to grow, it opened the door for agriculture! The reason to suspect that farming began in this place is because Southwest Asia had several types of wild grain that we still use today, like millet, barley, etc. The slow process of taking a plant from the wild and turning it into a farm crop is called **domestication**. Mesopotamian people used this technique and domesticated sheep, goats, cows, donkey, oxen, and pigs also.

Where Was Sumer And Who Were the Sumerians?

The land of Sumer was somewhat identical to modern day Iraq from the north of Baghdad to the Persian Gulf. Later it was known as Babylonia and eventually it became a lower part of Mesopotamia with an area of approximately 10,000 square miles. Its climate is very hot and dry; the land is flat and river-made, devoid of minerals and stones, and only reeds grow but no trees for timber. It all appears to be destined to extreme poverty and misery. But the people that inhabited it around 3000 BCE had remarkably creative intellect, adventurous and stubborn spirit. Historians claim that despite all that disadvantages, they transformed Sumer into a real paradise and developed the first high civilization in the history of humankind.

The inhabitants of Sumer had a rare talent for technological inventions: their idea of irrigation enabled them to collect and channel the rich silt-laden flood waters of the Tigris and Euphrates rivers to water their fields and gardens; for substituting minerals and stones, they learnt to bake the river mud and clay to make pots, plates, jars, and sickles; to make up the scarcity of timber for buildings, they cut swamp reeds, dried and tied them into bundles or interweaved them to make mats; and using mud-plastering designed them to build huts and cowsheds. Later, the Sumerians invented the brick moulds baking the abundant river clay thereby ending the building material problem. In addition, they also developed useful tools, skills, and techniques such as the potter's wheel, the wagon wheel, the plow, sailboat, arch, vault, dome, casting in copper and bronze, riveting, brazing and soldering, sculpture in stone, engraving, and inlay. Most importantly, they originated a system of writing on clay, which was used two thousand years all over the Near East.

Early Thoughts: Psychological vs Material

The Sumerians were also extraordinary for their ideas and values apart from their material progress and technological ingenuity. They were clear-sighted, level-headed and viewed life practically within the limits of their intellectual resources. They seldom confused fact with imagination, wish with accomplishment, or spiritual with bewilderment. Gradually, Sumerian sages developed a faith, and recognized and accepted the unavoidable earthly limitations, particularly helplessness before death and divine anger. On the material side, they gave importance to wealth and possession, rich harvest, well-stocked granaries, warehouses, bursting stalls of cattle, successful hunting, and good fishing. Spiritually and psychologically, they favored ambition and success, reputation, prestige, honor and recognition. They were fully aware of personal rights, and protested any violation whether by their king, or their superior, or their equals. It is not strange that Sumerians were the first to compose laws and codes to lay everything in black and white to avoid misunderstanding, misrepresentation, and uncertainty.

Although Sumer was very prosperous in grains, it lacked metals, stones, minerals, and timber. In order to obtain these essential commodities, it had to get them through trade or military force. Therefore, by 3000 BCE Sumer extended its culture and civilization to Mediterranean in the west, Ethiopia in the south, and Caspian in the north, and as far as India in the east.

It all occurred 5000 years ago, and it seems completely unrelated to the modern-day people. In reality, it does relate to modern day civilization and its culture. It is possible to find a prototype of ancient Sumer irrespective of whether he is a philosopher, poet, architect, sculptor, historian, lawyer, politician, or teacher. Undoubtedly, it is not possible to trace back the origin of the modern offshoot because the cultural diffusions are many, intricate, and complex. Even so, it is still obvious in the world literatures like the Mosaic Law (Law of Moses), in the Solomonic proverb (related to King Solomon), in the tears of Job (a biblical story of Job), in the Hesiodic cosmology (Hesiod was 800 BCE Greek poet), in Hindu myths, in an Aesopic fable (Aesopica is a collection of fables attributed to Aesop, a slave and storyteller who lived in ancient Greece between 620 and 564

BCE), in Euclidean theorem, in a zodiacal sign and a heraldic design, in the weight of a mina, the degree of an angle, the writing of a number. It appears all ancient literatures have the Sumer origin.

City

Eventually, when more people moved into these areas, villages and small towns began to appear. Researchers estimate that the world's first cities may have developed as early as 10,000 BCE in Damascus or Jericho. However, these individual cities do not qualify as a civilization because in order to be called a civilization, it needs to develop several cities and a common culture among all of the cities.

Some may argue that the city would have come into being even Sumer never existed. It may be true, or it may not be true because in Egypt - which also had a great ancient past - the city-state concept never originated there. And the same might have happened in other parts of the ancient world also.

A Short Timeline of Sumer/Mesopotamia

Pottery Neolithic Age: (7,000 BCE.) In this period extensive use of tools, clay pots, and an exclusive culture began to emerge in Mesopotamia, also called Fertile Crescent.

Copper Age: (5900 – 3200 BCE) Also known as The Chalcolithic Period. In this period several things happened: the transition from stone tools and weapons to copper made tools and weapons; the rise of cities, particularly in the regions of Sumerian cities. The cities Eridu, Uruk, Ur, Kish, Nuzi, Lagash, Nippur, Ngirsu, Elam, and Susa flourished. The earliest city is generally mentioned as Uruk (Iraq). Other occurrences in this period were the invention of the wheel (3500 BCE) and writing (3000 BCE) both by the Sumerians; the establishment of kingship to replace priestly rule; the first war in the world is recorded between the kingdoms of Sumer and Elam (3,200 BCE); the improved prosperity in the region gave rise to decorate temples and statuary; development of sophisticated pottery and figurines, toys for children; and the use of personal seals to signify ownership of property or sign for an individual's signature.

Early Bronze Age: (3,000 – 2119 BCE.) During this period, bronze displaced copper as the material from which tools and weapons were made. The appearance of the city-state set the foundation for economic and political stability which enabled the rise of the Akkadian Empire (2350 BCE). The Akkadian Empire of Sargon was the first multinational kingdom in the world, and Sargon's daughter, Enheduanna, was the first author of literary works known by name. The library at Mari contained over **20,000 cuneiform tablets (books)** and the palace was considered one of the finest in the territory.

Middle Bronze Age: (2119-1700 BCE) During this period, the development of the Assyrian Kingdom and the rise of the Babylonian Dynasty created an atmosphere favorable to trade as well as increased warfare. Hammurabi, King of Babylon (1792-1750 BCE), rose anonymously to conquer the kingdom and ruled for 43 years. His famous Code of Laws inscribed on the stone columns was one of his many accomplishments. Babylon became a leading center at this time for intellectual pursuit and high accomplishment in arts and literature. This cultural center was destroyed and looted by the Hittites.

Late Bronze Age: (1700-1100 BCE.) During this time the Kassite Dynasty from modern-day Iran conquered Babylon and expanded the culture and learning activities. Gradually Babylonian culture declined until Kassites were defeated by the Elamites. After the Aramaeans defeated Elamites, the Assyrian Empire was established and prospered under the rule of Ashurnasirpal II. Most Mesopotamian states were either destroyed or destabilized around 1200 BCE, heading to a brief dark age.

Iron Age: (1000 – 500 BCE.) After Bronze Age, the discovery of how to mine ore and make use of iron was learned and the Kassites and the Hittites used this technology in warfare. During this period the Babylonian King Nebuchadnezzar II destroyed Jerusalem and in 588 BCE he forced the people of Israel into Exile. He undertook many construction projects in Babylon, built famous buildings like the Ishtar Gate and the Great Ziggurat (Tower of Babel.) In 539 BCE, Cyrus II of Persia conquered and destroyed Babylonian culture in 539 BCE.

Classical Antiquity: (500 BCE – 700 AD). When Cyrus II conquered Babylon, the major portion of Mesopotamia became part of the Persian Empire. During this period Mesopotamian culture declined rapidly and the use of cuneiform script stopped. Again, the campaigns by Alexander the Great in 331 BCE ended Persian rule in this region. Hellenistic culture and religion spread in the region even though Alexander tried to restore Babylon's past glory. After Alexander's death, his general Seleucus took control of the region and founded the Seleucid Dynasty. They ruled Babylon until the land was conquered by the Parthians dominated by the Sassanians of Persian descent.

Bertman writes, "Under Sassanian domination, Mesopotamia lay in ruins, its fields dried out or turned into a swampy morass, its once great cities made ghost towns". By the time of Roman conquest in 116 AD., Mesopotamia lacked unity and had forgotten their old gods and the old ways. The Romans developed the infrastructure for their settlements drastically through the introduction of better roads and plumbing and imposed Roman Law to the land.

Muslim (From 651 **AD).** Sadly, the complete culture of Mesopotamia was brushed away when Muslim Arabs conquered the region in 700 CE resulting in imposition of Islamic law, language, religion, and culture. Bertman notes, "With the Islamic conquest of 651 CE the history of ancient Mesopotamia ends. Today the great cities that once rose along the Tigris and Euphrates rivers are largely unexcavated mounds or broken bricks on arid plains, and the once fertile crescent has steadily dwindled to a wasteland due to human factors (such as overuse of the land through agricultural pursuits or urban development) and to climate change."

The Emergence of Cultures (4000 BCE)

The first evidence for water transportation, a 4000 BCE model boat from the prehistoric cemetery has been discovered at Eridu, the south of Mesopotamia. Other developments of terra-cottas were impressive signs of progress.

The city of Eridu was the centre of the cult of the Sumerian god Enki. Initially a small, single-room altar, consisting of a rectangular building measuring 80 by 40 feet stood on an artificial terrace. It contained an offering table and a facade decorated with cupboards. Historians assume the temple on the terrace was probably designed to protect the building from flooding. But this type of religious structures was common in later Babylonia.

In order to extract information about life during 6000 BCE before the invention of writing, historians and archaeologists investigated four major sources like pottery, treatment of the dead, sculpture, and the designs on seals.

History

It was a disturbing phase for historians to reconstruct the history of Sumerians on the basis of weak, intangible, meagre, and partial character of the relevant source material. From the time of the Sumerians first settlements in Sumer from 4500 BCE and to 1750 BCE was a long period of 3000 years. They faced a very intricate question like how to get historical information and how trustworthy they are. The Sumerians themselves never wrote their history in a sensible manner. Their academicians and literates possessed no intellectual tools to explain historical assessment and to interpret events. Their world view was limited by obvious and noticeable truth. They believed that everything appeared as readymade, full-grown and full-blown gifts from god. Even their sages and philosophers never thought that their own territory of Sumer was once a deserted marshland and only by many generations' struggle and toil it became a bustling, thriving, complex community, and 'it was a human will and determination, man-laid plans and experiments, and man-made discoveries and inventions played a predominant role.'

Sumerians recorded the incidents not for their own sake, but for their kings and rulers of city-states, known as ensi's so that they could possess prosperity and long life for themselves by building, repairing and furnishing the temples of gods. Before the invention of writing, these royal building activities were not recorded in any way. After the cuneiform system of writing developed, it might have occurred to some temple priests to record all king's activities and rituals in writing. Historians suggest that this practice might have started in the second quarter of 3000 BCE laying a magnificent foundation for written history. 'The writing material utilized by our ancient historians was quite varied and diversified: stone and clay tablets, bricks, stones, and door sockets, bowls and vases, clay nails and cones, mortars and mace-heads, steles and plaques, statues and statuettes of stone and metal.' These recorded inscriptions became a prime source of political history for modern scholars.

Because the transactions and communications recorded in these documents needed a fixed time for practical purposes, the more inventive scribes started to plan a dating method as early as 2500 BCE. They did not name the years and months just by imagination, but they named them by outstanding religious and political events and listed all the year names and the reigns of their current rulers. This method helped modern scholars to estimate and identify the historical information of the primary value and to arrange the events in proper chronological order. King List is the most important document for their research.

Subarians

Later investigations reveal that long ago the Sumer was above the water and people lived long before Sumerians. But the name of these pre-Sumerian settlers of Sumer is unknown. They lived long before writing was invented and left no revealing records. There is some doubt that they were called Subarians in 3000 BCE. But they were the most important civilizing force behind ancient Sumer, its first farmers, cultivators, cattle raisers, and fishermen; its first weavers, leather-workers, carpenters, smiths, potters, and masons. This theory is based on linguistic analysis that provided the proof. According to the keenest mind scholar Benno Landsberger, a number of Sumerian words, which generally assumed to be Sumerian were not really Sumerian. He identified the words that consisted of two or more syllables (In Sumerian, the majority of roots are monosyllabic) and showed the same pattern as the words for Tigris, Euphrates, and the non-Sumerian city names. He concluded that they must belong to the language spoken by the pre-Sumerian people.

The first Sumerians might have arrived at Sumer probably in the second half of 4000 BCE and from where they came and where their first home was is not known.

Royal Correspondence

Another important historical evidence and source is "royal correspondence"; the letters (on clay tablets) exchanged between contemporary rulers and their administrators. The first letter is dated back to 2500 BCE and also many groups of letters have recovered with special historical significance. These letters display the motives, temptations, rivalries, and conspiracies which took place behind the scenes.

A straightforward, inventory-like document "Tummal inscription" is a unique compilation related to the restoration of the Tummal, the temple of the goddess Ninlil in Nippur and several parts of the building of Enlil temple. Another historiographic epic tale, "Gilgamesh and Agga of Kish" has a very special significance for the history of political organizations. It not only illustrates the murky period in which Sumerian people struggled with city-state conflicts, but also records the first known arrangement of political assembly to discuss and decide on the excruciating question of 'war or peace'; that is 4500 years ago!

Probably Sumer was first settled sometime between 4500 and 4000 BCE according to Near Eastern archaeologists. Noah Kramer writes, "... accumulation of all the earlier cultural remains down to virgin soil, that is, right down to the beginning of human habitation in Sumer. At that time, it was generally assumed, Sumer was a vast swampy marsh broken up here and there by low islands of alluvial land built up by the gradual deposit of silt carried by the Tigris, Euphrates, and Karun rivers. Before that, most of Sumer was presumably covered by the waters of the Persian Gulf, which extended much farther than they do today, and human habitation was therefore impossible." All this was accepted theory in archaeological circles until 1952.

The first ruler of Sumer is a king by the name Etana of Kish who ruled Sumer in 3000 BCE. According to recorded documents, he stabilized all lands, his reign represented a trustworthy tradition, his rule extended to distant parts of the land, and he was the first known empire-builder. Etana was a pious, god-fearing king, but he was childless to carry his name. His strong passion was to obtain "the plant of birth", which was found in heaven far from mortal reach. The legend says, 'In order to get to heaven, Etana got help from an eagle whom he had saved from a pit where it had been cast by a serpent whose friendship it had betrayed. This legend was very popular among the seal-cutters… a number of seals depicting a mortal climbing heavenward on the wings of an eagle.' All these legends tell that Etana was a powerful and impressive person whose life and deeds had occupied the imagination of the ancient writers and poets.

According to the King List, Etana was followed by seven rulers. Surprisingly, several of them were Semites rather than Sumerians. Some of the important king names are Enmebaraggesi, Meskiaggasher, Enmerkar, Lugalbanda, Dumuzi, Gilgamesh, Mesannepadda, Meskiagunna.

Some Prominent Kings of Sumer

Gilgamesh - Probably he existed between 2800 and 2500 BC

Gilgamesh was a popular ruler and was a supreme hero in Sumerian myth and legend. Gilgamesh and his adventures were praised, written and rewritten not only in Sumer, but in many other parts of western Asia. Gilgamesh was adventurous, brave, but he was a tragic figure symbolizing man's arrogance and endless drive for fame, glory, and immortality. His story is so enormous that modern scholars assume that he was a legendary figure rather than a real man and ruler. There are no contemporary records found about Gilgamesh, but historians say, 'there is some hope that the excavation now being conducted in Erech may uncover some information sooner or later.' In 1955, some light came in ten lines from a Tummal inscription about Gilgamesh. According to King List, Enmebaraggesi and his son Agga were contemporaries of Gilgamesh, the fifth ruler of Erech. Both parties carried a bitter fight for sovereignty over Sumer.

Tummal Inscription

Tummal is the name of a district in Nippur dedicated to goddess Ninlil. Two tablets of Tummal inscription text goes as follows (first 10 lines are missing):

11 For a second time, the Tummal fell into ruin,

12 Gilgamesh built the Numunburra of House of Enlil

13 Ur-lugal, the son of Gilgamesh
14 Made the Tummal pre-eminent,
15 Brought Ninlil to the Tummal.
16 For the third time, the Tummal fell into ruin,
17 Nanna built the "Lofty Park" of the House of Enlil.
18 Meskia-Nanna, the son of Nanna,
19 Made the Tummal pre-eminent,
20 Brought Ninlil to the Tummal.
21 For the fourth time, the Tummal fell into ruin,
22 Ur-Nammu built the Ekur.
23 Shulgi, the son of Ur-Nammu,
24 Made the Tummal pre-eminent,
25 Brought Ninlil to the Tummal.
26 For the fifth time, the Tummal fell into ruin,
27 From the year of Amar-Sin
28 Until (the year when) Ibbi-Sin, the kind,
29 Enamgalanna as the en of Inanna of Erech
30 Selected,
31 Ninlil was brought to the Tummal,
32 According to the word of Lu-Inanna, the Ashgab-gal of Enlil,
33 Ishbi-Erra built the kurraigigalla,
34 The storehouse of Enlil

First Historical Personalities

According to some authentic inscriptions, Enmebaragesi (2500 BCE), king of Kish, was the oldest Mesopotamian ruler. Two vase fragments inscribed with his name were found at Nippur and it is said that he built the first temple. A Sumerian poem, "Gilgamesh and Agga of Kish," describes the control of Uruk by Agga, son of Enmebaragesi.

Lugalannemundu

From the excavated inscriptions, it appears that Lugalannemundu was one of the powerful and dynamic rulers of Sumer as far back as 2600 BCE. The documents describe him as a "king of the four quarters, a ruler who made all the foreign lands pay regular tribute to him, who brought peace to the peoples of all the lands, who built the temples of all the great gods, who restored Sumer, and who exercised kingship over the entire world." (Known world at that point of time.)

The main part of the document describes a temple building of Enamzu, dedicated to the main deity mother-goddess Nintu; the temple had a Lofty Gate, Great Gate, Gate of divine decrees, Lofty Door, Door of Refreshing Shade, and so on. And then it continues to explain the sacrifices offered to goddess; "seven times seven" fatted oxen and fatted sheep; and high officials or sukkalmahs from Cedar Mountain land Elam, Marhashi, Gutium, Subir, Martu, Sutium, and Eanna (the old name for the kingdom of Erech (Iraq)) came with sacrifices and participated in the celebration in the Adab temple. This extraordinary inscription ends with a prayer to goddess Nintu to bestow long life to the inhabitants of these seven lands if they bring offerings and sacrifices to the Enamzu of Adab.

Mesilim

Around 2500 BCE, there was another Sumerian ruler Mesilim, who took the title of King of Kish and ruled the entire land. Several inscribed objects reveal that he was a great negotiator in a bitter boundary dispute between the kingdoms of Lagash and Umma.

Ur-Nanshe

In 2450 BCE Ur-Nanshe came to power and left some fifty inscriptions on tablets, plaques, door sockets, bricks and nails, which record mainly the building of temples, digging canals, and fashioning of divine statues. An inscription is translated as "The ships of Dilmun brought him (Ur-Nanshe) wood as a tribute from foreign lands," which suggests that he had control over a number of foreign lands beyond the Persian Gulf.

Eannatum

Ur-Nanshe's grandson Eannatum succeeded on the throne of Lagash and his military conquests made him the most powerful king of his day.

Enshakushanna

Later the land of Kish became weaker and Enshakushanna declared himself as "en of Sumer" and "King of the land"

Entemena

Entemena was the last ruler of ensi's of the Ur-Nanshe dynasty. A large number of administrative documents have been found and one letter addressed to Enetarzi by Luenna, the sanga (temple head) of Ninmar, reporting the defeat of a band of six hundred Elamites who attacked Lagash.

A sample letter from Luenna to Enetarzi:

"To Enetarzi, the sanga of Ningirsu, say: This is what Luenna, the sanga of (the goddess) Ninmar, says —

> Luenna, the sanga, fought with 600 Elamites who were carrying off booty (literally, "removable goods") from Lagash to Elam. He defeated the Elamites and took 540 Elamites prisoner. Ur-Bau, the man in charge of shubur (?) slaves, and Niglunutum, the ugula of the smiths, were among them, and they are in the Eninmar. He, Luenna recovered from them 5 vessels of pure silver, 20..., 5 royal garments, and 15 hides of food sheep (that is, sheep raised to be eaten rather than sheared for wood).
>
> As long as .. the ensi of Lagash liver and as long as Enannatum-sipad-zi, the agrig, lives, their... shall be brought to Ninmar."

Sargon the Great (2340 – 2284 BCE)

Akkadian from 2334 BCE.

The driving force of the Mesopotamian Empire was the Akkadians of the city called Akkad. Southern Mesopotamia was known as the land of Sumer, and Akkad is where the arts excelled to new heights. The names of several Akkadian scribes are found in the archives near Nippur in central Babylonia. In 2334 BCE the Akkadian leader Sargon conquered the Sumerians, creating the world's first empire. The empire last about two centuries and then crumbled into multiple smaller states. In the midst of hostility, the Akkadians admired and copied Sumerian culture and incorporated it with their native traditions.

Sargon's reign 2350 BCE

According to the Sumerian king list, the first five rulers of Akkad Sargon, Rimush, Manishtusu, Naram-Sin, and Shar-kali-sharri ruled for 142 years. According to the records, Sargon alone ruled for 56 years.

According to a fable, Sargon was a self-made man with ordinary background and presumed to be a son of a gardener. It is said that he was found as a baby floating in a basket on the river and the rumors were that his mother was a priestess. Rising without any help from significant relatives, he became a cupbearer to the ruler of the city of Kish, in Sumer. Slowly, he snatched the kingdom from Lugalzaggisi of Uruk. In that way, Sargon became king over all of southern Mesopotamia, the first great ruler of the Semitic tongue known as Akkadian. Sargon named himself Sharru-kin ("Rightful King")

Sargon gradually conquered the Sumerian cities - Kish, Uruk, and Ur and founded a capital city at Akkad. He then assumed a new title, 'King of the Nation'.

Another story about Sargon was that earlier Lugalzaggisi was an ambitious and military-minded ensi from Umma who occupied the throne by killing the king of Uruk mischievously. He burned, looted, and destroyed virtually all holy places of Lagash. Sargon made a surprise attack on the capital Erech, destroyed its walls and fought a fierce battle against Erech defenders. Lugalzaggesi was far away on a campaign at the time of attack and when he returned, he was defeated by Sargon. He brought Lugalzaggesi in chains and neck rock to the gates of Nippur. Eventually, Sargon conquered all the lands, washed his weapons at the shores of the Persian Gulf, and observed a ritual ceremony commemorating his victories.

He was a good negotiator too. Several merchants from an Anatolian city requested him to intervene in a local quarrel. According to one folktale, Sargon with a group of soldiers made a powerful journey to the unidentified city of Burushanda (Purshahanda) to settle the dispute.

During Sargon's rule Akkadian language was customized to the script to the Sumerian language, and the new spirit of calligraphy (In Greek kallos=beauty and *graphein*= to write) is visible on the clay tablets and also seen on contemporary cylinder seals. Also, there are tablets with beautifully arranged and executed scenes of mythology and festive life. It indicates that in Sargon's new capital, military and economic values alone were not important, but also the art and writing.

In the end, his conflicting actions caused rebels in the empire. The scholars believe that even though Sargon was an energetic ruler, the troubles might have been caused by the inability of one man to control that vast empire without a developed and well-trained administration. It is said that there is no evidence to conclude that Sargon was very harsh, nor that the Sumerians disliked him for being a Semite. The empire did not collapse completely because Sargon's successors were able to control their heritage. Subsequent generations honoured him as being the greatest name in their history.

Sargon's is the first Semitic dynasty in the history in which his civil servants used a script which is an important innovation in the history of writing. The cuneiform tablets discovered in Ebla prove the fact. One Italian team excavated a place called Tell Markikh in Syria and uncovered a pile of cuneiform tablets which belonged to Ebla's ruler of 2500 BCE. The first cuneiform tablets turn out to be part of a library amounting to some **15,000 items**. The evidence reveals that they were once arranged by subject on wooden shelves.

Some inscriptions describe Sargon waged war against the Sumerian cities of southern Babylonia, tore down city walls, took prisoners, and cleansed his weapons in the sea.

Sargon was one of the most remarkable rulers in the ancient Near East. He was a military leader of intelligence and an imaginative administrator and builder with a sense of the historic significance of his actions and achievements. 'His influence made itself felt in one way or other all over the ancient world from Egypt to India.' Hundreds of years later, Sargon became a legendary person on whom the writers and poets composed epics and marvellous stories - however based on the grain of truth. The author Kramer writes:

> "Fortunately, in the case of Sargon we have no need to go to these later chronicles and tales for our historical facts, since we have his own inscriptions recording his more important military conquests and achievements; for Sargon, as well as his two sons, Rimush and Manishtushu, who succeeded him, commemorated their victories by erecting in Enlil's temple at Nippur, inscribed statues of themselves, and also steles depicting themselves and their prostrated enemies."

He continues:

> "An anonymous scholar and researcher copied all the inscriptions on the statues and steles with the care and fidelity that would do honour to any modern archaeologist and epigrapher, even noting whether the copies of inscriptions came from the statue itself or from the pedestal with such phrases as '(this is) the inscription of the statue,' or' (this is) the inscription on the pedestal' or 'the pedestal is uninscribed." Just why he prepared these copies is altogether unknown; perhaps the temple and its monuments were in danger of being destroyed, and his purpose was to save them for posterity. If so, he succeeded almost better than he could possibly have anticipated; for his precious tablet was recovered almost in its entirety by the old Nippur expedition, and its contents have been made available to posterity by the two scholars Arno Poebel and Leon Legrain."

Sargon's conquests continued to reach far and wide; scholars assume that he may even have sent his armies to Egypt, Ethiopia, and India. To control his vast empire, he placed military battalions at various key colonies. He boasts, "5400 men ate bread daily before him." He built a city of Agada, where he had begun his job as a cupbearer. Within a short time, Agada became a famous city in the ancient world.

Sargon attributed his success to goddess Ishtar (goddess of war) establishing the city Agade. Later Mesopotamians considered Sargon as the founder of the military tradition that exists in history.

After Sargon, his son Rimush became the king and saw his kingdom fall apart by revolts and rebellions. He ruled only nine years and his twin brother Manishtushu came to power. Like his father, Manishtushu was a successful ruler. Manishtushu reigned fifteen years and was followed by his son Naram-Sin.

Enmeduranki

Sargon assigned one of his daughters as priestess of the moon-god in Ur. Her name was Enheduanna, a very gifted woman. Two Sumerian hymns composed by her have been preserved, and she is also credited to have collected songs dedicated to the temples of Babylonia. Sargon died at a very old age. The inscriptions preserved by his son Rimush are full of reports about battles fought in Sumer and Iran.

The original inscriptions and tablets that have been found are spread across the sites covering a distance of nearly 620 miles trailing the Tigris River. Even though it was not a part of Sargon's empire, it represents an impressive scope of his influence.

Naram-Sin (2564-2218 BCE) King of the Four Quarters

After the first kings of the dynasty had assumed the title as King of Kish, Manishtushu's son Naram-Sin assumed the title "King of the Four Quarters of the Earth". He also had his name written as "god" in cuneiform sign as if he were a divine entity. Moreover, he assumed another title as "god of Akkad." The king saw himself as the protector of the city and supporter of its safety and happiness. Documents from Girsu consist Akkadian dating methods like "in the year in which Naram-Sin laid the foundations of the Enlil temple at Nippur and of the Inanna temple at Zabalam." As verified by the dating procedures that was customary in Ur III, and in the Old Babylonian period, the use of such tradition suggests that the respective city identifies its ruler whose name it invokes.

Naram-Sin elevated the power and glory of Agade again only to see its end in tragedy: he subjugated a powerful alliance of disloyal kings of Sumer and surrounding lands; conquered other new territories as far as Mediterranean sea, and the Taurus and Amanus ranges; extended his authority into Armenia and installed his statue of victory near Dierbakir; converted Elam into a dependent-state and constructed number of buildings in Susa; and defeated renowned king Manium, Menes of Egypt and brought booty from Magan. No wonder he was powerful enough to call himself "king of the four quarters" and arrogant enough to deify himself as "the god of Agade."

Later, a disastrous calamity devastated Naram-Sin and the city of Agade. The Gutians, the ruthless barbaric crowd from the mountains of the east attacked the city of Agade. This story is written in a historiographic poem "The Curse of Agade: The Ekur Avenged." It was composed by a Sumerian poet living several centuries after the Gutian catastrophe when Agade had abandoned to ruin and desolation. According to this author of the poem,

> "Naram-Sin had sacked Nippur and committed all sorts of desecrating and defiling acts against Enlil's sanctuary, and Enlil had therefore turned to the Gutians and brought them down from their mountain abode to destroy Agade and avenge his beloved temple. Moreover, eight of the more important deities of the Sumerian pantheon, in order to soothe the spirit of their ruler Enlil, laid a curse upon Agade that it should remain forever desolate and uninhabited."

The ancient Sumerian historiographer writes his poem about Agade's rise, ruin and desolation that consumed it after its fall:

> "After, with following forehead, Enlil had put the people of Kish to death like the Bull of Heaven, and like a softy ox had crushed the house of Erech into dust; after, in due time, Enlil had given to Sargon, the king of Agade, the lordship and kingship from the lands above to the lands below. The city of Agade became prosperous and powerful under the tender and constant guidance of its tutelary deity, Inanna. Its buildings were filled with gold, silver, copper, tin, and lapis lazuli; its old men and women gave wise counsel; its young children were full of joy; music and song resounded everywhere; all the surrounding lands lived in peace and security. Naram-Sin, moreover, made its shrines glorious and raised its walls mountain-high while its gates remained open. To it came the nomadic Martu, the people who "know not grain" from the west, bringing choice oxen and sheep; to it came Meluhhaites, 'The people of the black land,' bringing their exotic wares; to it came the Elamite and Subarian from the east and north carrying loads like 'load-carrying asses'; to it came all the princes, chieftains, and sheiks of the plain bringing gifts monthly and on the New Year."
>
> Then came the calamity,
>
> "The gates of Agade, how they lay prostrate; .... The holy Inanna leaves untouched their gifts; the Ulmash (Inanna's temple) is fear-ridden since

she has gone from the city, left it; like a maid who forsakes her chamber, the holy Inanna has forsaken her Agade shrine; like a warrior with raised weapons she attacked the city in fierce battle, made it turn its breast to the enemy… in a short time…in not five days, not ten days, lordship and kingship departed from Agade; the gods turned against her, and Agade lay desolate; Naram-Sin sulked by himself, dressed in sackcloth; his chariots and boats lay unused and neglected."

How did it all happen? Ancient Sumerian author's version is that Naram-Sin, during first seven years in which his rule was securely established, had acted opposite to Enlil's word: he had allowed his soldiers to attack and destroy the Ekur and its orchards; he had thrashed the buildings of the Ekur with copper axes and hatchets, so that the houses stay like a dead youths. Furthermore, at the gate called 'Gate of No Grain-Cutting,' he cut grain; 'the Gate of Peace' he demolished with pickax'; he dishonoured the holy vessels and cut down the Ekur's groves; he grated its gold, silver, and copper vessels into dust; and he carried all the possessions of destroyed Nippur on boats and carried them to Agade.

After all these evil events, god Enlil lifted his eyes to the mountains and brought down the Gutians, "a people which brooks no controls; it covered the earth like the locust so that it could escape its power. Communication was impossible in Sumer whether by land or sea. The herald could not proceed on his journey; the sea-rider could not sail his boat… ; brigands dwelt on the roads; the doors of gates of the land turned to clay; all the surrounding lands were planning evil in their city walls."

Devoured with misery, want, death, and desolation, eight of the more important deities of the Sumerian pantheon - Sin, Enki, Inanna, Ninurta Ishkur, Utu, Nusku, and Nidaba - decided to calm the anger of Enlil. Hence, these eight deities 'turn their faces to the city and cursed for the destruction of Agade': (This is a translation of a composition by a Sumerian poet who lived several centuries after the Gutian catastrophe, the inscription found in excavation site was of approximately 2100 BCE.)

"City, you who dared assault the Ekur, who [defied] Enlil,
Agade, you who dared assault the Ekur, who [defied] Enlil,
May your groves be heaped up like dust …
May your clay (bricks) return to their abyss,
May your trees return to their forests,
May they become trees cursed by Ninildu.

.

.

Agade, instead of your sweet-flowing water, may bitter water flow,
Who says "I would dwell in that city" will not find a good Dwelling place,
Who says "I would lie down in Agade" will not find a good Sleeping place.

The curse really affected Agade and the eight dieties curse came true
Agade, instead of its sweet-flowing water, there flowed bitter water,
Who said "I would dwell in that city" found not a good dwelling place,
Who said "I would lie down in Agade" found not a good sleeping place.

Shulgi (2029 BCE – 1982 BCE)

Another famous emperor, Shulgi was a son of Ur of the Third Dynasty in Sumer. He ruled 48 years relatively in peace and prosperity. He extended his rule over Elam and Anshan to the east and also he dominated over nomadic peoples of the Zagros ranges. He also held a title "king of the four quarters" and had himself deified in his lifetime. His queen Abisimti was an energetic and active Semitic lady who survived Shulgi and continued as a (dowager queen) Queen Mother under Shulgi's three successors. Shulgi was followed by his son Amar-Sin who ruled only nine years.

Hammurabi (1792-1750 BCE)

Hammurabi, King of Babylon rose from somewhat anonymously to conquer the kingdom and ruled for 43 years. His famous Code of Laws inscribed on the stone columns was one of hi s many accomplishments. He attacked and defeated Rim-Sin of Larsa, Elam, Mari and Eshnunna and became the ruler of a United Kingdom extending from Persian Gulf to the Khabur River. With Hammurabi the history of Sumer ends and the history of Babylonia, a Semitic state built on a Sumerian foundation begins.

Other Rulers

Urukagina was renowned not for his military rule, but for his ethical aspects. He was the first pacifist who recommended social and ethical reforms, the earliest in the recorded history of humankind. Unfortunately, his reign was very brief.

The Sumerian City

The most important development in 4000 BCE was the beginning of the city. The concept of city started as a center for smaller settlements, consisting several temples with major deities, with extensive granaries, possessing an advanced stage of specialization in the crafts.

The earliest cities of southern Mesopotamia are Eridu, Uruk, Bad-tibira, Nippur, and Kish. The strong evidence of urbanization is found at Uruk (Iraq), with great increase in the size of the buildings. Uruk had rectangular buildings encompassing areas 275 x 175 feet. These buildings are illustrated as temples, and assembly halls for non-religious purposes also.

In Uruk they have excavated several masterpieces of sculpture, seal engravings, and wall decorations known as cone mosaics, bevelled-rim bowl, grey or red polished pottery, vessels of standard size for the measurement purpose called *sila*, meaning litre, probably used to distribute ration.

In 3000 BCE, Sumerian civilization was mostly urban in character. The territory of Sumer comprised around a dozen city-states, each containing a huge walled city enclosed by suburban villages and settlements.

Sumerian Socio-Economic Aspect

Temple: Sumer's great characteristic contribution to religious architecture is the notable feature of a main temple located on a high patio, gradually developed into a platform and ziggurat. Usually, the temple had a rectangular central cellar encircled by a number of chambers for the use of the priests. In the cellar there was a place for the god's statue, and an offering table made of mud brick in front of the statue. The temple was built mainly by mud bricks and the architects beautified the walls by regular indentations and braces. They also initiated mud-brick columns with zigzags, bars, and triangle patterns by inserting thousands of painted clay cones into the thick mud plaster. Inside the temple, walls were painted with the figures of animals and humans as well as various geometrical designs.

The temple used to be the largest, tallest and most important building in the city, and sometimes the entire city belonged to its main god.

Economy

Land: Practically, the temple owned some of the land, which it rented out to share-croppers and the remaining land was the private property of individual citizens.

Some scholars argue that Sumerian city-state was a totalitarian society and all the land was dominated by the temple. This is because the overwhelming majority of documents unearthed from 2400 BCE Sumer of pre-Sargonic era are inventory of documents from Lagash temple. But several documents unearthed in Fara and Bismaya indicate that the sale of real estate by private individuals was also in practice. A stone tablet records a sale of land by an individual to Enhegal, a king of Lagash, showing even a king must buy the land and not confiscate the property whenever he wants. Another stone record has been found showing a person called Lummatur, a son of Enannatum I, buying lands from various landowners and families. The temple land that could not be sold was divided into three classes: (a) *nigenna* - the land that was reserved for the maintenance of the temple; (b) *kurra* - the lands that were allotted to the farmers working the *nigenna* land and also to artists, administrative staff of the temple in payment for their services (this land should not be inherited or exchanged or confiscated by the temple administration whenever it decided to do so), (c) *urulal* - the lands that were allocated in exchange for a share of the crop of different individuals, but specifically to the staff of the temple to add to their income.

The documents show that the remaining part of the land, which did not belong to the temple in the territory of the city-state, was owned mainly by the nobility, that is princes and their families, palace administrators and important priests. And the rest of the land not owned by temples and nobility belonged to ordinary citizens.

In Sumerian city-sate the population consisted of four categories: nobles, commoners, clients, and slaves. (1) The nobility owned large part of real-estates and also they controlled the temple land, (2) the commoner who constituted the lower house of the assembly owned his own plot of land in the city state, (3) the clients consisted of the well-to-do dependents of the temple, temple personnel, and dependents of nobility. First two categories obtained a small plot of temple land temporarily and received rations of food and wool, and 4) probably slaves did not own any land.

Population: Priests, princes, and soldiers comprised only a small fraction in the city's population. Majority of people were farmers, cattle breeders, boatmen, fishermen, merchants, scribes, doctors, architects, masons, carpenters, smiths, jewellers, and potters. Obviously, there were a number of rich and powerful families who owned large property, but even the poor owned farms, gardens, houses, and cattle.

Slavery: Slavery was an accepted system in those days and temples, palaces, and rich estates kept slaves and abused them for their personal advantage. Many slaves were prisoners of war; sometimes freemen were reduced to slavery as a punishment for their crimes; parents could sell their children as slaves during hardships; or a man may offer his entire family to liberate from debt. The slave was considered to be a personal property of his master. He could be whipped and beaten and severely punished if a slave tried to escape. Slaves also had certain legal rights such as they could do business, borrow money and buy their freedom. 'If a slave, male or female, married a free person, the children were free. The sale price of a slave varied with the market and the individual involved; an average price for a grown man was twenty shekels, which was at times less than the price of a donkey.'

Marriage: The fundamental values of Sumerian society were the closely knitted families with love, respect, and mutual responsibilities. Marriage was arranged by parents, and the engagement was legally established as soon as the groom presented a wedding gift to the bride's father. Sometimes, the contract was inscribed on a tablet. A woman in Sumer had rights to own the property, engage in business, and was eligible for witness. But her husband could divorce for trivial reasons, and if she had no children, he could marry a second wife. Children were under the total control of their parents, who could disown them or even sell them into slavery. Normally, they had an affectionate relationship with love and at the parent's death they inherited all their property. Adopted sons were also treated with equal love, care and consideration.

Law

Written law in Sumerian society could be found in revealing documents. The inscriptions depict documents of 2700 BCE, the actual sales deeds of land, house, and slaves. One document demonstrates the constant struggle for freedom from tyranny and oppression. One document records a sweeping reform of a whole series of prevalent abuses, most of which could be traced to a ubiquitous and obnoxious bureaucracy consisting of the ruler and his palace coterie; at the same time it provides a grim and ominous picture of man's cruelty toward man on all levels-social, economic, political, and psychological.... There was also a bitter struggle for power between the temple and the palace and the citizens of Lagash taking the side of the temple.

Here are some selected comprehensible passages from Lipit Ishtar's Law Code written in 1900 BC: It is told that the first lines are in broken sentences.

8. If a man gave bare ground to another man to set out as an orchard and the latter did not complete setting out that bare ground as an orchard, he shall give to the man who set out the orchard the bare ground which he neglected as part of his share.
9. If a man entered the orchard of another man and was seized there for stealing, he shall pay ten shekels of silver.

10. If a man cut down a tree in the garden of another man, he shall pay one-half mina of silver.
11. If adjacent to the house of a man the bare ground of another man has been neglected and the owner of the house has said to the owner of the bare ground, "Because your ground has been neglected someone may break into my house: strengthen your house," and this agreement has been confirmed by him, the owner of the bare ground shall restore to the owner of the house any of his property that is lost.
12. If a slave-girl or slave of a man has fled into the heart of the city and it has been confirmed that he (or she) dwelt in the house of (another) man for one month, he shall give slave for slave.
13. If he has no slave, he shall pay fifteen shekels of silver.
14. If a man's slave has compensated his slave-ship to his master and it is confirmed (that he has compensated) his master two-fold, that slave shall be freed.
15. If a *miqtum* [servant] is the grant of a king, he shall not be taken away.
16. If a *miqtum* went to a man of his own free will, that man shall not hold him; he (the *miqtum*) may go where he desires.
17. If a man without authorization bound another man to a matter of which he (the latter) had no knowledge, that man is not affirmed (i.e., legally obligated); he (the first man) shall bear the penalty in regard to the matter to which he had bound him.
18. If the master of an estate or the mistress of an estate has defaulted on the tax of an estate and a stranger has borne it, for three years he (the owner) may not be evicted. Afterwards, the man who bore the tax of the estate shall possess that estate and the former owner of the estate shall not raise any claim.
22. If the father is living, his daughter whether she be a high priestess, a priestess, or a hierodule shall dwell in his house like an heir.
24. If the second wife whom he had married bore him children, the dowry which she brought from her father's house belongs to her children but the children of his first wife and the children of his second wife shall divide equally the property of their father.
25. If a man married his wife and she bore him children and those children are living, and a slave also bore children for her master but the father granted freedom to the slave and her children, the children of the slave shall not divide the estate with the children of their former master.

27. If a man's wife has not borne him children but a harlot from the public square has borne him children, he shall provide grain, oil and clothing for that harlot. The children whom the harlot has borne him shall be his heirs, and as long as his wife lives the harlot shall not live in the house with the wife.
29. If a son-in-law has entered the house of his (prospective) father-in-law and afterwards they made him go out (of the house) and gave his wife to his companion, they shall present to him the betrothal gifts which he brought and that wife may not marry his companion.
34. If a man rented an ox and injured the flesh at the nose ring, he shall pay one-third of its price.
35. If a man rented an ox and damaged its eye, he shall pay one-half its price.
36. If a man rented an ox and broke its horn, he shall pay one-fourth its price.
37. If a man rented an ox and damaged its tail, he shall pay one-fourth its price and so on.

Tax: In order to raise armies and supply them with arms and equipment, the rulers violated the personal rights of the man and imposed taxes on the wealth and property on citizens and even appropriated the property belonging to the temple. During the time of war rulers did not face any opposition. Once introduced, the palace authorities were unwilling to abandon the tax system even in peacetime as it was more profitable. Even for a small cause, citizens were thrown into the prisons for non-payment of taxes, debit or on charges of theft and murder.

A historian who lived more than 4200 years ago in Lagash narrates the abuse of people in the form of tax in three duplicating versions of his text and there may be more than that underneath the ground.

> "In the days preceding Urukagina, 'formerly, from days of yore, from the day the seed (of man) came forth," palace appointees practiced such abuses as seizing, presumably without right or warrant, property belonging to the citizens of Lagash - their donkeys, sheep, and fisheries. Other citizens were extracted money as a form of tax more or less indirectly of their goods and possession by being compelled to have their rations measured out in the palace, much to their disadvantage, or to bring their sheep to the palace for shearing (cropping) and to pay in 'cold cash' for the service, at least in certain specified cases."

"If a man divorced his wife, the *ensi* got five shekels, and his vizier got one shekel. If a perfumer made an oil preparation, the *ensi* got five shekels, the vizier got one shekel, and abgal got another shekel."

"The oxen of the gods plowed the *ensi's* onion patches; the onion and cucumber patches of the *ensi* were located in the god's best fields."

Death: Even in death, citizens were not free from taxes and levies. When a dead man was brought to the cemetery for burial, a number of officials demanded to pay a certain amount of barley, bread, date wine, and various furnishings from grieving families. The ancient reporter writes, 'From one end of the state to the other, there were the tax collectors.'

The Sumerian commentator writes: "The houses of the *ensi* and the fields of the *ensi*, the houses of the palace harem and the fields of the palace harem, the houses of the palace nursery and the fields of the palace nursery crowded each other side to side." So, it is not strange the palace was brimming fat and prosperous.

Reformist Urukagina (2350 BCE)

The Sumerian historian tells the story that a ruler Urukagina re-established the divine laws which had been abandoned and neglected by the previous rulers. He banned the systems like the seizure of donkeys, sheep, and fisheries belonging to the citizens, and demanding payment to the palace for measuring their rations and cropping their sheep. When a person divorced his wife, neither the ensi nor his vizier got anything. When a perfumer made oil, neither the *ensi* nor his vizier got anything. When a dead man was brought to the cemetery, officials received less than half of previous donations. Related to temple property which *ensi* had seized for himself, Urukagina returned it to the proper owner. The Sumerian historian writes, "From one end of the land to the other, there were no tax collectors."

Urukagina was also responsible for various other reforms. He stopped the injustice and exploitation suffered by the poor at the hands of the rich and powerful. Stable rations of food and drink were distributed to the craftsmen organizations, to certain blind laborers, and to other workers.

Artists and apprentices no longer had to beg for their food. To prevent the big men taking advantage of the poor people, he decreed two rules forbidding to force poor people to sell their donkeys or their houses against their will. Amnesty was granted to the citizens who were imprisoned for debt or failure to pay taxes. In cases of the orphans, widows, and helpless victims of the rich and powerful, "Urukagina made a covenant with the god Ningirsu that a man of power must not commit an injustice against them." Urukagina's court of law is a big document.

One Example of Court Document:

Akalla, the son of Luninshubur, and Urshuann were witnesses to the fact that Kaku, the son of Ninshubur, had bought 12 large date-palm saplings from Lunanna, the father of Urabu, for 3 shekels of silver as its full price. Urabu (however) repudiated the witnesses. Whereupon Kaku took an oath (that he had actually bought the saplings from the father of Urabu, Lunanna). Therefore, the garden was confirmed as belonging to Kaku.

Signed by:

Tiemahta - Mashkim

Lu-Shara and Ur-Sataran - the judges

Major Sumerian city-states included Eridu, Ur, Nippur, Lagash and Kish, but one of the oldest and most sprawling was Uruk, a thriving trading hub that featured miles of defensive walls and a population between 40,000 and 80,000.

The list of Sumerian rulers includes one woman. The list is a strange blend of historical fact and myth—one early king is said to have lived for 43,200 years—but it also includes Sumer's lone female monarch who supposedly took the throne in the city-state of Kish sometime around 2500 BCE Very little is known about Kubaba's reign or how she came to power, but the list credits her with making "firm the foundation of Kish" and forging a dynasty that lasted 100 years.

Along with inventing writing, the wheel, the plow, law codes and literature, the Sumerians are also considered as some of history's original brewers. Archaeologists have found evidence of Mesopotamian beer-making art dating back to the 4000 BCE. The brewing methods they used are a mystery, but their favoured content seems to have been a barley-based mixture. It was a very thick mixture, so they had very special kind of filtration straw to sip the beer. The Sumerians lauded the beer for its nutrient-rich ingredients and claimed that it endows happy heart and satisfactory liver. Even there was a Sumerian goddess of brewing called "Ninkasi," who is celebrated in a famous hymn as the "one who waters the malt set on the ground."

The Sumerians were particularly fond of lapis lazuli—a blue-coloured precious stone used in art and jewellery—and there is evidence that they may have travelled as far as Afghanistan to get it.

Material Aspect of Sumer

City: Studying incomplete and indirect ancient texts, it is estimated that the Sumerian population was around 100,000 in Lagash. When Ur was the capital of Sumer in about 2000 BCE, it is estimated that the population was some 360,000. Some historian estimate that it must be close to 200,000 in reality.

The Sumerian city was not so attractive in 4000 years ago. C.L. Woolley writes,

> "If the residential quarters excavated at Ur give, as presumably they do, a fair sample of the city as a whole, we see something that has grown out of the conditions of the primitive village, not laid out on any system of town-planning. The unpaved streets were narrow and winding, sometimes mere blind alleys leading to houses hidden away in the middle of a great block of haphazard buildings; large houses and small are tumbled together, a few of them flat-roofed tenements one storey high, most of them two storeys, and a few, apparently of three. Lanes sheltered by awnings and lined with open booths correspond to the bazars of the modern Middle Eastern town."

However, paragraphs in the "Lamentation over the Destruction of Ur" describe that the city was attractive: it had 'lofty gates', roads for walking and to celebrate feasts. And in an episode "A Scribe and His Perverse Son" and "Love Finds a Way", it appears that there was a public square.

House: The typical Sumerian house was a small one-storey, mud-brick structure having several rooms grouped around an open yard. The rich Sumerian people might have lived in two-story houses with more rooms, built by brick and plaster, probably mud plaster, and whitewashed both inside and out. The lower level of two-story house consisted a foyer, kitchen, lavatory, servant quarter, and a private worship place. The house had low tables, high-backed chairs, and beds with copper frames. Utensils were made of clay, stone, copper and bronze; baskets and boxes made of reeds and wood. Floors and walls were covered with reed mats, skin rugs, and woollen hangings. Although there were cemeteries outside the city, in some houses, there was a family grave where they buried their dead people.

Skills: Sumerians economic progress depended on highly developed skills of farmers, cultivators, artisans and craftsman. Early Sumerians did not develop any kind of science. But their thinkers classified the natural world into the following categories: domestic animals, wild animals, birds, fishes, trees, plants, vegetables, and stones. Interestingly, lists of all possible items in these categories were compiled in a text books in the *edubba*

(Edubba is a Sumerian house of tablets like a modern day library, and a place of learning where archives and literature were stored on clay tablets). Sometimes teachers added some definitions to the words to help students. For example, the "shepherd-bird" is described as

"The shepherd-bird says ri-di-ik, ri-di-ik,

The shepherd-bird has a variegated neck like the dar-bird,

He has a crest upon his head."

On cat's patience and mongoose' directness

"A cat - for its thoughts,

A mongoose - for its actions."

And so on.

Astronomy: Any kind of science was unknown to Sumerians except 25 stars. They might have observed heavenly bodies just for calendrical reasons, but they never recorded their observation.

The Sumerians divided the year in two seasons: *emesh* "summer" and *enten* "winter": Summer began in February-March and winter in September-October. The year may fall in April-May. The months were exactly lunar that began with the evening of the new moon and were 29 or 30 days in measurement. The name of the months named after certain deities, which differed from city to city. 'To take care of the difference in length between the lunar and solar years, an intercalary month was introduced at regular intervals. The day began with sunset and was twelve double-hours in length. The night was divided into three steps of four hours each. Time was measured by a water clock, or clepsydra, shaped like a cylinder or prism; the shadow clock or rod clock was also probably known.'

Sumerian Medicine: Only two Sumerian medical tablets were found. Kramer writes that one of these is a small piece of no importance. The other one is about 3 ¾ x 6 ¼ inches in size, inscribed with fifteen prescriptions. The tablet was inscribed around 2400 BCE and it is the oldest Medical Book known to humanity. 'Although the tablet was excavated in second half of 1800s, it was not known to public until 1940.

The prescriptions were divided into three classes according to the method of remedies applied. The first class consists of eight prescriptions in which the application is in the form of a poultice. The material in the inscription summarized as follows: "first a list of the herbs to be utilized in each prescription; then the direction to pulverize them and mix them with a liquid in order to form a paste which is to be fastened as a poultice to the sick part of the body after the latter has been rubbed with oil, an action performed either for its intrinsic therapeutic value or to keep the paste from clinging to the skin. The literal translation of the tablet follows here:

> Prescription No.4: Pulverize the anadishsha-plant, the branches of the "thorn" plant, the seeds of the duashbur, and... (names of at least two herbs destroyed);... pour water-diluted beer over it (the mass of pulverized herbs); rub (the sick spot) with vegetable oil, and fasten the paste formed by pouring the liquid over the pulverized herbs as a poultice.
>
> Prescription No. 5: Pulverize river mud and....; knead it with water; run with crude oil; and fasten as poultice.
>
> Prescription No. 6: Pulverize pears (?) and "manna," pour the lees of beer over it; run with vegetable oil, and fasten as a poultice.
>
> Prescription No. 7: Pulverize the lees of the dried vine, pine tree, and plum tree; pour beer over it, rub with oil, and fasten as a poultice.
>
> Prescription No. 8: Pulverize the roots of the....tree,... and dried river bitumen; pour beer over it; run with oil, and fasten as a poultice.
>
> And so on.

This Sumerian physician used botanical, zoological, and mineralogical sources for his medical practice. His favoured minerals were sodium chloride (salt), river bitumen, and crude oil. From the animal group he used wool, milk, turtle shell, and water snakes. But the majority of his medical source came from botanical class, from plants like thyme, mustard, plum tree, pears, figs, willow, manna plant, fir and pine, and processed products such as beer, wine, and vegetable oils.

In Sumer, a physician was known as the *a-zu* and the first doctor mentioned in the record was named as Lulu; 2700 BCE tablets containing the words "Lulu, the doctor" were excavated in Ur by Sir Leonard Woolley. There were also animal doctors, veterinarians, known as "the doctor of the oxen" or "the doctor of the donkeys."

Art: The Sumerian art involved in abstract and impressionistic nature. Author Kramer writes that the temple statues had great emotional and spiritual intensity rather than skill in modelling. Sculptors carved figures on steles and plaques, vases and bowls. It is from this sculpture historians have learnt a great deal about Sumerian appearance and dress.

Dress: Sumerian men used to be with both clean shaven and long beards, and their long hair divided in the middle. Most common dress was a kind of pleated skirt over which a long covering of wool or cotton fabric was worn. Later, there appeared the chiton or long skirt. "Covering the skirt was a big fringed shawl, which was carried over the left shoulder, leaving the right arm free. Women often wore dresses which looked like long tufted shawls, covering them from head to foot and leaving only the right shoulder bare. Their hair was usually parted in the middle and braided in a heavy pigtail, which was then wound around the head. They often wore elaborate headdresses consisting of hair ribbons, beads, and pendants."

Music: Sumerians were proficient in both instrumental and vocal music performance and some of the musicians played important roles in temples and palaces. Beautifully designed harps and lyres were excavated in the royal tombs of Ur. Percussive, which is striking with the hand, instruments like drum and tambourine, and pipes (flute) of reed and metal were also common in 4750 years ago in Sumer. Most of the recovered works are hymns to gods and kings to use in the temple and palace, but the evidence shows that music and dance were also used for entertainment in homes and marketplaces.

Sumerian Musical Instrument Lyre at National Museum of Iraq

Cylindrical Seal: Cylindrical seal is one of the most important Sumerian's original inventions and contributions to the art. Small cylinders of stone engraved with a design gave clear and meaningful art when rolled over on a wet clay tablet or clay jar, or other materials. The cylinder seal became a kind of Mesopotamian trademark; later it spread to Egypt, Greece, Anatolia (Turkey) and Cyprus. 'The earliest cylinder seals are carefully incised gems depicting rows of animals or fairy-tale creatures and monsters and such scenes as the kind on the battlefield and the shepherd defending his cattle against wild beasts.' Eventually, the seal designs developed as more decorative items.

Jewellers: The jeweller worked mainly on gold, silver and semiprecious stones such as lapis lazuli, carnelian, and topaz. His foundry contained three and four-piece molds; he hammered metal sheets over a wooden base and finished them with beating and inscribing. He also invented how to fix pieces of gold and silver with pins, how to solder, and how to frame and lace his creation.

Carpenters: Although there was a scarcity for wood in Sumer, a large number of carpenters worked to produce all kinds of furniture, boats, wagon, and chariots. As per one tablet, the carpenters built a podium of ivory weighing more than forty pounds. The Ibbi-Sin tablet describes that three old tabletops and four fir boxes were reused to make one table, two beds, and one small box.

Although Sumer lacked metal, stone, and timber, its artists were highly skilled in that ancient world. It is assumed that many of them came from foreign lands to display their skills in building temples and developing art.

Leatherworker: Excavated Sumerian tablets reveal that skins of bulls, calves, pigs, and sheep were used to make objects such as water-skins, bags, couples, saddles, tires for chariot wheels, and importantly, shoes and sandals. 'For tanning purposes, the leatherworkers used alkalis, sumac, and other still unidentifiable substances.' Fat was used to make the skins flexible and waterproof. "The leatherworker mentioned in Ur tablet made use of flour to finish off certain special skins and "powder of gold" to decorate some of the manufactured pieces."

Textiles: A large number of herds of goats, sheep and lambs were raised to obtain wool and cutting of wool was done by pulling and picking. A spindle rod was used to spin the wool, and weaving was done by horizontal and vertical looms. The woven cloth was soaked in an alkaline solution and then they compressed it by walking with their feet. In addition to wool, flax was also used to produce textile. Linen garments were used by certain priests and holy men.

Farmer's Manual: A tablet containing a farmer's manual discovered at Nippur starts with the following line: "In days of yore a farmer instructed his son." It contains all important procedures and labours that a farmer has to perform in order to get a successful crop. The manual deals with soil preparation, water management, removal of weeds, levelling the surface, smoothing the field, tilling, ploughing, sowing, etc., Also it deals with the essential tools such as whips, goads, hammers and other instruments. In the field the farmer is supposed to watch workers closely, but the farmer himself must follow some self-discipline and not to demand labourers for discipline.

When the buddings appear, the father should pray to Ninkilim, the goddess of field mice and vermin, otherwise, he thought, they harm the growing grain. The handbook tablet continues how much water to be fed level by level once crops start to grow. It is so astonishing to read how much understanding about agriculture they had 5000 years ago in Sumer.

Sumerian Farmer's Almanac: There are three Sumerian collections on farmer's almanac mentioning the principles and instructions:

1. The Farmer's Almanac,
2. The Instructions of Shuruppak to His Son Ziusudra,
3. No title but it seems to consist of applied cautions and moral and ethical practices.

The following is a part of a poem that was compiled around 2000 BCE. It was credited to King Shuruppak, who was the father Ziusudra and it begins with:

"Shuruppak gave instructions to his son,
Shuruppak, the son of Ubartutu,
Gave instructions to his son Ziusudra:
" "My son, I would instruct you, take my instruction,
Ziusudra, I would utter a word to you, give heed to it;
Do not neglect my instruction,
Do not transgress the word I uttered,
The father's instruction, the precious, carry out diligently." "

Here is the full translation of the document:

Farmer's Almanac Manual - 1700 To 1500 BCE Document

In days of yore a farmer instructed his son:

"When you are about to take hold of your field (for cultivation), keep a sharp eye on the opening of the dikes, ditches, and mounds, (so that), when you flood the field the water will not rise too high in it. When you have emptied it of water, watch the field's water-soaked ground so that it stays virile ground for you. Let shod oxen (that is, oxen whose hooves are protected in one way or another) trample it for you; (and) After having its weeds ripped out (by them) (and) the field made level ground, dress it evenly with narrow axes weighing (no more than) two-thirds of a pound each. (Following which) Let the pickaxe wielder eradicate the ox hooves for you (and), Smooth them out; Have all crevices worked over with a drag, and have him go with the pickaxe all around the four edges of the field.

"While the field is drying, let your obedient (household (workforce)) prepare your tools for you, make fast the yoke bar, hang up your new whips on nails, and let the hanging handles of your old whips be mended by the artisans. Let the bronze ..... your tools "heed your arm"; let the leather "headbinder", goad, "mouth-opener", (and) whip uphold you (in matters requiring discipline and control); let your *bandu*-basket crackle; (all this) will make a mighty income for you.

"When your field has been supplied with what is needed, keep a sharp eye on your work. After adding an extra ox to the plow-ox — when one is harnessed to another ox, their plow is larger than (an ordinary) plow – make them ..... one *bur*; they will make for you a ..... like a storm, so that three *gur* barley will be planted in that one *bur*. Sustenance is in a plow! (Thus) Having had the field worked with the *bardil*-plow – (yes) the *bardil*-plow – (and then) having had it worked over with the *shukin*-plow, repeat (the process). (After) Having had it (the field) harrowed, (and) raked three times and pulverized fine with a hammer, let the handle of your whip uphold you; brook no idleness. Stand over them (the field laborers) during their work, (and) brook no interruptions. Do not [distract] your field workers. Since they must carry on by day, (and by) Heaven's stars for ten, (days), their strength should be spent on the field. (And) They are not to dance attendance on you.

"When you are about to plow your field, let your plow break up the stubble for you. Leave your "mouth-cover" of the plow ....., (and) leave your ..... on a narrow nail. Let your mouldboards spread to the side, set up your furrows — in one *garush*, set up eight furrows. Furrows which have been deeply dug — their barley will grow long.

"When you are about to plow your field, keep your eye on the man who puts in the barley seed. Let him drop the grain uniformly two fingers deep, (and) Use up one shekel of barley for each *garush*. If the barley seed does not sink in properly, change your share, the "tongue of the plow". If the ....., (then) plow diagonal furrows where you have plowed straight furrows, (And) Plow straight furrows where you have plowed diagonal furrows. Let your straight furrows make your borders into *tulu*-borders; let the *lu*-furrows make straight your borders; (and) Plow *ab*-furrows where .....; (Then) Let all its clouds be removed; all its high spots be made into furrows; (and) all its depressions be made into low furrows — (all this) (It) will be good for the sprout.

"After the sprout has broken through (the surface of) the ground, say a prayer to the goddess Ninkilim, (And) shoo away the flying birds. When the barley has filled the narrow bottom of the furrow, water the top seed. When the barley stands up high as (the straw of) a mat in the middle of a boat, water it (a second time). Water (a third time)-its royal barley. If the watered barley has turned red, what you say is: "It is sick with the *samana*-disease." But if it has succeeded in producing kernel-rich barley, water it (a fourth time); (and) It will yield you an extra measure of barley in every ten (+10 %)

"When you are about to harvest your field, do not let the barley bend over on itself, (but) Harvest it at the moment of its (full) strength. A reaper, a man who bundles the mown barley, and a man who [sets up the sheaves] before him — these three (as a team) shall do the harvesting for you. The gleaners must do no damage; they must not tear apart the sheaves. During your daily harvesting, as in "days of need", make the earth supply the sustenance of the young and the gleaners according to their number (that is, presumably, he must leave the fallen kernels on the ground for needy children and gleaners to pick); (and) Let them sleep (in your field) as (in) the (open) marshland. After you have obtained ....., do not ....., (but) Roast (some of) the mown barley, (so that) the "prayer of the mown barley" will be said for you daily.

"When you are about to winnow the barley, let those who weigh your barley [prepare] for you (bins of) thirty *gur*. Have your threshing floor made level, (and) the *gur* (-bins) put in order (ready for) the road. When your tools have been [readied] for you, (and) your wagons put in order for you, have your wagons climb the (barley) mounds — your "mound-threshing" (is to take) five days. When you are about to "open the mound", bake *arra*-bread. When you "open" the barley, have the teeth of your threshing sledges fastened with leather and let bitumen cover the .....; When you are about to hitch the oxen (to the threshing sledge), let your men who "open" the barley, stand by with food (that is, the oxen's food).

"When you have heaped up the barley, say the "prayer of the (still) uncleaned barley". When you winnow the barley, pay attention to the men who lift the barley from the ground — two "barley-lifters" should lift it for you. On the day the barley is to be cleaned, have it laid on the sticks, (and) Say a prayer evening and night. (Then) Have the barley "unloose" (from the chaff) like (with) an overpowering wind; (and) The "unloosed" barley will be stored for you."

These are the instructions of Ninurta, the son of Enlil. O Ninurta, trustworthy farmer of Enlil, your praise is good. (Line 109-11).

The writer of this unique agricultural handbook was probably illiterate and had no time to prepare the manual. Without doubt it was written by a professor in the Sumerian school to teach the art and skill for successful farming. This composition is inscribed in numerous tablets and probably there are more in the ruins of Sumer.

Animal Husbandry: Like agriculture, animal husbandry was also a fundamental occupation to the Sumerian economy: Animals were the source of transportation, food and clothing. Tablet inscriptions explain elaborately about animals and their use.

Beverages: Most favourite drink of Sumerians was beer enjoyed by both gods and men. It also had medicinal value. Author Kramer writes, "The preparation of beer was closely related to the fabrication of cereal cakes from sprouted barley; it was this malting that gave a greater nutritional value to the grain that now had a large content of carbohydrates and protein. There was a special goddess in charge of beer preparation called Ninkasi, a name which seems to mean literally "the lady who fills the mouth." Although she was a goddess born in the sparkling-fresh water, it was beer that was her first love; and she is described in a hymn of glorification addressed to her by one of the devotees of the Inanna cult as the brewer of the gods:

who bakes with lofty shovel the sprouted barley,
who mixes the *bappir*-malt with sweet aromatics,
who bakes the *bappir*-malt in the lofty kiln, and
who pours the fragrant beer in the *lahtan*-vessel
which is like the Tigris and Euphrates joined.

To Sumerian poets and sages, even beer had divine and sublime qualities.

Religion: Theology, Rite, and Myth

Mesopotamia was renowned as a seat of learning since ancient times. Intellectual quests were vastly treasured across the region, and the schools dedicated mainly to the priests were supposed to be numerous. These schools attached to the temples taught reading, writing, religion, law, medicine, and astrology. It is estimated that there were more than 1,000 deities in the pantheon of the gods of the Mesopotamian cultures and many stories regarding gods and creation myths called Enuma Elish. The Mesopotamians believed that they worked with gods and the land was pervaded with spirits and demons.

Mesopotamians believed in the beginning there was a fight between gods and demons resulting the victory by the gods over the demons of chaos. They realized that even though the gods had won for the time being, demons would come again to create chaos. Mesopotamians thought that if they lead their life by daily rituals, devotion to the deities, proper funeral practices, and perform simple civic duties, they can defeat the demonic forces of chaos. Their belief also included to honouring the elders, treating people with respect, and honouring the gods by doing the jobs they were assigned.

According to the native legend, a half man-half fish Oannes and other divinities came out of the sea and told the story of the creation and brought civilization to the world.

In Mesopotamian mythology, Oannes **is** an amphibious creature who taught humankind wisdom. Oannes, as described by the Babylonian priest Berosus, had the form of a fish with the head of a man and under his fish's tail the feet of a man. (The legend says that Oannes is one of seven sages in Sumerian mythology.)

On the practical and functional level, the Sumerian priests and saintly men developed a variety of intricate rituals, rites, and ceremonies to please the gods. On the artistic level, the illiterate Sumerian entertainers and lyricists, and later their successors, poets and scribes created the richest mythology of the ancient Near East, which brought the gods down to human size. They did it with superb understanding, reverence, and imaginations.

Sumerian Theology: In relation to cosmogony and theology, Sumerian philosophers and thinkers had only rudimentary and superficial ideas about the nature of the universe and its methods of operation. Their untrained eyes saw the solid mechanisms of the universe, heaven and earth; they named it as *an-ki*, a compound word meaning "heaven-earth". In their opinion, tin was 'metal of heaven.' Between earth and sky they identified a substance called *lil*, probably they meant air, wind, breath, or spirit, or roughly atmosphere. The sun, moon, planets, and stars were made of the same substance as the atmosphere, but they were gifted with one more aspect 'luminosity.' Their entire visible sight, earth, sky, top, and bottom, is surrounded by an endless sea where the universe remains fixed and immovable.

Sumerian concluded that first there was the primeval sea; somehow this sea produced the universe consisting heaven and earth; between heaven and earth came moving and expanding atmosphere which separated heaven from earth; out of this atmosphere glowing bodies of moon, sun, planets, stars, and also astral bodies plant, animal, and human life came into existence.

Sumerian philosophers assumed that there is a group of living beings, humanlike in appearance, but superhuman and immortal in power, to operate, direct, and supervise this universe, guide and control the cosmos according to the well-established plans. They were invisible to mortal eyes. They thought every single thing, irrespective of their nature, was controlled by these superhuman beings. Obviously, they had a deity for each cosmic object and event.

This thought occurred to the Sumerian theologian probably because they saw everything, cities, palaces, fields and farms, all imaginable institutions were controlled, supervised and guided by living human beings; without them lands and cities will be abandoned, temples and palaces collapse, farmlands turn to wilderness. Thus, definitely this universe and its innumerable happenings also needed to be supervised, controlled and guided by living beings in invisible human form and they must be immortals. Otherwise, the universe will collapse when they die. 'It was each of these invisible, anthropomorphic, and at the same time superhuman and immortal beings that the Sumerian designated by his word *dingir*, which means the 'god.''

Sumerians tried to explain how these cosmic entities are operating the universe harmoniously without conflict and confusion, and designated a word *me*, the exact meaning of the word is not known to historians. But they guess it may imply rules and regulation assigned to each cosmic entity. The primary source of information about *me's* is the mythology "Inanna and Enki: The Transfer of the Arts of Civilization from Eridu to Erech." Kramer writes '*me'* appears hundreds of times in the myth.

Sumerian Gods

By the middle of 3000 BCE, hundreds of deities existed among Sumerians. Among them, four deities were most important: the sky god, An or Anu; the air god, Enlil; the water-god Enki; and the mother-goddess, Ninhursag.

Anu: Anu is the sky god.

Enlil, the air-god, was the most important deity in Sumerian pantheon. He was known as "the father of the gods," "the king of heaven and earth," "the king of all the lands." Kings considered that it is Enlil who has given the kingship of the land, who made the land prosperous for them, and who gave them all the lands to conquer by his strength. They also believed Enlil was a violent and destructive storm deity. Some hymns glorified him as a most friendly, fatherly deity who watches over the safety and well-being of all humans.

An ancient document recently acquired by Noah Kramer recites the hymn of Enlil:

"Enlil, whose command is far-reaching, whose word is holy,
The lord whose pronouncement is unchangeable,
Who forever decrees destines,
Whose lifted eye scans the land,
Whose lifted beam searches the heart of all the lands,
Enlil who sits broadly on the white dais, on the lofty Dais,
Who perfects the decrees of power, lordship, and princeship,
The earth-gods bow down in fear before him,
The heaven-gods humble themselves before him ….

The hymn continues on two pages.

Enki: Enki was the god of wisdom and he was the one who organized the earth according to the plans of Enlil. Enki executed Enlil's plans more skilfully. His legend "Enki and the World Order: The Organization of the Earth and Its Cultural Processes" explains the detailed story about Enki's creation activities, starting with natural and cultural occurrences, which were important to civilization. This myth gives a vivid illustration of the Sumerian's external idea about nature and its mysteries. They never tried to understand the fundamental origins of natural or cultural processes, but merely stated "Enki did it."

Ninhursag: Also known as Ninmah is the mother-goddess and fourth important deity. She was regarded as the mother of all living things. In one story, she created one man, and in another story, she gave several divine births. Previously, Ninhursag was worshipped as Ki, "Earth" and was a spouse of An, "Heaven".

Apart from the above four gods, there were many astral deities: the moon-god, Nanna-Sin, Nanna's son sun-god, Utu; and Nanna's daughter, the goddess Inanna. All made a group of seven deities: An, Enlil, Enki, Ninmah, Nanna-Sin, Utu, and Inanna; all had their own role on the earth.

Inanna: Inanna was a goddess of love, fertility and procreation. Every year in Inanna's temple in Erech, there was a practice of marriage ceremony between the king and a specially selected slave or a prostitute. It was according to the idea that the king of Sumer, no matter who he was or from what city he originated, must become the husband of the life-giving goddess of love, Inanna of Erech.

Man (Humans): In Sumerian thinker's world view, man was designed from clay and created to serve god by supplying them with food, drink, and shelter so that gods can have plenty of time to take care of the universe. His life was tormented with insecurity and chased by anxiety because they did not know what destiny would fall on by unpredictable gods. When he died, his weakened spirit arrived in the dark, depressing nether world where life was a miserable and worthless reflection of its earthly type.

The basic problem of Sumerian philosophers was that they never contemplated on the concept of free will. Surrendering to the decree without any argument, they accepted that the man was created by the gods to serve them, and the death was man's fate and only gods were immortal. 'All credit for the high moral qualities and ethical virtues that the Sumerians had evolved gradually and painfully over the centuries from their social and cultural experiences was attributed to the gods; it was the gods who planned it that way, and man was only following divine order."

According to their inscriptions and records, Sumerians cherished all good qualities like goodness and truth, law and order, justice and freedom, righteousness and straightforwardness, mercy and compassion, and obviously hated the opposite qualities like evil and falsehood, lawlessness and disorder, injustice and oppression, sinfulness and perversity, cruelty and pitilessness. A number of hymns are found claiming high ethical and moral conduct. One hymn to deity Lagashite goddess Nanshe describes:

"Who knows the orphan, who knows the widow,
Knows the oppression of man over man, is the orphan's mother,
Nanshe, who cares for the widow,
Who seeks out (?) justice (?) for the poorest (?),
The queen brings the refugee to her lap,
Finds shelter for the weak."

Another hymn describes what happens to the evil doers and how they suffer her displeasure.

Nanshe's social conscience is revealed as

"To comfort the orphan, to make disappear the widow,
To set up a place of destruction for the mighty,

To turn over the mighty to the weak…
Nanshe searches the heart of the people."

Did god notice the poor man's prostration and prayers and help him and fulfill his wishes? It is suspected 'probably not.' Sumerians thought gods are like mortal kings and they have other important things to attend to, so they needed a mediator to intervene on their behalf, one who is nearer to god to do favours. So there evolved personal gods to whom they disclosed their pain in prayer and supplication, and it was through those personal deities they found redemption. This is all in a pieced-together poetic essay, which deals with suffering and submission. It is important to know that this essay represents man's first recorded effort to manage the age-old problem of human-suffering.

It is evident from the thesis of this poem that 'in cases of suffering and adversity, no matter how seemingly unjustified, the victim has but one valid and effective option, which is to continually glorify his god and keep crying and lamenting before him until he turns a favorable ear to his prayers.' Ancient poet gives one example. It is a summarized version of a big poem:

> "Here is a man, who had been wealthy, wise, and righteous, and blest with both friends and kin. One day sickness and suffering overwhelmed him. Did he defy the divine order and blaspheme? Not at all. He came humbly before his god with tears and lamentation and poured out his heart in prayer and supplication. As a result, his god was highly pleased and moved to compassion; he gave heed to his prayer, delivered him from his misfortune, and turned his suffering to joy."

But, in fact, the man died while the hard-eyed Sumerian thinkers could see, and went to the world below never to return.

As for Sumerian cultural behaviour is concerned, the numerous royal burial tombs excavated with care and skill at Ur indicate that they are of great significance; early rulers of Sumer went to grave not only by their personal valuable possession, but also carried a sizable amount of human servants also. Shocking discovery of cuneiform documents proves that.

From the recovered and translated 4500 years old tablets of poems, we notice that there was a lot of suffering in humans. Most of the poems go like, 'although he had served gods well, they failed to stand by him in time of need; now was dead, and his wife and friends and supporters were filled with tears and lamentation.' Their philosophers had no answers except surrender to their personal gods.

Netherworld (Hell): According to scholars they have recovered one whole poem with reasonably good condition is "Inanna's Descent to the Nether World."

According to this poem, the nether world is a place where an individual raises and goes down through an opening or a gate located in Erech. (It is an imaginative location only.) It mentions about a place called "lapis lazuli Mountain" where its gates were locked and bolted and watched by gatekeepers under the supervision of Neti, their boss. The nether world had strict rules and regulations, one of those was its residents must be totally naked. Another strange rule was no one, even a deity, could leave above without a surrogate had been replaced to take its place.

In fact, the netherworld was believed to be another big galactic space below the earth just like the sky above, and souls of the dead people go down from graves through an opening and gate in Erech. There was a river through which the dead had to cross. The netherworld was ruled by Ereshkigal and Nergal and other associated gods; there was a palace with seven gates for Ereshkigal; and they also needed food, clothing, weapons, vessels, jewels, etc.

Rites: Even though devotion and piousness were important, Sumerian's world view required rites and ritual to please the gods. Because humans were created to serve the gods, it was their duty to perform the services satisfactorily to their masters.

Temples: Temple is a centre place where everything revolves around in Sumer. One of the earliest temples was excavated in Eridu, built in Enki. The temple is very simple measuring only about twelve feet by fifteen, but gradually it was extended large enough with brick walls. There was a niche for Enki's statue and an offering table of mud brick in front of it.

At Erech, they found another temple just like in Eridu dedicated to An, which was dated 3000 BCE. Here the platform was raised by an artificial hill rising some forty feet above the plain. A stairway facing northeast led to the peak where a small whitewashed temple stood. A numerous example of excavated temples with their features, how Sumerian architectural designs developed, how they started coloring the walls and floors, temple's size and measurements, how they decorated their walls with stones, geometrical shapes, etc.

Gudea Cylinders

The Gudea cylinders excavated in Lagash explain the building of a temple was accompanied by an abundant number of rites and rituals. The Gudea cylinders contain remarkable hymnal narrative poem composed by one of the poets of the Eninnu temple at Lagash.

The poem narrates that the deity Ningirsu appeared in Gudea's dream and ordered him to build a temple. Here is a paraphrased poem:

> "In the dream, Gudea saw a man of tremendous statue with a divine crown on his head, the wings of a lion-headed bird, and a "flood wave" as the lower part of his body; lions crouched to his right and left. This huge man commanded Gudea to build his temple, but he could not grasp the meaning of his words. Day broke -in the dream - and a woman appeared holding a god stylus and studying a clay tablet on which the starry heaven was depicted. Then a "hero" appeared holding a tablet of lapis lazuli (blue stone tablet) on which he drew a plan of a house; he also placed bricks in a brick mold which stood before Gudea together with a carrying basket. At the same time a specially bred male donkey was impatiently pawing the ground."

Gudea did not understand the meaning of the dream. Therefore, he went to consult the goddess Nanshe, who lived in Nina where one had to reach by canal. Nanshe interpreted the dream as follows: a) the man of tremendous statue was god Ningirsu, b) the woman holding the tablet was Nidaba, the goddess of writing, c) the man holding a tablet of lapis lazuli was god Nindub who was an architect of the temple plan, d) the male donkey stroking the ground impatiently is Gudea who is impatient to carry out the work.

Festivals: Sumerians observed festivals for many reasons. The temple cult included daily sacrifices consisting of animal and vegetable foods, libations of water, wine, and beer, and the burning of incense. The festivals were named as "The Month of the Eating of Barley of Ningirsu," "The Month of Eating of the Gazelles," "and "The Month of the Feast of Shulgi." There were also monthly festivals on the day of the new moon, fifteenth, seventeen, and the last day of each month.

Fertility: Inanna was a goddess of love, fertility and procreation. There was a practice of marriage ceremony between the king and specially selected slave or prostitute every year in Inanna's temple in Erech. It was according to the idea that the king of Sumer, no matter who he was or from what city he originated, must become the husband of the life-giving goddess of love, Enanna of Erech.

Priest: The managerial head of the temple was the *sanga*, and his duties were to keep the temple buildings and finances in good order. The spiritual head of the temple was the *en*, it could be women or men, depending upon the sex of the deity of the temple where their services are dedicated. So, the goddess Inanna had the male *en*, and the moon-god Nanna had female *en*.

Sumerian Mythology: Sumerian mythology played an important role in Sumerian religious practices later. They are literary and probing in character. The myths contemplate the creation and organization of the universe, the birth of the gods, their love and hate, their meanness and conspiracies, their blessings and curses, their acts of creation and destruction. Even though the Sumerian myths appear matured and sophisticated in approach to the gods and their activities, the mythographers were the direct descendants of the illiterate musicians and entertainers of earlier days, and their goal was to compile describing gods that would be appealing, inspiring, and entertaining. Their literary approach had not contained logic and reason but imagination and fantasy. While telling their stories, they invented motives and incidents without any rational and speculative thought. They even adopted legendary and folklore topics that had nothing to do with cosmological investigation and analysis.

The major characters included in these myths are very few in number: the air-god Enlil, the water god Enki, the mother-goddess Ninhursag (also known as Nintu and Ninmah), the god of the south wind Ninurta, the moon-god Nanna-Sin, the Bedu-god, Martu, the goddess Inanna, and her unlucky spouse Dumuzi.

The air-god Enlil was the most important deity in Sumerian gods, and he was also known as "the father of the gods," "the king of all the land." According to legend, Enlil separated heaven from earth, brought "whatever was needful" on earth, designed the axe for agricultural and building purposes, and gave it to the "black-heads", which is Sumerians or humankind in general. Enlil created "Summer and Winter", trees and grains, produced abundance and prosperity, and appointed "Winter" as the "Farmer of the Gods," in charge of life-producing waters and of all that grows. All other gods prayed for his blessing.

Even though Enlil was the most powerful god in Sumerian mythology, his power was also limited under certain situations. According to one myth, "When man had not yet been created and the city if Nippur was inhabited by gods alone, its young man was the god Enlil; its young maid was the goddess Ninlil; and it's old woman was Ninlil's mother Nunbarshegunu. One day, Nunbarshegunu evidently having set her mind and heart on Ninlil's marriage to Enlil, encourages her daughter Ninlil to make friendship with Enlil.

Enlil asks one of his attendants to bring a boat, and both Enlil and Ninlil sail on the stream and Enlil impregnates her with the moon-god Sin. By this act, the gods got angry by this immoral deed, and even though he is their king, they seized him and banished him from the city to the netherworld. One passage reads:

"The great gods, the fifty of them,
The fate-decreeing gods, the seven of them,
Seize Enlil in the Kiur saying:
'Enlil, immoral one, get you out of the city,
Nunamnir (a nickname of Enlil), immoral one, get you
Out of the city.'"

According to the decree Enlil departs towards Sumerian Hell. The pregnant Ninlil also follows him and refuses to remain behind. This bothers Enlil because his son Sin, who is destined to be in charge of the largest luminous body, the moon, would have to reside in the dark gloomy netherworld instead of in the sky. So, he devised a very complicated plan. On the way to the netherworld from Nippur, Enlil meets three individuals: the gatekeeper in charge of Nippur gates; the man of the netherworld river; and the ferryman, who ferries the dead across to Hell. Enlil transforms himself as these three men, the first known example of divine metamorphosis, impregnates Ninlil with three other netherworld deities as substitutes for their older brother Sin. Now, moon-god Sin is free to go to heaven.

A story about Enki is a more detailed Sumerian myth related to the organization of the universe by Enki, the Sumerian water-god and god of wisdom. Many myths are found on Enki. There is a myth concerned with the creation of man from clay. It begins with a description about the hardships of the gods in obtaining their food. The gods complain to Enki, who was supposed to help them, but he was lying in deep sleep ignoring their complaint. Then his mother, the primeval sea, the mother who gave birth to all gods brings the tears of the gods before Enki and says:

O my son, rise from your bed, from your… work
What is wise,
Fashion servants of the gods, may they produce their
Doubles (?).

Then Enki considers their prayers and directs to his mother, the primeval sea, to design and create servants to the gods:

"O my mother, the creature whose name you uttered, it exists,

Bind upon it in the image (?) of the gods;
Mix the heart of the clay that is over the abyss,
The good and princely fashioners will thicken the clay,
You, do you bring the limbs into existence;
Ninmah (another name for Ninhursag) will work above you,
The goddesses (of birth….will stand by you at
Your fashioning;
O my mother, decree its (the new-born's) fate,
Ninmah will bind upon it the mold (?) of the gods,
It is man …

THUS, MAN IS CREATED FROM CLAY.

The poem continues the creation of other imperfect human types, abnormal beings and so on.

The Sumerian mythologies laid the foundation for later religious scriptures for Jewish, Christianity, Islam and other civilizations.

Sumerian Occupation

In ancient Mesopotamia men and women both worked because it was fundamentally an agrarian society. The principal occupations were growing crops and raising livestock. Other occupations consisted of the scribe, the healer, artisan, weaver, potter, shoemaker, fisherman, teacher, and priest or priestess. The historian Bertman writes:

> "At the head of society were the kings and priests served by the populous staff of the palace and temple. With the institution of standing armies and the spread of imperialism, military officers and professional soldiers took their place in Mesopotamia's expanding and diverse workforce.
>
> "Women enjoyed nearly equal rights and could own land, file for divorce, own their own businesses, and make contracts in trade. The early brewers of beer and wine, as well as the healers in the community, were initially women. These trades were later taken over by men when it became apparent, they were lucrative occupations. The work one did, however, was never considered simply a `job' but one's contribution to the community and, by extension, to the gods' efforts in keeping the world at peace and in harmony."

Sumerian Buildings and Government

The temple was built at the centre of every city on a raised platform, which symbolized the importance of the city's deity worshipped by its communities.

Mesopotamia is considered to be the world's first cities which were chiefly built by sun-dried brick. Unlike Egypt, Mesopotamia was empty of stone and had to be quarried for construction from other regions. Therefore, the people used other natural resources that were available abundantly at proximity. With them, the Mesopotamians created the world's first columns, arches, and roofed structures. Unsophisticated homes were constructed from bundles of reeds smashed together, while more sophisticated homes were built by sun-dried clay brick. Cities and temple complexes were all built using oven-baked bricks of clay which were later painted.

The people assumed that the gods were present near them always and watching their planning and execution of any building project, so they offered specific prayers, recited in a set of order to the appropriate deity. It was considered as extremely important in the success of the project and the prosperity of the occupants of the home. This respect for the divinity was typified in the lives of both the worker and the king.

Literary and Other Historical Sources

Kathleen Kuiper writes, "Besides the peaceful pursuits reflected in art and writing, the art also provides the first information about violent contacts: cylinder seals of the Uruk depict fettered men lying or squatting on the ground, being beaten with sticks or otherwise maltreated by standing figures. They may represent the execution of prisoners of war. This does give the first evidence for the wars that are henceforth one of the most characteristic phenomena in the history of Mesopotamia."Bottom of Form

Sumerian Literature: The Sumerian Aesthetic Essays

The study of the Sumerian people's ancient past exposed in the excavations of prolonged buried cities and villages of Sumer, and articulating its material culture is absolutely fascinating. The archaeological findings consist basically of bricks and walls, tools and weapons, pots and vases, jewels and ornaments, statutes and figures. In Sumer, archaeologists have excavated literally ***tens of thousands of inscribed clay tablets***, which enable the modern people to understand the ancient culture. More than 90 percent of inscribed material contains economic and administrative documents. But a collection of five thousand inscribed tablets and fragments excavated are of literary works, and these would assist the historians to permeate to certain extent into the ancient Sumerian's hearts and souls. The Sumerian literary texts extend in size from large twelve-column tablets inscribed with hundreds of compactly written lines of text to tiny fragments with a few broken lines, and they rank high among the aesthetic creations of civilized man.

This extraordinary work of archaeologists and excavators and the people responsible for the recovery and restoration of this ancient and long forgotten literature is a major contribution to humanity.

Sumerian literature is limited to myths, epic tales, hymns, lamentations, history, long and short essays, dictums and proverbs. They probably began writing their literary works about 2500 BCE. Historians have found a solid clay cylinder inscribed with twenty columns of text, consisting of a myth related mainly to the god Enlil and his sister Ninhursag, and Inanna, Enki, and Ninurta. Its plot is still unintelligible, the individual words, phrases, and ideas show a style and structure very similar to the myths of a much later time, indicating continuous and consistent literary development was going on over the centuries. The Sumerian literary works were all religious in nature and that they were compiled and edited by priests for use in temple. Majority of Sumerian literature is in poetic form. The use of meter and rhyme was not discovered yet, but all other poetic devices and techniques such as repetition and parallelism, metaphor and comparison, and chorus were used with skill, imagination and effect.

Historians feel that all things considered, the Sumerian writers had failed to express the feelings for closely knit plot structure; their narratives deviated from the topic disconnecting the theme and were monotonous without emphasizing the theme. He continues that Sumerian poets were also imperfect in a sense of climax. Their myths and epic tales had no intensification of emotion and suspense and the last narration is more interesting than the first.

Sumerian historian Samuel Noah Kramer devoted twenty-five years of his life for studying Sumerian civilization and copying the unpublished Sumerian literary texts scattered throughout museums all around the world.

Some Sumerian Myths List: The recovered Sumerian myths, complete or large part, are as follows:

1. Two in which the god Enlil plays the major role:
   "Enlil and Ninlil: The Birth of the Moon-God" and
   "The Creation of the Pickax - axe;
2. Four in which the god Enki is the superman, a central character:
   "Enki and the World Order: The Organization of the Earth and Its Cultural Processes,"
   "Enki and Ninhursag: A Sumerian Paradise Myth,"
   "Enki and Nimmah: The Creation of Man, and
   "Enki and Eridu";

3. One concerning the moon-god, Nanna-Sin:
   "The Journey of Nanna-Sin to Nippur";
4. Two about Ninurta:
   "The Deeds and Exploits of Ninurta" and
   "The Return of Ninurta to Nippur;
5. Five in which the goddess Inanna plays the major role:
   "Inanna and Enki: The Transfer of the Arts of Civilization from Eridu to Erech,
   "Inanna and the Subjugation of Mount Ebih,"
   "Inanna and Shukalletuda: The Gardener's Mortal Sin,"
   "Inanna's Descent to the Netherworld," and
   "Inanna and Bilulu";
6. Four in which the god Dumuzi plays the major role:
   "Dumuzi and Enkimdu: The Wooing of Inanna,"
   "The Marriage of Dumuzi and Inanna,"
   "The Death of Dumuzi," and
   ""Dumuzi and the Galla's",
7. One myth concerned with god of the Martu, the Semitic Bedu living west of Sumer:
   "The Marriage of Martu"
8. The Flood myth, in which the identity of the deity who was the main character is still doubtful.

Enki and the World Order

"Enki and the World Order" is an excellent demonstration of the Sumerian mythological imagination. It is one of the longest and carefully preserved poems. The poet starts a myth with a hymn addressed to Enki, praises Enki's power and command for providing earth with prosperity and abundance and describes various rites and rituals. According to the myth, Enki advances From Sumer to Ur and blesses it with prosperity. From Ur he goes to Meluhha (Meluhha is an ancient name for India) and blesses it with trees and reeds, oxen and birds, gold, tin, and bronze genergly. He then goes to Dilmum and blesses its needs and so on. Here is the copy of the full poem just to get the idea that how the poets in Sumer wrote such a lengthy poem 4500 years ago using clay tablets and clay cylinders.

The following is the translation of the existing text of the poem (the first fifty lines are omitted because those fragments were unintelligible.)

When father Enki comes out into the seeded Land, it brings forth fertile seed,
When Nudimmud comes out to my fertile sheep, it gives birth to the lamb,
When he comesout to my seeded cow, it gives birth to the fertile calf,
When he comes out to my fertile goat, it gives birth to the fertile kid,
When you have gone out to the field, to the cultivated field,
You pile up heaps and mounds on the high plain.
[You]… the… of the parched (?) earth.

Enki, the king of the Abzu, overpowering (?) in his majesty, speaks up with authority:

"My father, the king of the universe,
Brought me into existence in the universe,
My ancestor, the king of all the lands,
Gathered together all the *ME'S* , placed the me's in my hand.
From the Ekur, the house of Enlil,
I brought craftsmanship to my Abzu of Eridu.

I am the fertile seed, engendered by the great wild ox, I am the first Born son of An,
I am the 'great storm' who goes forth out of the 'great below,' I am The lord of the Land,
I am the gugal of the chieftains, I am the father of all the lands,
I am the 'big brother' of the gods, I am he who brings full prosperity,
I am the record keeper of heaven and earth,
I am the ear and the mind (?) of the all the lands,
I am he who directs justice with the king An on An's dais,
I am he who decrees the fates with Enlil in the 'mountain of wisdom,'
He placed in my hand the decreeing of the fates of the 'place where The sun rises,'
I am he to whom Nintu pays due homage,
I am he who has been called a good name by Ninhursag,
I am the leader of the Anunnaki,
I am he who has been born as the first son of the holy An."

After the lord had uttered (?) (his) exaltedness,
After the great prince had himself pronounced (his) praise,
The Anunnaki came before him in prayer and supplication:

"Lord who directs craftsmanship,
Who makes decisions, the glorified; Enki, praise!"

For a second time, because of (his) great joy,
Enki, the king of the Abzu, in his majesty, speaks up with authority:
"I am the lord, I am one whose command is unquestioned, I am the
Foremost in all things,
At my command the stalls have been built, the sheepfolds have been
Enclosed,
When I approached heaven, a rain of prosperity poured down from
Heaven,
When I approached the earth, there was a high flood,
When I approached its green meadows,
The heaps and mounds were piled up in my words.

I built my house, a shrine, in a pure place, I called it with a good name,
I built my Abzu, a shrine, in a…, I decreed a good fate for it.
My house-its shade stretches over the snake-marsh,
My house, its . . wears a beard among (?) the honey-plants (?),
The carps wave the tail to him in (?) the small gizi-reeds,
The sparrows chirp in their… ,

The weapon-carrying….,
Came into my Enki's, the abgal's,
… [into my]….. . ,
The enkum and ninkum ….,
Sacred songs and spells filled my Abzu.
My magur-boat, the crown, the 'ibex of the Abzu'—
In its midst there is a great rejoicing.
The lofty marshland, my favorite spot,
Stretches out its arms to me, bends its neck to me.
The kara's drew on the oars in unison,
Sing sweet songs, cause the river to rejoice,
Nimgirsig, the ensi of my magur-boat,
Held the gold scepter for me,
I, Enki,… d the boat ibex of Abzu,
I, the lord…. .,
I, Enki….

(Approximately five lines are missing)

…I would watch over its green cedars (?),
The lands of Magan and Dilmum
Looked up at me, Enki,
Secured the Dilmun-boat to the ground (?),
Loaded the Magan-boat sky high;
The magilum-boat of Meluhha
Transports gold and silver,
Brings them to Nippur for Enlil, the kind of all the lands.

To him who has no city, to him who has no horse,
The Martu-Enki presented cattle as a gift,

To the great prince who came forth in his land,
The Anunnaki pay due homage:
"Lord who rides the great me's, the pure me's,
Who has charge of the universe, the widespread,
Who received the lofty 'sun-disk' in Eridu, the pure place, the most
Precious place,
Enki, lord of the universe praise!"

For the great prince who comes forth in his land,
All the lords, all the chieftains,
The incarnation priests of Eridu,
The "linen-weavers" of Sumer,
Perform the incantation ritesof the Abzu,
To (?) father Enki in (?) the holy place… they direct their step,
In the sleeping chamber, the princely house, they… ,
In the stations they call his name,
In (?) the lofty shrine, the Abzu they… ,
(about 36 lines are destroyed)
Ningirsig, the ensi of the magur-boat,
Held the holy scepter for the lord,
The lahama's of the sea, the fifty, did homage to him,
The kara's… d like a bird of heaven.
For the kind standing proudly, father Enki—in the Land -
The great prince who came forth in his Land,
Prosperity prevailed in the universe.

Enki decrees the fate:
"Sumer, 'great mountain,' 'country of the universe,'

Filled with enduring light, dispensing from sunrise to sunset the me's
To (?) the people,
Your me's are lofty me's, unreachable.
Your heart is profound, unfathomable.
The enduring…, you place where gods give birth, is untouchable
Like heaven.
The born king, who dons the enduring diadem —
The born lord, who puts crown on head —
Your lord is an honored lord, he sits with the king An on An's dais,
Your kind .. the 'great mountain,' Father Enlil,
Has . . d him for you by (?) the… like a cedar — the father of all the lands.
The Anunnaki, the great gods,
Have taken up their dwelling place in your midst,
Eat their food in your tree-planted giguna.
House, Sumer, may your many stalls be built, may your cows multiply,
May your many sheepfolds be erected, may your sheep be myriad,
May your giguna reach skyward,
May your enduring… lift hand to heaven.
May the Anunnaki decree the fates in your midst.

He proceeded to the shrine Ur,
Enki, the kind of the Abzu decrees its fate:
"City possessing all that is appropriate, water-washed, firm-standing ox,
Dais of abundance of the highland, knees open, green like a mountain,
Hashur-grove, wide of shade - he who is lordly because of his might
Has directed your perfect me's,
Enlil, the 'great mountain,' has pronounced your lofty name in the universe,
City whose fate has been decreed by Enlil,
Shrine Ur, may you rise heaven high."
He proceeded to the land Muluhha,
Enki, the king of the Abzu, decrees its fate:
"Black land, may your trees be large trees, may they be 'highland' trees,
May their thrones fill the royal palace,

May your reeds be large reeds, May they be 'highland' reeds,
May the heroes in the place of battle wield their weapons,
May your bulls be large bulls, may they be 'hindland' bulls,
May their cry be the cry of 'high' wild bulls,
May the great me's of the gods be perfected for you,
May all dar-birds of the highland wear carnelian beards,
May your bird be the Haia-bird,
May it calls fill the royal palace,
May your silver be gold,
May your copper be tin and bronze,
Land, may everything you have, increase,
May your people multiply,
May your .. go forth like a bull to his …"

…. the city of . .
He treated (?) like ….,
He cleansed, purified the land Dilmun,
Placed Ninsikilla in charge of it,
He gave . . as . . , he eats its… -fish,
He gave . . as a cultivated field (?), he eats its dates.

…. Elam and Marhashi…
Were destined to be devoured like…-fish;
The king (presumably Enki) upon whom Enlil had bestowed might,
Destroyed their houses, destroyed their walls.
Their precious metal and lapis lazuli and the contents of their storehouses,
He brought to Nippur for Enlil - the king of all the lands.
To him who builds no city, builds no house -
The Martu - Enki presented cattle as a gift.

After he had cast his eye from the spot,
After father Enki had lifted it over the Euphrates,
He stood up proudly like a rampant bull,
He lifts the genital, ejaculates,
Filled the Tigris with sparkling water,
The wild cow mooing for its young in the pastures, the scorpion infested stall,
The Tigris surrendered to him, as to a rampant bull.

He lifted the genital, brought the bridal gift,
Brought joy to the Tigris, like a big wild bull rejoiced (?) in its giving birth.
The water he brought is sparkling water, its wine tastes sweet,
The grain he brought, its checkered grain, the people eat it,
He filled the Ekur, the house of Enlil, with possessions,
With Enki, Enlil rejoices, Nippur is delighted.

The lord donned the diadem for lordship,
Put on the enduring crown for kingship,
Trod the ground on his left side,
Prosperity came forth out of the earth for him.
After he had placed the scepter in his right hand,
In order to make the Tigris and Euphrates "eat together,"
He who utters the . . word in accordance with his . . ,
Who carries off like fat the 'princely knee' from the palace,
The lord who decrees the fate, Enki the king of the Abzu,
Enbilulu, the inspector of canals,
Enki placed in charge of them.

He called the marshland, placed in it carp and…-fish,
He called the canebrake, placed in it…-reeds and green reeds,
(two lines missing)
He issued a challenge…
Him whose net no fish escapes,
Whose trap no… escapes,
Whose snare no bird escapes,
…the son of…
…a god who loves fish,
Enki placed in charge of them.

The lord erected a shrine (?), a holy shrine - its heart is profound,
Rected a shrine (?) in the sea, a holy shrine - its heart is profound,
The shrine - its midst is a …, known to no one,
The shrine - its station is the …iku constellation,
The lofty shrine, above (?) its station stand (?) by the chariot, constellation,
The…from the trembling… its melam's . .,
The Anunnaki came with prayer and supplication,

For Enki in the E-[engurra they set up] a lofty dais.
For the lord…,
The great prince . . , born ..,
The u-bird ….., (approximately three lines are missing)
Her who is the great inundation of the deep,
Who . . s the izi-bird and the lil-fish, who… ,
Who comes out from the zipag, who… ,
The Lady of Sirara, Mother Nanshe,
Of the sea, of its… places,
Enki placed in charge.

He called the "two" rains, the water of the heaven,
Aligned them like floating clouds,
Drives (?) their (?) breath of life toward the horizon,
Turns (?) the hilly ground into fields.
Him who rides the great storm, who attacks with lightning (?),
Who closes the holy bolt in the 'heart' of heaven,
The son of An, the gugal of the universe,
Ishkur . . , the son of An,
Enki placed in charge of them.

He directed the plow and the . . yoke,
The great prince Enki put the 'horned oxen' in the… ,
Opened the holy furrows,
Made grow the grain in the cultivated field.
The lord who dons the diadem, the ornament of the high plain,
The robust, the farmer of Enlil,
Enkimdu, the man of the ditch and dike,
Enki placed in charge of them.

The lord called the cultivated field, put there the checkered grain,
Heaped up it . . grain, the checkered grain, the innuba-grain into piles,
Enki multiplied the heaps and mounds,
With Enlil he spread wide the abundance in the Land,
Her whose head and side are dappled, whose face is honey-covered,
The Lady, the procratress, the vigor of the Land, the "life" of the black-heads,

Ashnan, the nourishing break, the bread of all,
Enki placed in charge of them.

The great prince put the "net" upon the pickax (axe), then directed the mold,
Fertilized the *agarin*, like good butter,
Him whose crushing pickax-tooth is a snake devouring the corpses,
....,
Whose . . mold directs... ,
Kulla, the brick-maker (?) of the Land,
Enki placed in charge of them.

He built stalls, directed the purification rites,
Erected sheepfolds, put there the best fat and milk,
Brought joy to the dining halls of the gods,
In the vegetation-like plain he made prosperity prevail.
The trustworthy provider of Eanna, the "friend of An,"
The beloeved son-in-law of the valiant Sin, the husband of holy Inanna,
The Lady, the queen of all the great me's,
Who time and again commands the procreation of the... of Kullab,
Dumuzi, the divine "*ushumgal* of heaven," the "the friend of An,"
Enki placed in charge of them.

He filled the Ekur, the house of Enlil, with possessions,
Enlil rejoiced with Enki, Nippur was joyous,
He fixed the borders, demarcated them with boundary stones,
Enki, for the Anunnki,
Erected dwelling places in the cities,
Set up fields for them in the countryside,
The hero, the bull who comes forth out of the *hashur* forest, who roars lion-like,
The valiant Utu, the bull who stands secure, who proudly displays his power,
The father of the great city, the place where the sun rises, the great herald of holy An,
The judge, the decision-maker of the gods,
Who wears a lapis lazuli beard, who comes forth from the holy
Heaven, the... heaven,

Utu, the son born of Ninga,
Enki placed in charge of the entire universe.

He wove the *mug*-cloth, directed the *temenos*,
Enki perfected greatly that which is woman's task,
For Enki, the people…d the… -garment,
The tiara (?) of the palace, the jewel of the king,
Uttu, the trustworthy woman, the joyous (?),
Enki placed in charge of them.

Then all by herself, having abandoned the royal scepter,
The woman,…, the main Inanna having abandoned the royal scepter
Inanna, to her father Enki,
Enters the house, and humbly weeping, utters a plaing (?):
"The Anunnaki, the great gods - their fate
Enlil placed firmly in your hand,
Me, the woman, why did you treat differently?
I, the holy Inanna, - where are my prerogatives?

Aruru, Enlil's sister,
Nintu, the queen of the mountain,
Has taken for herself her holy… of lordship,
Has carried off for herself her… and leeks,
Has taken for herself her inlaid (?) *sila*-vessel of lapis lazuli,
Has carried off for herself her holy, pure *ala*-vessel,
She has become the midwife of the Land,
In her hand you have placed the born king, the born lord.

That sister of mine, the holy Ninisinna,
Has taken for herself the bright *unu*, has become the hierodule of An,
Has stationed herself near (?) An, utters the word which fills (?) heaven.

That sister of mine, the holy Ninmug,
Has taken for herself the gold chisel and the silver hammer (?),
Has become the metalworker of the Land,
The born king, who dons the enduring diadem,
The born lord who puts crown on head, you have placed [in her hand].

That sister of mine, the holy Nidaba,
Has taken for herself the measuring rod,

Has fastened the lapis lazuli line (?) on her arm,
Proclaims all the great me's,
Fixes the borders, marks off the boundaries - has become the scribe
Of the Land,
In her hands you have placed the food of the gods.

Nanshe, the lady, the lord - the holy… fell at her feet,
She has become the fishery inspector of the sea,
Fish, tasty, and ….,
She presents to her father Enlil,
Me, the woman, why did you treat differently?
I, holy Inanna, where are my prerogatives?"
(approximately three lines are missing)
…his… ,
"Enlil… ,
Has adorned (?) for you ….,
You wear there the garment (?) 'might of the young lad.'
You have established the words spoken by the 'young lad,'
You have taken charge of the crook, staff, and wand of shephership,
Maid Inanna, what, what more shall we add to you?
Battles and onslaughts - of their oracles you give the answer,
In their midst, you who are not an *arabu*-bird, give and unfavorable answer,
You twist the straight thread,
Maid Inanna, you straighten the twisted thread,
You have fashioned garments, you wear garments,
You have woven *mug*-cloth, you have threaded the spindle,
In your… you have dyed (?) the many-colored . . thread.
Inanna, you have… ,
Inanna, you have destroyed the indestructible, you have made perish
The imperishable,
You have silenced (?) the . . with the 'timber of lament,'
Maid Inanna, you have returned the *tigi*- and *adab*-hymns to their house.
You whose admirers to not grow weary to look at,
Maid Inanna, you who know not the distant wells, the fastening ropes;
Lo, the inundation has come, the Land is restored,
The inundation of Enlil has come, the Land is restored."
(Remaining nineteen lines are destroyed)

Professor Noah Kramer writes that written epics of the Greek, Hindu, and Germanic heroic literatures date from much later period and comprise highly complex and sophisticated literary form and abridged versions. The three Indo-European epics show a number of striking similarities in the form and content. However, there are a number of outstanding differences that also exist between the Sumerian epic material and the Greeks, Indians, and Teutons (Germanic) literature.

The Author Noah Kramer evaluates the Sumerian and Indo-European literature: "The Sumerian epic poems consist of individual, disconnected tales of varying length, each of which is restricted to a single episode. There is no attempt to articulate and integrate these episodes into a larger unit. There is relatively little characterization and psychological penetration in the Sumerian material. The heroes tend to be broad types, more or less undifferentiated. Moreover, the incidents and plot motifs are related in a rather static and conventionalized style; there is little of that malleable, expressive movement that characterizes such poems as Homer's Iliad and Odyssey. Mortal women play hardly any role in Sumerian epic literature whereas they have a very prominent part in Indo-European epic literature. The Sumerian poet makes no use whatever of the meters or uniform line so characteristic in Indo-European epics. . … Since the narrative poetry of the Sumerians is by all odds the oldest of the four, it is not impossible that it was in Sumer that the epic genre first originated and that it spread from there to the lands around."

Sumerian Hymns: In addition to epics the hymnography was a prudently cultivated art in Sumer. Record numbers of hymns, ranging from 50 lines to 400 lines, have been discovered and Noah Kramer believes it is only a fraction that Sumerian poets have created. They are categorized as: 1. Hymns exalting the gods; 2) hymns praising kings; 3) hymns of victory to kings; and 4) hymns glorifying Sumerian temples.

The common word for Sumerian hymns is sir (Hebrews also use shir in place of sir, most probably similar to Hindu sri). They categorically included sir in their composition. For example, *sir-hamun* - "harmony hymns"; *sir-namnar* - musical hymns; *sir-namgala* - hymns of *gala*-ship; *sir-namursagga* - hymns of heroship; *and sir-namsipad-inanna-ka* - hymns of shepherd-ship of Inanna. They also had lamentation hymns.

Disputation: A composition "The Disputation between the Two School Graduates" consists about 140 lines which begins with a very arrogant address to the other graduate, "Old grad, come, let us debate." The competitor responds with the same arrogance, and the insults fly back and forth to the very end of the composition and closes with an insulting attack by one of the competitors consisting of 28 lines full of spiteful abuse. Another composition is a disputation between two ladies also about the vengeance.

Essay: The essays appear more gratifying than the compositions of disputation. Mostly they are in dialogue form and concerned with life and the value of education. A brief essay inscribed on a tablet describes a story about an evil and hated man Tani, who followed violence, hated righteousness and truth, and acted monstrously.

Sumerian Proverbs: Total number of Sumerian proverb materials contain approximately 700 tablets and fragments, and many of them were not identified until he wrote this book in 1963. These tablets contain more than a thousand proverbs. They show a deep evaluation of the human scene, the drives and motives, the hopes and desires, and the ironies and contradictions which encompass it. He provides more intelligible proverbs as translated by Edmund Gordon: (4000 year old proverbs!!)

1. Don't pick it now; later it will bear fruit.
2. He who eats much cannot sleep.
3. It's not the heart which leads to enmity; it's the tongue which leads to enmity.
4. Tell a lie; then if you tell the truth it will be deemed a lie.
5. Possessions are sparrows in flight which can find no place to alight.
6. Build like a lord - live like a slave; build like a slave - live like a lord.
7. Hand to hand - man's house is built; stomach to stomach - a man's house is destroyed.
8. Poorly fed - grandly living.
9. A scribe who knows not Sumerian, what kind of scribe is he?
10. A scribe whose hand moves as fast as the mouth, that's a scribe for you.
11. Friendship last a day; kinship lasts forever.
12. Who has much silver may be happy;
    Who has much grain may be glad;
    But he who has nothing can sleep.
13. A sweet word is everybody's friend.
14. A loving heart builds the home;
    a hating heart destroys the home.
15. A desert canteen is a man's life;

the shoe is a man's eye;
the wife is a man's future;
the son is a man's refuge;
the dauther is a man's salvation;
the daughter-in-law is a man's devil.

16. A singer whose voice is not sweet is a poor singer indeed.
17. Let what's mine stay unused;
    but let me use what is yours
18. You don't tell me what you have found;
    You only tell what you have lost.
19. Into an open mouth, a fly enters.
20. When walking, come now, keep your feet on the ground.
21. In a city without dogs, the fox is the overseer.
22. The fox trod upon the hoof of the wild ox, saying, "Didn't it hurt?"
23. A cat - for its thoughts! A mongoose - for its deeds!

Literary catalogue: The scholars have created the ancient Sumerian literary catalogues, which required the need of handling, storing, and recording the thousands of tablets that inscribed hundreds of literary compositions. Seven catalogues dating from the 2000 BCE have been excavated and are located in the following Museums:

1. One in Iraq Museum in Baghdad
2. One in Louvre, France
3. One in University Museum of the University of Pennsylvania
4. One in Berlin Museum
5. Two in Hilprecht Collection in the Friedrich-schiller University in Jena
6. One in British Museum .

Sumerian Education: The Sumerian School

He whose eyes are not open enters it,
He whose eyes are wide open comes out of it? (What is it?)
The Answer Is: It is The School.

– **Sumerian Riddle, ~2500 BC**

In the history of civilization point of view, Sumer's monumental achievements were the development of the cuneiform system of writing, and the standard system of education are its explicit contribution to the world. Had it not been anonymous Sumerian pundits and teachers who lived in 3000 BCE and their inventiveness and perseverance, the intellectual and scientific achievements of modern days would not have been possible. It was from Sumer that writing, and learning spread all over the world. In ancient Shuruppak, a large number of school "textbooks" dating from about 2500 BCE were excavated consisting of all kinds of subjects. *Tens of thousands* of clay tablets have been excavated and still hundreds of thousands of tablets could be excavated. Excavators have discovered hundreds of practice-tablets of exercises prepared by the students from first-grader to far-advanced students as a part of daily homework. The ancient professors and teachers themselves wanted to write about school life, and their essays on various subjects have been recovered. Based on all these resources, it is possible to imagine the Sumerian school, its purpose, aims, goals, its students and faculty, its curriculum and teaching techniques. It is a purely unique system in that early period of humankind's history.

The Sumerian school was known as *edubba, the* "tablet house." Within its walls flourished the scholar-scientists, the men who studied theological, botanical, zoological, geographical, mathematical, grammatical, and linguistic knowledge whatever existed in those days and later they added more to this knowledge. Most students became scribes.

In antiquity, education was not compulsory and not all children went to school. Large number of students came from wealthy families; the poor could not afford the time and money to go to school.

Sumerian School

The chief of the Sumerian school was called Ummia, professor was called "school-father" while the student was called "school-son", and alumnus "the school-son of days past." The assistant professor was known as "big brother." There was also a monitor who was responsible for maintaining discipline.

School teachers and staff also prepared all types of mathematical tables and mathematical problems. In the linguistic field, it is found that Sumerian grammar was inscribed in a long list of complex and verbal forms which indicate that a sophisticated grammatical approach existed. In the last quarter of 3000 BCE, ancient professors prepared oldest dictionaries.

Student's responsibilities:

> "It was only when the student had become well acquainted with the writing of the complex Sumerian vocabulary that he began to copy and memorize short sentences, proverbs, and fables, and also collections of 'model' contracts (essential for the edition of legal documents), which played a large role in the economic life of Sumer. Along with this linguistic training, the student was also given instruction in mathematics, which took the form of studying and copying meteorological tables, with the equivalence of measures of capacity, length and weight, as well as multiplication and reciprocal tables for computation purposes. Later the student was put to solving practical problems dealing with wages, canal-digging, and construction work."

Discipline: Discipline was a major problem in the Sumerian school. Using a rod is not restricted. Even though teachers inspired students to do good work by praising and awarding, they rested primarily on the cane for correcting student's mistakes and failures. Students also had no easy time: they attended school daily from sunrise to sunset; spent many years in the school; stayed in the school from their early youth to the day when they became young men.

School Building: The possible school buildings were uncovered during Mesopotamian excavation; one in Nippur, another in Sippar, and a third in Ur. For a long time it was doubtful to distinguish between a house and a school building. Around 1900, French excavated an ancient site at Mari and uncovered two rooms which definitely had physical features that were characteristic of a schoolroom.

A riddle of a school building on a tablet read as follows:

> A house which like heaven has a plow,
> Which like a copper kettle is cloth-covered,
> Which like a goose stands on a base,

He whose eyes are not open enters it,
He whose eyes are wide open comes out of it?

The Answer is: It is the School.

There are four better preserved essays related to school: (1) Schooldays, (2) School Rowdies, (3) A Scribe and His Perverse Son, and (4) Colloquy between an *ugula* and a Scribe. Each essay deals with a particular topic.

Dr. Samuel Noah Kramer narrates a translated Samarian essay of 4000 years old "Schooldays" as follows:

"The composition begins with a direct question to an old alumnus which reads: "Old Grad, where did you go when you were young?" the latter answers: "I went to school." The professor-author then asks: What did you do in school?" this is the cue for the old grad to recollect about his school activities thus:

I recited my tablet, ate my lunch, prepared my new tablet, wrote it, finished it; then my model tablets were brought to me; and in the afternoon my exercise tablets were brought to me. When school was dismissed, I went home, entered the house, and found my father sitting there. I explained my exercise-tablets to my father, (?) recited my tablet to him, and he was delighted, (so much so) that I attended him with joy.

The author now has the schoolboy turn to the house servants (it was evidently quite a well-to-do home) with these words:

I am thirsty, give me water to drink; I am hungry, give me bread to eat; wash my feet, set up my bed, I want to go to sleep. Wake me early in the morning, I must not be late lest my teacher cane me.

Presumably all this was done, for we next find our schoolboy saying:

When I arose early in the morning, I faced my mother and said to her: "Give me my lunch, I want to go to school." My mother gave me two rolls, and I went to school. In school the fellow in charge of punctuality said: "Why are you late?" Afraid and with a pounding heart, I entered before my teacher and made a respectful curtsy.

But curtsy or not, it was a bad day for the ancient pupil - at least as the old grad remembered it rather nostalgically - he had to take canings from various members of the school staff. Or, in the words which the author puts in the mouth of alumnus:

My headmaster read my tablet, said:

"There is something missing," caned me.

(two intelligible lines)

The fellow in charge of neatness (?) said:
"You loitered in the street and did not straighten up (?) your cloths (?)," caned me.
(two intelligible lines)

The fellow in charge of silence said:
"Why did you talk without permission," caned me.

The fellow in charge of the assembly (?) said:
"Why did you stand at ease (?) without permission," caned me.

The fellow in charge of good behaviour said:
"Why did you rise without permission," caned me.
The fellow in charge of the gate said:
"Why did you go out from the gate without permission," caned me.

The fellow in charge of the whip said:
"Why did you take . . without permission," caned me.
The fellow in charge Sumerian said:
"Why didn't you speak Sumerian," caned me.

My teacher (*ummia*) said:
"Your hand is unsatisfactory," caned me.
And so, I began to hate the scribal art, began to neglect the scribal art.
My teacher took no delight in me; even stopped teaching (?) me his skill in the scribal art; in no way prepared me in the matters essential to the art of being a "young scribe," or the art of being a "big brother."

In despair, according to our old grad, he turned to his father, saying: Give him a big extra salary, and let him become more kindly (?); let him be free for a time from arithmetic; when he counts up all the school affairs of the students, let him count me (too among them; that is, perhaps, let him not neglect me any longer).

From here on, the ancient author himself takes over describing the events thus:

To that which the schoolboy said, his father gave heed. The teacher was brought from school, and after entering in the house, he was seated on the "big chair." The schoolboy attended and served him, and whatever he learned of the scribal art, he unfolded to his father. Then did the in the joy of his heart say joyfully to the headmaster of the school:

> "My little fellow has opened wide his hand, and you made wisdom enter there; you showed him all the fine points of the scribal art; you made him see the solutions of the mathematical and arithmetical problems, you taught him how to make deep (?) the cuneiform script (?).

The ancient author now has the father turn to his household servants, saying:

> Pour for him irda-oil, bring it to the table for him. Make fragrant oil flow like water on his stomach and back; I want to dress him in a garment, give him some extra salary, put a ring on his hand.

The servants do as they are bidden, and the teacher speaks to the schoolboy:

> "Young fellow, because you hated not my words, neglected them not, may you complete the scribal art from beginning to end. Because you gave me everything without stint, paid me a salary larger than my efforts, and have honoured me, may *Nidaba*, the queen of guardian angels, be your guardian angel; may your pointed stylus write well for you; may your exercises contain no faults. Of your brothers, may you be their leader; of your friends may you be their chief; may you tank the highest among the school graduates, satisfy (?) all who walk (?) to and from in the palaces. Little fellow, you know your father, I am second to him; that homage be paid to you, that you be blessed - may the god of your father bring this about with firm hand; he will bring prayer and supplication to Nidaba, your queen, as if it were a matter for your god. Thus, when you put a kindly hand on the… of the teacher, and on the forehead of the "big brother," then (?) your young comrades will show you favor. You have carried out well the school's activities; you are a man of learning. You have exalted Nidaba, the queen of learning; O Nidaba, praise!"

Character: Psychological and Emotional Aspects of Sumerians.

So far we have dealt with Sumerian's social, political, economic, administrative, legal, religious, technological, artistic, and literary aspects. Now, let us look at the psychological points such as the character and personality of the people who created Sumerian civilization. Kramer has published two articles: 1. Rivalry and Superiority: Two Dominant Features of the Sumerian Culture Pattern," and 2. Love, Hate, and Fear: Psychological Aspects of Sumerian Culture. In the first article, he describes Sumerian behaviour as the drive for superiority and prestige emphasizing stress on competition and success. And in the second article he describes the role of love, hate, and fear as motivation emotional drives. There was a passion between male and female that usually ended in marriage, the love between husband and wife, between parents and children, between members of the family, between friends and associates, and the love between gods, kings, and people.

It was a custom that marriage in ancient Sumer was a practical arrangement where money prudently weighed more than love. However, there were many cases of clandestine love between lovers ending with marriage. One revealing example is provided by a Sumerian poem inscribed on a tablet in the Hilprecht Collection in the University of Jena, "Love Finds a Way" or "Fooling Mother". The two main characters in the poem are Inanna "Queen of Heaven," the Sumerian Venus and "Dumuzi". The poem is written by an ancient scribe *tigi.* It begins with a soliloquy by Inanna saying one day when she was naively singing and dancing, Dumuzi met her, took her hand, and embraced her; then she requested him to let go her because she did not know how to keep this love secret from her mother Ningal, wife of the moon-god Sin. Dumzi suggests deceiving Inanna's mother by telling her to say that she went to the market square with her girl-friend to watch some entertainment.

Love: Here are the poet *tigi's* own words in translation:

Inanna says:
"Last night as I the queen was shining bright,
Last night as I the queen of heaven was shining bright,
As I was shining bright, was dancing about,
As I was singing away while the bright light overcame (?) the night.
He met me, he met me,
The lord Kuli-Anna (Dumuzi) met me,
The lord put his hand into my hand,
Ushumgal-Anna (Dumuzi) embraced me.

Inanna pleads:
Come (?) now (?) set me free, I must go home,
Kuli-Enlil (Dumuzi) set me free, I must go home,
What can I say to deceive my mother!
What can I say to deceive my mother, Ningal!

Dumzi says:
I will tell you, I will tell you,
Inanna, most deceitful of women, I will tell you,

Say "My girlfriend, she took me with her to the public square,
There a player (?) entertained (?) us with dancing,
His chant, the sweet, he sang for us,
In sweet rejoicing he whiled away the time for us";

Thus deceitfully stand up to your mother,
While we by the moonlight take our fill of love,
I will prepare (?) for you a bed pure, sweet, and noble,
The sweet day will bring you joyful fulfilment."

After that night, Dumuzi agreed to marry her. It is said that the first para of the stanza has been destroyed. Inanna makes a joyful announcement to her mother and the poem ends with Inanna praising Dumuzi who is her future husband and also the future victim of her dreadful rage.

Inanna says:

"I (Inanna) have come to my mother's gate,
Walking in joy,
I have come to Ningal's gate,
Walking in joy,
To my mother he (Dumuzi) will say the word,
Will sprinkle cypress oil on the floor,
To my mother Ningal he will say the word,
Will sprinkle cypress oil on the floor,
He whose dwelling is fragrant,
Whose word brings joy.

My lord of pure and seemly limbs,
Ama-Ushumgal-Anna, the son-in-law of Sin,
My lord, sweet is your increase,
Tasty your plants and herbs in the plain,
Ama-Ushumgal-Anna, sweet is your increase,
Tasty your plants and herbs in the plain.

According to the myth, Damuzi comes to Inanna's house and asks for permission to marry Inanna. As per her mother's advice, Inanna bathes and anoints with fragrance, wears her queenly dress, decorates herself with precious stone ornaments, and opens the door for Dumuzi.

In another version, the permission of Inanna's father, the moon-god Sin, was essential and she sent a messenger to her father with a request to allow her to marry Dumuzi.

In Sumer not all marriages were for mutual benefit, but at least some instances were motivated by love and desire.

In some cases, the marriage was a burden on Sumerian man:

"Who has not supported a wife or child,

Has not borne a leash."

In some instances, the Sumerian husband was sometime neglected as one records shows:

"My wife is at the outdoor shrine,

My mother is down by river,

And here am I starving of hunger."

There are some incidents that the Sumerian man regretted his marriage:

"For his pleasure — marriage;

On his thinking it over — divorce."

Throughout Sumerian documents, the kings of Sumer are known as the beloved husbands (conceptual husbands) of Inanna, Dumuzi was identified as physically married to Inanna. According to the Sumerian mythographers, Inanna handed over Dumuzi to demons who carried him to the netherworld.

Love of the nation, patriotism, and predominantly love of the home town was a powerful moving force in Sumerian thought and action. The residents of a city were considered as 'sons' and had close relationships. They were very proud about their city, god, and ruler and were always ready to fight in defence of their city. A 2500 BCE royal hymns reveal, it was the king's sacred and patriotic duty to protect the land from enemies and maintain security and well-being of the land and of the people.

The love of the people for their city and state manifests in their heart-breaking lamentation poems in Sumerian poets who wrote the destruction of both city and state.

Hate: Where there is love, there is hate. One of the examples is about Gilgamesh's aphorism on beloved wife and the hated wife, the beloved son and the hated son:

"Kiss not your beloved wife,

Kiss not your beloved son.

Strike not your hated wife,

Strike not your hated son."

The god Hendursag is a king who loved justice but hated violence. Probably, in Sumer hatred played a dominant role in their behaviour because their political, economic and educational organizations demonstrate very aggressive competition for pride, prestige, superiority, and predominance. This must have produced a high degree of hatred, disrespect, and dislike.

The gods also displayed their hatred and anger. Examples are Enlil puts the people of Kish to death and crushes the houses of Erech into dust. Because his Ekur in Nippur was looted, he brings raging flood and barbarous mountain people Gutians to destroy Sumer.

Goddess Ninhursag was angry on Enki because he ate eight plants which she had created and pronounced a curse of death upon Enki.

God Ninurta furiously curses the stones who acted injuriously toward him in his struggle with the Asag demon.

Most important story of hate in Sumerian mythology is our great lover Inanna; the cruel, ambitious, aggressive and attractive goddess. When Damuzi put on a noble robe and sat high on his seat instead of crawling before Inanna, she became furious and sent him to the netherworld with the seven demons.

Ancient poet writes:

> "She fastened the eye upon him, the eye of death,
> Spoke the word against him, the word of wrath,
> Uttered the cry against him, the cry of guilt."

When a farmer took advantage of tired Inanna and raped her, she sent three destructive plagues against Sumer to locate her abuser. When Gilgamesh rejected Inanna's love application, she sent a vicious 'bull of heaven' to devastate his city of Erech. Even some hymns depict her as a goddess of bitter anger and frightful destructions.

Fear: Fear engulfed Sumerian people from birth to death and the fear was deep and dark in Sumerian way of life. They feared their parents, teachers, friends, and fellow citizens, superiors and rulers, the foreign enemy, the violence of nature, wild animals, vicious monsters and demons, sickness, death, and extinction. One Sumerian thinker dreams:

> "Once upon a time, there was no snake, there was no scorpion,
> There was no hyena, there was no lion,
> There was no wild dog, no wolf,
> There was no fear, no terror,
> Man had no rival."

Values: Love of life permeates Sumerian civilization that is fundamental in all cultures. Abundant number of prayer inscriptions dedicated to one or other god affirms to prolong their own life or for the life of close family members. The royal hymnal prayers are full of special prayers for the long life of the king. While other cultures cherished life and valued it profoundly, the Sumerians tenaciously gripped it because according to their theology that after death the feeble spirit descends to the dark netherworld where life was a miserable reflection of life on earth. They envisioned that there was no heart-lifting, soul-soothing hope of a life in paradise, though they believed that deserving good people will have happier destiny than the bad and evil people.

Some of the Sumerian proverbs illustrate the weakness, helplessness, and agony of the poor:

"When a poor man dies, do not try to revive him.

When he had bread he had no salt, when he had salt he had no bread,

When he had meat he had no condiment, when he had the condiment he had no meat.

Wealth is hard to come by, but poverty is always with us.

The poor have no power.

How lowly is the poor man; the edge of the oven is his mill.

His ripped garment stays unmended; what he has lost remains unsought for."

There was no hope and consoling promises of good days to the Sumerian poor. So, the pursuit of wealth played an important role in Sumerian life.

Ethics and Morals: The ancient documents disclose that the Sumerians treasured and valued goodness and truth, law and order, justice and freedom, wisdom and learning, courage and loyalty, in essence, all most suitable virtues and qualities. Even there are some glimpses of mercy and compassion in protective treatment to widows, orphans, and refugees as well as poor and oppressed.

Debate: There were many quarrelsome debates and contests in Sumer. Here is an example of copper addressing silver in "Copper-Silver" debate.

Copper:

"Silver, only in the palace do you find a station that is the place to which you are assigned.

"If there were no palace, you would have no station; gone would be your dwelling place.....

"In the ordinary home, you are buried away in its darkest spots, its graves, its 'places of escape' from this world.

"When Irrigation time comes, you don't supply man with the stubble-loosening copper mattock; that is why nobody pays any attention to you!

"When planting time comes, you don't supply man with the plough-fashioning copper adz; that is why nobody pays any attention to you!

"When winter comes, you don't supply man with the firewood-cutting copper ax; that is why nobody pays any attention to you!

"When the harvest time comes, you don't supply man with the grain-cutting copper sickle, that is why nobody pays any attention to you!

"Silver, if there were no palace, you would have neither station nor dwelling place; only the grave, the place of escape would be your station.

"Silver, if it were for these places, you would have no place to be assigned to! ……

"Like a god you don't put your hand to any useful work.

"How dare you then to assail me like a wolf? Get into your dark shrines; lie down in your graves!

The insults which mighty Copper had hurled against Silver made him feel wretched; the insults filled with shame and bitterness made him smart and wince like water from a salty well .. Then did Silver give the retort to mighty Copper…"

Dr. Kramer writes that silver's bitter address does not make sense at this point of time. Another wonderful debate is "Dispute Between Summer and Winter."

Evidently, the drive for superiority and prestige played an important role in Sumerian's education, politics and economics. Unfortunately, the passion for competition, superiority and prestige carried the seed of self-destruction and triggered the bloody and disastrous wars between city-states. It obstructed the unification of the country as a whole and exposed Sumer to foreign attacks, which finally overpowered the Sumer and annihilated the Sumerian civilization.

Heritage of Sumer

If civilization means anything to modern people living now, long-dead Sumerians may aim their fingerless point with pride towards their innumerable innovations, inventions, and organizations which they initiated. We may say, Sumerians or no Sumerians, all these would have happened anyhow regardless of Sumerians. But, the Sumerians were the first to originate these talents in human history and it is not unfair to give credit where it is due.

There are many significant contributions to the culture of humankind by Sumerians, particularly to their neighbour nations, near and far, in making history. An example of Aratta, a remote land in north-western Iran, which is grateful not to its own accomplishments but to the poets of Sumer, its craftsmen, artisans, its challenging god en, and its goddess Inanna of Sumer. Noah Kramer published a Sumerian poem "Enmerkar and the Lord of Aratta: A Sumerian Epic Tale of Iraq and Iran" from a well-preserved line of text pieced together from 20 tablets and fragments. These tablets are preserved in University Museum of the University of Pennsylvania at Philadelphia.

Sumerian Legacy

Bible: Everyone accepts the fact that Bible was written in the present form around 1000 BCE. , not before that. Sumerian influence entered the Bible through the Canaanite, Hurrian, Hittite, and Akkadian literatures through Akkadian language. There are numerous of Biblical parallels from Sumerian literature that indicate signs of Sumerian influence without a doubt. Here is only a list of those Sumerian parallels in Bible:

1. Creation of the Universe
2. Creation of Man
3. Creation Techniques
4. Paradise
5. The Flood
6. The Cain-Abel Motif
7. The Tower of Babel and Dispersion of Humankind
8. The Earth and Its Organization
9. Personal God
10. The Law
11. Ethics and Morals
12. Divine Retribution and National Catastrophe
13. The Plague Motif
14. Suffering and Submission
15. Death and the Netherworld

This is only a short list. Undoubtedly many other civilizations also have parallels from Sumerian literature and show the signs of its influence if studied carefully.

Political organization: The Sumer's legacy begins with the political organization like city-state developed in villages and towns in the second half of 4000 BCE. The city - with its free citizens and assembly, its nobles and priests, its clients, its slaves, its ruling god and his ministers, the king, farmers, its craftsmen, merchants, temples, walls, and gates - is found all over the ancient world from Indus to the western Mediterranean region. A few specific features may differ from place to place, but on the whole, there appears a strong resemblance to early Sumerian prototype. Some may argue that the city would have come into being even Sumer never existed. It may be true, or it may not be true because in Egypt - which also had great ancient past - the city-state concept never originated there. And the same might have happened in other parts of the ancient world also.

City-state: One of the most significant characteristic features of the Sumerian city-state in 3000 BCE was written law, starting with the writing of legal documents such as sales and deeds, and spreading of specially prepared law codes. Written legal documents and law codes are found all over the ancient Near East. "Even Greece and Rome would probably never have had their written laws had it not been for the Sumerian penchant for keeping a record of their legal transactions."

Mathematics: Regarding scientific achievement, in the field of mathematics Sumerians made their major contribution to future generation by inventing the sexagesimal (counting by sixtieths) system of place notation. The Sumerians mainly used a sexigesimal structure that was based around groupings of 60. This easily divisible number system was later adopted by the ancient Babylonians, who used it to make astronomical calculations on the lengths of the months and the year. The use of base-60 gradually decreased, but its legacy still lives on in the measurements of the both hour and the minute. Other traces of the Sumerian sexigesimal system exist in the form of spatial measurements such as the 360 degrees in a circle and the 12 inches in a foot, and in some of the weights and measures.

This system based on 60 explains why we have 60 seconds in minute and 60 minutes in an hour. They used a 12 month calendar with a 7 day week. Astronomers studied the stars and mapped the first set of constellations.

Since Babylonian education was restricted to the privileged people who were meant to fill all positions for which literacy was essential, the students received education with a broad curriculum. Establishments for all advanced study were placed in the schools. The curriculum included: Accountant, administrator architect, astrologer, clerk, copyist, military engineer, notary, priest, public scribe, seal-cutter, secretary, surveyor, teacher are just some of which have recorded on clay tablets.

Arithmetic was as important to Babylonian education as reading and writing. The art of working with figures that were taught and learned by them shows how Babylonians approached all forms of knowledge. The ability to manipulate numbers were more advanced in that ancient period. Their way of writing numbers was far superior to the Roman numerals. Here is the earliest known form the 'positional notation' just like the 'hundreds, tens and units' that we learn as children. It differed from our modern system only in that, using so-called Arabic numerals, we make each place to the left ten times larger, while the Babylonians made it sixty times. What they wrote in Hexagesimal with base 60 as 𒁹 𒁹 𒁹 𒁹 (1111) symbolized in our numerals as 216,000 + 3600 + 60 + 1 = 219,661.

Hexagecimal (Base 60)

𒁹	𒁹	𒁹	𒁹	
216,000 +	3600 +	60 +	1	= 219,661

Decimal (Base 10)

1	1	1	1	
1000	100	10	1	= 1111

Paul Kriwaczek

"As is well known, we still preserve the Babylonian number system, based on multiples of 60 when we speak of 95,652 seconds as 26 hours, 34 minutes and 12 seconds.

"Two signs they lacked were zero and the decimal point.... Dealing with a number base as large as sixty, rather than base ten was a stumbling block to school children trying to remember their times tables. They had very complicated methods and tables for solving like tables of reciprocal...Babylonian students were expected to be able to solve really quite advanced mathematical problems. They had solutions for linear equations – a method similar, modern mathematicians note, to Gaussian elimination – for quadratic and cubic equations, for calculating the hypotenuse of right-angled triangles (Pythagoras' theorem), for deducing the areas of polygons, for working with circles and chords of circles – they called them bowstrings. Their approximation for π, 'pi', was 3 1/8, which, at 3.125. is not so far from the value we use, 3.14159.

"If all the above looks fairly daunting, it is because it is expressed in the abstract language of modern mathematics. Babylonians educators put such problems much more accessibly. Like Victorian schoolbooks, they set them in entirely concrete, practical, situations. Just as our nineteenth century ancestors were confronted with questions like 'if 8 men in 14 days can mow 112 acres of grass, how many men can mow 2,000 acres in 10 days?', so Babylonian school boys struggled over: 'With a volume of earth of 90 I shall capture the city hostile to Marduk. From the foot of the earth-ramp I went forwards 32 lengths. The height of the earth-ramp is 36: what is the length I have to advance in order to capture the city?'

"Expressing moths in the form of apparently practical; problems extended even to complex algebra. Where today we might ask a student to find the value of x in the quadratic equation 11x2 + 7x = 6.25, a text from about 1800 BCE: 'I have added seven times the side of my square to eleven times its area, and it is 6 15.' In Babylonian hexagesimal numbers, six and fifteen sixths represent our 6.25 or six and a quarter. The problem implied here is to find the length of the side. Where a modern mathematician would apply the general quadratic formula, the Babylonian solution was reached this way:

> *You take 7 and 11. You multiply 11 by 6 15 and it is 1 8 45. You have 7 and obtain 3 30. You multiply 3 30 and 3 30. You add the result, 12 15 to 8 45 and the result 1 21 has 9 as its square root. You subtract 3 30, which you multiply by itself, from 9 and you have 5 30. The reciprocal of 11 does not divide. What shall I multiply by 11 so that 5 30 results? 0 30 is its factor. 0 30 is the side of the square.... .*"

Science

In ancient Babylonian period, the preference for the concrete over the abstract, for practice over theory, for specific examples over general principles, extended into every area of study, thought and intellectual life. For instance, Babylonian music-theory expected Pythagoras perception by more than a thousand years; but its ideas were conveyed in the form of practical instructions for tuning a musical instrument's strings.

In Mesopotamia, the foundations of science were laid long before Aristotle. At the source of all real knowledge stands observation and classification: classification must lead zoology. A correct account of the way the living world is organized must be established before a theory of evolution can be imagined. From the time of the invention of cuneiform writing, training in literacy had been based on word tables in Mesopotamia. These were long records of plants and animals, rocks and stones, human artefacts made of different substances, verbal expressions and grammatical forms. If students were to become totally literate, the lists had to be complete. The items listed were arranged according to the arrangements of their wedge-marks, their similarity of sounds, or classified by function, or arranged by shape, or size or material composition. Wow!!

They saw the world is based on laws and rules: they theorized that if this occurs, then that is likely to follow. To them events did not take place, as some religious believers argue, because God or the gods commanded from moment to moment that they should. Babylonians did not think that the world only exists from day to day by a miracle. Instead they noticed that there was an underlying order and logic to the universe, which can be disclosed with careful observation. Today we call that science.

Babylonian Astrology is undoubtedly a science – even though it is false. Seeking the future in the stars was definitely a study based on laws, on rules, on observation and deduction. And same with omens pursued in the livers of sacrificial animals, in the pictures formed by pouring oil on water, in shapes seen in rising smoke, in unusual configurations in the night sky, in the patterns of storm clouds, in abnormal births of humans or animals. We must accept that those early diviners were working with experimental observations. Predicting some false omens may be wrong, but observing the natural phenomena was important to brain development and it was the foundation for future science.

Babylonian Medicine

In Babylonia there were two kinds of doctors: the *ashipu*, who specialized in omens and exorcism, and the *asu*, who made physical diagnoses and prescribed remedies. Around the year 1800 BCE King Hammurabi's laws indicated the fees to be paid to physicians, depending on the condition of the patient. It also prescribed the punishments for a surgeon's failure in treating patients.

In Greek's view that illnesses were caused by an imbalance of the four bodily nature – blood, black bile, yellow bile and mucus – would torment the practice of medicine for more than two millennia. But Babylonia was far ahead of Greeks. A letter from the King of Mari to his wife, which was discovered in late nineteenth century, shows how European practitioners were astonished to know: "I have heard that the lady *Nanname* has been taken ill. She has many contacts with the people of the palace. She meets many ladies in her house. Now then, give severe orders that no one should drink from the cup in which she drinks, no one should sit on the seat where she sits, no one should sleep in the bed where she sleeps. She should no longer meet many ladies in her house. This disease is contagious."

Paul Kriwaczek writes:

> "a collection of translation of Babylonian medical texts published in 2005 noted that the Mesopotamian treatments were often appropriate because they had evolved through hundreds of years of careful experimentation and observation: 'Some are still in use, such as surgically draining the pus that sometimes develops between the lungs and chest wall of pneumonia patients. Their precise instructions to make an opening in the fourth rib with a flint knife' to insert a lead drainage tube, pretty well match present-day procedures.
>
> "Most treatments were, necessarily herbal and dietary – pills and potions, rectal and private organ pills, skin patches and plasters – but none the worse for it. Some even accord with modern medicine's prescriptions. "A couple of tablets describe night blindness when a patient can see in daylight but is blind at night,' say the authors of medical text collection, "They talk about cutting off a piece of liver and having the patient eat it. Night blindness, we now know, is caused by Vitamin A deficiency, and liver is loaded with Vitamin A." Babylonians also seemed to have obsessed that date kernels contained what we now call estrogen. Symptoms of the condition they called *Nahshatu* included abnormal uterine bleeding. To treat this, "You char and grind date kernels, wrap them in a tuft of wool and insert the result into her private organ."

It would not be surprising to guess that Mesopotamia had many more remedies that we have not yet known.

Technology: In the technological field, the potter's wheel, the wheeled vehicle, and the sailboat are all perhaps Sumerian inventions. Although metallurgy was not Sumerian origin, the products of the Sumerian metalworkers are distributed all over the ancient Near East, and even reached Hungary and Central Europe.

Architecture: Architecture was the most important art of Sumer from earliest times, particularly the construction of temples with their stone foundations and platforms, inner chamber of temples, painted walls and altars, mosaic-covered columns and impressive elevations. It is not an exaggeration to say that some of these architectural techniques have diffused all over the ancient world.

Religion, Education, and Literature: Sumerians left deep impressions in the matter of religion, education, and literature on the ancient Hebrews and the Bible.

Writing: All people of western Asia borrowed the cuneiform script to inscribe their own records and writings. The learned teachers and scribes were imported from Sumer to the schools of the neighbouring countries, and some travelled to Sumer for special instruction to its more famous academies. As a result, there occurred a wide spreading of the Sumerians cosmology, theology, ethics, and system of education permeating all the knowledge and writings of Sumerian people.

The Word Sumer

It is said that there is no mention of the name Sumer in the Bible even though it has so much influence on it. The question is if the Sumerians were a people of such an outstanding literary and cultural importance for the ancient Hebrew men of scholars, why is it that there is no trace of them in the Bible? Assyriologist Noah Kramer mentions that his teacher Arno Poebel made an important deduction and published it in one of the journals. To understand Poebel's explanation, Dr. Kramer writes, the reader 'will have to bear in mind a rather curious and generally accepted Sumerian phonetic law which is essentially an intelligent approach to the problems involved.' He writes:

> "This phonetic law, the Sumerian final consonants were not pronounced in speech unless followed by a grammatical particle beginning with, or consisting of, a vowel. Thus, for example, the Sumerian word for field, *ashag*, was pronounced *asha* (without the final g). But when this same word appeared in the Sumerian complex *ashag*-a, "in the field," in which the -a is a grammatical element equated with the English "in," it was pronounced ashag, not asha. Similarly, the Sumerian word for "god," *dingir*, was actually pronounced *dingi*, with the final r silent. But in the complex, *dingir*-e, "by god" in which the -e stands for the English "by" the word was pronounced *dingir*, not *dingi*."

So, in the case of Sumer also, the same phonetic law applies. The name Shem is used profusely in the Bible and many other ancient books. At a passage of time, Sumer might have become Shumer, Shem, and so on. The name Sumer may be found in many literatures with a slight modification throughout the world.

Without a doubt, many civilizations throughout the world have assimilated much of the Sumerian culture, civilization, and their way of life. In China, there was a tradition to call ordinary citizens as black-haired commoners. In Sumer also, we see calling blackheads for ordinary Sumerian people.

Samuel Noah Kramer lists 39 Firsts in his book, "*History Begins at Sumer*", which are recognized as the Sumerian culture that created them. Included in these Firsts are The First Schools, The First Farmer's Almanac, The First Pharmacopeia, The First Library Catalogue, First Cosmogony and Cosmology, The First Moral Ideas, First Epic Literature, The First Case of Library Borrowing, The First Legal Precedent, The First Aquarium, and The First Proverbs and Sayings and so on.

The Assyrian Empire maintained and developed Mesopotamian art and literature, theology, science, mathematics and engineering to new heights, and masterminded the introduction of the age of iron into the Mesopotamian world. Assyria emperors improved the welfare and equality of their citizens in methods no previous administration had ever attempted. Beside the Hebrew Bible, the commitment to refrain from work every seventh day is first introduced in Assyria. Finnish scholar Simo Parole writes that "Assyrian religious beliefs and philosophical attitudes are still very much alive in Jewish, Christian, and Oriental mysticism and philosophies."

Harappans & their Mesopotamian links

MT.Saju@timesgroup.com

TALE OF TWO CIVILISATIONS: Excavation of a large number of carnelian beads known as 'long barrel cylindrical beads' from Chanhudaro was a turning point in establishing Harappan's link with the Mesopotamian

Chennai: While the links between the Indus Valley Civilisation and Mesopotamian civilization were known when Harappan remains were discovered, their extent of their close links were established over a period of time, said V N Prabhakar, who heads the excavation branch of the Archaeological Survey of India (ASI), New Delhi. "The contacts that Harappans had with Mesopotamia were ascertained as early as 1924 when John Marshall announced the discovery of the Indus Civilisation. But a chronology was not established with the finding. It was after the publication of a number of Harappan seals and other objects from Harappa and Mohenjo-daro that paved the way for identification of similar finds from sites in Mesopotamia and Susa, thus establishing a link between these two great civilisations. Some of the earliest finds that were compared with Harappan antiquities came from Kish and included a typical unicorn seal with Harappan signs, long-barrel cylindrical beads of carnelian, and etched carnelian beads. These findings helped in placing the hitherto unknown Indus Civilisation in a proper chronological horizon," he said.

Speaking on "the 3rd Millennium External contacts of the Harappan Civilisation" at the department of ancient history and archaeology at the University of Madras recently, Prabhakar highlighted a subsequent excavation at Chanhudaro by John Henry Mackay which brought to light a large number of unfinished carnelian beads known to us as 'long barrel cylindrical beads'. He said Chanhudaro was a famous centre for bead-making. "This was an important discovery which proved beyond doubt that similar finds from Mesopotamia were actually manufactured in the Indus Valley and exported by the Harappans. Harappan Civilisation is also identified with 'Meluhha' of the cuneiform records of Mesopotamia. The mention of 'Meluhha' is made for the first time in the cuneiform inscriptions of the Early Dynastic Period of the mid-third millennium BC," he said. Prabhakar said scholars identified Dilmun with the Island of Bahrain and the near shores of the Arabian Peninsula, Magan with Oman, and perhaps part of the Iranian coast around the Straits of Hormuz, and Meluhha with the Greater Indus region including the Harappan civilization. The contacts Harappans established with the Mesopotamian world are further strengthened by the presence of Harappan pottery, seals, ornaments like ivory combs, segmented silver beads, etc., from sites in Oman.

Sumerian civilization helped as a model for all future empire-builders: there is direct continuity between the Sumerian, Assyrian, Babylonian, Persian, Hellenistic and Roman empires. This empire was the channel through which a great deal of Mesopotamian knowledge and culture was directed to Greece and spread across the world.

It is not a surprise that Harappa and Mesopotamian civilizations had many links because the land was connected from Sumer to Harappa making it easy to exchange their culture and trade relationships. In ancient times, Egypt, Mesopotamia, Greece, Turkey, Iran, Afghanistan, and Harappa (modern Pakistan) were all connected by land and busy with trading, making wars with each other and making alliances with each other. The civilizations also spread, taking many forms.

That is why it is called Indus Valley Civilization, not Ganges Valley civilization.

4

India

But, after all, who knows, and who can say whence it all came, and how creation happened? The gods themselves are later than creation, so who knows truly whence it has arisen? Whence all creation had its origin, he, whether he fashioned it or whether he did not, he, who surveys it all from highest heaven, he knows - or maybe even he does not know.

– Rigveda (10:129)

Some foolish men declare that a Creator made the world. The doctrine that the world was created is ill-advised, and should be rejected. If God created the world, where was He before creation? How could God have made the world without any raw material? If you say He made this first, and then the world, you are faced with an endless regression. Know that the world is uncreated, as time itself is, without beginning and end. And it is based on the principles.

– The Mahapurana, Jinasena (9th century, India)

The study of the distribution pattern of Paleolithic sites in different parts of India has shown that there was habitational preference for certain regions. The region characterized by semi-arid monsoonal climate with suitable physiographic setting in the form of fertile upland, flat surface by riverside, and sparsely forested savanna type of vegetation was preferred for settlements.

A group of Indo-French researchers has discovered that the prehistoric Indians were skilled at crafting stone tools like hand-axes, cleavers and flakes, which they used for digging roots and tubers. They also knew woodworking besides butchering and skinning large animals.

The team recovered 3528 stone tools from excavations at Attirampakkam, an open-air Paleolithic site situated near a tributary of the river Kortallaiyar, northwest of Chennai. Known as Acheulian tools, they indicate the ancient stone tool making industry of early humans in India. Analysis of Tamil tools suggest that they were made between 1.07 and 1.5 million years ago by Homo erectus.

Ancient India - Early Habitation in India

The Bhimbetka rock shelters are located in Madhya Pradesh. The Bhimbetka shelters illustrate the primitive marks of early human life in India. Some of the Stone Age paintings found at the Bhimbetka rock shelters are approximately 30,000 years old.

Mehrgarh Site and Its Four Periods (7000-2600 BCE)

The site of Mehrgarh, which is in present day Pakistan area on the Kachi Plain of the Indus Valley, is a major archaeological discovery about India. It is an area of over 495 acres. The site was discovered by a team of French archaeologists headed by Jean-Francois Jarrige together with the Pakistan Department of Archaeology. Excavations have shown that the area was never totally settled at any one time. There are seven periods within the boundaries of the site, dated by a series of radiocarbon dates. According to UNESCO, it is one of the earliest sites with evidence of farming and herding in South Asia.

Bhimbetka rock paints in Madhya Pradesh. 30,000 years old.

Period I: Neolithic (New Stone Age) (7000–5500 BCE)

Mehrgarh I was a small village consisting of farmers and herders covering the area of 7 to 10 acres. Houses and cubicle buildings and granaries were found in the area. Storage facilities of this type began in Period I. As agricultural production increased, their number and sophistication were also developed. The houses were simple and built by mud-brick structures. Ovens and hearths were commonly found in the corners of rooms, and signs of their use are revealed in marks of smoke on the walls. The technology of Mehrgarh I was simple. A small amount of copper (not smelted) appears to be of the native variety. The bed of the Bolan River holds cobbles of light brown flint from which tools were shaped and some sickle blades were occasionally polished. For food processing ground-stone tools were also found. Slabs of bitumen with basket impressions, a small amount of pottery, unbaked clay figurines appear toward the end of Period I.

There was a rich bone industry: awls, spatulas, a bone needle, and two highly polished bone pendants with round holes were found in the area.

The animal economy was dominated by twelve species of large game animals. Richard Meadow refers to the first inhabitants of a ceramic Mehrgarh I exploited not only the surrounding hills but the Kachi Plain also. The chaff-temper (separating outer seed cover from grain) technology appears between 6000 and 5500 BCE

Period II: Burj Basket Marked Phase (5500–4500 BCE)

Evidence of manufacturing activity, more advanced techniques, terracotta beads and images were found in this period. Images of females were decorated with paint and had varied hairstyles and ornaments. Two flexed burials with a covering of red ochre on the body were found. The button seals, geometric designs from terracotta and bone were produced. Technologies included stone and copper drills, upward ovens, large pit ovens, and copper melting crucibles. The discovery of several semi precious stones such as blue beads of lapis originally from Badkshan shows that there was a long-distance trade in period II.

Period III: Togau (4500–4000 BCE)

Period III Togau remnants cover an estimated 170 acres. The distinguishing feature in this period is further development of craft activities. Evidence of use of metallurgy appears first at this time. The other noticeable feature is the evolution of the ceramic industry in Mehrgarh. It is dominated by fine red ware and wheel-made vessels.

A shell industry using conch shells existed in Period II shows a bangle fragment decorated with carving parallel lines. Evidence for melting, refining, and smelting copper came from a domestic structure. Ceramics are the most ubiquitous evidence for craft production at Mehrgarh.

Craft production expanded significantly in Period III at Mehrgarh. Development of pyrotechnics and pottery production, copper and gold metallurgy occurred in this period and the basic bead-drilling technology was invented. By the end of Mehrgarh III, the technology used by the Harappa civilization and long-distance trade already existed on the plains of the Indus River.

Period VII: Damb Sadaat (3,200–2,600 BCE)

Sometime during the Period VII, occupation of another major settlement was established at Naushahro , next to Mehrgarh. Mehrgarh was gradually abandoned and the new settlement of Naushahro was occupied paving the way to a more mature urban phase of Harappa civilization when the Indus Valley Civilization was in the development stage.

The elephants roamed free from Assam to the western reaches of Mehrgarh. It has been recorded that in the Pleistocene period there were seventeen varieties of Indian elephants.

Indus-Valley Civilization

Harappa & Mohenjo-Daro (3,000 BCE)

In pre-Harappan period there existed small peasant states, each self-contained. There is no evidence of any uniform arbitrary standards accepted or imposed throughout the territory. But, later the Harappa civilization developed a system to build Empires. Diversity is replaced by uniformity. A sophisticated and technologically advanced urban culture was formed in the Indus Valley Civilization making them the first urban centers in the region.

A first major civilization of the subcontinent India was located in the valley of the Indus River and flourished between 2500 BCE and 1500 BCE It was centered about two great cities, Harappa and Mohenjo Daro. The Harappa civilization was highly developed. Excavated remains indicate connections with the ancient culture of Mesopotamia and Harappa influence on Indian culture persists today. Harappa's major cities were carefully laid out in a rectangular pattern. They had elaborate municipal drainage systems, great granaries, and public buildings of impressive size. Tools of bronze and copper were used, and clay seals and bronze images of high artistic quality were produced. There was an active trade with the ancient Near

East. Presumably the Harappa people were predecessors of the Dravidian people of southern India.

Indus Valley cities also maintained an active commerce and close cultural contacts with Sumerian and Persian Gulf region.

Amaury de Reincourt, a French Historian, writes about the glory of Harappa civilization:

> "Archeological evidence shows a huge irregular triangle area with the sides measuring 950 by 700 by 550 miles. From end to end of this region, some forty settlement sites containing pottery vessels of identical mass-produced types have been excavated; houses are built from baked bricks of standard dimensions; stamp seals are used, and a uniform script, as yet unread; a standard system of weights is recognizable. While some sites are villages, others are small towns. Two cities, probably twin capitals of an Empire, stand 350 miles apart each covering at least a square mile of ground. To a British archeologist the inevitable parallel is the Roman Empire.
>
> "The gigantic Empire, twice the size of Old Kingdom Egypt, had two enormous metropolises: Harappa in the North and Mohenjo-Daro in the South. Towns were no longer laid out for military defense as in the old pre-imperial days because a universal type of peace prevailed throughout the "civilized" world of those times. The extremely advanced stage of standardization indicates the existence of a universally accepted commercial code and uniform technique of production controlling the sizes of bricks, the capacity of pots, and so on. Agricultural output was under municipal control, and huge granaries similar to those of the contemporary Egyptian Civilization dotted the landscape. For centuries street-frontage regulations were strictly observed.
>
> "The amazing efficiency of the Harappa Civilization was linked to a remarkable cultural stagnation. Its uniformity was expressed in time as well as in space. There were at least nine phases of rebuilding at Mohenjo-Daro, and all indications are that there was no change in the people's way of life. The script, with its 270 characters, essentially hieroglyphic as in contemporary Egypt, remained identical throughout the entire period. This urban and literate Civilization, known to us only in its mature form, was undoubtedly the heir to the Culture whose scattered remnants are strewn over Sind and Baluchistan.
>
> "Who were the people dwelling in the Harappa Empire? There is evidence of two main racial strains: the first, belonging to the long-headed "Mediterranean" type which spreads from Spain to India. The second belonged to the "Australoid" group with their thick lips and coarse noses, probably the original natives of the land. If we include brachycephalic (flat head) and the Mongoloid hill people of the Himalayan foothills, we have a complex ethnic situation where white, brown, dark and yellow races lived side by side within the compass of

a great cosmopolitan Civilization. But the majority must have belonged to a stock very similar to the modern dark-skinned Dravidians of southern India.

"The colossal size of the capital cities reminds one of Imperial Rome. The sheer size of the Citadel, the impressive Great Bath, the Collegiate Building, the Pillared Hall, all these great monuments indicate that Mohenjo-Daro was a center of religious and administrative life on a grand scale. The city itself, with its countless shops and residential districts, was laid out like a gridiron of large avenues cutting each other at right angles, dividing the city into large rectangular blocks. The large houses of the wealthy people were provided with doormen, elaborate bathrooms, and rubbish chutes running through the outside walls into bins probably cleared by the municipal authorities. A complex drainage system under the streets was connected with the house drains. There seems to be no doubt that the general standard of health and sanitation were remarkably high. Large sections of the town were laid out for the workers; depressingly uniform rows of cottages lined narrow streets. Massive wooden mortars, large granaries, metal worker's furnaces, everything suggests a high degree of semi-industrialization. In fact, archeology claims that the Harappa Civilization attributes the first really organized industry in Western Asia.

"Little is known about the Harappa religion, although archaeological research suggest the widespread cult of a Mother Goddess—undoubtedly the direct ancestor of the Grama-Devatas who are still worshipped in countless Indian villages to this day and whose priests are outcastes, remnants of the pre-Aryan population of India. Archaeological excavations have also found prototypes of the future god Siva seated in the position of a yogi, as well as evidence of phallic worship. And, the important of all, the Harappa people buried their dead, the symbolic gesture of men concerned with duration in sharp contrast to the succeeding Aryans.

"From 2700 BCE to 1700 BCE, this great Civilization flourished in relative peace. But like all Civilizations, it seems to have become completely sterile and ossified as time streamed by. Even technologically, it became backward. Although Harappa men were at the time the sole inventors and users of saws with undulating teeth and although they made ample use of copper and bronze, they did not know iron; and whereas from the millennium onward Mesopotamians knew how to fashion tools with sockets for handles, Harappa ignored this technical revolution. Harappa, it seems, had not domesticated the horse. Inevitably, this great Civilization was the mercy of barbarians who were technologically more advanced. When those barbarians appeared, sometime in the first half of the second millennium BCE on the northwest passes of Lak Phusi, the Bolan and the Gaj Valley, the great Civilization of Harappa collapsed for all time and faded from the memory of man until archaeology began to unearth its impressive remains in the twentieth century CE."

Indus Valley cities also maintained an active commerce, and probably had close cultural contacts with Sumerian and Persian Gulf regions.

In the Gangetic Plain there were settlements of people who made a crude ocher colored pottery and perhaps combined hunting with primitive agriculture. In the Deccan the flint tools were in use side by side with artifacts of bronze and copper. In the far south there was a complex megalithic culture that may have had links with Mediterranean megalithic culture.

Aryan Civilization (1700 BCE)

Aryan Invasion Theory

Aryans first literary work, Rig-Vida, is a unique source of information. It gives us the atmosphere of this period with a wealth of hymns, chants, prayers, songs and magic spells sometimes sublime and sometime childish. It is a colorful and invaluable document on the wars between Aryan invaders and native dwellers Dasyus of the Indus Valley region. The hymns reflect the feelings of victorious and warlike masters of a huge fertile land and a scared local population. The picture which emerges from a careful scrutiny of the Rig Veda is as follows:

"The tall, fair-skinned Aryan appeared into the broad plains of the Indus Valley mounted on horses, dressed in heavy coats, with weapons made of iron and military equipment which the men of Harappa did not possess. Looking down at dark-skinned, flat-nosed Dasyus, the victorious Aryans (Bharatas, Yadus, Anus, Purus, etc.) gradually occupied a large part of India. There was a fierce struggle between the Aryan chieftain Divodasa and the Dasyu ruler Sambara. The Indra, the prominent god of Rig Veda, was a destroyer of "forts" (purandara), a wrecker of cities."

The Rig-Veda provides many glimpses of the social life of those times. Life was exclusively rural; the great cities of the Harappa period had completely disappeared. The word "city" (nagar) is never mentioned in the Rig-Veda. In the most powerful military-based society, the feudal lords lived in their purs (forts). War and agriculture were the chief occupations of the times even though there was a certain amount of trade. The art of writing, fully developed in the Harappa Civilization, have become completely lost after the Aryan invasions. The early literature of the Aryans was not written down but transmitted orally. Nevertheless, those ages were also ages of youth and hope, of dynamic vigor, the childhood of a new Culture. The early Vedas are full of this enthusiasm for life which is the privilege of youth, new outlook on life, and rebirth.

Vedic India was split into an unknown number of independent states (Rashtras) and by kings (Rajas). In the early days, the Aryan leaders checked the power of the rajas through their assemblies (samiti or sabha) and, gradually these assemblies discontinued when the power of the royal rulers became more autocratic.

Non-Aryan Invasion Theory

The Aryan invasion theory is one of the most controversial historical topics for over a century in India. The Aryan invasion theory is based upon the idea that the name Aryan represents a specific group of people. In the traditional view of the Aryan invasion, the Aryans are a particular ethnic group, speaking a particular language. However, in Vedic literature Aryan is not the name of the Vedic people or their descendants. It is a title of honor and respect given to certain groups for good or dignified manners. In this regard even the Buddha calls his teaching Aryan or Arya Dharma. The Jains also call themselves Aryans, as did the ancient Persians.

Another vital point in this regard is that nomadic people do not use chariots. Some argue that an invasion of India from Central Asia required crossing mountains and deserts, a chariot is useless for such an exercise; therefore, the Aryan invasion theory is false.

According to Bal Gangadhar Tilak's theory, the North Pole was the original home of Aryans during the pre-glacial period. They had to leave their place due to the ice surge around 8000 BCE and had to migrate to the Northern parts of Europe and Asia looking for lands and for new settlements. Supporting this theory, Tilak has given certain Vedic hymns, Avestic passages, Vedic chronology, and Vedic calendars with interpretations in detail in his book, 'The Arctic Home in the Vedas.' When it was mentioned this to a prominent scholar in Vedic knowledge, he disqualified this theory.

The New Model

The New Model of ancient India has surfaced from the collapse of the Aryan invasion theory. This new model suggests that an indigenous civilization existed in ancient India at Mehrgarh site during 6500 BCE. The people in this tradition were the same ethnic groups as in India today, with their basic form of languages: Indo-European and Dravidian. Later Harappa civilization 3100-1900 BCE shows massive cities, complex agriculture and metallurgy, sophistication of arts and crafts, and precision in weights and measures. Post-Harappa civilization 1900-1000 BCE shows the abandonment of the Harappa towns due to ecological and river changes without a break in the continuity of the culture.

Therefore, the new model declares throughout these changes, traditions, culture and languages continued without a break.

Vedic Period (1500-600 BCE)

Initially, in ancient Indian cities, people worshipped a mother goddess like any other civilization; they also had a male divinity, represented in one of the typical attitudes of yoni, surrounded by animals. For Aryan's, most important divinities were male. They had an important class of priests who were very skilled in composing hymns for use at the sacrifices and in memorizing the hymns composed by others.

The word Veda is derived from the Aryan root vid; that is, "seeing," vision (in Latin, video). The early Vedic poets, the rishis, called themselves the seers of the hymns. They looked upon the universe and thought it is absolute, indisputable, and having existed for all eternity. The Vedas were the brilliant product of instinctive insight and understanding, though it may not be of the logical intellect. It was passed on orally by word of mouth from master to disciple.

The Vedic Period deals with the age of the settlement of the Aryans and the steady development and spread of the Aryan culture and civilization. It was the time which witnessed the growth of the forest universities, where the sublime idealism of India was evolved. They described their thoughts through Mantras or the hymns, the Brahmanas and the Upanishads. Their views presented in this process are not philosophical in the technical sense of the term. It was the time of probing, examining and investigating the nature of the universe, where superstition and thoughts were contradictory.

The oldest Vedic deities were the Dyaus, the glittering God of Heaven and Prithvi, the Earth Goddess. Later appeared innumerable Gods: Varuna, (god of sky, of water), Vayu (god of wind, air or atmosphere), Agni (god of fire), and Surya (the sun God). Stars, mountains, rivers, human qualities and faults, all had their controlling deity.

Some scholars implicate the Vedic hymns to 3000 BCE, and some others to 4500 BCE, 6000 BCE and so on. Dr. S. Radhakrishnan assigns 1500 BCE so that the date will not be challenged as being too early.

Rig-Veda

The Rig-Veda is the oldest noteworthy existing text of India. It is a collection of 1028 Vedic Sanskrit hymns and 10,600 verses, organized into ten books. The hymns are dedicated to Rigvedic gods. The books were composed by sages and poets from different priestly groups over a period of about 500 years. The ten rishis or the composers of Rig-veda: Angirasa, Kanva, Vasishta, Vishvamitra, Atri, Bhrgu, Kashyapa, Grtsamada, Agasthya, Bharata.

There are strong linguistic and cultural similarities between the Rig-Veda and the early Iranian Avesta, obtained from the Proto-Indo-Iranian times, frequently associated with the Andronovo[1] culture. The earliest horse-drawn chariots were found at Andronovo sites near the Ural Mountains which date to 2000 BCE.

Rig-Veda also deals with other subjects, like the procedure of wedding, the foolishness of gambling, etc. About two-thirds of Rigveda is about the gods Agni (Fire) and Indra (King of gods). Other Rigvedic gods include Rudra (destroyer), the two Ashvins (two horsemen, who are sons of cloud and sun), Savitar (solar power) and Surya (sun), Varuna (water), the Maruts (winds} and the Ribhus (rays of the sun). There are references to a divine creeper, the Soma, whose juice was an energizer. Some animals, rivers, and even implements (like mortar and pestle) were sanctified. Rigveda contains a sense of intimate communion between Nature and the Rishis or visionaries.

In this period, new deities began to join the Vedic gods: Vishnu and Shiva became powerful deities but the most metamorphosis among the gods was that of Brahman (from the root Brh, to swell or to grow). Brahman was regarded as the creative principle of the universe.

Yajur Veda

It is said that theYajur-Veda (Veda of sacrificial formulas) consists of ancient mantras. In this Veda some parts of verses are borrowed from the Rig-Veda. Yajurveda refers the acts of worship like sacrifice made to Agni or Fire. It has two branches: Krishna or Black and Shukla or White. The literary value of Yajurveda is mostly for its prose, which consists of short concise sentences full of meaning and intonation.

Sama Veda

The Sama Veda is the Veda of chants or knowledge of melodies. Its purpose is liturgical and practical, and a priest who sings hymns from the Sama-Veda during a ritual is called an *udgat*. The methods of chanting are important to the liturgical use of the verses. Therefore, the verses need to be sung in specifically indicated melodies using the seven svaras or notes. Such songs are called Samagana and in this sense Samaveda is really a book of hymns.

It contains verses addressed to the three gods Agni (Fire), Indra (King of Gods) and more on Soma (Energizing Herb).

AtharvaVeda

Atharva Veda means the Veda of the wise. It is related to the name of the ancient poet Atharvan. According to the tradition, the Atharva Veda was composed by two groups of rishis: Atharvana and the Angirasa. Atharvaveda contains unique poetry coming from visionary poets, much of it being glorification of the curative powers of herbs and waters. Many poems are related to diseases like cough and jaundice, to male and female demons that cause diseases, to sweet-smelling herbs and magic things, which drive diseases away. There are poems relating to sins and their punishments, errors in performing rituals and their penalty acts, political and philosophical issues, and a magnificent hymn to Prithvi or Mother Earth.

Vedic cosmology

The authors of the hymns are greatly concerned with the origin of the universe. They suggested that the world emerged from a golden embryo at the beginning of time. They concluded that really nobody, not even the gods themselves, knows certainly how the creation came out.

On creation Rigveda says:

> But, after all, who knows, and who can say whence it all came, and how creation happened?
>
> The gods themselves are later than creation, so who knows truly whence it has arisen?
>
> Whence all creation had its origin, he, whether he fashioned it or whether he did not,
>
> he, who surveys it all from highest heaven, he knows - or maybe even he does not know.
>
> — Rigveda (10:129)

In fact, the sacrifices are now conceived as repetitions of the first great sacrifice due to which the universe was created, and the creative process is symbolically repeated again and again, and the universe is being renewed.

It is assumed that the caste concept started in the Rig Vedic period. In those days, caste was the expression of the talent of Indian Civilization: Once it was like a labor union, enforcing certain rigid social security and the extreme and social expression of Civilization's specialization. Every member of a given caste was trained for a particular function from the day the child is born. It enforced democratic equality with the group, provided a particular religious framework according to their psychological nature for the particular caste members, and yet instilled respect to all Indians for multitudes of other forms of worship. Unfortunately, it became a national menace and causing wide problems of discrimination and prejudice.

Upanishads (800-400 BCE)

The word Upanishad comes from the Sanskrit verb *sad* (to sit) and the two prepositions: *upa* (near), *ni* (below) *sad* (to sit), sitting down near the teacher to obtain Vedic knowledge. Upanishads are Hindu sacred texts of spiritual and philosophical nature. Vedic literature is divided into Karmakanda containing *Samhitas* (hymns) and *Brahmanas* (commentaries); and Gyana-kanda containing knowledge in the form of the *Aranyakas* and *Upanishads*. Thus, each Upanishad is associated with a Veda, Isha-upanishad with Shukla Yajurveda, Kena-upanishad with Samaveda, and so on.

It is estimated that the earliest Upanishads have been composed between 800 and 400 BCE The major Upanishads are ten: Isha, Kena, Kattha, Prashna, Mundaka, Mandukya, Taittiriya, Aitareya, Shwetashwatara, Chhandogya and Brihadaryanyaka.

In ancient India, complete freedom of thought was observed as Indians were free to contemplate upon all the great spiritual and metaphysical problems in unconditional liberty. No Indian was put to death because his opinions did not meet with fellow thinkers, nor was there any investigation or examination of their thinking.

Maha Janapadas (700-300 BCE)

Early Vedic texts indicate several Janas or clans of the Indo-Aryans living in a semi-nomadic tribal state and fighting among themselves, and with other Non-Aryan tribes for cows, sheep and green pastures. These early Vedic Janas later came together into the Janapadas of the Epic Age.

The Pre-Buddhist north-west area of the Indian subcontinent was divided into several Janapadas distinguished from each other by borders. According to Panini's interpretation, *Janapada* means country and *Janapadin* for its citizenry. Each of these Janapadas was named after the Kshatriya tribe, who had settled therein.

The Buddhist and other texts occasionally refer to the following sixteen great nations of Mahajanapadas, which were in existence before the time of Buddha:

1. Anga (East Bihar)
2. Kosala (Oudh)
3. Kashi (Benares)
4. Magadha
5. Vajji/Vriji) (Near Bihar)
6. Malla (Gorakhpur)
7. Chedi (On the Jamuna)
8. Vatsa (Allahabad)
9. Kuru (Delhi)
10. Panchala (Bareilly)
11. Machcha/Matsya (Jaipur)
12. Surasena (Mathura)
13. Asmaka (Godavari)
14. Avanti (Malwa)
15. Gandhara (Peshawar)
16. Kamboja (South Kashmir and Kafristan

Epic Period (600 BCE-200 A.D)

The Epic Period extends between the early Upanishads and the Darshanas (a sense of seeing or beholding), a metaphysical system of Indian philosophy. The epics of the Ramayana and Mahabharata conveyed the new message of the heroic and the pious nature in human relations. The religious systems of Buddhism, Jainism, Shaivism, and Vaishnavism belong to this age. The development of abstract thought in the schools of Indian philosophy, the darsanas, also belongs to this period. Most of the systems took shape early in this period, and they expanded side by side through many centuries.

Mahabharata

The Mahabharata is one of the two major Sanskrit epics of India. Apart from narrative stories of Kauravas, Pandavas, and Kurukshetra War, Mahabharata contains philosophical and devotional material.

The authorship of the Mahabharata is attributed to Vyasa. Scholars have made attempts to determine its historical growth and compositional stages. The text most likely reached its final form by the early Gupta periods, 400 CE. The original form of Mahabharata consisted of 24,000 verses and was called Bharata. Later, it is extended up to one hundred thousand verses. According to Howard Spodek and Amartya Sen, the Mahabharata is roughly ten times the length of the Iliad and Odyssey combined. W. J. Johnson has compared the importance of the Mahabharata to world civilization to the Bible, the works of Homer, Greek dramas, the Quran, and the works of Shakespeare. The Mahabharata has acquired an iconic and culturally talismanic significance that is reflected in its assessment of itself: 'what is here may be found elsewhere, what is not here is nowhere at all'."

Research on the Mahabharata has put an enormous effort to recognize and date of various stages within the text. Some incidents of the present Mahabharata can be traced back to Vedic times. The background to the Mahabharata suggests the origin of the epic occurs after the very early Vedic period and before the first Indian Empire was to rise in the third century BCE Unlike the Vedas, which have to be preserved letter-perfect, the epic reciters would inevitably conform to changes in language and style. It is estimated that the Sanskrit text probably reached a final form by the early Gupta period around the 4th century CE.

Outline of the Story

The center of the story of Mahabharata is a dynastic struggle for the throne of Hastinapura, the kingdom ruled by the Kuru clan. The Kurus were an Indo-Aryan tribe. Their kingdom existed in the Vedic period of India and later became a republican part of Mahajanapada. Kurus formed the first political center of the Indo-Aryans in Punjab after the Rigvedic period. It was there that the codification and revision of the Vedic texts began. Archaeologically, they correspond to the Black and Red Ware Culture of the 12th to 9th centuries BCE At this time, iron first appeared in western India. Panchala was the second urban center of Vedic civilization because its focus moved to east from Punjab.

The two divisions of the family that fought for the throne were the Kauravas and Pandavas. Although the Kaurava was the senior branch of the family, Duryodhana, the eldest Kaurava was younger than Yudhisthira, the eldest Pandava. Both Duryodhana and Yudhisthira claim to be first in line to inherit the throne.

The struggle concludes with the war between Kauravas and Pandavas in the battlefield of Kurukshetra, and ultimately Pandavas turn out to be victorious. The battle creates complex conflicts between kinship and friendship, family loyalty and duty, right and wrong.

Ramayan

The Ramayana is a Sanskrit epic and it is one of the two great epics of India. It describes the duties of relationships with characters like the ideal father, ideal servant, ideal brother, ideal wife and the ideal king. It explains the doctrines of human existence and the concept of righteousness. Ramayana has greatly influenced on Indian life and culture.

The Ramayana consists of 24,000 verses in seven sections (kāṇḍas) and narrates the story of Rama.

The names of the characters Rama, Sita, Dasharatha, Janaka, Vasishta, and Vishwamitra were all known in late Vedic literature. According to some modern academic view, Vishnu who incarnated as Rama is not Vedic deity, and he came first into prominence with the epics and also during the Puranic period of the later 1st century CE.

Valmiki's Ramayana is an epic poem of about 50,000 lines. Later Ramayana, like the Mahabharata, is a gradual growth for centuries.

Outline of the Story

The Epic is divided into several major kāṇḍas or sections that deals chronologically with the major events in the life of Rama—Bala Kanda, Ayodhya Kanda, Aranya Kanda, Kishkindha Kanda, Sundara Kanda, Yuddha Kanda and Uttara Kanda. The Bala Kanda describes the birth of Rama, his childhood and marriage to Sita. The Ayodhya Kanda describes the preparations for Rama's coronation and his exile into the forest. The Aranya Kanda, describes the forest life of Rama and the kidnapping of Sita by demon king Ravana. The Kishkindha Kanda describes the meeting of Hanuman with Rama, the destruction of the vanara king Vali and the coronation of his younger brother Sugriva to the throne of the kingdom of Kishkinda. The Sundara Kanda narrates the heroism of Hanuman, his flight to Lanka and meeting with Sita. The Yuddha Kanda describes the battle between Rama and Ravana's armies. The Uttara Kanda describes the birth of Lava and Kusha to Sita, their coronation to the throne of Ayodhya, and Rama's final departure from the world.

Puranas/Mythologies 300-1200 CE.

The Puranas are classic literary texts, written in Sanskrit verses and their composition dates back from the 300 CE to about 1,000 CE. The word

"Purana" means "old". Some scholars consider that composing of Puranas started around the time that the composition of the Mahabharata came to end around 300 CE. Certainly, in its final form the Mahabharata shows puranic features. The special subject of the puranas is the powers and works of the gods. An ancient Sanskrit lexicographer Amarasinha of fifth or sixth century CE. defined a purana as having five characteristic topics or *pancha laksana* (five qualities):

(1) The creation of the universe.

(2) Its destruction and renovation.

(3) The genealogy of gods and patriarchs.

(4) The reigns of the Manus, forming the periods called Manvantaras.

(5) The history of the Solar and Lunar races of kings.

When the puranas began to be composed first, the belief in particular deities, which is one of the principal marks of the Hindu faith, had been established. And to some degree the puranas can be depicted as a form of sectarian literature. Some puranas exhibit devotion to Shiva; in others, the devotion to Vishnu predominates.

There are eighteen major puranas and a similar number of minor or subordinate puranas. One method of the classification of puranas organizes the traditional three divisions of the gunas or qualities which tend toward purity (*sattva*), passion (*rajas*), and impurity or ignorance (*tamas*),

Puranas assisted in the transition from Brahmanism to Hinduism, particularly Hinduism that was friendlier to common folks with popular forms of devotion and worship, and arts, crafts, and sciences. The Puranas contain the stories about the gods who had become the objects of devotion as well as the modes of worship of these gods. These gods were no longer Vedic gods, but the gods form the Hindu trinity. In addition, the Puranas describe the battle between devas and asuras, and one can undoubtedly understand the struggle within each person between the forces of light and darkness. Though the Puranas are a vast repository of Hindu religious practices — yoga, puja, prayers, sacrifices, customs and traditions - they are not without a sense of humor and irony. They harmonize the metaphysical severity of the Upanishads, the magical and sacrificial knowledge of the Atharva Veda, and the orthodoxy of the Rig Veda.

Puranas consist of narratives of the history of the universe from creation to destruction, genealogies of kings, heroes, sages, demigods, descriptions of Hindu cosmology, philosophy, and geography.

Vyasa, the narrator of the Mahabharata, is traditionally considered the compiler of the Puranas. However, the earliest written versions date from the time of the Gupta Empire (third-fifth century CE) and much material may have been added in the succeeding centuries. They existed in oral form before being written and then incrementally modified later on.

According to American mythologist Joseph Campbell, the mythologies (Puranas) should not be taken as a literal description of historical events happening in our current understanding of time and space, but as a metaphor for the rise of man's cognitive consciousness as it evolved from a prior animal state. In 1924, Joseph Campbell traveled to Europe with his family. On the ship back, he encountered Jiddu Krishnamurti. They discussed about Asian philosophy, which sparked interest about Hindu and Indian mythology in Campbell.

Function of Myth - Campbell

Campbell often described mythology as having a fourfold function for human society: Metaphysical Function, Cosmological Function, Sociological Function, and Psychological Function.

1. **The Metaphysical Function: Awakening a sense of awe before the mystery of being.** According to Campbell, the absolute mysteries of life cannot be captured directly in words or images. The first function of mythology is to organize waking consciousness to the *mysteries* of this universe *as it is*.
2. **The Cosmological Function: Explaining the shape of the universe.** Myth also functions as a *proto-science*, bringing the observable (physical) world into accord with the metaphysical and psychological meanings rendered by the other functions of mythology. Campbell noticed that the modern dilemma between science and religion on matters of truth is actually between science of the ancient world and that of today.
3. **The Sociological Function: Validate and support the existing social order.** Ancient societies had to conform to an existing social order if they were to survive at all. This is because they evolved under "pressure" from necessities much more intense than the ones encountered in our modern world. Mythology confirmed that order and enforced it by reflecting it into the stories, often describing how the order arrived from divine intervention.
4. **The Psychological Function: Guide the individual through the stages of life.** As a person goes through life, many psychological challenges will be encountered. Myth may serve as a guide for

successful passage through the stages of one's life. For example, most ancient cultures used rites of passage as a youth passed to the adult stage. Later on, a living mythology taught the same person to let go of material possessions and earthly plans as they prepared to die.

Evolution of Myth

Campbell's view of mythology was by no means static and he describes how mythologies evolved through time, reflecting the realities in which each society had to adjust. Various stages of cultural development have different, yet identifiable mythological systems. In brief these are:

The Way of the Animal Powers: *Hunting and gathering societies.*

At this stage of evolution of religion was animistic, as all of nature was seen as being infused with a spirit or divine presence. At center stage was the main hunting animal of that particular culture and a large part of religion. It focused on dealing with the psychological tension that came from the reality of necessity to kill vs. the divinity of the animal. This was done by presenting the animals as springing from an eternal source and coming to this world as *willing victims*, with the understanding that their lives would be returned to the soil or to the Mother Earth through a ritual of restoration. The act of slaughter then becomes a ritual where both parties, animal and humankind, are equal participants.

The Way of the Seeded Earth: Early agrarian societies.

In the beginning, the practice of agriculture spread along with a new way of understanding humankind's relationship to the world. At this time the earth was seen as the Mother, and the myths focused on her life-giving powers. The plant and cultivation cycle were mirrored in religious rituals which often included human sacrifice, symbolic or literal. The main figures of this system were a female Goddess Mother Earth, and her ever-dying and ever-resurrected son/consort, a male God. At this time, the focus was to participate in the repetitive rhythm as the world expressed as four seasons, the birth and death of crops and the phases of the moon. At the center of this motion was the Mother Goddess from whom all life springs and to whom all life returns. This often gave her dual functions as both mother and destroyer.

The Way of the Celestial Lights: The first high civilizations.

As the first agricultural societies evolved into the high civilizations, the observation of the stars inspired them with the idea that life on earth must also follow a similar mathematically predetermined pattern in which individual beings are but mere participants in an eternal cosmic play. The king was symbolized by the Sun with the golden crown as its main metaphor, while his courts were the orbiting planets. The Mother Goddess remained, but her powers were now fixed within the rigid framework of a clockwork universe. But for the largest part the focus was heavily shifted toward the masculine god Indra or Zeus.

Campbell believed the religions of the world to be the various culturally influenced "masks" of the same fundamental, transcendent truths. All religions can bring one to an elevated awareness above and beyond a dualistic conception of reality, or idea of "pairs of opposites" such as being and non-being, or right and wrong. He quotes from the Rig Veda in the preface to The Hero with a Thousand Faces: "Truth is one; the sages speak of it by many names."

From 200 CE. -Scholastic Period

The Scholastic period also dates from the second century A.D and continues to the present. Noisy controversialist indulging over subtle theories and twisting arguments and fighting seriously over the nature of logical universe could be found here. Many Indian scholars' theories more often confuse us. Instead of thought, one can find words. Obscurity of thought, subtlety of logic, and intolerance of disposition mark the dreadful kind of commentators. None would deny their acuteness and enthusiasm.

Indian Philosophies

Jainism (900 BCE)

According to scholars, Parshvanatha was an historical person who lived in the 9th century BCE. In the 6th century BCE, Vardhamana Mahavira became one of the most prominent Jainism teachers. He organized a large group of disciples and taught them an ascetic doctrine in order to achieve enlightenment. The disciples referred to him as Jina, which means "the conqueror".

Jainism prevailed even before Parshvanatha or Vardhamana. It is said that the Yajurveda mentions the names of three Tirthankaras-Rsabha, Ajitanatha and Aristaneme. The Bhagavata endorses the view that Rsabha was the founder of Jainism.

Deciphering of the Brahmi script by James Prinsep in 1788 enabled the reading of ancient inscriptions in India and established the antiquity of

Jainism. The discovery of Jain manuscripts has added significantly to revise Jain history.

Jains have successfully sustained this longstanding religion to the present day and have significantly influenced and contributed to ethical, political, and economic sectors in India. Jains have the highest degree of literacy for a religious community in India. Jain libraries are the oldest in the country.

Karma Theory in Jainism

According to Jains, karma is of material nature. They perceive that thoughts and ideas affect our character and create or modify the tendencies of our souls. Karma is a material force, matter in a subtle form. It is a kind of matter, which is in the subtle form of particles to manifest karma, fills all cosmic space. It has the peculiar property of developing the effects of merit and demerit. The soul by its interaction with the outer world becomes literally penetrated with the particles of subtle matter. These become karma and build up a special body called karma sharira, which does not leave the soul till its final emancipation. The karmic matter retards the radiance of

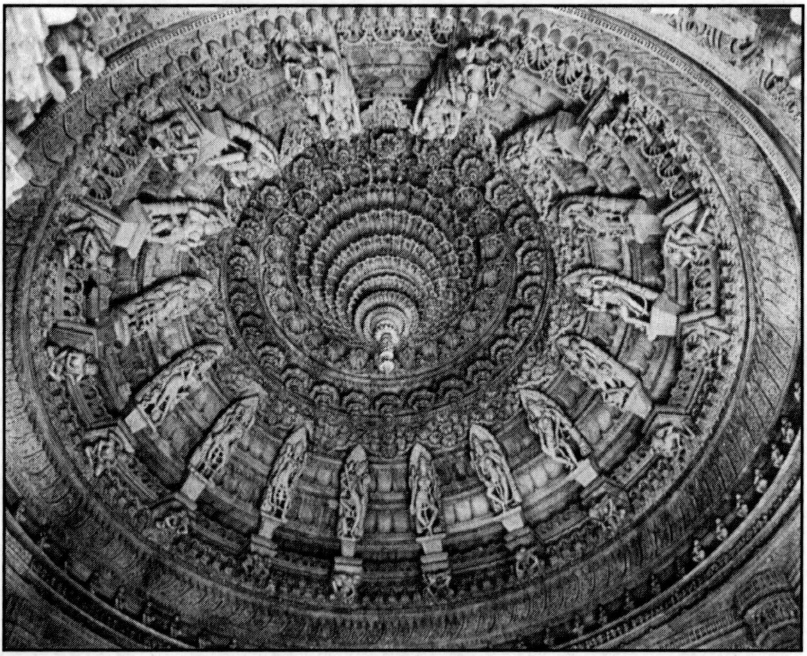

Highly decorated ceiling of Vimal Vasahi Jain temple at Mt. Abu in Rajasthan

the soul. Karma works in such a way that every change which takes place leaves a mark which is retained and built into the organism to serve as the foundation for future action. It is present and acting in the nature of the human souls. To obtain liberation from karma, Jainism emphasizes that one has to try to transgress this karma cycle.

Customs and Practices

Jains are strict vegetarians. They prevent eating root vegetables in general because cutting root from a plant kills other parts of the plant. In addition, according to Jain texts, root vegetables contain a huge number of microorganisms called nigodas. They eat before the night falls. They filter water to remove any small insects that may be present and boil the water before the drinking.

Jain monks and nuns practiced strict ascetism and attempt to make their present birth is their last one to escape from the cycle of transmigration. Jain monks and nuns walk barefoot and sweep the ground in front of them to avoid killing insects or other tiny beings.

Buddhism (600 BCE)

Vardhamana of Jainism and Gautama Buddha of Buddhism were contemporaries. Guerinot has highlighted the date and the birth of Vardhamana and Gautama Buddha. Vardhamana was born at Vaisali about 599 BCE while Gautama Buddha was born at Kapilavastu about 567 BCE Vardhamana died at Pawa in 527 BCE while Gautama died at Kusinagar about 483 BCE

Two major branches of Buddhism are recognized: Theravada, "The School of the Elders" and Mahayana, "The Great Vehicle".

Buddhism was born in India by Gauthama Buddha's life and his teachings. Buddha. His teachings are the revelations to the people who are suffering from the pain of birth and death cycle. He spread this knowledge for the sake of humanity. Three things are necessary to take refuge in Buddhism. They are the Buddha, the Dharma, and the Sangha.

As a prince, Gauthama was never exposed to pain, suffering, old age, or any illness. Since an oracle told that Gauthama would become a sanyasi (saint) if he saw a sick person, old men or any kind of suffering, his father arranged a strict atmosphere so that Gauthama could never come into contact with any suffering. At the age of twenty-one years, accidentally he encountered a dead body, an old man, and a beggar on his way back from a retreat. Then, Siddhartha Gauthama determined to find the way out from suffering, renounced the family, all worldly pleasures, and entered the forest in search of salvation. There, he observed rigorous penance. After six years of strict mental and physical discipline, he attained Enlightenment under the Bodhi-tree. He realized the cause of pain and suffering. Gauthama Buddha's teachings are the four Noble Truths:

1. Life is full of suffering.
2. The cause of suffering is human desire.
3. Cessation of suffering (*nirvana*) is attainable.
4. The discipline of morality, meditation, and wisdom is the path to attain *nirvana*.

Gautama's doctrine contained no theology, no metaphysics: it was essentially logic, psychology, and practical ethics. What is important is not the knowledge of the structure of the universe but one's relations to the universe. His teaching was essentially psychological, dedicated to the liberation of the individual human being alone.

Buddhist architecture. (Photo Courtesy: Archaeological Survey of India)

According to Buddha, the cause of human-suffering is not from outside, but humans themselves. A person commits *karma*, the cause of suffering, by thoughts, words, and deeds through his body, mind and intellect. People are self-creating themselves by desire for life, for pleasure, for power, for possession since whatever a person thinks that he becomes. The deeds performed through thinking good, speaking good, and doing good produce good *karma*, that is *punya*; and deeds performed through bad intentions produce bad *karma* that is papa. Both kinds of people have to experience their *karma* according to their deeds. Good merits produce happiness, such as good health, high status, long life, wealth, power, pleasure, taking birth in heaven, and bad merits produce unhappiness such as poverty, poor health, untimely death, and taking birth as subhuman beings. A person is born as a human being due to his past *karma* and accumulates merits for his future births. According to Buddha's worldview, there are several levels of life, like god, animal, ghostly and human forms. Below the earth is the hell and above is heaven.

Buddha said, through meditation, the meditator attains selfless state and understands the real nature self and the world. This is Enlightenment. Buddha called it *nirvana*. The ultimate goal of Buddhism is *nirvana*, freedom from suffering.

This moral perfection and *nirvana* cannot be attained in one life, and it may take many lives. Buddhism offered a panacea, a progression from offering (*dana* or donation) to morality to meditation. Respect and service to holy monks develop morality. Eventually, morality leads a person to be able to live the monastic life which is full of moral purity and meditation. In one's life, a person may not attain *nirvana*, but he will be born again to perpetuate his unfinished journey, ultimately reacheing *nirvana*.

Buddha travelled throughout the northeastern part of India to spread his message and died in 483 BCE at the age of 80 in Kushinagar.

Hindu Philosophers

Sankara (788-920 CE) : By the fifth century, the South Indian religious outlook was different because of several religions existing together with Vedic sacrifice and non-Vedic traditions like Buddhism and Jainism. There existed Hindu schools of Philosophy, Sankhya, Vaisheshika, Buddhism, Carvaka and Jainism. A sentiment of Buddhism or Jainism domination provoked Hindus and a large Hindu revival movement reached its peak in the seventh century.

Adi Shankaracharya was an Advaita philosopher who had a tremendous influence on the growth of Hinduism through his non-dualistic (monism) philosophy. He promoted the greatness and importance of the Hindu scriptures, the Vedas, Upanishads and gave new life to Hinduism at a time when Buddhism and Jainism were achieving popularity. Shankara was a brilliant dialectician and his teachings soon became the standard philosophy of intellectual Hinduism.

Basaveshwara (1132 -1196 AD): Basaveshwara was a philosopher, revolutionary, and a social reformer, who fought against caste system, gender inequalities and blind beliefs, besides increasing honor to work culture. His teachings and preachings are universal and go beyond all belief systems. He was a great philosopher in his time and started a literary revolution through Vachana Sahitya in Kannada language. Basaveshwara fought against the inhuman practice of the caste system, which discriminated against people based on their birth. He spread social awareness through his poetry, popularly known as Vachanas. These are rational and progressive social thoughts including established perception of God in Hindu society. Basaveshwara did not preach to people the intricate aspects of spirituality; but, he taught how to live happily in a rational social order, later came to be known as Veerashaiva Dharma or Lingayata Dharma. The Anubhava Mantapa founded by Basaveshwara promoted social democracy. Basaveshwara believed that man becomes noble not by his birth but by his action in the society. He declared that all individuals are laborers. Some may be intellectual laborers and others may be manual laborers. He also taught the dignity of manual labor by maintaining the work as worship. Basaveshwara arranged people's committees representing various professions such as agriculture, horticulture, tailoring, weaving, dyeing, and carpentry. All vocations were regarded with equal value and its members belonged to all types of professions.

Basaveshwara taught his followers a lesson of self-purification. He tried to improve the moral level of the public life in the country and insisted that the same rules of conduct be applied to the administrators as well as the individual members of the society.

Basaveshwara's chief teaching to humankind is -

> Do not steal, do not kill, do not utter lies;
> Do not lose your temper, do not detest others;
> Do not glorify yourself, do not blame others;
> This alone is purity within, this alone is purity without;
> And this alone is the way to please our Lord Kudalasangamadeva.

Basaveshwara created controversy by his radical actions and actively ignoring the social rules associated with the caste system, which he always wished to abolish. He allowed untouchables to have lunch at his residence and praised the marriage of a high caste woman and an untouchable man which made orthodox Hindus very furious. He was a great humanitarian and preached a new way of life regardless of gender, belief, tradition, religion, caste, social status.

Ramanuja (1200 AD): Theistic philosopher Ramanuja of eleventh and 12th century CE initiated the Sri Vaishnava movement and advocated *Jnanayoga,* the way of knowledge. He promoted devotion to god. According to Ramanuja, salvation could be gained by unconditional surrender to god and humbly waiting for his grace. Ramanuja's god was personal. In Ramanuja's theory, although an individual is a fragment of god, he is never completely identical with god. In the highest level, the soul is personally joined with him, but not one with him, and retains some degree of self-consciousness. Thus, the liberated soul is one with God but yet separate! Hence, Ramanuja's philosophy is known as qualified monism, *Vishishtadvaita.*

Madhwacharya (1300 AD): Madhwacharya of the 13th century promoted a doctrine of devotion, *dwaita* philosophy (monotheism/dualism). According to Madhwa, God, souls, and matter are eternally distinct. He did not teach salvation as union with God, but salvation is dwelling near god forever. According to him, god saves his devotees by his grace; without his grace, intense devotion and strict morality are of no use. But God's grace is showered without fail on those who lead the righteous path. Evil souls are expelled to eternal damnation. This concept contradicts popular belief that all souls have a chance to rise again. A. L. Basham says Madhwa philosophy is influenced by Christianity.

Theism has great inspiration on Hindu reformers. The teachings of the Vedas, Upanishads and works of great masters were in Sanskrit. Only educated Brahmins could be able to study and understand them. It was the hymnodists who composed devotional songs in local languages and carried the message of devotion to the people. A common man understands the doctrine of *moksha*, liberation through the stories and songs written in regional languages. Thus, hymnodists changed the way of Hinduism.

Kabir: Among these and other religious masters, Kabir was an important reformer. At his time, India was dominated by Muslims and they opposed image worship. His goal was to unite both the Hindu and the Muslim and convince them that they were the children of the same Father. He touched the most controversial practices like caste, idol worship, pilgrimage, and reverence for sacred places and tried to bring them into a common community by saying,

> If God be within the mosque, then to whom does this world belong?
>
> If Ram be within the image which you find upon your pilgrimage, then who is there to know what happens without?
>
> Hari is in the East; Allah is in the West;

Look within your heart, for there you will find both Ram and Karim.
All the men and women of the world are his living forms.

There is nothing but water at the holy bathing Places;
And I know that they are useless,
For I have bathed in them.
The images are all lifeless, they cannot speak;
I know, for I have cried aloud to them,
The Purana and the Koran are mere words;
Lifting up the curtain, I have seen.
Kabir gives utterance to the words of experience;
And he knows very well that all other things are untrue.

(Kabir Poems - Translated by Rabindranath Tagore)

His hymns were welcomed by both theist and non-theist because they had universal appeal.

Aurobindo tried the modern evolution method. He proclaimed the ancient idea that there is an eternal self and consciousness. All beings are united in that one eternal self but are separated by ignorance. To prove this, he used the evolutionary theory. "Evolution is the process by which it liberates itself. Consciousness appears in matter, and once having appeared, it grows higher and higher towards greater perfection. Life is the first step of this release of consciousness; mind is the second. But, evolution does not end with mind; it awaits release into something greater, a consciousness which is spiritual and supramental." He argued that by following certain disciplines one can reach this state.

Empires

Magadha Empire (684 BCE – 550 CE)

Among the sixteen Mahajanapadas, the kingdom of Magadha became an important Empire under a number of dynasties. During Ashoka Maurya's leadership, the kingdom of Magadha had emerged as a major power and possessed an unparalleled military.

The kingdom of the Magadha approximately represents the modern districts of Bihar, Nalanda, Aurangabad, Patna, Gaya, and parts of Bengal in the east. On the north it was surrounded by the river Ganges, on the east by the river Champa, on the south by the Vindhya Mountains and on the west by the river Sone.

Magadha Empire ascended to world dominion during 7th and 6th century BCE A few centuries later Magadha became a classical world as equal to

Rome. The founder of Magadha Dynasty was Bimbasara, a contemporary of Gautama Buddha. Magadha state was situated across two of the greatest international trade routes of the Indian world: navigation through river streams on the Ganges and the land route through important meeting place of Gaya. An enthusiastic military man, Bimbasara, was the first ruler to discover the fighting potential of the armored war-elephants, the heavy tanks of those days.

Ajatshatru even built a huge fort around his capital Pataliputra. With an unmatched military force and advanced forms of weaponry, the Magadha Empire conquered neighborhood places and extended its territories.

After the death of King Udayan, the Magadha Empire started to decline very rapidly. Internal disturbances and corruption within the kingdom led to its decline. Finally, the Magadha Empire was taken over by the powerful Nanda Dynasty who ruled the kingdom until Mauryas replaced their Empire.

Although the Magadha nation was as old as the later Vedas, it remained a small state for many centuries far away in the east, remote from the great centers of Kurus and Panchalas where Indian Culture was in full development. It was considered as a barbarian country because its population was mixed, partly Aryanized and incompletely Brahmanized. However, economic efficiency seems to have been the defining factor of Magadha life: roads and pathways, irrigation canals and dams, granaries, everything was built faster and on a larger scale than other states. Because of their cultural inferiority consciousness, many young men from Magadha were sent to Takshashila faraway in the north-western state of Gandhara to acquire education.

Maurya Dynasty (324-184 BCE)

Chandragupta Maurya**:** In 321 BCE Chandragupta Maurya established the Maurya Dynasty after defeating the Nanda king Dhana Nanda.

In 326 BCE Magadha was the most powerful state in India. Chanakya Kautilya met a young man of great energy and ability, Chandragupta Maurya, while they both were hiding in the vindhya forests. Forming forces, fusing penetrating thought and forceful action, they raised an army of outlaws, fanning the anti-foreign feeling of the Indians in western India. They went to war against the small Macedonian fortified military regions left behind by Alexander, and soon became masters of the lower Indus Valley. In a short period of time, the Mauryas conquered the whole of western India and then turning east, defeated the Magadhan army led by the Bhadrasila. Thus, Chandragupta Maurya became the emperor not only of Magadha, but also for almost united India for the first time in history. At first time as an Emperor, he concluded a treaty with Alexander's successor, Seleukos, according to which he received the entire territory of modern Afghanistan and Baluchistan.

Using Gandhara as his base, Chandragupta led a rebellion against the Magadha Empire and ascended the throne at Pataliputra in 321 BCE. There are no Indian records of Chandragupta Maurya and almost all that is known is based on the diaries of Megasthenes, the ambassador of Seleucus at Pataliputra, as recorded by Arrian in his Indika. Chandragupta's son Bindusara expanded the kingdom Turkestan down to modern Mysore and comprised most of northern India and the Deccan. Only Kalinga remained independent.Chinese travelers came to India on pilgrimages. It is known from Fa Hien who visited Pataliputra in the fifth century CE. describes that the magnificent palaces built seven hundred years before by Ashoka were still existed. The Greeks in the third century BCE had judged them to be the finest in the world, and the Chinese who visited them in Gupta times felt nothing but awe and admiration. A comparison between the Greek and Chinese descriptions about life in India seven hundred years apart reveals great admiration about the remarkable civilization displayed during their visit. It can be noticed by their documentation that the severe system of government of Mauryas with its countless spies and secret service seems to have softened somewhat by the time of the Guptas.

One of the remarkable characteristics of that period was the frequent contacts between India and China – India sending Buddhist missionaries to China, China sending back pilgrims to India.

Megasthenese's Indica

Concerning the condition and organization of the vast Maurya Empire, the Greeks have provided India with a considerable body of valuable information. Until Akbar comes to picture, there is not much information about India. India was struggling for its existence fighting with invaders, one after another, losing its identity.

Megasthenes[2] was a Greek historian and an ethnographer in the Hellenistic period. He was born in modern day Turkey and came with Alexander the Great as an ambassador of Seleucus. He was an author of the book 'Indica' in which he wrote his experiences about India, its geography, its people, its culture, and manners.

It is said that the original book 'Indica' of Megasthenese was lost. But, parts of his writings were recovered and have been preserved by various ancient authors both in Greek and Roman. Those fragments were collected by Dr. Schwanbeck and translated by J.W. McCrindle and presented in "Ancient India" as described by Megasthaenese and Arrian. It gives a picture of India in 300 BCE during Maurya's period.

The following excerpts are gathered from "Ancient India" and from "The Cambridge History of India, Vol. I" and produced here to get a glance of India as Megasthanese and Arrian saw it in 300 BCE:

> India has many huge mountains which abound in fruit-trees of every kind, and many vast plains of great fertility, but all interconnected by a multitude of rivers. The greater part of the soil is under irrigation, and consequently bears two crops in the course of the year. At the same time, it is abundant with animals of all sorts —beasts of the field and fowls of the air —of all different degrees of strength and size. As its soil supplies food in generous surplus, India is abundant with elephants, which are of monstrous bulk making these animals exceed in strength those that are bred in Libya. Since they are caught in great numbers by the Indians and trained for war, they turn to the extent of victory most of the time.
>
> The inhabitants, having abundant means of subsistence, exceed in consequence the ordinary stature, and are distinguished by their proud bearing. They are also found to be well skilled in the arts, as might be expected of men who inhale pure air and drink the very finest water. And while the soil bears on its surface all kinds of fruits, which are known for cultivation, it also has numerous underground veins of all sorts of metals, like gold and silver, copper and iron in no small quantity, and even tin and other metals, which are used in making articles and ornament, as well as the implements and accessories of war.

On Caste System

The whole population of India is divided into seven castes, of which the first is formed by the collective body of the Philosophers. In number they are lesser to the other classes, but in point of dignity they are greatest overall. For the philosophers, being exempted from all public duties, are neither the masters nor the servants of others. However, they are engaged by private persons to offer the sacrifices due in lifetime, and to celebrate the funeral rites of the dead for they are believed to be most dear to the gods and to be the most conversant with matters pertaining to Hades (lord of the dead). In return to such services they receive valuable gifts and privileges. To the people of India at large they also render great benefits. At the beginning of the year, they forewarn multitudes about droughts and wet weather, and also about propitious winds, and diseases, and other topics capable of profiting the hearers. Thus, the people and the sovereign, learning beforehand what is to happen, always make adequate provision against a coming deficiency, and never fail to prepare beforehand what will help in a time of need. The philosopher who makes mistakes in his predictions suffers humiliation and then he observes silence for the rest of his life.

The second caste consists of the Farmer, who appears to be far more numerous than the others. Being exempted from fighting and other public services, they devote the whole of their time to tillage. No enemy would do any harm to a farmer at work on his land because these men of this class are regarded as public benefactors and are protected from all injury. The land, thus remaining unravaged, and producing heavy crops, supplies the inhabitant with all that is requisite to make life very enjoyable. The farmers themselves, with their wives and children, live in the village, and entirely avoid going into town. They pay a land-tribute to the king, because all India is the property of the crown, and no private person is permitted to own land. Besides the land-tribute, they pay into the royal treasury a fourth part of the produce of the soil.

The third caste consists of the Herdsmen and Shepherds, and in general of all herdsmen who neither settle in towns nor in villages but live in tents. By hunting and trapping they clear the country of noxious birds and wild beasts. As they apply themselves eagerly and assiduously to this pursuit, they free India from the pests with which it abounds,—all sorts of wild beasts, and birds which consume the seeds sown by the farmers.

The fourth caste consists of the Artisans. Of these some are armorers, while others make the implements which farmers and others find useful in their different occupation. This class is not only exempted from paying taxes, but even receives maintenance from the royal exchequer.

The fifth caste is the Military. It is well organized and equipped for war, holds the second place in numbers, and gives itself up to idleness and amusement in the times of peace. The entire force—men-at-arms, war-horses, war-elephants, and all—are maintained at the king's expense.

The sixth caste consists of the Overseers. It is their province to inquire into and superintend all that goes on in India, and make a report to the king, or, where there is not a king, to the magistrates.

The seventh caste consists of the Councillors and Assessors, —those who deliberate on public affairs. It is the smallest class, looking at numbers, but the most respected on account of the high character and wisdom of its members. From their ranks the advisers of the king are taken, and the treasurers of the state, and the arbiters who settle disputes. The generals of the army also, and the chief magistrates, usually belong to this class.

Such are the parts into which the body of politics in India is divided. No one is allowed to marry out of his own caste, or to exercise any work or art except his own: for instance, a soldier cannot become a farmer or an artisan, a philosopher.

Megasthenese has divided the people of India into seven Castes. Herodotus, however had divided the people of Egypt into seven castes, namely priests, soldiers, herdsmen, swineherds, tradesmen, interpreters, and steersmen. It is a curious fact that, from the time of Alexander's expedition to a comparatively recent date, geographers and others have continually drawn analogies between Egypt and India.

On Administration

Indian officers are appointed even for foreigners, whose duty is to see that no foreigner is wronged. If any one of them loses health, they send physicians to attend him, and take care of him. If he dies, they bury him and deliver such property to his relatives. The judges also decide cases in which foreigners are concerned, with the greatest care, and come down sharply on those who take unfair advantage.

On Manners of the Indians

The Indians live sparingly, especially when in camps. They dislike a great undisciplined multitude, and consequently they observe good order. Theft is of very rare occurrence. Megasthenese says that those who were in the camp of Sandrakottos (Chandragupta[3]) with 400,000 men, found that the thefts reported on any one day did not exceed the value of two hundred drachmae (currency used in Greece), and this was among the people who had no written laws, and are ignorant of writing. Nevertheless, they live happily enough remaining simple in their manners with meager resources. They never drink wine except at sacrifices. Their beverage is liquor composed from rice instead of barley, and their food is principally rice. The simplicity of their laws and their contracts is proved by the fact that they seldom go to law. They have no suits about pledges or deposits, nor do they require either seals or witnesses, but make their deposits and are faithful to each other. They generally leave their houses and property unguarded.

These things indicate that they possess good, calm sense; but other things they do which one cannot approve: for instance, that they eat always alone and they have no fixed hours when meals are to be taken with all in common, but each one eats when he feels inclined. The contrary custom would be better for social and civil life.

Their favorite mode of exercising the body is by friction, applied in various ways, but especially by passing smooth ebony rollers over the skin. Their tombs are plain, and the mounds rose over the dead lowly. In contrast to the general simplicity of their style, they love fine clothes and ornament. Their robes are worked in gold and ornamented with precious stones, and they wear flowered garments made of the finest muslin. Attendants walking behind hold up umbrellas over them: for they have a high regard for beauty and use every device to improve their looks. Truth and virtue they hold alike in esteem. Hence, they accord no special privileges to the old unless they possess superior wisdom. They marry many wives, whom they buy from their parents, giving in exchange a yoke of oxen. Some marry hoping to find in them willing helpmates; and others for pleasure and to fill their houses with children. The wives prostitute themselves unless they are compelled to be chaste. No one wears a crown at a sacrifice or libation, and they do not stab the victim, but strangle it so that nothing mutilated, so that it could be presented to the deity with full form.

On Punishment

A person convicted of bearing false witness suffers mutilation of his extremities. He who mutilates any one not only suffers the loss of the same limb in return, hut his hand also is cut off. If he causes an artisan to lose his hand or his eye, he is put to death.

On King

The care of the king's person is entrusted to women, who also are bought from their parents. The guards and the rest of the soldiery attend outside the gates. A woman who kills the king when drunk becomes the wife of his successor. The sons succeed the father. The king may not sleep during the daytime, and by night he is obliged to change his couch from time to time, with a view to defeat plots against his life.

The king leaves his palace not only in time of war, but also for the purpose of judging cases. He remains in court for the whole day, without allowing the business to be interrupted, even though the hour of rubbing with a cylinder of wood arrives. He continues hearing cases while the friction, which is performed by four attendants, is still proceeding. Another purpose for which he leaves his palace is to offer sacrifice; a third purpose is to go hunting, for which he departs in Bacchanalian fashion. Crowds of women surround him, and outside of this circle spearmen are ranged. The road is marked off with ropes; anyone passing within the ropes is a death, for man and woman alike. Men with drums and gongs lead the procession. The king hunts in the fields and shoots arrows from a platform. At his side stand two or three armed women. If he hunts in the open grounds he shoots from the back of an elephant. In case of women, some are in chariots, some on horses, and some even on elephants, and they are equipped with weapons of every kind, as if they were going on a campaign.

On Elephants

India possesses a vast number of huge elephants, which far surpass those found elsewhere both in strength and size. The period of gestation is at shortest sixteen months, and at furthest eighteen months. Like mares, they generally bring forth one young at a time, and give milk to the young for six years. Most elephants live to be as old as an extremely old man, but the most aged live two hundred years.

A private person is not allowed to keep either a horse or an elephant. These animals are considered to be the special property of the king and persons are appointed to take care of them.

The manner of hunting the elephant is like this. Round a bare patch of ground is dug a deep ditch about five or six stadia in extent, and over this is thrown a very narrow bridge which gives access to the enclosure. Into this enclosure are introduced three or four of the best-trained female elephants. The men themselves lie in ambush in concealed huts. The wild elephants do not approach this trap in the daytime, but they enter it at night, going in one by one. When all have passed the entrance, the men secretly close it up. Then, introducing the strongest of the tame fighting elephants, they fight it out with the wild ones, whom at the same time they weaken with hunger. When the latter are now overcome with fatigue, the boldest of the drivers dismount unobserved, and each man creeps under his own elephant, and from this position creeps under the belly of the wild elephant and ties his feet together. When this is done, they provoke the tame ones to beat those whose feet are tied until they fall to the ground. Then, they bind the wild ones and the tame ones together neck to neck with thongs of raw ox-hide. To prevent them shaking themselves in order to throw off those who attempt to mount on them, they make cuts all round their neck and then put thongs of leather into the incisions, so that the pain obliges them to submit to their fetters and to remain quiet. They reject the elephants, which are too old or too young to be serviceable, and the rest were taken away to the stables. Here they tie their feet one to another and fasten their necks to a firmly fixed pillar and tame them by hunger. Afterwards, they restore their strength with green reeds and grass. They next teach them to be obedient, by soothing them, some by coaxing words, and others by songs and the music of the drum.

Some of them take up their drivers when fallen in battle and carry them off to a safe place from the battlefield. Others, when their masters have sought refuge between their forelegs, have fought in their defence and saved their lives. If in a fit of anger, they kill either the man who feeds or the man who trains them, they pine so much for their loss that they refuse to take food, and sometimes die of hunger.

Most of them live as long as men who attain extreme longevity and some live over two hundred years. They are liable to many infectious viral diseases and are not easily cured. The remedy for diseases of the eye is to wash it with cows' milk. For most of their other diseases black wine is administered to them. For the cure of their wounds they are made to swallow butter, for this draws out iron.

On Kalanos and Mandanis

Megasthenese says that self-destruction is not a doctrine of the philosophers, but committing that kind of acts are regarded as foolish of those who with severe temper stabbing themselves, or throwing themselves down from a peak, or those reluctant to pain drowning themselves, or those capable of enduring pain strangling themselves, or those of obsessive temperaments throwing themselves into the fire.

Kalanos was a man of this brand. He was ruled by his passions and became a slave to Alexander. On this account, he was condemned by his countrymen. But, Mandanis was applauded because when messengers from Alexander invited him to go to the son of Zeus (Alexander), with the promise of gifts if he complied, and threats of punishment if he refused, he did not go. Alexander, he said, was not the son of Zeus, for he was not a master of the larger half of the world. For himself, he wanted none of the gifts of a man whose desires nothing could satiate; and as for his threats he did not have any fear. He knew that if he lived, India would supply him with enough food and if he died, he would be delivered from the body of flesh now afflicted with age, and would be translated to a better and a purer life. Alexander expressed admiration of the man, and let him have his own way.

Kalanos followed the Makedonian army from Taxila. According to Plutarch, his real name was Sphines, and he received the name Kalanos among the Greeks because when saluting persons, he used the Sanskrit word êáëå (kalyan or good) instead of the Greek ÷áéñå (hail or jai).

Beyond Palibotra[4] is Mount Maleus on which shadows in winter fall towards the north, in summer towards the south, for six months alternately. In that region the Bears are seen but once a year, and not for more than fifteen days. Those living near the river Indus in the regions that flow southward are scorched more than others by the heat, and the complexion of the people is visibly affected by the great power of the sun. The mountains are inhabited by the Pygmies.

But those who live near the sea have no kings. The Pandaean nation is governed by females, and their first queen is said to have been the daughter of Hercules.

Heracles begat a daughter in India whom he called Pandaia. To her he assigned that portion of India which lies southward and extends to the sea. He distributed the people subject to her rule into 365 villages, giving orders that one village should bring to the treasury the royal tribute each day.

On Brahmins

The Brahmins have the greatest prestige, since they have a more consistent rigid system. As soon as they are conceived in the womb, men of learning take charge of them. These go to the mother and ostensibly sing a charm tending to make the birth happy for mother and child, but in reality convey certain virtues, counsels aid suggestions; the women who listen most willingly are held to be the most fortunate in childbearing. After the birth, the boys pass on from one set of teachers to another in succession, the standard of teachers rising with the age of the boy. The philosophers spend their days in a grove near the city, under the cover of an enclosure of right size, on beds of leaves and skins, living sparely, practicing celibacy and abstinence from flesh· food, listening to grave discourse, and admitting such others to the discussion as may wish to take part. He who listens is forbidden to speak, or even to clear his throat or spit, on pain of being ejected from the company that very day as incontinent. When each Brahman has lived in this fashion for thirty-seven years, he departs to his own property, and lives now in greater freedom and luxury, wearing muslin robes and some decent ornaments of gold on his hands and ears, eating flesh, so long as it is not the flesh of domestic animals, but abstaining from pungent and highly-seasoned food. They marry as many wives as possible to secure good progeny; for the larger number of wives, the larger the number of good children is likely to be. Since they have no slaves, they depend all the more upon the administrations of their children as the nearest substitute. The Brahmins do not admit their wives to their philosophy.

The chief subject on which the Brahmins talk is death; for this present life, they hold, is like the season passed in the womb, and death for those who have cultivated philosophy is the birth into the real, the happy, life. For this reason they follow an extensive discipline to make them ready for death.

They say none of the accidents, which befall on men, are good or evil. If they were, one would not see the same things causing grief to some and joy to others - men's notions being indeed like dreams - and the same men grieved by something which at another moment they will turn and welcome. Their teaching about nature is in parts naive for they are more admirable in what they do than in what they say, and the theoretic proofs on which they base their teaching are mostly fable.

In many points however their teaching agrees with that of the Greeks- for instance, that the world has a beginning and an end in time, and that its shape is spherical; that the Deity, who is its Governor and Maker, interpenetrates the whole; that the first principles of the universe are different, but that water is the principle from which the order of the world has come to be; that, beside the four elements, there is a fifth substance, of which the heavens and the stars are made[5]; that the earth is established at the centre of the universe. About generation and the soul their teaching shows parallels to the Greek doctrines, and on many other matters. Like Plato too, they interweave fables about the immortality of the soul and the judgments inflicted in the other world and so on.

On Palace

The palace is a walled building, with women's apartments, gardens, and tanks in the rear. In front of these is the innermost court, where the king on awakening is saluted by the various domestic officials and, according to Aelian[6] also by an elephant. The next is the station of a sham bodyguard of dwarfs, hunchbacks, wild men, etc.; the outermost of all, communicating with the exterior, is occupied by armed attendants, by ministers and associates.

Everything bespeaks precaution. The structure of the palace itself includes mazes, secret and underground passages, hollow pillars, hidden staircases, collapsible floors against fire, poisonous animals and other poisons creatures. There are diverse specifications, including trees, which snakes avoid; parrots and sarika birds, which cry out on seeing a serpent;

other birds which are affected by the sight of poison. Everyone has his own apartments, and none of the interior officials are allowed to communicate with the outside. The women are carefully watched by attendants, male and female; not even their relatives are admitted to them, except in time of childbirth or illness. All employees coming from outside, such as nautch women (dancers) need to undergo bath and massage and change their dress before admission. Material objects, as they pass in and out, are placed on record and under seal. The king changes his apartment every night.

The kitchen is in a secret place, and there is a multitude of tasters. The signs of poison in the delicious food and in the demeanor of the persons are carefully noted. Medicaments must pass similar test. The instruments of the shampooer and others must be handled by the bodyguard, and the persons themselves to be bathed. Articles of ornament and apparel are inspected by female slaves. Cosmetics are first tried on those who apply them. If actors are admitted, the orchestra and other accessories separate them from the spectator.

The king rides or drives in the company of high officials. When he embarks upon a ship, the same is the ease; no other vessel must be near, and troops are stationed on the shore. Similar precautions apply in the hunt also.

On Administration

Foreign emissaries are received in durbar. The king inspects his armed troops, mounted on elephant or horse. As he progresses, the roads are lined on both sides by police who keep away all armed persons. Whenever ascetics and cripples enter a procession, banquet, festival, or wedding, attendants should take them away apart.

On Other Things

Their customs are very strange when compared with our own, but the following are still more strange; for Megasthenese states that the tribes inhabiting the Kaukasos[7] have intercourse with women in public, and eat the bodies of their relatives, and that there are monkeys which roll down stones. Herodotus has noted the existence of both practices among certain Indian tribes.

The Indians neither put out money at usury, the lending of money, at exorbitant interest rates, nor know how to borrow. To perform a wrongdoing is contrary to established usage for an Indian; therefore, they neither make contracts nor require securities.

Megasthenese, in the second book of his Indica says that when the Indians are at supper, a table like a tripod is placed before each person. Upon it a golden bowl is placed, into which they first put boiled rice and then they add many delicates prepared according to Indian recipes.

Ashoka the Great (304–232 BCE)

The Maurya Empire was inherited by Bindusara's son Ashoka the Great, grandson of Chandragupta Maurya. Emperor Ashoka's remarkable achievements are known mainly through numerous inscriptions carved on rock and stone. He extended the Empire up to Tamil Land and proved that he was one of the great emperors of all times.

According to legend, after noticing the massacre in the Kalinga war, he renounced bloodshed and converted to Buddhism following the policy of non-violence or ahimsa. Ashoka spread Buddhism across the entire East Asia and South-East Asia.

Ashoka was exceedingly tolerant in matters of religion and fallowed absolute faithfulness to the Eightfold Path prescribed in Buddhism. He started social welfare duties like digging wells and irrigation canals; construction of roads, hospitals, and public gardens all over the Empire. Widows, orphans and the disabled were looked after and supported financially by the administration. State warehouses in the countryside, filled with provisions for the relief of unexpected famines. He created a special department for the benevolent administration of aboriginal tribes, endowed many schools and universities, improved the taxation system, included the income of his own private estates in the state budget and spread economical justice all over India.

Amaury de Reincourt writes, "Gradually artistic inspiration had been overcome by engineering skill in Maurya India. Technological progress from the seventh century BCE onward must have been remarkable and suggests the possibility of a real industrial revolution. Complex irrigation works had multiplied – a vast network of canals with sluices spread all over northern India, varied water rates being levied on the customers. Roads and large highways, in no way inferior to those of the Roman Empire, connected all important cities. One great highway ran from Taksasila in the northwest to distant Pataliputra. Pillars marking distances, caravansaries and rest houses, store houses, lined all the main highways. Life was full of bustle and activity, trade flourished, education was widespread, and it is highly probable that there was a higher percentage of literacy among the population than that existing at present. The immense bureaucracy worked with precision and efficiency, taxing, regulating, inspecting – all under the personal supervision of the emperor."

The dependable source of events and occurrences in Ashoka's life known from his own inscriptions are as follows:

(1) In the ninth year after his coronation he began the conquest of the Kalinga country, i.e. Orissa. The slaughter and suffering caused by the conquest produced a lasting impression and it was the turning-point in his mind and career. Thereafter, he joined the Buddhist order as a lay disciple.

(2) His devotion to Buddhism faith began two and a half years later, about the end of the eleventh year from his coronation. When he became a member of the Sangha, or order of monks, he travelled from place to place like the wandering Buddhist and Jain brothers displaying energy, as he phrases it. This energy took the form of visits and gifts to Brahmins, ascetics, and old people, instructions and discussions relating to the Buddhist Dharma or religious rules and principles.

(3) At the end of this tour he issued the first of his religious proclamations, a slogan to his officials to adopt the principles of energetic action and he also ordered that this message should be engraved everywhere, upon rocks and on stone pillars. The practice of carving Buddhist sentiments in this manner on noticeable objects became wide practice. It is still visible in Tibet, Central Asia, China, and throughout the Buddhist world.

(4) 'During the thirteenth and fourteenth year, Ashoka's activities must have been at its height. He issued nearly sixteen memorandums of which fourteen are found engraved throughout his empire. In these records, which are engraved in his fourteenth year, Ashoka gives an account of the administrative and other measures which he had adopted. He instructed to dig wells by the roads, to provide medical aid for men and animals, to open animal hospitals, to propagate medical or useful plants not only in his own territories, but in neighboring territories also like independent and quasi-independent states of South India and the north-west frontier, even as far as the Greek kingdom of Antiochus and beyond. Then he had made regulations restricting the slaughter of animals for food and especially on occasions of festivals and public shows. He had issued persuasive appeals for kindness and consideration in family relationships, in dealings with Brahmins and teachers, in the mutual attitudes of different sects. He had

condemned what he regarded as excess of profitless (i.e. Brahman) ceremonies in public and private life, which had instilled economic burden.

(5) In his thirteenth year, he instituted quinquennial (every five years) circuits of the leading officials for the purpose of proclaiming the moral law as well as for the discharge of their normal functions.

(6) In the fourteenth year he appointed high officials, entitled *dharma mahamatras* with the duty of instilling piety, rectifying misfortune or wrong, organizing charitable endowments and gifts. Some of these officers stood in special relation to the establishments and benevolences of his various endowments, and the operations of others extended even to the foreign countries.

At the same time he gave instruction for the periodical public recitation of these admonitions, and repeats his intention of instituting quinquennial circuits for the benefit of the Kalinga officials. His sons, the Viceroys in Taxila and Ujjain, followed a similar practice at intervals of three years.

(7) In his thirteenth and again in his twentieth year, he dedicated cave-dwellings in the Barabar hills for the use of monks of the Ajivika sect.

Ashoka Pillars:
Single Lion capital at Vaishali

A Standing Pillar, 300 BCE

(8) In his fifteenth year he enlarged the stupa of the Buddha Kanakamuni, and during the twenty- first year, he personally visited this site and that of Buddha's own birth-place.

As regards to the aged and the poor, they are placed under the care of religious officials. Here we see the greatness of Ashoka who implemented a system to take care of the aged and poor when there was no 'poor law' that existed anywhere in the world.

Guptas

The Gupta Dynasty was one of the largest political and military Empires in ancient India. This period has been called the Golden Age of India because of its accomplishments in science, mathematics, astronomy, engineering, religion, philosophy, art, literature, dialectic, literature, logic, trade, technology that developed the essentials known as Hindu culture. The peace and prosperity created under the leadership of Guptas enabled us to pursue scientific and artistic endeavors in India.

The cultural creativity of magnificent architecture, sculpture, and painting was accomplished in this period. The Gupta period presented great scholars such as Kalidasa, Aryabhata, Varahamitra, and Vatsyayana who made great advancements in many academic fields.

CHESS is said to have originated in this period. Early form of Chess in the 6th century was known as Chaturanga, which means four divisions of the military. Infantry, cavalry, elephants, and chariots in the game represent the modern pawn, knight, bishop, and rook, respectively.

The Earliest Buildings

Buildings in primitive India, as among the poorer classes of to-day, the materials most commonly used were mud or mud bricks, bamboo canes, and other kinds of wood. The simplest kinds of dwellings were constructed of screens of bamboo woven with palm branches or the like, the roofs being flat or arched. The bamboos were lashed together at the apex and tied in near the lower end, thus forming a singularly strong framework of curvilinear form, while the walls were strengthened to resist the outward thrust. In other cases, the walls were constructed from unbaked brick or mud, and the subsequent material was also used as a covering for the flat roofs or for plastering the screens of the walls on the wattle and daub principle. At a later date cut timbers came to be used in the flashier dwellings, and provided opportunities for the development of that exuberant surface decoration in which the genius of India has always excelled.

These materials left their character deeply and permanently impressed on Indian architecture. From the use of the bamboo came the curvilinear type of roof which later was reproduced in cut timber and subsequently in stone, and from which the familiar chaitya arches used over doorways and windows were evolved. Log capitals[8] were imitated in stone, and the more finished timbering of walls, roofs, and gateways in stone including every detail down to the nail-beads were copied with care and accuracy by the masons of later days.

As a precaution to protect against destructive insects, wooden poles were set in jars of earthenware as a pot and foliage base (probably insect repellent herbal plants), so beautifully developed in the Gupta age. An outstanding illustration of the influence used by wood in contrast with brick construction is to be found in the pillars of the cave temples. In the earliest examples, the stone pillars are noticeably copied from wooden prototypes and are relatively slender, though sufficiently thick enough for their purpose. In the later examples, the pillars are heavy and cumbersome, not because extra strength was required, but because they were copied from the brick-in-mud pillars of famous viharas, which required much thicker in proportion to their height than columns of stone.

Middle kingdoms of India (230 BCE – 1279 CE)

Middle kingdoms of India refer to the political entities in India from the 2nd century BCE after the decline of the Maurya Empire and the parallel rise of the Satavahana Dynasty. This was a classical period of India having the largest economy in the world. Middle Kingdoms survived for 1,500 years and ended in the 13th century CE.

In the Northwest of India, following the breakdown of the Mauryan Empire, the Indus Valley and Gangetic plains of the north-west attracted a chain of invaders between 200 BCE and 300 CE. Eventually the invaders became Indianized as they were influenced by society and philosophy across the Gangetic plains. This period has featured both intellectual and artistic achievements inspired by cultural diffusion of the new kingdoms across the Silk route.

Gandhara (600 BCE)

Gandhâra is the name of an ancient kingdom located in modern day northern Pakistan and eastern Afghanistan. Its main cities were Purushapura (modern Peshavar) literally meaning City of Man, and Takshashila, modern Taxila.

The Gandhara people were settled on the banks of Kabul River down to its confluence with the Indu since the Vedic times. Later Gandhâra included parts of northwest Punjab. Gandhara was located on the northern trunk road and was a centre of international commercial activities. Trunk Road was built by the Maurya Empire in 3rd century BCE who had trade connections between India and Greek world Taxila being a central place. Taxila (Takshashila) was well connected by roads with other parts of the Maurya Empire. According to the Magasthanese, Chandragupta Maurya's army maintained an ancient highway from Pataliputra (Patna) to Takshashila. It was an important channel of communication with ancient Iran, India and Central Asia.

The region shows southern Central Asian culture in the Bronze Age and the Gandhara grave culture, likely corresponding to immigration of Indo-Aryan speakers and the center of Vedic civilization. Gandhara had played an important role in the epic of Ramayana and Mahabharata. Great scholars such as Panini and Kautilya lived in this cosmopolitan environment.

Persian and Greek conquests (600-500 BCE)

Much of the northwestern subcontinent, present-day eastern Afghanistan and Pakistan, came under the rule of the Persian Achaemenid Empire in 520 BCE

In 326 BCE Alexander the Great conquered Asia Minor and the Achaemenid Empire, reaching the northwest frontiers of the Indian subcontinent. There he defeated King Porus and conquered much of the Punjab. Alexander's march towards the east placed him in confrontation with the Nanda Empire of Magadha. His army, exhausted and frightened by the possibility of facing larger Indian armies at the Ganges River, refused to march further. Plutarch writes the concerns of Alexander's army:

> "As for the Macedonians, however, their struggle with Porus blunted their courage and stayed their further advance into India. For having done all they could do to repulse an enemy who mustered only twenty thousand infantry and two thousand horse, they violently opposed Alexander when he insisted on crossing the river Ganges also, the width of which, as they learned, was thirty-two furlongs, its depth a hundred fathoms, while its banks on the further side were covered with multitudes of men-at-arms and horsemen and elephants. For they were told that the kings of the Ganderites and Praesii were awaiting them with eighty thousand horsemen, two hundred thousand footmen, eight thousand chariots, and six thousand fighting elephants."

Alexander convinced recognizing his army's sentiments to go back to their homes and agreed to return back.

The Persian and Greek invasions had important repercussions on Indian civilization. The political systems of the Persians influenced future forms of governance on the subcontinent, including the administration of the Mauryan Dynasty. In addition, the region of Gandhara, or present-day eastern Afghanistan and northwest Pakistan, became a melting pot of Indian, Persian, Central Asian, and Greek cultures. It also gave birth to a hybrid culture, Greco-Buddhism, which lasted until the 5th century CE. and influenced the artistic development of Mahayana Buddhism.

The Indo-Greeks ruled various parts of northwestern India until the end of the 1st century BCE and then they were conquered by the Scythians and Kushans.

The Indo-Scythians Sakas (200 BCE-400 CE)

The Indo-Scythians are the offshoot of Sakas (Scythians), who migrated from the middle of the 2nd century BCE crossing southern Siberia into Bacteria, Sogdiana, Arachosia, Gandhara, Kashmir, Punjab, and into some parts of Western and Central India, Gujarat, Maharashtra and Rajasthan. The first Saka king in India was Moga who founded Saka rule in Gandhara and gradually extended dominance over north-western India. Their rule in India ended in 395 CE.

The Yavanas (100 BCE – 400 A.D)

The Yavanas were living beyond Gandhara. Yavanas, Sakas, Pahlavas, and Hunas were all considered as Mlechhas. This name was used to refer to their cultural differences with the Vedic culture that prevailed in the Kuru Panchala kingdoms. The Mahabharata compliments the all-knowing Yavanas as the architects of vimanas (aerial vehicles, even though it is questionable). It is said that in the ports of southern India, the early Tamil poems speak about the settlement of the Yavanas.

Old Persian inscriptions of Darius show that the Yavanas and Persians applied to all Greeks without distinction and they are the name of the Ionians of Asia Minor who were conquered by Cyrus in 545 BCE Therefore, Greeks were known in India at a time when a large portion of the northwest was still under the Persian rule. The occurrence of the word Yavana in a grammatical rule of Panini (IV, 1.49) is a clear indication that it had been adopted into Sanskrit before the middle of the 4th century BCE Its Prakrit equivalent, Yona, is used in the inscriptions of Ashoka to describe the

Hellenic sovereigns of Egypt, Cyrene, Macedonia, Epirus, and Syria. There is no doubt that in all Indian documents earlier than the third century CE. , the term Yavana denotes a person of Greek descent. In spite of the fact, like other foreign settlers in India, many of the Yavanas had become Hinduized and had adopted Indian names. At a later date, foreigners generally are classified as Yavanas.

Gangetic Plains and Deccan

Following the decline of the Mauryan Empire, the Gangetic area broke up into several states. In the Deccan, the Chalukyas began developing a strong nation and spreading the cultural and military power that was in the hold of the Indo-Gangetic Plain.

The Satavahanas (230 BCE – 220 CE)

The Satavahana Empire started as feudatories to the Mauryan Empire. They became independent and declared independence some time after the death of Ashoka. The Satavahanas originally ruled in the areas of current Telangana and other coastal Andhra areas as well as Pune. They fought against Sungas, Kanvas and protected their territory from Sakas, Yavanas and Parthivas. Four or five Kings of Satavahana Dynasty ruled the Empire until 220 AD., and it declined following the rise of its feudatories.

The Satavahanas created a cultural bridge between Indo-Gangetic Plain and southern part of India, and played an important role in trade and transfer of ideas and culture. The Satavahanas influenced South-East Asia by spreading Hindu culture, language and religion. They contributed a great deal towards the development of art. They spoke Telugu and Maharashtra Prakrit.

Northeast India

- 350 – 650 CE. The Varman Dynasty: The Varman Dynasty ruled Kamarupa (Assam), founded by Pushya Varman in the 4th century CE.
- 650- 900 CE. Mlechchha Dynasty: The Mlechchha dynasty ruled Kamarupa (Assam) from their capital at Hadapeshvar in the modern day Tejpur after the decline of Varman Dynasty. The rulers were aboriginals.
- 900 – 1100 CE. The Pala Dynasty of Kamarupa: The Pala Dynasty of Kamarupa (Assam) succeeded the Mlechchha Dynasty and ruled until the end of the 12th century CE.

- 250 – 500 CE. The Vakatakas: The Vakataka Empire was the contemporaries of the Gupta Empire and the descendants of Satavahanas. Vakatakas were famous for encouraging arts, architecture and literature. The stone-built Buddhist viharas and chaityas of Ajanta Caves were built under the sponsorship of the Vakataka rulers. Ultimately, they were defeated by the Chalukyas.

Harsha Vardhana (606–647 CE)

After the collapse of the Gupta Empire, the Gangetic plains divided into several small states. Harsha Vardhana of Kannauj was able to unite them together under his rulership briefly. This unity did not last long beyond his reign and his Empire was divided again soon after his death in 647 AD.

Harsha was a Mahayana Buddhist. He was a tolerant ruler and supported all faiths: Vedas, Buddhism, and Jainism. The great Indian mathematician Brahmagupta lived in the Empire of Harshavardhana.

According to the Chinese Pilgrim Xuanzang, who visited Harsha's kingdom in 636 AD, Harsha built several stupas in the name of Buddha. Harsha was also a supporter of art and literature. He contributed numerous endowments to the University of Nalanda.

Harsha himself was a famous author. He composed three Sanskrit plays – Nagananda, Ratnavali, and Priyadarsika. Bana, in his first historical poetic work in Sanskrit language, composed Harsha Charitha, which describes India's natural environment and vitality of life at that time.

The Rajputs (600 – 1950 A.D)

The Rajputs were of Hindu origin who ruled the region stretching from the Gangaetic plains to the Afghan mountains. Their dynasties made the transition from Buddhist ruling dynasties to Hindu ruling dynasties.

After the collapse of the Gupta Empire, the first Rajput kingdoms rose to power in 5th and 6th centuries CE. They ruled the Indian subcontinent from 6th century to 20th century CE. , and Southeast Asia from 9th to 15th centuries. Nepal was the last Empire of Rajputs which ended in 1950. At the time of India's independence in 1947, Rajputs ruled in the princely states of Rajasthan and Saurashtra.

Rajput kingdoms competed against Arabs, Moguls, Mongols, Afghans and Turkic people. They gained their reputation by fighting these battles with rules of polite conduct rooted in their staunch adherence to tradition. The Rajput Kings protected their kingdom against Arabs and other Central Asian Empires for several centuries. A few Rajput Kings did convert to

Islam and eventually an alliance was formed with the Mughals. Eventually they had to face Muslim invasion.

During the British Raj, after the third Anglo-Maratha War in 1817-1818, Rajputs entered into a subsidiary alliance with the East India Company and became princely states under the British Raj.

The Palas (750–1174 A.D)

Pala Empire was a Buddhist Dynasty that ruled north-eastern region of India. The Palas were followers of the Mahayana and Tantric systems of Buddhism. The first ruler Gopala, a son of a warrior, came to power in 750 CE. in Gaur by a democratic election according to Tibetan scholar Taranatha. This event is recognized as one of the first democratic elections in South Asia since the time of Mahajanapadas. Gopala unified Bengal territories and brought peace and prosperity in the region. The period of anarchy ended with his election. Palas constructed many temples and works of art, and supported the Universities of Nalanda and Vikramashila. Somapura Mahavihara built by Dharmapala is the famous Buddhist Vihar in India.

The Pala kings devoted themselves in public welfare and social reform. They adopted the policy of religious tolerance and co-existence of Buddhists and Hindus. Pala kings won the heart of the people by welfare activities like constructing lakes and establishing towns.

The earlier version of Bangla language was born at the time of Palas. The Buddhist works of Charyapada, mystical poems are the earliest forms of Bangla language. Texts on every type of knowledge were compiled during the Pala Rule:

- **On philosophy**: Agama Shastra by Gaudapada, Nyaya Kundali by Sridhar Bhatta, Karmanushthan Paddhati by Bhatta Bhavadeva;
- **On Medicine**: Chikitsa Samgraha, Ayurvedidvipika, Bhanumati, Shabdachandrika, Dravya Gunasangraha by Chakrapani Datta;
- **Shabda-Pradipa,** Vrikkhayurveda, Lohpaddhati by Sureshwara;
- **Chikitsa Sarsamgraha** by Vangasena;
- Sushrata[9] by Gadadhara Vaidya;
- Dayabhaga, Vyavohara Matrika and Kalaviveka by Jimutavahana and so on.
- Atisha compiled more than 200 texts.
- The great epic Ramacharitam written by Sandhyakar Nandi, the court poet of Madanapala was another masterpiece of the Pala

literature. The Pala copperplate inscriptions were of excellent literary value. These distinctive inscriptions are in Gaudiya Style.

Palas created excellent art and sculpture monuments, a distinctive form of Buddhist art known as the Pala School of Sculptural Art.

Southern India

In the early period of history, Southern India saw various small kingdoms rise and fall, and the spread of Buddhism and Jainism up to the southern end of India. After the fall of the Gupta Empire, there was a gradual shift of balance of power from the northern states to the southern states, both in military and in culture.

Southern India in those days had a high regard in the world for its booming Civilizations. The southern areas had a great geopolitical advantage over the northern regions. Northern regions were repeatedly devastated and weakened by the foreign invasions, while south was safe from outside invaders. Therefore, they were more prosperous and freer to devote themselves to cultural pursuits and remained distinct from the rest of the subcontinent.

The Deccan known as South Land (dakshinapatha), stretching down to south of the Vindhya mountain ranges to the Tungabhadra River, was covered with dense jungles and populated by aboriginal tribes akin to the old Dasyus (the known enemies of the Vedic Aryans). Penetration across the thickly forested Vindhya Mountains was extremely difficult and hazardous, but the powerful Aryans overran the Deccan in increasing number from 7th century BCE They civilized the aborigine tribes; they gave their languages and literatures, their artistic styles and technology, their social structure and political ideas. But, Fa Hien, a Chinese pilgrim who traveled India in 399 BCE wrote the Deccan was still sparsely populated and dangerous, swarming with leopards, tigers, snakes and monkeys.

The history of Deccan comes to light after the collapse of the Maurya Empire, when the Dravidian-speaking Andhras, founded an enduring state that included most of the Deccan and survived almost five hundred years. When northern India was overrun by the Yueh-chis and Huns devastated northern India, the Deccan became an asylum for many northerners. Buddhists and Hindus lived side by side peacefully until Islam came to dominate India.

Brahmins and Buddhists penetrated the formidable Venkata Hills and entered Tamil Land where they met strong powerful kingdoms that would not submit to the northern rule. In the Tamil Land, large states existed even before Ashoka's reign and had great wealth and prosperity due to the amazing growth of foreign trade that was taking place at the time. Approximately at the same time, the great cultures in China, India and Greeco-Roman world were passing into Civilization. Foreign trade was becoming an economic factor of paramount importance. Megasthanese[10] has mentioned the power of the Pandya state (modern Madurai) in his Indica. A generous nature provided these southern states with many riches for which the rest of the world thirsted such as pearls, corals, rice, pepper, ginger, sandalwood, cinnamon, and ivory. As early as 450 BCE, rice and peacocks had been sent to Greece from the south. The fabulous wealth of Tamil Land became an epitome all over the known world; gold poured into South India in exchange for spices. Vast numbers of Roman coins have been found at Madurai, and Roman colonies and mercenaries were numerous all over the south.

When northern India descended into cultural sterility, South India provided Indian Civilization with a remarkable cultural rebirth. One after another, great dynasties arose in South India. All noteworthy Indian thinkers between the seventh and thirteenth century came from the south: Shankara from Malabar (Kerala), Ramanuja from Kanchi, and Madhva from South Canara.

Tamil Nadu's history dates back to pre-historic times and archaeological evidence indicates that this area was one of the longest steady habitations in India. In Adichanallur, 24 km from Tirunelveli, archaeologists from the Archaeological Survey of India excavated 169 clay urns including human skulls, skeletons and bones, in addition to husks, grains of rice, charred rice, and Neolithic celts, providing evidence to confirm that they belonged to the Neolithic period, 3800 years ago. The archaeologists have suggested that the script used at the site is a very rudimentary form of Tamil Brahmi.

Long before the beginning of the Christian era, the Dravidian South had developed a considerable culture of its own, and its inhabitants had possessed powerful kingdoms, some of which carried a thriving trade with Western Asia, Egypt, and later with the Greek and Roman empires.

The Pandya Dynasty (500 BCE – 1345 CE)

Pandya kingdom seems to have been founded in the 5th century BCE by Pandya, a person of the agricultural class. The word Pandya is derived from the Tamil word "Pandi" meaning bull. Bull is a sign of masculinity and valor. Pandya became the nickname of the first Pandyan king of Madurai, Kulasekharan Pandya because he was built like a bull and was used as a personification of masculinity.

The Pandyas and their capital city Madurai were well known to the ancient Greeks and Romans. Megasthenes, a Greek ambassador of Seleukos at the court of Chandragupta Maurya mentions about the Pandyan kingdom around 300 BCE. and gives an elaborate report of the Pandyan kingdom, which according to him was governed by women. He mentions that Heracles was the ruler of a southern country and Pandyan queen at the time, *Pandaia* was a daughter of Heracles. He says, "Heracles begat a daughter in India whom he called Pandaia. To her he assigned that portion of India which lies to southward and extends to the sea while he distributed the people subject to her rule into 365 villages, each of which was expected to meet the needs of the royal household for one day in the year." Since a story Silappadikaram refers to an example of a cowherdess who says that it was her turn of the day to supply ghee to the royal household of Madurai, Dr. Devakunjari maintains that this statement was probably a kind of payment to the queen.

Emperor Augustus of Rome at Antioch was aware of the Pandyan and met a Pandyan ambassador with letters and gifts from this ancient Tamil Kingdom. Strabo, a Greek historian, geographer and philosopher, wrote that an ambassador from a South Indian King known as Pandyan visited Emperor Augustus Caesar. Records indicate that the Pandya kingdom was described as *Pandyan Mediterranea* by *Periplus* and *Modura Regia Pandyan* by Ptolemy.

Ptolemy shows great knowledge of the interior of the Tamil country and mentions a number of inland cities of the Pandoonoi, namely, Tainour (Thenur), Peringkarei (Perunkarai), Korindiour, Tangala or Taga and Akour. Madurai, the capital of Pandyans was in the south far away from the coast. They also had extensive trade links with the Southeast Asian countries.

There were constant wars and conflicts between Cholas, Pandyas and Pallavas. The kingdoms were conquered and replaced by each other several times.

In the 8th century A.D Pallavas were replaced by the Pandyas. During the 13th century Marco Polo mentioned Pandyan Kingdom as the richest Empire in existence at that time. Meenakshi Temple at Madurai is the best example of Pandyan Temple architecture. The Pandyas excelled in both trade as well as literature and they managed the pearl fisheries along the South Indian coast, between Sri Lanka and India, which produced some of the finest pearls known in the ancient world.

The Cheras (300 BCE – 600 A.D)

The early Cheras ruled parts of Kerala (Malabar) state, Kongu Nadu, Salem, and Dharmapuri from time immemorial. Cherans, who spoke Tamil language, ruled from the capital of Karur in the west and traded significantly with West Asian kingdoms.

In Sanskrit Kera means 'coconut' and Keralam (Kera Alam) means Kera kingdom. Pliny, the Roman historian of the first century, who most likely visited Kerala, called the area *Caelobothras* in his Natural History. The Periplus of the Erythraean Sea states that Chera as *Cerobothra* whose capital was Karur.

The Chola Dynasty (300 BCE-1300 CE)

The Chola Dynasty was a Tamil Dynasty. The earliest records of this Hindu Dynasty could be found from the inscriptions from the 3rd century BCE of Ashoka. Pillars of Ashoka inscriptions mention Cholas among other kingdoms that existed on friendly terms with him although independent of Ashoka. Cholas continued to rule various territories until the 13th century CE. The origin of the Chola Dynasty can be found in ancient Tamil literature, inscriptions and Sangam period literature.

There are also brief notices on the Chola country and its towns, ports and commerce furnished by the Periplus of the Erythrean Sea[11] (*Periplus Maris Erythraei*). Greek Geographer and Astronomer Ptolemy has described the Chola town of Kaveri Poompattinam, also known as Poompuhar as an important sea port that had trade connections with the Roman Empire and China. Roman coins from the early centuries have been found near the Kaveri delta.

By the 9th century under Rajaraja Chola and his son Rajendra Chola, the Cholas emerged again as a prominent power in south Asia. Their Empire extended as far as Bengal. Rajaraja Chola conquered most of South India and parts of Sri Lanka. Rajendra Chola's navies moved forward and occupied the coasts from Burma to Vietnam, the Andman and Nicobar Islands, Lakshadweep, Sumatra, Java, Malaya, and Pegu islands. He conquered Mahipala, the king of Bengal, and celebrated victory building a new capital Gangaikonda Cholapuram (City of Gangas conquered by Chola).

Under Cholas, the Tamil excelled in art, religion, and literature. Monumental architecture in the form of majestic temples and sculptures in stone and bronze reached an elegance and refinement.

The age of the Medieval Cholas (850–1200) was the golden age of Tamil culture and literature. Jain and Buddhist authors flourished as well. Cholas were the staunch followers of Hinduism. Throughout their history, they were never persuaded by Buddhism or Jainism influence.

The Kadambas (345 – 525 CE)

The Kadamba Dynasty was an ancient royal family of Karnataka that ruled from Banavasi, Uttara Kannada district. At the peak of their power under King Kakushtavarma, they ruled large parts of Karnataka. The Kadambas were the first indigenous dynasty to use Kannada, the language of the natives at an administrative level. In the history of Karnataka, this period is a starting point in the study of the development of the region as an enduring geo-political entity and Kannada as an important regional language. The dynasty was established by Mayurasharma in 345 CE. The Kadambas were contemporaries of the Western Ganga Dynasty of Talkad.

Also there were Badami Chalukyas, Pallavas, Eastern Chalukyas, Rashtrakutas, Western Chalukyas, Yadavas, Kakatiyas, and Hoysalas, who ruled southern kingdoms.

Vijayanagara Empire (1336–1646 AD)

The Vijayanagara Empire referred as the Kingdom of Bisnaga by the Portuguese was a South Indian Empire located in the Deccan Plateau of modern day Karnataka. The Empire was established by Harihara I and his brother Bukka Raya I in 1336 CE. The Empire, named after its capital city of Vijayanagara (City of Victory), is now a World Heritage Site in Karnataka state. The writings of European travelers such as Domingo Paes, Fernao Nune, Robert Sewell and Niccolo Da Conti and the literature in local languages provide important information about its history. Archaeological excavations at Vijayanagara have discovered the Empire's power and wealth.

The founders of Vijayanagar Empire Harihara I and Bukka Raya I originated from Kuruba community and were related to the Kakatiya kingdom. They were controlling northern parts of the Hoysala Empire at the end of their rule. Those brothers were supported and inspired by Vidyaranya, a sage at the Sringeri monastery and his brother Sayana to fight Muslim invasion in South India. It was more defensible and secure for its location between the 14th and 16th century. They designated varaha (boar) as their emblem.

Before the rise of the Vijayanagara Empire in the early 14th century, the Hindu kingdoms of the Deccan were repeatedly invaded by Muslims from the north. The Hoysala Empire was the only remaining Hindu kingdom preventing Muslim invasion. After the death of Hoysala King Veera Ballalla III during a battle against the Sultan of Madurai in 1343, the Hoysala Empire merged with the emerging Vijayanagara Empire. Ultimately, the Empire came under the rule of Krishnadevaraya, the son of Narasa Nayaka of Tuluva community.

Vijayanagara Empire dominated Southern India and defended their kingdom from Deccan Sultanates. The Empire reached its peak during the rule of Krishnadevaraya. It captured the areas, which were under the Sultanates in the northern Deccan and the territories in the east.

After Krishnadevaraya, the Empire gradually declined and feudatories of the Vijayanagar Empire - Mysore, Keladi Nayakas, Nayaks of Madurai, Nayaks of Tanjore, and Nayakas of Chitradurga - declared independence.

Writings by foreign travelers and recent excavations in the Vijayanagara have unearthed information about Vijayanagar Empire's history, fortresses, scientific developments and architectural innovations.

The kings of the Vijayanagara Empire followed the methods to govern their provinces developed by their predecessors, the Hoysala, Kakatiya and Pandya kingdoms and maintained the well-functioning administrative schemes.

The kingdom's economy mainly depended on agriculture. Its capital city was a thriving business centre that included a flourishing market in large quantities of precious gems and gold. Lavish temple-building provided employment to thousands of masons, sculptors, and other skilled artists.

Merchants from many nations including Arabs, Persians, Northwestern Iran, and Afghanistan were settled in Calicut, attracted by the booming business. Shipbuilding prospered and ships sailed to the Red Sea ports of Aden and Mecca with Vijayanagara goods and sold as far away as Venice. Cotton yarn was exported to Burma and indigo to Persia. Chief imports from Palestine were copper, quicksilver (mercury), vermilion, coral, saffron, colored velvets, rose water, knives, colored camlets[12], gold and silver. Persian horses were imported, and silk arrived from China. Spice trade was very popular in India, especially Pepper, which was highly valued. Therefore, the workers on shipping vessels were prevented from having pockets on their dresses presuming that they may steal this black gold! A mineral rich region, Machilipatnam was the main source for high quality iron and steel exports. The Kollur region dealt in diamond mining business.

Most of the information on the social life in Vijayanagara Empire is known from the writings of foreign visitors and from research in the Vijayanagara area. The Hindu caste system was prevalent and untouchability was part of the caste system. The Muslim communities were represented by their own group in coastal Karnataka. But the caste system did not stop distinguished persons from being promoted to high ranking posts in the army and administration. In civil life, Brahmins enjoyed a high level of respect. Most Brahmins concentrated on religious and literary matters. Free from material wealth and power made them ideal arbiters in local judicial matters.

Although it was voluntary, the practice of Sati was common in Vijayanagar and commonly observed among the upper classes.

Women were actively involved in matters such as administration, business and trade, and involvement in the fine arts. Until then it was considered as the monopoly of men.

Portuguese visitor Domingo Paes was at Vijayanagara during the reign of Krishnadevaraya . He gives invaluable information on the walls, gates, streets and markets of the city, major temples of the city, including the Virupaksha at Hampi, and its row of pillars bazaar. Paes describes the Mahanavami festival beginning with the preparations within the king's palace where ceremonies were held at the House of Victory, all decorated with precious cloths. According to Paes, the festival included numerous processions of animals, warriors and courtly women, as well as wrestling matches, fireworks and other entertainments.

Rich men wore the Peethambara Kulavi, a tall Turban made of silk and decorated with gold. Jewellery was used by men and women and records tell the use of anklets, bracelets, finger-rings, necklaces and earrings of various types. During celebrations, men and women adorned themselves with flower garlands and used perfumes. In contrast to the commoners whose lives also were modest, the lives of the kings and queens were full of ceremonial pomp in the court. Queens and princesses had numerous attendants who also lavishly dressed and adorned with fine jewellery.

Domingo writes:

> "The city of Bidjanagar is such that the pupil of the eye has never seen a place like it, and the ear of intelligence has never been informed that there existed anything to equal it in the world.

The Vijayanagara kings were tolerant of all religions and sects as understood by writings by foreign visitors.

Roy gave orders for the entertainment of mussulmans in his service; allotted those jaghires, erected a mosque for their use in the city of Beejanuggur, and commanded that no one should molest them in the exercise of their religion. He also ordered a Koran to be placed before his throne, on a rich desk, so that the mussulmans might perform the ceremony of obeisance in his presence, without sinning against their laws. Physical exercises were popular with men and wrestling was an important male preoccupation for sport and entertainment.

Gymnasiums have been discovered inside royal quarters and records write about regular physical training for commanders and their armies during peacetime."

During the rule of the Vijayanagar Empire, poets, scholars and philosophers wrote in Sanskrit and in the regional languages, Kannada, Telugu and Tamil. Their literature consisted of subjects like religion, biography, fiction, music, grammar, poetry and medicine. The Telugu language became a popular literary medium, reaching its peak under the rule of Krishnadevaraya.

Vijayanagara architecture is a brilliant combination of the Chalukya, Hoysala, Pandya, and Chola styles. The previous temple building traditions in South India came in the Vijayanagara Architecture style. The combination of all faiths and vernaculars inspired architectural innovation of Hindu temple construction using the local granite. The Empire's support enabled fine arts and literature to reach new heights in the languages of Kannada, Telugu, Tamil and Sanskrit. Carnatic music also prospered.

A feature of Vijayanagara architecture shows the multi-ethnic trend of the great city is the presence of many secular structures bearing Islamic features. While political history describes the ongoing encounters between the Vijayanagara Empire and the Deccan Sultanates, the architectural record shows a more creative interaction. Vijayanagar kings had employed many Muslims in their army and court, some may be Muslim architects. This harmonious exchange of architectural ideas must have happened during the periods of peace between the Hindu and Muslim kingdoms. The "Great Platform" popularly known as Mahanavami Dibba has carvings that illustrate a broad range of royal figures receiving guests, enjoying entertainments, and hunting expeditions.

Kannada, Telugu and Tamil languages were used in the Empire. The Empire minted coins at Hampi, Penugonda and Tirupati with Sanskrit, Kannada and Telugu legends usually carrying the name of the ruler. Gold, silver and copper were used to issue coins called Gadyana, Varaha, Pon, Pagoda, Pratapa, Pana, Kasu and Jital. The coins contained the images of various Gods including Balakrishna, Venkateshwara, Goddesses such as Bhudevi and Sridevi, divine couples, animals such as bulls and elephants and birds. The earliest coins featured Hanuman and Garuda.

Mughal Empire

UNTIL about the tenth century, Indians enjoyed the Indian Civilization without any interruption. All previous invaders Greek, Persians, Kushans, and Huns had been absorbed into Indian life and culture and digested the customs and tradition, and completely ceased to exist as separate entities.

Muslim domination in India started when the Turks appeared on the scene of Indian history. In 986 CE. Amir of Ghazni Sabuktagin attacked India and defeated the Hindu ruler, Raja Jaipal of Bathindah in Punjab. Muslims destroyed the areas under their control and instilled terror in the hearts of Hindus.

At the end of the thirteenth century, the Slave Dynasty was replaced by Turko-Afghan Khiljis, who extended their empire southward. Early in the fourteenth century, Ala-uddin crossed the Vindhya Mountains and entered into the Deccan and started to conquer the peninsula. Hindu states were unable to unite themselves against the foreign invaders and ultimately, the whole of India plunged under the wave of the Turko-Afghan conquerors.

The Moghal period started from 1556 CE. with the ascent of Jalaluddin Mohammad Akbar, known as Akbar the Great. During the period, the Mughal Empire had a highly centralized administration connecting different provinces. All of the important monuments of the Mughals are distinguished by Persian cultural influence with exceptional literary, artistic, and architectural innovations.

The name *Mughal* is derived from the original Central Asian plains conquered by Genghis Khan known as Moghulistan, the Land of Mongols. For centuries thereafter, generation after generation of Hindus saw the Muslim conquests. Amaury de Reincourt writes the pitiful condition of Indians during that period:

> "The breakdown of the Universal Empire of Mauryas left India with a Universal Society, not a Universal State. That was the final political and social form in which its life stream was gloomy and survived until alien civilizations challenged and overpowered it. Its political philosophy never attempted to overcome the pessimism and distrust of Kautilya's Arthashastra. In India politics is considered as a replica of the lawless world of the jungle. Most of the rulers followed Kautilya's harmful, malicious, mischievous traits. This attitude of indifference toward all worldly matters was mainly responsible for the collapse of the Indian world into an anarchic combination of unstable and quarreling states. When their country was conquered by aliens, Indians did not care. They turned their attention inward selfishly, and

intellectual communities completely submerged in the religious mysticism and ceremonies neglecting the world of politics and history. "Alberuni described the Hindus' pride and their unwillingness to communicate their culture and knowledge to foreigners. He wondered at their religious tolerance and lack of systematic and rational study of religion among pandits, and their reluctance to risk their lives for their ideals. Indians did not concern themselves with the events taking place west of Hakra River, the historical boundary between Sind and Hind. For all practical purposes, the area occupied by the Arabs remained unholy ground to the Hindus, and the mainland of India moved on living unconcerned. It is only in the days of Mahmud of Ghazni's invasion, the Hindu hostility began. For centuries thereafter, generation after generation, Hindus wept as they heard the pitiful tale of the Muslim conquests, and then drying their tears, and went to work for their Muslim masters losing their identification."

Mahmud of Ghazni (971-1030 A.D)

Mahmud was a son of a Turkish slave. At the age of 27, he became a ruler of Ghazni in 998 CE. demonstrating remarkable administrative capability and rulership.

His main opponent in northern India was Jaipal, the ruler of Punjab. When in 1001 Mahmud rallied against India with 15,000 horse troops, Jaipal confronted him with 12,000 horse troops, 30,000-foot soldiers, and 300 elephants. In a battle near Peshawar, the Indians, though superior in numbers and equipment, were defeated under the attack of the Muslim horses, leaving 15,000 soldiers dead. As Raja Jaipal could not endure his defeat, he climbed to his own funeral pyre and ended his life.

His son Anandpal with the help of other Indian kings waged war against Mahmud. In the middle of an aggressive fight, Anandpal's panic-stricken elephant departed from the battlefield. The Indian army believing that their leader was returning back ran away from the battlefield. This unexpected victory enabled Mahmud to move forward into the center of India. After annexing the Punjab, he returned with enormous booty.

On April 30, 1030, Mahmud caught malaria and died in Ghazni at the age of 59.

Alberuni

Alberuni accompanied Mahmud of Ghazni to India around 1010 CE. and stayed in Punjab for many years and studied the Sanskrit language very deeply.

Alberuni was regarded as one of the famous scholars of the medieval Islamic period and was knowledgeable in mathematics, astronomy, physical and natural sciences, and also renowned geographer, historian, chronologist and linguist. He made a thorough study of Sanskrit and Hindu literature and wrote a profound description of India in his famous work Tahkik-i-Hind (An Enquiry into India). In this document one can find a mine of information about India and its people.

The book "Indica of Alberuni" provides us a rare insight into the habits, customs, beliefs, religion, philosophy, literature, geography, laws, chronology, astronomy, and astrology of Hindu India as Alberuni saw it in 1030 CE.

His biographer informs that "he never had a pen out of his hand, or his eye ever off a book, and his thoughts were always directed to his studies, with an exception of two days in a year." He was beyond comparison, superior to every man of his time in the art of composition, in scholarly accomplishments, and in the knowledge of geometry and philosophy, and above all he had "most firm regard for truth."

Alberuni explains that art and science require the protection of kings. "For they alone could free the minds of scholars from the daily anxieties for the necessities of life, and stimulate their energies to earn more fame and favor, the yearning for which is the pith and marrow of human nature."

To Alberuni the Hindus were excellent philosophers, good mathematicians and astronomers, although he considered himself superior to them. He never concealed whatever he considered wrong and unpractical with them, but he duly appreciated their mental achievements and took maximum care to correct his views. Whenever he ran into something that was noble and grand both in science and in practical life, he never failed to place it before his readers with warm-hearted words of admiration. Speaking of the construction of the ponds at holy bathing-places, he said, "In this they have attained a very high degree of art, so that our people (the Muslims), when they see them, wonder at them, and are unable to describe them, much less to construct anything like them".

Alberuni felt a strong affection towards Indian philosophy. Probably he thought that the philosophers both in ancient Greece and India are an ignorant, image-loving crowd. Eventually he realized that in reality they have very same ideas as his own, that is pure monotheism. He realized that originally all people were alike, pure, and virtuous, worshipping one sole Almighty God. But, in the course of time, the dark passions of the group of people had given rise to the difference of religion, of philosophical and political persuasions, and of idolatry. "The first cause of idolatry was the desires of commemorating the dead and of consoling the living; but on this basis it has developed and has finally become a foul and pernicious abuse".

He contrasted the democratic equality of people in his country with the castes of India, the matrimonial law of Islam with degraded forms of it in India, the cleanliness and decency of Muslims with filthy customs of the Hindus. With all this, his recognition of Islam was not without a hidden secret. He dared not to attack Islam, but he attacked the Arabs. In his work on chronology he criticizes the ancient Muslims having destroyed the civilization of Iran, and makes us to understand that the earlier Arabs were certainly no better than the Zoroastrian Iranians. Whenever he spoke of a dark side in Hindu life, he turned round sharply to compare the manners of the ancient Arabs, and declared that they were quite as bad, if not worse. This could only be meant as a hint to the Muslim reader not to be too arrogant towards the poor bewildered Hindu, trodden down by the savage hordes of King Mahamud, and not to forget that the founders of Islam were not angels.

He was a strict judge both of himself and of others. He himself was perfectly sincere and it was the same sincerity he demanded from others. Whenever he did not fully understand a subject, or only understood a part of it, he would tell the reader accordingly, either asking the reader's pardon for his ignorance, or promising to continue his hard work and to publish its results in time, as if he were acting under a moral responsibility to the public.

He did not like those who hate to admit their ignorance by frankly saying, "I do not know", and he was provoked to strong annoyance whenever he encountered a lack of sincerity.

If Brahmagupta teaches two theories of the eclipses, (1) the popular about the Rahu consuming the luminous body, and (2) the scientific one, Alberuni considers Brahmagupta committed the sin against conscience by undue concessions to the priests of the country. It was the fear of a fate like that which happened to Socrates when he came into conflict with the beliefs of the majority of his countrymen.

In the works of Varahamihira, he found honest scientific work sentences which sound to him "like the ravings of a madman", but he gently suggested that behind those passages, perhaps there may be an esoteric meaning, unknown to him. However, when Varahamihira seems to exceed all limits of common sense, Alberuni regarded that "to such things silence is the only proper answer."

He sincerely hated the verbosity of Indian authors or rhyme writers, who used lots of words where a single one would be sufficient. He called it "mere nonsense—a means to keep people in the dark and throw an air of mystery about the subject. This superficial and abundance of words offer painful difficulties to those who want to learn knowledge resulting in absolute waste of time".

When a man from Kanoj came and lectured on chronology, the serious scholar smiled and remarked, "I used great care in examining every single one of them, in repeating the same questions at different times in a different order and context. But Lo! What different answers did I get! God is omniscient".

He did not blindly accept the traditions of former ages; he wanted to understand and criticize them. He wanted to filter the wheat from the chaff, and discard everything that alleviates against the laws of nature and of reason.

He criticized manuscript tradition like a modern philologist. Sometimes he doubted that the text was corrupt and inquired the cause of the corruption and proposed to make corrections. He criticized different translations and complained the carelessness and ignorance of the copyists. He was aware that Indian works, badly translated and carelessly copied by the successive copyists will be very soon degenerate to such a degree that an Indian author would hardly recognize his own work, if it were presented to him in such a garb.

He wrote, "My book is nothing but a simple historic record of facts. I have already translated two books into Arabic, one about the origins and a description of all created beings, called Samkhya, and another about the emancipation of the soul from the shackles of the body by Patanjali.

Some of his comments on Indians are - The Hindus believe that there is no country but theirs, no nation like theirs, no kings like theirs, no religion like theirs, and no science like theirs. They are by nature niggardly in communicating that which they know, and they take the greatest possible care to withhold it from men of another caste among their own people, still much more, of course, from any foreigner ... Their haughtiness is such that, if you tell them of any science or scholar in Khorasan and Persis, they will think you to be both an ignoramus and a liar. If they traveled and mixed with other nations, they would soon change their mind, for their ancestors were not as narrow-minded as the present generation is."

In the book "Alberuni's India", he covered every aspect of Indian knowledge in 79 chapters.

Cultural Contributions of Deccan Sultanates

All five Deccan sultanates have contributed tremendously in the fields of art, music, literature and architecture.

Deccan sultanates developed Dakhni Urdu language, copying resources from Arabic-Persian, Marathi, Kannada and Telugu. It helped administrative purposes as well as literary development. The Deccani miniature painting flourished in the courts of Ahmadnagar, Bijapur, and Golconda making major cultural contributions by the Deccan Sultanates. The architectural grandeur of Deccan, like Char Minar and Gol Gumbaz, belongs to this period. The religious tolerance demonstrated by the Nizam Shahi, Adil Shahi and Qutb Shahi rulers is admirable.

The major architectural activities of the Barid Shahi rulers are the garden tombs. The tomb of Ali Barid Shah is the most famous monument in Bidar, in Karnataka state.

The Adil Shahi rulers contributed greatly in the fields of art, architecture, literature and music. Bijapur developed into a cosmopolitan city, and attracted numerous artists, musicians, scholars, and Sufi saints from Rome, Iran, Iraq, Turkey, and Turkestan.

Other major architectural works in Bijapur sultanate are the unfinished Jami Masjid. The greatest monument in Bijapur is Gol Gumbaz, the tomb of Muhammad Adil Shah.

Fortified city of Golconda is one of the architectural achievements of the Qutb Shahi Dynasty. Muhammad Quli Qutb Shah constructed one of the unique monuments in Deccan, the Char Minar.

The Qutb Shahi rulers were great supporters of literature and invited many scholars, poets, historians and Sufi saints from Iran to settle in their sultanate. Ibrahim Quli Qutb Shah supported Telugu literature also. Muhammad Quli Qutb Shah was not only a great patron of art and literature, but also a poet by himself. He wrote in Dakhani, Persian and Telugu. In addition to praise of God and the Prophet, he wrote on nature, love and contemporary social life. The Qutb Shahi rulers invited Persian artists to their court, which left a profound impact of different phases of Iranian art on the miniature paintings in this period.

Babar (1526-1530 CE.)

Zahir ud-din Muhammad Babar from Central Asia rose to power at Kabul, the modern day Afghanistan. He established the Mughal Empire in India after defeating Ibrahim Lodhi in the Battle of Panipat in 1526 CE.

Humayun – (1530 -1556 CE)

Nasir ud-din Muhammad Humayun was a son of Babar and the second Mughal Emperor who ruled modem day Afghanistan, Pakistan and some parts of northern India. For fifteen years in the middle of his reign, from 1540-1555, he lost his kingdom, but he regained it again by Persian help. In a noticeably short time, Humayun expanded his Empire conquering central plateau around Delhi and left a significant legacy for his son Akbar. Akbar - 1556-1605.

Jalaluddin Muhammad Akbar was the third Mughal Emperor. At the end of his magnificent reign in 1605 CE., the Mughal Empire covered most of northern and central India.

Humayun died in 1556 CE. His son Akbar was thirteen years old when he ascended the Mughal throne in Delhi. During his leadership, he eradicated military fear from powerful Pashtun descendants of Sher Shah Suri and in the Second Battle of Panipat, he defeated the Hindu king Hemu. Within two decades, he consolidated his power and brought all parts of northern and central India under his rule.

Akbar was a great conqueror, but an idealistic one. Completing the work started by Babar, he strengthened his control over northern India, and made allies with Rajputs. Preoccupied by the dream of an All-India Empire, he marched towards the Sultanates of the Deccan and integrated the peninsula to his Empire. Akbar was an astonishing ruler, who not only consolidated the political power of his Empire, but also significantly influenced the artistic and cultural life of India.

During the early years of his rule, Akbar had an intolerant attitude towards Hindus and the other religions. He had committed cruel atrocities on Hindus and massacred Hindus and destroyed temples. But later he became tolerant of other races and religions. All discrimination against Hindu religion was banned and the tax on unbelievers of Islam was eliminated. From the beginning of the Islamic intrusion, a special tax was imposed on non-believers of Islam. This special tax, called the *jizya,* was obnoxiously opposed by all during the Muslim rule in India. Besides, they levied a pilgrimage tax on unbelievers travelling to various Hindu pilgrimage centers. Akbar eliminated this tax in 1564 CE. He encouraged marriages between Mughals and Hindu women.

Akbar was curious to understand the various manifestations of the human mind, mainly through the religions of the Hindus, Parsees, and Christians, anticipating to understand the ultimate truth. In a special building, called the 'Home of Worship', he organized discussions on religion and philosophy. In 1582 A.D he proclaimed a new religious system, called 'Din Idaho', the 'Divine Faith.' But the new religion of Akbar never became popular.

Akbar regularly held debates and discussions with Jain scholars and was intensely impressed by their teachings. Convinced by their logical arguments about vegetarianism and non-violence preached by the Jain monks, he stopped eating meat and became vegetarian, prohibited slaughter of animals and birds on Jain festivals, and gave up fishing and hunting.

Early in the Akbar's rule, Hindus could not construct temples without the emperor's permission. In the beginning, his army was responsible for the demolition of rich Hindu temples, which had gold deities in the Doab region between Ganga and Yamuna rivers. Later, he eventually made amendments to his policy by donating a golden umbrella to cover the deity at a temple which had been demolished, and allowed the reconversion of a mosque into Hindu temple at Kurukshetra.

Akbar's rule largely influenced art and culture in the country. He was a great supporter of art and architecture. Since he had huge interest in painting, he decorated the walls of his palaces with murals. Akbar promoted a lively literary culture and encouraged translations from Sanskrit to Persian and Persian to Sanskrit and Hindi. Also, religious literature was translated into Persian language from other languages, like Chaghatai Turkish, Sanskrit and Arabic. Akbar suffered from stomach ailment and died on 27 October 1605.

Prominent Muslim rulers in India were Jahangir, Shah Jahan, Aurangzeb, and Hyder Ali.

Military Rocket Innovations

Although the Rocket technology was already in use when Hyder Ali's father served Mysore, it was Hyder who enhanced them further and significantly expanded their use in the military. Technological innovations included the use of high-quality iron casting for the combustion chamber, enabling the use of higher-powered explosive charges. He also organized bands of rocket men who were proficient in aiming rockets based on the size of the rocket and the distance to the target. Rockets could also be mounted on carts that improved their mobility and enabled them to fire a large number of them simultaneously. Professor Roddam Narasimha in his lecture on the curious history of rockets mentions:

> "The Mysore rockets of this period were much more advanced, than what the British had seen or known, chiefly because of the use of iron

tubes for holding the propellant; this enabled higher bursting pressures in the combustion chamber and hence higher thrust and longer range for the missile. The rockets consisted of a tube (about 60 rom[13] diameters and 200 rom long), fastened to a sword or 3 m bamboo pole, and had a range of 1-2 km. In the famous battle of Pollilur (1780) in which the British were defeated - a scene celebrated on the walls of Darya Daulat Bagh in Srirangapatna - a strong contributory cause is thought to have been the explosion of Colo Baillie's ammunition tumbrils[14], touched off by Mysore rockets. Rockets were used in the 3rd and 4th Anglo-Mysore Wars as well; although they caused much confusion and fear especially when used against massed troops or cavalry, they were too inaccurate to tilt decisively the fortunes of battle in favor of Tipu."

Hyder Ali engaged in wars constantly to increase his power.

Tipu Sultan - 1750 – 1799 CE.

Tipu Sultan was a son of Hyder Ali and was born in Devanahalli near Bangalore, Mysore state.

During Tipu's childhood his father Hyder Ali rose to power in Mysore; after his father's death, Tipu assumed the leadership of the kingdom. He was a successful ruler, a scholar, a soldier, and a poet. He was proficient in many languages. He was a pious Muslim, but the majority of the people were Hindus. He used French trained army in many of his battles. On request of French, he built the first church in Mysore. He built roads, public buildings, and ports on the Kerala seashore. His trade extended to countries which included Sri Lanka, Afghanistan, France, Turkey, and Iran. Unlike his father, Tipu hated Christians. He treated Catholics in a very heinous manner.

These experiments led the Royal Woolwich Arsenal to begin a rocket research and development program in 1801 based on Mysorean technology. According to William Congreve's report in Notes & Records of the Royal Society:

"The Indian war rocket that inspired his efforts was a product of military reform in the armies of Mysore, India, during a period of prolonged war. From 1767 to 1799 the armies of Hydar Ali and his son Tipu Sultan fought the British, who sought to extend their dominion over southern India after gaining control of the east at the battles of Plassey and Buxar.

The use of military rockets, or *baana*, had flourished in India since the reign of the Mughal emperor Akbar in the second half of the sixteenth century. Under Haidar and Tipp, production expanded in Mysore, probably in the fort of Thirthahalli, in the northern part of their kingdom. Rockets consisted of bamboo sticks or wood steel blades attached to iron cases, about eight inches long and weighing from six to twelve pounds, charged with one to two pounds of gunpowder. Rocket making was skilled work, undertaken by specialized artisan castes, whose expertise reflected long Indian traditions of working the high-quality iron ores and saltpetre[15] deposits found in India. By the end of Tipu's reign, some 5000 Mysorean troops fired off huge volleys of rockets against the enemy, although, as in Britain, rockets served other functions besides the military. Like McCartney, Tipu deployed his best technologies as diplomatic gifts, sending rockets to the Ottoman sultan, Abdülhamid I, on an embassy to Constantinople in 1783 the sultan was impressed and sent a tiger throne to Tipu in return. Rockets were also used as a measuring unit in India, and in Mysore they were subject to the princely practice of 'name-changing', whereby the prince signaled his power by creating new names for things. To *Mir Miraan*, the commanding officers of his armies, Tipu 'presented dresses of gold embroidery ... and jeweled gorgets. About this time the sultan changed the names of the different arms, as for instance ... a *ban*, or rocket, *Shuhab*.'

He engaged in wars constantly to increase his power, which included: (1) Second Mysore War, (2) Third Mysore War, (3) Fourth Mysore War apart from several other minor wars. Like his father, Tipu sultan used rockets in the military extensively with improved technology.

During the Fourth Mysore War, Tipu Sultan died defending his capital on May 4, 1799. Tipu was buried near the tomb of his father. In the midst of his burial, a great storm broke with massive winds and rains. Lieutenant Richard Bayly of the British 12th regiment wrote on May 5, 1799:

> "... I must relate the effects and appearance of a tremendous storm of wind, rain, thunder, and lightning that ensued on the afternoon of the burial of Tipu Sahib. I had returned to camp excessively indisposed. About five o'clock a darkness of unusual obscurity came on and volumes of huge clouds were hanging within a few yards of the earth, in a motionless state. Suddenly, a rushing wind, with irresistible force, raised pyramids of sand to an amazing height, and swept most of the tents and marquees in frightful eddies far from their site. Ten Lascars, with my own exertions, clinging to the bamboos of the marquee scarcely preserved its fall. The thunder cracked in appalling peals close to our ears, and the vivid lightning tore up the ground in long ridges all around. Such a scene of desolation can hardly be imagined; Lascars struck dead, as also an officer and his wife in a marquee a few yards from

mine. Bullocks, elephants, and camels broke loose, and scamperd in every direction over the plain; every hospital tent blown away, leaving the wounded exposed, unsheltered to the elemental strife. In one of these alone eighteen men who had suffered amputation had all the bandages saturated, and were found dead on the spot the ensuing morning. The funeral party escorting Tipu's body to the mausoleum of his ancestors situated in the Lal Bagh Garden, where the remains of his warlike father, Hyder Ali, had been deposited, were overtaken at the commencement of this furious whirlwind, and the soldiers ever after were impressed with a firm persuasion that his Satanic majesty attended in person at the funeral procession. The flashes of lightning were not as usual from far distant clouds but proceeded from heavy vapors within a very few yards of the earth. No park of artillery could have vomited forth such incessant peals as the loud thunder that exploded close to our ears. Astonishment, dismay, and prayers for its cessation were our solitary alternative. A fearful description of the Day of Judgment might have been depicted from the appalling storm of this awful night. I have experienced hurricanes, typhoons, and gales of wind at sea, but never in the whole course of my existence had I seen anything comparable to this desolating visitation. Heaven and earth appeared absolutely to have come in collision, and no bounds set to the destruction. The roaring of the winds strove in competition with the stunning explosions of the thunder, as if the universe was once more returning to chaos. In one of these wild sweeps of the hurricane, the poles of my tent were driven to atoms, and the canvas wafted forever from my sight. I escaped without injury, as also my exhausted Lascars, and casting myself in an agony of despair on the sands, I fully expected instant annihilation. My hour was not, however, come. Towards morning the storm subsided; the clouds became more elevated, the thunder and lightning ceased, and nature once more resumed a serene aspect. But never shall I forget that dreadful night to the latest day of my existence. All language is inadequate to describe its horrors. Rather than be exposed to such another scene, I would prefer the front of a hundred battles...."

Influence of Mughal Rule on India

The Mughal period is famous for its multiple cultural developments. The Timurids had a great cultural tradition. Their ancestral kingdom at Samarkand was the meeting place of the cultural traditions of Central and West Asia. The Mughals brought with them Muslim cultural traditions from Turko-Iranian areas, which eventually stimulated the evolution of the Indo-Muslim culture, a combination of two cultures: Central-West Asia and Turko-Iranian cultures.

Turks were supporters of arts and education. They had poets, amateur painters, calligraphers, singers, and instrumentalists. They were fine warriors, capable of handling a sword as a pen. They loved palaces, gilded tents, fine clothing, and rich garnishes. They were collectors of books and paintings eagerly seeking new kinds of luxury.

Major contributions of Mughals to India are their exceptionally ingenious architecture. A number of monuments were built by the Muslim emperors throughout their Indian occupation. Particularly Shah Jahan's contributions to architecture and painting are outstanding. His most monumental work includes Taj Mahal, which is regarded as a World Heritage Site. Other World Heritage Sites include the Humayun's Tomb, Fatehpur Sikri, Red Fort, Agra Fort, and Lahore Fort.

The palaces, tombs, and forts built by Mughal Dynasty are situated in Delhi, Aurangabad, Fatehpur Sikri, Agra, Jaipur, Lahore, Kabul, Sheikhupura, and many other places of India, Pakistan, Afghanistan, and Bangladesh.

Mughal's influence on political and cultural could be found in areas like:

- Smaller kingdoms were brought together under a centralized and stately government system.
- New trade routes were built to Arab and Turkic lands.
- Persian art and culture combined with Indian art and culture.
- Mughal cuisine was introduced to Indian subcontinent. For example, Aloo ka Raita, various kinds of koorma, Chole or Chana masala, Tikkas, Naan, Palak Paneer, Kababs, Tandoori, Biryani, Pulao, Keema, Malai Kofta, Navratan korma, Samosa, Barfi, Gulabjamun, Kalakand, Kulfi, Sheer korma, Badam Halwa, etc.
- Magnificent gardens
- Mughal miniature paintings

Urdu language

Even though Persian language was the leading official language of the Empire, the language of the elite developed into a form of Hindustani known as Urdu. Compared with Hindi, the Urdu language derives more vocabulary from Persian and Arabic than from Turkic languages. Hindi derives its vocabulary from Sanskrit profoundly. Modern Hindi uses Sanskrit-based vocabulary along with Urdu borrowed words from Persian and Arabic, and it is mutually understandable with Urdu.

Astronomy

Mughal astronomers made improvements in observational astronomy and produced about a hundred Zij[16] treatises.

The instruments and observational techniques used at the Mughal observatories were primarily derived from the Islamic tradition. Two most remarkable Mughal Celestial seamless Globes were invented during Mughal's rule. The second celestial globe exhibits 1018-star positions marked by inlaid silver points and 48 constellation figures drawn in outline apartment from usual circles. The interesting feature of this globe is that it is bilingual. It includes the names of the Zodiac signs, lunar mansions, and other constellations in both Arabic and Sanskrit scripts. The graduations are also numbered in two systems. The ecliptic is graduated in single degrees and each fifth is labeled in Arabic and Sanskrit numerals.

Another remarkable work is a metallurgical seamless Globe invented in Kashmir by Ali Kashmiri ibn Luqman in 998 CE. Another famous seamless celestial globe was produced using a lost-wax casting method in the Mughal Empire around 1630 CE. with Arabic and Persian inscriptions. Mughal metallurgists established the method of wax casting to produce seamless globes.

Technology

Fathullah Shirazi, a Persian-Indian Engineer who worked for Akbar the Great in the Mughal Empire, invented a multi-barrel gun with gunpowder. Unlike polybolos and repeating crossbows used in ancient Greece and China, Shirazi's gun was a rapid-firing gun, which had multiple gun barrels that fired hand cannons loaded with gunpowder. He also invented a primitive auto cannon.

Tipu Sultan of Mysore, the Nawab in the south of India, experimented with war rockets, invented iron-cased and metal-cylinder rocket artillery.

Colonial India (1510 – 1954 CE)

INDIA had experienced numerous invasions over thousands of years of its long historical existence. But all of them had come by land routes, coming down into the Indo-Gangetic plains from the rugged mountain passages of the northwest, which was the only defenseless border of a land. Otherwise, India is perfectly isolated from the rest of the world. All kinds of invaders

– Aryans, Yueh-chis, Kushans, Huns brought no culture of their own with them, but all were gradually absorbed into Hindu society. Then Muslims came and retained their separate identity up to a point. But, in the fifteenth century, an entirely different type of invader arrived from the sea, a tiny European group and made their landfall on India's shores.

The first European power, which came to India, was the army of Alexander the Great in 327-326 BCE. His established satraps in the northwest collapsed after he left. Later, trade was conducted between Indian states and the Roman Empire by Greeco-Roman and Egyptian sailors reaching India by sail on the Red and Arabian Seas. The spice trade between India and Europe was one of the main driving forces of the world economy in those periods.

In 1498 A.D, a Portuguese sailor Vasco da Gama's three small ships and hundred and sixty men landed in the spacious harbor of Calicut.

European culture that was started around the tenth century was bursting with energy, creative imagination and constructive visions. Europeans were inspired by a strong feeling of historical destiny that was unknown to other civilizations. They had an unshakable belief in the perfectibility of man and of human conditions. Compared with the refined Asians, they were crude and rough: but they had tremendous vitality and faith, and a bold determination to make their views available to all human races. They believed that life and creation has a purpose, humans are on earth to make sure that the message was delivered, and they were going to ensure that it would be fulfilled.

Many Asians understood that these strange Europeans who came from other sides of the globe had some inner mainspring which gave them mysterious power, a kind of psychological strength. It was a personal skill and individual initiative, a strength and continuity of purpose that made the difference.

Unlike early invaders in India, European's purpose to come to India was trade. So, one company after another came into being: The English East India Company secured a trading monopoly from 1600 CE. Portuguese East India Company (*Companhia da Índia Oriental)* came into existence in 1628. The United East India Company of Netherlands was incorporated in 1602; The Danish came in 1616; the French East India Company was formed in 1664; Austrian Ostend East-India Company was established in 1722; the Swedish East India Company was followed in 1722.

Colonial India refers to regions of the Indian Subcontinent and Maharajahs under European power through trade and conquest.

The search for the wealth and prosperity of India by Europeans led the discovery of the Americas by Christopher Columbus. But, at the end of the 15th century Portuguese sailor Vasco da Gama arrived in India by circumnavigating Africa and re-established direct trade links after Roman period.

Trading competition brought other European powers to India. Because Mughal Empire collapsed in the early 18th century, and then the Maratha Empire was destabilized after the third battle of Panipat, the unstable Indian states were progressively controlled by the Europeans through dependent Indian rulers.In a nutshell Portuguese were in India from 1510-1961 AD; Dutch from 1605-1825 AD; Danish from 1620-1869 AD; and French from 1674-1954 AD.

British India -1612 – 1947

By the middle of the 19th century, the British had achieved direct or indirect control over almost all of India. India was the most populous and valuable colony of the British Empire. The important characteristics of the colonial world were the overwhelming importance of India in the whole scheme of European imperialism with and without the British Empire. India, with its great resources, hundreds of millions of human beings, and high standards of civilization, weighed twice as much as all other colonies put together. In order to protect themselves on the Indian subcontinent, the British were ambitious to conquer the entire India. Then, in order to protect this whole political complex, the British were motivated to absorb India's neighbors – Ceylon, Burma, some Himalayan states, the northwestern part of the Pathans and Baluchistan. Also they sent military expeditions to Afghanistan and Tibet and brought them within the British realm of influence. The British was determined to occupy a great part of the coast of Arabia, the Persian Gulf, and southern half of Persia. And then moving towards the east coast of Africa, they occupied Zanzibar and its African surrounding, and established themselves securely in South Africa in order to protect one of the routes of India. In the east, they occupied Malaya and Singapore, and some parts of Borneo, the whole of it attached to the huge continent of Australia. The huge Indian Ocean itself had become a British lake becoming a steely triangle of South Africa, India and Australia. Then approaches to the Indian Ocean had to be guarded: the British clung tenaciously to Gibraltar, and Malta, acquired Cyprus and occupied Egypt, and control of the Suez Canal. In this whole scheme the central position of India was so well acknowledged that most consular and many diplomatic posts in the Orient were employed by and financed by British India. It became the 'Jewel of the Crown' to British.

British life

After 1770 CE. the British people developed garden suburbs marked with large Palladian mansions. Although English residents in Indian cities, often consisting of wealthy officers with elaborate lavish lifestyles, lack of resistance to tropical disease had succumbed to early death. In places like Park Street Cemetery, Calcutta, they erected towering monuments to announce their dominance.

Two settlements were created between European and 'natives.' One was a settlement of Anglo-Indians, near the railway stations. Anglo-Indians were often seen as an embarrassment to the British, but a place for them was established in railway employment because their loyalty could be trusted. The second colony was with Bengalis, whose numbers grew in upscale cities and towns as their literacy provided them an advantage in government employment.

Beyond their separate urban residential areas, the British went further from disease-infested land escaping to the Himalayas in the north and Nilgiri Hills in the south. In 1865, John Lawrence as a viceroy made Simla the regular summer capital of British India.

There were many hill schools. But, European children were sent home for schooling whenever funds permitted. The colonial British themselves returned home after their retirement.

Life under British

There were many developments by the early 1880s. A new middle-class of Indian people had arisen and increased in number across the country. This hope came from the success in education and its benefits such as employment in the Indian Civil Service. Queen Victoria's proclamation of 1858 in which she declared, "We hold ourselves bound to the natives of our Indian territories by the same obligation of duty which binds us to all our other subjects" also boosted hope in Indian educated class. More importantly, the encouragement came from the works of contemporaneous Oriental scholars like Monier-Williams and Max Müller, who were portraying ancient India as a great civilization.

On December 28, 1885, professionals and intellectuals from this middle-class - many educated Indians at the new British established universities in Bombay, Calcutta, and Madras, and familiar with the ideas of British political philosophers - founded the Indian National Congress in Bombay. Alan Octavian Hume was one of the founders of the Indian National Congress; a political party that later led the Indian Independence

Movement. He called for more Indian participation in provincial legislative councils and improved Indian access to civil service jobs.

After retiring from the civil services, Hume felt that the people of India had developed a sense of hopelessness and decided to do something.

Hume attempted to start an organization by reaching out to selected alumni of the University of Calcutta. He wrote his inspiring thoughts in his letter in 1883,

> "If only fifty men, good and true, can be found to join as founders, the thing can be established, and the further development will be comparatively easy … And if even the leaders of thought are all either such poor creatures, or so selfishly wedded to personal concerns that they dare not strike a blow for their country's sake, then justly and rightly are they kept down and trampled on, for they deserve nothing better. Every nation secures precisely as good a Government as it merits. If you picked men, the most highly educated of the nation, scorning personal ease and selfish objects, make a resolute struggle to secure greater freedom for yourselves and your country, a more impartial administration, a larger share in the management of your own affairs, then we, your friends, are wrong and our adversaries right, then are Lord Ripon's noble aspirations for your good fruitless and visionary, then, at present at any rate all hopes of progress are at an end and India truly neither desires nor deserves any better Government than she enjoys. Only, if this-be so, let us hear no more factious, peevish complaints that you are kept in leading strings and treated like children, for you will have provided yourself such. Men know how to act. Let there be no more complaining of Englishmen being preferred to you in all important offices, for if you lack that public spirit, that highest form of altruistic devotion that leads men to subordinate private ease to the public weal – that patriotism that has made Englishmen what they are – then rightly are these preferred to you, rightly and inevitably have they become your rulers. And rulers and task-masters they must continue let the yoke gall your shoulders never so sorely, until you realize and stand prepared to act upon the eternal truth that self-sacrifice and unselfishness are the only unfailing guides to freedom and happiness."

Also, he published a poem in Calcutta in 1886 summarizing his feeling:

Sons of Ind, why sit ye idle,
Wait ye for some Deva's aid?

Buckle to, be up and doing!
Nations by themselves are made!

Are ye Serfs or are ye Freemen,
Ye that grovel in the shade?
In your own hands rest the issues!
By themsclves are nations made! ...

Awakening the Consciousness of Indian People

Slowly, Indian people started to recognize their inability to defend themselves. As a consequence, activities to protest British government began in many parts of India.

In the year 1915 Mohandas Karamchand Gandhi returned to India from South Africa. Gandhi followed the advice of his mentor Gopal Krishna Gokhale. Undertaking the challenge of holding the community together and confronting the colonial authority, Gandhi created a technique of nonviolent resistance called *Satyagraha*. He opposed the British government through Ahimsa or nonviolence to obtain freedom.

In 1920, when British government resisted, Gandhi started his campaign of noncooperation, provoking many Indians to return British awards and honors, to resign from civil service, and to boycott British goods. Besides, Gandhi reorganized the Congress, converting it into a mass movement and opening its membership to the poorest Indians also.

Gandhi started the Quit India movement in August 1942, demanding the immediate withdrawal of the British from India or face nationwide civil disobedience. Along with other Congress leaders, Gandhi was imprisoned and the country exploded in violent demonstrations conducted by students and after by peasant political groups in Bihar and Bengal.

Widespread agitation forced Britain to make a decision about India's independence.

English Education

The awakening of India's head and heart took place at a time when India was firmly under British control. This awakening was ignited by the association between European culture and India's solidified civilization. Indians were impressed by recognizing that European culture was in full development and had generated the Industrial Revolution.

The awakening took place in an Anglo-Indian atmosphere and expressed itself in a relatively new linguistic medium: English replaced Persian as the universal language of India (before Persian had replaced Sanskrit); the local vernaculars developed an entirely new group of autonomous literatures in various provinces.

A Company civil servant, Charles Grant, thought of idea of establishing a new educational network to teach English and impart European culture to Indians, thinking that the old Indian education was responsible for India's apparent decadence. Christian missionaries followed up his suggestion, and many great educational establishments started to teach English in humble fashion. Subsequently, any effort made by the Anglo-Indian government to encourage Indian learning was opposed by enlightened Indians. Chief among them was Rajaram Mohan Roy, whose powerful protest against the establishment of a Sanskrit College in Calcutta is considered as a classic. Reiterating this decision in a petition to Governor General Lord Amherst, he wrote that "The Sanskrit system of education would be the best calculated to keep this country in darkness if such had been the policy of British legislature. But as the improvement of the native population is the object of the Government, it will consequently promote a more liberal enlightened system of instruction, embracing mathematics, natural philosophy, chemistry and anatomy….."

Englishmen were aware of the dangers of a new English education system. They always feared that to train the Indians the new civilization of the West in English with its newly attained and progressively developing mastery over the forces of nature was extremely threatening to their existence. They believed that keeping Indians in dark within the narrow boundaries of their traditional culture is the secured way of longevity of the British Empire in India. Sir Richard Temple compared the potential discontent in the hearts of the educated natives and contrasted it with the loyalty of the uneducated Indians.

Consequently, Missionaries like Alexander Duff, administrators like Lord Bentinck established the Medical College in Calcutta. From 1835 onwards, European learning through the medium of English language revolutionized the whole educational system of India. The result was a great gap between the small English-educated classes and the great illiterate or vernacular-educated masses. The gap was also widened between the Hindu middle classes and the Hindu upper classes, who remained faithful to their traditional learning, and the Indian Muslims, who remained aloof from Western education altogether. To a large extent, this awakening of India was due to the result of evolution of liberalism in Europe itself — historic changes in Britain, such as, the Catholic Emancipation Act (1829), the Reform Bill (1832), the Abolition of Slavery (1833), and the New Poor Law (1834) had passed.

The other side of the benefit was that it gave India something it had missed since the days of Ashoka: cultural unification and linguistic unity. Although English influence affected about only1 per cent of the population, it enabled these small elites to have free intellectual communication. Future Indian Nationalists to come were born in English language atmosphere. The Indian press in English had already developed to a remarkable extent in the nineteenth century and early in the twentieth century. More than a thousand books in English were published each year. All major discussions and controversies on technical or political took place in English.

Three points must be made about this early group of the English educated.

First, English educated people were representatives of the old professional elites in each region. It had a long-term consequence throughout the country on non-elites, for example non-Brahmins in the west and south. Best and highest opportunities were afforded to the small percentage of Brahmins who had acquired western education.

Secondly, English connected people across India. It was a necessary component for creating political ties and movements because English was the cosmopolitan language throughout the world. A large portion of the English-educated men and women had experience in the areas like government, law, and journalism.

Thirdly, the English-educated people better understood the new phrases of liberal politics and provided competition to the traditional notables. When electoral politics were introduced, frequently they took part in elections.

The gap between the British-educated upper classes and the rest of the population increased gradually. Yet, it is this education and the use of the English tongue that gave real rational unity to India. If this had not happened, if the British had concentrated on developing the vernaculars, there would not have been one Indian nationalism, but many; local loyalties of Bengalis and Punjabis, Marathas and Gujratis, Tamils and Telugus, Kannadas would have taken the upper hand and destroyed the fabric of all-Indian unity. Regardless of the whole thing, modern India was shaped by this European education and strongly united by the use of English.

Rabindranath Tagore gave a remarkable description of the alteration in sentiment that had taken place in his generation: "As I look back on the vast stretch of years that lie behind me, I am struck by the change that has taken place… our direct contact with the larger world of men was linked up with the contemporary history of the English people… the educated of those days had recourse to English language and literature, their days and nights were eloquent with the stately declamations of Burke, with Macaulay's long rolling sentences, discussions centered upon Shakespeare's drama and Byron's poetry and above all upon the large-hearted liberalism of the nineteenth century English politics. At the time, though tentative attempts were being made to gain our national independence, at heart we had not lost faith in the generosity of the English race….."

The true expression of modern India flourished in the vernacular languages, before it was commonly used for oral communication and poetic expression. Here again, the leader was Rajaram Mohan Roy, who promoted European culture and yet made Bengali a literary language. Even the vernaculars made a strong imprint on English models and patterns rapidly blooming to life by the impact of English culture. One after another, the vernaculars became alive during the nineteenth century, offering new mediums of expression to scholars, novelists, dramatists, philosophers – the novelist Bunkim Chandra Chatterji, the dramatist Dinabandhu and the poet Rabindranath Tagore in Bengali and many more in Marathi, Gujarati and so on. It dragged the new Indian middle classes out of their lethargy.

Certainly, these vernacular literature began to invigorate the sleeping nationalism of the Indians. One advantage in this awakening of nationalism was to kindle Indian interest in history.

Social Reformers

Earlier civilizations who invaded India were able to assimilate Indian culture and were not able to preserve their separate identity for a long time. But, the British wanted to maintain their identity separately. The most intelligent Indians were profoundly puzzled at the view of British Empire whose heart was located at the other end of the earth, and kept pumping new blood into the imperial arteries to avoid a fatal dilution.

British organized with remarkable efficiency of the whole banking system, the new transportation network of rail and road, the extraction of minerals, the erection of power plants, the building of dams and digging of irrigation canals, while the Indian world went on weaving its endless and purposeless dreams, undisturbed with this western impact.

But while the more concrete-minded, practical people of the Far East felt the physical impact of Western power with agonizing keenness in the nineteenth century, the Indians felt the cultural impact with the same agonizing keenness, only much earlier. In those days, every scheme of British was overwhelmed by the thoughtful Indians with a sense of the absolute superiority of the West: its complete monopoly of scientific knowledge in basic research and in technological application, the exuberant artistic creations, the vigorous literature, the dynamic outlook on life that contrasted so sharply with the complete stagnation that had solidified India's old Civilization. A few farsighted Indians, who began the process of India's awakening started to promote full integration of India. The awakening took two different but complementary aspects: first an awakening of the head, and then an awakening of the heart – corresponding respectively to the two revolutionary activities of Rajaram Mohan Roy and Ramakrishna. The keynote in both cases, philosophical and religious, intellectual and emotional, was the required agent of a fusion between East and West.

Rajaram Mohan Roy ***Keshavachandra Sen*** ***Ravindranath Tagore*** ***Dayanand Saraswati***

The general view of India during the Colonial Era was widespread. Even though it sounds erotic, it demonstrates the reality in some situations and circumstances. 18th century social reformers worked hard to change this view considerably.

- Indians are inherently incapable of adventurous behavior and do not venture beyond the boundaries of the Indian subcontinent (Kalapani syndrome).
- Indians are incapable of original, rational, and creative ideas.
- Indians are incapable of independent thinking and are unquestioning in their adherence to authoritarian dogmas such as those in the Vedic texts and are only capable of rote learning.
- Indians fundamentally have no intention in making progress and advancing in the modern world and are lost in an ancient mind set.

- Everything good and worthwhile in the Indian subcontinent has been imported by the invaders, and the only indigenous characteristics are those like caste is natural to the Indian civilization.
- Indian is pessimistic and will not make an effort to change his destiny which is written in stone the moment he is born.
- Caste system is an artifact of the Indian religious belief system, and that India is inherently opposed to egalitarian ideas and is wedded to the racial and ethnic stratification of its own society.
- Indian is egregious in the manner in which he exploits his fellow Indian.
- Indian is lazy and sluggish.
- India has no sense of history and is even poorer at keeping records of his historical past.
- Religious beliefs of Indians are the root cause of their misfortunes.
- As a consequence of the above, India is socially backward, morally corrupt, and always dependent upon the west to reform the problems in Indian society.

Macaulay argued that Indians could be transformed through the systems of law, free trade, and education. He believed that Britain's mission was not to create just a class of Indians sufficiently well versed in English to help the British to rule the country, but to create the Indians with English in taste, in opinions, in morals and in intellect. As a result, he visualized, Indians would become independent and exemplify the imperishable empire of English arts, their morals, their literature and their laws in time.

Rajaram Mohan Roy (1772 – 1833 CE)

Rajaram Mohan Roy was a writer, educationist, journalist, philosopher, politician, social reformer, theologian, and humanist. He fought to liberate India from darkness, superstition, and ignorance.The great awakening was introduced by Rajaram Mohan Roy late in the eighteen century. His fantastic knowledge and amazing life symbolized this blend of East and West for which he worked hard all his life. Sunken in both Hindu and Muslim cultures, fluent in Arabic, Persian, Sanskrit, English, Hebrew, Greek and Latin languages, expelled by caste and family, lived for years thereafter in Benares and Tibet. He finally returned home in 1796. Campaigning vigorously against the monstrous distortions of centuries of sloth, corruption and inertia, which had inflicted on Hinduism, he tackled every social, political and cultural problem of his time.

Rajaram Mohan Roy was an Indian religious, social, and educational reformer who questioned traditional Hindu culture and suggested different alternative methods of progress for Indian society during British rule. Influenced by the European Liberalism, he concluded that radical reform was necessary in Hinduism and in the social practices of the Hindus. Therefore, along with Dwarkanath Tagore and other Bengalis, he founded the Brahma Samaj, an influential Indian socio-religious reform movement to fight against social evils. 'There is only one God, None equals Him. He has no end. He is present in all living beings' is the message of Brahma Samaj. It emphasized the idea of universal brotherhood. It did not acknowledge the differences of caste, creed, or nationality. Also, it believed that in order to worship Him, fixed place or time is not necessary.

Rajaram Mohan Roy fought for the reformation of Hindu Law, conducted the protest against restrictions on the press, rallied against the oppressive landlords, and favored the English system of education in India.

His influence on politics, public administration, education, and religion was widely popular. He worked tirelessly to abolish the practice of sati, the Hindu funeral practice in which the widow immolates herself on her husband's funeral pyre. He demanded property inheritance rights for women.

Ramakrishna Paramahamsa – (1836-1886 CE)

Ramakrishna Paramahamsa was a famous mystic of 19th-century India. His religious school of thought led to the formation of the Ramakrishna Mission by his main disciple Swami Vivekananda. Both were prominent persons in the Bengal Renaissance and Hindu renaissance during the 19th and 20th centuries

Swami Vivekananda (1863-1902 CE)

One among Ramakrishna's chosen disciples was a remarkable man Swami Vivekananda, who eventually transformed Ramakrishna's mission into the language of service and brought his master's greatness to the attention of the world.

Swami Vivekananda was the chief disciple of Sri Ramakrishna Paramahamsa and the founder of Ramakrishna Order. He introduced Hindu philosophy of Vedanta to America and Europe and raised the status of Hinduism during the end of the 19th century.

Vivekananda considered service to humanity is the most efficient way to worship God.

On his way to Chicago, Vivekananda visited Japan in 1893.

It was a period of military build-up in Japan, which led to the Sino-Japanese War and the Russo-Japanese War. Noticing ongoing preparations in Japan, Vivekananda wrote,

> "The Japanese seem to have fully awakened themselves to the necessity of the present times. They have a thoroughly organized army equipped with guns that one of their own officers has invented and which is said to be second to none. Then, they are continually increasing their navy."

> About the industrial progress he observed,

> "The match factories are simply a sight to see, and they are bent upon making everything they want in their own country."

Vivekananda's philosophy of life started to widen gradually as he traveled all over India like a wandering monk. Wherever he went, he became increasingly conscious of the need for modernization, for breaking with the past and for awakening the dormant potentials rather than destroying them. Inevitably, something new emerged in him, a crying need for a new dimension of human understanding that had always been sorely lacking in Indian consciousness: historical consciousness, the bold facing of historical reality – not just the prophetic instinct, but the detached, objective and scientific precision with which western culture was in the process of reusing humankind's history

Contrasting the speedy development of Japan with the situation back in India, he appealed his countrymen to come out of their narrow holes and have a look abroad as following:

> Only I want that our young men should pay a visit to Japan and China every year. Especially to the Japanese, India is still the dreamland of everything high and good. And you, what are you? .. talking twaddle all your lives, vain talkers, what are you? Come, see these people, and then go and hide your faces in shame. A race of dotards, you lose your caste if you come out! Sitting down these hundreds of years with an ever-increasing load of crystallized superstition on your heads, for hundreds of years spending all your energy upon discussing the touchable or untouchableness of this food or that, with all humanity crushed out of you by the continuous social tyranny of ages – what are you? And what are you doing now?.. promenading the sea-shores with books in your hands – repeating undigested stray bits of European brainwork, and the whole soul bent upon getting a thirty rupee clerkship, or at best becoming a lawyer – the height of young India's ambition – and every student with a whole brood of hungry children cackling at

his heels and asking for bread! Is there not water enough in the sea to drown you, books, gowns, university diplomas, and all?"

After his memorable work in the west, Swamy Vivekananda arrived at Colombo on January 15, 1897. While in the west he gave speeches on India's spiritual tradition. On return to India, his speeches were about upliftment of the masses, eradication of superstition and caste virus, promotion of studies in science, industrialization of the country, removal of poverty, and the end of colonial rule. His speeches are well recorded in his fabulous book 'Lectures from Colombo to Almora'. These lectures havc nationalistic passion and spiritual ideology. His speeches had tremendous influence on the Indian leaders as well as common people.

After visiting America (Lectures from Colombo to Almora):

"On the other hand my mission to America was not to the Parliament of Religions. That was not only something by the way, it is only an opening an opportunity, and for that we are very thankful to the members of the Parliament; but really, our thanks are due to the great people of the United States, the American nation, the warm hearted hospitable, great nation of America, where more than anywhere else, the feeling of brother-hood has been developed. An American meets you for five minutes on board, a train, and you are his friend, and the next moment he invites you as a guest to his home and opens the secret of his whole living there. That is the character of the American race, and we highly appreciate it. Their kindness to me has passed all narration; it would take me years yet to tell you how I have been treated by them most kindly and most wonderfully."

After visiting England (Lectures from Colombo to Almora):

"No one ever landed on English soil with more hatred in his heart for a race than I did for the English, and on this platform are present English friends who can bear witness to the fact; but the more I lived among them and saw how the machine was working – the English national life – and mixed with them, I found where the heart-beat of the nation was, and the more I loved them. There is none among you here present, my brothers, who love the English people more than I do now. We have to see what is going on there, and you have to mix with them. As the philosophy, our national philosophy of the Vedanta, has summarized all misfortunes, all misery, as coming from that one cause, ignorance, here in also we must understand that the difficulties that arise between us and the English people are mostly due to that ignorance; we do not know them, they do not us."

Vivekananda asked Indian people to shun superstitions and follow true Hinduism in his "Lectures from Colombo to Almora".

"At the same time we must not forget that what I mean by the conquest of the world by spiritual thought is the sending out of the life-giving principles, not the hundreds of superstitions that we have been hugging to our hearts for centuries. These have to be weeded out even on this soil, and thrown aside, so that they may die for ever. These are the causes of the degradation of the race and will lead to softening of the brain. That brain which cannot think high and noble thoughts, which has lost all power of originality, which has lost all vigor, that brain which is always poisoning itself with all sorts of little superstitions passing under the name of religion, we must beware of."

"I would rather see every one of you rank atheists than superstitious fools, for the atheist is alive and you can make something out of him. But if superstition enters, the brain is gone, the brain is softening, and degradation has seized upon life. Avoid these two. Brave, bold men, these are what we want. What we want is vigor in the blood, strength in the nerves, iron muscles and nerves of steel, not softening namby-pamby ideas.

"Come, be men! Kick out the priests who are always against progress, because they would never mend, their hearts would never become big. They are the offspring of centuries of superstition and tyranny. Root out priest craft first. Come, be men! Come out of your narrow holes and have a look abroad. See how nations are on the march! Do you love man? Do you love your country? Then come, let us struggle for higher and better things; look not back, no, not even if you see the dearest and nearest cry. Look not back, but forward!

He spoke numerous times at the Parliament on topics connected to Hinduism. All his speeches at the Parliament stressed religious tolerance.

Two leaders are among many people who sacrificed their life to earn freedom from British Rule: M.K. Gandhi and Jawaharlal Nehru.

M.K. Gandhi (1869–1948 CE)

Gandhi studied law in London (1888–91). Unable to find a job in Bombay, he practiced law in South Africa from 1893 to 1914. There he fought for the rights of South Africa's Indian residents and devised the ideas of *Satyagraha* movement. On his return to India Gandhi made Ahmedabad as his center and launched peasant and labor protests in Bihar and Gujarat. In 1919, he conducted India-wide protests against the Rowlatt Acts. In

September 1920, he obtained support of the Indian National Congress for his strategy of non-violence and non-cooperation with the British government. In 1930, he launched the salt march to protest against salt tax. In 1931, signing the Gandhi– Irwin Pact, Gandhi represented the Congress at the second round table conference in London. He was responsible for gaining Independence through his ideas and missions. He was assassinated by a Hindu on 30th January 1948.

M.K. Gandhi

Jawarharlal Nehru

Jawaharlal Nehru (1889 -1964 CE)

Pandit Jawaharlal Nehru took active part in the Non-Cooperation Movement. He was one of the prime leaders of Indian freedom struggle. He was the trusted disciple of Mahatma Gandhi and later he became the first Prime Minister of India in 1947. He is widely regarded as the architect of modern India.

After the independence, Jawaharlal Nehru effectively managed the difficult situations and challenges of that time like the disorders and mass exodus of minorities across the borders of India and Pakistan, the integration of princely states into the Indian Union, the forming of a new constitution, establishing the political and administrative infrastructure for a parliamentary democracy, and drafting five year plans for the development of new independent India.

Jawaharlal Nehru played an important role in building modern India. He set up a Planning Commission, encouraged development of science and technology, and launched three successive five-year plans. His policies led to a substantial growth in agricultural and industrial production. Nehru also played a major role in developing independent India's foreign policy.

To Jawaharlal Nehru India's current existing danger was within India. Since independence, wherever he went across the country, hc appealed for national unity. His mission was "Integrate or perish." He thought it was a historic mission to conquer the widespread challenge – a challenge created by many major languages, each well-established in its own historic provinces, with tens of millions of speakers connected to age-old scripts. This is a challenge to a central authority to process and to conduct smooth administration in parliamentary. He feared that this critical challenge will create a problem sometime in the future and the unity achieved by opposing British will slip away.

While differences of culture and language threatened the unity of the new nation, Nehru established programs like the National Book Trust and the National Literary Academy which encouraged the translation of regional literatures between languages. In order to unify India, he warned again and again reminding his slogan - Integrate or Perish.

Education and Social Reform

Jawaharlal Nehru was a passionate advocate of education for India's children and youth, believing it is essential for India's future upliftment. His government directed the establishment of many institutions of higher learning, including the All India Institute of Medical Sciences, the Indian Institutes of Technology, the Indian Institutes of Management, and the National Institutes of Technology. Adult education centers, vocational and technical schools were also organized for adults, especially in the rural areas.

A system of reservations in government services and educational institutions was created to eliminate the social disparities and hardships faced by the scheduled castes and scheduled tribes. Nehru also advocated secularism and religious harmony, increasing the representation of minorities in the government.

Nehru was a writer in English and wrote several books like, The Discovery of India, Glimpses of World History, and his autobiography, Toward Freedom.

Independent India-1947

Exhausted by recently concluded World War II and realizing that no consent at Britain, any international support, and increasing restlessness in India, the Labor government in Britain decided to end the British rule in India. In early 1947, Britain announced its intention of transferring power. On August 14, 1947, the new Dominion of Pakistan came into existence. Muhammad Ali Jinnah sworn in as Pakistan's first Governor General in Karachi. The following day, August 15, 1947, India became an independent country. In New Delhi Jawaharlal Nehru assumed the office of the Prime Minister.

All agreed that the new India will be based on democratic values with universal suffrage, freedom of press and speech. Concerned by the persisting discrimination against untouchables and other disadvantaged groups, the Congress Party took action to ensure that these groups have a voice in the new constitutional order. It appointed an untouchable leader Dr B. R. Ambedkar to chair the drafting committee for the constitution. The new constitution outlawed untouchability gave greater importance to the reservation of seats in the legislatures for the former untouchables and depressed forest tribes.

India after Independence

Ambedkar, a graduate of Columbia University in New York, had never agreed with Gandhi's idealism. Calling 'Hinduism is a veritable chamber of horrors', he argued that all Gandhism has done was to 'smoothen its surface and give it the appearance of decency and respectability'. Before his death in 1956, Ambedkar converted to Buddhism.

Nehru's earnest wish in 1947 was that India to shed 'the burden of the past'. But the past remained contested. The sharpest divide was that between secular liberals and supporters of Hindutva. Each possessed a vision of India's past that it cherished and attempted to propagate.

Such an idealized past had a powerful appeal in India. The liberal economist Amartya Sen writes his views in *The Argumentative Indian,* a vision of India in which the values of forethought and diversity lay at the heart of its past. His heroes included ancient Buddhist ruler Ashoka and the Mughal emperor Akbar, Gandhi and Nehru. Sen wrote, Akbar championed 'pluralist ideals', and even 'the politics of secularism'.

By contrast, the proponents of Hindutva designed a vision of India that it is fundamentally Hindu nation from ancient times. Hindutva historians devoted plenty of time towards proving that Aryan peoples who were indigenous to northern India, not migrants from Central Asia, are descendants of the country's original inhabitants from time immemorial despite a good deal of evidence to the contrary.

Indian Legacy

The entire South-East Asia received most of its culture from India. Early in the 5th century B.C. migrants from Western India settled in Ceylon, which was eventually converted to Buddhism in the sovereignty of Ashoka. Then, a few Indian merchants had probably travelled to Malaya, Sumatra, and other parts of South-East Asia. They were followed by Buddhists monks and brahmanas radically influencing the indigenous culture. There arose great civilizations, capable of organizing large maritime empires and of building such wonderful monuments to their greatness as the Buddhist stupas of Borobudur in Java or the temples of Angkor Wat in Cambodia. Other cultural influences came from China and Islamic world to South-East Asia, but the primary motivation to civilization came from India.

The Indian colonies were peaceful ones, and the Indianized kings of the territory were native chieftains who learnt what India taught them.

In the North, Indian cultural influence spread through central Asia to China. Contrary to South-East Asia, China did not integrate Indian ideas in every aspect of her culture except Buddhism, but the whole of the Far East is in India's debt for Buddhism, which helped to shape the distinct civilizations of China, Korea, Japan and Tibet.

India has offered many practical benefits on the world at large apart from her special gifts to Asia: notably rice, cotton, the sugar cane, many spices, the domestic birds, the game of chess, and most important of all, the decimal system of numeral notation early in the Christian era. The extent of spiritual influence of India on the ancient West is much debated. The heterodox Jewish sect followed monastic practices in some respects similar to those of Buddhism. Parallels may be found between passages in the New Testament and Pali scriptures. Similarities between the teachings of western philosophers and mystics from Pythagoras to Plotinus and those of the Upanishads have been spotted. However, none of these similarities is close enough to confirm with certainty because there was no evidence that any ancient philosophers had a deep knowledge of Indian religion. Only possible fact is that there was always some contact between the Hellenic world and India after Alexander's campaign, intermediated first by the Achaemenid Empire, then by the Seleucids, and finally, under the Romans through Indian Ocean. It is established that there were Indian merchants and Buddhist colonies at Alexandria in Egypt. The possibility of Buddhist influence on Christianity cannot be ruled out.

Supplement - 1

Ashoka

2260 years ago, a great emperor Ashoka, the one "Without Sorrow", ruled united India nearly forty years. Ashoka unified the country under one government, transformed a minor religious group Buddhism into a world religion, and introduced moral values whose impact on Asia can be sensed even today. Ashoka was the first ruler to build India into a single nation. In addition, before Mahatma Gandhi, Emperor Ashoka advocated non-violence and introduced the absolutely original concept of victory by moral force alone. Probably he was the first ruler in history to establish a welfare state!!

Ashoka's edicts and inscriptions, which were written in Brahmi, as Ashoka's Song. They were carved on thousands of rocks and on numerous polished pillars of stone throughout the Indian subcontinent. This colossal work made his song could be heard loud and clear from Kandahar to Irrawaddy (Irrawady is a river that flows from north to south through Myanmar, also called Burma) and from Cape Cormorin (Kanyakumar) to the Himalayas. From this mainland, the message spread out in ripples on all sides until it was heard in the remotest corners of Asia.

Today, only a few precious edicts have survived in readable form due to passage of time and humane violence. Nearly 26 rock and pillar inscriptions have survived in moderate form that can be attributed to Ashoka. But it is astonishing to know that these extraordinary songs and its composer were lost for about two thousand years.

Initially, British historians and archaeologists blamed Muslim conquests for the decline of Buddhism. No doubt it was true, but long before Mahmud Ghazni crossed Indus in the year 1008 AD, Buddhism was weakening. First Huns destroyed many Buddhist places and then it was unable to compete with Adi Shankaracharya and his followers.

The most stunning proof of Hindu hostility towards Buddhism comes in the form of silence; Buddhism was removed from the historical record. It was this simple act of omission, the Ashoka's song was silenced, and the Emperor Ashoka himself had been erased from India's history.

Rediscovery of Ashoka

The brighter side of the story is it became an instrument to rediscover India's lost pre-Muslim history in the late eighteenth century and early nineteenth century. It is an astonishing saga of painstaking detective work instigated by European Orientalists who were criticized by many people.

Allen writes, "Yet anyone who values advancement and learning has cause to be grateful for these pioneers… In recounting how the rediscovery of Ashoka and his world came about I hope that even the most ardent Indian nationalist will accept that these foreign enthusiasts and scholars played a progressive role in the advancement of modern India, for all that some were part of the colonial exploitation of India."

The first generations of Orientalists were very few in number and they had no idea what they were looking for, they had no tools other than their enthusiasm, and the driving force of reason. But there were clues, thrown like pieces of jigsaw puzzles all over the Indian landscape. Their work was finding these pieces and clues, recognizing them, and painstakingly piecing them together. They had to face many false starts and blind passages to reconstruct India's pre-Islamic history. It took more than two centuries to understand who Ashoka was, what he was like and how important a figure he had been in the molding of Asia.

In the process, mainly they consulted ancient texts in three interrelated languages Prakrit, Sanskrit and Pali and two main alphabets Brahmi lipi and Kharosthi.

The Emperor Ashoka became known throughout the Buddhist world as Ashokadharma or Asokhadhamma and he used the word repeatedly in his Pillar and Rock Edicts. The word Dharma or Dhamma is closely related with the name of Ashoka and Buddhism but has its roots in the Proto-Indo-European verb dhr, 'to hold', used to describe the cosmic law supporting the universe. It can also be called Moral Law. Hindus, Buddhist, Jains, and Sikhs use the word to describe the proper practice of one's religion and ultimate reality.

Around 1194 AD, two hundred armed horsemen of Khilji slaves crossed the Ganges River at Varanasi looking for booty. Muhammad Bakhtiyar was an impetuous, bold, sagacious, and expert military commander in the army of Sultan of Muhammad of Ghor, also known as World-Burner. Persian Sadruddin Muhammad Hasan Nizami has recorded Sultan's cruel and heinous deeds in detail, the disaster how sultan purged the land of Hind from impurity of idol-worship from his sword and left not even one temple standing. All the idol temples were converted into mosques. After making a heinous disaster in Benares, he proceeded towards Bihar. He and his army were not aware that there is a place where people believed in the oneness of god like they (Islam) did. That place was the Mahavihara or Great Monastery of Nalanda, known as the Dharmaganja or Treasury of the Moral Law.

Nalanda was the most important learning place in Asia. It contained a large repository of Buddhist knowledge in the world storing in multi-storied library buildings: (1) the Ratnasagara, Sea of Jewels; (2) the Ratnadadhi, Ocean of Jewels; and (3) the Ratnaranjaka, Jewels of Delight. Most gifted scholars came here to study and teach the Buddhist knowledge.

Muhammad Bakhtiyar successfully conquered the Bihar fortress and then turned his attention to Nalanda. But before attacking, he sent his army men to check whether the library contained any copy of the Quran. After knowing that the library did not contain the Quran, he ordered to the destruction of the Great Monastery and all its treasure.

In a chronicle Minhaj-ud-din recorded what happened during the attack noting that the large number of occupants in that place were Brahamins and they were all killed by the army. First, they saw a great number of books in the library. They attempted to enquire Hindus about the books and what knowledge they contain. Minhaj-ud-din wrongly thought the inhabitants of Nalanda were Hindus. In reality, they were mainly Buddhist monks and a few Brahmins. Minhaj-ud-din ordered the burning of the entire library, which was resting on many acres of land. It took them several months and the smoke from burning manuscripts dangled like a dark cloud over the hills.

There were three major Buddhist learning centers in Bihar and two more in Bengal. Nalanda was the first one to succumb to fire and then other monasteries of Odantapuri, Vikramashila, and Nuddia. Then he applied fire and sword to Buddhist great monasteries at Sompura and Jagadalala on the banks of Ganges River. Apart from this, numerous small monasteries were destroyed.

Charles Allen says burning Nalanda library is more tragic than Alexandria library. Thus, India's Buddhist past was gone and very soon forgotten.

Sultan Firoz Shah had a fascination for pillars to build a victory tower at Hisar, hundred miles north-west of Delhi. By chance a readymade handsome tower, approximately thirty feet high, cut by a single block of stone was found on some abandoned place north of Delhi. Happily, he erected the tower in the prayer hall of a new mosque he was building.

Another time while he was hunting near the village Topra between the Jamuna and Ganges rivers, the sultan found another standing magnificent pillar. It was also cut from a single chunk of stone, but it was more impressive than the first. It weighed more than twenty five tons and forty two feet in length. It was in good condition with sparkling and polished red surfaces shining like gold. He found another pillar like the same at Meerut near Delhi. Luckily, Firoz Shah did not destroy them, but wanted to understand their significance. He searched for Brahmin pandits who can explain their significance and made exhaustive enquiries. One pandit told, "Bhim of Mahabharata used them as walking sticks. When he died these two columns were left standing as memorials to him."

Firoz Shah himself supervised and transported the pillar to Delhi with great care and re-erected. He named it Minara-I zarin or Column of Gold. One witness recorded the event as "Directions were issued for bringing parcels of the cotton. Quantities of this cotton were placed round the column, and when the earth as its base was removed, it fell gently on the bed prepared for it. The cotton was then removed by degrees, and after some days the pillar lay safe upon the ground…The pillar was then encased from top to bottom in reeds and raw skins, so that no damage might accrue it. A carriage, with forty-two wheels, was constructed, and ropes were attached to each wheel. Thousands of men hauled at each rope, and after great labor and difficulty the pillar was raised on to the carriage."

He erected one of these pillars in his worship place near his palace. The second stick went through the same process and re-erected in a hunting pavilion to the north of Firozabad.

After a long time, when Tamur visited the place, he was carried away with full of admiration for the twin columns and proclaimed that 'in all the countries he had travelled he had never seen any monument comparable to these.'

Around 1610, an English traveler William Finch described the pillar at hunting lodge as higher than twenty-four foot having a globe and half-moon at the top. And it also had inscriptions.

In fact, Sultan Firoz Shah with curiosity had made exhaustive efforts to know the meaning of the inscriptions. Many Brahmans and Hindu devotees were invited to read them and no one could read it. They did not know what was written on the pillars and who made it. Firoz Shah's biographers had written how they found the pillar, how they transported and installed it, and how Firoz Shah himself wrote poems describing the grandeur of the pillar. But, no information about the inscriptions.

Eventually William Finch and his friends inspected the pillar of gold and concluded that incoherent letters may be some form of Greek, most likely installed by Alexander the Great to mark his victory.

Then Finch travelled to Prayag and he found another same type of pillar in Allahabad fortress. Here also they thought it was installed by Alexander.

In 1670, another Englishman, John Marshall recorded the existence of more monumental stone pillars in the northern parts of India. In response to news about an interesting standing pillar, he walked 18 miles northwards to see the stone pillar. On top of this pillar, there was a neatly engraved Tiger. He wrote this finding in his diary and presented it to the Archaeological Survey of India (ASI).

Around 1769, an Italian Father Marco Della Tomba reported the existence of two stone pillars near Varanasi. He wrote, "They stand 27 cubits (40 ft.) high, on top of which there is a lion.... The column seems to consist of a single stone. These two columns are as if covered with certain writing, which I traced on paper and then sent to the Hindu Academy of Benares and to some Tibetan scholars; but not one of them could read or understand a word of them...These characters appear to be some ancient Greek."

Next Englishman working on the inscriptions was William Jones. He was the son of mathematician. This child prodigy was gifted with an incredible capacity for learning languages. Jones was fluent in thirteen languages and familiar with another twenty-eight languages by the time he graduated from Oxford in 1768. He came to Calcutta on September 1783 as the embodiment of European Enlightenment. He carried two lists in his coat pocket. He set out sixteen 'Objects of Enquiry during the Residence in India', while the second concentrated on how those objectives might be achieved; and other objectives were to establish a learned body modelled on the Royal Society, mission to enquire into man and nature in general and Asia in particular; investigate the records and traditions of those nations, who from time to time have peopled or desolated it; to bring to light their various forms of government with their institutions, civil and religions, etc.

A new chapter in India's history had begun. The light of reason would now be brought to bear on each of Jones's sixteen objects of inquiry, leading to a new understanding of Mother India as 'the nurse of sciences, the Inventress of delightful and useful arts, the scene of glorious actions, fertile in the productions of human genius'.

As a senior judge of Calcutta's Supreme Court, William Jones had easy access to Governor General Warren Hastings. Both men co-founded the Asiatic Society by which every kind of information gathered, centralized, cross-referenced, examined and interpreted, and the results distributed through the Society's journal Asiatic Research. Soon they found out that they were dealing with a people crushed by centuries of oriental disposition and shackled by superstition, their minds untaught by learning and experience, unstored by science and literature, and uncheered by warm and benevolent religions.

A few freethinkers volunteered to offer their support. A small group of people joined the innovative discipline of sharing the results of their research in the form of papers read at monthly meetings. Slowly a long-lost India began to disclose itself.

Jones and his wife Anna embraced all things Indian with openness. He admired Indian music, literature, and epics. That admiration led him to read those texts in original. He learned Sanskrit from Pandit Ramlochan. He soon learned to pronounce Sanskrit precisely what the Brahmins maintained for a long time and he found out that Sanskrit has a close similarity to Latin and Greek, 'So strong, indeed, that no philologist could examine all three without believing them to have sprung from some common sources." With the help of Pandit Ramlochan and Pandit Radhakanth, Jones brought a vast arena of sacred and semi-sacred Indian books unknown to the western world.

It is Jones' self-imposed mission to shed light on India's pre-Muslim history. The first obstacle he faced was the absence of historical records. He was familiar with Al-Biruni's Indica and Persian historian Firishta. Brahmins offered a collection of eighteen Puranas, which means ancient times. These Puranas included genealogical lists of numerous gods and humans ruled over the Indian subcontinent, previously called as Jambudwipa or 'Blackberry Island'. These genealogies enabled Jones to assemble a concise version of Indian Chronology.

This chronology showed sixteen Janapada kingdoms were there, Magadha was one of them. According to Puranas, Magadha was ruled by the main monarchs Chandragupta, Bindusara, and Ashoka as the Maurya dynasty. Puranas did not consider Ashoka as an important figure and also not interested in knowing why he was great.

The information about Buddhism has dispersed in Europe since the return of Marco Polo. Buddha was rarely mentioned in Indian texts, and also there were no Buddhists, Buddhist literature, or Buddhist monuments in India.

Later, they discovered more number of inscriptions cut and carved onto the rocks at Nagarjuni and several caves. The unreadable inscriptions were written in some thirty or so characters looking like Greek. Jones' Brahmin companions declared the script to be Brahmi lipi.

Jones established that the alphabets used on Firoz Shah's golden pillars and some copies made from Ellora of Bombay were the same found in Nagarjuni caves.

Search for Ashoka

Jones received very conflicting views about Buddha. Some Pandits viewed that Buddha was a heretical leader of a false sect, but also the ninth incarnation of god Vishnu. It was very controversial. To him Buddha was following the doctrines contained in the Vedas through his good nature although he criticized cattle sacrifice and some other ancient books. It led him to think there were two Buddhas, the first one being a revolutionary one who attempted to overturn the old system of Brahmins and the second Buddha came later with conventional character. He published his findings in Asiatic Research magazine. They triggered a flood of responses from friends and journalists from all over including Sumatra, Madras, Ceylon, Calcutta, Mirzapur, and Bengal. These journalists were able to mention ancient Buddhist texts obtained in countries outside India, some written in Sanskrit and others in Pali language.

All these foreign texts concurred that Buddhism originated in India in Magadha which was a center place of learning, civilization, and trade about two thousand years ago. The founder of Buddhism was a historical figure called Shakyamuni or Gautama Buddha who died in late fifth century BCE. In spite of being branded as heretic and atheist religion, Buddhism survived until the twelfth century in some parts of India.

Bodhagaya

Supporting evidence for Buddhism's Indian roots emerged from several places beginning with an inscription found in an abandoned temple known as Buddha-Gaya. In Varanasi surprising evidence emerged suggesting that at one time Buddhism was contending with the most orthodox Hindu cities also.

With all these findings Jones could not solve the mystery of pillars, inscriptions, and the creator of pillars. So he wanted to know some name tied to European history. His attention turned to Alexander the Great and wanted to know which kings he encountered in the course of his invasion to India.

From Greek Source - Chandragupta in Megasthanese's Indica

Sisikottos/Sisocostus was one such Indian mercenary fighting for the Greeks. His qualities of leadership recommended him to Alexander as a man worthy of confidence. The ambassadors of Alexander and Seleukos are Megasthanese and Deimachos: Megasthanese was present at the court of Sandrakoptos (Chandragupta). Both ambassadors provided a valuable source of information for Arrian, Diodorus, Pliny, and Strabo to write the history of India. The ambassadors observed Indian society at first hand. Like all good diplomats, they gathered intelligence, taking careful note of the administration and how it worked, the strength of its army, the class structure of the country, its economy and natural resources. All this he found in Megasthanese's book Indica.

Here Jones found some information from the Greeks side. Now he had to link the desired part of synchronicity to new material emerging from his research in Sanskrit records. He understood the war between Seleukos and Sandrokoptos took place around 305 BCE. He connected an Indian prince with the contemporary personality Seleukos and declared the common fixed point in history.

Major James Rennell, known as the 'father of Indian geography' was a geographer, mapmaker and oceanographer. He was badly attacked and injured by local people while surveying Bhutan and returned to London. When Jones was searching a missing link between India and ancient Greece, he received a letter from Rennell about the identity and location of ancient Palimbothra (Pataliputra or modern-day Patna). This was the city Megasthanese had written elaborately in such detail. Jones and his pandit companions searched for Palimbothra and they could not find it. Another letter from Rennell came mentioning that he learned from local people that an ancient city named 'Patelpoot-her' once stood there. It was indeed the one and the same site of Greek's Palimbothra and ancient India's Pataliputra.

This discovery led to link two Sanskrit texts, which was written by a poet Somadeva. It told the story of revolution of Pataliputra beginning with Nanda and also about the coronation of Chandragupta. He now confirmed that Greek Sandrokoptos was the Indian king Chandragupta. The final confirmation came with identifying two other names Sisikottos and Sandrokoptos, both Greek versions of the same name. Sisikottos was a Greek version of Sashigupta, which also means the moon-protected.

Today it seems obvious, but in Jones' time it was a big breakthrough. He was able to date some events also. Alexander the Great died in 323 BCE. By the time Seleukos campaigned against India in 305 BCE, Chandragupta was already established as a great emperor. He must therefore have won the throne before Alexander's death.

According to Puranas

According to the Puranic 'Table of the Kings of Magadha', Chandragupta ruled twenty-four years from about 317 to 293 BCE. His son Bindusara had ruled twenty five years from 292-268 BCE. His son Ashoka had ruled for thirty-six years from 267-230 BCE. The Maurya dynasty lasted a total of 137 years.

Jones who had come to India to serve a term of ten years was completed and by which time Jones and his wife Anna were seriously ill. But he stayed a little longer to complete his Digest of Hindu and Muslim Law. He considered giving 24 million of Indian people their own law is more flattering than the thanks of the King. Unfortunately, a year later he died in 1875. His works on discovering Ashoka also halted. It was a great loss to Asiatic Society.

One of Asiatic Society's dispersed contributors James Hoare presented a book of drawings of the Firoz Shah's Pillars in Delhi and Allahabad together with eye-copies (eye-copy is made by hand as seen by the eye (not carbon copy or Xerox copy!)) of their inscriptions. It was fortunate because just a month after the military engineer of Colonel Kyd who was the enemy of Hindustani architecture uprooted the pillar in Allahabad and left it broken into pieces by the roadside.

Ajanta Discovered

In September 1803, the army brought their wounded soldiers to the little village of Ajanta where a small mud-walled fort was set to use as a field hospital. While the army stayed for a month, rumors reached them that there are many wonderful things to be seen in the caves less than a mile where a small river valley is situated. Locally it was called Tiger Valley and people avoided going there. Probably that was the reason why the caves and their contents had remained undisturbed for centuries. Meanwhile, a peace treaty was signed, the army returned back, and the caves of Ajanta were forgotten. It has to wait another twenty-one years for James Alexander to finish the work.

Fort William College, Calcutta

Wellesley assumed that the best method to understand is to acquire knowledge of manners and customs of the natives of India. By 1818, hundreds of Indian linguists were employed at Fort William College, Calcutta. The college also had the finest oriental library in the world housing almost twelve thousand printed books and manuscripts. Wellesley did not anticipate the impact of his college on Bengal. It paved the way to Bengal Renaissance inspiring men like Raja Ram Mohan Roy to work for social reforms that would eventually end the British rule in India.

In Mysore

One closely associated with Fort William College was Henry Colebrook, Professor of Sanskrit and Hindu Law. He assisted many people to continue William Jones work. John Leyden was one among them and he was sent to survey Mysore. He carried on inquiries concerning the natural history of the country, manners and languages, etc. of the natives of Mysore. In the course of his duties, Leyden learned thirteen Indian languages in a few months. After completing the translation of Babur's autobiography Baburnama, he was sent to Java as an interpreter to Lord Minto. In Java he visited a library, which had a reputation of having Indian manuscripts and collected rare Indian manuscripts. Three days after returning from Java, Leyden died due to fever.

Next Henry Colebrook appointed Horace Hayman Wilson in place of Leyden. First, Wilson's duty was to translate William Jones's Sanskrit translations. Desiring to understand better, he searched for Sanskrit-English dictionaries and found there were none. This led him to write his own dictionary. It took several years to finish the work, but he gained a mastery of the Sanskrit language.

One among many Wilson's achievements was establishing a Sanskrit college in Calcutta in 1824 equivalent to Benares. His other important works are Sanskrit Grammar, translations of a number of ancient dramas, and his work on the eighteen Puranas.

Sources from Kashmir

Wilson also discovered and translated a long-forgotten document Rajatarangini, a chronicle of the kings of Kashmir written by a Brahmin poet named Kalhana. In his work, Kalhana had drawn earlier historical sources to write about Kashmir prior to the Muslim invasions. According to his writings, Buddhism was a dominant religion in that region.

Ashoka Established the City of Srinagar

According to Rajarangini, Buddhism was introduced to Kashmir by a king named Ashoka. The King Ashoka had established the city of Srinagar, built a number of temples and spread Buddhism to adjacent countries. But the author displayed a striking hostility towards Ashoka in his book than his son Jalauka and grandson Damodara. Wilson came to the conclusion that if this Ashoka was the one who brought Buddhism to Kashmir and is the same as listed in the dynastic table in Purana as a third ruler of the Mauryan of Magadha, then he must be a powerful ruler. But the mystery for Wilson was that the names of Ashoka's son and grandson Jaluka and Damodara were not listed in any of the Puranic tables. Later he came to know that the authors of Rajataragini and puranas disliked Buddhism. Then Wilson lost his interest in his work and the scheme fell apart for lack of a directing force.

In spite of all this, The Asiatic Society was receiving many unknown religious texts from China, Ceylon, and Burma, all canonical works and collections of Buddhist tales 'Divyavadana'. All this shed light on the fact that Gautama Buddha, emerging from the realms of myth, was actually lived in the kingdom of Magadha, attained enlightenment, preached his message of Dharma or 'Moral Law' for forty-five years, and died in the year 544 BCE.

Buddhagaya

Francis Buchanan surveyed Bihar and found some more facts about Ashoka finding the ruins of great antiquity. He found a dilapidated Hindu temple surrounded by scores of stone images. A Burmese pilgrim told that it is the temple of Buddha-Gaya built by Ashoka and both the platform and the papal tree were the works of Ashoka. Upon examination he found most of the stone images worshipped even today are the same as seen in Burma and Kathmandu. On more research, it was found out that indeed Buddha-Gaya was a Buddhist temple built by Ashoka.

Buchannan's survey work continued towards Bihar and westwards where he found an immense mass of ruins consisting of foundations of many brick walls, buildings, and temples. Later he discovered the ruins of the Great Monastery of Nalanda, once a famous Buddhist University.

Another engineer and map-maker Colin Mackenzie was making advances in Jain study in South India. He found a Jain textbook Parisisthaparvam, the work of Acharya Hemachandra. This shed the light on the founder of the Mauryan dynasty, a detailed account of Chandragupta and Chanakya. According to this book, Chandragupta came to power 155 years after the death of Buddha.

Sources from Andhra Pradesh

Mackenzie received a report from a local raja in Andhra Pradesh, which uncovered a large antiquity while collecting the building material. This place is called Amaravathi. The site was surrounded by a ring of large marble pillars and slabs, carvings of bas-relief sculptures that showed exceptional artistry and sophistication, perhaps the finest Buddhist monument ever erected in India. He and his companions had no idea what to make of the iconography shown on its magnificent sculptures. Unfortunately, many decorated slabs had been recycled, turned over and new scenes carved on their backs, so that the earlier scenes were hidden from view.

Sri Lanka

First English translation of the Sri Lankan epic, the Great Dynastic Chronicle in Pali language stated that India had a history of strong connection between a Sri Lankan king named Petissa II and an Indian monarch King Darmasoca of Jambudwipa. Because of these two royal friendships, Buddhism had been established in Sri Lanka. The Great Dynastic Chronicle of Ceylon had devoted several chapters to the Indian Monarchs who had ruled Magadha from the time of Buddha to Darmasoca. It described how Chandragupta's son Bindusara chose his eldest son Prince Sumana and there was also a son called Priyadase. This single chapter proved a clear link that no one at the time noticed that it was that King Bindusara's eldest son by his second queen was named Priyadase, also called 'Asoca'!

Inscriptions

Colin Mackenzie came to see the Elephant's cave inscription and recognized the writings to be the identical characters on the pillars at Delhi. He made

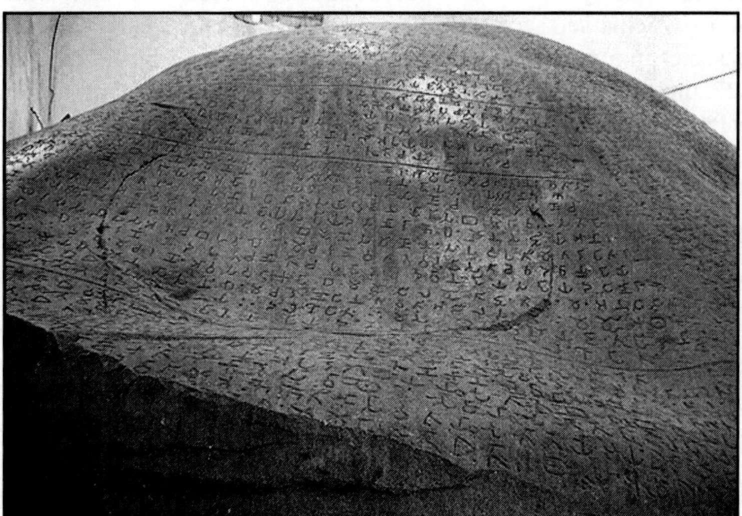

Ashoka Inscriptions on a rock

an eye-copy of inscriptions noting that the same writings were reported from a number of ancient monuments scattered all over India. He clarified that any reader who takes some trouble to compare the writings on inscription on the pillars of Firoz Shah Lat at Delhi and other monuments will find that the characters are identically the same.

On the mountain of Girnar there was a huge hemispherical mass of dark granite shaped like a kneeling elephant, almost its entire surface covered in writing. It was like a book on a rock because it was covered with characters so uniform and implicated that it has to be the work of one man. But who was that man?

Henry Colebrook delivered his society's goal, declaring that 'since the origins of Western civilization were to be found in Asia, and England's success as a world power owed so much to India, England had a duty to repay this debt. This included making a study of Asia in all its aspects.'

Ajanta Revisited

In 1824, James Alexander took leave to go for hunting and entered a tiger-infested place Ajanta escorted by a local guide ignoring resident's warnings about tigers. He entered the cave holding a brushwood torch. What he saw was breathtaking. The wall and ceilings were decorated with paintings of astonishing quality, displaying the dresses, habits of life, pursuits, and features of native Indians probably two thousand or two thousand five hundred years ago, and well-preserved Buddhist sects. This extraordinary discovery remained secret for the next five years and Alexander revealed the secret in a speech to Sandhurst Military Academy in 1828. Then in 1827, first notice of the Ajanta cave was published in Journal of the Asiatic Society of Bengal.

In Which Language the Inscriptions Were Written?

James Princep painstakingly tried to analyze the inscriptions and its alphabetical signs, which he found over all parts of India. He presumed that the alphabets must have been derived from Devanagari script. He compared five basic vowel sounds 'a','e','i','o','u' (e.g., a, aa, e, ee, u, uu, etc.) found in Sanskrit and other Indo-European root languages. He drew a chart showing all the radical letters with their inflections and found that twenty-nine characters were used and he thought it might be an early form of Sanskrit script. After extensive research with various books including Ceylon works, he found out that the language was Pali, early Magadhan Prakrit. It appeared that Pali and Sanskrit scripts were derived from the same source Magadhan Prakrit.

He went on highlighting a group of fifteen characters that were occurring in the beginning of every paragraph of the inscription. He retrieved other eye-copies of inscriptions collected from various places where each paragraph began with the same group of fifteen letters. Princip contemplated to find out whether it is a mark of victory of some raja, or the boundary pillars, or religious doctrines. It was important to discover the language to solve the mystery.

According to the Great Dynastic Chronicle, found in Ceylon, Ashoka played a key role in spreading Buddhism in India and abroad. Wilson said it is nonsense because it is well-known that Ashoka was a worshipper of Shiva and declared Dynastic chronicles unreliable.

Ashoka in Great Dynastic Chronicle (Thervada Version)

Turmour translation of Great Dynastic Chronicle gave details about how Ashoka came to power having killed 99 brothers born to different mothers and how he ruled over Jambudwipa.

It documents a report that because of some rumor that Ashoka intended to murder his father Bindusara and occupy the throne for himself, he was sent away to rule the Avanti, its capital being the Ujjain. On the way he met a beautiful girl named Devi, the daughter of a merchant. Later he married her. A son Mahindo and a daughter Sanghamitta were born to them.

A decade later, Ashoka receives the news that king Bindusara is dying. Suddenly he goes to Pataliputta to see his father for the last time. After Bindusara's death, Ashoka occupied the throne killing all his 99 brothers, born to different mothers, except his biological brother Tisso. It took four years to take the position of the throne. He appointed Tisso as his deputy. However, Ashoka's violent behavior brings him the name 'Chand Ashoka' 'Angry Ashoka'.

He then begins to have religious doubts noticing some dreadful behavior and alarming practices. He orders representatives of all religions to come before him and answer some of his questions as well as their principles. While this inquiry was going on, he saw through the window a calm young Buddhist monk passing by. The boy's name was Nigrodha, and he happened to be the orphaned son of Ashoka's eldest half-brother Sumana, whom Ashoka killed to rise to power. Ashoka invites him and questions on matters of Buddhist doctrines until he is satisfied. Then he comes to the conclusion that Buddhism is the true faith.

Ashoka Converts to Buddhism

Ashoka becomes a believer of Buddha and he replaces sixty thousand Buddhist monks in place of Brahmins in his court. Maggaliputta becomes King Ashoka's teacher and remains a dominant figure in Ashoka's life.

Discovering that there are eighty-four thousand discourses on the tenets of Buddhism, Ashoka ordered to build stupas and monastic institutions in eighty-four thousand places throughout his empire.

Ashoka makes friendship with the king of Anuradhapura in Lanka and both exchange royal gifts. Along with the gifts including sacred water of Ganges, he sends the gift of pious advice to King to take refuge in Buddhism. The Great Dynastic Chronicle spends a great deal of space on Ashoka's children Mahinda and Sangamitta's mission to Lanka. In Lanka, the King received the missionaries and converted himself to Buddhism along with his family and his court. Lankan King sends a request for a branch of the Bodhi tree. Ashoka was very much worried to harm the tree. After a complex ceremony, a cutting from the tree was sent to Lanka with Sangamitta. Other relics like Buddha's alms bowl, collarbone and tooth were also sent.

After Ashoka's Buddhist queen Asandhimitra died, he married an attendant of his former wife. The new wife was jealous of her husband's devotion to Buddhism and complained that the King loves Bodhi tree more than me. After four years of their marriage, she poisoned the Bodhi tree with the tooth of a toad. After this event, Ashoka's miserable days began. Ashoka dies soon after.

This source of story is according to Theravada.

Decoding the Inscriptions

Lt. Markham Kottoe tried to track new inscriptions in Oria. When he was searching near a place of worship, he was distracted and told that there was no such thing there. He was returning a mile or so and met a Hindu mendicant from Benares who helped him to find what Kottoe was looking for. When they returned back to the same spot by torchlight, they saw the inscription, which was completely hidden.

The problems faced by Indian archaeologists who want to dig and examine old ruins are either religious prejudices or it is perceived as someone is seeking buried treasure or anything inscribed on rocks and pillars must have the secret to those treasures.

Kittoe returned to the rock the next morning to copy the inscription and also documented many more inscriptions from various places. He noticed virtually everyone ended in the same two letters: a snake-like scribble formed by six straight lines, followed by inverted capital letter T with a dot on one side. After complex concentrated study, he found that the snake-like character represents the sound 'da', the inverted 'T' represents the sound 'na', and the dot the 'm', together forming the word 'danam'.

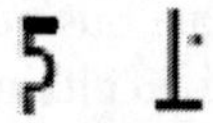

After this single most important advancement in the study of Indian history, Kitto needed to prepare a source for the alphabet to make a complete translation of the Firoz Shah Lat inscription.

The written language of the Magadhan was the ancestor of most of India's modern languages and alphabets. Later it was termed as Brahmi lipi. The earliest form was referred to as Ashoka Brahmi.

Once he comprehended how the Brahmi alphabet functioned, Princip was triumphantly ready to translate all Sanchi stupas and names of their donors. Next, he translated Indo-Bactrian coins bearing Greek letters. Then a number of short inscriptions from Bodhgaya followed. Then he translated Firoz Shah's Lat and other inscriptions found in Delhi, Allahabad, Girnar, Dhauli etc. Almost all inscriptions started from

"Devanampiya piyadasi laja hevam aha"

Here the laja means raja. That gives them the starting phrase: "Beloved-of-the-Gods beloved king", hevam aha - translated as 'spake thus':

"Thus spake King Piyadasi, Beloved-of-the-God"

Princip had gone through all Hindu genealogy tables and had found no one by the name of Devanampiya. Here also he does painstaking research to find out who was this Devanampiya.

Ashoka Found

One day Princep received a dramatic response from George Turnour in Columbo. While normally turning the pages of translation of the Great Dynastic Chronicle, Turnour hit a new passage relating to the identity of Piyadasi. It read: "Two hundred and eighteen years after the beatitude of Buddha was the inauguration of Piyadasi who, the grandson of Chandra-gupta, and own son of Bindusara, was at that time Viceroy of Ujjayani." He was the Indian King Ashoka! Thus, the identity of the originator of all the rocks and pillars was ashoka maurya is established beyond doubt.

What Was in Decoded Inscriptions?

In his Rock Edict 2 (RE2), he emphasized to give respect for all living things and to provide medical aid for both humans and animals, to dig wells, to plant trees beside roads for the benefit of the people. In RE3 he instructed his subjects to respect their parents, show generosity to others and live with moderation. He was very keen on administration. In RE6 he orders his executives to report state business affairs whether he is eating, or in women's quarters, or in bed, in chariot, or in the park or wherever.

He preached religious tolerance in RE7 emphasizing that his desire was that all religions should prevail everywhere. So, he summons all religions for self-control and purity of heart. In RE13, he expresses his strong emotion of the Kalinga war and its consequences.

(At the end of this summary, translation of all his Rock Edicts, Pillar Edits will be posted.)

First Buddhist scriptures were written in Brahmi script around 100 CE. Later the southern Buddhists adopted Pali and northerners adopted more defined language Sanskrit.

In Theravada version of Great Dynastic Chronicle Ashoka was described as a supporter and propagator of Buddhism and father of Mahinda and Sangamitta. Maggaliputta Tissa was guiding Ashoka to spread Buddhism in Ceylon and beyond.

Ashoka in Divyavadana (Mahayana Version)

Burnouf was able to obtain a Sanskrit text Divyavadana or Divine stories of the lives of Buddhist saints. One of these avadanas was Ashokavadana or The Legend of King Ashoka about his life and death. This Sanskrit text belonged to Mahayana school of northern India. Divyavadana portrays Ashoka in a different way than the Great Chronicles. It does not mention the great slaughter at Kalinga or his remorse and conversion. It is completely quiet on the subject of propagation of Buddhism abroad.

According to this book Divyavadana, Ashoka meets Buddha in his previous life and offers a handful of dirt. It lists the kings of Magadha but completely omits Chandragupta mentioning Bindusara is a son of Nanda. Ashoka's mother was Subhadrangi, a daughter of a Brahmin. Their first son was named Ashoka, 'without sorrow' because Subhadrangi herself had suffered much in her life due to vengeance of Bindusara's other wives. Bindusara neglects his son Ashoka because he was born with some skin disease having rough and unpleasant touch. The book relates this as a direct consequence of his offering dirt to Buddha in his previous birth. Ashoka grows as an unruly prince. An astrologer predicts that Ashoka will succeed his father to the throne. But Bindusara liked his eldest son Sushima and wanted him to be his successor. At the same time, a revolt against the King breaks out in Taxila. King takes an opportunity and sends Ashoka to Taxila to defeat the enemies with the army but without any arsenal. Nevertheless, Ashoka solves the situation and establishes the peace. On the way back, he makes friendship with two powerful mountain warriors, possibly Greek local rulers and soldiers.

In the meantime, Sushima insults Chief Minister Chanukya who turns all ministers including his own son Radhagupta against Sushim and in favor of Ashoka. Again, a second rebel rises in Taxila and Bindusara sends Sushima to deal with it and soon Bindusara falls ill seriously. King orders to recall Sushim from Taxila commanding Ashoka to go in his place. However, the ministers apply turmeric on Ashoka's body to make him look like too sick to travel. When it is confirmed that Bindusara is dying, Ashoka emerges dressed in full royal ornament and asks his father to make him temporary ruler. This incident makes Bindusara so furious and vomits blood and dies.

Once Ashoka was crowned, he demonstrated his unkind nature. He built a prison, which contained all the tortures of hell.

One day a Buddhist hermit Samudra walks into Ashoka's hell while begging for offering. When the hell-manager Chandagirika finds Samudra unbending to his cruelty, he reports it to the king. Ashoka himself comes to see the hermit. Samudra explains that he is free from the mundane world - suffering from birth and death - grateful to Sakhyamuni Buddha. He continues to tell that the Buddha has predicted that hundred years from now a great king named Ashoka will rule the Pataliputra. He will be a Chakravarty, 'Wheel-turning Monarch' like Buddha turning the wheel of the Dharma. He will also be a Dharmaraja, 'Righteous King' who distributes the relics of Buddha worldwide. That is what Buddha has predicted, Samudra asks, "But instead, your Majesty, you have built this place that resembles the hell where thousands of living beings have been killed."

Now Ashoka regrets his deeds and promises to fulfill Sakhyamuni Buddha's forecast. Then he converts to Buddhism, demolishes the hell along with Chandagirika. He declares Buddhism as an official religion of the country.

Then he builds eighty-four thousand monuments containing Buddha's relics throughout his empire. After completing pilgrimage to many holy places, Ashoka returns to Bodhgaya and finds the Bodhi tree is dying. This was caused by his queen, Tishyarakshita. She was jealous because the king is abandoning the family religion. He becomes emotional and faints. Then the queen realizes her mistake and waters the tree roots with a thousand jugs of milk a day until the tree recovers. Then Ashoka multiplies his service by honoring the monks and appoints them to preach the true religion throughout his empire.

When Ashoka's son Dharmavivardhana was born, he overcomes with joy seeing the child's eyes and names him Kunala after a Himalayan bird called kunala. Later, Ashoka's queen Tishyarakshita falls in love with Kunala. When he refuses her ambition, she plans to take revenge by destroying him.

Again, when an agitation started in Taxila, Kunala was sent to subdue the mob. In the meanwhile, Ashoka falls seriously ill. He sends a message to Kunala to return and take over the Kingdom. Tishyarakshita fears that if Kunala becomes king, he may put her to death. So in order to find a cure for king's illness, she appoints servants to search and find a person with the same kind of illness. One such person was found and brought to the palace. She kills him, cuts the body and detects a large worm in his stomach. She experiments with various medicines to kill the worm, nothing works. Finally, when she used onion, which was prohibited as unclean by Brahmans and Kshatriyas, the worm died. Then she treats the king with onion and cures him. As a reward she asks the king to rule the country for a week. Then, she sends messengers to Taxila ordering to blind Kunala.

After all these events, Ashoka preaches his younger brother Vitashoka about Dharma and proclaims him as a Buddhist monk. After some time, a cowherd spots Vitashoka who has grown a beard and hair and thinks he must be a blasphemer. The cowherd then kills Vitashoka and brings his head to the king to claim the reward. Ashoka recognizes his brother and is deeply saddened. His preacher Upagupta explains that it is all due to Ashoka's cruelty. One time, an enemy of Buddhism was distributing a painting of himself where Buddha was sitting at his feet. This annoys Ashoka.

As stated by the Legend of King Ashoka, the monarch's last days were not happy. As his illness increased, he became obsessively inclined to give donations to Buddhist temples. It reached a point that the state treasury was near empty. Prince Kunala's son Sampadi was appointed as heir to the throne and on advice of his ministers he stopped the state treasurer to release any more funds. The emperor Ashoka starts donating his personal belongings like tableware, gold dishes, silver plates, copper plates until it reaches the food being served on rough earthenware. He offers his last gift a cherry blump fruit with these words:

He who previously ruled the earth
Over which he spread his umbrella of sovereignty
And warmed the world like the noonday sun at it zenith
Today that king has seen his fortunes cut off
Deceived by his own karmic acts, he finds his glory gone
Like the setting sun at dusk.

On his last day, Ashoka mashed the cherry plum fruit and mixed it into a soup and distributed it to a group of monks at his favorite Cock monastery. He asked his lifelong friend and minister Radhagupta "who is the lord of the earth?" and Radhagupta declared Ashoka is the lord of the earth. And then he moved around the ground each point of the compass and with a sign of offering he announces that he is giving the whole earth 'to the community of the Blessed One's disciples.' He had documented these words already, seals with his teeth and dies. With whatever remained in the state treasury, the minsters brought back some assets from Buddhist Sangha and Ashoka's grandson Sampadi was coronated.

Later Ashoka's great-great-grandson Pushyamitra wanted his name to be renowned equal to Ashoka and asked his Brahmin priest how it could be accomplished. He says there are two ways: One way is like Ashoka build eighty-four thousand stupa and the second way of doing is to destroy all those stupas. Pushyamitra chose the second one and goes to Cock monastery with his army, and tells the monks to choose between saving themselves or the monastery. Monks offered themselves to sacrifice, but Pushyamitra destroyed both monks and monastery. He did not stop there; he went on a campaign against all Buddhist institutions and declared reward for the head of every monk. Finally, a yaksha crushes him under a mountain. So ends the Maurya dynasty with the death of Pushyamitra.

This source of story is according to Mahayana.

Ashoka in Tibetan Lama Taranath – From Russian Source

As Burnouf was completing his work, another source about early Indian Buddhism came from Russia. They emerged from the Department of Mongolian Language at the University of Kazan on the Volga River, a handwritten text translated from the original Tibetan entitled Gya-garChos-byung or The History of Buddhism in India, the work of a Tibetan Lama named Taranath.

Although Taranath's history was dismissed by scholars, the author writes certain things to be considered when reconstructing the Ashoka and his time. It describes Ashoka as the son of Nemita, king of Champaran in the north Magadha and a daughter of a merchant. Ashoka was leading a simple life. When Kashmir and Nepal revolted, Ashoka was sent there to deal with it. When Ashoka was successful in his endeavor, he was made governor of Pataliputra. When king Nemita dies, his ministers make Ashoka as the ruler of Pataliputra. Ashoka worshipped various mother goddesses. He kept 500 women in his harem and was Kama Ashoka.

Ashoka kills all his half-brothers, becomes very cruel and finds peace of mind when performing violent actions and earning the name 'Ashoka the Wrathful'. As explained in Theravada story, a Buddhist arrives in torture house and reforms Ashoka. Taranath's history somewhat resembles Legend of King Ashoka.

Fa Hian (Faxian) and Hwan Thsang (Xuanzang)

Taranath's History of Buddhism was known in Russia and Germany only. But, Orientalists, Indologists, archaeologists, philologists, and epigraphists working in India were occupied with two different texts.

(1) The first one was "Jean-Pierre Abel-Remusat's 'Foe Koue Ki, ou Relations des Royaumes Bouddhiques" (Record of Buddhistic Kingdoms), a French translation of Chinese Buddhist pilgrim FA HIAN (Faxian) on his pilgrimage to India around 400 CE.

(2) The second was "Histoire de la vie de Hiuen-tsang et de ses voyages dans l'Inde depuis I'an 629 jusqu'en 645" (History of the Life of HIUEN-TSANG (Xuanzang) and his Travels in India Between the Years 629-645).

James Princep was happy to know about these publications and he was longing to see the books desperately. Unfortunately, before this happened, he was fatally incapacitated by recurrent headaches and lever problem. He returned to England in poor condition and did not recover and died at the age of 40. After him, Captain Markham Kittoe and Captain Alexander Cunningham continued his work.

Fa Hian (Faxian)

In August 1966 during China's cultural Revolution a group stormed an ancient seven storied Dayan Ta or Wild Goose Pagoda shouting "Smash the old world, build a brand-new world.' They broke down doors, shoved aside the monks, and tied ropes around Buddha and Bodhisattva statutes to bring them down. At this time, the Cultural Relics Bureau came and stopped the damage. But they did not stop burning the collection of ancient Buddhist sutras and texts. They all were gathered and thrown into a pyre. Maybe they would have provided more information what these people were looking for.

Trailing the upper pathway of the Indus River with great difficulty, a Buddhist monk Faxian arrived to Buddhist kingdom from northern Pakistan in the spring of 402 CE. There he noticed a Buddhist demi-paradise where 'the Law of Buddha' was thriving. Then he moved to Gandhara, and noticed the Hinayana Buddhism was flourishing there.

Throughout Gandhara, Faxian saw numerous memorial mounds having relics of Buddhist monks known as stupas. Faxian was delighted to see two stupas at Purushapura (Peshawar) built by Kushan King Kanishka. One stupa contained an alms bowl of Buddha brought back from India by Kushans as a war booty.

Before Kanishka, a king known to Chinese as 'Wayou Wang' or 'The King Not Feeling Sorrow' was responsible for bringing Buddhism to China. He was also called Chakravartin or "Wheel-turning Monarch." Wayou Wang's name appeared throughout Faxian's India travel. After six months in Gandhara, his companions returned to China and Faxian continued his journey and reached Punjab where the people were firm believers in Dharma. They were not Buddhists but respected Buddhist monks.

Defeating Kushans, Guptas were ruling the country. During the time of Faxian's visit to India, Vikramaditya, also known as Chandragupta II of Gupta dynasty (not Maurya dynasty) was a ruler. Even though he worshiped Hindu god Vishnu, he patronized all forms of religious faith.

In his 'Record of Buddhistic Kingdoms', Faxian reports at Sankisa the great monarch King Wuyou had built a monastery 'with a standing image, sixteen cubits (24 feet) in height. Behind the monastery he had erected a stone pillar about fifty cubits (75 feet) high with a lion on top of it.' This is the earliest known mention of the stone column accredited to Ashoka.

After visiting many Buddhist places, he traveled to Pataliputra, the city of flowers from where the King Wuyou ruled India. He writes, "Indeed his palace and his halls were still to be seen, and his towering city walls and gates still stood, all inlaid with sculpture-work carved in a way which no human hands of this world could accomplish." King Ashoka had built an artificial hill inside the city to his younger brother who wished to spend his time in solitude taking refuge in Buddhism. Faxian writes many other great works done by Ashoka in Patliputra. Besides, he spent three years learning Sanskrit, copied a number of sutras to take back to China.

In his writing he adds a full chapter devoted to Ashoka beginning with how Ashoka as a small boy in his previous birth offered earth (dirt) to the begging bowl of Buddha. As a result, he received huge landmass and became a king of the iron wheel to rule the Jambudvipa.

In the year 407 AD, Faxian travels to Singhala, the Lion Kingdom (now Sri Lanka). After the departure of Faxian from India, Hunas, a group of Central Asian nomads, came to power after driving out Gupta rulers. Their rule ended when Persian Sassanid emperor joined nomadic tribes and forced out White Hunas. Nevertheless a small group of isolated Huns stayed, adopted the local culture, accepted the religious authority of the Brahmans, underwent various purification rites, emerged as self-proclaimed Rajputs and Kshatriyas of the warrior caste. One of the Rajput kings was Raja Harshavardhana who ruled India from 606 to 647 CE. was a powerful ruler and ruled the country for some forty years.

Hwan Thsang (Xuanzang)

Inspired by Faxian, nearly 236 years later another Chinese pilgrim Hwan Thsang (Xuanzang) came to India in the year 636 in search of Buddhist sutras . He noticed the Buddhist monks who had survived Huns' destructions. In Bamiyan he saw two great standing images of Buddha and hundreds of monasteries with several thousand monks. Even then, the Gandharan summer capital Kapisha was governed by Buddhist king.

Hwan Thsang (Xuanzang) travels to eastern part of India and gives a detailed description of the reality of the region. He observed that Buddhism in India was in decline. In Faxian's time Purushapura (Peshawar) was flourishing, but now it is all abandoned, its Buddhist monuments are in ruins. Kanishka's most prized Buddhist trophy, the Buddha's bowl, had been carried off to Persia. In Malakand mountain range too everything lay in ruins: 'Along the two sides of the Subhavastu River [Swat River] formerly there were one thousand four hundred monasteries, but most of them are now in desolation." Then he goes to Taxila. There also the same story of ruination. He identifies the location where Kunala's eyes were removed.

Hwan Thsang (Xuanzang) travels to Kashmir as a guest of honor of its Buddhist ruler. Here he observes the influence of Wuyou Wang (Ashoka). He writes an interesting story. When Ashoka came to know that five hundred monks are following unorthodox teachings of a Buddhist, he ordered them to be drowned in the Ganges. The monks escaped to Kashmir and refused to return. Then the king personally comes and apologizes for his ill-treatment and orders to build five hundred monasteries in Kashmir to accommodate them.

Hwan Thsang Meets Harshavardhana

Hwan Thsang (Xuanzang) arrived Kannouj. He visited king Harshavardhana and was questioned about his own country. Afterwards he met the king several times. He was greatly impressed by Harsha's character and principles he was using to rule the country. His rule illustrated the principles based on Wuyou Wang's (Ashoka's) instructions. Harsha was not a Buddhist but all values were according to Ashoka's.

Xuansang continued his journey to every part of Uttar Pradesh and Bihar and many other places and the physical evidence of Buddhist was irrefutable. The glorious events of the past, the monuments and monastic institutions have been ruined, deserted, and abandoned. At almost every stage the legacy of the Wheel-turning Monarch Wuyou Wang was there.

In Pataliputra he saw the mighty city was all abandoned: 'Of the monasteries, deva-temples and stupas, there are several hundred remnant sites lying in ruins; only two or three remain intact.'

Xuansang's next visit was to Bodhgaya where he was shocked to see the temple and Bodhi tree was surrounded by drifting sand mounds. He writes that some old people predicted that when the statutes of Bodhisattva disappear, the Buddha-dharma will come to an end. He can see the prediction was already happening. He writes:

"When King Wuyou had just ascended the throne, he believed in heretical doctrines and destroyed the sites left by the Buddha. He sent his troops and went in person to cut the Bodhi tree. He chopped the roots, stalks, branches, and leaves into small pieces and had them heaped up at a spot, where fire-worshipping Brahmans were ordered to burn the pile as a sacrifice to their god. But before the smoke and flames had vanished, two trees grew out of the furious fire and luxurious and verdurous leaves." It seemed a miracle to him. (High oxygen producing peepal tree generates its roots very easily.)

On seeing this miracle, with great regret king Wuyou irrigates the tree roots with milk with full devotion. After some time, his wife wants to destroy the tree:

"The queen, being a heretical believer, secretly sent a man to fell the tree after nightfall. When King Wuyou went to worship the tree at dawn, he was incredibly sad to see only the stump of the tree. He prayed earnestly and irrigated the stump with sweet milk, and in a few days the tree grew up once again. With deep respect and astonishment, the king built a stone enclosure to the height of more than ten feet around the tree, which is still in existence."

The Bodhi tree once again came under attack by King Sasanka of Bengal, who murdered Harshavardhana's elder brother. Sasanka was a devotee of Shiva and enemy of Buddhism. He had destroyed many monasteries in Bengal and Bihar and made Bodhi tree his next target. He first cut down the tree, set the fire and dug the roots and soaked them with sugarcane juice to prevent them from regrowing. The last descendent of Magadha, king Purnavarman heard this event, he said with a great regret, "The Sun of Wisdom has sunk, and only Buddha's tree remained in the world; now that the tree has been destroyed, what else is there for living things to see?"

Again, King Purnavarman irrigates the leftover roots of the tree with milk from thousands of cows and the tree grows ten feet. He then builds a new arena round the tree to the highest twenty-four feet. Xuanzang concludes, "Thus the Bodhi Tree at present is behind the stone wall with over ten feet of its branches growing out over the wall."

Hieun-Tsang in Nalanda

Then the Chinese pilgrim goes to Nalanda, the greatest hub of learning attracting students from all over Asia. According to Xuanzang, all the students were brilliant scholars of high learning, whose reputation was known to foreign lands. The results of centuries of Buddhist thought and philosophy were held in Nalanda and its sister monasteries. It shows that by the time Xuanzang returned to China in 640, Nalanda was prospering and thriving. He was able to carry many Sanskrit works and manuscripts and thorough knowledge of 'Yogacara' or consciousness of Buddhist teaching that spread through China, Korea, and Japan.

In 1842, Captain Alexander Cunningham triumphantly demonstrated the accuracy of Faxian's version by using several examples. He declared that East India Company has a duty to India to protect its ancient monuments, and sooner the better. 'The discovery and publication of all the existing remains of architecture and sculpture, with coins and inscriptions, would throw more light on the ancient history of India, both public and domestic, than the printing of all the rubbish contained in the …."

Inscription with Two Different Characters

In a village called Shahbazgarhi, they found two faces of a large rock. After several days of cleaning the sides of the rock, they made the eye-copy of the impressions. The letters found on it were slightly different from Brahmi. After a great difficulty of reading, it was confirmed the word 'Devanamapiya'. The important difference was that the word was written not from left to right, as in Pali and Sanskrit, but from right to left, as in Aramaic. Previously Princep had mentioned this as Kharosthi writing. This made them to realize that two different branches of characters had co-existed together in the north-west part of India. Most of the inscription was on the eastern face of the rock and the final part contains five Greek kings, in western face. First the rock was mistaken as a shapeless rock, but actually it was a seated elephant.

Approximate Date of Ashoka's Coronation

Solid rock at Dhauli and Sankisa have been cut or carved with outstanding knowledge. They were in excellent condition. Cunningham wrote, "I find the Khalsi text to be in a more perfect state than any of them, and more specifically in that part which contains the names of the five Greek kings - Antiochus, Ptolemy, Antigonus, Magas, and Alexander." He investigated who these five kings referred to attending king Ashoka's inauguration as king. So, Cunningham makes detailed calculations to find out in which date these five kings were alive. Here is the list of five kings ruling period:

Antigonus II (319-239 BCE)
Antiochos II (262-246 BCE)
Ptolemy II (283-246 BCE)
Magas (277-255 BCE)
Alexander II (272-254 BCE)

So, Ashoka became Chakravarty between 274-267 BCE.! What a precise calculation!

Missing Link between Ashoka and Taxila

The missing link between Ashoka and the city in Taxila where he spent as his father's governor came in the form of an inscription written in Aramaic, inked and overcut on a stone slab was stuck onto the wall where it had been used as a building material for a Greco-Bactrian king Demetrius in about 200 BCE. Half of each line was missing but the contents matched to his other inscriptions in RE 3 and 11.

After a long period of excavation and hard work, the bounty Cunningham found in Bharhut was remarkable. He made a decision to move everything he found to Indian Museum in Calcutta. His contemporaries in England condemned him as an act of vandalism. But Cunningham wrote, 'I am willing to accept the blame since I have saved all the more important sculptures. Of those that were left behind at Bharhut every stone that was removable has been carted away by the people."

Cunningham, in collaboration with the leading epigraphists like Ramakrishna Gopal Bhandarkar in Bombay, Rajendra Lal Mitra in Calcutta, Georg Buhler and Max Muller in Oxford published his "Inscriptions of Ashoka."

Another Archaeological Surveyor by name Burgess was focusing on architecture rather than archeology, particularly in cave temples of western India and their inscriptions.

Inscriptions Found in Mysore State

Benjamin Lewis Rice was born in Bangalore in 1836 and in 1860 he became a headmaster of a high school. Later he became Inspector of Schools and Director of Public Instruction for Mysore State. During his duties, to explore the state he travelled on horseback and came to know many inscribed stones scattered all over. In order to decipher those inscriptions, he took help from Sanskrit and Kannada scholars and collected nearly nine thousand inscriptions in Mysore state. After his retirement, he was appointed as Mysore State's director of archaeology.

He discovered 3 minor rock edicts in Mysore State: the Brahmagiri, Jaina-Ramesvara and Siddapur in Chitraduraga. All three were worked by one man named 'Capada' in Kharosthi script who labelled himself as a scribe. It implies that he probably came from Taxila. Rice wrote: 'The inference is that the scribe may have been an official transferred from the extreme north to the extreme south of the empire, which implies a freer inter-communication that has been generally supposed to exist at that period."

Saranath Sculpture

Charles Allen expresses his admiration that of all the discoveries made so far, the Saranath sculptures stand more sophisticated and it is no exaggeration to say it is the work of Mauryan Michelangelo. Its craftsman's mastery was equivalent to anything produced by the Assyrians, the Persians or the Greeks. There were no known such sculptures or constructions in earlier times in India before Ashoka. But, wood and bricks were used abundantly. This new eloquence must have come from somewhere and it steers to Seleucid Bactria and Greco-Persian craftsmen. It makes sense because Ashoka's royal family including his grandfather Chandragupta had intimate ties and relationships with their western neighbors. It suggests a team of sculptors and stonemasons arrived from there replacing wood to stone, which is only possible to accomplish by royal command and patronage.

A question arises that if this master sculptor experienced the patronage of Ashoka, why is it there are no sculptures of Ashoka? In Ashoka's time, no iconic images were allowed, even to Buddha. Mauryas prohibited images of any kind, even for themselves. Maybe there were some images of Ashoka, but they did not survive. The first sculptors and stonemasons appear to have come from the north-west and established workshops at Mathura and Varanasi supported by royals, which laid the foundation for native Indian school of sculpture. He also writes that it is viewed by Indians with suspicion on Greek influence because it is too much for their patriotic sentiments.

Marshal recognized the significance of massive findings in Saranath, applied for more funds and built India's first onsite museum to house them. He did the same thing in Sanchi and Taxila for next twenty-five years.

Even after 100 years of emergence of Ashoka's discovery, this great monarch was still unknown in his own country whereas he was recognized outside the country.

H.G. Wells in his book 'The Outline of History' writes about Ashoka:

> "In the history of the world there have been thousands of kings and emperors who called themselves 'their highnesses, 'their majesties,' and 'their exalted majesties' and so on. They shone for a brief moment, and as quickly disappeared. But Ashoka shines and shines brightly like a bright star, even unto this day."

Dr. Radhakumud Mukerji wrote about Ashoka in the context of renowned historical figures:

> "In his efforts to establish a kingdom of righteousness after the highest ideals of a theocracy, he has been likened to David and Solomon of Israel in the days of its greatest glory; in his patronage of Buddhism, which helped to transform a local into a world religion, he has been compared to Constantine in relation to Christianity; in his philosophy and piety he recalls Marcus Aurelius; he was a Charlemagne in the extent of his empire and, to some extent, in the methods of his administration, too; while his Edicts, 'rugged, uncouth, involved, full

of repetitions,' read like the speeches of Oliver Cromwell in their mannerisms. Lastly, he has been compared to Khalif and Emperor Akbar, whom also he resembles in certain aspects."

After Mukerji, many post-independence Ashokan scholars raised presenting Ashoka as a ruler uncontaminated by foreign influence, down-played Pali source, and ignored the evidence of Ashoka's commemoration in Sanchi gateways presented by John Marshal and Alfred Foucher.

Rock Edicts in Karnataka

It is remarkable to know that Ashoka's edicts appear as a new Invention because they showed out from nowhere. Probably in the beginning Kharosthi and Brahmi script were tested on palm leaves and some on cloth at Taxila. Taking the clue from Persians and Greeks, Ashoka began the practice of writing inscriptions on stone to convey his messages on his own indigenous script Magadhan Prakrit to enable people to read these inscriptions throughout his empire. His stirring sentiments shaped the culture in the utmost corners of Asia.

Many people lament, "The nation that admires Rama, who said to be ruled eleven thousand years ago had no time to Ashoka: the one man who first mustered India into a single nation; the first Indian ruler with a distinctive, identifiable voice, the pre-Gandhian pioneer of non-violence; the first proponent of conquest by moral force alone, whose words remain absolutely, unequivocally unique among rulers as a statement of governing principles."

Nehru Honors Ashoka

Inspired by Ashoka, Nehru named his daughter 'Priyadarshini' and considered Ashoka is equal to Jesus. When he became the first Prime Minister of India, he selected two images directly linked to Ashoka: the twenty-four-spoked wheel known as Dhamma Chakra or 'Wheel of Law', and the national emblem of four lions of Ashokan capital excavated at Saranath.

Rise and Fall of Ashoka Dharma

In essence the story of Ashoka begins with his grandfather Chandragupta and his mentor Chanukya from Taxila. Taxila was occupied by Achaemenid Empire during the period of Cyrus the Great (576 – 530 BCE). By the fourth century BCE, it became a great learning place attracting high-caste Brahmin youths from all over India to study law, medicine and military science and Kshatriyas the art of war. It was also a place to exchange goods and ideas by merchants and general the public which influenced social, economical and cultural aspects.

One of Chanukya's teachers may be Panini, who formulated the rules for Sanskrit language. After his studies, he headed towards Pataliputra and offered his service to King Dhana Nanda. Something happened and he had to run for his life. Later he was helped and supported by Ajivikas and Jains. He was searching for a boy entitled to supreme power and found Chandragupta. Chandragupta was a son of chief of a hill-town called Moriyanaga, 'peacock mountain'. From peacock came the dynasty name Maurya.

Chandragupta

Chandragupta was a horseman of warrior caste. Chanukya saw him in a group of cattle and took responsibility to mold him. It was very much like Aristotle who taught Alexander of Macedonia. It is so remarkable that two most powerful men in the ancient world received education from the world's two greatest thinkers. Chanukya strategically removed the Nanda line and replaced Chandragupta. Then he found time to write Arthashastra. Chandragupta adopted Chanukya's teachings to rule the country.

During his campaign Alexander knew Chandragupta as Sisikottos - Sashigupta, an Indian mercenary and leader of cavalry. The young Chandragupta played an important role in Alexander's subjugation of Chandragupta's own mountain people, Mahaban. As Meroes 'the Mountain Man', Chandragupta further justified Alexander's faith in him by bringing King Poros over to Alexander's side.

With the guidance of Chanukya, Chandragupta launched a lightning strike against Dhana Nanda and defeated him thoroughly. He was anointed as a king in 322 BCE He married Dhana Nanda's daughter Dhurdara who gave birth to Bindusara.

After Alexander, the new ruler Seleukos came to reclaim Alexander's lost Greek territories east of the Indus. Chandragupta repulsed, easily launching a counterattack and pushed back across the Indus and all the way into his own lands. As a result, Seleukos required giving back Gandhara including modern day Kabul, Ghazni, Kandahar, Herat and Baluchistan. In return Chandragupta gave five hundred war elephants and their charioteers. The third element of the peace treaty was the marriage. Chandragupta married Seleukos daughter who was eligible for marriage when Chandragupta was 40 years old.

Chandragupta's wife Dhurdhara unknowingly takes poison in her last stage of pregnancy. Chanukya had to cut open her womb and keep the embryonic Bindusara draped in a cord of freshly slaughtered goat until the child was strong enough to survive on his own. That is how he gets the name Bindusara or 'Blood spotted'.

Chandragupta Converts to Jainism

In spite of Megasthanes' service as ambassador to both Chandragupta and Bindusara, no information is available in Indian texts about the transition of power from father to son, why Chandragupta became Jain, and reason for his journey to Shravanabelagola in Mysore District. Probably there was a dispute within the royal family. It appears that the transition took place smoothly and peacefully under the supervision of Chanakya according to Arthasasthra. (It is hard to believe because Chandragupta was an undisputable emperor and he had no rival in the family. It could be his repentance and dispassion towards the worldliness). Jain texts document that Chandragupta followed his Jain guru Bhadrabahu. Due to twelve years of famine in Magadha, Bhadrabahu had migrated to south. Twelve years after the death of Bhadrabahu, Chandragupta died by self-starvation at Shravanabelagola in Mysore district.

Perhaps Chanakya was not happy about these events to see his favorite student to become a Jain sanyasi. He stayed in Pataliputra and continued to offer his advice to Bindusara for fifteen more years until his death. Chanukya's grandson Radhagupta played a key role in helping Ashoka to ascend to the throne.

Bindusara extended his father's empire across the Deccan to include the Mysore region, except the powerful kingdom Kalinga. He maintained relations with his western neighbors, helped Ajivikas. He had several queens and 101 children: the eldest being Sushim and the youngest being Vitashoka (Tissa). According to Theravada tradition, Bindusara's son Ashoka's mother was Dharma, whose father was Ajivika named Janasena. According to Mahayana tradition, Ashoka's mother was Subhadrangi, daughter of a Brahman of Champaran.

There were no other marriage relationships with Greece except Chandragupta's marriage to Seleukos' daughter. Because of her, there was a continued Greco-Persian presence in Bindusara's court.

Ashoka's Endeavour to Spread Moral Law

Ashoka started an endeavor to establish eighty-four thousand stupas, pillars, and monastic institutions in eighty-four thousand places in three years knowing that there are eighty-four thousand discourses on the tenets of Buddhism. Three years may be an exaggeration, but it was indeed a huge project. We can imagine how it might have carried out with a huge army of craftsmen and workforce to exhaust all possible regions, resources, and locations. There is evidence that Ashoka himself went with his royal family to give his messages to be crafted. He wanted them to be heard by all and to be persisted for future generations. So, he advances to build stupas, pillars, and monasteries.

Before Ashoka, no religious structures had been constructed other than wood, mud and plaster. Now, bricks, mortar and stone buildings were soaring up all over the empire. This transformation had a profound effect on Indian landscape whatever Ashoka's intention was.

He needed a written language to convey his message through a medium to survive. Ashoka's own dialect was Prakrit, the Magadhan spoken language and now it was designed in a newly formalized alphabet to write. It was better expressed than Kharoshti script. Since the writing system itself was new in India, it was less perfect and ambiguous, incoherent, and naïve. Ashoka dictated the messages undoubtedly and scribes did not have courage to ask questions. But, without doubt they have come right from the heart of Ashoka.

More important things to observe in his inscriptions are Social Welfare, Non-violence, Respect to Parents, Freedom of Religious Expression, and so on. All human values he wanted to inscribe.

After Ashoka

Buddhist monasteries and stupas were abandoned and depilated due to hostilities from Huns, Muslims, and others in India. Gradually after the decline of Buddhism, some of the most famous temples were converted as Hindu temples with Buddhist structures, often installing images of deities or lingams. Giving historical and archaeological evidence, the author gives four likely examples - selected simply because they come from four corners of the continent: (1) North: the Badarinath shrine, (2) East: the Jagannath temple at Puri, (3) South: the Ayyappa shrine at Sabarimalai and (4) West: Vittala shrine at Padharapur.

1. Badrinath

Buddhist vihara type architecture of the temple and padmasana posture of the deity suggests it was a Buddhist temple before.

2. Jagannath

Jagannath temple has Kalinga Buddhist architecture style.

Vivekananda narrates in his "Lectures from Colombo to Almora" that there was a belief that Jesus Christ came to Jagannath temple to study with the Brahmins. Later Russian archeologists proved that there was not even one Brahmin there in the temple because it was a Buddhist temple at the time of Jesus. Vivekananda writes, "To any man who knows anything about Indian history the very statement proves that the whole thing was fraud, because the temple of Jagannath is an old Buddhist temple. In Jagannath, there was not one Brahmin there then, and yet we are told that Jesus Christ came to study with the Brahmins there." Vivekananda also writes about the degraded Buddhism. It is very sad.

3. Sabarimalai

(a) A Chinese traveler, who visited India in the 6th century (Probably Xuanzang) mentions about a temple of Avalokiteœvara, a Bodhisattva, located in Sabarimala Hill, which at that time known as Churulimala. Based on this theory the Sabarimalai was originally the temple of Avalokiteœvara.

(b) The Mudra displayed by the idol of Ayyappa and the yogic position also may have a connection to Vitarka mudra and Lotus position in which Buddha is depicted.

(c) The chants of 'Sharanam' recited by worshippers of Sabarimalai is identical to the Sharanathrayam (Buddham Sharanam, Sangham Sharanam, etc.) of Buddhist disciples and not used in any other Hindu temples.

4. Pandharapur

Some suggest that Pundalika might have been a Jain or a Buddhist, since Varkari tradition is a combination of Jain and Buddhist morals, and Vithoba is viewed as Vishnu in his form as Buddha.

B. R. Ambedkar, an Indian political leader and Buddhist convert, suggested that the image of Vithoba at Pandharpur was in reality the image of the Buddha.

Ashoka's Rock Edicts - Re# 1

Beloved-of-the-Gods, King Piyadasi, has caused this Dhamma edict to be written. Here in my domain no living beings are to be slaughtered or offered in sacrifice. Nor should festivals be held, for Beloved-of-the-Gods, King Piyadasi, sees much to object to in such festivals, although there are some festivals that Beloved-of-the-Gods, King Piyadasi, does approve of.

Formerly, in the kitchen of Beloved-of-the-Gods, King Piyadasi, hundreds of thousands of animals were killed every day to make curry. But now with the writing of this Dhamma edict only three creatures, two peacocks and a deer are killed, and the deer not always. And in time, not even these three creatures will be killed.

Ashoka's Rock Edicts Re# 2

Everywhere within Beloved-of-the-Gods, King Piyadasi's domain, and among the people beyond the borders, the Cholas, the Pandyas, the Satiyaputras, the Keralaputras, as far as Tamraparni (modern day Tirunelveli) and where the Greek king Antiochos rules, and among the kings who are neighbors of Antiochos, everywhere has Beloved-of-the-Gods, King Piyadasi, made provision for two types of medical treatment: medical treatment for humans and medical treatment for animals. Wherever medical herbs suitable for humans or animals are not available, I have had them imported and grown. Wherever medical roots or fruits are not available I have had them imported and grown. Along roads I have had wells dug and trees planted for the benefit of humans and animals.

Ashoka's Rock Edicts Re# 3

Beloved-of-the-Gods, King Piyadasi, speaks thus: Twelve years after my coronation this has been ordered — Everywhere in my domain the Yuktas, the Rajjukas and the Pradesikas shall go on inspection tours every five years for the purpose of Dhamma instruction and also to conduct other business. Respect for mother and father is good, generosity to friends, acquaintances, relatives, Brahmans and ascetics is good, not killing living beings is good, moderation in spending and moderation in saving is good. The Council shall notify the Yuktas about the observance of these instructions in these very words.

Ashoka's Rock Edicts Re# 4

In the past, for many hundreds of years, killing or harming living beings and improper behavior towards relatives, and improper behavior towards Brahmans and ascetics has increased. But now due to Beloved-of-the-Gods, King Piyadasi's Dhamma practice, the sound of the drum has been replaced by the sound of the Dhamma. The sighting of heavenly cars, auspicious elephants, bodies of fire and other divine sightings has not happened for many hundreds of years. But now because Beloved-of-the-Gods, King Piyadasi promotes restraint in the killing and harming of living beings, proper behavior towards relatives, Brahmans and ascetics, and respect for mother, father and elders, such sightings have increased.

These and many other kinds of Dhamma practice have been encouraged by Beloved-of-the-Gods, King Piyadasi, and he will continue to promote Dhamma practice. And the sons, grandsons and great-grandsons of Beloved-of-the-Gods, King Piyadasi, too will continue to promote Dhamma practice until the end of time; living by Dhamma and virtue, they will instruct in Dhamma. Truly, this is the highest work, to instruct in Dhamma. But practicing the Dhamma cannot be done by one who is devoid of virtue and therefore its promotion and growth is commendable.

This edict has been written so that it may please my successors to devote themselves to promoting these things and not allow them to decline. Beloved-of-the-Gods, King Piyadasi, has had this written twelve years after his coronation.

Ashoka's Rock Edicts Re #5

Beloved-of-the-Gods, King Piyadasi, speaks thus: To do good is difficult. One who does good first does something hard to do. I have done many good deeds, and, if my sons, grandsons and their descendants up to the end of the world act in like manner, they too will do much good. But whoever amongst them neglects this, they will do evil. Truly, it is easy to do evil.

In the past there were no Dhamma Mahamatras but such officers were appointed by me thirteen years after my coronation. Now they work among all religions for the establishment of Dhamma, for the promotion of Dhamma, and for the welfare and happiness of all who are devoted to Dhamma. They work among the Greeks, the Kambojas, the Gandharas, the Rastrikas, the Pitinikas and other peoples on the western borders. They work among soldiers, chiefs, Brahmans, householders, the poor, the aged and those devoted to Dhamma — for their welfare and happiness — so that they may be free from harassment. They (Dhamma Mahamatras) work for the proper treatment of prisoners, towards their unfettering, and if the Mahamatras think, "This one has a family to support," "That one has been bewitched," "This one is old," then they work for the release of such prisoners. They work here, in outlying towns, in the women's quarters belonging to my brothers and sisters, and among my other relatives. They are occupied everywhere. These Dhamma Mahamatras are occupied in my domain among people devoted to Dhamma to determine who is devoted to Dhamma, who is established in Dhamma, and who is generous.

This Dhamma edict has been written on stone so that it might endure long and that my descendants might act in conformity with it.

Ashoka's Rock Edicts Re #6

Beloved-of-the-Gods, King Piyadasi, speaks thus: In the past, state business was not transacted nor were reports delivered to the king at all hours. But now I have given this order, that at any time, whether I am eating, in the women's quarters, the bed chamber, the chariot, the palanquin, in the park or wherever, reporters are to be posted with instructions to report to me the affairs of the people so that I might attend to these affairs wherever I am. And whatever I orally order in connection with donations or proclamations, or when urgent business presses itself on the Mahamatras, if disagreement or debate arises in the Council, then it must be reported to me immediately. This is what I have ordered. I am never content with exerting myself or with dispatching business. Truly, I consider the welfare of all to be my duty, and the root of this is exertion and the prompt dispatch of business. There is no better work than promoting the welfare of all the people and whatever efforts I am making is to repay the debt I owe to all beings to assure their happiness in this life, and attain heaven in the next.

Therefore, this Dhamma edict has been written to last long and that my sons, grandsons and great-grandsons might act in conformity with it for the welfare of the world. However, this is difficult to do without great exertion.

Ashoka's Rock Edicts - Re #7

Beloved-of-the-Gods, King Piyadasi, desires that all religions should reside everywhere, for all of them desire self-control and purity of heart. But people have various desires and various passions, and they may practice all of what they should or only a part of it. But one who receives great gifts yet is lacking in self-control, purity of heart, gratitude and firm devotion, such a person is mean.

Ashoka's Rock Edicts - Re #8

In the past kings used to go out on pleasure tours during which there was hunting and other entertainment. But ten years after Beloved-of-the-Gods had been coronated, he went on a tour to Sambodhi and thus instituted Dhamma tours. During these tours, the following things took place: visits and gifts to Brahmans and ascetics, visits and gifts of gold to the aged, visits to people in the countryside, instructing them in Dhamma, and discussing Dhamma with them as is suitable. It is this that delights Beloved-of-the-Gods, King Piyadasi, and is, as it were, another type of revenue.

Ashoka's Rock Edicts - Re #9

Beloved-of-the-Gods, King Piyadasi, speaks thus: In times of sickness, for the marriage of sons and daughters, at the birth of children, before embarking on a journey, on these and other occasions, people perform various ceremonies. Women in particular perform many vulgar and worthless ceremonies. These types of ceremonies can be performed by all means, but they bear little fruit. What does bear great fruit, however, is the ceremony of the Dhamma. This involves proper behavior towards servants and employees, respect for teachers, restraint towards living beings, and generosity towards ascetics and Brahmans. These and other things constitute the ceremony of the Dhamma. Therefore a father, a son, a brother, a master, a friend, a companion, and even a neighbor should say: "This is good, this is the ceremony that should be performed until its purpose is fulfilled, this I shall do. "Other ceremonies are of doubtful fruit, for they may achieve their purpose, or they may not, and even if they do, it is only in this world. But the ceremony of the Dhamma is timeless. Even if it does not achieve its purpose in this world, it produces great merit in the next, whereas if it does achieve its purpose in this world, one gets great merit both here and there through the ceremony of the Dhamma.

Ashoka's Rock Edicts - Re #10

Beloved-of-the-Gods, King Piyadasi, does not consider glory and fame to be of great account unless they are achieved through having my subjects respect Dhamma and practice Dhamma, both now and in the future. For this alone does Beloved-of-the-Gods, King Piyadasi, desire glory and fame. And whatever efforts Beloved-of-the-Gods, King Piyadasi, is making, all of that is only for the welfare of the people in the next world, and that they will have little evil. And being without merit is evil. This is difficult for either a humble person or a great person to do except with great effort, and by giving up other interests. In fact, it may be even more difficult for a great person to do.

Ashoka's Rock Edicts - Re #11

Beloved-of-the-Gods, King Piyadasi, speaks thus: There is no gift like the gift of the Dhamma, no acquaintance like acquaintance with Dhamma, (no distribution like) distribution of Dhamma, and no kinship like kinship through Dhamma. And it consists of this: proper behavior towards servants and employees, respect for mother and father, generosity to friends, companions, relations, Brahmans and ascetics, and not killing living beings. Therefore, a father, a son, a brother, a master, a friend, a companion or a neighbor should say: "This is good, this should be done." One benefits in this world and gains great merit in the next by giving the gift of the Dhamma.

Ashoka's Rock Edicts - Re #12

Beloved-of-the-Gods, King Piyadasi, honors both ascetics and the householders of all religions, and he honors them with gifts and honors of various kinds. But Beloved-of-the-Gods, King Piyadasi, does not value gifts and honors as much as he values this — that there should be growth in the essentials of all religions. Growth in essentials can be done in different ways, but all of them have as their root restraint in speech, that is, not praising one's own religion, or condemning the religion of others without good cause. And if there is cause for criticism, it should be done in a mild way. But it is better to honor other religions for this reason. By so doing, one's own religion benefits, and so do other religions, while doing otherwise harms one's own religion and the religions of others. Whoever praises his own religion, due to excessive devotion, and condemns others with the thought "Let me glorify my own religion," only harms his own religion. Therefore contact (between religions) is good. One should listen to and respect the doctrines professed by others. Beloved-of-the-Gods, King Piyadasi, desires that all should be well-learned in the good doctrines of other religions.

Those who are content with their own religion should be told this: Beloved-of-the-Gods, King Piyadasi, does not value gifts and honors as much as he values that there should be growth in the essentials of all religions. And to this end many are working — Dhamma Mahamatras, Mahamatras in charge of the women's quarters, officers in charge of outlying areas, and other such officers. And the fruit of this is that one's own religion grows and the Dhamma is illuminated also.

Ashoka's Rock Edicts - Re #13

Beloved-of-the-Gods, King Piyadasi, conquered the Kalingas eight years after his coronation. One hundred and fifty thousand were deported, one hundred thousand were killed and many more died (from other causes). After the Kalingas had been conquered, Beloved-of-the-Gods came to feel a strong inclination towards the Dhamma, a love for the Dhamma and for instruction in Dhamma. Now Beloved-of-the-Gods feels deep remorse for having conquered the Kalingas.

Indeed, Beloved-of-the-Gods is deeply pained by the killing, dying and deportation that take place when an unconquered country is conquered. But Beloved-of-the-Gods is pained even more by this — that Brahmans, ascetics, and householders of different religions who live in those countries, and who are respectful to superiors, to mother and father, to elders, and who behave properly and have strong loyalty towards friends, acquaintances, companions, relatives, servants and employees — that they are injured, killed or separated from their loved ones. Even those who are not affected by all this suffer when they see friends, acquaintances, companions and relatives affected. These misfortunes befall all (as a result of war), and this pains Beloved-of-the-Gods.

There is no country, except among the Greeks, where these two groups, Brahmans and ascetics, are not found, and there is no country where people are not devoted to one or another religion. Therefore, the killing, death or deportation of a hundredth, or even a thousandth part of those who died during the conquest of Kalinga now pains Beloved-of-the-Gods. Now Beloved-of-the-Gods thinks that even those who do wrong should be forgiven where forgiveness is possible.

Even the forest people, who live in Beloved-of-the-Gods' domain, are entreated and reasoned with to act properly. They are told that despite his remorse Beloved-of-the-Gods has the power to punish them if necessary, so that they should be ashamed of their wrong and not be killed. Truly, Beloved-of-the-Gods desires non-injury, restraint and impartiality to all beings, even where wrong has been done.

Now it is conquest by Dhamma that Beloved-of-the-Gods considers to be the best conquest. And it (conquest by Dhamma) has been won here, on the borders, even six hundred yojanas away, where the Greek king Antiochos rules, beyond there where the four kings named Ptolemy, Antigonos, Magas and Alexander rule, likewise in the south among the Cholas, the Pandyas, and as far as Tamraparni. Here in the king's domain among the Greeks, the Kambojas, the Nabhakas, the Nabhapamkits, the Bhojas, the Pitinikas, the Andhras and the Palidas, everywhere people are following Beloved-of-the-Gods' instructions in Dhamma. Even where Beloved-of-the-Gods' envoys have not been, these people too, having heard of the practice of Dhamma and the ordinances and instructions in Dhamma given by Beloved-of-the-Gods, are following it and will continue to do so. This conquest has been won everywhere, and it gives great joy — the joy which only conquest by Dhamma can give. But even this joy is of little consequence. Beloved-of-the-Gods consider the great fruit to be experienced in the next world to be more important.

I have had this Dhamma edict written so that my sons and great-grandsons may not consider making new conquests, or that if military conquests are made, that they be done with forbearance and light punishment, or better still, that they consider making conquest by Dhamma only, for that bears fruit in this world and the next. May all their intense devotion be given to this which has a result in this world and the next.

Ashoka's Rock Edicts - Re #14

Beloved-of-the-Gods, King Piyadasi, has had these Dhamma edicts written in brief, in medium length, and in extended form. Not all of them occur everywhere, for my domain is vast, but much has been written, and I will have still more written. And also there are some subjects here that have been spoken of again and again because of their sweetness, and so that the people may act in accordance with them. If some things written are incomplete, this is because of the locality, or in consideration of the object, or due to the fault of the scribe.

Kalinga Rock Edicts - Kre #1

Beloved-of-the-Gods says that the Mahamatras of Tosali who are judicial officers in the city are to be told this:[30] I wish to see that everything I consider to be proper is carried out in the right way. And I consider instructing you to be the best way of accomplishing this. I have placed you over many thousands of people that you may win the people's affection.

All men are my children. What I desire for my own children, and I desire their welfare and happiness both in this world and the next, that I desire for all men. You do not understand to what extent I desire this, and if some of you do understand, you do not understand the full extent of my desire.

You must attend to this matter. While being completely law-abiding, some people are imprisoned, treated harshly and even killed without cause so that many people suffer. Therefore your aim should be to act with impartiality. It is because of these things — envy, anger, cruelty, hate, indifference, laziness or tiredness — that such a thing does not happen. Therefore your aim should be: "May these things not be in me." And the root of this is non-anger and patience. Those who are bored with the administration of justice will not be promoted; (those who are not) will move upwards and be promoted. Whoever among you understands this should say to his colleagues: "See that you do your duty properly. Such and such are Beloved-of-the-Gods' instructions." Great fruit will result from doing your duty, while failing in it will result in gaining neither heaven nor the king's pleasure. Failure in duty on your part will not please me. But done properly, it will win you heaven and you will be discharging your debts to me.

This edict is to be listened to on Tisa day, between Tisa days, and on other suitable occasions, it should be listened to even by a single person. Acting thus, you will be doing your duty.

This edict has been written for the following purpose: that the judicial officers of the city may strive to do their duty and that the people under them might not suffer unjust imprisonment or harsh treatment. To achieve this, I will send out Mahamatras every five years who are not harsh or cruel, but who are merciful and who can ascertain if the judicial officers have understood my purpose and are acting according to my instructions. Similarly, from Ujjayini, the prince will send similar persons with the same purpose without allowing three years to elapse. Likewise from Takhasila also. When these Mahamatras go on tours of inspection each year, then without neglecting their normal duties, they will ascertain if judicial officers are acting according to the king's instructions.

Kalinga Rock Edicts - Kre #2

Beloved-of-the-Gods speaks thus: This royal order is to be addressed to the Mahamatras at Samapa. I wish to see that everything I consider to be proper is carried out in the right way. And I consider instructing you to be the best way of accomplishing this. All men are my children. What I desire for my own children, and I desire their welfare and happiness both in this world and the next, that I desire for all men.

The people of the unconquered territories beyond the borders might think: "What is the king's intentions towards us?" My only intention is that they live without fear of me, that they may trust me and that I may give them happiness, not sorrow. Furthermore, they should understand that the king will forgive those who can be forgiven, and that he wishes to encourage them to practice Dhamma so that they may attain happiness in this world and the next. I am telling you this so that I may discharge the debts I owe, and that in instructing you, that you may know that my vow and my promise will not be broken. Therefore, acting in this way, you should perform your duties and assure them (the people beyond the borders) that: "The king is like a father. He feels towards us as he feels towards himself. We are to him like his own children."

By instructing you and informing you of my vow and my promise I shall be applying myself in complete fullness to achieving this object. You are able indeed to inspire them with confidence and to secure their welfare and happiness in this world and the next, and by acting thus, you will attain heaven as well as discharge the debts you owe to me. And so that the

Mahamatras can devote themselves at all times to inspiring the border areas with confidence and encouraging them to practice Dhamma, this edict has been written here.

This edict is to be listened to every four months on Tisa day, between Tisa days, and on other suitable occasions, it should be listened to even by a single person. Acting thus, you will be doing your duty.

The Seven Pillar Edicts - Pe #1

Beloved-of-the-Gods speaks thus: This Dhamma edict was written twenty-six years after my coronation. Happiness in this world and the next is difficult to obtain without much love for the Dhamma, much self-examination, much respect, much fear (of evil), and much enthusiasm. But through my instruction this regard for Dhamma and love of Dhamma has grown day by day, and will continue to grow. And my officers of high, low and middle rank are practicing and conforming to Dhamma, and are capable of inspiring others to do the same. Mahamatras in border areas are doing the same. And these are my instructions: to protect with Dhamma, to make happiness through Dhamma and to guard with Dhamma.

Pillar Edicts - Pe #2

Beloved-of-the-Gods, King Piyadasi, speaks thus: Dhamma is good, but what constitutes Dhamma? (It includes) little evil, much good, kindness, generosity, truthfulness and purity. I have given the gift of sight in various ways. To two-footed and four-footed beings, to birds and aquatic animals, I have given various things including the gift of life. And many other good deeds have been done by me.

This Dhamma edict has been written that people might follow it and it might endure for a long time. And the one who follows it properly will do something good.

Pillar Edicts - Pe #3

Beloved-of-the-Gods, King Piyadasi, speaks thus: People see only their good deeds saying, "I have done this good deed." But they do not see their evil deeds saying, "I have done this evil deed" or "This is called evil." But this (tendency) is difficult to see. One should think like this: "It is these things that lead to evil, to violence, to cruelty, anger, pride and jealousy. Let me not ruin myself with these things." And further, one should think: "This leads to happiness in this world and the next."

Pillar Edicts - Pe #4

Beloved-of-the-Gods speaks thus: This Dhamma edict was written twenty-six years after my coronation. My Rajjukas are working among the people, among many hundreds of thousands of people. The hearing of petitions and the administration of justice has been left to them so that they can do their duties confidently and fearlessly and so that they can work for the welfare, happiness and benefit of the people in the country. But they should remember what causes happiness and sorrow, and being themselves devoted to Dhamma, they should encourage the people in the country (to do the same), that they may attain happiness in this world and the next. These Rajjukas are eager to serve me. They also obey other officers who know my desires, who instruct the Rajjukas so that they can please me. Just as a person feels confident having entrusted his child to an expert nurse thinking: "The nurse will keep my child well," even so, the Rajjukas have been appointed by me for the welfare and happiness of the people in the country.

The hearing of petitions and the administration of justice have been left to the Rajjukas so that they can do their duties unperturbed, fearlessly and confidently. It is my desire that there should be uniformity in law and uniformity in sentencing. I even go this far, to grant a three-day stay for those in prison who have been tried and sentenced to death. During this time their relatives can make appeals to have the prisoners' lives spared. If there is none to appeal on their behalf, the prisoners can give gifts in order to make merit for the next world, or observe fasts. Indeed, it is my wish that in this way, even if a prisoner's time is limited, he can prepare for the next world, and that people's Dhamma practice, self-control and generosity may grow.

Pillar Edicts - Pe #5

Beloved-of-the-Gods, King Piyadasi, speaks thus: Twenty-six years after my coronation various animals were declared to be protected — parrots, mainas, aruna, ruddy geese, wild ducks, nandimukhas, gelatas, bats, queen ants, terrapins, boneless fish, vedareyaka, gangapuputaka, sankiya fish, tortoises, porcupines, squirrels, deer, bulls, okapinda, wild asses, wild pigeons, domestic pigeons and all four-footed creatures that are neither useful nor edible. Those nanny goats, ewes and sows which are with young or giving milk to their young are protected, and so are young ones less than six months old. Cocks are not to be caponized, husks hiding living beings are not to be burnt and forests are not to be burnt either without reason or to kill creatures. One animal is not to be fed to another. On the three Caturmasis, the three days of Tisa and during the fourteenth and fifteenth of the Uposatha, fish are protected and not to be sold. During these days animals are not to be killed in the elephant reserves or the fish reserves either. On the eighth of every fortnight, on the fourteenth and fifteenth, on Tisa, Punarvasu, the three Caturmasis and other auspicious days, bulls are not to be castrated, billy goats, rams, boars and other animals that are usually castrated are not to be. On Tisa, Punarvasu, Caturmasis and the fortnight of Caturmasis, horses and bullocks are not be branded.

In the twenty-six years since my coronation prisoners have been given amnesty on twenty-five occasions.

Pillar Edicts - Pe #6

Beloved-of-the-Gods speaks thus: Twelve years after my coronation I started to have Dhamma edicts written for the welfare and happiness of the people, and so that not transgressing them they might grow in the Dhamma. Thinking: "How can the welfare and happiness of the people be secured?" I give attention to my relatives, to those dwelling near and those dwelling far, so I can lead them to happiness and then I act accordingly. I do the same for all groups. I have honored all religions with various honors. But I consider it best to meet with people personally.

This Dhamma edict was written twenty-six years after my coronation.

Pillar Edicts - Pe #7

Beloved-of-the-Gods speaks thus: In the past kings desired that the people might grow through the promotion of the Dhamma. But despite this, people did not grow through the promotion of the Dhamma. Beloved-of-the-Gods, King Piyadasi, said concerning this: "It occurs to me that in the past kings desired that the people might grow through the promotion of the Dhamma. But despite this, people did not grow through the promotion of the Dhamma. Now how can the people be encouraged to follow it? How can the people be encouraged to grow through the promotion of the Dhamma? How can I elevate them by promoting the Dhamma?" Beloved-of-the-Gods, King Piyadasi, further said concerning this: "It occurs to me that I shall have proclamations on Dhamma announced and instruction on Dhamma given. When people hear these, they will follow them, elevate themselves and grow considerably through the promotion of the Dhamma." It is for this purpose that proclamations on Dhamma have been announced and various instructions on Dhamma have been given and that officers who work among many promote and explain them in detail. The Rajjukas who work among hundreds of thousands of people have likewise been ordered: "In this way and that encourage those who are devoted to Dhamma." Beloved-of-the-Gods speaks thus: "Having this object in view, I have set up Dhamma pillars, appointed Dhamma Mahamatras, and announced Dhamma proclamations."

Beloved-of-the-Gods, King Piyadasi, says: Along roads I have had banyan trees planted so that they can give shade to animals and men, and I have had mango groves planted. At intervals of eight krosas, I have had wells dug, rest-houses built, and in various places, I have had watering-places made for the use of animals and men. But these are but minor achievements. Such things to make the people happy have been done by former kings. I have done these things for this purpose, that the people might practice the Dhamma.

Beloved-of-the-Gods, King Piyadasi, speaks thus: My Dhamma Mahamatras too are occupied with various good works among the ascetics and householders of all religions. I have ordered that they should be occupied with the affairs of the Sangha. I have also ordered that they should be occupied with the affairs of the Brahmans and the Ajivikas. I have ordered that they be occupied with the Niganthas. In fact, I have ordered that different Mahamatras be occupied with the particular affairs of all different religions. And my Dhamma Mahamatras likewise are occupied with these and other religions.

Beloved-of-the-Gods, King Piyadasi, speaks thus: These and other principal officers are occupied with the distribution of gifts, mine as well as those of the queens. In my women's quarters, they organize various charitable activities here and in the provinces. I have also ordered my sons and the sons of other queens to distribute gifts so that noble deeds of Dhamma and the practice of Dhamma may be promoted. And noble deeds of Dhamma and the practice of Dhamma consist of having kindness, generosity, truthfulness, purity, gentleness and goodness increase among the people.

Beloved-of-the-Gods, King Piyadasi, speaks thus: Whatever good deeds have been done by me, those the people accept and those they follow. Therefore they have progressed and will continue to progress by being respectful to mother and father, respectful to elders, by courtesy to the aged and proper behavior towards Brahmans and ascetics, towards the poor and distressed, and even towards servants and employees.

Beloved-of-the-Gods, King Piyadasi, speaks thus: This progress among the people through Dhamma has been done by two means, by Dhamma regulations and by persuasion. Of these, Dhamma regulation is of little effect, while persuasion has much more effect. The Dhamma regulations I have given are that various animals must be protected. And I have given many other Dhamma regulations also. But it is by persuasion that progress among the people through Dhamma has had a greater effect in respect of harmlessness to living beings and non-killing of living beings.

Concerning this, Beloved-of-the-Gods says: Wherever there are stone pillars or stone slabs, there this Dhamma edict is to be engraved so that it may long endure. It has been engraved so that it may endure as long as my sons and great-grandsons live and as long as the sun and the moon shine, and so that people may practice it as instructed. For by practicing it happiness will be attained in this world and the next.

This Dhamma edict has been written by me twenty-seven years after my coronation.

The Minor Pillar Edicts - Mpe #1

Twenty years after his coronation, Beloved-of-the-Gods, King Piyadasi, visited this place and worshipped because here the Buddha, the sage of the Sakyans, was born. He had a stone figure and a pillar set up and because the Lord was born here, the village of Lumbini was exempted from tax and required to pay only one eighth of the produce.

The Minor Pillar Edicts - Mpe #2

Beloved-of-the-Gods commands: The Mahamatras at Kosambi (are to be told: Whoever splits the Sangha) which is now united, is not to be admitted into the Sangha. Whoever, whether monk or nun, splits the Sangha is to be made to wear white clothes and to reside somewhere other than in a monastery.

Minor Rock Edicts - Mre #1

Beloved-of-the-Gods speaks thus: It is now more than two and a half years since I became a lay-disciple, but until now I have not been very zealous. But now that I have visited the Sangha for more than a year, I have become very zealous. Now the people in India who have not associated with the gods do so. This is the result of zeal and it is not just the great who can do this. Even the humble, if they are zealous, can attain heaven. And this proclamation has been made with this aim. Let both humble and great be zealous, let even those on the borders know and let zeal last long. Then this zeal will increase, it will greatly increase, it will increase up to one-and-a-half times. This message has been proclaimed two hundred and fifty-six times by the king while on tour.

Minor Rock Edicts - Mre #2

Beloved-of-the-Gods speaks thus: Father and mother should be respected and so should elders, kindness to living beings should be made strong and the truth should be spoken. In these ways, the Dhamma should be promoted. Likewise, a teacher should be honored by his pupil and proper manners should be shown towards relations. This is an ancient rule that conduces to long life. Thus should one act. Written by the scribe Chapala.

Minor Rock Edicts - Mre #3

Piyadasi, King of Magadha, saluting the Sangha and wishing them good health and happiness, speaks thus: You know, reverend sirs, how great my faith in the Buddha, the Dhamma and Sangha is. Whatever, reverend sirs, has been spoken by Lord Buddha, all that is well-spoken. I consider it proper, reverend sirs, to advice on how the good Dhamma should last long.

These Dhamma texts — Extracts from the Discipline, the Noble Way of Life, the Fears to Come, the Poem on the Silent Sage, the Discourse on the Pure Life, Upatisa's Questions, and the Advice to Rahula which was spoken by the Buddha concerning false speech — these Dhamma texts, reverend sirs, I desire that all the monks and nuns may constantly listen to and remember.[38] Likewise the laymen and laywomen. I have had this written that you may know my intentions.

Jawaharlal Nehru considered Ashoka was equal to Jesus. Indeed, he was equal to Jesus and Buddha.

Supplement - 2

Jawaharlal Nehru and his Discovery of India

Nehru wrote the book "Discovery of India" in Ahmednagar jail during the Independence Movement in India gathering material from the letters he wrote to his daughter Indira Gandhi which was published as '*Glimpses of World History.*' It was an attempt to discover the past in its relation to the present. Behind that writing, there was a quest for knowledge and yearning for discovery.

In fact, Nehru narrates the history of the world in this fascinating story of India from ancient times of the Vedas to the on-going Second World War.

Nehru was educated at home by private governesses and tutors. His tutor Ferdinand T. Brooks initiated interest in science and theosophy. Then he was introduced into the Theosophical Society at the age of thirteen by Annie Besant. Theosophy made him study the scriptures of Buddhism and Hinduism. But Nehru was not interested in theosophy and left the society.

Nehru went to Cambridge and graduated in Natural Science. During this time, he also studied politics, economics, history, and literature. He was influenced by Karl Marx and Lenin and they helped him to view history in a different light.

Western educated Jawaharlal Nehru had an intense love and hope for India. Although he took intense pride in India's rich heritage, he always emphasized that we cannot live in the past. His dreams and hopes for India were a forward looking, modern and tolerant nation promoting peace and cooperation in the world.

He writes how he saw India returning from England. Even though he loved India and it was in his blood, he approached her as an alien critic, full of dislikes for the present and for many of the relics of the past he saw. He was eager and anxious to change her outlook and appearance and wanted to give her the garb of modernity.

He saw a stillness and everlastingness about the past and how it maintains its dignity unaffected by the storms and upheavals of the present. He wanted to scrap a great deal from Indian life to give a modern outlook. But he faced a great problem in doing so. He started to think if India was able to continue this cultured existence for thousands of years, it may possess something very vital and long-lasting virtue, something that was worthwhile. What was this something?

He writes, "The roots of the present lay in the past and so I made voyages of discovery into the past, ever seeking a clue in it, if any such existed, to the understanding of the present."

Nehru wanted to know not only about a few centuries of Indian history, but he wanted to take a panoramic view through the ages from the Indus Civilization to the present conditions of history.

So, he started his investigation standing on the mounds of Mohenjo-Daro in the Indus Valley. Around him there were houses and streets of the ancient city that is said to have existed over five thousand years ago. Even 5000 years ago, it was considered as an old and well-developed civilization.

Then he visited old monuments and ruins of Ajanta, Ellora, the Elephanta Caves, and other places. He also saw the lovely buildings of a later age in Agra and Delhi, where every stone told its story of India's past.

At Sarnath, he envisioned Buddha preaching his first sermon and some of his words came like a distant echo. Ashoka's pillars of stone with their inscriptions spoke to him in their brilliant language and Nehru wondered how Ashoka, though an emperor, was greater than any king or emperor.

He realized that unless there are vital links between the past and the present, it is not a life. It is a kind of art without the passion and the urge to action. He writes, "Without that passion and urge, there is a gradual oozing out of hope and vitality, a settling down on lower levels of existence, a slow merging into non-existence. We become prisoners of the past and some part of its immobility sticks to us."

He noticed that the finer physical types were among the upper castes, who were a little better off in the economic sense. He questioned, "Sometimes, as I was passing along a country road, or through a village, I would start with surprise on seeing a fine type of man, or a beautiful woman, who reminded me of some painting of ancient times. And I wondered how the type endured and continued through ages, in spite of all the horror and misery that India had gone through. What could we not do with these people under better conditions and with greater opportunities opening out to them?"

In his book he writes the impact of Hinduism, Buddhism, and Jainism in India.

He writes about the cultural exchange between India and China, the works of Kumarajiva in 401 AD, Nagarjuna, and Jinagupta, 600 CE. Jinagupta went to China and also translated thirty-seven original Sanskrit works into Chinese. Among the best known Chinese who left records of their journeys to India are Fa Hien (or Fa Hsien), Sung Yun, Hsuan-Tsang (or Chwen Chuang), and I-Tsing (or Yi-Tsing). Fa Hien was a disciple of Kumarajiva in China.

Nehru found an interesting Tamil inscription of 1088 CE. which refers to a 'Corporation of the Fifteen Hundred.' Obviously, this was a union of traders who were described in the inscription as 'brave men, born to wander over many countries ever since the beginning of the Krita age, penetrating the regions of the six continents by land and water routes, and dealing in various animals such as horses, elephants, and precious stones, perfumes, and drugs, either wholesale or in retail.'

Those traders had connections with Malay Peninsula, Cambodia, Malaysia, and Sumatra. At the peak of its power it included Malaya, Ceylon, Sumatra, part of Java, Borneo, Celebes, the Philippines, part of Formosa, and Siam. Jayavarman united smaller states in the ninth century and built the Cambodian Empire with its capital at Angkor. Cambodia's great builders were Jayavarman, Yashovarman, Indravarman, and Suryavarman.

He briefly writes about Aryabhata, 476 AD, Bhaskara I 522 AD, and Brahmagupta 628 CE. Brahmagupta was a famous astronomer and mathematician who specified the rules for applying *shunya* or zero.

He proudly presents that Algebra and Zero originated from ancient India. Zero is defined as a - a = 0; a + 0 = a; a - 0 = a; ax0=0; and a 0 becomes infinity.

He elaborately discusses Akbar. He describes Akbar was a symbol of India's unity because he tried to unify all religious people despite Muslim opposition.

He identifies the relationship between Iran and India. He writes that this relationship goes back even to the beginning of Indo-Aryan civilization because it was out of some common stock the Indo-Aryans and the ancient Iranians separated and took different ways. Their old religions and languages also had a common background. The Vedic religion had much in common with Zoroastrianism, and Vedic Sanskrit and the old Pahlavi of Avesta closely resemble each other. Classical Sanskrit and Persian developed separately but many of their root-words were common. Persian art appears to be connected with the soil and scenery of Iran. The Indo-Aryan artistic tradition and ideals grew out of the snow-covered mountains, rich forests, and great rivers of north India.

Nehru compares Ancient India and Greece in many ways and finds out that even though they are so different, they have so much in common. He believes that their background of life was very similar. He mentioned that the Peloponnesian war might in some way be compared to the Mahabharata war. But Greece never recovered from these shocks, although Greek civilization flourished in the Mediterranean and influenced Rome and Europe. In India there was a remarkable recovery after the Mahabharata war, and thousand years from the Epic Period and Buddha onwards there was a full of creative energy. Innumerable great names in philosophy, literature, drama, mathematics, and the arts continued.

In spite of all her past glory, greatness and stability, he could not tolerate to find India as a slave country, an appendage of Britain. His desire was to revitalize India again.

He writes, "These journeys and visits of mine, with the background of my reading, gave me an insight into the past. In this and other ways I tried to discover India, the India of the past and of the present."

He describes and writes about the ghastly famine in India. He remembers how warm-hearted men and women in England and America came to India's help in spite of governmental obstruction, and China even though it was poor in its own resources, its own difficulties, and having bitter experience for itself of famine how it gave generous help to India.

His wife Kamala Nehru was in the Sanatorium in Germany during the Nazi period. When Kamala Nehru's condition was serious, British government released Nehru from prison to be with his wife. He stayed in Germany until Kamala breathed her last.

When Nehru was in Germany, he was invited by Nazi government to visit Mussolini even after knowing Nehru's opposition to Nazism. He declined the invitation with thanks. Later, when he was planning to return to India, he received a letter from Nazi government to meet Mussolini second time. Again, he rejected the invitation even though he was curious to know what kind of man Mussolini was. While he landed in Rome on the way to India, a high official handed him a letter from Mussolini fixing that evening for the interview for the third time. All that Mussolini wanted to do was to shake hands with Nehru and to personally convey his condolences to his wife Kamala's death. After arguing stressfully for a full hour, he decided not to go for the interview. He sent a letter to Mussolini expressing his regret and thanking him for his message of sympathy.

Nehru regretfully writes about Jinnah's role in the Independence movement. He understood that different persons take different views of truth, and each individual is powerfully influenced by his own background, training, and impulses. But truth is at least for an individual what he himself feels and knows to be true. He painfully narrates Jinnah's separation from Congress, "He left the Congress not because of any difference of opinion on the Hindu-Moslem question but because he could not adapt himself to the new and more advanced ideology, and even more so because he disliked the crowds of ill-dressed people, talking in Hindustani, who filled the Congress. His idea of politics was of a superior variety, more suited to the legislative chamber or to a committee-room. For some years he felt completely out of the picture and even decided to leave India for good. He settled down in England and spent several years there."

When Nehru was a Congress president, he wrote to Mr. Jinnah on several occasions and requested him to tell exactly what he would like Congress to do. After a long hesitation Jinnah said he will return to India only after Congress recognized publicly that the Moslem League was the sole representative organization of the Moslems of India, and the Congress is purely Hindu organization. It was an unsolvable situation because

Congress could not ignore many other Moslem organizations in the country, which were strongly associated with them.

Mr. Jinnah's demand was based on two nations, Hindu and Moslem. From Mr. Jinnah's two-nation theory the conception of Pakistan was developed.

Nehru writes several things about political issues and British rule in this book. Most importantly our politicians should read this book to understand how much struggle our leaders have gone through to free India.

He writes, "Though books, old monuments and past cultural achievements helped to produce some understanding of India, they did not satisfy me or give me the answer I was looking for."

What Nehru was looking for and what were his ambitions will be seen? As he said before, "The roots of the present lay in the past and so I made voyages of discovery into the past, ever seeking a clue in it, if any such existed, to the understanding of the present", he made the voyage and realized the strength and weaknesses of India.

He recognized the human relationships were not ignored in the old and wise civilizations of India and China. With all their faults, they developed patterns of social behavior which indeed gave poise to the individual. He noticed that poise was not in evidence in India today.

He believed that in the past, there was an urge to adventure and the overflowing of life, which led to distant colonization and the transmission of Indian culture in far lands. All these disappeared and narrow orthodoxy taboos, even the crossing of the seas, emerged. A rational spirit of inquiry, so evident in earlier times, which might have led to the further growth of science, is replaced by irrationalism and a blind idolatry of the past. Indian life became a sluggish stream, living in the past, moving slowly through the accumulations of dead centuries. It is not surprising that in this condition of mental stupor and physical weariness, India deteriorated and remained rigid and immobile, while other parts of the world marched ahead.

He did not believe in the negation or abstention from life. He loved life and that very desire led him to play with life to look over its boundaries.

Any religion as practiced and accepted even by thinking minds did not attract Nehru. It seemed to be closely associated with superstitious practices and rigid beliefs based on uncritical dependence on the supernatural.

But he accepted the fact that religion has provided some inner need of human nature. It has produced many fine types of men and women. It has given a set of values to human life, and though some of these values have no application today are still the foundation of morality and ethics. At the same time, it has produced intolerant, narrow-minded, cruel tyrants also. Ethical approach to life strongly appealed to him.

He observed that Vedas are the unfolding of the human mind in the earliest stages of thought. He writes, "And what a wonderful mind it was! The Vedas (from the root *vid,* to know) were simply meant to be a collection of the existing knowledge of the day. There is no idolatry in them, no temples for the gods. The vitality and affirmation of life pervading them are extraordinary. The early Vedic Aryans were so full of the zest for life that they paid little attention to the soul."

He observed Buddhism and Jainism emphasized the abstention from life. Perhaps the ideas of renunciation and life-negation are caused by a feeling of frustration due to political and economic factors.

He thought that if people believe Mythology in the real content of these stories, the whole thing was absurd and ridiculous. But if people stop believing and see in a different way, they appear in a new light, a new beauty, a wonderful flowering of a rich imagination, and full of human lessons. No one believes in the stories of Greek gods and goddesses. Believing in them is a burden and often we miss their beauty. Indian mythology is richer, vaster, exceptionally beautiful, and full of meaning. He wondered what type of men and women they were who gave shape to these brilliant dreams and lovely fancies and out of what gold mine of thought and imagination they dug them.

He warns, "Looking at scriptures as a product of the human mind, we have to remember the age in which it was written, the environment and mental climate in which it grew, the vast distance in time and thought and experience that separates it from us. We have to forget the trappings of ritual and religious usage in which it is wrapped and remember the social background in which it expanded."

The Upanishads are instincts with a spirit of inquiry, of mental adventure, of a passion for finding out the truth about things. Even though the search for this truth is not by the methods of modern science, there is an element of the scientific method in the approach. He understood that the dominating characteristic of the Upanishads is the dependence on truth. And the famous invocation is for light and understanding: 'Lead me from the unreal to the real! Lead me from darkness to light! Lead me from death to immortality.'

He writes, "Therefore with the temper and approach of science, allied to philosophy, and with reverence for all that lies beyond, that we must face life. A blind reverence for the past is bad and so also is contempt for it, for no future can be founded on either of these. The present and the future inevitably grow out of the past and bear its stamp, and to forget this is to build without foundations and to cut off the roots of national growth.'

He says that we have to get rid of that narrowing religious outlook, that obsession with the supernatural and metaphysical speculations, that loosening of the mind's discipline in religious ceremonial and mystical emotionalism, which come in the way of our understanding ourselves and the world. We have to come to grips with the present, this life, this world, this nature which surrounds us in its infinite variety. Some Hindus talk of going back to the Vedas, some Moslems dream of an Islamic theocracy. He reminds that it is all idle fancies for there is no going back to the past; there is no turning back even if this was thought desirable. There is only one-way traffic in Time.

He urges that India must therefore lessen her religiosity and turn to science. She must get rid of the exclusiveness in thought and social habit which has become a prison to her, stunting her spirit and preventing growth. The idea of ceremonial purity has erected barriers against social interaction and narrowed the sphere of social action. The day-to-day religion of the orthodox Hindu is more concerned with what to eat and what not to eat, who to eat with and from whom to keep away, than with spiritual values. The rules and regulations of the kitchen dominate his social life. The Moslem is fortunately free from these inhibitions, but he has his own narrow codes and ceremonials, a routine which he rigorously follows, forgetting the lesson of brotherhood which his religion taught him. His view of life is, perhaps, even more limited and sterile than the Hindu view, though the average Hindu to-day is a poor representative of the latter view, for he has lost that traditional freedom of thought and the background that enriches life in many ways.

Nehru insists that we should search for wisdom and knowledge and friendship and comradeship wherever we can find them, and cooperate with others in common tasks, but we are no suppliants for others' favors and patronage. Thus, we shall remain true Indians and Asiatic, and become at the same time good internationalists and world citizens.

He inspires Indians to think critically and act intelligently. Here are some quotes, which describe Nehru's views on Religion, Philosophy, and Science. He sums up all three subjects as follows:

"Religions have helped greatly in the development of humanity. They have laid down values and standards and have pointed out principles for the guidance of human life. But with all the good they have done, they have also tried to imprison truth in set forms and dogmas and encouraged ceremonials and practices which soon lose all their original meaning and become mere routine. While impressing upon man the awe and mystery of the unknown that surrounds him on all sides, they have discouraged him from trying to understand not only the unknown but what might come in the way of social effort. Instead of encouraging curiosity and thought, they have preached a philosophy of submission to nature, to established churches, to the prevailing Social order, and to everything that is. The belief in a supernatural agency which ordains everything has led to a certain irresponsibility on the social plane, and emotion and sentimentality have taken the place of reasoned thought and inquiry. Religion, though it has undoubtedly brought comfort to innumerable human beings and stabilized society by its values, has checked the tendency to change and progress inherent in human society.

"Philosophy has avoided many of these pitfalls and encouraged thought and inquiry. But it has usually lived in its ivory tower cut off from life and its day-to-day problems, concentrating on ultimate purposes and failing to link them with the life of man. Logic and reason were its guides and they took it far in many directions, but that logic was too much the product of the mind and unconcerned with fact.

"Science ignored the ultimate purposes and looked at fact alone. It made the world jump forward with a leap, built up a glittering civilization, opened up innumerable avenues for the growth of knowledge, and added to the power of man to such an extent that for the first time it was possible to conceive that man could triumph over and shape his physical environment. Man became almost a geological force, changing the face of the planet earth chemically, physically, and in many other ways. Yet when this sorry scheme of things entirely seemed to be in his grasp, to mold it nearer to the heart's desire, there was some essential lack and some vital element was missing. There was no knowledge of ultimate purposes and not even an understanding of the immediate purpose, for science had told us nothing about any purpose in life. Nor did man, so powerful in his control of nature, have the power to control himself, and the monster he had created ran amok. Perhaps new developments in biology, psychology, and similar sciences, and the interpretation of biology and physics, may help man to understand and control himself more than he has done in the past. Or, before any such advances influence human life sufficiently, man may destroy the civilization he has built and have to start anew." (I wonder what he would say about the advancement of science today.)

A Biography of World Civilizations

A Biography of World Civilizations

Volume - III

Europe, The Middle East , Maya and Aztec, United States of America

Jaya S. Nagendra

GYAN

Published, 2021
Published by

Gyan Publishing House
5, Ansari Road
Daryaganj, New Delhi-110002
Phone: 011-47034999, 9811692060
www.gyanbooks.com
E-mail: books@gyanbooks.com

Printed at: Gyan Press, Delhi.

Cataloging in Publication Data—DK
Courtesy: D.K. Agencies (P) Ltd. <docinfo@dkagencies.com>

Nagendra, Jaya S., author.
A biography of world civilizations / Jaya Nagendra.
volumes cm
Includes bibliographical references and index.
Contents: volume I. Migration of people, ancient Egypt, Sumerial education, India — volume II. Greece, China, Persia, Rome — volume III. Europe, The Middle East, Maya and Aztec, United States of America.
ISBN 9788121220101 (set: HB)
ISBN 9788121220361 (vol. III)

1. Civilization. I. Title.

LCC CB69.N34 2020 | DDC 909 23

Contents

9

Europe

"European History is whatever the historian wants it to be. It is a summary of the events and ideas, political, religions, military, pacific, serious, romantic, near at hand, far away, tragic, comic, significant, meaningless, anything else you would like to be. There is only the limiting factor. It must take place in or derive from the area we call Europe. But as I am not sure what exactly that area is meant to be, I am pretty well in a haze about the rest."

– ***European journalist Mr. A.J.P. Taylor***

In the beginning, there was no Europe. All there was a long, graceful peninsula positioned like an image of a ship on the world's largest land mass with no name. To the west sat the ocean which no one had crossed. To the south sat two surrounded and knitted seas, scattered with islands, bays, and peninsulas of their own. To the north sat the great polar icecap, expanding and contracting through the eons like some monster. To the east sat the land-bridge to the rest of the world, waiting for all civilizations to come.

In the gaps between the Ice Ages, the Peninsula received its first human settlers approximately 30,000 years ago according to DNA, a genetic Marker Chromosome Y M173. Before that the humanoids of Neanderthal, and the cave people of Cro-Magnon, must have arrived there with some ideas. But it cannot be known who they really were. They can only be recognized faintly from their drawings, their artefacts, and their bones. Twelve thousand years ago after the last drain of the ice, the Peninsula received new waves of migrants. Anonymous pioneers and prospectors moved slowly towards the west, rounding coasts and crossing the land. Their greatest surviving masterwork, like the Stone Age was built on the edge of human habitation on a remote, offshore island. But no amount of modern speculation can tell for certain what inspired those master architects.

By tradition the ancient Greek Hellenes took control of the seacoasts towards the end of 2000 BC. conquered islands between the coasts of Peloponnese and of Asia Minor and absorbed the prevailing culture of the mainland

Origin of the name "Europe"

Later when children asked where humankind had come from, they were told about the Flood and about Europa. Europa was the subject of one of the most respected legends of the classical world. Europa was the mother of Minos, Lord of Crete, and therefore the most eccentric ancient branch of Mediterranean civilization. But in Greek mythology 'Europa and the Bull,' she is immortalized as an innocent princess seduced by the Father of the Gods, Zeus. When she was wandering with her friends along the shore of her native Phoenicia, she was abducted by Zeus in the disguise of a snow-white bull.

In historian Herodotus' view, the abduction of Europa was just an incident in the age-old wars over women-stealing. The Legend of Europa has many implications. But in carrying the princess to Crete from the shores of Phoenicia (now south Lebanon), Zeus was certainly transferring the bounties of the older Asian civilizations of the East to the new island colonies of the Aegean. Phoenicia belonged to the circle of the Pharaohs. Europa's journey provides the mythical link between Ancient Egypt and Ancient Greece. Europa's brother Cadmus, who roamed the world in search of her, was attributed with bringing the art of writing to Greece.

Europa's tour also represents the important impatience of those who followed in her way. Contrasting the great river valley civilizations of the Nile, Indus, Mesopotamia, and China, the civilization of the Mediterranean Sea was accelerated by continuous movement. Movement caused uncertainty and insecurity. Uncertainty nourished a constant ferment of ideas. Insecurity encouraged energetic activities. Crete was the first naval power in Mediterranean region. The ships transported people and goods and culture, promoting exchanges of all kinds with the lands to which they navigated. The minds of those ancient seafarers were constantly triggered for new ideas like flickering in the breeze.

The Hellenes used "Europe" as a name for their new territory to the west of the Aegean. At the beginning of European history, the known world stayed in the east. It paved the way to the founding of a new civilization that would ultimately bear Europa's name and would spread to the whole Peninsula.

Basically, European history begins with a great Roman Empire intensely designed by its unique type of administration.

While Alexander wanted to conquer the whole world and impose Greek civilization all over, it is the European civilization which practically accomplished that vision. It achieved this ambition by various means like by conquest and settlement; by its economic power; and by the power of its ideas. Initially science was a European invention and today every country on earth uses most of its discoveries of science and technologies that originate from it. It took ideas of philosophy, art, literature, maths, science, medicine and politics from ancient Greece.

A leading historian of Australia, John Hirst explains the life in Greece and the Europeans cultivated their civilization by learning Greek. All Greeks aspired to belong to a state as modern day people and liked to belong to an organization. In Greece, male citizens used to gather in one place and talked about public affairs on various subjects such as laws, voting, senator, public policies, etc. Previously, Italy was a small country, and Romans were very backward people. They met Greeks and eventually learned more from them that laid the foundation for Roman civilization. Greeks also learned more from Egypt.

Even though Romans were more advanced than the Greeks at fighting, law, and engineering, they acknowledged Greeks superiority and copied every aptitude from them. It was a fashion to a Roman to send his son to Athens University or hire a Greek slave to teach his children at home.

Greeks were very bright in Geometry and demonstrated how geometry works beginning with basic definitions. It starts with a few basic definitions and builds on them.

- First, the starting spot is a point, which the Greeks defined as having a location but no size. Of course, it does possess the size because there is the width of the dot on the page, but geometry is a type of make-believe world, a pure world.
- Second: a line has length but no width.

- Third, a straight line is defined as the shortest line joining two points.

From these three definitions a circle can be created: Basically, it is a line making a closed figure. But, how to make roundness? Roundness is very hard to define. It can be defined by saying there is a point within this figure from which straight lines drawn to the figure will always be of equal length.

So, "Along with circles, there are parallel lines that extend forever without meeting and triangles in all their variety, and squares and rectangles and other regular forms. These objects, formed by lines, are all defined, their characteristics revealed and the possibilities arising from their intersection and overlapping explored. Everything is proved from what has been established before. For example, by using a quality of parallel lines, you can show that the angles of a triangle add up to 180 degrees."

Geometry Is Beautiful!

The Greeks considered that geometry is a simple, elegant, logical system, very satisfying, and beautiful. Beautiful? The fact they found it beautiful is a clue to the Greek mind. Their geometry was not like we do for practical uses in surveying or navigation. They recognized geometry as a model to the fundamental nature of the universe. If we look around us, we discover the variety of different shapes and different colours. The Greeks believed that underneath all these varieties, there must be some logical, regular, and simple explanation. Something like geometry.

To understand the science, the Greeks did not make experiments with hypotheses and tests. They believed if we got our mind into a wheel of thinking and contemplated hard, we would get the right answer. So, they proceeded by a system of inspired guesses. One Greek philosopher said all matter is made up of water, which shows how desperate they were to get a simple answer. Another philosopher said all matter is made up of four things: earth, fire, air, and water. Another philosopher said all matter is actually made up of little things which he called atoms – and hit the jackpot. He made an inspired guess which came back to in the twentieth century.

Even though the Greeks were often very wrong in their guesses, their fundamental guesswork that the answers would be simple, mathematical, and logical turned out to be right. This is the greatest legacy that European civilisation still owes to the Greeks.

The Greek view was that the world is simple, logical and mathematical; the Christian view was that the world is evil, and Christ alone saves; and the German warrior' view was that fighting is fun.

Women in European Culture

The attitude of protecting and honouring ladies was a long-lasting custom in European culture. After the tradition of knights disappeared, it became the attitude of a 'gentleman'. A gentleman showed respect for women by standing when women came into the room, by refusing to be seated while women were standing, and by touching his hat to women.

Forms of Government I

Democratic state was invented by ancient Greeks. They also invented the word politics, which comes from the word for city, *polis*. Greeks another invention was the government formed by discussion among all citizens and selecting leaders by majority voting. In their Direct Democracy, all citizens collected in one place to discuss, debate, and determine policies, but not all the Greek states were democratic. In Athens democracy lasted for 170 years with some interruptions. During this time, men born in Athens had the right to participate in government, but women and slaves had no rights.

Socrates, Plato and Aristotle, the great Athenian philosophers had severe doubts about Athenian democracy, and they criticised the system. They complained that the people were unreliable, ignorant, and indecisive and were easily persuaded. Government is a fine art that requires wisdom and judgement, which is not the property of all citizens. Probably those philosophers would be much happier with our system of representative democracy because no matter what we say about our representatives, they are usually better educated and better informed than the people as a whole. In our democracy, our political leaders are guided by a civil service in which there are many intelligent people. Therefore, the people do not rule directly and there is a contribution from those who are trained and thoughtful about the whole business of government.

Direct Democracy required a great loyalty and commitment from the people and a great faith in the people. The principles of Athenian democracy were laid in an Athenian leader, Pericles, in a speech he delivered on the occasion at a burial of soldiers killed in a war. This speech was recorded by an Athenian historian Thucydides (460 BCE). Thucydides' manuscript of history was preserved in Constantinople. During the Renaissance period, 1800 years after it was written, it reached Italy where it was translated into Latin and then into several European languages. Here are some extracts from Thucydides, (460 BCE) speech:

> "Our constitution is called a democracy because power is in the hands not of a minority but of the whole people. When it is a question of

settling private disputes, everyone is equal before the law; when it is a question of putting one person before another of impositions of public responsibility, what counts is not membership of a particular class, but the actual ability which the man possesses.

"When our work is over, we are in a position to enjoy all kinds of recreation for our spirits. There are various kinds of contests and sacrifices regularly throughout the year; in our own homes we find a beauty and good taste which delight us every day and which drive away care.

"Here each individual is interested not only in his own affairs but in the affairs of the state as well; even those who are mostly occupied with their own business are extremely well informed on general politics — this is a peculiarity of ours: we do not say that a man who takes no interest in politics is a man who minds his own business; we say that he has no `business here at all."

The idea of open, cultivated society with committed, engaged citizens was an attractive ideal to those who cared about democracy, even though the Athenian leisure and beauty was at the expense of slavery. An English scholar and radical George Grote argued that democracy and the high culture were inter-connected, and one cannot neglect one and accept the other. This was Pericles' contribution to the origin of democracy in England.

Republic - Rape as a Root Cause of Republic

In the beginning, Rome was ruled by kings. When Romans overthrew the king Tarquin the Proud in 500 BCE, the republic was established. The Roman historian Levy writes this story in his book. A single copy of his book has been preserved which was discovered in the sixteenth century. The cause of revolt was ignited by a rape, which resulted in establishing republic in Rome. The rapist was a son of king Tarquin, Sextus Tarquinius. His victim was Lucretia, the wife of Collatius. The head of the revolution that ousted the king was Brutus, who was a nephew of the king.

It happened when all sons of the king were away from Rome fighting in a war. In the tent, a conversation started discussing their wives and each boasted that his wife is the best. According to Collatius' suggestion, they came to an agreement to test what their wives are doing and resolve the matter by riding back to Rome. They found all princes were enjoying the party merrily, but Collatius' wife Lucretia was working hard at spinning. So Collatius had won the argument. After a few days, Sextus, the son of the king returned to visit Lucretia without the knowledge of Collatia. The author writes the story:

"He was hospitably welcomed in Lucretia's house, and after supper, escorted like the honoured visitor to the guest chamber. Here he waited till the house was asleep and then, when all was quiet, he drew his sword and made his way to Lucretia's room determined to rape her. She was asleep. Laying his left hand on her, 'Lucretia,' he whispered, 'not a sound. I am Sextus Tarqunius, I am armed - if you utter a word I will kill you.' Lucretius was in terror. He urged his love, begged her to submit, pleaded, threatened, and used every weapon that might conquer a woman's heart. But all in vain; not even the fear of death could bend her will. Sextus cried, 'If death will not move you, dishonour shall. I will kill you first, then cut the throat of a slave and lay his naked body by your side. Then everyone will believe that you have been caught in adultery with a servant and paid the price.' Even the most resolute chastity could not have stood against this dreadful threat. Lucretia yielded. After raping, he rode away, feeling proud of his success.

The unhappy girl wrote to her father in Rome and to her husband in Ardea, urging them both to come at once with a trusted friend and quickly, for a frightful thing had happened. Her father came with Valerius, her husband with Brutus, with whom he was returning to Rome when he was met by the messenger. They found Lucretia sitting in her room in deep distress. Tears rose to her eyes as they entered and to her husband's question, 'Is it well with you?' she answered, 'No, what can be well with a woman who has lost her honour? In your bed, Collatius, is the impression of another man. My body only has been violated; my heart is innocent, and death will be my witness. Give me your solemn promise that the adulterer shall be punished. He is Sextus Tarquinius. He is who last night came as my enemy disguised as my guest and took his pleasure of me. That pleasure will be my death — and his too if you are men.'

The promise was given. One after another they tried to comfort her; they told her she was helpless and therefore innocent, that he alone was guilty. It was the mind, they said, that sinned, not the body; without intention there could never be guilt.

'What is due to him,' Lucretia said, 'is for you to decide. As for me, I am innocent of fault, but I will take my punishment. Never shall Lucretia provide a precedent for unchaste women to escape what they deserve.' With these words she drew a knife from under a robe, drove it into her heart and fell forward, dead. Her father and her husband were overwhelmed with grief. While they stood weeping helplessly, Brutus

> drew the bloody knife from Lucretia's body and holding it before him cried: 'By this girl's blood — none more chaste till a tyrant wronged her — and by the gods I swear that with sword and fire and whatever else can lend strength to my arm, I will pursue Licius Tarquinius the Proud, his wicked wife and all his children, and 'never again will I let them or any other man be king in rome.'

Brutus fulfilled his promise by defeating the king and launched the Republic because of an outrageous crime committed by a prince, and because a Roman woman valued highly her honour more than her life. But not everyone in Rome wanted Taraquin to be out of power. So, a conspiracy to bring the king back emerged. The culprits were caught and brought before the seat of judgment. Brutus was sitting in the public assembly when the names of the conspirators were brought before him. On the plotters list, two of his son's names were there. It was Brutus' term to punish the conspirators. People at the crowd shouted that Brutus does not have to punish his family members and he can pardon them. But Brutus would not yield; he applied the same rule to his sons like everyone else. He watched his sons stripped naked, flogged, and then beheaded. Such was Brutus' devotion to the Republic.

This is the spirit of devotion to the Republic: Leave all personal and private attachment aside and serve the public good. Romans called it Virtues, republican virtue. It is necessary if the republic was to survive without the king. Isn't it inhumane that Brutus sitting there and watching his sons die? In a way this republican virtue created monsters.

This Roman republic survived for about 200 years and then it began to fall into disorder. In 27 BCE, Augustus, an adopted son of Caesar, became the emperor of Rome.

Customs in Some Cultures

All know that holding hands together is a position to pray. But Christians prayed, extending their hands and facing towards the east where they believed that Christ would return with triumph. The position of prayer indicates that one's loyalty to lord. In Roman society, if a person wanted to survive, he needed a supporter or a donor. At that time, kings and emperors were considered that they were representatives of gods or they themselves were gods. So, the ritual of prayer originated. As the dominance of the empire declined, people began looking for a strongman to protect them. As such the bond between warriors and their chief created a ritual by kissing the hand. It was a ritual started by Germans.

A subject gave his loyalty by kneeling down and raising his fastened hands and the king would put his hands around him. Then the subject would promise to be the king's man to serve him. After the commitment was sworn, the subject would stand, and the subject and king, both kissed each other. This was a ritual of both obedience and equality, which indicated the nature of the relationship: the subject promised to be loyal so long as the king protected him.

Forms of Government II

The basis for creating state was that the king (a leader, later became a king) distributed lands to his followers and in return the followers were expected to provide him fighting force. So, the king collected his army without taxation. Land held in this way was called a fief (from the word *feudum* in Latin, and the English word for 'feudal'.)

Feudal monarchs relied heavily on what their great landowners could provide, which made them weak monarchs. Theoretically landowners kept control of the land they had been given, but in reality, the land became private property and was passed down from father to son. The great landowners owed commitment to the king, but they could also disobey or ignore him. They controlled armed forces to assist the king whenever he needed, but that same force could be used against the king. Landlords lived in castles and could defend themselves against any rivals and their king.

Emperors and Popes

European history begins with a Roman Empire taking much from its history.

The rule of Augustus in Rome began in 27 BCE and the empire he founded lasted for 500 years. Around 400 CE the empire was permanently divided into east and west and the eastern empire survived another thousand years until 1453 CE. The barbarians who conquered the Western Roman Empire accepted the emperor of the eastern empire. Clovis, the first Christian king of the Franks, received the title 'Consul' from the emperor in the east. The pope, who survived in Rome, also accepted the eastern emperor. Despite all the barbarian invasions and the downfall of the empire in the west, major parts of the old order were still unbroken. There was a pope and a Christian Roman emperor in Rome. Those two authorities, the pope and the emperor, jointly controlled Christendom.

Charlemagne (747 AD)

The king Charlemagne significantly extended the province of the Frankish kingdom. His lands extended across the Pyrenees into Spain; midway in

Italy including the land his father had allotted to the pope; in the east to Austria and into modern Germany. Since the fall of Rome, there has been no single European state that was so extensive except for the short-lived empires of Hitler and Napoleon.

In 800 CE Charlemagne (800 CE). 2. The Christian Church preserved Greek and Roman learning and used it to construct its own doctrine. They copied and recopied them again and again right through the Middle Ages. It is said that the church borrowed what it wanted from this literature, reassembled the bits it had taken, put them with passages in the Bible, and constructed a Christian theology. 3. Farmers made civilization possible.

In the year 800 CE Charlemagne visited Rome and attended mass on Christmas Day in the cathedral. After the mass, and apparently with no earlier notice, the pope placed a crown on Charlemagne's head and declared him to be Roman emperor.

Charlemagne's empire was a very different empire from the Roman, and he was a very different ruler among Roman emperors. Basically, he was still a barbarian king and he was educating himself: he had learnt to read Latin but had difficulty in writing. Until the end of his life he kept a little wax plaque beside his bed in order to practise his writing, but he never really got the skill of writing. But he did have a clear understanding of the empire as a civilising force, something he learnt from the Roman example. Saint Augustine, who lived in the last days of the Roman Empire in the west, wrote in his City of God: "If there is no justice, what are kingdoms but great robberies?" Charlemagne knew of this work and understood this point because Saint Augustine was one of his favourite authors. He made sure that the subjects were ruled impartially.

Charlemagne though poorly educated himself, encouraged education and became a supporter of learned men. He ordered them to find and copy the ancient manuscripts. Almost all the Latin works that have survived were copied in Charlemagne's time. Without him, the classical inheritance would have been very little and would have been lost.

Charlemagne confronted enormous obstacles. He had no bureaucracy, communications were poor; there was little trade; towns were tiny; and there was a great amount of chaos. His mode of government was to appoint accountants and dukes throughout his kingdom to keep the local lords in order and to ensure that they gave their loyalty to Charlemagne. There was no institutional base to this empire; its government depended on the personal power of its leader.

After building up this huge empire with such great effort, Charlemagne decided that after his death, it should be subdivided among his sons. But, only one of his sons survived. So, the division of the empire occurred among his grandchildren. The grandsons fought among themselves and Charlemagne's empire fell into three parts. Ultimately, the western part became modern-day France; the eastern part became the basis of Germany.

During the fights among his grandchildren and the Norse invasions at the same time, Charlemagne's methods of control disappeared. The Counts and Dukes began themselves as local strongmen declaring loyalty to whoever the king.

The Catholic Church was the great international institution of the Middle Ages, but kings and local power brokers wanted to control the bishops in their own territory.

Church's Contributions to Books

Christian churches continued Greek and Roman learning. Actually, it was a functioning process of preservation; not merely placing the smart books on a cabinet and leaving them there untouched. They have survived so long, and anyone can read them now because the church copied and recopied them again and again right through the Middle Ages. In antiquity, there was no printing: books rot and perish. It was the monks in the monasteries who preserved much of the treasures of Greece and Rome by copying systematically.

If these books are read in their own expression, these literatures provide a philosophy, a system of values, an attitude towards life, which are pagan ideas according Christianity. But the church in the Middle Age was able to maintain a command over intellectual life that no-one ever looked at this literature in its own terms. It is said that the church borrowed what it wanted from this literature, reassembled the bits it had taken, put them with passages in the Bible, and constructed a Christian theology. So Greek philosophy, Greek learning, and Greek logic were all pressed into service in support of Christianity.

Renaissance (1300-1700 AD)

The Renaissance is frequently portrayed as the discovery or rediscovery of Greek and Roman learning.

Renaissance - Photo of Raphael's School of Athens, 1509.

The Greeks and Romans had been greatly concerned with people and their doings on this earth rather than with their life after death. They celebrated human's capacity and powers, and they had not dwelled on their immorality. It was a very open-minded world. There were enormous types of views among the ancient philosophers and moralists on how best to live

Age of Enlightenment

Age of Enlightenment

and what best to think. Their discussions and assumptions had not been carried on within the guidelines that the church had imposed on thinking.

The Church's aim was to control all of life and thoughts of people in the name of religion. Once that control had been broken, European thought became much more adventurous, more broad-minded.

Romanticism (Idealism) (~1800 CE)

In the Renaissance period, people of one culture and tradition judged themselves with another culture and tradition. Once it is done, people will never be the same again. Nothing ever seems as certain and fixed as they were taught before. As a result, European thinkers had jumped out of their own skin.

The source for Renaissance art, which inspired Michel Angelo and others, that the human body as a thing of beauty and perfection is a Greek invention. The goal of the Greeks was not to demonstrate a particular form of body. They toiled to find perfection in the body and used their mathematics to confirm the proportions that are most pleasing and beautiful. Michelangelo in the Renaissance demonstrated his David figure as a human form of perfection: man, an individual, as the embodiment of something high-spirited, noble, and beautiful.

Enlightenment (~1800 AD)

The start of the Enlightenment was strongest in France. The scholars of the Enlightenment perceived the world is ruled by ignorance and superstition. They found that two great irrational forces in the society were the church that is the Catholic Church, and the king, the absolute monarch of France. They proclaimed that church and king preserved their positions by depending on the ignorance of the people. The church sold stories of miracles and punishment to their sins in hell to keep the people in order. The kings honoured the claims that they were appointed by God and it was irreligious to question their authority. So people had no choice but to obey.

The Enlightenment was not a revolutionary undertaking. It was a collection of scholars, writers, artists and historians who held that as reason and education increased, superstition and ignorance would decrease, and people would stop to believe in such nonsense as miracles. They believed once people are educated, enlightenment will follow. But, the leading persons of the Enlightenment were not democrats; they were comfortable to see an enlightenment ruler begin to implement their plans for a society governed by reason. It is said that some of the kings of the eighteenth-century in Europe were enlightened dictators. They got rid of barbaric punishments and torture and codified their laws; they began to do something about educating the people.

One of the great works of the French Enlightenment was the production of an encyclopaedia. Contrasting to modern-day encyclopaedia, it was a radical encyclopaedia because it employed reason to everything. All knowledge was treated in the same way and was subjected to the same test. The encyclopaedia warned: 'the manner of adoring the true God ought never to deviate from reason, because God is the author of reason....'

One example of the Enlightenment period radical Encyclopaedia contained the story of Noah's Ark, a bible story about the ship built by Noah to save his family and two of every kind of animal from the great Flood. It begins by asking how big Noah's Ark was. It must have been very large because it had to accommodate two of each of the animals from all over the world. Two of each animal were not enough because to stay in the Ark (ship) for a long time, they needed food to stay alive. Two sheep would not have been enough in order to feed the lions; so there would have to have been hundreds of lambs. Yet two pairs of each species require a huge ship. But the Bible says only four people worked to make it. Apparently to make a genuine inquiry, the encyclopaedia proved the story to be illogical.

In a nutshell, the message of the Enlightenment was that religion is superstition. So religion, which was once central to European civilization, had to be excluded and Reason had to take Religion's place. They realized that if we follow reason and science, there will be progress. And that progress was a new idea. The ancients did not believe in progress because they believed that there is a cycle of growth and decay; that institutions and society would be fresh and vigorous in the start and then a process of corruption would emerge naturally. The church also did not believe in progress by human efforts independent of God, because it is believed that humans were basically wrong and evil. It believed humans guided by reason only could never produce a perfect society.

Romanticism (~1800 CE)

The Romantic Movement believed in feelings, emotions, and all the passions. It was exactly opposite to the Enlightenment ideas. It was a Europe-wide movement, but strongest in Germany. These Romantic Movement people did not want reason to control their emotions and passions. They considered a great writer or a great artist should not be rewriting old themes from the classics in an elegant way; instead a writer or an artist should be exposing his soul, bringing his passions, his anguish, and his misery to the forefront. They believed the art should be emotional, expressive, and highly thrilling.

The Germans affirmed that one should not discuss people and society in abstract because humankind is different depending on the country, they live in. Romantics said that we are shaped by our language and our history; they are embedded in us. They declared that Germans are always going to be different from the French having their own history and their own language. They did not believe in universal reason, which intellectuals in French gatherings believed in. They said we are Germans and we want to find out about the German's of being German. The German Romantics wanted to know what the German warriors were like before they got mingled with civilizations of Rome and Christianity. They were pulling the Germans away from the mix. They liked the men of the woods, their vigour and vitality, and their crudity. They did not want to follow weak intellectuals. They honoured Germans who lived close to the soil, and who knew what being German was about.

Modern interest and respect for culture begins when intellectuals first began to collect folk culture. The German Romantics' response was, "The answer to the prattle about reason by arrogant French intellectuals was to put on your boots and go hiking. Go to the German people, go to the peasants, record their stories and songs: that is where you will find true enlightenment. The message of Romanticism was that civilization is artificial; that it cramps and constrains us. It is within traditional culture that life is fully lived."

Surprisingly, this view has been strong in Western society ever since. There was a great eruption of it in the 1960s. Cry for liberation was one of its forms. They exclaimed, "let us not have any rules, let us live in a simple, direct, plain way, let us grow our own food and weave our own clothes. Let us wear our hair long, let us live in communes, and let us be frank with our own feelings and frank in our dealings with each other. And let us borrow from more authentic people – from workers or peasants or noble savages."

Romanticism presented an ideology of nationalism claiming that distinct peoples, who have their own culture and languages, must live together and have their own government. This formal thinking remains a big force in today's modern world. It believes that if the leadership is not by the government of its own people, it cannot be a good government. In that sense, Serbs must live together and have a Serbian government; Croats must live together and have Croatian government, and so on. In a country where Serbs and Croats live together, they cannot fully express them. For example, Serbs cannot flourish unless they have their own country: this is the ideology of nationalism.

The Romantic Movement believed in emotion, culture, nationalism and liberation, which is like an arrow moving in the opposite direction to reason, science and progress.

Renaissance, the Reformation, the Scientific Revolution, the Enlightenment, the Romantic movement; all in different ways reduced the authority of the church. Every enlightened person believes that birth control is a good thing, but the pope says it is against god's teaching.

In today's world what is people's reaction if somebody suggests dropping biology and evolution and teaching the bible or scriptures in schools? They would say, 'No, no' because they are enlightened, progressive people now. This is the education they are talking about.

Socrates, Plato, and Aristotle lived in Athens in a democratic society in the fifth and sixth centuries BCE. Socrates believed that 'if our mind is clear and sharp, we could reach the truth. We do not have to seek it out or conduct research. The truth exists; we have to cultivate our mind to grasp it.'

Romans established guilt or innocence by the examination of evidence and witnesses, whereas the Germans established the guilt by trial by test of fire, water, or battle. For example, to test whether a suspect is guilty or not, (1) his arm was placed in boiling water. If the arm was not healed after three days, they decided the suspect was guilty. (2) Suspects were thrown into water: if they floated, they were guilty; if they sank, they were innocent. (3) Two parties in dispute over land would be set to battle and the winner declared to be the right.

The Germans became Christians soon after the invasion by Romans, renouncing their own gods and their Arianism. Arians believed that since

Jesus was the son of God, he must be a lesser person and could not be the equal to God.

Then the Islamic rule appeared in Europe. The Muslims were cruel conquerors of Christians, but gentle rulers. They allowed Christians to continue their worship, but as non-believers they had to pay tax; Muslims paid no tax. This was an incentive to convert to Islam.

In the Middle Ages Spain became the most civilized part of Europe under Muslim rule. On their journeys of conquest, the illiterate Arab tribesmen became educated and cultured from the people they conquered: from Persians, who nourished a highly cultivated civilization, and from Greeks in the Byzantine Empire.

In the 1400s, two transforming developments of modern Europe occurred: The Renaissance and the Reformation.

Renaissance began in the northern cities of Italy where city-states such as classical Greece's small cities. The Italian cities were competitors militarily and culturally: they waged war with each other, and they wanted to excel each other with the grandeur of their art. Their talented people concentrated in one place. The nobility had nothing to do with their estates as their natural home; they lived in the cities too. The diversity and strength of city life branded whole societies. These places conceived and carried out the project of reconstructing the ancient world.

Although the position of the emperor carried no power, the Holy Roman Empire survived. Voltaire, the leader of the Enlightenment, mocked the Holy Roman Empire as neither holy, nor Roman, nor an empire, but its survival was always rather magical, carrying a name and an idea in a very odd form. A new emperor had to arrive to abolish this strange system. He was Napoleon Bonaparte, who took charge of France in 1799. Ten years after, the revolution began.

Napoleon Bonaparte (1769 –1821 AD)

French Revolution began by declaring liberty, equality, and fraternity. Napoleon Bonaparte partially started the revolution and became a general in the revolutionary wars that France had waged against the monarchical powers of Europe. He was a son of the Enlightenment, a believer in the principles of the revolution, excluding the right of the people to govern themselves. Since the French had failed that task since 1789, Bonaparte's method of approach was very appealing. He was the most seductive of tyrants. He desired no group to enjoy special privileges. In his view all citizens were to be treated as equals; all children were to have the chance of education provided by the state; all positions were to be open to people of ability. He collected men of great talent into his government irrespective of what party they had participated during the revolution, whether as monarchists or republicans, supporters of the Jacobin terror or its opponents. He gave them the responsibility of making France an orderly and rational system of government.

Napoleon established a team of experts. Their important work was the development of the Civil Code in a single document in which the law on every topic was laid down. Basically, it was an imitation of the code of Emperor Justinian.

The Roman example was important to Napoleon. Like the Romans, he planned to create a big empire where the principles of republican France would be the basis for a just and orderly society. He continued to wage wars with the great powers of Europe that extended the boundaries of France, and beyond France he redesigned territories and kingdoms and placed his brothers in charge of them. All over the continent he removed medieval rights, privileges, and anomalies and launched his new rational order. He was pleased to know that his Napoleon Code survived throughout Europe even after his life in exile on Saint Helena in the South Atlantic — which still survives. What did not survive was the Holy Roman Empire. Napoleon eliminated it in 1867 when he regrouped several small states in Germany into the Confederation of the Rhine.

Napoleon was a non-believer in god; but he was a great believer in chance and destiny. He understood how strongly people were devoted to their faith and how useful religion was in preserving morality and good order. The early revolutionaries of the Enlightenment did not have this respect for organized religion. The revolutionaries confiscated church land and set up a competing national church, which the pope refused to recognize. Napoleon decided to end the bitterness and division that this had caused. He achieved an agreement with the pope, a Concordat, which acknowledged that the catholic faith was the religion of the great majority of the French people.

The Pope was present in Notre Dame Cathedral when Napoleon was crowned as emperor. He anointed Napoleon and his empress, Josephine; he blessed the imperial ceremonial objects: orb, hand of justice, sword and sceptre. But Napoleon himself put the crown on his head.

Languages

In the Roman Empire there were two universal languages: Latin in the west and Greek in the east.

Now, no country or land on earth has Latin as its common language. Latin is considered as a dead language. It was spoken only by the people in Rome at first and in small regions of country around it. As Roman rule expanded, Latin speaking also expanded. Eventually, after hundreds of years it was being spoken throughout the western empire. Latin was the language of administration, of law, of the army, and of trade.

Greek is still spoken in Greece and Greek settled areas around the eastern Mediterranean and in the wider Greek migration areas. Now the spoken Greek may be in a different form.

Latin, Greek, Slavonic, and Germanic languages are all derived from a common origin, named Indo-European. Linguists are trying to understand some of its elements by working back from the commonalities in the languages. They argue that somewhere in the east, Indo-Europeans were located. They call that language is Indo-European because the Indian languages Sanskrit and Iranian languages are also derived from it.

The discovery of Indo-European language occurred in the eighteenth century. Until then Europe had presumed that all languages had arrived from Hebrew, spoken by Jews and by proposition that it was the language of Adam and Eve, the first people. Hebrew is an entirely different language from European languages. As a consequence, the pursuit of Hebraic origins completely ended. During the age of Enlightenment in the eighteenth century, scholars ignored the Biblical framework and developed new theories. The breakthrough of Indo-European theory was made by William Jones, an English judge in India. He detected similarities in the basic vocabulary of Sanskrit and European languages — the words for numbers, parts of the body and family members, etc.

For example, here are the words for brother:

Brother (English)
Bhratr (Sansrkit)
Broeder (Dutch)
Bruder (German)
Phrater (Greek)
Brat (Russian)
Brathair (Irish)

Jones considered that these similarities were more than accidental and concluded that these languages had a common ancestor that no longer exists today. Therefore, the reconstruction of Indo-European began.

The Common People

People see ordinary common people as dirty, smelly, and not attractive to look at because they are under-nourished, worn down and tainted by disease, beaten and blemished by hard work in all weathers. Century after century they live the same way and most of them grow food.

Approximately 90 percent of the people were living in the countryside/villages in the Roman Empire. There were great cities in the empire, predominantly in Rome itself, but they comprised only 10 percent of the population. The villages delivered grain to the big cities, but grain is a heavy product and could not be carried far by land. The grain for Rome came from Egypt by sea, which was the cheapest mode of transport. In the beginning Rome was like a Third-World city of today, and it was unable to provide a living for all the people who clustered there. During the celebration of festivals, along with free bread, Rome provided regular shows in the Colosseum to its citizens.

The trade in the Roman Empire was light, but valuable luxury goods could afford a long transport. Just like Europe until the nineteenth century, in the Roman Empire most people survived on what was grown locally: their food, drink, clothes and shelter were all local products. Old cottages in Europe had thatched roofs because they were cheap material. So, in case of economy, the Romans were not a changing force; their innovation rested in connecting an empire together by a single law and with a military organization that was exceptionally efficient. The Roman roads were designed by army engineers for the prime purpose of allowing soldiers to march quickly from place to place. That is the reason they are straight. If they were designed for horse and carts, the gradients would have been gentler.

In the last two centuries of the Roman Empire, the cities were losing population because the German invaders attacked them. As a result trade narrowed and local self-sufficiency became more crucial. After the German invasions, Muslims invaded Rome in the seven and eighth centuries; Vikings in the ninth and tenth centuries spread great chaos. Peace came in the eleventh and twelfth centuries and trade and town life began to recover. Some towns had almost completely disappeared after the fifth century.

Farming in Ancient Times

During the nineteenth century, in Italy, southern France and Spain, ploughing was the same as in Roman times. The ploughing was very primitive; it was like a split stick with a cutting blade at its bottom; an oxen or horse pulled the plough; the ploughman held and directed it and the blade entered not far below the surface. It was somewhat like scratching the surface.

Wheeled plough is one of the great inventions of the early middle ages. The inventor is unknown. This was more effective for the heavier soils of northern France, Germany, and England. Actually, it was the same type of modern ploughs, but it was pulled by animals and held by humans. The sharp cutter cut the soil and a mouldboard lifted and turned the soil that had been cut. This produced channels in place of scratches and the channels all ran the same way, parallel to each other. In the heavy soil, water could run off down the channels. Ploughing was hard work. If a farmer does not hold it firmly with his shoulders and arms, it would fall over instead of cutting the soil. After ploughing the land, seed must be spread. Then with a kind of rake, the seed was covered.

Harvesting was done with the sickle, a curved blade with a handle. Archaeologists find them in the most ancient human settlements. The same sickles were still the standard harvesting mechanism in Europe up until the early twentieth century. The communist revolution in Russia in 1917 chose its new flag to honour the workers: it carried the hammer and sickle, the hammer for urban workers and the sickle for the country.

In the past, the ploughing was not like today's farmers sitting in air-conditioned tractors and driving over the land. Peasants were plodding, bending, straining over every inch of ground year after year.

If the grain did not ripen or bad weather spoiled the grain before it was harvested, then the whole community had to suffer. In that situation, grain would have to come from elsewhere and it would be very expensive. In times of shortage of grain, the price of commodities would be doubled or tripled. This was not like one item in the supermarket. It was the cost of the whole food intake that was doubling or tripling.

Farmers Made Civilization Possible

The 85-95 percent of those who worked on the land made civilization possible. If peasants had grown enough food for themselves only, there would not have been any cities or lords, priests or kings, or armies. All individuals depended on farmers to grow their food. Whether they wanted or not, the peasants had to supply food to other people.

Initially, governments took money from peasants and used it on the military. Collecting money from peasants is the foundation of civilization. Probably they might have enjoyed paying their taxes or complained about it. No one likes to pay taxes, but we get the benefit of the services that the government provides us. But the peasants get no services. Previously, Governments did not run schools or health systems and even they did not look after the roads. Romans looked after the public health of their cities by providing water and sewerage systems, but they did not do anything for the village side. Until recently, 80 or 90 percent of tax collected was spent on the armed forces. So, did the peasants benefit from the foreign enemy being kept at bay? It appeared to them that the government and the church are exploiting, and the money taken from them was a robbery.

French Revolution

Until the French Revolution, the peasant riots were always crushed. The French Revolution became more radical and as a result, a new constitution was created, and all dues and obligations were cancelled. The peasants became full owners of their land, completely free of their landlords.

Agricultural Revolution

The introduction of a modern commercial relationship between the landlord and occupant in England allowed a huge jump in agricultural productivity that is called the Agricultural Revolution. Not everything was the king's: this is the foundation of European liberty and its prosperity.

The upsurge in agricultural productivity contributed to cities to grow. In general, a smaller segment of people was able to provide food for the whole community. England was the first large modern state to make this jump.

Industrial Revolution

After the mid-eighteenth century, the Industrial Revolution moved along with the Agricultural Revolution in England. Previously, cotton and wool were spun and woven by workers in their cottages. Due to the Industrial Revolution, that task was transferred to factories where new inventions powered first by water wheel and then by steam engines did the work.

The Agricultural and Industrial Revolutions produced shocking changes in the society. But it promised that the common people, who were suffering so much for mere survival, will get an unimagined prosperity.

Declaration of the Rights of Citizens

John Hirst writes that after French Revolution, the Declaration of the Rights of Man and of the Citizen was passed by France's National Constituent Assembly in August 1789. It is a most important document of the French

Revolution, which emphasized on human and civil rights. Basically, the declaration was directly influenced by Thomas Jefferson along with General LaFayette, who introduced it. Also, it was influenced by the principles of "natural right", the rights of people are held to be universal: lawful at all times and in every place, relating to human nature itself. It became the foundation for a nation of free individuals protected equally by law.

The leaders of the assembly were men of Enlightenment; they had very clear liberal, egalitarian, and democratic principles. Their motto was liberty, equality, and fraternity. The assembly issued its manifesto under the title Declaration of the Rights of Man and of the Citizen. (Maybe they should change the word 'Man' to people). These rights were not just for the French, but rights for all humankind. The summary of its chief articles:

- Men are born and remain free and equal in rights.
- These rights are liberty, property, security, and resistance to oppression.
- Sovereignty resides in the nation.
- Liberty consists in the freedom to do everything which injures no-one else.
- Every citizen has a right to participate personally or through a representative in making the law.
- No person shall be accused, arrested or imprisoned except by process of law, which shall provide only punishments that are strictly necessary.
- No-one shall be disturbed on account of his opinions, including his religious views.
- Every citizen may speak, write and print with freedom but will be responsible for abuses of this freedom as defined by law.
- A constitution without the separation of powers is no constitution at all.

It is a glorious document, the founding document of modern democracy.

China Vs Europe

For a long period, Chinese civilization was more advanced than European. Europe learned printing, papermaking, the compass, gunpowder and locks for canals from China directly or indirectly. However, it was in Europe that the steady economic growth and the Industrial Revolution happened, and it was Europe that first developed representative government, individuals' rights, and other brands of modernity. What is it about Europe?

In 1480 the Ming emperor of China declared that foreign exploration and trade were prohibited; merchants who continued to trade were proclaimed as smugglers and the army was sent to destroy their settlements and burn their boats. No European king ever used such a self-denying regulation. For centuries the danger to the king's control came from the strongest group of his subjects. Ultimately, they were suppressed. But subjects were strong enough to acquire security of private property.

European monarchs taxed a regular, moderate way so that they did not kill the goose that laid the golden egg. Rulers of Asian countries were more indiscriminative, levied penalizing taxation or just confiscated the goods of merchants and traders if they were short of money.

Despite the fact that Europe was divided, it was one civilization known as Christendom. In Europe, the power was split, and the high culture was fused, and not firmly bound to secure rule. The Chinese were very knowledgeable, but their knowledge never got widespread; they never transferred their innovations. The openness of European society goes a long way back. The vitality of its economy and the turbulence of its intellectual life in the modern period originate from the fact that no single power was responsible in shaping it for good or ill. Its varied legacy could be fully explored and extended. The Greek mathematics was comprehended during the Scientific Revolution, which created a new source for technological innovation.

A question being posted by Economic historians that why Europe was the first to industrialize it while other societies also had the same opportunity and why Europe reached the goal first? Probably it is because Europe had curiosity and inquisitiveness.

Destructive Forces

Europe consisted a group of states and they always fought each other. There were two dreadful wars in the twentieth century in Europe in which both soldiers and civilians were killed on a mass scale.

Two forces nationalism, which originated from intellectual origins in Germany and industrialization, which began in Britain played a large part:

Nationalism intensified the affection of people to their country and motivation to fight for their country. This was a great source of conflict in the countries of Central and Eastern Europe.

Industrialization magnetized people from the countryside and far from villages into the more unknown place of towns. People gathered together as never before and populations increased quickly. They began to learn to read. They began to learn about their society in schools and from newspapers, which were processed cheaply on machinery run by steam. In the twentieth century they were listening to the radio and watching films; old social ties weakened and the church became less important; national feelings instilled in schools and spread by new media helped people to knit together. Nationalism replaced religion giving individuals a place in an everlasting community. Anthems and flags began to appear, heroes and heroines were born, sacred moments and places emerged to secure attachment to this new faith.

Ironically, nationalism produced war, industrialization made war more terrible because the new iron and steel factories were able to produce larger and more destructive weapons in greater quantities.

In Europe there was a new kind in human affairs: mass production, mass society; mass slaughter.

Communist Movement

Industrialization created a fear in Europe. Before, farmers had regularly rioted and had easily been suppressed. But now workers worked and lived more closely together in the new industrial towns and as they learnt to read and write, they began to understand the powers that controlled them. Therefore, they created organisations and made their claims for a better life, and their input in the administration of their society had to be considered.

Eventually employees organized protest movements to claim political rights, foremost among them was the right of all men to vote. They organized trade unions to fight their employers for better wages and conditions. They founded political parties, removed bosses with the intention to run the industry for the good of those who did the work. It was a motto and program of socialism. They planned a revolution to get rid of bosses and to establish a worker's state. This communist movement had no permanent success in Europe, but they succeeded in Russia. Their role in Russia triggered the fear in Europe. Nationalists hated communists because communists claimed that workers should not fight for their countries; they said, workers should co-operate and fight only for their bosses and the governments that protected their bosses.

Industrialization also increased the grades of the middle class, merchants, bankers, manufacturers and the professional people who served them. Once trade and industry started to grow, they became important. Before, absolute monarchs drew people on their wealth and had appointed them into their service. One may speculate did industrialization lead to revolution.

The Condition of the Working Class in England

Hirst writes, in Britain, the Industrial revolution was unplanned and there was no planning in the cities that developed around the new workshops. To accommodate the workers, old houses were rented from attic to cellar; one room was the living place for a whole family. New row houses built were crowded together, back to back, had a front door but no back door or back windows. The roads were unpaved; there were no sewers or gutters; waste of every kind amassed in the streets.

In the 1840s Friedrich Engels came from Germany to England to check his father's business that manufactured sewing threads. Inspecting the conditions of England, he authored a book, *The Condition of the Working Class in England.* He wrote that no people on earth had ever lived like the English lived then. Manufacturing goods by machinery had polarised society: there were only two classes in the new towns: the middle-class owners of the factories and the workers. The work itself was dull and repetitious and humiliating; the workers had nothing but their work to live in destitute; it was like to experiment 'in how little space a human being can move; how little air he can breathe; how little of civilization he may share and yet live.' Engels foresaw that this situation may not last long.

Karl Marx - The Communist Manifesto

Karl Marx, a German philosopher turned revolutionary journalist read Engels' book when he published in German. In 1848 Marx and Engels jointly published The Communist Manifesto, which claimed that history was leaning to the situation that Engels had explained in England. It noted that just like the middle class had struggled against the aristocracy, so is the workers' state. 'The history of all hitherto existing society,' said the opening words of The Communist Manifesto, 'is the history of class struggle.' Its final advice to workers was that by overturning society they would lose nothing but their chains. It exclaimed that the law and religion in existing societies operated only to oppress them. Individual rights, what we now call human rights, are fraud too; they are benefiting the bosses and not the workers. Their little book was the most influential political pamphlet. According to the theory, the workers' revolution would happen first.

Many changes happened after England's revolution in the seventeenth century and produced a constitution in which the king was controlled by parliament; voting rights were given, including some women over thirty to vote. As a result, workers' living standards were improved. Thus, the leaders of Britain handled the social disorder of the industrial revolution without political disorder.

1. Industrial revolution. 2. Holocaust. 3. Napoleon Bonaparte (1769 –1821 CE). 4. Karl Marx. 5. Adolf Hitler

There was no industrial revolution in France. The textile industry became mechanized, but the coal and iron industries did not expand fast. Throughout the nineteenth century France was an agricultural society, lands owned by peasants because of the 1789 revolution. The Paris Commune was the last and most determined effort of the people of Paris to make a revolution of their own. The cruel control of the Commune stopped the working-class threat to French society. However, people had democratic republic and voting privileges.

Germany had its industrial revolution late in the second half of the nineteenth century. It was a third stage industrial revolution with industries in chemical, electrical, textiles, coal and iron. German industrial workers supported the largest socialist party in Europe, which followed Karl Marx teaching for a long time. This made them opposed to war that owned the most efficient war machine in Europe.

Britain's control over the seas was important for the survival of its empire as well its own survival because it did not grow enough food to feed the country. It was frightened by German's shipbuilding and went forward to prove that it could excel at it.

Europe Fought Two World Wars

Europe fought two World Wars: World War 1 from 1914 to 1918 and World War 2 from 1939 to 1945.

President Wilson of the United States had a difficult job to take his country to participate in the war in Europe. It was a strong tradition of the United States to stay away from quagmire with wars of Europe. When it became necessary to join hands with Europe, he declared that US participation in war is not about conquest and vengeance; it was a war to make the world 'safe for democracy'. He listed his principles for the people in "Fourteen Points" to assure the future peace to endangered ethnic groups becoming separate nations; secret treaties between nations; and a new world body to settle disputes.

Hitler

In the 1920s, Hitler's party was limited to a small group. It was called the National Socialist Party. It is Socialist because he wanted to appeal to workers, National because he wanted to limit the internationalism of Marxian socialism. Hitler was angry about Marx's statements that workers had no country; that their first loyalty should be their class; and that they should divide their country with class warfare. Hitler did not attack big businesses, because it had to do the work of rearming Germany. He desired workers to have a job, live comfortably in better housing and with more holidays. But they were prohibited to have unions.

The plan was more National than Socialist. Hitler wanted an end to party division; to create a united Germany under his leadership strong enough to abolish the restrictions of Versailles to which the weak politicians had agreed; and to claim German nation to the east occupied by the substandard Slavs: the Poles, Ukrainians and Russians. He intended that the internal enemies of the Reich should be eliminated: the internal enemies were Marxists, both socialists and communists, and the Jews. Hitler believed that there was a worldwide Jewish conspiracy to degrade the higher races that were the carriers of civilization. Marx was a Jew and some leading Bolsheviks in Russia were Jews. Hitler believed the Jews were responsible for WWI and thought so much suffering could have been avoided if they had all gassed.

In Europe there was a longstanding prejudice against Jews, and they thought they were the killers of Christ. As race-thinking became stronger in the nineteenth century, anti-Semites began to see Jews as an immediate and dangerous threat to racial health. They believed that Jews inter-breeding with the higher race would damage their prospects in the struggle of existence. These concepts were broadly shared by many and not only in Germany. Also, they were backed and endorsed as scientific. Hitler was so paranoid about the danger and so he became absolutely inhuman in finding a solution for it.

Nazi Party

Hitler was not the founder of the Nazi Party, but he was a member of the party. In January 1919 Nazi Party began in Munich in southern Germany under the name German Workers' Party. Eventually, he became the undisputed leader, banned committees and ruled that the party platform was never to be debated again. He acquired this power because of his extraordinary ability as a speaker; he could entrance, persuade, excite and energise his audiences. This demobilized soldier, who had been a drop-out and wanderer before the war, had found his profession. Hitler's abilities made this tiny party into a significant player in Munich's political life and he also won the support of some influential people.

During a brief exchange of gunshots, four police and fourteen of Hitler's men were killed and Hitler was captured. Hitler was put on trial on the charge of treason and got a light sentence of five year's imprisonment.

Mein Kampf (My Struggle)

Hitler was imprisoned not in a jail but comfortably in an old castle used for political prisoners. He had the leisure to read, think and write. He produced a long tedious book called Mein Kampf (My Struggle), which became the Bible of his movement. It was a mixture of his life history, his political views, the history, and the future of racial struggles. None of the ideas were original; the original passages recorded his discoveries on how to get a crowd to change its mind. According to him 'mass suggestion' and 'mass effect': Speaking was vital; print was too cool a medium; reasoning would not work; your will must conquer over the multitude of individual wills; the time and setting for meetings were important: night rather than day; some halls would work and some would not. Hitler was freed in less than a year.

Later Hitler advanced from Munich beer halls to leading over huge outdoor rallies, very carefully staged and choreographed. He knew why they worked: when the lonely, uncertain individual becomes part of a larger community, the morale of the community soars.

The Nazi Party invited people from all classes: workers, clerks, shopkeepers, students, farmers, middle-class, and upper-class people. The other parties exemplified a class or a faith or a region; the Nazi Party alone was truly national. Within the party its highly distinct members were of equal standing, which was an unusual practice in a society, which was still very status conscious. Its members were equal in their love of country, their membership was in the superior Aryan race, and their obedience to the Fuhrer who was an ordinary man, as the party propaganda boasted.

The Nazi government moved on Jews more cautiously. Boycotts of Jewish business shocked people and caused economic disruption. Then the law in 1935 was decreed that the Jews were denied of citizenship and prohibited to marry or have sexual relations with Germans. In 1938 the Nazis gave orders to their followers for an attack on Jewish shops, businesses and synagogues. For the first time Jews were sent to concentration camps because they were Jews rather than members of political organizations. Then the orders were issued that took property from Jews, kept them out of public places, and expelled their children from school. Emigration of Jews was encouraged.

Hitler had accomplished his promise to abolish the restrictions of the Versailles Treaty within a few years of taking office and increased the army five times larger than Versailles. He marched German troops in the demilitarized Rhineland. Britain and France were not eager to wage war to stop him. They did not want to see the recurring of the horrors of WWI and particularly in Britain.

At last when Hitler invaded Poland in September 1939, Britain and France declared war on Germany.

Concentration Camp and Holocaust

For Hitler the battle in the east was bigger. He made it into a campaign of mass murder so that the lands of Slavs and Jews can be used for the settlement by the superior race. First, he ordered the Jews making them stand in line. But, as this was a slow process and unpleasant, the Nazis constructed a factory-like killing machine in which Jews were gassed and their bodies burnt in ovens. Once this system was operating, Jews were brought from all Nazis occupied territories and destroyed them systematically. The collection and transport of Jews continued even as the fighting was going against Hitler. For Hitler the purging of Jews had become top priority, necessary to secure Germany's future and a fit punishment for the race that in his opinion had caused this war as they had done in the last war. It is estimated that about six million Jews died in what has been named the Holocaust. Even though the Nazis thought this destruction was for the best, they did not advertise what they were doing. But many thousands of Germans inside and outside the Nazi Party did know of it because they directly involved.

The United States did not join the war until Japan, an ally of Germany, launched an attack on the US navy at Pearl Harbour in Hawaii in December 1941. President Roosevelt obviously declared war on Japan, but he did not declare war on Germany. But Hitler immediately declared war on the US, making an enemy of the world's greatest power.

It was the Russians who fought their way into the centre of Berlin where Hitler and his group were hiding in a bunker. Hitler was unaffected by the destruction that his war had brought to Germany. He committed suicide rather than be captured.

Hitler was unsuccessful to destroy Russian communism. Instead, he brought the Red Army into central Europe. The Russians installed communist governments in the territories they had liberated from the Nazis: Poland, Czechoslovakia, Hungary, and the Balkan states except Greece.

European Union

Old enemies Germany and France agreed to combine their resources of coal and iron and stop being competitors in the making of steel. From this start came the European Common Market, this was a grouping of six European countries with France and Germany as its core. Germany was accepted back into the community of nations and tied into peaceful relations because of those economic arrangements. Economic co-operation grew into the European Union, a political organization that was a European federation in making.

When the Soviet Union started to restructure itself in the later 1980s and stopped to support the communist regimes of Eastern Europe, those governments dissolved quickly. The ex-communist countries applied to join the European Union and were accepted. The collapse of communist regimes liberated millions of people from dictatorship. It also liberated Europe from the poisonous doctrine that civilization was simply a system of oppression and that a ruthless dictatorship would create a workers' condition as a state of perfect equality.

John Hirst writes, "The constitution of the European Union, in the usual way carries a preamble. In a civilisation of mixed origins there was naturally an argument over what it should contain. The pope wanted Christianity acknowledged: but France the home and nurturer of

Enlightenment fiercely opposed. So, it is not Christianity that is acknowledged but more vaguely Europe's religious inheritance, which is joined to humanism from the Renaissance and to its culture generally. Enlightenment is the dominant influence, for a Europe committed to 'the universal values of the inviolable and inalienable rights of the human person' is to follow the path of 'progress and prosperity'. And nationalist will be transcended for 'while remaining proud of their own national identities and history, the peoples of Europe are determined to transcend their former divisions and, united over more closely, to forge a common destiny'."

10

The Middle East

"People between 600 and 300 BC, in remote and seemingly unrelated lands achieved major spiritual and intellectual breakthroughs. This was the time of Confucius and Lao-Tse in China, Buddha in India, Zoroaster or his major disciples in Iran, the prophet in Israel, and the philosophers in Greece. These were to a very large extent unknown to one another. There seems to have been some activity in the Middle East by Buddhist missionaries from India, but it is little known, and appears to have had no effect on each other."

– ***The German philosopher and historian Karl Jaspers***

The Middle East is a modern English term for the most ancient area of human civilization. Before Christianity, the Middle East referred to Arabia, the Gulf, Persia (Iran), Egypt, Turkey, Mesopotamia (Iraq), Afghanistan, and most likely Meluha (Harappa). There are numerous references in Sumerian clay tablets about the trade transactions between Sumer and Harappa.

The common usage of the Middle East should not allow us to lose sight of its past distinguished civilization and culture. It was far advanced than Western Europe except for the last five hundred out of the five thousand or so years. The Nile Valley and Delta; Mesopotamia, the land of the twin rivers, the Tigris and the Euphrates, can claim superiority as the cradle of human civilization, but it is their joint role in the development of humankind which matters.

Hammurabi, King of Babylon in the 1800 BCE, devised the first all-inclusive code of law which has survived even today. Akhenaten, Pharaoh of Egypt in the 1400 BCE had the first idea of a single all-powerful deity. Rameses II the Great founded an empire which covered most of the Middle Eastern region. In this huge range of territory, a good deal of human history was made.

1. Confucius, 2. Lao-Tse, 3. Buddha, 4. Zoroaster

Middle East before Christianity

Before Christianity, the western half of today's Middle East from Bosphorus (Northwest of Turkey) to the Nile Delta in Egypt belonged to Roman Empire eliminating all their ancient civilizations. The eastern half of the region belonged to Persia, which was also called Iran.

The ancient cultures that had survived until the beginning of the Christian era preserved their old identity and their old language, particularly Egypt. Even though Egyptian language and writing had undergone many changes over the period, it survived until Christian period and was replaced by Coptic, the latest form of ancient Egyptian language. Gradually Coptic language disappeared gradually and survives only in Coptic Church.

The Middle East had many names before it was called Middle East:

1. EGYPT: The name Egypt was used by Greeks and the Romans and today's modern world; it was not the original Egyptian name. The second syllable in Egypt is probably from the root 'Copt' who spoke Coptic language.
2. MESOPOTAMIA: The south, the center, and the north of today's Middle East belonged to the people who spoke the languages of Sumer and Akkad, Assyria, and Babylonia, which was also called Mesopotamia.
3. PERSIA: The south and center places of today's Middle East as far as Baghdad were under the control of Persians. The name Baghdad means "God gave" (Bagh+dad) in Persian language.
4. ASSYRIA: The origin of the name Syria is not traceable. Herodotus explains it as Assyria, but modern scholars dispute the place. The name Syria, Suriya in Arabic, appears in some writings.
5. CANAAN: The Mesopotamian (also called Fertile Crescent) countries were called in Hebrew Bible and other ancient writings as Canaan.
6. ISRAEL: After the Israelites conquered the region and settled in the area, they described it as 'land of the children of Israel.'
7. JERUSALEM, JUDAH, SAMARIA: After the breakdown in 1000 BCE, the southern part was called Judah and Jerusalem as the capital. North was called Israel, later Samaria.
8. PHOENICIA AND PHILISTIA: The north and southern coastal areas were known as Phoenicia and Philistia.
9. YEHUD: After the Persian conquest in 600 BCE, the area was resettled by exiles and named as Yehud.
10. The south, center, and north of the country are called Judaea, Samaria, and Galilee.

The main languages in Mesopotamia and Syria were Semitic with several different subdivisions of the language. Then they were replaced by several later languages like Hebrew, Carthaginian, and Canaanite languages.

Aramaic became an international medium of communication. Later, Aramaic was replaced by Arabic.

Turkey did not obtain its name until the middle ages when the Turks or Mongols arrived from the Far East. The usual names used in earlier times were Asia or Asia Minor, and Anatolia. Anatolia has the origin from a Greek word meaning 'sunrise', in Latin 'Orient', and in Italian 'Levant'.

Name Modification from Asia to Middle East

(1) When Mediterranean people came to know that there is a vast land of Asia in remote East, they renamed their region as Asia Minor.

(2) When they discovered Indus River in the East some centuries later, it became Near East.

(3) And when they became aware of more distant eastern countries, they changed their region as the Middle East.

According to Bernard Lewis, Persia was not the name of a country, but it was the name of a province. Because their regional language was Pars or Fars, their land was known as Persia. They always used the name Iran for their country implying the name derived from the ancient Persian Aryanam, "the land of the Aryans," which dates back to the early migrations of the Indo-Aryan people.

Religions - Monotheism and Jews

Both Christian and Islamic civilizations have common roots in Jews, Persians and Greeks and the idea of monotheism in these religions was not completely new. It was perceived by pharaohs of Egypt sporadically in 1400 BCE. But, the first to make the ethical monotheism as an essential part of their religion seriously were Jews recording their outlook in their Hebrew Bible. Believing in monotheism, one god, among their idol-worshippers and polytheistic neighbors isolated Jews from the rest of the region. Even in modern times, those who believe that they are in a unique position of acquiring the truth do agree that the discovery of monotheistic truth was Jew's achievement. For the pious devotees of idol-worshippers in ancient times, this line of monotheistic thoughts would have been terribly disrespectful to their faith.

However, Jews were not the only people who believed in one god. On the highland of Iran, the people of Medes and Persia believed in a single supreme deity, the fundamental power of good. The origin of this religion was associated with Zoroaster. During 600-500 BCE, Zoroastrian religion was very active.

In 586 BCE, the king of Babylon Nebuchadnezzar captured Jerusalem and destroyed both the kingdom of Judah and Jerusalem temple, and sent captivated people to Babylonia. Some decades later, 'Cyrus the Great' of Persia conquered Babylonia and authorized the Jews to return to the land of Israel from Babylonia. He also gave orders to build the temple in Jerusalem at the government's expense. Cyrus was perceived as their shepherd with great respect.

Pivotal Age

The German philosopher and historian Karl Jaspers exclaims that the period between 600 and 300 BCE was an 'Axial Age' in the history of humanity. He writes,

> "People in remote and apparently unrelated lands achieved major spiritual and intellectual breakthroughs. This was the time of Confucius and Lao-Tse in China, Buddha in India, Zoroaster or his major disciples in Iran, the prophets in Israel, and the philosophers in Greece. These were to a very large extent unknown to one another. There seems to have been some activity in the Middle East by Buddhist missionaries from India, but it is little known, and appears to have had little effect."

The productive mutual relation between Jews and Persians starts from the date of Cyrus and his successors, around 550 BCE. Cyrus' successors came into contact with Greeks and thus established the lines of communication between Greek civilization and Persian Empire. The Greek's brilliance was philosophical and scientific rather than religious. The visions realized by Greek philosophers and scientists have a deep impact on the later religious civilizations of the Middle East.

The Zoroastrian faith and priesthood achieved great power, but subsequently after much political turmoil, its priestly establishment was destroyed along with the Persian Empire. Zoroastrians reached a long decline in Islamic times. A renowned British-American historian Bernard Lewis writes,

> "Religious resistance was offered to the advance of Islam in Iran came not from the orthodox Zoroastrian priesthood but rather from Zoroastrian heresies, that is, from those who were accustomed to opposition and repression, not from those accustomed to the exercise of authority."

The children of Israel, later the people of Judaea, became the Jews. The Jews failed in political resistance before Greece and Rome. They revolted against mighty Rome and were crushed and reduced to slavery and their kings and high priests became Roman pawns. Jews began another revolt in 66 CE. In spite of a long and bitter fight, the rebels were conquered and captured, and destroyed the second temple in Jerusalem, which had been built by the exiles returning from Babylonia. Jews did not end their struggle and continued to rebel against Rome. In 135 AD, Romans decided to get rid of these troublesome people once and for all and sent a large part of the population of Jews into captivity and exile. This time there was no Cyrus to protect them. Jerusalem was renamed Aelia Capitolina, and the temple of Jupiter built on the site of the destroyed Jewish temple. The names Judaea and Samaria were eliminated, and the places renamed Palestine.

A few centuries later, a second major religion Islam ascended in the same region. With two world religions living side by side in the same region, it was inevitable that they would clash one day.

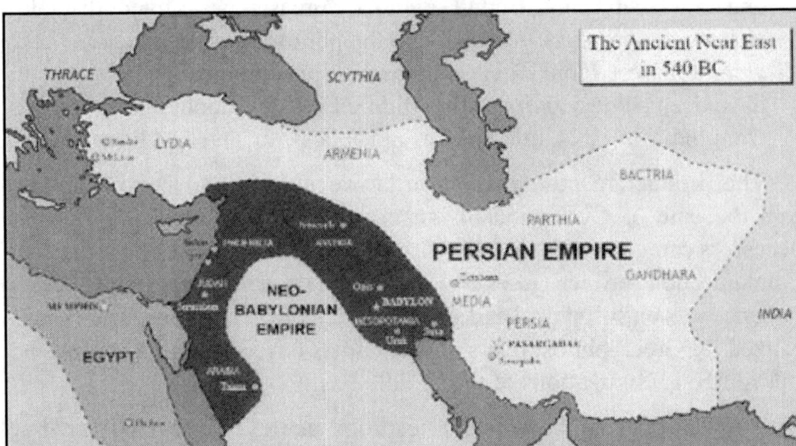

The Ancient Near East in 540 BC

Middle East Before Islam

Six hundred years between the period from Christianity and Islam, the region was shaped by a several major developments both in the form of incidents and in the movement of civilizations. The first was the rise of Christian religion which was submerged by all ancient religions except the Jews and the Persians. For some time, classical Greco-Roman paganism remained. After the conversion by the emperor Constantine (311-337 CE) Christianity spread all over the Roman Empire.

The second important change was the shifting of the capital of Roman Empire from Rome to Constantinople. The name generally called as

Byzantine is derived from the name of the settlement previously existed on the location of the city of Constantinople.

Both Roman rulers and Christian Churches were influenced by the Hellenistic traditions and philosophies and the Christian scriptures and the New Testament were written in Greek language. Even the Old Testament was translated into Greek.

Persia

During the first six centuries of the Christian dominance, Iranian Empire instigated two stages: The first being the Parthians and second the Sassanid. The first Sassanid ruler Ardashir (226-240 CE) launched a new type of war against Rome, and his successor Shapur I succeeded in capturing the Roman emperor Valerian in a battle. It was a great accomplishment and he victoriously carved this story on several stone monuments in Iran. The depicts are still seen as the Shah of Persia on horseback, the Roman emperor at his feet,. and Shah's feet on the emperor's neck.

The long and endless series of wars between Perso-Roman and later Perso-Byzantine destroyed one of the rivals and weakened the other. Shapur III (383-388 CE) made a peace agreement with Rome and stayed mainly calm until 628 CE with minor clashes. Shortly a new power was lingering at the corner that would dominate both aggressive enemies.

Recently, the modern historians have found the reason behind the wars other than territorial claims, which was about the control over the trade routes between East and West. To the Mediterranean World, two major imports were particularly important from east: Silk from China and spices from India and Southeast Asia. Because of these two commodities, Roman and Byzantine empires were in touch with these two civilizations. There were no regular relations with these countries, but the recorded documents indicate a very few exchanges and it seems both empires paid the gold coin in exchange. Persians made enormous profit as middlemen dominating the silk trade from China.

Turks and Arabs

Previously, the Turks and Arabs were people of insignificant frontiers in the history, remaining in barbarous or semi-barbarous plains and desert lands. Even Romans and Persians did not show any interest to conquer these desert lands and stayed away from their vicinity. One Syrian historian Ammianus Marcellinus in 400 CE writes about the desert dwellers:

> "The inhabitants of all the districts are savage and warlike, and take such pleasure in war and conflict, that one who loses his life in battle is regarded as happy beyond all others. For those who depart from this life by a natural death, they assail with insults as degenerate and cowardly.
>
> "The Saracens… whom we never found desirable either as friends or as enemies."

Therefore, realizing that to defeat such people by armed forces was expensive, difficult, and dangerous, they kept them satisfied by flattering and providing financial and other small things to retain their good will. These tribal chiefs learned to exploit taking advantage of their goodwill leaning sometimes one side and sometimes on the other side. They accumulated wealth by the caravan trade and established their own cities and kingdoms with their own political system. Gradually they started to become partners with imperial powers.

In the distant south of the Arabian Peninsula, South Arabia was very different from the semi-desert region of the north. It had well cultivated lands and cities ruled by dynasties and monarchs. But these monarchies collapsed becoming a battleground for Persians from the east and Ethiopians from the west.

By the third century, the economic decline occurred due to vanishing of trade in the region. Roman coins became fewer and fewer and there were virtually none of the Roman coins found in India after 217 CE. Arabia descended to a kind of Dark Age between the fourth and sixth centuries. Its fertile lands diminished and became sedimentary centers, and camel nomadism came into existence. This situation was brightly remembered in early Muslim stories which soon saw the advent of Islam.

The reason for this decline in Arabia was due to the negligence of two imperial powers Rome and Persia. They were not interested in Arabia and its long, expensive, and hazardous trade routes that passed through the deserts. Some of the inhabitants in the desert migrated elsewhere or assumed nomadic life again. The evaporation of trade and declining standard of living left Arabia still more isolated from the civilized societies in the world. Nomadism was always a norm in Arabian society. Now it became permanent and predominant. Muslims call this period as 'Jahiliyya,' the Age of Ignorance, and comparing the period of Islam as the Age of Light. In the neighboring countries peace was maintained by Byzantine and Persia without any wars for more than a century.

Prophet Muhammad (571 AD)

Everything changed again in the sixth century when Muhammad was born. The main reason was the eruption of conflicts between Byzantine and Persia resulting in continuous war. Arabia once again materialized as the main actor in the struggle and enjoyed the experience of flatter and honor. Actually, in peacetime the more convenient way of trade was by water. During war time, these routes were closed to rival parties, which enabled Arabian Desert routes to be more desirable.

In the early years of the Prophet Muhammad's life, Yamen was under Persian control governed by a satrap establishing the Persian power defeating the Byzantine power. It opened a trade route to the east and also a major development happened in the region. For a long period of time, the manufacture of silk was secretly guarded in China and export of silkworm faced capital punishment. In 552 CE two Nestorian monks were able to achieve smuggle silkworm eggs from China to Byzantine. By the 700 AD, sericulture was fully established in Asia Minor. Author writes, "Chinese silk was still valued for its superior beauty and quality, but the Chinese world monopoly had ended."

The Persians tried to survive for a while, but they also were terribly weakened by dispute over succession and by religious problems emerging within the Zoroastrian faith.

Byzantine had their own problem including the great church disputes which shook Byzantine Christianity.

All these changes had a significant effect in the Arabian Peninsula. Apart from political changes, a number of foreigners came to Arabia, as colonists and refugees; they brought new ideas, artefacts and new ways of life. Because of Byzantine-Persia conflicts, new trade routes opened resulting in significant movement of merchants and commodities.

All these developments produced a great materialistic power to Arabs. They learned the use of arms and weapons, military secrets, which were the most important training and lessons that were to occur in the future. They also learned to enjoy the taste of more civilized societies previously not known to them. There was also some intellectual and spiritual reaction as Arabians started to learn the religion and culture of their sophisticated neighbors. They learned writing, created a script, and began to write their own language. They absorbed new ideas and disliked their primitive paganism religion seeking something better. Majority of the people were prepared to abandon paganism but did not like to accept the contending religious doctrines of that time. They were the first converts to the newly budding religion of Islam.

Origin of Muhammad

According to Bernard Lewis, the early life of Prophet Muhammad and the origin of Islam are understood only from the Muslim scriptures, traditions, and historical recollections. After some time, these events came to the attention of the outside world and were recognized by external observers. The Islam resembles many popular religions of humankind, like Judaism, Christianity, and Zoroastrian.

According to the Muslim belief, a signal for Prophet-hood came to Muhammad, the son of Abdallah, when he was about the age of forty. The narration follows thus:

> "On a night in the month of Ramadan, the Angel Gabriel came to Muhammad as he slept in solitude of Mount Hira and said, 'Recite!' Muhammad hesitated, and three times the Angel nearly choked him until Muhammad asked, 'What shall I recite?' Then the Angel said, 'Recite in the name of thy Lord who created all things, who created man from clots of blood. Recite, for the Lord is the most generous, who taught by the pen, who taught man what he did not know.' These words form the first four verses of the ninety-six chapter of Muslim scripture, known as the Quran."

Quran is an Arabic word which joins the meaning of 'reading' and 'recitation'. According to Muslim belief, the revelations in the book were given by God.

According to the legend, Muhammad was born around 571 CE in the family of Arab tribe of Quraysh in Hijaz of western Arabia. The region was mainly empty desert with rare oases and crossed by a few travelers. Most of its people were nomads, lived their life by raising sheep, goats, and camels. Some also lived by cultivating lands occasionally and some by commerce.

In the beginning of his mission Muhammad earned a number of followers, first in his own family, and then in broader circle. Initially, his new ideas and new movements were perceived in suspicions and as a threat to the existing order. In the year 622 AD, the prophet made an agreement with a small town called Yathrib and Mecca. The people in Yathrib invited Muhammad and his followers to their city and asked him to be an arbitrator in one of their disputes. Muhammad and sixty of his followers migrated from Mecca to Yathrib known as Hijra in Arabic. Hijra means literally the migration, which was defining moment in Muhammad's evangelistic activity. When Muslim calendar was established, this migration day was counted as the beginning of the Arabian year in which the Hijra happened. Later Yathrib was renamed as Al-Madina – the City.

In Mecca, Muhammad had to face the hostilities of the local rulers. But, in Medina, he himself became a ruler controlling political, military, and religious authorities. Muslim community involved in warfare with the pagan rulers of Mecca, and eventually Muhammad conquered Mecca and established Islamic faith converting idol-worshipers of the region.

The difference between the Muhammad and previous religious leaders Moses and Jesus is described in the writings of his followers:

> "Moses was not permitted to enter the Promised Land and died while his people went forward. Jesus was crucified, and Christianity remained a persecuted minority religion for centuries, until a Roman emperor, Constantine embraced the faith and empowered those who upheld it. In contrast, Muhammad occupied his promised land, and while alive he achieved victory and power in this world, implementing both political and religious authorities. As a messenger of God, he narrated religious revelations and at the same time he imposed laws, offered justice, collected taxes, handled diplomacy, made war, and peace."

When the Prophet died on 8 June 632 AD, his mission was accomplished. The duty of his followers was to restore the true monotheism, abandon idolatry, and to follow God's revelations exemplifying the true faith and the holy law. According to Muslim belief, Muhammad was the last prophet and there will be no more prophets and no more revelations. Likewise, the spiritual search was completed, and spiritual function remained as maintaining and defending the Divine Law and spreading it to the entire world.

They needed to choose a leader for their community soon. The Muslim community chose one of the inner circle followers, Abu Bakr. The title used for Abu Bakr as a leader was Khalifa, an Arabic word, which combines the concept of both successor and deputy. He was Khalifatu Rasul Allah 'the successor of the Prophet of God'; according to some others, he was Khalifat Allah, 'the Deputy of God'.

Within a century after the Prophet's death, the entire western part of Asia was transformed. It was certainly a dramatic change in the whole of human history. By the late 700 AD, the Muslim empire extended its domination as far as the borders of China and India in the east, Mediterranean coast to the Atlantic in west, Africa in the south, and Europe in the north. The Persians in the east having their powerful state destroyed and their priestly system was powerless recognized a structure and meaning in Islam. And in the center, Aramaic speaking people of Mesopotamia and Coptic-speaking people of Egypt found their new masters more tolerant and more welcoming than the old rulers. All learned the Arabic language and liked the Arab tastes, attitudes, and ideas.

Transition to Islam was quite easy for these countries: Arab taxes were lower than those collected by the Byzantines for both Muslims and general populations.

One of the driving forces of the Arab conquests was the burden of overpopulation in the unfertile land of Arabian Peninsula. Consequently, the Arab influence radiated into the nearby areas and gradually further and further.

Shia

By 656 CE many Caliphas had been murdered by Muslim followers and installed Prophet's cousin and son-in-law to a key position. As a husband of the Prophet's daughter Fatima, Ali had no special claim of attention because such relations did not count much in polygamous society. As the Prophet's relative, he was eligible to become a candidate for the succession to some political and religious authority. Ali's personal qualities attracted the support of many Muslims and kindled the hope that he might bring opponents back to original true message of Islam. Their party was called Ali, Shiatu, or simply Shia.

Sunni

The name Sunni is derived from the phrase "Ahl al-Sunnah" or "People of the Tradition." The tradition refers to practices based on what the Prophet Muhammad said, did, agreed or condemned.

Karbala

A religiously and historically significant incident occurred in 680 CE. A son of Ali and a grandson of the Prophet, Husayn conducted a mutiny in Iraq. On the tenth day of the month of Muharram, Husayn, his family, and his followers faced an Umayyad army in the battle and were defeated. As per the documented records, some seventy people were killed in the battle. But the sole survivor was the sick son of Husayn who was left lying in a tent. The massacre of Karbala became central to the Shite perception of

Islamic history, and the tenth day of Muharram a major event in the Shiite religious calendar.

The massacre of Karbala transformed Shias from a political party to a religious sect. Their main perception of god was, "God is one, without a partner, without a companion." In this stanza it rejects the Christian doctrine of the Trinity.

The 800, 900, and 1000 CE had experienced a great intellectual expansion in cultural life in the Middle East. During that period, the economic progress encouraged the development of cities and allowed the urban population to enjoy leisure, taste, and curiosity. The Greek scientific and philosophic literatures were translated into Arabic introducing a time called "The Renaissance of Islam." Recognizing the Greek learning and Persian worldly wisdom, Islam renewed and enhanced the old Arabic humanities. But this cultural development was impermanent and unstable because this art was limited to only city people. It was not compatible with tradition to the Islamic way of religious life which was very strict in tradition.

In Islamic society many internal weaknesses were appearing by 1100 CE. The relationship with Egypt, Byzantine and Sassanid Iran was deteriorating, the economic life was weakening, the profitable trade with China decreased, and trade with Russia that flourished in the eighth, ninth and tenth centuries was also diminished.

The religious institutions of Sunni caliphate had carefully guarded their privileges in the disciplines of doctrine, law, education, and social institutions according to its own inner logic. Even though it had some advantages, it produced dangerous organizational conflicts in the harmony of state. The tension between state and religion increased.

Steppe People

During the 1100 and 1200 AD, the empire was exposed to a series of attacks by internal and external enemies of all sides. The most important of all was the wave of invaders from the east, the Altaic peoples of Asian steppes. The Muslims first imported Turks from the eastern borders as slaves who were trained in the military, later they called them Mamluk, meaning 'owned' to separate them from simpler slaves hired for domestic and economic purposes. Gradually, the Turkish troops became commanders and established their dominations. In 868 AD, a dynasty of Muslim Egypt was founded by a Turkish military slave. In Iran, national dynasties of Samanids depended on Turkish soldiers and eventually Turks displaced Samanids and established Turkish dynasty by Ghaznavids who was a Turkish slave. The single soldier or a group of soldiers entered the Muslim states and replaced them.

The unique character of Turkish people is that they surrendered themselves to new religion Islam. Except for a few folk poetry and genealogical legends, the civilizations, states, religions, and literature of the pre-Islamic past of Turks were erased and forgotten.

Mongolia & Genghiz Khan

A new more deadly external threat to Islam was brewing in the north-eastern corner of Asia from warring nomadic tribes of Mongolia. In 1206, Genghiz Khan invited all his Mongolian tribes on the bank of Onon River and unfurled his white banner with nine horsetails and demanded their loyalty to him. They unanimously offered their loyalty and there began Mongol Empire. By 1218, almost northeast Asia was at his feet and by 1219 his army marched towards the lands of Islam, and by 1220 the cities Bukhara, Samarqand and other places were under his control.

Even though the death of Genghiz Khan in 1227 gave some break, his grandson Hulagu moved westward to conquer all the territories of Islam and as far as Egypt. Within a few months, the long-haired Mongol troops roared through Iran facing all mighty resistance. *Lastly, the Mongol soldiers occupied Baghdad in January 1258.*

In place of caliphates, the sultanate gained the recognition of the jurists and religious institutions, and they claimed religious titles and rights for themselves previously reserved to the caliphs. The sudden attacks of Mongols were obviously crushing, and the whole areas were devastated, depopulated, and destroyed. But Egypt, the chief center of Arabic culture was never conquered by the Mongols and was not affected at all.

In Iran, Mongol khans provided political stability, encouraged industry and trade, reconstructed town life, assisted Islamic literature and learning. In fact, the Mongol conquests actually helped to instill new life into the staggering civilization of the Middle East. Meanwhile, they began renewed contacts with Europe and provided opportunities to non-Muslim rulers to explore the land routes to China. Regarding this new approach, a Persian historian, basically a Jewish converted to Islam, Rashid al-Din, who was also a physician, scholar and wazir was delegated to compile a universal history. The author Bernard Lewis writes, "He assembled a team of collaborators, including two Chinese scholars, a Buddhist hermit from Kashmir, a Mongol specialist in tribal tradition, and a Frankish monk, as well as some Persian scholars. Incidentally, in attempting a universal history going beyond their own civilization, Rashid al-Din and his patrons anticipated Europe by half a millennium."

After the destruction of the caliphate, Mongols completely controlled the Middle East and it became a great cultural zone. In these countries, Arabic language remained the language of religion, tradition, law, theology, and science. Literary and artistic life was dominated by Muslim Iran of Turkish dynasties and achieved a fresh renaissance under the Mongols and their descendants. Persian language remained a spoken and cultural language in Iran. The regions in the east and west of Iran, Central Asia, Anatolia, were immensely influenced by Persian classics. Turks or Mongols were leading powers everywhere and their dynasties ruled all countries from Mediterranean to Central Asia and India and even Egyptian Empire.

Sufism

In this period of political and cultural diversity, the unifying factor was religion, particularly the new *Sufi form, which was based on the cooperation between mysticism and orthodoxy founded by al-Ghazali.* The author Bernard Lewis writes,

> "The Sunni revival of the eleventh century had gone far to revive and reunite Islam, but its task was not completed. The country folk and the nomads remained outside, and the latter were of great importance in an age when civil government was collapsing and whole peoples were on the move. The Turkish tribes in particular were deeply affected by Sufism. They had first converted to Islam by wandering monks and mystics, mostly Turkish, whose faith had little in common with the complex dogmatism of the schools. The compromise of al-Ghazali prepared the way for the interpenetration of mysticism and theology. The shock of heathen conquest and rule drove the theologians and the people into each other's arms. Henceforth, both Sufi and dogmatist professed the same orthodox Sunni religion, although with considerable variation of worship and belief, and not infrequent conflict."

From the thirteenth century, Sufism became the media for the main expression of religious sentiment and loyalty, and the binding force of Islamic unity. Eventually, it also became a source of intellectual culture and political power sometimes. Both Turkey and Iran were profoundly affected by Sufi ideals and organizations.

After the Mongol conquests and annihilation of the caliphate, three major powers, Iran, Turkey, and Egypt, emerged in the Middle East, Iran as the main center of power. The Mongol khans of Iran were called

1. al-Ghazali and Sufism: Sufi form, which was based on the cooperation between mysticism and orthodoxy was founded by al-Ghazali.

2. Rashid al-Din, a Persian historian, basically a Jewish converted to Islam, who was a physician and scholar was delegated to compile a universal history. So, he assembled a team of collaborators, including two Chinese scholars, a Buddhist hermit from Kashmir, a Mongol specialist in tribal tradition,a Frankish monk, also some Persian scholars and attempted to write a universal history going beyond their own civilization.

Il-Khans who provided equal tolerance and opportunity to people of all faiths before their conversion to Islam. The Mongolian Berke Khan was the first ruler who embraced Islam along with his Turkish population. The fight between Iran and Egypt continued even after the conversion of Ghazan Khan to Islam.

Christians Converted to Islam

Ottoman Empire that took the name from its founder Osman entered into Europe and within a few years established its military power. Regional expansion continued and victoriously conquered the Greeks, Serbs, Hungarians and Christian Crusaders under the leadership of Murad II (1421-1444 and 1446-1451). Towards the end of 1400 AD, they heavily recruited Christian population into the Ottoman army and state service. The following quote indicates the method of recruitment that was well described by the 1600 Ottoman historian and translated by English scholar William Seaman:

> "The most renowned King...entering into consultation with his ministers of State, the result hereof was, that for the time to come,

> there should be choice made, of valiant and industrious youths, out of the children of unbelievers, fit for the service, whom they should likewise immobilize, by the faith of Islam; which being a means to make them rich and religious, might be also a way to subdue the strongholds of the unbelievers. In prosecution hereof, there were several persons deputed by the king, for this business; with order to recollect in several countries, about a thousand of the unbelievers children, whom they should discipline and train up in the way of Auxiliaries…they by this means being conversant with the light of Islam may penetrate their hearts, and they may be cleansed from the pollution of false worship: likewise their desires fixed upon that which is of worth, and their hopes placed upon degrees of advancement; they may perform with faithfulness, their duties, and services. Their wages were ordained to be at first, one Asper a day, and so to be augmented, according to their abilities, and merits: and they were commonly known by the name of Janissarie [the new army]. Those valiant men in expeditions of war and fighting of battles have been so skillful that by their assistance, the Most renowned Kings have gotten much fame. Likewise they having by their worthy services attained to Eminent advancements; others in contemplation here of (with their hearts, and souls) were desirous, and did petition to have their children accepted: so that by this means, there were in a short time some thousands of unbelievers made glorious by the faith of Islam."

In this way, the spirits, strengths and vitalities of the Christian population were harnessed for the service of Ottoman dynasty.

In the Ottoman period the Islamic religion reached its maturity and integrated into Sunni polity. Islam represented a real religious organization with a structure of professional and academically trained men of religion with defined functions and powers greatly recognized as Holy Law of Islam. Ottomans gave a status, authority, and power to its scholars and judges they had never known before.

Ottomans launched attacks on Mamluks in Egypt and Safavid dynasty of the shahs of Iran and eventually they were conquered and brought to power by a radical Shiite movement, and created a united and powerful state comprising the whole area between the Mediterranean lands, and established the contacts to Central Asia.

Conquest of Europe

After subjugating Persians and Mamluks, Ottomans prepared to wage war against Europe. During the rule of Suleiman the Magnificent (1520-1566

AD), the Ottoman Empire was on its top in power. Here is the description of how Ottomans shattered the kingdom of Hungary in Europe:

> "With flashing swords like burning flames they charged the doomed but stout-hearted infidels, in glorious squadrons resembling tulip-strewn mountains. In a festival of battles, they were at once dyed red like goblets of wine, their heads like the flower of the Judas tree, their eyes like shining cornelian, their hands like coral... [The battle continued] until the rim of the heavenly hippodrome was tarnished by the bloodstains of sunset... the evil-doing [Hungarian] king... Advanced into the battlefield, amid a cloud of dust that shrouded both east and west... undaunted by the fire of guns and muskets, with a stout heart impervious to fear, he led a charge of his headlong cavalry, charging at one bound against the janissaries, the bravest of brave soldiers... he reached the batteries, where the musketeers greeted him with a deadly hail of fire that withered the flowers in the garden of the evildoing enemy's unavailing existence...
>
> At the Sultan's command, the janissary musketeers fired volleys against the enemy... and in an instant sent hundreds, or rather thousands, of them straight to Hell... the scroll of [the king's] time was folded, the circuit of his days of command was concluded, the record of his transient life was sealed with the loss both of this world and of the next."

Elizabeth historian Richard Knolles expressed the common feeling of Europe as "the present Terror of the World."

Table Turned - Maritime Power

The sixteenth century is the highest watermark of the Turkish tide and also the beginning of its receding tide. Ottomans always ruled on the land by waging war against their enemies, but they were not ready to face Portuguese and other Western warships with maritime naval power in Europe. Finally, as Ottomans were totally unprepared for oceanic warfare, they were defeated in Europe.

The greatly criticized Ottoman's devshirme tax had some positive sides in Europe (The **devshirme tax** system began in the late 14th century. Christian boys were recruited by force to serve the Ottoman government. The boys were usually taken from their families and raised in order to serve the country, converted to Islam, and conducted a series of examinations to determine their intelligence and capabilities.) It enabled the humblest villager to rise to the highest and most powerful offices in the state. Many brought their families with them, which was impossible in the aristocratic societies of the contemporary Christian world.

The Ottoman Empire influenced Europe in a number of ways. Mostly it was feared as a dangerous enemy, but for merchants, manufactures and financiers, it was a rich and progressively open market. The alienated populous and ambitious people were attracted by the opportunities provided by Ottoman. Many traitors in European's view and *muhtadi (*who has found the true path) in Muslim's view made brilliant careers in the Ottoman service. The oppressed peasants regarded the enemies of their masters optimistically. Martin Luther King in 1541 CE warned that the poor people oppressed by greedy princes, landlords, and citizens, might choose to live under the Turks instead of Christians. A vast majority of European literature deals with the merits of the Turkish order and the wisdom of imitating it.

Muslim Ideologies

As recorded in Muslim literature, the Prophet Muhammad wrote letters from his home in Arabia to the kings and princes of the non-believers, notifying his revelations and inviting them to accept Islam. Many kings, rulers, governors, and bishops including Roman Caesars received such letters.

The Arab invaders of Persia and Byzantium abolished the old order and created their own dominant institution. But the later invaders who entered and conquered the regions of Islam behaved very differently. The Turks and Mongols after their conversion, preserved the institution of the Islamic faith and the structure of the caliphate and sultanate, and used them for their own purpose. The Arabic and Persian languages were preserved and cherished by the new rulers.

Just like any other governments, Muslims also collected taxes and made wars. They participated in their religious activities far more than any others. Earlier times, the ruler was a king, priest, and even considered as a god. For the prophet and his followers and in Muslim teachings there was no king or god. In their opinion, God was the head of the state, and on his behalf, Muhammad preached and ruled the nation. As Prophet, he had no successor.

The Caliphate was described as a religious institution and his duty was to safeguard the heritage of the Prophet and to impose the Holy Law. Caliph had no significant or priestly function, and he did not require any education or professional experiences as *ULEMAS*, the Muslim scholars. His duty was neither to develop nor explain the faith, but he was supposed to protect and preserve the faith among citizens in order to lead a good Muslim life in this world and to prepare them for the life after death. To accomplish this task, he had to protect and maintain the Holy Law given by God within the Islamic state. He can also extend and reach the boundaries of all the nations in the world until they open their doors to the light of Islam to spread. In the beginning, the Muslim conquests were designed by an Arabic word *FUTUH* means 'Opening'.

Sultan means authority and rule and was used from early times to denote the government or authorities.

The surviving documents of the initial caliphates explain that the local administration was carried on like before the conquests with the old bureaucracies of Persian in Iraq and Iran, Christian in Syria and Egypt. The Umayyad caliph Umar II tried to interrupt the growth of bureaucracy. According to an early historian, one day the Caliph's clerk asked him to provide more papyrus:

> "Umar replied, 'Sharpen your pen and write less. It will be more swiftly understood.' The caliph also wrote to another official, who had written asking for papyrus and complaining that he had very little of it. 'Cut your pen fine and your words short, and make do with what papyrus you have..."

Some Administrative Facts

According to Islamic Law, Muslim governments were required to maintain two separate treasures: one for general, the other assigned as *khassa* (special). Probably, the *khassa* (special) indicates that the finance could be drawn in times of deficits. The special treasury had to meet the expenses of pilgrimages to Mecca, to maintain the fortresses, to pay the salaries for religious functionaries to uphold the Holy Law, to maintain the courier system, to provide ransom of captives, to the reception of ambassadors, and to allocate rewards generously to poets.

The tax was derived as specified by Holy Law. These were the *kharaj*, the land tax; the *jizya*, poll tax paid by non-Muslims; and the *zakat*, paid by Muslims. Revenues were assessed and collected both in cash and in kind.

There is a disagreement in Muslim approach: In one way, as per religious principles, the tax system was divinely proclaimed organization required to maintain the order in the society and to meet the God's purpose. In another way, it was perceived as a kind of evil for those who participated to carry the tax collection work as it was a contamination and dangerous to involve in such kind of works. According to the sayings of Prophet, government and paradise cannot be combined. The establishment of government unavoidably involves evil-doing and sin.

> "One story tells of a discussion at the court of the caliph al-Mansur as to the true nature of happiness. The caliph himself was asked how he would define a truly happy man, and he answered, 'I don't know him, and he doesn't know me.' The meaning is clear: the less one has to do with the government, the happier one is likely to be."

The medieval Muslim perceptions of the nature and purpose of government are explained in some proverbs:

> "Islam assigns four things to government: justice, booty, the Friday prayer, and the jihad.
>
> Islam, the government, and the people are like the tent, the pole, the ropes, and the pegs. The tent is Islam, the pole is the government, the ropes and the pegs are the people. None will do without the other.
>
> Chosroes said: 'do not stay in a country which lacks these five things: a strong rule, a just judge, a fixed market, a wise physician, and a flowing river.'
>
> Umar ibn al-Khattab said: 'He alone is fit to rule, who is mild without weakness and strong without harshness.'
>
> The most eloquent statement by an unnamed king concerning his subjects: "in their hearts I stored respect untainted with hate and love untainted with disrespect."

Economies

Historians write that the economic history of the Middle East is not investigated and very little is known. The main reason is the lack of historical studies in these regions. At the same time the medieval Western Europe progressed into the nations of modern Europe, and their old documented histories and achievements were preserved until modern times and they became a precious resource for the historians. In contrast, the countries of the medieval Middle East, except Ottoman Empire, were defeated and destroyed by internal turmoil and external invasions, and their records were ignored, disappeared and lost.

Up until the expansion of Western influence and administrative techniques in twentieth century, the Ottoman Empire was the only state that continued its leadership until the early twentieth century without any abruption in its political and administrative systems. The Ottoman archives endured the dangerous times up to the new age for historical study. These valuable archives throw light on the history of the Middle East in Ottoman period, and even some dark places in previous centuries. Since the literature is so daunting and immense in volumes, historians need to study them thoroughly.

On the basis of available information, historians were able to study the evolution of Middle Eastern economies and societies.

From the time immemorial, agriculture is the most important economic activity in the Middle East as any other part of the world. Its agricultural economies were of two types: river-valley economy and rainfall economy.

The distinct feature of the region is the lack of forests and as a result the lack of timber. During the Islamic Middle Age, the Middle East was importing timber from Africa, India, and Southeast Asia.

Rice!

The most important produce was cereals. They had barley, millet, and some primitive forms of wheat. But by medieval times, wheat dominated the area. Rice was introduced to the Middle East from India and its cultivation spread to Iran, Iraq, Syria, and Egypt.

An Arab storyteller who was with the army during the conquest tells an interesting story about rice:

> "Some Persian pickets whom an Arab force surprised in the marshes took flight, leaving behind them two baskets, one containing dates, and the other what they afterwards learned to be unhusked rice. The Arab commander told his men: 'Eat the dates, but leave this other thing, for it must be poison which the enemy has prepared for you.' They therefore ate the dates and avoided the other basket. But while they were eating, one of their horses broke loose and started to eat the rice. They were about to slaughter the horse, so that they could eat it before its flesh was also poisoned, but the horse's owner told them to wait, and said that he would see to it in due course. The following morning, finding that the horse was still in excellent health, they lit a fire under the rice and burned off the husks, and their commander said: 'Pronounce the name of Allah over it and eat.' 'And they ate it, and they found it a most tasty food.'

Later, along with rice, they also cultivated other cereals, notably sorghum, chickpeas, beans, peas, lentils and the like – even now a prominent food in many parts of the Middle East to Egypt.

Very important oil producing oleaginous plants were grown was oil being required for food, lighting, and toiletries of various kinds, particularly soap. The chief oil producing plant was the olive. Oil was also extracted from other various types of oilseeds.

From east, sugar cane was introduced to produce sugar during the period of Arab-Muslim rule. In Persia it was known as 'sheker' and 'qand'. In Greco-Roman period, sugar was not known and not used and occasionally sugar was used for medicinal purposes. They sweetened their food and drink with honey. In the course of Islamic Middle Ages, the cultivation and refining of sugar extended to Egypt and North Africa, Muslim Spain, Atlantic islands and to the New World, and sugar became a major export.

In many parts of the Middle East, spices were cultivated and also imported from South and Southeast Asia. Before the invention of refrigerators, food perished rapidly in hot climates. To preserve the food, it was salted and pickled in various ways using spices and condiments.

For clothing purposes, Flax, cotton, mulberry and silkworm were cultivated.

Very important crop was the papyrus, a reed from the banks of the Nile which provided the chief writing material of the eastern Mediterranean region until the arrival of parchment, and then the paper.

Fruits and vegetables like vines, figs, and dates were widely grown. Vegetables like spinach, eggplant and artichoke were introduced by the Persians.

The sweet Orange was introduced to the Middle East from India and China by Portuguese merchants at the beginning of the sixteenth century. In most Middle Eastern languages, the orange is called *'bortaqal'* in Arabic, *portakal* in Turkish, probably it is because Portuguese introduced it to them. Citrus fruits were known in the Persian Empire as *turunj*. Also it was called *narang* in Persian. The cultivation of the lemon and the lime spread rapidly in the Middle East and Europe.

The Portuguese and West Europeans introduced American plants, tobacco, maize, potatoes and tomatoes to the Middle East. The Turkish historian Ibrahim Pechevi writes:

> "The fetid and nauseating smoke of tobacco was brought in the year 1600-1 CE by English infidels, who sold it as a remedy for certain diseases of humidity. Some... pleasure-seekers and sensualists... became addicted, and soon even those who were not pleasure-seekers began to use it. Many even of the great *ULEMA* and the mighty fell into this addiction."

Tea and Coffee

Two more important plants which had the impact on economic as well as social life were Tea and Coffee. An Arab traveler describes the mysterious land of China:

> "The king has the exclusive right to the income from salt and from an herb which they drink with hot water. It is sold in every city at high prices, and it is called *sakh*. It has more leaves than a clover and is slightly more scented, but is somewhat bitter. Water is boiled and then poured on it... The total receipts of the public treasury come from poll-tax, salt, and from this herb."

Tea drinking was introduced to Iran by the Mongol conquerors in the thirteenth century. But the extensive shift to tea drinking happened in Iran in the early nineteenth century, when it was reintroduced from Russia. The large-scale cultivation of tea started in the twentieth century by rulers of Iran and Turkey to cut the craving on coffee, which they could not grow.

Coffee

Another important beverage was the introduction of coffee. Coffee originated in Ethiopia and it may have taken its name from the Ethiopian territory of Kaffa, where the coffee plant grows wildly even now. An Egyptian writer proclaims, "At the beginning of the sixteenth century, the news reached us in Egypt that a drink called *'qahwa'* had spread in the Yemen, and was being used by Sufi Shaykhs and others to help them stay awake during their devotional exercises..."

The writer continues to explain how a traveler from Yamen brought coffee from Ethiopia:

> "After he had returned to Aden he fell ill and remembering [*qahwa*] he drank it and benefited by it. He found that among its properties was that it drove away fatigue and lethargy and brought to the body certain liveliness and vigor. In consequence, when he became a Sufi, he and other Sufis in Aden began to use this beverage... then the whole people – both the learned and the common – followed his example in drinking it, seeking help in study and other vocations and crafts, so that it continued to spread."

Undoubtedly, the use of coffee spread. By 1511 AD, coffee drinking was certified in the holy city of Mecca and from there the returning pilgrims and merchants carried the habit to Egypt, Syria, Central Ottoman lands and to Iran. When the western world had easy access to Tea from China and India, coffee remained a Middle Eastern monopoly for some time.

A Venetian ambassador in Istanbul writes about the earliest European references to coffee:

> "All these people are riff-raff, of bad habits and of no inclination to work, so that they spend most of their time in the greatest idleness. They sit around almost all day, and for entertainment it is their practice to drink publicly, both in shops and in the streets, not just common folk but also some of the great ones, a black liquid as boiling hot as they can endure extracted from a seed which they call Cavee, and which they say has the quality of keeping a man awake."

George Sandys, an English visitor to Turkey in 1610 CE writes mockingly, "There [in their coffee-houses] they sit chatting most of the day and sippe of a drinke called 'Coffa'... as hot as they can suffer it: black as soote, and tasting not much unlike it..."

It is not difficult to comprehend why Middle Easterners liked tea and coffee so fondly. Unlike other religions, Islam bans alcoholic beverages. Although there are evidences of widespread drinking in Muslim poetry and narratives, drinking was behind the high walls of a private home, or amidst non-Muslim subjects. Anyway, the coffeehouse and tea-houses filled this void.

The method of cultivation in the Middle East was still primitive. They used a simple ancient type of wooden, wheel less plough, which is used even today in some places. It was used without a mouldboard and yoked to oxen or to mules or buffalos.

Agriculture and Universities

The reason for lack of technological innovations in the Middle East could be the dearth of monasteries and educated farmers. In European societies educated and dedicated men in monasteries spend their time growing crops by innovating new methods. European educated farmers used their techniques to grow the crops and obtained successful results. The author writes,

> "The type of the English country gentleman, for example, who studied at the university and then worked and managed his own farm, applying a trained mind to the problems of agriculture, had no equivalent. Educated gentlemen in the Middle East, with few exceptions, did not bother with farming. Farmers were not educated. The combination of intellectual discipline, technical skill, and actual involvement in agriculture needed to produce technological improvement was, in general, lacking."

The Middle Easterners' real ingenuity was in irrigation. They organized and maintained an enormous number of ditches, reservoirs, and canals to preserve and distribute the flood waters of the huge rivers. Also, the Middle East faced very severe erosion problems throughout history.

Another reason for the decline in agricultural output is the low self-esteem. Historically, the people who cultivated the earth were owned by the government and sometimes by religion. In Muslim tradition, there is a great respect for commerce and city dwellers, but not for agriculture and farmers. The Holy Law is concerned with lives and problems of city-dwellers and provides assistance by regulating rules. In contrast, apart from taxes, farmers were totally ignored. 'The situation was surely worsened by the increasing tendency towards the state direction of the economy, and the control of agricultural land by military officers with no great knowledge of agriculture and no great interest in the long-term prosperity of their domains.'

Animals

As the Middle East region contains mostly dry lands, it is not suitable for agriculture or even for grazing large cattle. But whatever they grow is enough to support sheep and goats. Besides meat, wool, and hides, they provided yogurt and cheese, the basic food of the Middle Eastern diet. Camels existed from prehistoric times as a means of transport and horses were very few but regarded highly known by name and pedigree. Horses and ponies were important for nomadic people. The pigs were not a part of the economy in the Middle East. Egypt devised a technique for poultry which surprised the westerners. A French traveler Jean de Thevenot visited Egypt in 1655 CE and observed and wrote:

> "The first of these extraordinary things I saw at Cairo, was the artificial way of hatching Chickens; one would think it a Fable, at first, to say that Chickens are hatched without Hens sitting upon the eggs; and a greater, to say, that they are sold by the Bushel: Nevertheless both are true, and for that effect, they put their Eggs in Ovens, which they heat with so temperate a warmth, which imitates so well the natural heat, that Chickens are formed and hatched in them... They heat them with a very temperate heat, only of the hot ashes and Camels-dung, or the like, which they put at the mouth of each Oven, and daily change it, putting fresh hot dung into the same place... Many think that this cannot be done but in Aegypt, because of the warmth of the climate; but the Great Duke of Florence having sent for one of these men, he hatched them as well there as in Aegypt: the same also (as I was told) had been done in Poland."

Later this method of incubation was introduced to Europe and it spread all across the world.

Minerals

Minerals such as gold, silver, unalloyed copper, bronze were found in the Middle East from historic times. Bronze was used in Mesopotamia in 3000 BCE. Tin was imported from Cornwall; iron came from north. Industrial techniques remained primitive. The reason for the lack of progress in generation of energy is the lack of suitable materials like firewood, coal, and charcoal as used by Western Europe. Yes, undeniably petroleum was there, but it had to wait for a long time to know the secret of its extraction. In ancient times it was used to keep the sacred flame in the temples, and some parts to make mixtures for weapons of war.

Until 1800 AD, wheeled carts were not used in the area. A French traveler observed:

> "It is noteworthy that in the whole of Syria no wagon or cart is seen; this is probably due to the fear lest they should be seized by the government's men, and a heavy loss should be suffered in a moment."

Usually the available transportation at that time was by animals or by water. The camels domesticated in 2000 BCE were able to carry up to 1200 pounds, cover 200 miles in a day and they can travel for 17 days without water. Camels die in moist climates, but in dry climates they are the most cost-effective animals.

Documents from medieval Egypt show that flax workers were employed for daily wages and the most important commodity was *tiraz*. T*iraz* in Arabic is a kind of brocade or embroidery on clothing. It was worn only by rulers and whom the king honored. The *tiraj* became a system of honors and decorations.

Emancipation of Slave Trade

Islamic legislation humanized the misery of large-scale and long-range commerce of human beings. In ancient times, the vast majority of the people were used as slaves and as a commodity and recruited locally. A number of ways were used to fill the job as slaves: to subjugate criminals and debtors; adaptation of children abandoned by their parents as slaves; by those who sold their children; and those who offered themselves into bondage.

Islamic law ended this practice. According to the code formulated by the Muslim jurists and Muslim rulers, the natural condition of humankind is freedom. "Freeborn subjects of the Muslim state, whether Muslims or followers of permitted religions, could not be enslaved either for debt or for criminal offences other than armed rebellion. Abandoned children must be presumed to be free unless they could be proved to be slaves. The children of slave parents were born and remained slaves unless and until they were released from the slavery. Free persons could only be enslaved if they were infidels captured in a holy war...The price of slaves, especially young female slaves, was high...The price of young male slaves could be greatly increased by castration to meet the demand for eunuchs to serve in palaces, in the wealthier homes, and in some religious sites. The law of Islam forbids mutilation, and eunuchs were therefore 'manufactured' on the frontiers before entering Islamic territory."

They brought slaves from Europe, Eurasia, and Africa, and very rarely from India and China.

Decline

The commerce was high in Islamic Middle East in the late middle ages leading ahead of Europe in every aspect. It was richer, larger, better organized with more commodities to sell and more money to buy with a large network of trading connections. But by the end of middle ages, the positions were reversed. Portuguese, a small country in Europe dominated with its extraordinary naval power and commercial strength. No Middle Eastern powers were able to compete with Portugal. The disturbances in trade and technological, financial, and commercial advances in Western Europe all contributed to decline of Middle East strength.

The Elites

As in any civilizations, Islamic civilization also has distinctions between privileged groups and non-privileged groups. In Arabic language they denote the terms *KHASSA* and *AMMA*. In fact, Islam is a democratic and egalitarian system, and it does not recognize superiority over one believer over another by birth or ancestry, race or nationality, or social status. Classical Islam adopted a fundamental inequality between man and woman, freeman and slave, believer, and non-believer, and applied inferior status on non-believers according to the Holy Law. Apart from these inequalities, Islam does not distinguish infidels in any way. They considered only self-righteousness and good actions to bring respect because self-righteousness and good actions replace all wealth, power and noble birth.

Practically, in all societies, all privileged groups who possessed wealth and power wanted to pass their fortune to their children. Literary proofs like earlier books, letters, and other documents indicate that Islamic history was influenced by two factors: bureaucracy and religious men. An 800 CE bureaucrat writes to another bureaucrat:

> "God... made you secretaries in the most distinguished positions, men of culture and virtue, of knowledge and discernment. By your means the excellences of the Caliphate are well-ordered, and its affairs uprightly maintained. By your counsel God fits government to the people, and the land prospers. The king cannot do without you, nor can any competent person be found, save among you. You are, therefore, for kings the ears with which they hear, the eyes with which they see, the tongues with which they speak, and the hands with which they strike."

The medieval Islamic realm created two kinds of literate and educated classes: One is called *ADAB* and *BELLES-LETTRES. ADAB* consisted of poetry and history and a huge literary work explaining what a cultured man was expected to know and appreciate. The other was called *'ILM*, means knowledge, basically about the religious tenets, the Qur'an and its teachings, the tradition of the Prophet, theology and law, which were the dominion of the *ULEMA*.

Madrasa

Madrasa was a magnet for drawing together government and religious personalities. In earlier times, Madrasa was a type of college or university which became the major center of Muslim higher education in religious and other fields. Those centers were supported by rulers and private individuals. Some large centers had libraries, which were available to students and scholars. Bernard Lewis writes, "There were also semi-public libraries which contained books on non-religious subjects such as mathematics, medicine, chemistry, philosophy, and music. In the early 900 AD, the 'Abbasid caliph al-Ma'mun founded the famous 'House of Wisdom' in Baghdad. It was modelled on the older academy of Gondishpur in Persia, a center of Hellenistic sciences....."

In 1100 AD, the madrasa appeared in its classical form, sometimes attached to a mosque, sometimes as an independent center with a small place of worship. Later it developed like an organized school with a syllabus and timetable to study, a permanent faculty and staff, funds and facilities for students. Basically, the madrasas were concentrated on teaching religion and law. But, after some time, like the colleges and universities of the West, they began to produce educated class. (Now, it seems the Madrasas are teaching religion only.)

Islamic Ideologies

Another significant group of elites were the men of the pen, the poets. They composed songs and eulogies which could be easily memorized and rapidly distributed. They also prospered by wealthy private individuals celebrating births, marriages, and other events. In the age when there were no mass media, poets and poetry played a role in the publication of news.

Islamic teaching favored commerce from the beginning. Even though Qur'an approved trade, it banned money lending business. The notable passages in Quran deals with the lawfulness of honest trading, the use of fair weights and measures, the honest payment of debts, the fulfillment of contracts, etc., some teachings even defend the luxuries honestly. The prophet said, "When God gives wealth to a man, he wants it to be seen on him." There is an interesting story told by a Shiite imam. Once, an Imam was approached by a disciple wearing fine attire while his ancestors had worn crude, simple clothing. The imam defended his disciple saying that his ancestors had lived in a time of scarcity, while he lived in a time of plenty, and it was appropriate to wear the clothing of one's own time. This narrative clearly justifies the luxurious living instead of the stress of asceticism. Muhammad al-Shaybani argues:

> "The earning of a livelihood is not merely permitted but is an obligation for Muslims. Man's primary duty is to serve God. But in order to do this properly, he must be adequately fed, housed, and clothed. This he can only achieve by working and earning money. He need not limit himself to provide the bare necessities of life, since it is also permissible to buy and use items of luxury." The point is that the money earned by trade or handicrafts is more pleasing in God's eyes than money received from the government.

Another Arabic classical author al-Jahiz writes in praise of merchants. He emphasizes the security, dignity, and independence of merchants in contrast with the uncertainty, humiliation, and sycophancy of those who serve the ruler, and he upholds the righteousness and techniques of business against their critics.

Islam dejects the privileges by descent, birth, status, wealth, or race, but emphasizes the grade and honor are decided only by piety and good action according to Islam.

Religion and Law

Ever since the formation of Islamic Domain in the mid 700 AD, Islam is a dominant religion in the Middle East and they became prominent people in most of the region. Caliph Umar ordered that in Holy Land Saudi Arabia, only Islam should be permitted and everyone else should leave the place. This decree did not apply to southern Arabia where Christianity survived for some time. Judaism still exists there.

In North Africa, Christianity vanished. The Zoroastrians in Persia, without support from their neighbors, suffered badly. Some escaped to India where small communities live known as Parsees, even today.

After the advent of Islam, the fate of Persia was very much threatened. Not only Persia's distant provinces, but its own capital and the whole kingdom were captured and incorporated into the new Arab Islamic world. The people from Syria and Egypt could go to Byzantium, but Zoroastrians of Persia had no place to go, but to stay under Muslim rule or to seek refuge in the only place that was open to them, India. During the early centuries of Muslim rule in Iran, the old language and its old script was gradually forgotten except a small minority who preserved their heritage.

ISLAM: In Arabic, the verb Islam means 'surrender' to God. The active participle of the same verb 'Muslim' means one who surrenders. Therefore, the Muslim is the one who surrendered to only one God in contrast to polytheists that prevailed in pagan Arabia during that time.

As a matter of fact, Muslim tradition was not an innovation, but continuation of the long struggle between monotheism and polytheism. Both Judaism and Christianity believe in one God as stated revelations in the New Testament and Bible. Muhammad incorporated the messages whatever the truth they contained in those two scriptures. The not incorporated materials were considered to be unworthy and untrue.

Mosque: In Arabic, 'masjid' means a place of prostration, where worshippers kneel before God. A mosque is a building, a place of worship, for meeting and study. No other activities are performed there. In earlier times, prostration could be performed in private houses, in public places, in open air, and in the very earliest time in conquered religious places. When Turks conquered Anatolia, they converted a Christian temple of 'Santa Sophia' in Constantinople into an imperial mosque. They mounted a crescent on the dome and added four minarets, one at each corner, from which the muezzins could announce the unity of God and the teachings of Muhammad. Inside the building, they removed Christian images and symbols or covered them with Qur'anic verses and other Islamic texts.

The mosque contains no altar and no sanctuary because Islam has no rituals and priesthood. Muslim public prayer is a disciplined, communal act of submission to the creator, to the universal and immaterial God. There will be no drama, mystery, music, or poetry, and any kind of art. Sculptures are rejected. In their place, they used abstract and geometrical designs and inscriptions. For Muslims the Quran is divine and reading and writing of it is the act of worship. Because of this practice, the art of calligraphy achieved an intricate and complex beauty. The Muslim population had totally forgotten their ancient heritage of art and law that were practiced by Greeks and Romans, and it was an astonishing news when it is presented to them.

Mirza Abu Talib, a Muslim visitor to England in eighteenth century wrote about his visit to the House of Commons. The author explains his reaction:

> "…described a visit to the House of Commons, and his astonishment when it was explained to him that its functions and duties included the promulgation of laws and fixing of penalties for wrongdoers. Unlike the Muslims, he explained to his readers, the English have not accepted a divine law revealed from heaven, and were therefore reduced to the expedient of making their own laws 'in accordance with the necessities of time and circumstance, the state of affairs, and experience of judges.
>
> "In principle, the Islamic legal system was totally different from that which the traveler found and described in England. For Muslims the sole valid law was that of God made known through revelation, manifested in the Quran and hadith, and then amplified and interpreted through the work of the later-jurist-theologians. Where the law itself is seen as enacted by God and promulgated by the Prophet, jurists and theologians follow different branches of the same profession…. The *QUADI*, appointed by the state, administered justice in his court. His task was to apply the law, not to interpret it. That function belonged to the mufti, juris consult whose opinions or rulings, called fatwa, from the same root, could be cited as legal authorities though not as law."

Friday: Just like Jews' Saturday and Christians' Sunday was dedicated to prayers, Muslim's Friday was a day of public and communal prayer, and increased public activity in the markets and elsewhere. But, not a holiday from work.

Hajj: Another aspect of Islam is pilgrimage to HAJJ. It is an obligation to every Muslim to visit Mecca and Medina in his life time. The hajj festival is observed every year between the seventh and tenth days of the month of Dhu'l-Hijja of Muslim calendar and concludes with sacrifices and the circumambulation of the Kaaba, the cube-shaped building in Mecca. The Mosque contains the venerated Black Stone.

The effects of the pilgrimage have a vast impact on social, cultural, and economical levels. Bernard writes,

> "This level of physical mobility... involved important social, intellectual and economic consequences. The pilgrim, if wealthy, was often accompanied by a number of slaves, whom he might sell on the way to pay the expenses of his journey. If he was a merchant, he might combine his pilgrimage with a business trip, buying and selling commodities in the places through which is passed, and thus learning to know the products, markets, merchants, customs and practices of many lands. If he was a scholar, he might take the opportunity to attend lectures, meet colleagues, and acquire books, thus participating in the diffusion and exchange of knowledge and ideas."

The knowledge of the pilgrimage produced a rich literature of travel, gave information about faraway places and enhanced understanding of belonging to a greater whole.

Fasting: The fourth pillar of Islam is fasting. All adult Muslim, both men and women, are required to fast during Ramadan, the ninth month of the Muslim calendar. They are supposed to fast from sunrise to sunset. The old people, children, and sick people have exemptions, but those who are travelling or involved in jihad may postpone the fast.

Jihad: Another obligation for Muslims is jihad prescribed by Muslim jurists and theologians. Jihad's real literal meaning is striving, as per Quranic phrase 'striving in the path of God.' The majority of early writers interpret and discuss jihad in military terms. Warriors in the holy war ordered not to kill women and children unless they pose any danger; not to torture or injure prisoners; give warning about the consequences to hostility; and to respect agreements. The Holy Law also endowed winners' huge rights over the property, persons and families of the losers.

The Muslim jihad is considered as infinite and ongoing responsibility to continue until the entire world accepts the Muslim faith or Muslim rule. The Quran promises abundant rewards in both worlds - loot in this world and pleasures in paradise in heaven for those who participate in the act of jihad.

During the peak of Arab expansion, the armies of Islam thought that they were doing the work of God and believed that this work would be completed within a predictable time in the future, and the whole world would be brought under the rule of Islam.

The act of jihad did not get universal support all the time. Ottoman historian Esad Efendi of early 1900 CE narrates a story about a dervish (Dervish is a member of Sufi religious order):

"...went among the Muslim troops when they were encamped from the night, and went from soldier to soldier saying: 'Hey, you fools, why do you squander your lives for nothing? Shame on you! All the talk you hear about the virtues of holy war and martyrdom in battle is so much nonsense. While the Ottoman emperor enjoys himself in his palace, and the Frankish king disports himself in his country, I cannot think why you should give your lives fighting on the mountaintops!"

Zakat: *Zakat* is a tax paid by Muslims for charitable purposes.

Sufi: Sufism started exclusively based on individual mystical experience and became popular among the general public. Sufis promoted brotherhood of all people, recognized in Arabic as *tanqa*, in Turkish as *tarikat*. Different from Islamic ideology, their faith was mystical and insightful, and their worship was adoring and ecstatic. Sufis used music, song, and dance to achieve mystical union with God.

Muhammad al-Ghazali (1059-1111 CE) was responsible for bringing Sufi teachings into the Islamic mainstream. Bernard Lewis explains that Ghazali was a great theologian and philosopher of medieval Islam and his ideas had a great impact on later development of Muslim religious sciences. He was from Iranian province of Khurasan and he studied in the colleges of Nishapur and Baghdad, and later he became a professor in the madrasa. After four years, he resigned his teaching profession, abandoned all public functions, and immersed himself in solitude to contemplate on fundamental problems of religion. He studied exuberantly theology, philosophy, and law, and travelled extensively to Mecca, Jerusalem, Damascus, and Alexandria. He wrote an outstanding autobiography where he explains how he failed to find the answer to his satisfaction in scholastic theology, in rational philosophy, in Shiite doctrines; and declares how he found truth in Sufism. Later he returned to his birthplace and established a Sufi lodge in 1106 AD.

The author Bernard Lewis writes that certain Sufi principles and dogmas were the subjects of suspicion because they show disrespect to the established law and traditions. The traditional Muslims accused the acts of holding pantheistic doctrines, worshipping saints, and holy places, which is the violation of the Islamic ban on idolatry. The more common complaint was that Sufis were indifferent to God's law and also, they encouraged such negligence in fellow citizens too.

Culture

The land of the Middle East belongs to an ancient civilization among the most ancient civilizations in the world. But compared to other two major ancient civilizations, India and China, it differs in two unique features: diversity and discontinuity.

Even though many changes have occurred through thousands of years in Chinese history, there is a component of continuity in its existence from the beginning to recent times. For example, ancient China and modern China use the same language with some familiar modifications, use the same scripts with some alternatives, and observe the same religion and philosophy similar to its fundamental precepts.

In India also we see the same continuity. Although it may not be completely similar and homogenous as China, it retains the same interconnected and united force in its existence. The Hindu religion, the Sanskrit classics, and scriptures have a powerful factor in Indian civilization and the knowledge of their ancient heritage itself is a continuing entity.

In the Middle East, from the ancient to modern time, there is no such unity or continuity. From the beginning it is very diverse with no common binding factor like Chinese, Sanskrit, philosophy, or beliefs. Its civilization evolved in different places and in different types and retained their significant differences of culture, belief and way of life. While India and China even now revere and study the scriptures of their ancient past in an unbroken way, the Middle East's ancient past was literally forgotten and buried. Its languages were dead, its writings bolted in unreadable scripts that no one can read. Their gods and worships are known only to a small number of scholars, experts, historians, and professionals. The Middle East even has no shared name like India and China to identify its past. Bernard sadly writes,

> "That indeed is why in our century it has come to be known, first in the Western world, and finally among the peoples of the region itself, by shapeless, formless, colorless, and entirely relative designations, such as 'Middle East' – designation that obviously lack the dignity, the stature, the evocative power of names like India and China."

The Middle East went through several stages in their history beginning from the ancient Mesopotamians world, and then a series of catastrophic changes of Hellenization, Romanization, Christianization and Islamization. Christianity tried to use its language Latin in the area as a common dialogue. But the Muslim Arabs who conquered Christian Roman Empire and North Africa brought their own religion - Islam, their own language - Arabic, and their own scripture - the Quran, and they established their own imperial state clearly marking a new society.

There are some examples of adaptation of lexical from Greek vocabulary to Arabic. Some recognizable words: kimiya (chemistry), falsafa (philosophy), shurtha (the police force), askar (army) from Latin exercitus. Sirat (Roman road strata, similar English word street), kharaj (Aramaic karaga, Greek khoregia). A more interesting example is a nickname applied to Mecca, "Umm al-Qura", "the mother of towns" (Greek 'metropolis': metera=mother + polis=town).

Musicians and composers of songs were slaves or other non-Muslims. After the Islamization of the area, gradually there were more Muslim artists and architects. The artists also played different roles as organizers and administrators using more authority providing some basic needs of government, religion and the city to people: palaces and fortresses for the first; mosques, convents, and colleges for the second; bridges and bathhouses, markets and inns, and dwellings of various kinds for the third.

Whether it was a palace or a private building, the Middle Easterners did not use furniture in their domestic interiors. In the ancient Middle East, tables and chairs were used commonly, but not in the middle ages. In its place, people used wool and leather readily available from nomadic people. Usually their furniture consisted of carpets and mattresses, hassocks, and cushions. They used a wide range of metal, glass, and earthenware objects – trays, lamps, bowls, dishes, and a variety of utensils. Engraved and carved metalwork, painted ceramic, and glass made an important part of industrial arts in medieval Islam.

Muslim rulers did not put their faces on coinage or on postal stamps. In 1721, a Muslim Ambassador went to Paris and writes his experience in a report, "The custom of these people is that the king gives ambassadors his own portrait adorned with diamonds as a gift. But I explained that pictures are not permitted among Muslims; I was therefore given instead a diamond-studded belt." The Ambassador was amazed to see the European tapestry on the walls. Impressed by the realistic representation of their art, he describes:

> "One appears laughing, to show his joy; another sad, to show his sadness. One is shown trembling with fear, another weeping, and another stricken by some disease. Thus, at first glance, the condition of each person is known. The beauty of these works is beyond description and beyond imagination."

Even though there was a ban on music, all kinds of poetry flourished in ME, sad, love, separation, etc. In spite of ban on alcohol in Islam, wine appears very notably in Arabic poetry. Making, selling, and drinking wine were prohibited to Muslims, but were permitted to the non-Muslim subjects in the Muslim state. If Muslims wanted a drink, they had to go to non-believers house to get it.

The major portion of composition of classical prose literature was intended to be to inform and instruct and not for amusement. It was written to preserve and transmit the knowledge about history, biography, and literary history of the past. Muslim rulers wanted their actions to be recorded and left for later generations. Almost every dynasty and every ruler of Islam left records and chronicles of some kind. They considered an accurate knowledge of history was supremely important because it provides authoritative guidance in the fields of both religion and law.

Islam did not encourage translating the Quran into any other language because some Muslim authorities condemned such translations, and considered it is impious. Some informal translations are available in the guise of commentaries, but Muslims were required to study the Quran only in Arabic whatever their native language is.

The magnificent Arabic dictionaries of the middle ages, listing the different meanings of words and illustrating them with examples of their occurrence in classical texts were remarkable achievements. They produced geographical dictionaries or gazetteers, lengthy essays on the towns, countries, geographical features and a wide range of biographical dictionaries, arranged by country by century, or by profession or vocation.

Middle Easterners Contribution

Another important achievement is the development of scholarship of science and learning, which was the work of translators who worked on major Greek writings on mathematics and astronomy, physics and chemistry, medicine and pharmacology, geography and agronomy, and a wide range of other subjects including philosophy. Some of these works were preserved by the local non-Muslims, and others were imported from Byzantine. Many important Greek works which were lost in the barbarous and uninterested West became known through Arabic translations, from which Latin versions were made. Interestingly, most of the translators were non-Muslims, Christians, and Jews. Medieval Islamic scientists immensely enriched the modern world by their efforts and contribution. Greek science inclined to be theoretical, while Medieval Middle East science was more practical in medicine, chemistry, astronomy and agronomy. They were clarified by the experiments and observations. The Arabic numerals, positional numbering with a sign for zero came from India, but it was Middle Easterners who, in the ninth century made it the starting point of a new arithmetic. Islamic geometry was founded on Greek and influenced by Indian teachings.

In the medical field, Middle Eastern contribution to Western medicine is remarkable. In 1717 AD, Lady Mary Worley Montagu from Edirne describes the method of smallpox vaccination used by Turks:

> "A propos of Distempers, I am going to tell you a thing that I am sure will make you wish yourself here. The Smallpox so fatal and so general amongst us is here entirely harmless by the invention of engrafting (which is the term they give it). There is a set of old Women who make it their business to perform the Operation. Every autumn in the month of September, when the great heat is abated, people send to one another to know if any of their family has a mind to have the smallpox. They make parties for this purpose, and when they are met (commonly 15 or 16 together) the old Woman comes with a nutshell full of the matter of the best sort of small-pox and asks what veins you please to have opened. She immediately rips open that you offer to her with a large needle (which gives you no more pain than a common scratch) and puts into the vein as much venom as can lye upon the head of her needle, and after binds up the little wound with a hollow bit of shell, and in this manner opens 4 or 5 veins.... Then the fever begins to seize them and they keep their beds for 2 days, very seldom 3... and in 8 days' time they are as well as before their illness.... Every year thousands undergo this operation, and the French Ambassador says pleasantly that they take the Smallpox here by way of diversion as they take the Waters in other Countries."

After Arabs captured some Chinese paper makers, the development of literature, learning, and education was immensely helped by the introduction of paper, a Chinese invention. They introduced the skill of paper making to Islamic world and then the manufacture of paper spread westwards.

Islamic society resisted another Chinese invention printing. Printing was forbidden by the order of Sultan Bayezid II issued in 1485 CE. This new technology of book production was introduced by Jewish refugees from Spain.

The Islamic civilization of the Middle East made remarkable progress in human achievements along with other civilizations at the time like India and China, and to a lesser extent in Europe. But eventually, it was the poor, unsophisticated, monochrome culture of Christian Europe that progressed from strength to strength, while the Islamic civilization suffered a loss of creativity, energy and power.

Challenges to the Islamic World

Usually, it is comprehended that the beginning of modern history in the Middle East and other parts of the world is European imperialism from the west, and its arrival and presence in these countries initiated the process of transformation.

All the lands where Islam law dominated was called as Dar al-Islam, the House of Islam. All of its surrounding areas were encircled by the Dar al-Harb, the House of War, resided by non-believers who had not accepted the Muslim faith or surrendered to Muslim rule. In the east and the south of the Islamic world, there was no threat to the Islamic caliphate as a world power. Those infidels were both civilized and barbarous and they were potential recruits to the Islamic world. Bernard Lewis writes,

> "The great civilizations of China and India never seriously challenged, still less threatened, the Islamic world. The one great pagan invasion from the East that of the Mongols, despite its immense impact, was eventually absorbed with the conversion and assimilation of the conquerors themselves, who became a part, and indeed an important part, of the Islamic world."

There was a different situation in the north-western border of Islam in the European Christian states, both Greek and Latin. Here, Muslims encountered the rivals whose religion also believed that they were the keepers of God's revelations and had the responsibility to spread it to all humanity. In the early centuries Muslims neglected Europeans thinking them as primitive and had nothing to offer. Muslims never feared or respected the barbarous non-believers of northern and western Europeans. They were not fit for anything except for enslavement. This perception began to change. In the struggle between Muslims and Christians, Muslims had a strong hold nearly a thousand years.

The Muslims contribution to Europe is huge in its own inventions, reproducing, reworking, and adapting from other civilizations from eastern Mediterranean and from remote parts of Asia: Muslims preserved and improved Greek science and philosophy, which were forgotten and neglected by Europeans; borrowed and reproduced Indian numbers and Chinese paper; introduced oranges and lemons, cotton and sugar, and a wide variety of other plants including the techniques of cultivating these plants.

European contributions to the Middle East were in the form of material and technical. Muslims were not interested in European arts and writing, science and philosophy because they rejected everything that was not in accordance with the Islam and considered they are all insignificant things belonged to primitive society. But Europeans were skillful in their hands and produced many useful things, which Muslims liked and adopted. Around 1500 AD, European inventions like clocks and watches to measure time, eyeglasses and telescopes to enhance vision were very attractive. Even though it is insignificant, a few food plants were imported from west including peas, maize, potato, tomato, and most important commercial crop, tobacco. Unfortunately, another most important contribution of the west to Islamic world is weaponry.

From time to time there were some, in both church and state, who condemned and tried to stop this traffic of weapons of war. Governments denounced other governments for condoning and even encouraging it. The church was very clear. Papal edicts of the sixteenth and seventeenth centuries, encouraged to 'excommunicate and condemn… all those who take to the Saracens, Turks, and other enemies of the Christian name, horses, weapons, iron, iron wire, tin, copper, bandaraspata, brass, Sulphur, and all suitable for the making of artillery, and instruments, arms and machines for offence, with they fight against the Christians, as also ropes and timber and other nautical supplies and other prohibited wares.'

Ironically, this trade of weapons and the efforts to stop it continued.

Maritime Power

In the course of passage of time, the Spaniards and the Portuguese, freed from Muslim rule, began their voyages through Asian waters. When Portuguese encountered Muslim rulers in Turkey, Egypt, Iran and India, their main opponents failed to stop them. After Portuguese, the Spaniards, the French, the Dutch, and the English followed their maritime journey.

By the sixteenth century the Islamic Middle East came under the grip formed by the expansion of Europe. The Russian army came from the north crushing both Turkey and Persia, the West Europeans came first circumnavigating Africa and crossing the Mediterranean, they reached the Arab world.

Change

By the nineteenth century the Middle East had become weaker and declined from its great days of the sixteenth century. Several factors caused this situation of deterioration starting with high price weaponry and war. Its internal economy was unfavorably changed by inflation and the upsurge in prices was unstoppable. Their foreign trade suffered from the development of transoceanic trade routes and the Middle East lost its importance. "Another element in the situation was the continuing unfavorable balance of trade of the Ottoman Empire with the countries to the east of it and the steady flow of gold and silver eastwards to Iran and India. These processes were accelerated by a lack of technological progress in agriculture, industry and transportation within the Middle east." Another change was a sudden drop in population. It is estimated that the population in Turkey, Syria, and Egypt was lower in 1800 than they had been in 1600.

The Middle East faced technological backwardness in shipbuilding and weapons. There was no intention to improve the network of roads and canals. Until the beginning of the 1900 AD, wheeled transport was almost unknown in the area. Only a few important personages used carriages in the cities, and a few peasants used the carts in villages. For any transportation, people used animals on roads and boats on rivers.

Most importantly, the decrease of the Ottomans was their inability to keep pace with the fast development of the West in science and technology, their failure to overcome the great established ideological barriers, and acceptance to new ways and new ideas.

In the course of the seventeenth century, Ottoman government funded training schools to teach the techniques of warfare and employed European instructors. Previously, Muslims neglected Europeans as barbarous, now they were required to learn their languages and read their books. The other change is the almost complete disappearance of the traditional values, standards and tastes that were trademarks in Ottoman buildings. The Dolmabahce palace is an example that illustrates its design as a wedding-cake architecture and unique mixture of styles imported from Europe.

Along with European weapons and technology came European ideas and helped the growth of personal communications through education, diplomacy, trade, and diffusion of ideas.

In the middle ages, Europe had nothing to offer to the far developed and sophisticated societies of Islam. Europeans' intellectual communication level was zero. By the time Europe reached intellectual and material power, Islamic world neglected anything coming from Christendom and refused to open its mind.

In Ottoman Empire, the European literature was negligible; the major movements like the Renaissance, the Reformation, the Enlightenment, and the Scientific Revolution were ignored because Islam itself had its own Renaissance with considerable effect on Europe.

The French Revolution began to change the process of thoughts and ideas in the minds of the Middle East. What happened to its rich civilizations like Sumer, Mesopotamia, Persian, Greek, and Egyptian?

Discovery of Oil

One of the most important changes in the history of the Middle East is the discovery, adventure, exploitation and use of petroleum, generally called Oil. The first drilling process began in Russian ruled part of the Apsheron peninsula of the Middle East in 1848. The first refinery was built in Baku in 1863 and from Apsheron to Baku, a pipeline was built in 1877-8. Later the oil of the Middle East was exploited by British, French, Dutch and American under royalty agreements with Middle Eastern governments. Gradually, oil fields mushroomed in Iran, Iraq, Arabia and the other parts, and Middle East became one of the major oil-producing places in the world.

Changes

In many ways, Muslims accepted the European style social and cultural changes. The first change was in the traditional arts. As early as 1800, the old traditions of tiny paintings in books and interior decoration in buildings were evading. They were replaced by a new art and architecture that were influenced by European patterns.

The customers in any part of the world café do not look very different from the café in Europe, particularly in Middle East Europe. But it does look very different from their predecessors 50 or 100 years ago. The changes that are prevailing at present, like the appearance, the manner, the dress, the behavior are almost completely of European origin.

The changes in the Middle East originated from outside. A scene in a restaurant people sitting in the chair at the table, reading a newspaper, and drinking coffee captures the changes that have transformed people's life from their parents – how they look, what they love, how they dress, all symbolize the immense changes coming from the West and have affected all modern time people.

The first visible change is their dress, the kind of clothes they wear, which indicates western style. Probably some people are wearing the traditional dress occasionally, but it is becoming less and less in major cities. Clothes have tremendous importance in one's own identity; it is not simply a way of keeping warm or cold, and to maintain decency.

Even some scriptures mandate to wear their traditional dress or otherwise "god will punish 'all such as are clothed with strange apparel.' Jewish and Muslim writings say, 'Do not dress like the infidels lest you become like them.' In some areas, even today each ethnic group has its own distinct dress code according to its religious value.

Initially, change in dress began with the military. Sultan Mohammad, one of the first major reformers of the nineteenth century, told, "We want to wear civilized clothes." Why should the clothes of much more ancient civilizations be considered uncivilized? For him, civilization meant modern that is Western civilization.

The style in the restaurant sitting on the furniture, a chair next to the table is also of western influence. Even though tables and chairs were there during Roman times, they disappeared when Arabs arrived. The Arabs came from a land where trees were few, and wood was a rare commodity. They had abundant wool and leather, which were used for clothes and other furnishings like reclined dewanas, etc.

The customers smoking cigarettes in the restaurant were imported from the west, which has the American origin.

Coffee - 1600 AD

Coffee originated in Ethiopia. In the sixteenth century it was introduced to southern Arabia, and afterwards to Egypt, Syria, and Turkey. As stated by a Turkish journal, it was brought by Sultan Suleiman to Istanbul around 1550 CE by two Syrians, one from Aleppo and the other from Damascus. They opened a coffee house, which became very popular and enormously fashionable. It is said that a coffee-house owner from Aleppo earned five thousand gold pieces in just three years. (1550 AD!)

The development of coffee houses raised concerns among religious and political authorities fearing that it may cause some form of plotting of agitation and lawlessness to Islamic Law. In 1633, Sultan Murad IV ordered the prohibition of both coffee and tobacco and commanded to execute smokers and coffee drinkers. After defending arguments between supporters and opponents, tobacco was declared lawful. This decision was taken due to belief in Islamic Law which ordains that all that is not forbidden is permitted. Thus, Coffee and Tobacco came back again.

Newspapers

Reading the newspaper in a restaurant or in the house was one of the most explosive and influential changes that was affecting an individual and society in those days. The art of writing was used in the Middle East since ancient times. Designing the alphabets was the invention of ancient the Middle Eastern and valuable contribution to the world, which enabled other scripts to develop by making modifications and improvements to the original alphabets. It was a huge change from the art of writing system of signs and pictures which had existed in the past.

But, paper making and printing were other major inventions from China. Although the Mongol rulers of Persia first printed bank notes and paid their employees in paper and insisted tax be paid in gold, it failed. Even though China invented printing technology, it did not come from China, but it came through the West and spread throughout the world. Among other artefacts, skills and ideas, they brought printed books and the knowledge of how to produce them.

In orthodox Muslim societies, rulers were bringing the news to the public about important changes in two ways: the inscription on the coinage and the Friday sermons. During sermons, citizens would know if there is a change of ruler by succession or rebellion, or a transfer of loyalty. They also announced the new measures and policies, removal, and imposition of taxes – along with inscriptions in public places. The praises of the ruler were sung by court poets, which were disseminated providing a kind of public relations.

The introduction of local press in the Middle East was the work of two great reforming rulers, Muhammad Ali Pasha of Egypt and Sultan Mahmud II of Turkey. The Egyptian rulers started an official journal in French and Arabic and the Turkish sultan in French and Turkish. The Turkish editorial announced the purpose of the newspaper, "The aim of the newspaper is to make known to the subjects the intentions and orders of the government."

The history of the newspaper in the Middle East reached its decisive turning-point with the Crimean War when the telegraph was introduced as a means of communication. People were addicted to newspapers more than ever, even more than coffee and tobacco.

In most parts of the world when illiteracy was a major problem, the introduction of newspapers and books had a revolutionary impact.

Photography

Mere presence of a person's picture on the wall was a radical change in Muslim world. According to their tradition, pictures are not permitted among Muslims. Islam has no place for music or poetry, painting, or sculpture. Instead, Muslim artists used conceptual and geometrical design by using inscriptions. Stanzas or the entire chapters of Quran are used to decorate the walls and ceilings of mosques including homes and public places.

Western paintings and sculptures also appeared in the Middle East, which had banned its ancient tradition of magnificent paintings and sculptures for a long time.

Western innovation of Cinema, Radio, TV, and Telephone also entered the Middle East and they are overwhelmingly successful. Writer notes that Egyptian film industry is the third largest in the world after the USA and India.

Eyeglasses

Among many other western innovations, the author refers to the eyeglasses: If a man in the coffee-house is an educated class and has damaged his eyesight by reading, he may be wearing a European invention eyeglasses; the coffee house may have a clock on the wall; the customer may be wearing a watch; may be playing board games; and on and on... These changes were overwhelming and probably irreversible.

There are many who see the impact of Western civilization as the greatest tragedy ever occurred on their region.

This new commodity affected the world in several ways. The author writes, "The use of the internal combustion engine transformed overland communications. It was now possible to link major centers and move persons, commodities, printed matter and ideas on a scale and at a speed undreamt of in earlier ages. The replacement, on a massive scale, of the horse, donkey and camel by car and truck, coupled with rapid economic development and the spread of such other Western means of communication as printing, newspapers, cinema, radio and television, began a far-reaching social transformation and made visible to all."

Unfortunately, once unified Middle Eastern countries are being engaged in war and destruction, which was anti-Islam in nature. And also according to the basic principles of the Arab League, no Arab state should take up arms against another Arab state to settle a dispute. Bernard Lewis writes:

> "These powers will, at most, act to defend their own interests... markets and oil, and the interests of the internal community, that is to say, a decent respect for the basic rules of the United Nations. Otherwise, the peoples and governments of the Middle East, for the first time in two centuries, will determine their own fate. They may produce new regional power, perhaps acting in concert, perhaps contending for regional hegemony. They may go the way of Yugoslavia and Somalia, to fragmentation and internecine chaos – and there are movements and individuals in the region who have made it clear that they would choose this rather than compromise on what they believe to be their religious duties or national rights.... They may unite – perhaps as some urging, for a holy war, a new jihad which, again as in the past, might

well evoke the response of a new Crusade. Or they may unite for peace–with themselves, their neighbors, and the outside world, using and sharing their spiritual as well as their material resources in the search for a fuller, richer, freer life. For the moment, the outside world seems disposed to leave them in peace, and perhaps even to help them to achieve it. They alone – the peoples and governments of the Middle East – can decide whether and how to use this window of opportunity while, in an interval of their troubled modern history, it remains open."

Very strong message!

11

Maya and Aztec

A millennium before Europeans were willing to divest themselves of the Biblical idea that the world was a few thousand years old, the Mayans were thinking of millions and the Hindus billions.

– ***Carl Sagan***

The Maya civilization had been hidden from the human eye until 1521 CE. Only about 500 years ago, it came to light to the outer world and was soon destroyed by Spaniards.

Background

The first hunter-gatherers arrived in America around 21,000 BCE and the city Tenochtitlan and the Aztec builders' culture was the product of more than 22,000 years of human activity. They left monumental symbols of their ingenuity in great cities of La Venta and San Lorenzo in 12,000 BCE, the Zapotec architects of Monte Alban in 500 BCE, and Toltec founders of Tollan in 950 CE. Maya also built their remarkable jungle cities in the east of Mexico.

Mesoamerica

Geographically, Mesoamerica runs from the Valley of Mexico across Guatemala and Honduras to Western Nicaragua and Costa Rica. Historically, it includes all occurrences between the arrival of the first human settlers in 21,000 BCE and the arrival of Spanish invaders in 1521 CE. Mesoamerica's civilization covers Mexico and Central America's ancient native peoples such as Olmec, Maya, Chichimec, Huastec, Zapotec, Toltec, Mixtec, Totonac, and Aztec. This remarkable land and civilization were not known to the world until 1521 CE.

In 1521 AD, when Hernan Cortes sent a shipment of gold, leatherwork and other rare treasures from Mesoamerica to the court of Roman Emperor Charles V in Spain, a great excitement spread in Europe. A German artist who saw the collection wrote in his journal, "I have seen nothing that has so thrilled my heart as these artifacts for I saw in them strange and wonderfully worked objects and marveled at the subtle genius of men in far-off lands."

After six hundred years of his remarks and more than a century of excavations and interpretation, the history of ancient Mesoamerican civilization is known to the world. Previously, a good deal of Mesoamerican mythology and history was transmitted orally from generation to generation and never written down although they had developed outstanding hieroglyph scripts, mathematics, and astronomy.

After Spaniards captured Tenochtitlan in 1521, they vandalized the city, broke images of gods, melted down gold and other treasures into nuggets to send to Europe, destroyed buildings and used the materials for the foundations of their New Spain colonies. They also burned many bark-paper scrolls. They interpreted that those manuscripts contained nothing but evils and false information. So they burned them all. The conqueror's belief that the native's books and religious rites were evil led to a terrible cultural loss.

A surviving book contained a prophecy and myth of a Maya seer who was said to have predicted the arrival of 'bearded men of the east who would bring violence and force the Maya to speak another language.'

Maya hieroglyphs were phonetic. Different signs represented combinations of vowels and consonants and they were used to spell out words. 20th century onwards, scholars were able to read and recognize the inscriptions that contained a great deal of information about the ritual calendar and astronomy. In the beginning they thought the Maya were peaceful people guided by priestly astronomers. But later scholars who could decipher the writings started to understand that the inscriptions were about the kings and sacrificial victims, usually rival kings were put to ritual death after defeat.

When Alberto Ruz was excavating a great royal tomb under a mortuary monument in the Maya city of Palenque, he found a vast Temple of Inscriptions and he curiously lifted one of the slabs on the temple floor. Then he discovered a narrow stairway leading downward. The stairway was purposefully blocked with debris, which Alberto painstakingly cleared them for four years. In June 1952, the stairway took him to a chamber and a 30' x 23' tomb. The carving on the tomb indicated that it was the tomb of king Pacal of Palenque.

In a deep rainforest of Mexico, they discovered a three room building in 1946 whose walls were decorated with a remarkable series of murals containing gaudy images of life at a Maya royal court in the 800 CE. The paintings portrayed royal succession, battles, musical performance, and deadly ceremonials.

History

According to historians, Mesoamerica's magnificent architectural and cultural accomplishments comprises nearly 3000 years. They suspect the first inhabitants of Mexico might have arrived from Siberia to North America. Radiocarbon dating of bone fragments found in a city of south-east Mexico City gives evidence that by 21,000 BCE people were living there. For some 14,000 years they remained as hunter-gatherers as the climate was cooler than now, and large cattle and animals flourished on that opulent grassland vegetation. Around 7000 BCE, temperature rose worldwide causing a major climate change, which changed the lifestyle for Mesoamericans because many grassland areas became deserts or tropical jungles. They had only small dogs and turkeys. Because there were not many animals and hunting became more difficult, people turned to cultivate more food products. So, they gradually began to develop farming skills and domesticate the plants. Since Mesoamericans had no oxen or horses, they did not develop wheeled vehicles and had no benefit of animal-drawn vehicles for moving food and materials.

There emerged different types of civilizations like Olmec, Maya, Chichimec, Huastec, Zapotec, Toltec, Mixtec, Totonac, and Aztec each having remarkable history of religions, culture, architecture, cities, buildings, crafts, and arts.

Jungle Cities of Maya

The Maya's sacred book 'The PopolVuh' explains how the sky and sea gods created the Earth from the primordial waters at the beginning of the time. (The PopolVuh is the book of the creation myth of the Quiche Maya peoples, the Book of Victories and the Book of Community, and a guidebook to the ancient myths of Mayan civilization.) The sky and sea gods just uttered 'Earth' and it rose up like a great mist, uncovered and displayed the mountains and the plain. Thick vegetation spread all over. The holy book compares the creation just like a farmer measures a field, "it was a fourfold siding, fourfold cornering, measuring, fourfold staking, halving the cord, stretching the cord, in the sky, on the earth, the four sides, the four corners." Farmers throughout Maya used a measuring technique like this. The other places like Guatemala used different techniques to measure the land.

First Settlement Models

Farmers conventionally practiced 'slash and burn' agricultural systems in the jungle. In the dry season, a farmer used a stone axe to clear the thick growth of trees and set them ablaze. Then he measured his land with the fourfold cornering and sowed the seeds of maize and other crops in the ash-filled earth in the beginning of the rainy season, in May or early June. For ten years he used the land and cultivated grains. After ten years, he moved to another place to clear, slash, and burn the land in the forest to sow the seeds and to start all over again. On hilltops the volcanic earth was deeper and richer, so farmers did not need to move their fields periodically.

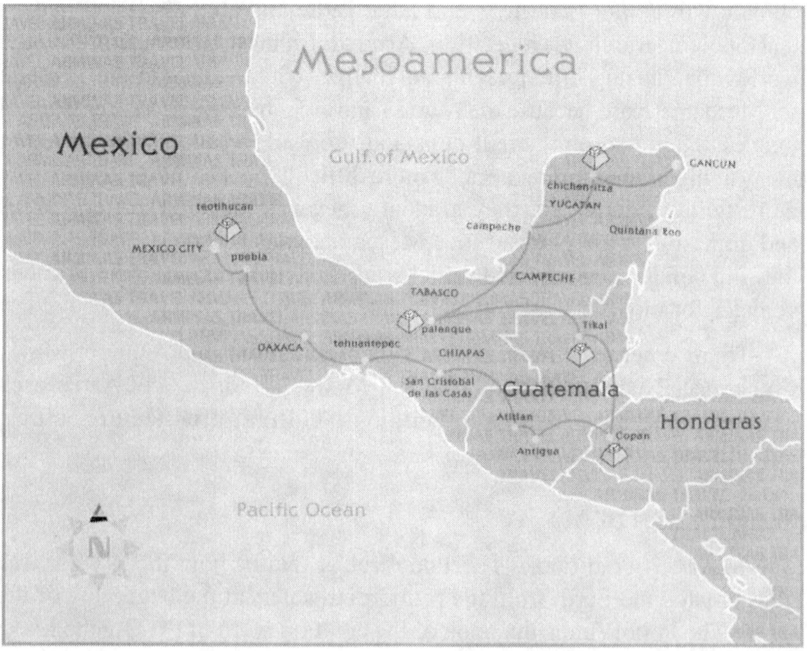

It seems that by the 8th century, the Maya had cleared the forest almost completely. Historians and scholars believe that this forest clearing process contributed to the 'Maya collapse' resulting in the abandonment of the cities of the area in the 9th century indicating the end of the Maya Classic period. The overuse of the land caused the ecological catastrophe because there was no land to go around slashing and burning and sowing the seeds.

Cenotes

In the Yucatan peninsula the land is porous limestone; water runs through the rocks and collects below ground. In some places the land collapses forming about 200 feet wide and 100 feet deep vast holes, which are called cenotes. The earliest settlers constructed cities around these cenotes and drew water building staircases. They used one of these cenotes as a 'Well of Sacrifice' for sacred ritual purposes. According to Bishop de Landa, the Maya performed sacrifices to the rain god Chac during famine, in which priests hurled human victims into the well with offerings of precious gold and jade. A legend describes that beautiful virgins were tossed into its water to please rain god Chac. In 1901, when the well was searched, they found precious offerings and the remnants of humans including skulls of men, women, and children. The American traveler and archaeologist John Lloyd describes how the Maya moved down over fragile rock deep into the earth by using the light of pine torches and a long ladder made from sheets of wood tied together with earthen pots for carrying the water fastened to their back and heads.

In some places the Maya made their own lakes because there were no rivers, springs, but plenty of rainfall. They coated natural valleys with clay padding and left them to dry in the sun to create a water-tight area! They added a walkway or boardwalk across the lake that also worked as a dam! The Maya also built wells that collected rainwater as it ran off the roofs of houses and ceremonial buildings. The wells also had covers to avoid evaporation of the precious water during hot weather.

Sacrifices to Please Gods

Maxtla was a dominant ruler of Azcapotzalco. In 1428 he was defeated by a party of three coalition rulers and taken as a prisoner. Later he was put to death in a ritual death ceremony and blood sacrifice to maintain political power and safeguard the natural order in Mesoamerica. In Mesoamerican culture, the sacrifices had a number of symbolic meanings and they were gross and sickening. First, it was linked to fertility. They believed the offering of the victim's lifeblood would safeguard the richness of the soils, guarantee the return of the rains, and therefore promote a good harvest. Second, the ceremony was a rebirth of the state, authenticating the power of the ruler, and keeping order in the realm. Third, the killing of Maxtla was an act of respect, because Mesoamericans considered it was shameful for a warrior or ruler to be captured and kept alive. Instead it was an honourable act to kill him as a human sacrifice.

For Mesoamericans, it was necessary to offer human blood sacrifice in a sacred religious function to sustain the world order, to maintain the fertility of land, and to safeguard the power of rulers. They thought that humans, gods, and the natural world were part of a cosmic pattern of energy in which the energy was recycled and passed on through rituals and sacrifices. Their ritual methods included removing the heart, burning, throwing down, and so on.

It is so graphic and appalling to read and write these rituals. But it is important to understand because these kinds of practices were prevalent in the ancient world all over. Here are some simple examples:

> "The extraction of the heart was performed with great ceremony on a special sacrificial block known as a quauhxicalli ('Stone of the Eagle'). The stone was pointed in the centre, so that a victim thrown down on it would be forced to arch his back and so thrust up his chest ready for the sacrificial knife."

To prepare this sacrifice the naked victims were collected at the temple steps and a priest came down with an image of the god. Then he showed the deity to each victim, saying 'this is your god'. Six priests (chachalmua) performed each sacrifice: four to hold the victim's feet, one to hold his throat and one to cut his chest.

BURNING SACRIFICE was performed for honoring the fire god Xiuhtecuhtli. Victims were sacrificed to the gods of planting and vegetation and they were shot with arrows so that their blood flowed into the earth like life-giving waters. They practically called human blood 'precious water.' The body was slashed, and a priest would wear the skin in honor of the god. This ritual was meant to split the seeds that make it possible the growth of new vegetation each spring.

The sacrificial targets were regarded with utmost respect calling him, 'Here I find my well-loved son'. The victim also declared, 'Here I met my well-respected father.' A story of warriors describes this concept. A soldier Tlahuicole captured by Aztec army was spared his life and made him a commander in a campaign against one of their battles. Tlahuicole accepted the role and when he returned back from the battlefield, he asked to be put to ritual death, because he felt that living alive in captivity was a shame to him. Instead, sacrifice to god would bring honor he had worked so hard to win. The killed victims in ritual sacrifice were considered as messengers to the gods and it was a way of honoring the divine presence on Earth. The sacrifice celebrations provided magnificent entertainment to the public.

"Priests were bedecked in splendid costumes and feather headdresses, and flowers adorned the temples. Musicians performed on conch-shell trumpets, flutes made from bones or reeds, drums and rattles. Dancers wore gold and silver bells that made a high ringing sound and blood flowed in a bright river from the steep temple steps and the bodies of the slain piled high at the temple front."

To Maya people, bloodletting was considered as a mystical act, an effort to achieve an ecstatic state in which a devotee could communicate with ancestors or gods.

"A carving in a cave demonstrates some lady drawing her blood by pulling a thorn cord across her tongue, while her husband holds a flaming torch above her head. The second carving shows that her devotions deliver her to a visionary state. The blood she has produced has been collected on a piece of bark paper and set alight producing a swirl of smoke in whose coils she can see the awesome Vision Serpent.... the serpent has two jaws through ancestors or deities can make..."

The Maya had many rituals for various purposes to make amendments by performing bloodletting rituals. They also had a scapegoat tradition, in which a certain individual took the punishment on behalf of the whole community's wrongdoing, often an elderly woman.

Mesoamericans believed that time was sacred and the experts in sacred rites can read the events of the future. Some claimed that they were able to decipher patterns of future events in the moving light on an obsidian mirror or on water in a pot. Others claimed that they can see what is coming in the lines made by a handful of grains of maize when they throw them on a robe. They worshiped sacred bundles that contained materials pertaining to a god or ancestor. It may be a tradition of nomads who packed up their gods during migration. According to their holy book 'Popol Vuh', the Maya priests brought holy parcels with them on their migrations and worshiped it in honor of their revered ancestors and gods. The bundles contained the mantles of the gods, jaguar skins, pieces of jade, jewels, and other precious items. In the homes Maya kept life-size clay idols for religious rites.

Death and the Afterlife

For Mesoamericans, life expectancy was low, child mortality was high, wars were frequent, and a continuous demand for a stream of human victims for sacred religious sacrificial rituals was high. To them death, its ceremonies, assumptions and speculations about the life after death were abundant as much as other civilizations. Their search for the human spirit's fate after death is similar to the ancient Egyptian and the Tibetan Book of the Dead.

Cosmology

The Aztec and Maya cosmology envisioned many layered universes with thirteen levels of heaven above the Earth and nine levels beneath. The underworld was a place of darkness and fear and endless misfortune. Its rulers were the skeleton god Mictlantecuhtli, Lord of the Dead, and his serpent-skirted spouse Mictacacihuatl. According to the Aztecs only a few selected people go to the happy realms above. Those who died a natural death would go to the underworld, but soldiers killed in battle, women who died in childbirth and even those who took their own lives were excluded from the underworld.

Funeral: All people, rich and poor, were buried with supplies to help their afterlife journey. Poorer Maya were laid beneath the floor of their

In a deep rainforest of Mexico, they discovered a three-room building in 1946 whose walls were decorated with a remarkable series of murals containing gaudy images of life at a Maya royal court in the 800 CE. The paintings portrayed royal succession, battles, musical performance, and deadly ceremonials.

house while nobles, royal and priestly elite were buried in grand tombs with lavish supplies and even assistants.

Usually, the Aztecs were cremated. The corpse was dressed in best clothes, tied in a squatting posture and wrapped in cloth before setting fire. An important person might have a number of servants and even wives cremated along with him so that they could escort him to the underworld.

War

For Mesoamericans war was a way of life. They waged war to secure resources, raw materials, and slave labor. They also thought waging war was a religious duty to return energy to the universe and to offer lifeblood to gods. The inscriptions and old texts suggest that Aztecs and Maya were hungry for live prisoners; ordinary common people were considered as slaves and the noble prisoners of war were reserved for sacrifice on the temple-pyramids.

According to one document, the rulers needed a plentiful supply of sacrificial victims for an inauguration function of a temple in Tenochtitlan. They decided that there is no need to wage war: one can simply enter a convenient market to find a victim. At this market, the army could buy victims like tortillas or french-fries. The market should be nearby, because the flesh of distant peoples was not good.

In 1487, a re-dedication of a great Temple took place in which as many as 80,000 victims had been sacrificed demonstrating the mighty power of Aztec rulers. Interestingly, they used to offer only well-built, good-looking, praiseworthy young people for sacrifice to gods.

Structure of Power

The rulers of classic period Maya were dynastic leaders and honored as 'holy kings.' The holy kings inscribed stelae, thrones, wall panels, door lintels and other monuments recording their date of birth, accession, major anniversaries, duration of rule, military triumphs, and significant ritual sacrifices and so on.

"The evidence suggests that a woman could succeed her father in the royal palace only as a wife. Her husband would be 'adopted' by her father and become the rightful heir in her place. Their children would then inherit the throne."

"Among the Aztecs, succession was not hereditary. An election was held among the nobles of the highest ranks to determine who should succeed the tlatoani and the new ruler was then blessed, following complex coronation rites, by the high priest. However, essentially the election was a token. The old ruler would nominate a successor and it would usually have been clear who this would be…"

Coronation

Aztec and Maya kings dressed in big grandeurs to demonstrate themselves as gods. They wore wooden frames on their backs to support more than a metre large headdress. The frame and headdress were covered with elaborate decorative designs using shells, carved jade, feathers and clothes. They usually contained sun god or rain god images. The long bright quetzal bird was a precious symbol of sovereignty.

Some kings wore the stick bundles indicating that the king was literate and had high status. Coronation ceremony was conducted very pompously and spectacularly with dance, drums, and rituals including a vast human sacrifice.

The Mayan Law, Time Concept, Mathematics, & Hieroglyph

In the Mesoamerican empire, there were three main players; Tenochtitlan, Texcoco and Tlacopan, who created a victorious coalition and made a Triple Alliance and divided the loots among themselves. The kings of the Triple Alliance used a legal code or a list of punishments to rule their domains. They all agreed to what comprised good behavior. According to Bernardino de Sahagun, righteous Aztecs were obedient and honest, treating their fellow citizens with respect and showing discretion in their dealings with others. Righteous men and women worked hard, no matter where they worked such as in the fields, sewing, preparing food, workshops, or in the marketplace.

Charles Phillips writes, "They brought energy to their works, without overindulging in sleep but rising early and laboring for long hours. They ate and drank in moderation; drunkenness was particularly disliked. They did not make a great noise when eating, thought carefully before speaking and were circumspect in what they said. They dressed and behaved with modesty. Children were raised to understand and follow this code."

Punishment

The punishments for wrongdoers varied in Aztec and Maya territories. Punishments for wrongdoers comprised jailing and execution by strangulation, at the pole, or stoning. Theft was punished by strangulation. Drunkards were punished with a sliding scale of penalties. The alcoholic drink was allowed only for nobles, for those who were sick, or aged over 52 years. The warriors could drink pulque as a reward for their brevity.

In one occasion when judges failed to follow required procedures and conducted cases in their private quarters, they were put to death by strangulation.

The Zapotec, one of many Mesoamerican civilizations (700 BCE - 1521 CE) that flourished in the Valley of Oaxaca.

The Maya imposed severe penalties for those who threatened social order like murder or adultery. They considered that the bad things will not happen accidentally because every event is the fulfillment of patterns that were set in motion by the gods and it could be studied in the stars. According to their view, "A hunter who killed another man by accident in the forest was just as guilty of murder as a man who killed another before witnesses in a quarrel over food. The unfortunate hunter must have been chosen by the gods to meet this end." If someone loses someone else's goods, it was considered as a crime and he must compensate for the owner of the property. Those who had no wealth were forced to slavery and would be freed once they had worked off the money they owed to the victim.

The punishment for murder was death. When couples were caught committing adultery, the man was dragged on the street and handed over to the husband of the women to take revenge. The usual method was dropping a heavy rock on the adulterer from a height.

Theft was also considered a serious crime. The Maya did not put thieves, murders or adulterers in jail. They kept only the captives from war in jail for sacrifice during the festivities.

Maya Social System

The Maya managed two blood groups: the matrilineal group, derived from the mother, and patrilineal group, derived from the father. Each person had a name given by and inherited from the mother and another taken from the father. Children could inherit the property only from the father. The members of the father's side were expected to help one another in time of trouble like to buy out a relative who had been put into slavery because of debt or crime. According to one historian, each family was allocated 400sq feet of land to cultivate. As per marriage arrangements, a man could marry his mother's brother's daughter or his father's sister's daughter, but he would be banned from making other different marriages.

About class divisions, it was extremely prestigious to a noble family to be able to trace the lineage on both mother's and father's side back across many generations. Actually, the word for a noble, *almehen* means 'a man whose bloodline can be read on both sides.' Nobility included wealthy farmers, prosperous merchants, priests, leading warriors, councilors, judges, and governors. The most important positions were filled by close members of the ruler's own blood group.

The statues of the warriors and column ruins on the top of a temple in the Toltec archaeological site of Tula, Mexico.

Importantly, scribes occupied a high social position and these literates were leading members of the king's staff. Probably many cities had a school for scribes or writers where royal and noble children went and learnt the complex skills of reading and writing Maya hieroglyphs.

For the general population, literacy was not widespread. Scholars estimate that probably one in four in Maya could read and few could write. 'Archaeologists have found attempts at writing by non-elite scribes at minor settlements or on the bricks are not understandable because those non-elites had not mastered the difficult technique required to write. All they could manage was a crude imitation of the fine calligraphy found on carvings and ceramics produced by the elite scribes.'

Slaves

Some people worked on the lands of the wealthy. Most of them were captured in war. While poorer prisoners were put into slavery, the noble prisoners were reserved for the sacrifice. Others were people form Maya homelands who were entrusted to slavery because of wrongdoings, or debt, or poverty. There was also a system of slave trade across Mesoamerica. For most of them, there was no chance to escape from that condition including their children. But it was possible to anyone to buy an individual out of slavery. Female slaves worked as drawing water from wells, dyeing cloth and grinding maize. Male slaves worked as fishermen and movers for merchants.

The kings and nobles lived in the center of the city, close to temples and markets. Around this area were palaces and homes of the elite nobles; merchants and professionals lived in small residences; and humble homes of the working class were far away.

The Aztec society was also highly classified as nobility, commoners, artisans according to their positions and wealth.

The Time Concept in Mesoamerica

For Mesoamericans, TIME was not an orderly sequence from past to the future, from the beginnings of the visible world to its end. Instead, they believed time is recurring and cyclical. For example, the Aztecs believed that we live in the Fifth Sun or Age, and our age would end at a certain time. They also believed that time was sacred, energized with the power of the gods. Its movements could be fluid and unpredictable and could be directed as gods wanted. Their gods could take many forms simultaneously including the form of time itself. People depended on priests to interpret time.

A time span of 52 years was produced by the intersection of the two calendars used by the Aztecs and their Mesoamerican associates since they were separated by centuries and by miles. The inhabitants of Copan used a 365-day solar calendar to celebrate religious festivals together with a 260-day calendar for discovering the future. "The first day of the 365-day calendar and the first day of the 260-day calendar intersected only once every 52 years. The Aztecs called this time span a 'bundle of years' while the Maya version is usually the 'the Calendar Round'."

Mathematics

The Maya used an extremely sophisticated mathematical notation to write a very large number in manuscripts. They were the first people along with the ancient Babylonians, the Chinese and the Hindus in India to develop the concept of zero and a symbol for it. Maya 'Zero' was not represented by an empty circle (0), but by an image of a shell ( )

Dots and Bars: The author writes,

"The Maya did not have the familiar decimal system based on 10, instead a count based on 20 (called a vigesimal system). Scholars suggest that the unit of 20 may have been used because it matches the number of fingers and toes in the human body. The Maya scribes and craftsmen wrote the numbers 1 to 4 with simple dots. One dot meant 1, two dots 2, three dots 3 and four dots 4. The number 5 was written with a horizontal bar, and 6 was a single bar with a dot above it. They were able to write numbers up to 19 with a combination of horizontal bars and dots. For example, 17 were written with three bars making 15, and two dots."

"To write large numbers they used these same symbols arranged in vertical columns. The bottom line showed units (1 to 19), the line

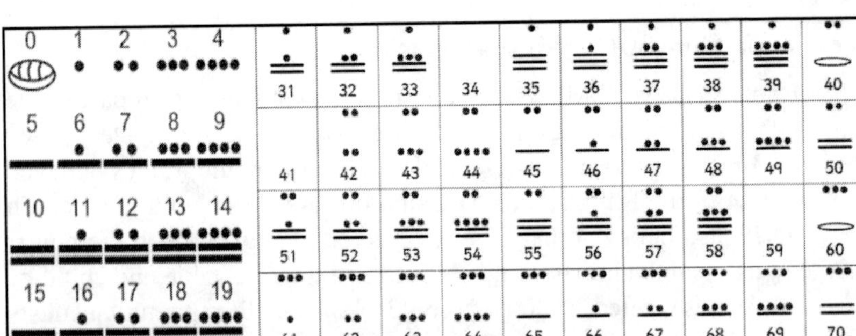

Mayan Numerals

above it numbers of twenties, the line above it numbers of 400s (20 units of 20), the line above that numbers of 8000s (20 units of 400) and so on. A single bar in the first line, with a dot in the line above, two bars in the line above and one bar in the line above represent (1x5) plus (1x20) plus (10x400) plus (5x8000), which makes 5+20+4000+40,000=44,025."

A brilliant naturalist and traveler-writer Constantine Rafinesque (1783-1840) made a breakthrough deciphering this Maya bar and dot numerical system. Observing the frequent use of bars and dots in the Maya texts, he deduced that these symbols were being used as numbers. He noticed that the dots never appeared in groups of more than four and guessed that the bar stood for 5 and the dots for single units. Afterwards an archivist found out that the Maya scribe's use of a shell symbol to represent 0.

Some scholars believe the system possibly dates back to 1500 BCE - 400 BCE.

Calendars

The Aztec's 365-day calendar contained 18 months of 20 days, and five days at the year's end that were regarded as inauspicious. This calendar was used for religious festivals and for indicating the seasons. Another Aztec 265-day calendar contained the numbers with 20 names of creatures, house, wind, flint knife, jaguar and reed. When the calendar was written down, each day's name was denoted by hieroglyphs showing the object, animal or force, and each number was shown by dots. The cycle was called TONALPOHUALLI (the counting of the days): 1-Crocodile, 2-Wind, and 3-House. The thirteenth and fourteenth names in the cycle were reed and jaguar, but there was no fourteen in the number sequence. After 13-Reed, the cycle proceeded to 1-Jaguar and so on.

Each 20-day month was related to a religious festival. Some of them are linked to the agricultural year. One group worshiped the sun, the land and maize. And so on.

The 20 Aztec Day names were:

1. Crocodile,
2. Wind,
3. House,
4. Lizard,
5. Serpent,
6. Death,

7. Deer,
8. Rabbit,
9. Water,
10. Dog,
11. Monkey,
12. Grass,
13. Reed,
14. Jaguar, (1)
15. Eagle, (2)
16. Vulture, (3)
17. Movement, (4)
18. Flint knife, (5)
19. Rain, (6)
20. Flower (7)

Scholars do not understand why the Mesoamericans used a 260-day calendar. Some modern scholars speculate that the 260-day cycle may be based on human rhythms. Midwives may have been used to measure, counting 260 days from the date of a woman's last menstrual period to predict when a baby would likely be born.

Mayan Calendars

Here is an example of how they arranged their festivals in a 20-days month (western dates are used for practical purposes.)

Aztec Month 1 (14 February - 5 March)

Festival Name

1. Atlacaualo (The Ending of Water)
2. Cuauhitleua (The Lifting of Trees)

Gods/Goddesses Honoured

1. Tlaloc (Rain And Fertility)
2. Chalchiuhtlicue (Goddess Of Springs, Rivers And The Sea)
3. Chicomecoatl (Maize Goddess)
4. Quetzalcoatl (Storms, Wind and Rain God)

Rites

1. Offerings to maize divinities, including the sacrifice of children; banners erected in homes and temples.

   In the same way, all Maya months had festivals to concerned gods with rites and sacrifices. Each festival was elaborate and pompous, and at the same time gruesome human sacrifices also.

   The Maya also had another very complex calendar called Long Count. The author writes, "The Maya Long Count calendar counted days in units of 20 and used a 'year' of 360 days. Its five units were:

   1. The BAKTUN (144,000 days),
   2. The KATUN (7,200 days),
   3. The TUN (360 days),
   4. The UINAL (20 days) and
   5. The KIN (1 day).

Dates were carved in this order, with units separated by full points.

For example, the date 3.3.2.1.1 would be

1. 3 BAKTUNS (432,000 days),
2. 3 KATUNS (21,600 days),
3. 2 TUNS (720 days),
4. 1 UINAL (20 days) and
5. 1 KIN (1 day)

It makes a total of 454,341 days after the Zero date of 11 August 3114 BCE.

Well, we all know what happened to this calendar. The fact of the matter is December 20, 2012 was not the End of the World. It was the End of the Era (End of the Fifth Sun according to their calendar.)

Forecasting the Future

Aztec priests consulted the long screen-fold ritual calendar TONALAMATL to foretell the future. These books were made from bark paper coated with a white mineral paste for recording purposes.

The calendars contained a rich mixture of mysterious meanings. Each number in the TONALPOHUALLI (day count) was under divine influence. Each of the 13 lords of the day was associated with a butterfly or bird. Each of the day-names also had its associated deity. A further cycle of nine lords of the night influenced the calendar. The influences that were in place at the start of each 13-day period remained a powerful force throughout.

Priests observed the movements of celestial bodies. Priest-astrologer-fortune tellers would find the best days for planting, harvesting and other daily activities. Maya planting books instructed farmers which day is good to plant during the months of Chen and Yax.

Merchants took priests advice for planning their departure and arrival dates for their business travels. Rulers consulted astronomer-priests to attack enemies, to observe festivities and other ceremonies. Venus was a war god.

Reading Stars

It is said that in Mesoamerican latitudes, Venus shines brilliantly in the morning sky as large as a tennis ball. This planet takes an important role in the religion and mythology of Mesoamerica. As per astronomers, "Venus follows a near circular orbit around the sun. One orbit around the sun takes 225 days. It goes through a number of phases: one cycle of phases takes 584 days." The Mesoamerican astronomers knew this because they had constructed observatories in Mayapan and Chichen Itza and measured it. They knew that Venus goes through four phases.

- Phase 1: It rises first in the morning sky and is visible as the morning star for 236 days.
- Phase 2: Thereafter it disappears into the light of the sun and is lost to sight for 90 days.
- Phase 3: At the end of this period it rises in the evening sky and is visible as the evening star for 250 days.
- Phase 4: In its fourth phase, it is invisible for eight days before reappearing as the morning star." = 584 days.

The Maya connected the disappearance of Venus for eight days in the fourth phase with the journey to the underworld or spirit region to claim the bones of fishmen, the people of a previous world-age. After returning from his journey successfully, he rose in the sky as a morning star. The author writes, "Every Maya ruler was thought to travel to the underworld after death and if he passed successfully through the trials he faced there, would rise into the sky as Venus." The appearance of Venus as a morning star was considered as the king's immortality and a celebration of the victory.

Maya Observatories

Maya Observatories

Excerpt from the book Aztec & Maya

"Maya star-watchers, who had no specialized astronomical equipment, predicted the rising of Venus as morning star and evening star with astonishing accuracy; to within one day in 6,000 years. The tower-observatory in the Maya city of Chichen Itza tells of the dedication with which Maya priests plotted celestial movements. The tower is known in modern times as the Caracol, from the Spanish for snail, because it has spiral passageways. It was built for observation of Venus. Three passages leaving the Caracol line up precisely with the spots in the western sky where Venus can be seen as the evening star, among them the most northerly and southerly point at which it sets. At Palenque, the square tower that rises above the palace is decorated with a Venus glyph and appears to have been used as an observatory for plotting the planet's movements, while at Uxmal, the Governor's Palace must have been used for astronomical observation. It is aligned with a mound above which Venus would have risen at the most southerly point in its cycle."

Written Records

The honor of developing first written scripts in Mesoamerica belongs to the Olmec people in the Gulf Coast of Mexico in 1500 BCE - 400 BCE.

Interestingly, it seems like Olmec was already using screen-fold books (written on a long sheet of amate bark paper to make a book with many sheets). A ceramic bowl dated as early as 1200 BCE is carved with two objects that resemble this kind of book. The Olmec people might have had some kind of communicating system though it was not as we think.

After the downfall of Olmec culture, the Zapotec craftsmen were the next to develop the art of writing in Mesoamerica around 600-200 BCE. They carved images of male figures with hieroglyphic signs representing the name of the image. But the scholars are unable to decipher these inscriptions and carvings.

Another system of writing, 'Isthmian' script was used in the 2nd century CE and they are in the Smithsonian Institution, Washington, DC. The script used only 150 signs and the scholars think that these signs probably represented whole words instead of phonetic elements.

Royal Scribes and Scrolls

In Mesoamerica, the scribes always belonged to royal and elite societies. They were the sons and daughters of nobles and royal families. Many kings knew how to write and read. They were displayed on vases showing a bundle of pens in their hair, which was a respected high-ranking mark of scribes. The most important scribe in the classic Maya period was AK K'U HUN (guardian of the sacred books).

A chief scribe had many administrative jobs apart from artistic scribe jobs: he was a manager of royal ceremonies, a negotiator of royal marriages, a record keeper, and a teacher in scribal schools. Probably the Maya scribe painted the images with words. The scribes who produced calligraphy and paintings were awarded a title as AH TS'IB (he of the writing); those who produced hieroglyphic inscriptions and images were honored as YUXUL (sculptor). They were awarded to both men and women, mostly men.

At scribe schools, students had to follow long and demanding courses of study for reading and writing Maya hieroglyphs and required great knowledge and skills.

The four surviving Maya codices or manuscripts deal mainly with priestly rituals and tables for calculating astronomical events. "Writing on carved bones and jade and on the pots and other ceramic goods left with deceased royals and nobles in their graves mostly gives the name and titles of the deceased and sometimes contains dedications to the gods. Some also name the artist who drew them."

Mythology & the Destruction of Maya Civilization

Like any other culture, Mesoamerica has a very interesting mythology. Its concept of creation varies from one part to another. They saw a world full of dangerous sacred power that demanded ritual worship; they believed this power could take many forms shifting between human, animal or symbolic forms as they wish. They passed this belief from culture to culture, generation to generation. Their stories explained: why things are as they are; once upon a time gods and goddesses walked on the Earth and controlled the world; now, they control the world in spirit form.

1. POWER: Mesoamerican cosmology envisions that "At north, south, east and west of the Mesoamerican universe stood four pillars, or trees, that supported and connected the three levels of the cosmos. In the center was a fifth tree, whose roots were in the underworld, but its topmost branches touched the very highest of the celestial planes. The four other trees at the points of the compass were in fact outgrowths of the main cosmic tree. The trees stood on hollow hills and were themselves hollow, and within them the power of the underworld and of the heavens was always flowing, powering the repeating movements of time, of the seasons, of the sun, moon, stars, and planets and of the energy recycled in acts of blood sacrifice. Only after the creation of the four trees of north, south, east and west could time be measured and sacred events honored through use of the ritual calendar."
2. Another version of the creation myth says that in the primordial era, the earth and sky were not separated, but were mixed in wetness and darkness. The earth was merely a mixture of water and muddy, wet and dark. The creator god Lord Nine Wind arose from the dark and separated the waters from the earth, raising the waters up to form the sky. And ....
3. Another myth says the earth was born from the conversation of the gods.
4. Myth on Birth of the Gods elaborately describes many stories.
5. Myth on Man of Mud: The creators tried to make a human being from mud. But they could not make the body hold together no matter how they tried. It kept falling apart and melting into a watery mess. Its face was not good and although it could talk, it did not make any sense.
6. Myth on Man of Wood: The creators consulted two ancient shaman-divinities and asked whether human beings could be made from wood. The two divinities, also called grandfather and

grandmother, performed a divination using kernels of corn and coral seeds and declared that wood was a suitable material for making people. Eventually after many trials, they made men from the wood of the coral tree and the women made from the core of bulrushes (a tall water plant). The wooden people multiplied and formed families. Although they could speak, their hearts and minds were empty. They did not remember their creators or counting of the days and did not worship the gods at proper time. Besides, their skin was dry and flaky because they had no sweat, and their bodies distorted in the heat because they had no blood to keep them moist. So, gods decided to destroy wooden people and sent powerful rain and thunderstorms and drowned them. Next, some wooden people survived and transformed to monkeys. Still, the gods are determined to keep trying to make human beings.

7. Myths on Jaguar Sun, The Wind Sun, The Rain Sun, The Water Sun, and so on and on …

The Maya Collapse

The cities of southern cities of Maya Lowlands began to collapse in the 9th century. Indeed, it was a human tragedy. Within four or five generations, an entire great civilization disappeared. The scholars argue that intensifying war between the city-states competing for land and also to capture prisoners of war in order to conduct lavish sacrifices to bring back the old time of plenty is the main cause of collapse.

A Kingdom Defeated, a Kingdom Triumphed - Arrival of the Spaniards

In 1509 AD, a comet appeared in the sky over Lake Texcoco. It stretched into the sky like a tongue of flame and seeped a rain of small hot burning drops. The priests and astronomers could not interpret the meaning or reason. The Texcocan king Netzahualpilli who was said to be able to see the future, declared that terrible events will happen in the future that would end in the destruction of cities and their empire.

The Aztecs must have known the European visitors through the word of mouth and through the merchants because the Spaniards had already landed in Mexico by 1492. In 1518, a laborer came to king's court and reported that he had seen mountains floating on the sea, meaning the large Spanish ships. When king Moctezuma sent investigators to the coast, they discovered men with long beards and fair skin, fishing vessels and floating mountains.

Return of the God

The most fascinating part of these reports was that they believed that they were omens of the return of the god Quetzalcoatl, the Plumed Serpent. According to myth, the said god had departed by sea heading east and had vowed to return from that direction in order to lead a new age. When Moctezuma heard this news in April 1519 that the ships had landed in the region, it confirmed his impression that Spanish conquerors landed at the exact place where Quetzalcoatl departed.

The Aztec empire was no more, and it ended on 13 August 1521.

Welcome Visitors?

The Spanish expedition was conducted by Hernan Cortes and came to Mexican border from the Spanish colony in Cuba. Now, Moctezuma was confused whether to treat the incomers with reverence as gods or with violence as invaders. First, he sent supplies together with magnificent offerings including large coins of gold and silver representing the sun and moon, and ritual costumes. The food he sent was ritualistically soaked with the blood of a sacrificial victim as it was a custom in the Aztec region. Because Cortes rejected the offerings, Moctezuma changed his mind and sent sorcerers and magicians to recite incantations capable of keeping the intruders in their place. But the Spaniards proved that they were unaffected by local magic and Cortes proceeded inland from the coast towards the capital and attacked the empire. As part of a plan designed by Moctezuma, the Cholulians invited the army into the city. Hidden soldiers were supposed to emerge and kill the foreigners. But the plan was disclosed to the Spaniards by the inner circle and they slaughtered the Cholulian chiefs and everyone.

When the Spanish army came to Tenochtitlan, Moctezuma went to meet Cortes on a palanquin carried by four noblemen and greeted the Spaniard with the highest respect. He gave Cortes a necklace of snail shells and shrimps made of solid gold and received a string of Venetian glass-beads from Cortes in return. Then in an inauspicious moment Moctezuma invited Cortes to his Aztec capital.

The guests were lodged in the palace near the ritual arena at the center of the city. But the Spanish team thinking that the plot that had failed in Cholula might be tried again acted swiftly. Showing simplicity and boldness, they took the Aztec emperor prisoner and kept him in a guarded room in the palace. The Aztec nobles wanted to resist Spanish, but Moctezuma advised cooperation.

When Cortes went to Cuba to put down an insurgent, the Spaniards attacked and slaughtered a group of Aztec nobles to eradicate any conspiracy. To take revenge, the Aztecs attacked the Spanish. Moctezuma climbed to the palace roof and shouted for peace, but even though they obeyed their emperor, they lost their respect for him at that moment. They elected his brother Cuitlahuac and attacked Spanish army once again. Again, Moctezuma climbed the palace roof and called for peace. This time, Aztec people greeted his words with boos and then with a storm of arrows and stones. Eventually, Moctezuma died. Then Cortes army stormed the Great Pyramid, set fire to the shrines, and threw down the Aztec's most respected idols. After attacking and destroying Aztec palaces, Cortes army captured tlatoani Cuauhtémoc and his army when they attempted to flee to a new place. Finally, Aztecs made a dignified surrender. The Aztec empire was no more, and it ended on 13 August 1521 AD.

To Spaniards, conquering the more dispersed Maya region was harder than Aztecs. With their control over gunpowder, they unleashed a storm of gunshots that crushed the Maya and terrified the remaining defenders. The last container of Maya sovereignty was conquered ending a great civilization without a trace.

12

United States of America

America will never be destroyed from the outside. If we falter and lose our freedoms, it will be because we destroyed ourselves.

– ***Abraham Lincoln***

Do not pray for easy lives. Pray to be stronger.

– ***John F. Kennedy***

In 1867 Mark Twain, as a newspaper reporter, was travelling through the countryside of France in a railway carriage. He suddenly felt that he was in a highly civilized country France and began to compare it with America of 1867 that looked like rural and unsophisticated at that time:

> "What a bewitching land it is! Surely the leagues of bright green lawns are swept and brushed and watered every day and their grasses trimmed by the barber. Surely the straight, smooth, pure white turnpikes are jack-planed and sand-papered every day. How else are these marvels of symmetry, cleanliness, and order attained? It is wonderful. There are no unsightly stone walls. No dirt, no decay, and no rubbish anywhere-nothing that even hints at untidiness. All is orderly and beautiful.
>
> ...and American atmosphere was like, "hog-wallows, broken fences, cow lots, unpainted houses, mud, absence of cleanliness, potholes and inequality of surface.... ."

America Discovered

On a beautiful morning of April 1607, the history of America began when Captain Christopher Newport anchored his three storm-beaten ships near the estuary of Chesapeake Bay. He sent a group of people to browse the area. John Percy, a member in the ship, records how they found noble forests, the ground carpeted with flowers; fair meadows, large tall trees with fresh waters; fine strawberries, four times bigger and better than in England's; oysters very large and delicate in taste; stocks of turkey nests and many eggs; and an Indian town, where the tribal Indian brought them cornbread and tobacco smoked in clay pipes with copper bowls. He also records the delight of seeing richly coloured birds, the fruits and berries, the fine fish, and the pleasant scenery.

The other side of English settlers' story was more pathetic in the beginning: Local Indian attacked them on all sides creeping from hills like bears; men were caught by cruel diseases, such as swellings, instabilities, burning fevers; people, mostly male, died by famine. Their bodies were pulled out of their cabins like dogs to be buried.

The Establishment of the Colonies & the Natural Topographies of North America

Establishing a new nation in America was not a joyful mission like a holiday picnic. Working in eastern side was ugly, dirty, laborious, and dangerous. It was a great shabby and disorganized continent covered with pathless forests; its mountains, broad rivers, lakes, and plains were all on grand and impenetrable measure. Everything was humongous. Its Northern parts were brutally cold in winter; southern parts were burning hot in summer; and occupied with wild beasts and warlike, cruel, and dangerous people still in the Stone Age culture. In reality, it was a forbidden land. It was reachable only by a sail and it was so hazardous that ships were buried as many as they landed. In spite of all its disadvantages, it was suitable to become the home of an energetic and thriving people.

North America is a rich, multi-coloured and well-watered area. Here the climate is healthy with a warm summer that allows fine crops and a cold winter that encourages people to action. Europeans adjusted to this climate and settled without any problem as they brought their chief food crops like wheat, rye, oats, beans, carrots, and onions. They discovered two more remarkable foods, maize and potatoes. Everywhere wild animals were abundant; the deer and bison wandering in millions, the flight of pigeons darkening the sky with their herd. The coastal waters were rich in fish. The land contained more iron, coal, copper, and petroleum than any other country and it had practically boundless forests. Peoples from all parts of Western Europe intermixed in it to become a great pool in which a new democracy and a new American sentiment developed.

They discovered that the far west had high plains and Rocky Mountains with dry climate. Gold and other minerals attracted a crowd of adventurous pioneers. Trailing the buffalo hunters, the cattle breeders occupied the whole plains and the population gradually increased as the railroads brought the materials needed for the conquest of the treeless land. It brought barbed wires, windmills, lumber, and agricultural implements. By 1890 the Wide Wild West no more existed.

1. Christopher Columbus

2. Mayflower Ship

Since the Indians were small in numbers in North America, it was a good opportunity for the white settlers to colonize. The Indians gave some troubles, but they never stopped foreigners completely. When the first Europeans arrived, the Indians in Mississippi were around 200,000 and the whole continent in north of Mexico did not exceed 500,000. Possessing only the bow and arrow, tomahawk/hatchet, the war club, and unaware of any military skills, Indians were no match for well-equipped and ever alert Europeans. Indians lived mainly by hunting and fishing not showing any interest in conquering nature.

After a long struggle with European invaders, Indians found European allies finally. Some of the Northern clans combined with the French; some of the Southern clans received arms and encouragement from the Spaniards. English-speaking settlers took a friendly attitude and gave active aid in campaigns against the French. Finally, the aggressive Indians were once and for all defeated.

An assembly of English Calvinists (Reformed Protestants) who had established in Holland were thinking to move to the New World. These people were ill-treated because they rejected the priestly supremacy of the king and wanted to set up a separate church of their own. They had three leaders with outstanding ability: the teacher John Robinson, a learned, broad-minded, generous-hearted graduate of Cambridge; William Brewster, also a Cambridge man; and William Bradford, sharp, influential, and idealistic. They possessed integrity, industry, sobriety, courage and determination. They had sustained hostility in England and also they had tolerated loneliness and difficulties in Holland. Obtaining an entitlement to settle in America, a group of 102 pilgrims prepared to face the rigidities of wilderness on a ship named "Mayflower" with a stockpile of provisions. They landed on the Massachusetts coast on December 11, 1620. The following winter more than half of them died of cold and scurvy[25]. The following summer they raised good crops and a new ship arrived with more pilgrims.

Roger Williams courageously taught the separation of Church and state with other radical views and founded Providence in Rhode Island as a place of perfect religious toleration. Another notable colony Maryland was founded under the guidance of the liberal-minded Cecilius Calvert, second Lord Baltimore. A large number of ships carried numerous numbers of things from London: hundreds of livestock, furniture with thousands of settlers. The great majority of emigrants to Massachusetts and Virginia were yeomen, mechanics, shopkeepers, and clerks of moderate means; in other parts of America were bonded servants. Their real wealth lay in their sturdy integrity, self-reliance, and energy.

The Emergence of Self-Government

Wherever the colonists went, they carried and maintained the philosophy of the rights of freeborn Britons, accepting the custom of the English struggle for liberty. They announced that the settlers were to have all the liberties, licenses, and protections as if they had been within the jurisdiction of England. They were supposed to have the protection of Magna Carta and the common law. But to make it effective the settlers had to exhibit continuous care and if needed to be ready to wage war. From the beginning, they started to nurture their own framework of constitutional government, competing for a stronger representative system, control of the money, and complete assurance of personal liberty.

Church and State in the Colonies

Virginia Church was neither a prosperous organization materially nor one which influenced settlers spiritually and intellectually. As the thirst for political freedom grew in America, the spirit of religious tolerance also grew. Social and economic conditions were unfavourable to settlers. Small churches spread out over large parts of thinly populated territories. Following the river banks closely, the boundaries of territories were about thirty to sixty miles in length. Those who wanted to go to Church had to travel long distances over dreadful roads or to row strenuously for hours on rivers. Obviously, attendance was irregular. As the church minister's salary was low, they made bitter complaints.

With meagre salaries, insecure jobs, and many hardships to meet, it was difficult to find enthusiastic pastors with ability and piety. The best priests would not migrate to America from England because they could find better opportunities at their homeland. Those who migrated were, most of the time, dull of mind, lazy of body, or untrustworthy in morals. So complaints started to emerge as 'a pack of scandalous fellows,' 'many vices not agreeable to their coats,' and 'addicted to swearing, drunkenness, and fighting.' Consequently, reform movements were undertaken and a William and Mary college were founded in 1603 in Williamsburg, Virginia, primarily as a training school for young church ministers and priests. In all respects the church played a major role in early history of America.

Massachusetts' two great messengers of religious liberty were Roger Williams and Anne Hutchinson. Williams, a highly educated man who had graduated from Cambridge in England, and a most pious Christian, was a radical opponent of the whole Puritan idea of theocracy, a system of government in which priests rule the country in the name of a god. He argued that Church and state should be entirely separated; that it was wrong to try to compel men to attend church; and that nonconformists should be calmly tolerated; that the government should protect all well-behaved people equally. Noticing William's radical movements, Massachusetts's government ordered him to return to England. But he escaped through the snows to Rhode Island where he applied his principles.

Anne Hutchinson preached doctrines similar to transcendentalism. She said that it was the duty of every individual to follow the instigations of inner supernatural voice; and it was the presence of the Holy Ghost within, which really saves an individual, but not any amount of good work or beatification or dedication or blessing can save. Toleration became the rule throughout the middle colonies.

Colonialism to Americanism

Two main elements distinguished the distinctive American nationality. One element was an amalgamation of people from different nationalities. The other element was a new country, which was rich and empty. It demanded new people to bring courage and hard work. By 1775 a distinct American society with its own social, economic, and political features was emerging closely resembling the European pattern. English language and English institutions were dominant everywhere making the country to possess a general unity. Even though Germans and French had a choice to set up a separate colony, they mingled with the first British comers, adopting their language and outlook.

The second element shaping a unique American nationality was the enormous and bountiful land. The early settlers were undoubtedly inexperienced, and they thought that they could live in newfoundland just like in London streets. But they had to adjust to the cruel, primitive wilderness or prepare to die. First, they learnt from Indians how to plant and fertilize corn, to cook local dishes, to make canoes and snowshoes, to hunt, to tan deer skins, and to learn woodcraft. By hard work, they became hunters, farmers, and fighters all in one. There was no icing on the cake of American society. As commoners, they hated the aristocrats who had acquired large land grants or who made fortunes from trade and guesswork. But irrespective of how poor, the average person felt in America a sense of opportunity and independence that he was not known in Europe. This feeling was born in the wide spaces and abundant natural wealth of the country. Only the rich people stayed in Europe; ordinary and poor people migrated to America. Everything that inclined began to regenerate them here: new laws, new mode of living, new social system; here they found a sense of individuality. A French gentleman St. John Crevecoeur wrote in his eloquent passage in 1759:

> "A European, when he first arrives, seems limited in his intentions as well as in his views; but he very suddenly alters his scale. He no sooner breathes our air than he forms new schemes, and embarks on designs he never would have thought of in his country. There the Plenitude of society confines many useful ideas, and often extinguishes the most laudable schemes which here ripen into maturity.... He begins to feel the effects of a sort of resurrection; hitherto he had not lived, but simply vegetated; he now feels a man, because he is treated as such; the laws of his own country had overlooked him in his insignificancy; the laws of this cover him with their mantle. Judge what an alteration there must arise in the mind and thoughts of this man! He begins to forget his former servitude and dependence, his heart involuntarily dilates and glows, and his first swell inspires him with those new thoughts which mark an American."

Gradually, colonies such as the New England colonies, the Middle colonies, the Southern colonies were founded. By the year 1750, thirteen colonies had secured a strong base and contained 1,500,000 people. Virginia passed laws to create large towns requiring each county to erect a house in Williamsburg. In 1732 apart from the top man of the place, it had only one merchant, a tailor, a smith, an ordinary-keeper, and a lady who acted both as doctor and coffee-house custodian. Maryland, Virginia, and South Carolina were generally faced towards some river or creek which allowed water transportation. Each had its family mansion with brick or stone, its storehouses, blacksmith shop, handyman, and other outhouses and bumpy huts for black slaves (Previously black people were called Negroes. Nigger or Niger means black). Many large houses for VIPs were beautifully designed and finished. Inside were large halls, fine staircases, and large rooms. The best houses included beautiful mahogany furniture made in America and imported from England, heavy silver amenities with London seal, silk or velvet hangings, good family portraits, engravings, and most importantly libraries. Robert Carter of Nomini Hal had more than 1500 volumes of books and William Byrd had more than 4000 volumes. Some planters were also criticized for the lack of intellectual tastes. But they took a passionate interest in politics, held most of the elective offices, spoke and wrote on government with extraordinary ability, and surprisingly a number of gentlemen were interested in science.

The lowest layer of white society in the South was made by separate lines. Some convicts, released debtors, and indentured servants who came from Europe were made up a mass, illiterate, vulgar, and lazy, who were hated by even black people. London authorities transported convicts even for a small offence, and interestingly some people intentionally committed crimes to come to America and were sold to the highest bidder. The southern states acquired a large number of vagabonds, criminals, and turbulent folk, who made lazy farmers and poor citizens. The black slaves were brought mainly from the west coast of Africa. Many other emigrants of high character paid for their way to come to America by giving bond service. They included cabinetmakers, tailors, silversmiths, jewellers, gunsmiths, and the like. Many escaped from prisons in London by assistance to reach America.

Moving to the Interior Parts of the Wilderness

In the beginning most of the settlers built their cities and houses in coastal areas and borders of huge river areas. In the eighteenth century there came a time to spread to the back country supervised by the militia organization Green Mountain Boys, first established in the late 1760s. Forest clearing tasks were undertaken where rude, simple, and fearless people, purely American looking people lived.

Buying cheap land at one or two shillings per acre, they cleared the regions in the wilderness, burned the bushes, and planted corn and wheat among the other things. They built rude cabins of hickory, walnut, or persimmon logs, notching the timbers into each other at the four corners, filling the gaps with clay, laying timber floors, and making windowpanes of paper soaked in fat or bear grease. The men dressed in homemade hunting shirts and deerskin socks, the women in clothes made on the spinning wheel and loom erected in every home. They attached their chairs and tables together from wooden slabs; ground their meal in homemade blocks of mortars; they ate with spoons made from pine tree branches; they walked with barefoot or skin shoes. Their food was pigs, corn, beef, turkey and fish. To guard against Indians the settlers built a fort, at some places with bulletproof blockhouses and fences.

The Success of Hard Work

Although the interior parts of the country lands were full of peril and hardship, the area had irresistible uniqueness and fascination. William Byrd describes the beauty of land as 'the sweet grapes, both black and white, stooping all over the trees; the wild turkeys, buzzing away in flocks on every hand; the multitude of pigeons, clouding the skies as they passed sometimes breaking down the larger limbs of mulberries and oak trees; fat bears, swimming awkwardly across the rivers; the tree-dwelling opossums, feeding on wild fruits; the wolves, which entertained them a great part of the night; and the slow-grazing buffalos. He continues telling that the shelves of purple and white marble, the clear streams pouring over sandy beds where mica gleamed in the sun like gold, the rich forests of oak, hickory, and locus, the distant peaks glimmering against the western sunset; the thrill of approaching upon an Indian encampment, and observing the grave, dignified manner of the braves, often with something great and venerable in their countenances, and the charm of the copper-colored maidens, neither very clean nor very chaste, but bashful before the white men.' Once the joys of the wilderness had been tasted, many explorers felt it is preferable to any other environment.

Culture

Culture was starting to thrive heroically in privileged communities. Particularly in New England, great emphasis was laid on education. Since the colonies were still in the infant stage, they made elementary school compulsory. A number of grammar schools existed. Two prosperous colleges, Harvard and Yale, had been established. Harvard had spacious brick buildings, a library of five thousand volumes, and good scientific equipment, and the instruction in theology and philosophy. Unlike European universities, the Classics slowed behind.

Only Maryland had a public education system although it was ill-organized; Pennsylvania had many private schools; New York had some good town schools. In the South, education was mainly in private hands. Clergymen and others kept good private schools. Virginia principal took twenty pounds per boy as tuition fees. Rich planters in Virginia and Carolinas hired private tutors from Great Britain and the Northern colonies who taught reading, writing, practical mathematics, and Latin and Greek. Only two free schools existed in Virginia and South Carolina. A number of colleges were founded in the middle and lower colonies - William and Mary in Virginia, which trained Thomas Jefferson; the College of Philadelphia, where Franklin did so much to set up; the college at Princeton; and King's College, now Columbia University in New York, which trained Alexander Hamilton. Some Wealthy families in New York and the South sent their sons to the British universities.

Newspapers, magazines, and almanacs were being published in the colonies. The oldest printing press in America was established in 1639 at Cambridge. At the time of Revolution, Boston had five newspapers and Philadelphia three. Bookdealers became important emigrant figures, and a number of libraries were established. Boston library was established in 1656. In 1771, one Philadelphia publisher imported a thousand sets of Blackstone's Commentaries (Blackstone's Commentaries is the book on the Laws of England, which sold more books in America except the Bible.) Other prominent writers enriched American culture by publishing volumes and volumes of books on science, theology, philosophy, history, literature, astronomy, mathematics, botany, medicine, and agriculture. Good artists were also creating history in the colonies.

Benjamin Franklin

Benjamin Franklin has described in his Autobiography a graphical idea of the way in which cultural applications increased. Born in Boston in 1706 in a family of thirteen children, Franklin was basically self-educated. His father, who had come from England, had a little library. At the age of twelve, he got training in printing and obtained other books and some ancient classics in translation. With a few cents he bought a volume of Addison's

Spectator, which inspired him a desire to write essays. He went to Philadelphia to study more, and found literature is taking root in the city.

Franklin established a "club of mutual improvement," with nine members. He walked strenuously through a circulating subscription of the library in 1731, the first in America, which rapidly expanded. He founded an academy which grew into the university.

He writes how luxuries such as china and silver crawled in to replace plain crockery and pewter (tin and lead); how inoculation for smallpox was introduced. Science always interested him; he was performing the famous experiment sending up a kite into the thunderclouds. Overall, 'Franklin's profession illustrated both how much could be made of the cultural resources of the colonies and how much an able leader could do to strengthen them.'

Colonial Heritage

Author Allen Nevis writes that part of the heritage that colonies left to the young nation can be noticed. The English, as a common language, had immeasurable value. It was one of the great binding factors which made a true nation possible. The respect paid to fundamental civil rights was another important factor in the heritage because colonists had a firm belief in freedom of speech, of the press, and of assembly as they had in England. The rights were not completely protected, but they were cherished. The religious toleration, protection of every faith under the British flag, spirit of racial toleration for people of different blood - English, Irish, German, French Huguenot, Dutch, and Swedish - mixed and intermarried without any difference. All in all, these colonial heritages were a treasure worth far more than shiploads of gold or domains of diamonds. In the New World, they anticipated to establish a society in which every person should not only have a chance, but a good chance in which he could rise from the bottom to the very top of the ladder. This need for equality of opportunity was to bring changes in the social structure of America, breaking down all kinds of special privileges. It was to produce noticeable changes in education and intellectual life, making America the 'most common-schooled' nation in the world. It was to produce vast political changes, providing the ordinary a more direct control of government. This commonwealth, the energy of the people and the atmosphere of freedom exposed an aggressive self-confidence. Along with this idea of democracy, it gave American life freshness, breadth, and cheerfulness that was incomparable to anywhere. The new land was a land of promise; land of hope, and of steadily widening of horizons.

Conflicts with French and Spaniards

After Columbus's discovery of the New World, Spaniards had a stronghold on North America. In 1519, a stubborn Spanish soldier Hernando Cortez came to Mexico with a small army and defeated Aztec emperor Montezuma and occupied the country. Twenty years after this event another gentleman from Spain, Hernando De Soto arrived in Florida, conquered the Indians, and with six hundred men roamed tirelessly across Southern states going as far as Oklahoma and Texas. Another group of Spanish explorers marched towards north from Mexico in search of mythic places like Seven Cities, which had jewel-studded doorways and whole streets of busy goldsmiths. A Jesuit missionary explored Lower California and Arizona, built churches and baptized the admiring Indians. Finally, in 1769 a force of Spanish soldiers occupied California.

In 1608 a French soldier and sailor Samuel de Champlain laid the foundations of Quebec, the first permanent settlement in New France. Eventually, the king of France made him royal geographer. The Europeans introduced Christianity to millions of primitives; trained them new skills, better agriculture, and some preliminary European education; made their lands productive with millions of cattle; established universities for the study of the classics.

The French came to America only in small numbers. They were not interested in silver, gold, or estates. All they wanted were fish and furs. They entered deeply into a chilly and inhospitable land to get more furs. They established weak agricultural settlements in order to penetrate farther and farther into the wildness trailing the main river paths. British colonies and French colonies differed in various ways.

The conflicts among British, French, and Spanish went about seventy years and finally a treaty of peace was reached in 1763. England took parts of Canada from France and Florida from Spain. North America, from Atlantic to the Mississippi except New Orleans, became British.

Seeds of Revolution

Finally, America was a fertile soil for republican rule in character. For a century and a half, the population had been living in the environment of democracy or at least aspiring. Economic differences were few and opportunities were equally open to all. The farmers, the Scotch-Irish and German immigrants, the labourers and mechanics of the cities, always contended against the older merchants and planters. The groundwork for Revolution was taking place.

The leaders of Revolution against England fall in two categories: One was a group of educated men, writers, and thinkers such as John Adams, Samuel Adams, Alexander Hamilton, Benjamin Franklin, Thomas Jefferson, George Mason, and several others. They were supported by a group of radicals of poor education or no education, originated from the mechanics and carpenters. The second group was reckless, angry, and ready to take radical views of the government. They liked a pure democracy. They derived their inspiration from intellectuals like Jefferson and Sam Adams, but their Revolution movement started with brutal energy. To start the movement, the first group was much more important. The educated leaders used voice and pen sincerely, distributed bundles of pamphlets, stuffed the newspapers with essays, and spread their political views by public meetings.

These early American writers and leaflet distributors were aware of powerful British thinkers and they copied their arguments from Sidney, Milton, and importantly from John Locke. Locke upheld that the supreme function of the government is to protect life, liberty, and property to which everyone is eligible. He said that the political authority is held in trust for the benefit of the people only. When the natural rights of citizens are violated, the people have the right and duty to eliminate and change the government. Locke also wrote in his Letter of Toleration that the Church and state belong to two different spheres and should be kept apart. His argument was that the healthiest character of the Church is a voluntary organization, supported by its members and not by the taxing power of the government. Locke and other thinkers of England were overwhelmingly venerated by all educated Americans interested in politics.

Misunderstanding

The author Henry Steele writes that British never desired to oppress or dictate America. Their efforts to solve the local Indians problem, to fortify the colonies for their own protection, and to strengthen the customs service appeared fair and moderate to administrators in London. But to American people these steps appeared like closely monitored oppression.

The revolt against British government was well-planned by some of the most active spirits on the land. The first step in the movement was the appearance of sporadic and unconnected rioting in resistance to the British measures. They protested the Stamp Act of 1765. The second step was the introduction of economic boycott by groups of merchants. The third step was the formation of a system of local and intercolonial committees of correspondence. The fourth step was the creation of revolutionary legislatures. Conducting the first Provincial Convention on August 1, 1774, a revolutionary movement was born in the colonies.

George Washington

Under the leadership of George Washington, America became independent on July 4, 1776. Congress chose George Washington as a leader without any knowledge of his capacities, but he proved his best patriotism and as a best guide. He was criticized for narrow military grounds because he never handled a large army; he made many mistakes and was defeated again and again. Nevertheless, he became the spirit of the war at the age of forty-three. The author writes,

> "George Washington, a Virginia planter was America's main spirit during Revolution because of his untiring patriotism, his calm wisdom, his serene moral courage; because in the gloomiest hours he never lost his dignity, poise, or decision; because he knew how to combine plan and caution; because his integrity, elevation, and magnanimity never failed and his fortitude never faltered. He knew how to wait his hour to strike, so that his patient vigilance gave him the title of 'Fabius', a Roman statesman.

"He could lose his temper fiercely when provoked beyond endurance, as the traitorous Charles Lee learned at the battle of Monmouth; but in general he had an iron self-control, so complete that when in later years the news of Wayne's terrible defeat at the hands of the Indians was brought him at a presidential dinner party, he betrayed no emotion to his guests. Scrupulous in everything, he drove his troops hard and punished army offenses severely, but his justice and devotion to his men won their utter loyalty. When he began his address to the unpaid and discontented troops at Newburgh with the words, 'Gentlemen, you will permit me to put on my spectacles, for I have not only grown gray, but almost blind in the service of my countrymen,' many shed tears. It was characteristic of him that he accepted nothing but his expenses for his Revolutionary services and kept account of these expenses with minute care. When war was over, he thought of going back to his beloved farm, which he wished to make the best in America; 'Agriculture has ever been the most favourite amusement of my life,' he wrote. But he remained at the call of duty. Less humanly appealing than some other heroes of the republic, he has remained preeminent in the massiveness of his character, the fixed elevation of his arms, and the wisdom and breadth of his mind. Three finest things in the Revolution 'are the character of Washington, the behaviour of his army, and the devotion of the better class of loyalists."

Independence- July 4, 1776

A committee of five, for whom Thomas Jefferson held the pen, sketched a formal Declaration of Independence, which Congress adopted on July 2 and proclaimed on July 4, 1776. Jefferson wrote the principles of government:

> "That all men are created equal, that they are endowed by their creator with certain unalienable Rights that among these are Life, Liberty and the pursuit of Happiness. That to secure these rights, Governments are instituted among men, deriving their just powers from the consent of the governed; that whenever any form of government becomes destructive of these ends, it is the Right of the People to alter or to abolish it, and to institute new government, laying its foundation on such principles and organizing its powers in such form, as to them shall seem most likely to affect their Safety and Happiness."

Here the philosophy of democracy, the truth that all men/women are created equal and are equal in the sight of god and before the law is evident. But as even Jefferson identified many inequalities in America: the inequality of rich and poor, of men and women, of black and white. But the failure of a society to follow that ideal does not nullify the ideal; the idea of equality once proclaimed worked as a substance in American thought.

Another significant truth proclaimed in the Declaration of Independence is that men (women) are endowed with unalienable rights - which are life, liberty, and the pursuit of happiness. These are not bestowed by some compassionate government by mercy, but they are the rights with which all are born and which they cannot lose forever. This principle worked as ferment in the minds of American altering their attitude toward authority. Here lies a magnificent compact theory of government: Once upon a time people lived in a wild state of natural atmosphere, in that state they continuously faced the dangers of various types. In order to protect themselves, they came together and designed certain forms of governments; allowing those governments just enough power to protect their lives, their liberty, and their property. In summary, people made governments to do good, not evil; made it to protect them, not to injure them. The instant that the government failed to perform its responsibilities, it no longer deserved the support of people or loyalty to them. If people could make governments, they could unmake them because it is their right to change or abolish a bad government and to establish a new one.

The Growth of Democracy

Externally America had accomplished a memorable revolution, but internally an equally important change was taking place. Separation of England had provided an immediate gain in political democracy. When British evacuated Charleston, a convoy of a hundred ships departed with British loyalist that was both magnificent and tragic. After their departure, the unattractive, hard-working farmers, shopkeepers, and craftsmen were free to create a civilization following their own sentiments. Dignity, leisure, and culture counted less afterwards; energy and rude self-statement counted more. The forcing trader and speculator were more prominent in American society. Everyone was considered equal, everyone was in a rush, and everyone thought more of the dollar. As Jefferson said in his Notes on Virginia, 'the province was thus given a set of great aristocratic families, who were formed into an upper-class order, distinguished by the splendor and luxury of their establishments.' Thomas Jefferson led an attack on primogeniture (the unjust claim of firstborn children of the same parents) and succeeded in abolishing those laws. Some argued that the eldest son should get at least a double share. Jefferson retorted, "No, unless he eats a double allowance of food and does a double amount of work." As a consequence, according to a French traveler, the distinction of classes began to disappear. Similar things happened to the huge lands of the rich for a democratic system of small holders.

Religious aristocracy was also brought under control and guarantee of religious toleration was introduced. Madison wrote, "All men are equally entitled to the free exercise of religion." Some solicited that the commonwealth has to pay a moderate tax or contribution for the support of the Christian religion or church. But the opposition was raised to halt the measures and the bill was postponed allowing the liberal leaders to wage a movement of education.

Education

Enormous measures were taken in various states to strengthen the foundations of education. The disagreement had a disturbing effect upon private schools and colleges: Yale College, King's College, and Columbia colleges were closed for some time. During 1797, the president of William and Mary was teaching a group of barefoot boys; in 1800 the Harvard University had a president, three professors, and four teachers.

The Revolution had one happy impact in increasing the general demand for public schools. Leaders recognized that the democratic self-government required an educated electorate. Governor George Clinton of New York wrote in 1782: "It is the peculiar duty of the government of a free state where the highest employments are open to citizens of every rank to endeavor by the establishment of schools and seminaries to diffuse that degree of literature which is necessary to the establishment of public trusts." Jefferson wrote: "Above all things, I hope the education of the common people may be attended to; convinced that in their good sense we may rely with most security for the preservation of a due degree of liberty." In the beginning poverty obstructed the state governments, but in time resulted in providing good elementary education than before the war. Widespread importance was given by allocating millions of acres of public land as an endowment for public schools.

The future of the young republic was hopeful and progressive. One dark side was that the thirteen states had never established a true national government. The Revolution had provided American people an independent place in the family of nations. It had given them a different kind of social order, in which heredity, wealth, and privilege counted far less and human equality more; the standards of culture and manners were temporarily reduced, but justice and fairness were raised.

Crafting the Constitution

All agree that the United States has one of the most original and effective constitutions ever written. The story of how it came into existence is of an extraordinary and remarkable thing. Gladstone wrote, "As the British Constitution is the most subtle organism which has ever proceeded from progressive history, so the American Constitution is the most wonderful work ever discovered by the brain and purpose of man." The making of the Constitution is a very interesting process in which enormous brains and hard work were put together by the magnificent founding fathers of America. All sections of government Executive, Judiciary, and Legislative branches were deliberately discussed for a prolonged period of time, manuscripts were written and rewritten, quarrels and compromises were made, innumerable amendments were made, leaders spent sleepless nights and tiresome days. Finally, the small states were given equal representation with the large in the Senate, but in the House of Representatives the seats were to be based upon population. Allan Nevins writes,

> "When it came to the executive, the greatest difficulty lay in fixing upon a mode of election. Should the President be chosen by Congress? That would go far toward making him dependent on the legislative branch, and so upsetting the balance of power. Should he be chosen by popular vote? The people of the United States were scattered over an immense and expanding area, and communications were poor. It would, therefore, be difficult for them to concentrate upon one or a few

candidates; a great number of choices would be made, and no one man would have any approach to a majority of votes. It was finally decided, therefore, to set up an electoral college, each state having as many electors as it had Senators and Representatives."

The inventiveness as well as the wisdom of the authors of the Constitution is remarkable. They established the most complex government not conceived thus far, and also the most nicely balanced and secured. Even though each of the three branches was independent and organized, it was checked by the others.

Federal government hold the power: to lay taxes, to restore its credits, authority to coin money, to fix weights and measures, to grant patents and copyrights, to establish post offices and roads, to maintain army and navy, to regulate interstate commerce, to maintain international relations, to wage war, to naturalize foreigners, and thus became a strong national government.

State governments also remained strong. They kept the powers of local government under their control and regulated most of the daily affairs of the people. Schools, local courts, policing, the chartering of towns and cities, the incorporation of banks and stock companies, the care of bridges, roads, and canals and other stuffs were in state hands. The original text contained 4 pages and all four pages of the original U.S. Constitution are written on parchment[26].

Even though Franklin did not approve all parts of the Constitution, he was surprised to see it was almost nearly perfect. He requested, actually begged those who did not like some features of the constitution to accept the document. Spirited young Alexander Hamilton also made the same type of appeal. He desired a more centralized and more aristocratic form of government, but, he questioned, how could a true nationalist hesitate between anarchy and imprisonment on one side, and order and progress on the other? Delegates on behalf of twelve states came forward to sign. Many appeared depressed by the sombreness and Washington sat with deep thinking.

But Franklin, indicating to the half sun painted in brilliant gold on the back of Washington's chair, said that artists had always found it difficult to distinguish between a rising and a setting sun.

"I have often and often, in the course of the session, and the vicissitudes of my hopes and fears as to its issue, looked at that behind the President, without being able to tell whether it was rising or setting; but now, at length, I have the happiness to know that it is rising, and not a setting, sun."

American Constitution

Ratification: For many the newly scripted constitution appeared full of dangers. They feared that the strong central government would dictate over them, oppress them with heavy taxes, and pull them into foreign wars. The struggle over ratification started and the press was overloaded with for and against arguments. The papers written by Alexander Hamilton, James Madison, and John Jay became a classic work on politics. Metal-workers, mechanics, lawyers, merchants, and farmers considered the constitution as a victory. After some agitation, all gave their approval.

Philadelphia organized a great procession on July 4, 1788 to celebrate the acceptance of the new form of government. The Constitution was ready to take its navigation on the high seas. Arrangements were made to select the President. 'One name was on every man's lips for the new chief of state, and Washington was unanimously chosen President.' On April 30, 1789 four million people attended Washington's Inauguration ceremony in New York's Wall Street on the balcony of Federal Hall. People shouted, "Long live George Washington, President of the United States!"

Life in New America

It was robust America that was ready to begin its new job. The population was almost rural in a tremendously vast country. Communications were poor and slow, roads were wretched, carts and carriages uncomfortable, the sailing vessels uncertain. But turnpike companies began to form, canals were dug. Majority of people lived in isolated places with poor schools, few books, and infrequent newspapers. European travellers had the impression that America was rude, discomfort, rough manners, and weak culture along with independence and unlimited self-confidence.

As the country was growing strongly, immigration from Europe was pouring in. Sometimes Americans think that half of western Europeans are moving into the land. Fertile lands could be purchased for a small amount; labour was huge and well-paid. Washington liked the idea of bringing expert farmers from Britain to teach better agricultural methods to Americans.

Manufacturers are also growing. Massachusetts and Rhode Island were laying the foundation for textile industries; Connecticut was making tin-ware and clocks; Middle States paper, glass, and iron. However, there were no big factories in America; all materials were produced in households. During winter, farmers were making coarse cloth, leather goods, pottery, simple iron implements, maple sugar, and wooden gadgets. When factories and mills started, usually owners also joined their hands.

Shipping flourished and vessels were built in great numbers in the coastal areas for trade, cod-fisheries, whaling, and for carrying breadstuffs, tobacco, lumber, and other goods to Europe.

The greatest impulse of American energy was westward. The sound of clearing of the oak trees, shrubs, and pine from Ohio to Georgia, woodsman's axe resonated in the forests. Up to the long slopes of the Alleghenies climbed the white-topped wagons of the emigrant trains; through the Cumberland Gap into Kentucky rolled the buckskin-dressed hunters and the pioneers with carts of furniture, seeds, simple farm materials, and domestic animals. Ohio and Mississippi saw more American groups and flatboats floating downward to New Orleans with grain, salt, meat, and potash. On the way, Indian warfare, malaria, wild beasts, the roving robbers of the remote borders, and other hardships had to be faced; difficulty, poverty, and disease took a heavy toll. But still streams of settlement dispersed into the wilderness.

The Republic

Washington's leadership was indispensable to the new government. 'Politically, he was not a man of imagination or brilliant initiative; he was a stiff writer and a poor public speaker.' Responsible men of every party and section trusted his fairness, breadth of view, and wisdom. Allan Nevins writes,

"Always dignified, his republican court was marked by serious formality. At receptions he would enter dressed in black velvet and satin, with diamond knee buckles, his powdered hair tied in a bag, his military hat under his arm, and a dress sword in a green scabbard at his side. In his relations with Congress and administrative officers he held aloof from party or infighting, attempting to represent the national idea alone though his sympathies were with the Federalists. Vigilant and laborious as ever, he worked by fixed schedules for long hours. He toiled successfully to give the government elevation and principle and to impress upon the country the warning which he put into his Farewell Address in 1796: "Be united - be American."

Alexander Hamilton

As revolutionary America had produced two impressive personalities, Washington and Franklin, the youthful republic produced two brilliant men, Alexander Hamilton and Thomas Jefferson, whose reputation spread beyond the sea. They represented two different powerful and crucial tendencies: while Hamilton's tendency was towards closer union and a stronger national government, Jefferson's tendency was towards a broader and freer democracy.

Alexander Hamilton was born in Nevis to a Scottish father and French mother. As explained by a writer, Hamilton grew up a man of ambitious, generous, devoted, proud, and quick to take offense and to forgive, of flashing mind and inexhaustible energy. All his achievements were the combination of brilliancy, self-confident ambition and hard work. Since his father failed in business, he had no money to go to college. When a terrible hurricane destroyed his native place, Hamilton wrote a description of it which attracted so much attention. Later his aunts sent him to America. He came to King's College in New York which turned out to be a lucky one. At the age of eighteen, he published two long essays, at twenty he became captain of an artillery company, and he illustrated omnivorous mind by taking books to campus for studying throughout the night.

Besides brilliancy and ambition, Hamilton had other qualities which served him well. He possessed great personal attractiveness. With reddish-brown hair, bright brown eyes, fine forehead, and firm mouth and chin, he was exceptionally handsome, his face animated and pleasant when he talked, sincere and thoughtful when he was at work. He liked a lively dinner party and excelled in any circle which offered good wine, intellectual companions, and clever talk. .... he had a great quality of doing the right thing at the right time. His speech took him to President Washington's notice and made him the general's chief advisor. He had remarkable talents as an executive and organizer. He wrote and spoke with admirable dash and vigour. Nevertheless, he also displayed striking defects. He was short-tempered and emotional. Once, in the middle of the battle, when Washington criticised General Charles Lee for withdrawing, Hamilton jumped from his horse, drew his sword, and cried, 'We are betrayed!' Washington silenced him quietly commanding: 'Mr. Hamilton, mount your horse.' His hot impulsiveness, his readiness to enter hastily upon a quarrel, and his moody arrogance of spirit disrupted Washington's administration, brought harsh conflict with Jefferson and James Adams, and others.

The important public profession of Hamilton was his love of efficiency, order and organization, a dominant instinct which explains his unforgettable service to the young nation. He hated disorder. As Washington's secretary, he was the instrument through whom the commander-in-chief conducted most of his business.

Hamilton introduced a set of measures that made him the greatest finance minister in American history. His program was not only impressive in amount but creative in character.

Thomas Jefferson

Historians describe that Jefferson was a man of thought. While Hamilton talents were executive, Jefferson's were thoughtful and theoretical. Hamilton enjoyed creating strong machinery and watching its perfection; Jefferson's enjoyment was in people and seeing them happy whether perfect or not perfect. As a political thinker and writer, he was no match anywhere in the world in his generation. He proposed to record the inscription on his gravestone his three major contributions of thought and not to record his offices or achievements. The stone reads:

HERE WAS BURIED THOMAS JEFFERSON
AUTHOR OF THE DECLARATION OF AMERICAN INDEPENDENCE
OF THE STATUE OF VIRGINIA FOR RELIGIOUS FREEDOM
AND FATHER OF THE UNIVERSITY OF VIRGINIA

Jefferson grew up in the free, friendly, and carelessly intellectual atmosphere of Virginia. In his childhood he enjoyed dancing, entertainments, and picnic; in his young age he was fond of riding, observing wildlife, and playing the violin; he read novels of prominent authors. Later his varied interest in nature, books, and men, simply intensified his intellectual versatility. He obtained the knowledge of half a dozen languages, mathematics, surveying, mechanics, music and architecture, and law and government.

He enthusiastically collected a large library and a remarkable collection of prints. He wrote about plants and animals, about history, politics, and education, all with originality and insight. He himself designed his famous house at Monticello and the magnificent halls of the University of Virginia. He was a lover of deep, broad, and many-sided best conversationalists of his time. In his house at Monticello, he would have fifty people as guests from a well-educated Blackman to a European nobleman displaying courtesy and warmth. (There are some allegations about treatment of black people. But later in his life, Jefferson changed his attitude.) In his entire life, he loved freedom, leisure, and large contacts.

When he was a minister to France, he urged for repayment of the loans to America. He realized that a strong national government has to have respectful relations with foreign nations, yet he did not want it to be too strong in many other respects. He thought that a strong government would restrict people. He was an egalitarian democrat. He did not like cities, great manufacturing interests, and large banking and trading organizations thinking they promote inequality; but later he admitted that industrialism is necessary to give the country an independent economy. Still he believed that America would be happiest if it remained chiefly a rural nation.

Hamilton's great ambition was to give America a more efficient organization; Jefferson's great ambition was to give individual men a wider liberty. The country needed both influences. It needed a stronger national government and it also needed the liberal and unrestricting government.

In 1801, Thomas Jefferson assumed the presidency in the new capital Washington where the ceremonies were held and also it marked the fact that democracy came to power. Then the Washington area was a plain forest village on the north bank of the Potomac River; had muddy roadways built through bushes and across swamps; had only dilapidated houses, most of them small and miserable huts. One cabinet member mocked saying, "We want nothing here but houses, cellars, kitchens, well-informed men, amiable women, and other trifles of this kind, to make our city perfect" implying that Washington is not fit for capital.

Most part of Jefferson's inaugural speech was about much-needed appeal for reconciliation. 'He begged the citizens to remember that political intolerance is as bad as religious intolerance and to unite as Americans in preserving the Union, making representative government effective, and developing the national resources.

Jefferson was elected as a president for two terms that greatly encouraged democratic procedures throughout the country. He abolished all the aristocratic accessories; weekly receptions were cancelled; court etiquette was rigidly trimmed, and titles of honour like "Excellency" were abandoned. Jefferson understood the plainest citizen was as worthy of respect as the highest officer. He instructed his assistants to remember that they are merely trustees for the people. He promoted agriculture and encouraged land settlements by purchasing from Indians and helped them to migrate westward. Believing that America should be an asylum for the oppressed, he encouraged immigration by a liberal naturalization law. He always worked hard to keep peace with foreign nations because war means more government actions, more taxes, and less freedom.

Louisiana Purchase

Louisiana was in a very strategic place at that time and it belonged to Spain. The city New Orleans is the major port for the shipment of American products grown in the Ohio and Mississippi valleys. Napoleon wanted to eliminate the weak Spanish government and take it back to France. Jefferson thought that if France took possession of Louisiana, America must join British to fight against France. Napoleon was certain that the United States and Britain would attack. Therefore, discouraged by the fact, he decided to fill his treasury by keeping Britain out and making friendship with America by selling the region. For $15,000,000 that huge area went to the republic. Author writes, "Jefferson 'stretched the Constitution till it cracked' in buying it, for no clause authorized the purchase of foreign territory, and he acted without Congressional consent."

Chief Justice John Marshall

Another important architect of America was John Marshall. He became a chief justice just before Washington entered presidency and was in office until his own death in 1835. Previously, the court had been weak and had no respect and esteem. John Marshall changed it into a powerful and majestic court leading it as important as the President. His manners included simple friendly planter society; dressed plainly; carried his own dinner; loved cards and boisterous game of horseshoes. His unforgettable decisions with penetrating mind demonstrated that he was directed by two fundamental principles: one, the sovereignty of the Federal government; the other the sanctity of private property.

Marshal was a distinguished judge. His judgements were written with a masterly logic: simple in style supported upon a remarkable learning and a thorough analysis. Historian Allan eloquently writes, "His habit was first to establish his major premise fully; then to go on to the deductions, demolishing every objection to them; and finally state his conclusion, amply supported by citations and illustrations."

Nearly 100 cases he dwelt with involved constitutional issues and made judgements on the basis of a well-matured political philosophy. They related all the important parts of the Constitution. When he completed his long service, the Constitution was in great degree considered as the 'Constitution as Marshal interpreted it.'

Nationalism was overwhelmingly growing. A national literature was being born; the Hudson River school of painters were celebrating the new American scene although it was strongly under European influences. Jefferson proficiently adapted Italian and classical architecture to American requirements, and he built the University of Virginia presenting a harmonious architecture.

A good national land system was established. The law of 1820 reduced the price of government held lands from $2 to $1.25 per acre!!! Commerce was strengthening the American people; as national unity advanced with many improvements, democracy also advanced.

Andrew Jackson

The election in 1828 Andrew Jackson defeated John Adams in a bitter campaign. His inauguration was regarded as opening a new age in American life. Washington witnessed an inauguration that was never seen before. Some compared it with the invasion of Rome by the barbarians. People had come from five hundred miles to see their hero made president, and they felt like the country had been rescued from danger.

Jackson was one of few Presidents, whose heart and spirit were totally with the ordinary people. He was born in utter poverty. His father was a Scottish linen merchant and died when Jackson was still unborn. His mother became a housekeeper to a brother-in-law. The boy was raised in hardship and insecurity, dressed in cheapest clothes, and exposed to a kind of nervous disease, and most likely humiliated again and again. His childhood sense of inferiority may be the reason for his lifelong sympathy with the oppressed. After studying law, he bought and sold land, traded horses and slaves, and for some time he owned a general store.

Jackson had many bitter experiences as a frontier lawyer, planter, and merchant, and felt that East had victimized him. He realised the Western faith that the common man is capable of uncommon achievements. Author writes 'Westerners believed that an upstanding man who could command a militia company, run a plantation, and make a good speech was fit for any office. They did not believe even for a minute that the great prizes of public life were reserved for the rich, the well born, and the educated. For them, the racoon hunter had as good a right as the Harvard graduate.' Jackson had seen many examples of achievements made by several people. He understood the tremendous energy of the West and its strength of character. He summarized: faith in the common man; belief in political equality; belief in equal economic opportunity; hatred of monopoly; special privilege and the intricacies of capitalistic finance.

As soon as he came to power, Jackson vigorously introduced his main ideas into practice.

Democratic Tendencies

Many changes occurred in the administrative system during Jackson's period spreading democratic wave throughout the country. In a way he accepted the rule described by William L. Marcy of New York: "To the victors belong the spoils."

The manners were becoming less conventional and sloppy, and more democratic. Foreign visitors were horrified to see the general tobacco spitting, the speedy eating at table, the disrespectful curiosity, the common arrogance and boasting, and the nervous panic. The American culture appeared as recklessness and violence. Since it was a fast-developing country, the job at hand appeared more important than human life. Steamboats and railroads paid no attention to safety and in the South and West, family disputes, use of knives and pistols, were common. In spite of all that, actually the average level of manners was not lower than in the early days of the republic.

On one side there were democratic and humanitarian men, intelligent workers; and on other side there were aristocrats, conservatives, many planters and farmers and teachers in private schools. Even religion became democratized as it moved westward. Literature also disclosed democratic tendencies. These are the effects of Jackson's influence on democracy.

The West and Democracy

Shaping of America happened when people began to move to the frontiers of American vast land towards the west, whose meagre population, were not more than six people per square mile. They toiled mainly in clearing and breaking land and building homes. Moving across the landmass of the country as the population increased, it extremely affected the American character. Actually, it was more than a borderline - it was a social process.

It inspired people's initiative; it coarsened manners; it destroyed conservatism; it raised a spirit of local self-determination along with respect for national authority.

(1) **The First Group** of adventurous settlers were usually a diverse group of individuals. In front of the migration group hunter or trapper of wild animals marched. An English tourist describes briefly the wilder kind of pioneers, usually unmarried:

"A daring, hardy race of men, who live in miserable cabins, which they fortify in time of war with the Indians, whom they hate but much resemble in dress and manner. They are unpolished but hospitable, kind to strangers, honest and trustworthy. They raise a little Indian corn, pumpkins, hogs, and sometimes have a cow or two, and two or three horses belonging to each family. But the rifle is their principal means of support."

(2) **The Second Group** of settlers was a mixed group of hunters and farmers. Instead of a cabin, they built a log house, which had glass windows, a good chimney, and partitioned rooms, and was as comfortable as an English farm cottage; instead of using a stream, they dug a well. A hardworking man would speedily clear land of timber, burn the wood for potassium to use in agriculture and let the bases decay. Growing their own grain, vegetables, and fruit, reaching the woods for beef, wild turkeys, and honey, fishing in the nearest streams, they never cared over the loneliness and roughness of their life. Some business minded people purchased the land while it was cheap, sold their acres when land value rose, and moved forward giving way to the third group of people.

(3) **The Third Group** of settlers were not only famers, but also doctors, lawyers, storekeepers, editors, preachers, mechanics, politicians, and land investors - all needed materials to provide the fabric of a dynamic society. But the farmers were the most important.

Several different kinds of peoples mixed their blood in the new West. People in the West had to stand on their own feet. They were respected not for family, inherited money, or years of schooling, but they were respected for what they could do. People could get farms and lands not beyond their reach. Around 1820, government land could be bought for $1.25 per acre and after 1826, for simply settling on it. This equality of economic opportunity raised a sense of social and political equality. 'Initiative, courage, individual vigour, and common sense were the requirements of a good innovative hunter, farmer, or sailor.

Frontier Merits and Evils

European visitors noticed the dramatic change in the independent attitude of American people. The observers saw that workmen did not tilt their hats and said "Sir" to earn a shilling. A European traveller mentioned that American servants did not wear uniforms and usually ate with the family and they were called "help" not servants. He saw only two beggars in America, and both were foreigners. He writes that a typical ordinary Yankee (New Englander) man from West turns farmer, storekeeper, land dealer, lawyer, Congressman, judge, a jack-of-all-trades, always standing on his feet. He gives a real example of W.T. Sherman, who was a military student, became a soldier in Mexican war, banker in San Francisco, lawyer in Leavenworth, manager in Kansas, head of a military college, and then soldier again.

These frontiers had virtues and at the same time it had evil effects also. The frontier people were usually unruly, impatient of discipline, and too aggressive. During the war of 1812, the military had to suffer many defeats because people disliked the training and subordination. Frontier trained American military wanted to do everything quickly and clumsily. Many things that needed careful finishing appeared a waste of time to those people. They hurried up rough frame houses instead of durable stone and brick structures; they built rough roads, made makeshift bridges, stripped rather than cultivated the soil. Railroad collisions and steamboat explosions were everyday events. Obviously, no attention was paid to manners or culture; the frontier had no leisure for them. And worst of all, the frontier life was full of criminality. Mainly the scum of other parts of the society rolled out to the border. Men developed uncontrollable tempers and like to settle the regional disputes with guns and pistols. "Officers of justice had to have iron nerves and a quick trigger finger."

These undisciplined men's characters clashed with the American Indians because they constantly encroached their lands, destroyed their game on which Indians depended for food and clothing, and were ready to kill any redskins on sight.

Transportation

The first major highway to the West was the Cumberland road. Starting from Cumberland, Maryland, the highway passed over the mountains to Ohio, Indiana, and finally reaching Vandalia in Illinois. When completed, its length was about six hundred miles, sixty feet wide. Upon this road ran the Western mails with special postage. Along the way, hotels and guesthouses leaped up, hundreds of families migrated to the west with ease and comfort.

However, the most famous highway to the West was the Erie Canal, which linked the Hudson River and Atlantic Ocean with the Great Lakes, providing a water road straight into the heart of the continent. This canal's contribution to western growth is more important. When completed in 1825, it was the second longest canal in the world (363 miles) after the Grand Canal in China (1115 miles). It was responsible for remarkable expansion in the American population and saved the Union. Many canals were built, and they used rivers and canals to pull boats, cargo, and passengers by stream.

The Annexation of Texas

In the beginning, Texas was a part of the Mexican Republic and as large as Germany inhabited by a few farmers and hunters. It was easily reachable to the southern states. The Mexican government was inefficient, corrupt, and tyrannical. In 1835 the immigrants revolted against the government and won their independence. For some time, the United States was reluctant to annex the land, but gradually changed their minds. There were many reasons for this change of mind: they thought that it was a duty to expand over the unpeopled and undeveloped West; they wanted Texas people to remain under the American flag; they were afraid of Great Britain, which may intervene in Texas and establish their sovereign. Texas was annexed to America in 1845. Next came the acquisition of California and New Mexico.

Slavery

One New York observer writes about a typical slave life in Mississippi:

> "He found a large and handsome mansion; nearly 1400 acres planted to cotton, corn, and other crops; and two hundred pigs. Of the 135 slaves, nearly 70 worked in the fields, three were mechanics, and 9 were house or stable servants. They labored from dawn to dark, with Sundays and sometimes Saturdays free.... The food allowance was corn and four pounds of pork per person each week, supplemented by vegetables, eggs, and poultry grown by the slaves themselves. Every Christmas molasses, coffee, tobacco, and calico were generously distributed. The black people got their own fuel for their little cabins from a wooded swamp."

Critics accused slavery because of the over work, occasional beating, the cruel disturbance of families by sales, the denial of education and advancement. Defenders praised it because it protected the worker in unemployment, sickness, and old age; because it Christianized a pagan people and gradually uplifted them, because it made masters courteous and servants loyal. As an economic organization, slavery had both critics and defenders. The slave population was great where the climate was hot, the soil was flat and rich, and it was less in mountainous and barren lands.

Around 1830 slavery question took a hard line and clashes between Southern and Northern states began. Northern free-land men argued that slavery must not expand even one inch further. Meanwhile, in the South several leaders declared slavery is for a positive good. They even pointed towards ancient Athens and argued that slavery offered the strongest basis for a splendid culture.

Harriet Elisabeth Beecher

Harriet Beecher's came from a renowned religious family, and her best-known novel *Uncle Tom's Cabin (published in 1852)* described the harsh conditions for subjugated African Americans. The book became influential in the United States and Great Britain, stimulating anti-slavery sentiments in the North, at the same time infuriating widespread anger in the South. Mrs. Beecher Stove had lived in Cincinnati doing full justice to the many humane and generous slave-holders. She described how slavery was so close to cruelty and how basically incompatible were free and slave societies. Her book was translated into many languages and sold more than a million copies in the British Empire. The voters in the North were deeply provoked by it.

Several Northern States passed "personal liberty laws." When Anthony Burns, a slave from Boston, was captured, some of the city's most prominent leaders rushed to save Anthony. All angry men from eastern Massachusetts gathered and filled the streets. It required city police, national army, and navy to pull one poor black man back into slavery. It shows how much North was against slavery.

A poet-editor William Cullen Bryant wrote, "If....wherever our jurisdiction extends, it carries with it the chain and the curse — wherever our flag floats, it is the flag of slavery. If so, that flag should have the light of the stars and the lines of morning red erased from it; it should be dyed black, and its device should be the whip and the shackle. Are we to accept, without question, these new readings of the Constitution...? Never! Never!"

The North and South were growing very differently and widely unlike, economically, socially, and politically. The south was nearly rural with considerable city, New Orleans. Majority of Northern parts had become urbanized. Almost all of the substantial flood of European immigration stayed in the North and West, the Irish settled in the cities, many Germans and Scandinavians going to the farms, the British spreading everywhere. Railroad construction was better improved in the North. Generally, the North, in spite of growing extremes of wealth and poverty, was more democratic than the South.

Numerous Northern politicians, editors, clergymen unpleasantly exaggerated the evils of slavery and the purpose of slave-owners. Several Southerners also vehemently exaggerated the evils of industrial society and the goals of the free-landers. Southern extremists were demanding Congress to pass laws protecting slavery in the regions. North complained about the Southerners and their terrible abuses at prisons. But Northern sites were also not so good either: favouritism, fraud, and corruption thrived in both parts. Washington became full of dishonest contractors, speculators, and lobbyists.

Civil War

As a result of long-standing controversy over slavery, civil war broke out in April 1861 shortly after Abraham Lincoln was inaugurated as U.S. President.

The war between North and South was a historical event. In the South, there was a memorable hero Robert E. Lee and in the North Abraham Lincoln. Lee was a cavalier of commanders. The brilliance of his leadership, the vigorousness of his service, the humanity he portrayed throughout the conflict, and his nobility in accepting defeat and urging the Southern people to be loyal partners of their enemies always arouses admiration. At the end of the war Lee had to accept the defeat, which enabled Lincoln to issue Emancipation Proclamation in 1862.

Abraham Lincoln

Lincoln was rough-looking Western lawyer, homely, awkward, and ill-schooled. One time his second Secretary called him a gorilla - but later he declared Lincoln was a great leader ever lived - the harsh media called him as a blockhead. But slowly it started to recognize his deep wisdom, originated upon careful study and hard thinking, his extreme love of truth, his unlimited patience, and his infinite kindness of spirit. Allan writes,

"If he seemed at moments to hesitate and fluctuate, time always proved that he had known how to wait for the national advantage, how to combine strength with tact. Understanding the American people, he knew when to pause for public sentiment to crystalize and when to move forward boldly. He was the most honest of leaders and, though a skilful politician never resorted to unfair measures. He constantly appealed to the intelligence, never the ignorance, of the electorate. He was so charitable in thought and deed that during all the agony of the conflict, he never uttered a vindictive word against the Southern people. He was anxious above all to weld the country together as a union not of force, but of hearts; and even as the Union armies were winning their last victories, he proposed to pay the South handsomely for its slaves. His foreign policy showed dignity, integrity, and firmness.... His Gettysburg address, the Second Inaugural Address, and some of his letters are among the finest treasures of English prose."

Famous Gettysburg Address

"Four score and seven years ago our fathers brought forth on this continent, a new nation, conceived in Liberty, and dedicated to the proposition that all men are created equal.

1. George Washington (1732-1799). First President of the USA, 2. Benjamin Franklin (1705-1790) was one of the founding fathers of America., 3. Abraham Lincoln (1809-1865).4. Hamilton, 5. Thomas Jefferson, 6. Theodore Roosevelt

"Now we are engaged in a great civil war, testing whether that nation or any nation so conceived and so dedicated, can long endure. We are met on a great battlefield of that war. We have come to dedicate a portion of that field, as a final resting place for those who here gave their lives that that nation might live. It is altogether fitting and proper that we should do this.

"But, in a larger sense, we cannot dedicate — we cannot consecrate — we cannot hallow — this ground. The brave men, living and dead, who struggled here, have consecrated it, far above our poor power to add or detract. The world will little note, nor long remember what we say here, but it can never forget what they did here. It is for us the living, rather, to be dedicated here to the unfinished work which they who fought here have thus far so nobly advanced. It is rather for us to be here dedicated to the great task remaining before us — that from these honored dead we take increased devotion to that cause for which they gave the last full measure of devotion — that we here highly resolve that these dead shall not have died in vain — that this nation, under God, shall have a new birth of freedom — and that government of the people, by the people, for the people, shall not perish from the earth."

Abraham Lincoln
November 19, 1863

His murder on April 14, 1865 was a stunning stroke to the nation, a tragic misfortune to victor and vanquished. As James Russell Lowell wrote:

> "Never before that startled April morning did such multitudes of men shed tears for the death of one they had never seen, as if with him a friendly presence had been taken from their lives, leaving them colder and darker. Never was funeral panegyric as eloquent as the silent look of sympathy which strangers exchanged when they met that day. Their common manhood had lost a kinsman."

Lincoln had hoped that it would have been better if the abolition of slavery could have taken place gradually and with due compensation to slaveholders. That action would have given time to educate the blacks in their new place in society. It would also have saved six hundred thousand brave young men who lost their lives in the war, and the millions of children they would have brought into the world.

It was accepted mainly because the idealistic division of the party wished to protect black people, and the materialistic division hoped to occupy the South for votes, offices, and power.

After Emancipation

What did the end of slavery mean to the previous slaves? Some people worried, but most people felt great joy. One liberated black man said, "I won't wake up some morning to fin dat my mammy or some ob de rest of my family am done sold." Separated families hunted eagerly to find their kins. And the beating was over! Everybody went wild shouting, "We was free, Just like that, we was free." There was a great eruption of singing freedom songs. Some ran into the forests telling again and again, "I'se free, I'se free!" An old black man of Virginia reached a barn, jumped madly on straw stack to straw stack and screamed and screamed.

Unfortunately, their joy and freedom also had bad effects. Now, the white population who had bad relations with black people could injure, stab, torture, burn and kill black people who had no masters to answer and protect them. It was a long journey to obtain full freedom and a place in the society.

Reconstruction Reforms - Fourteenth Amendment

It was recognized that private prejudice could not be avoided, but discrimination could be prohibited in every public activity introducing laws by prohibiting discrimination at the polls, in public places, on public transport, and in education. In order to maintain the law, they passed the Fourteenth Amendment in 1968. Sweeping and powerful phrases are extremely important weapons in social reform and in providing legality to the ambition of minority groups.

Other Reconstruction leaders decreed major reforms. They granted the South its first system of public schools; the right to vote in elections to men free of property qualification was passed and imprisonment for debts ended. Farmhouse laws promised poor men a minimum amount of property safe from attachment for debts; standard election of county officials replaced the previous authoritarian system of appointment; salaries were given to public officials; the number of crimes punishable by death was reduced; taxes were rearranged so as to bear on plantation owners instead of landless individuals.

Segregation

After emancipation, the cities were populated by half white and half black. It was a question faced by all administrators what was to be done with all these people? Should they be sent to school when they are young, taken care of in hospitals when sick, cared for in old age homes when they are old, just like whites? What kind of jobs would they be given? How about crime and punishment, the police, and courts? The immediate familiar response was segregation with regard to jobs, housing, public facilities as street-cars and buses, hotels, and restaurants. But an unfamiliar response was the exclusion to public services like hospitals, schools, asylums, and organizations for the physically handicapped. Because the cities were poor and it was hard for them to take care of even white citizens, they refused this burden that ascended on them with the ending of slavery. After radical Reconstruction started, Republican city officers began providing facilities for black people and opening existing establishments to them for the first time - however, on a segregated basis. This minimum provision of services is considered as a victory. In 1869, the Fifteenth Amendment granted blacks voting rights.

Voting Right for Women

The women were also citizens of the United States and they questioned when Fourteenth Amendment says, "no State shall make or enforce any law which abridges the privileges or immunities of citizens of the United State," didn't laws restrict the vote to men only? A courageous feminist Susan B. Anthony led the strike. She joined Elizabeth Cady Stanton and founded the National Woman Suffrage Association. In 1872, on the claim of Fourteenth Amendment, she registered to vote in Rochester, New York. She was arrested and imprisoned for breaking the law, and also, she refused to pay a $100 fine charged on her. In 1875, the US Supreme Court said, "If the law is wrong, it ought to be changed; but the power for that is not with us." In 1878 Senator Aaron Sargent of California proposed constitutional amendment: "The right of citizens of the United States to vote shall not be denied or abridged by the United States or by any State on account of Gender." At that time nothing happened, but forty-two years later the exact sentence became the Nineteenth Amendment.

Scientific Racism

When the Northern educated class had more moral concern for the wellbeing of black Americans, a new situation of opinion was developing. Science and rationalism were overpowering and Charles Darwin's 'The Origin of Species' obtained tremendous recognition. It described that natural selection is a system in which less fruitful and reproductive species will be doomed to extinction. One author wrote an article, 'Essay on the Inequality of Races' in 1860, mixing races will always produce offspring of the lower race. One unproven quality was that lower race species produce children abundantly, while the more intelligent species had few children. Many educated Northern Anglo-Saxon took that lesson seriously and thought the same concept apply to human society also. They believed that the Anglo-Saxon race is in danger and proper steps need to be taken. Conservative Northerners developed a distaste of strange-looking, dirty, illiterate immigrants with their huge families crowding into their seaports.

At the same time, another line of reasoning also was developing. Some people argued that although blacks are not equal to the whites at present, according to the evolution theory, they might potentially be equal sometime in the future. For them, social Darwinism notions of natural selection and survival of the fittest appeared logical, and it indicated long-range improvements. But such progress would take a long time as the counter argument; at present circumstances, blacks are not ready for the responsibilities of ballot, important professions, and social leadership, they said.

Southerners argued that it is the idea of enlightened white to take away the votes from blacks now and start slowly and carefully to train them for full citizenship. This required schools for instruction in practical, simple arts instead of the liberal arts and the traditional training for future elites.

Several whites were influenced by the British social scientist Herbert Spencer's book First Principles (1862) that had wide American readers. In theory,

> "It was Spencer who devised from Darwin's theories the concept of survival of the fittest. Though he later made a place for education, in First Principles he held that the 'social order is fixed by laws of nature precisely analogous to those of the physical order.' Therefore, 'the most that man can do… by this ignorance and conceit is to destroy the operation of social laws.' In short, people should leave social problems entirely alone. Avoid public-health measures, so that diseases will sweep away the unfit. Avoid even the building of lighthouses, for dangerous reefs will kill off the unfit seamen. Let the laws of nature operate. Strong government is a curse, for it will always be misinformed and will make mistakes, thus disorganizing nature's wise plans."

The idea is plain. Their understanding of science was to prove conclusively that the black race was not equal to the white. Whatever happens without government interference is the best even though it is oppressive. They looked at everything calmly and unemotionally. Moral arguments are unnecessary because they are unscientific and government involvement is harmful. It was their conclusion.

Railroad Surge and the Changed Economy

Railroad explosion energised the flourishing economy in late nineteenth century America. A vast marketplace extended across the country. Industrialists and farmers had more productive capacity and created more goods that choked the market; so, overproduction created a long price decline. The railroads were built badly to grab each other's trade; merchants gave rebates and special favours. Small producers protested bitterly because the railroads refused to give rebates to them while giving liberally to large corporations. Therefore, railroad owners had to plan to bring some order out of chaos. So, they adopted a technique: 'Counting Everything' - cars, amount of freight, distances travelled, costs, wages, and every other business expense. This required central business offices to be established where statistics concerning foreign and passenger movements could be gathered, analysed, and used to figure costs and fair rates. This new technique laid the foundation for the modern business with its reliance on centralized, analytical, bureaucratic methods.

The Agricultural Transformation

The effect of the Industrial Revolution hit American agriculture with full force after the Civil War. Whether the work was planting trees, caring for livestock, or raising flowers, a stream of inventions revolutionized the process. Mechanical refrigeration and assembly-line slaughtering changed the meat-packing industry. In the 1870s, agricultural chemists began encouraging farmers to use fertilizers on a large scale. In the 1880s, inspection for plant diseases introduced the use of pesticides, which largely increased the production and saved the industries.

The American Indians

Americans who marched across the plains to the Far West created devastation for many Indian tribes in those areas. Endless lines of wagons, stretching from one end to the other, forced away buffalo, scattered roads with discarded equipment, destroyed grass, and spread diseases. Cholera spread like a wildfire in the wagon trains spreading to the Indians and destroyed the whole tribal population. Indian survivors thought that it was intentionally introduced to extinguish them.

In 1859, gold rush and the settlement of Colorado established permanent wagon roads across the plateaus. The government relocated Indians to large reservations in Oklahoma and the Dakotas. By the 1880s, the massive buffalo population of the plains, which had given life and independence to the Indians, were totally wiped out. In fact, slaughtering of the buffalo was done by local smaller tribes, who sold hides, tongues, and meat to the whites and received guns and other goods. However, it was white hunters who killed most buffalo. It is estimated that in the 1860s there were still thirteen million buffalo roaming the plains in large groups. Then they discovered that buffalo skins could be converted into fine valuable leather and started killing buffalo in a large scale. Very soon the buffalo population disappeared. A museum mission searched for specimens in 1883 and they could find only 200 buffalo in the entire West.

Indian Acculturation

Indians were virtually helpless without buffalo. It was the question to the government to think what was to be done with them? Eastern reformers suggested with uproar for more humane treatment and insisted that the only chance was to give civilization for Indians. They did not understand that the Indians could live happily and productively within their own tribes rather than spreading in American society. An anthropologist Lewis Henry Morgan argued that the only way to solve the problem was to teach the tribes with white man's methods. Some observers advised that Indians settle as farmers, learn English, and adopt white values. Helen Hunt Jackson's two books on behalf of Indians, "A Century of Dishonour (1881)" and the novel "Romana (1884)" triggered a national sensation and approved with the idea of acculturation. This required fixed settlement, dividing tribal lands into individually owned plots (severalty) and learning the arts of agriculture. The left-over surplus land was sold to whites. The Dawes Act of 1887 included these policies in permanent form.

The Growth of Big Business

The beginning of a national market transformed business life in eastern states. In the early 1900s, the economy no longer consisted of small markets; instead it was dominated by a small number of large companies who sold their merchandise nationwide and worldwide. Europeans were astonished at the fast growth of American industry, which exceeded their own industries in size and wealth. Even though the reason was the country was large and had huge resources, there were many other factors, which influenced its economy. One example was that businessmen in America were surrounded by a friendly cultural environment. In Europe, ancient governments controlled by landlords with strong powers crushed businessmen. Preventive laws obstructed business operations, and governments favoured stability instead of change. In contrast, in the United States, the government hardly existed. A district or county or a state had only a few employees, but corporations hired thousands of employees. Businessmen were honoured and admired; young boys were trained in getting ahead; everything was measured on practical standards. People had the confidence and convinced themselves that "If they jumped forward, the future will catch them."

Nation in Crisis

The population in more than 100 American cities increased rapidly during the 1840s, which was the urbanizing period in American history. American farm workers found that rural life was toil, distressing, loneliness, primitive living conditions and low income. So, they flocked to the cities where they found neighbours, busy streets, newspapers, theatres, saloons, and most importantly jobs with good pay.

1880 onwards America was receiving a great wave of millions of immigrants, roughly 55 million people, from European countries. The native born American also grew rapidly. It caused a new clash in American life and the cities faced huge problems. City corporations had to build miles of streets, drain off sewage, and clear garbage. To shelter the flow of people, inflammable or balloon frame houses were built. They were made of light, cheap lumber, inexpensive, and quickly built. They provided ordinary Americans a standard of housing better than the average European housing. But in the most crowded cities, tight apartment buildings were built, which lacked light, air, water, heat, or sanitation.

Diseases devastated the slums. People died due to smallpox, typhoid, fever, etc. Because medical facilities were not yet proficient at that time, only fittest people survived. The only solution was to encourage cleaning up every source of contamination. Most important improvement was collecting pure public water that reduced the death rate significantly and it enabled a flow of water to take away wastes. In the 1880s, the germ theory of disease attracted proponents of health. Hospitals were built in cities and a medical profession with a new sense of responsibility began to give attention to the poor. By the 1890s health codes in municipal offices required the selling of food under hygienic circumstances, the pasteurization of milk, the wrapping of bread, and the use of refrigeration. In 1906 the federal government passed pure food and drug laws. Overall, even though the urban poor were still misused, at least they survived, ate better, and lived in housing suited to human needs.

Labour Conflicts

In the late nineteenth century, labour conflicts elevated, and industrial fighting exploded. In fact, salaries increased at a rate close to the rise in worker's productivity, most of which was created by heavy investments by employers in machines that increased output. Even though their wages and earnings rose remarkably, the gap between rich and poor was enormous. When workers were living their simple lives, capitalists were not only making enormous fortunes, but also were displaying them ostentatiously. In America, expectations were rising high and asking what was America if it was not a life of prosperity and ease. Employees watched the wealthy few building their luxurious mansions, and watched the middle class moving to spacious suburban homes. In front of this affluence, the fate of workers seemed pitifully small, particularly who worked twelve hours a day for six or seven days a week.

Labouring classes organized huge protests in the 1870s and they had one powerful leader, Samuel Gompers. The president of the American Federation of Labour Samuel Gompers inspired workers lecturing as, "What shall the workers do? Sit idly by and see the vast resources of nature and the human mind be utilized and monopolized for the benefits of comparative few? No. The labourers must learn to think… that only by the power of organization and common concert of action can either their manhood be maintained, their rights to life, work to sustain, be recognized, and liberty and rights secured. Join together, hang together; do not trust the government, that instrument of the wealthy and the patronizing middle class, to do the job. Let strong unions fight for simple, realizable goals: better pay, better hours, and better working conditions. Let the capitalists do their thing, we will do ours. Do not let the 'intellectuals' and their airy theories do our thinking for us; don't expect middle-class 'reformers' ever to understand what workers do, how they have to live, or what they need. Organize." That was the slogan of Gompers.

Gompers advised workers not to radicalize. He fought bitterly to prevent the socialists and revolutionary Marxist temper control of the labour movement. He understood that the government takeover of all means of production and distribution was industrial nonsense. It doesn't work. Violence is also nonsense. It doesn't work. The enemy of workers was too powerful with too much control of the police, the military, the army, and private spies and guards. Above all, violence simply aggravated the American public and this was fatal because industrial workers were a small minority; they needed the respect and support of all communities. Since Gompers was Jewish, some people did not appreciate his anti-revolutionary thinking. But in the end employers had to recognize the representative of their workers, bargain with them, accept their power.

Women and the Family In 1800s

It was disturbing news that the birth-rate in American white was declining because American women had been reducing the size of their families. The main motive for this decision was the desire to secure more independence for themselves within the family. Of course, there were also economic reasons. Outside the home, jobs were available, and the more income was valuable to the family. Women postponed marriages for some years to work for some time.

The author Robert Kelly writes,

> "Working outside the home, however, was for women a complex and often cruel business. For single women it was not so bad: they were often encouraged to work for a time, learning of the world before marriage and helping the family support itself. But married women were not supposed to work, and few did so systematically enough to be counted in the census. Their place was in the home, raising children and caring for the husband. Schools would not hire married women as teachers, nor would business use them as stenographers. If they simply had to work to live, therefore, they had to take the jobs no one else wanted: scrubwoman, janitor, laundress, being a maid or a servant. Or they worked at home, secretly, doing piecework sewing. The important thing was to stay inside. It was shameful for a married woman to have to work, especially a woman of the middle class."

Highly restricted jobs were available even for single women like store clerks, saleswoman, typists (a growing women profession in 1880s), bookkeepers or cashiers. Occupations of power were available to only males. After the Civil War, teaching and nursing became women's job.

19th Century: National Debate

In the late nineteenth century a debate began to identify what is America all about, what is to be done, and where it should be headed. Since the beginning of the nation, American people have had a divided mind about themselves, a contradictory mixture of self-praising delight and anxious disappointment. Writers like Mark Twain called the years of President Ulysses Grant as the Gilded Age (the Golden Age). They perceived the period as a time of hypocrisy, shallow glitter, dollar chasing, and political irresponsibility. To them American political leaders were greedy, cunning, and indifferent to the public affairs. Their motto was "Survival of the fittest"; nothing was done to those who fell behind. Boyce wrote, "Everything in America tends to make the individual independent and self-reliant. He goes early into the world; he is left to make his own way alone; he tries one occupation after another if the first or second venture does not prosper; he gets to think that each man is his own best helper and adviser."

However, in the Gilded Age Americans were also intensely concerned over public welfare and they passionately argued about what to do about it. Some good politicians paid attention and respected that huge powerful force called 'public opinion', which is the fountain of public policy in America. The United States government was everyone's matter and they watched it constantly. Bryce wrote, "They have unbounded faith in what they call the People and in a democratic system of government. They are certain that the truth and justice are sure to make their way into the minds and conscience of the majority."

Cultural Governments

In America, politics is run not only by economic self-interest, but also by broad, powerful cultural forces. Americans went to vote at the polls in great numbers not merely to get benefits, but they cared about what was happening to their country and they felt responsible for it. As a result, two powerful parties emerged as Republicans and Democrats.

Republican Party Culture

The Republicans were motivated by a dream that under the leadership of their party America would become a unified, homogenous, hard-working, religious (Protestant type) people moulded in Yankee's reflection. They desired to see America as a community and did not want it to be a collection of lonely individuals. Team spirit to see the nation as a whole and continued focus on common goals was the Yankee way of thinking about America. They believed that the government should control the moral life of the community at large.

Democratic Party Culture

The Democratic Party was a party of individualism, and it had no trust in government. They believed the government is the tool of the wealthy. Since the Gilded Age, its famous members were white Southerners who wholly hated the Yankees of North, Catholics from Ireland, Germany, Italy, Poland and other European catholic countries. And others whom Yankees thought as un-American were anxious about Democratic Party. They were Jews, French-Canadians, Mormons, the irreligious, the free living and the sceptical, and those who believed Jefferson's nature 'that people's morals should be their own affair, and that churches should stay out of politics.'

Because most of the immigrants were from Catholic countries, Democratic Party grew fast.

Prohibitionism

Among many issues that separated these two parties the prohibitionism, a nationwide constitutional ban on the production, importation, transportation, and sale of alcoholic beverages, was the most turbulent. Favourite drinks for Irish were whisky, beer for Germans, and wine for Italians and Spanish people. The drinking problem of booming immigrant's influx made a great threat to social fabric of America: threats to morality exhibited every side in city streets, theatres, dance halls, houses of prostitution, bars, and saloons. As a matter of fact, alcoholism was a real comforter and curse for poor working people.

Republicans, as the party of puritanism, supported the prohibition with the same spirit as they condemned slavery and other similar issues. Democrats, as the party of personal liberty and the immigrants, attacked back with bitterness. It seemed to them meddling with other people's business.

Women in Public Life

Remarkably, women took initiative to fight against alcoholism. At that time people preferred that women stay out of public affairs. In the late nineteenth century, technological improvements transformed women's life in cities and towns. 'Hot and cold running water drastically reduced one big job for women: the weekly wash. Before it was taking a ¾ part of the housewife's time to pump water from the well, carry bucket after bucket to the kitchen, lift up and down the heavy wash tubs from the stove, sitting and heating it slowly. Washing machines with indoor plumbing and flowing tap water was a miracle of labor saving. Electricity made each day longer with artificial lighting and refrigerators provided immediate help to women. The telephone eliminated hours of travel by horsecar and cart, electric elevators made the apartment buildings possible, hot water heaters in winter, tile floors and walls, central heating, disposal of garbage, repair men at hand to fix the plumbing or electrical connections, and elevator men to help with heavy packages. Due to all these efficient technological housing, housewife's time expanded and had plenty of time to think and do something useful.

After the 1870s, commercial canning of fruits and vegetables enabled a rich variety of readily available foods and refrigerated railway carts for fresh meat eliminated laborious tasks. New bakeries also eliminated the work for women to prepare bread and cakes. Washers for laundry and dishes are other conveniences. Another innovation departmental store was open to shop, meet friends, and spend the day in. In cities middle-class women had a great deal of leisure time. Looking for a job in their free time was out of question. Even women did not want to work; they preferred to care for people, nurture them, and provide a shining model as a virtuous woman. Ideal childbearing, raising children with love and affection became very popular after the Civil war. They claimed that because their husbands were men who are basically animals, needed taming and that was also the pious woman's duty. They were supposed to tame the society also. Social critics wrote that because women were pure in thought and heart, loved beauty, expressed unselfish devotion, they were desperately needed for the turbulent nineteenth century America.

Surprisingly, it is said that women were unfit to work because of physical weakness. Experts maintained that women were highly nervous and sensitive during their periods and they do things irrationally. Even women also took this seriously. To face the situation, women's colleges were built to train the students to make them strong enough to handle the strain. Historian Sheila M. Rothman writes, "women were at once incompetent and competent, broken and whole, to be pitied and to be emulated."

Many high school and college educated women coming from the middle-class wanted to do something important in the world in order to civilize American life and make the home safe with their leisure time. All they needed was a great medium like the women's club movement. First this club was started for educational purposes - discussing books and listening to lectures - and then soon started to attack on social ills like alcohol that threatened their families. Those women found their channel through Women's Christian Temperance Union (WCTU) founded by Willard's Frances in 1873.

WCTU's main target was the liquor trade. It wanted to eliminate drinking, which was a curse to families, and also to attack on prostitution, which was also a curse to women and danger to loving marriages and families.

Frances Willard

Frances Willard grew up as a child of harsh puritan Yankee, hated house work, and enjoyed hunting and shooting. A voracious reader and college educated, she became a teacher. She liked independent life. That means remaining single. So, she did remain single. In the mid-1870s crusade on alcohol exploded as a "woman's cause" and an association "Women's Christian Temperance Union" (WCTU) was formed. Willard jumped into it and soon became a main spirit of the movement. Willard was a beautiful woman - small, erect, graceful - and a gifted politician. Like a magnet she attracted millions of women followers and they adored her. As a shrewd strategist, she retained the WCTU in her hand even though husbands, brothers, fathers, sons, and literally every other male person criticised vehemently at her followers. During that time for American women simply to be active in public life was a sign of liberation. For doing so, they were rebuked and ridiculed.

Enrolling into WCTU meant tossing all restrictions on women's life. Willard fought not only on the alcohol and drinking problem, but also for women's suffrage - voting rights, the labour movement and socialism. She believed in women's potential for changing and civilizing society. She conducted national conventions which were on the front pages of all national newspapers. Her followers, liberated in spirit, demanded equality everywhere, worked for civic reform. A sense of importance in American politics for women began with Willard. She kindled middle-class women's consciousness and got them out of the home and into public speaking, taught them how to organize, and provided a new model.

Until then the world had never seen such a big women's movement in history. Soon after Willard's death in 1898, her statue appeared in the Capitol building in Washington; bridges, streets, schools, and hospitals were named after her; four states made her birthday a school holiday in 1915. When the alcohol prohibition act passed in the 1930s, thousands exclaimed her name-also blamed her.

Imperialism

Internal conditions and the world situation influence a nation's foreign policy. While a country is in an isolated location and its economy is agricultural, it cares little about the outside world, unless it is threatened by foreign countries. It was the situation for America in 1880s seventy years after the war and the world was also relatively calm. It had to worry about the North American continent only. Then America was considered as a poor and minor power by Europeans. Its large navy built during the Civil War was crumbled due to the nation's non-involvement in world politics policy.

In the 1880s all this non-involvement policy changed, and the sentiments grew that the United States must overcome the minor power status and obtain pride and dignity. In the 1890s the United States responded shockingly to a string of incidents: it almost went to war with Germany over a dispute related to Samoa; it almost annexed Hawaii in 1893 after a revolt by local Americans against its Hawaiian Queen; it spoke about war with Italy and Chile over minor crisis; it unnerved Britain over a controversy in Venezuela; went to war with Spain in 1898 and emerged with an empire consisting of Puerto Rico, Guam and the Philippine Islands together with Cuba; and it annexed Hawaii in 1898.

Subsequently, the United States was a courageous, ambitious, aggressive, even a covetous nation in its foreign relations. It crushed a bloody revolution in the Philippines; converted the Caribbean an American lake by helping to build the Republic of Panama, building a canal, and establishing territories over Haiti, Nicaragua, the Dominican Republic, and Honduras. President Theodore Roosevelt declared America's right to interfere anywhere in the Western Hemisphere whenever it discovered persistent wrongdoing. At the same time, it entered Chinese markets by proclaiming its support of an Open Door policy and recognized Japan silently for mutual influence. With incomparable speed, a nation that was considered as a minor power in international politics became a world power.

How did this all Happen?

Because Germany, Japan, Russia and France were challenging supremacy by the1870s, Britain was no longer the dominant world power. These emerging new nations were prepared with armies, navies, industry, and dynamic commerce. Importantly, German Empire astonished everyone. Its brilliant universities and advanced social welfare programs attracted the admiration of intellectuals and reformers. But, its aggression and hostility, tyranny, and dictatorship together with confrontational "blood-and-iron rulers" pronouncements were frightening. Many in America and Britain were convinced that conflict with Germany is inevitable in the future. There was a rumour in 1895 that British are encircling the United States, from Canada down to Latin America with the intention to invade Latin America. Some argued that if British were not challenged, France and Germany would not be far behind.

Kelly writes, "Many felt demeaned by the fact that America was remaining inactive while others were gobbling up the huge empires. What glory was America winning? Progress was on the advance everywhere, it seemed; barbarism was being replaced by European law and order. How could the United States hold up its head when other nations were carrying the 'white man's burden'?"

The power of making foreign policy is in the hands of the president in America. He has an enormous power to act on his own. 'His advice on foreign policy comes not only from his secretary of state but also from many public groups, a body of men called Foreign Policy Community. This group consists of the general population who focus on foreign affairs as their essential interest and pursue by writings and speeches to bring the president to form his opinion. Its members include politicians, intellectuals, newspaper editors and publishers, heads of major corporations, organizations officials, international bankers, and military figures.'

This kind of foreign policy elite was formed in the 1880s and 1890s. Intellectual descendants of Alexander Hamilton were interested in talking about "the nation," "national power," and "national destiny." Democrats were purely concerned with local matters and did not pay any attention to the outside world. The Republicans foreign policy elite usually travelled significantly abroad, kept transatlantic contacts, read constantly about world affairs, and were disappointed that their country had so little military and naval power, and had no weight in world politics.

Alfred Thayer Mahan said that the national power lies in foreign trade and in the wealth, it creates and expanding foreign commerce is the key to strength and prosperity. Security lies in American ships protected by a strong American navy. In order to accomplish this goal, some specific steps to be taken: American vessels should cut the limited Atlantic basin; the construction of an American controlled canal through Central America to be built; such a canal would reach the markets of the Far East; to protect the canal, some form of American control should be established over Cuba and the other Caribbean islands; coaling stations and naval bases to be obtained in Hawaii, Guam, Wake Island, and the Philippines; and the American government should build a large merchant marine.

Progressive Age: New Way of Thinking

Sometime in the 1890s, a nationwide revolutionary change in American life began to spur. It was a Progressive period in American history full of energy. Civil War was undoubtedly an earthquake in American life because nothing can be compared to emancipation of slavery. Freeing of slaves was not enough to combat other national issues like, establishment of protective tariffs, national currency, banking system, corporate greed, etc. The progressive age touched every point and changed it. After 1916, American way of living changed significantly. They created a new agenda for their national life, including a new relationship between government and the economy, new types of government and a new ideology with a new name.

Every part of the nation was a new dialogue about the New Woman, the New Journalism, New Nationalism, and the New Freedom. A stream of new innovations produced amazing improvements in public life.

In 1900, a historian Edward W. Byrne imagined how America looked 100 years back. He dreamt travelling backward for a century and wrote:

> "We lose air engines, stem-winding watches, cash-registers and cash-carriers, the great suspension bridges, and tunnels, canals, iron frame buildings, monitors and heavy ironclads, revolvers, torpedoes, magazine guns and Gatling guns, linotype machines, all practical typewriters, all pasteurizing, knowledge of microbes or disease germs, and sanitary plumbing, water-gas, soda water fountains, air brakes, coal-tar dyes and medicines, nitro-glycerine, dynamite and guncotton, dynamo electric machines, aluminium ware, electric locomotives, Bessemer steel with its wonderful developments, ocean cables, enamelled iron ware, Welsbach gas burners, electric storage batteries, the cigarette machine, hydraulic dredges, the roller mills, middling's purifiers and patent-process flour, tin can machines, car couplings, compressed air drills, sleeping cars, the dynamite gun, the McKay shoe machine, the circular knitting machine, the Jacquard loom, wood pulp for paper, fire alarms, the use of anaesthetics in surgery, oleomargarine, street sweepers, Artesian wells, friction matches, steam hammers, electroplating, nail machines, false teeth, artificial limbs and eyes, the spectroscope, in Kinetoscope or moving pictures, acetylene gas, X-ray apparatus, horseless carriages, and — but enough! (The Progress of Invention in the Nineteenth Century [1900])

It was an amazing feeling to pass through all these innovations even before Newton and Einstein. This innovative work is still going on exponentially and changing the destiny of the world rapidly. American thinkers realized that there is some powerful force of process behind all this *work* of progress, improvement and intelligence. The task was to find out the secret of the process, which is enabling technical revolution, and apply the same process to make social and economic policy.

Progressive Movements

American reformers watched the Old World to collect ideas. To Americans British reforms excited and appealed. Britons and Americans read the same reformist books and exchanged them enthusiastically between two countries. As soon as a new idea appeared in London, American youth were broadcasting them in their own country. If the subject is about city reform, Americans prepared long bibliographies of British books on city reforms. If the subject is slum reform, American youth spent strenuous years to work in settlement houses in London, then returned back to build the same type of organizations in America.

German examples were also as important as Britain to Americans. In Germany the standards of the welfare state had fully developed. Thousands of Americans studied in German universities and brought socialist views to their country. Some wanted to transform American civilization from English model to German type. Chambers of Commerce advised German methods of industrial efficiency on businessmen; city planners sketched the idea of German beautification of cities.

Efficiency

Robert Kelly writes that the word Efficiency spread throughout the Anglo-American world. First, Sidney Webb publicised the term 'Efficiency' in London in 1902, a young Princeton professor Woodrow Wilson started writing articles on the theme in America. Personalities like Theodore Roosevelt were eager to make America a strong and efficiently organized nation.

Universities' Role

The fountain of the progressive consciousness stayed in the American middle-class. It was learning new ideas and new ways of doing things in the new universities, which developed in the last part of the nineteenth century. Since 1850, higher education was rising in American life. There were 550 institutions in higher learning with 5,500 faculty members and around 50,000 students. In 1900 there were about 1000 colleges and universities with 24,000 professors and 240,000 students undertaking a major role never seen before in American life. For example, in 1850 only 1 out of 60 youngsters was receiving higher education; in 1900 the number was 1 out of 25. Gradually, Americans realized the value of academic training for social and political governance, more income, and good standard of living. Achieving this goal meant civilizing the United States of America because it was a crude, disorganized, violent country. It required order and the inspiring effects of education. The slow, rural, unsophisticated ways of farming society needed to be abandoned, and a new national culture had to be built: it needed to be active, industrialize city-centred, well-educated, and linked to the outside world.

In fact, the blueprint for modern America was already planned by the Republican Party during Civil War time. The Morrill Act of 1862 provided lavish aid for building a national system of land-grant-supported state colleges and universities. It was not astonishing because New England had been the land of schools and colleges. The new universities helping to spread Yankee values nationwide were growing. The Yankee values were learning cultivated and disciplined mind; serving the community; and searching for new knowledge. For 1880s and 1890s, they were the driving motivation for well-educated and public-spirited reformers.

Bertman writes,

> "Traditional Yankee culture, for all its elitism, was also meritocratic: That is, it believed that those who had talent and energy should be encouraged to get ahead not simply those who came from good family or were aristocratic in background. The old colleges had admitted students only from certain faiths, families, or social classes. The new university, by contrast, was open to everyone as long as he or she had ability and energy. (Minority groups, however, were excluded by poverty, language difficulties, and social prejudice.) Its inner spirit was classically Yankee: a blend of hard work, time consciousness, and systematic performance, driven by completion."

Locally trained lawyers and doctors had to be retrained in the universities and they were urged to adopt an ethic of social service. The other new professions going out to the world from universities: economists, architects, biologists, scientifically trained agriculturists, chemists, public health specialists, social welfare workers, and teachers of all kinds. We perceive the emergence of a special kind of activist group of professionals who want to devote their life and time to social reform with a strong sense of mission. They gave birth to the Progressive movement.

Inner Characteristics of the University

Before 1850s, colleges were small, four-year, church-connected institutions that offered bachelor's degrees only, and their main purpose was to shape the moral character of their students. The curriculum of their studies was fixed for generations, the faculty were priests, who were trustees and presidents also. Each student took the same courses as others; all students were supposed to learn by memory; and they were kept under close discipline.

On contrast, a different type of institutions had developed in Germany. It was interested basically with creating and spreading knowledge, not morals. At the end of 1800s, dissatisfied with their education in America, more than 9000 young Americans went to Germany for advanced studies. After their education, they returned back and became presidents of esteemed colleges like Harvard, Yale, Columbia, and transformed them into modern universities. Others went to John Hopkins, and the like.

Professors were hired for their knowledge about the subject, not because they were of the right faith and had a strong will to discipline students. The new code was that a university was supposed to create knowledge and pass it on to the next group. They were supposed to participate in the international conversation of scholars and scientists by leading creative intellectual lives outside and inside the classroom. Training to learn by rote was replaced by the German method of lecturing, where professors brought their own research to classrooms. Ph.D., an ancient German degree indicating the highest level of advanced scholarly accomplishment was introduced in American universities. Graduate students learned to question, analyse and conduct their own research by conducting seminars.

Even though these universities were designed according to the German practices, the whole effect was completely American. Universities in Germany were located in a nation governed by strong militarized aristocrats, and they taught knowledge alone, not community need. In the state universities in America, the atmosphere was extremely public spirited and practical. It is reported that 'Engineering students, trained to meet the country's practical needs, were the most characteristic students of the new regime. For this reason, industrialists began making large gifts to universities, even endowing them: Ezra Cornell, whose gifts helped to create (1865) a combined private and state university for New York; Cornelius Vanderbilt and Leland Stanford, the universities bearing their names (1875 and 1885); and John D. Rockefeller, the University of Chicago.'

America wanted to fulfil many needs and greatly expanded its course offerings ending its restricted curriculum like mathematics, classics, rhetoric, and music only. At Harvard, President Eliot stunningly introduced an individualistic idea of the elective system, where students could choose their own courses of study. The idea of major fields of study appeared. Even though the new universities were not any more church-dominated institutions, the American people continued to think of college as a place where the character and mind of the pupil was sculpted.

Revolt against Conservative Social Darwinism

In American universities, all science faculties completely embraced Darwinism and teaching accordingly, which traditional Americans did not like. Charles Darwin, in his book, "Origin of Species" stated that all life evolved into its countless number of species in the present form by a long process of 'evolution,' propelled by the force of 'natural selection.' This theory was against the Biblical teaching that God created all plants, animals, and humans as they are now, in the present form, and in six days. Some people easily accepted this evolutionary view. The author writes, "The difficult part of Darwin's evolution to accept, (it bothered even Darwin) was that the mindless process, 'natural selection' is what governs evolution.... species periodically have offspring whose characteristics are changed from those of the parents. Mutations like this simply happen, apparently by chance. They involve a change in what we now call the gene material - DNA. The organism so modified may be better equipped in the struggle for survival and procreation, and if so the new forms crowd out the old ones. Change chance? Few could accept that. Where is God in such a process? Surely the changes are planned by him? Surely there is guiding intelligence?" Conservative people questioned and looked for answers.

Some other people concluded that the 'struggle' is the basic fact of life and out of 'struggle' comes progress to both species and plants. This bitter and pitiless version of evolution was called Social Darwinism. The sad part is it is justified that the country should be ruled by the powerful races, by the wealthy and privileged. Because the evolution states 'survival of the fittest,' it is the doctrine of doing nothing whatsoever to help the unfortunate.

To compassionate youth educated in the new universities, this negative thinking was awfully upsetting. When they wanted to help the unfortunate poor, to serve the society, how could they pursue their ideals in situations like this? So, many students changed their subjects taught in the universities as a way of unselfish lives opting for medicine, social work, teaching, and government services. As a result, 'The building of hospitals and the discovery of anaesthesia and antisepsis surfaced in the 1880s as a subject of charitable endeavours.

The staunch advocates of social reforms looked for a new philosophy to rationalize reform. Lester Frank Ward, one of the most extraordinary scholars and creative thinkers, wrote a massive work 'Dynamic Sociology,' published in 1883 targeting to destroy conservative social Darwinism. In it Ward stated,

> "...that people had forgotten humanity's unique possession - its mind. Whereas plants and animals might evolve, as Darwin had said, without conscious action, humanity had been given a reasoning brain with which to consciously improve its situation. Natural evolution is aimless without goals. Social movement must be planned, not left to haphazard influences."

In the new Universities, professors all over the country picked up Ward's ideas and started to teach to their students. Their motive was 'Search for the life of service'. One outcome of this temper was the beginning of social work as a medium through which youth can serve their communities. Jane Addams stands as a symbol of this new category.

Jane Addams

Jane Addams wanted to serve the community but did not know how. She discarded the idea of joining missionary work. Medicine was emerging as a popular profession. She started medical studies, but her health failed.

Jane Adams discovered her inspiration in England where Settlement Houses were growing. Started in the 1880s, the Settlement Houses project was a group of educated people posted in the slum areas to help the working poor to understand their problems by giving education in schools. It decreased disease by raising awareness in cleanliness; opened a channel to violent youngsters by training in athletics, games, arts, and crafts; and provided clinics after training in professional skills; opened various organizations to provide skills like kindergarten jobs for working women, literacy, and the pleasure of arts, playgrounds for healthy exercise and the learning of teamwork.

Inspired by this model, Jane Addams founded Hull House in Chicago. She became an inspiration for young women and men. To fight against Social Darwinism, she created a counter philosophy saying that people should not be isolated as atoms and cut off from each other. Instead the future for America depends on reviving the sense of community, the collective responsibility, of human warmth, interaction and love. She said, "The real curse of industrialism lay in its shattering of the net of associations that had formerly bound people together. Women especially should not care only for their individual families: they should launch out into the community and help ro build a better, more humane human family." She emphasized that the healthy self grows not in seclusion, but it grows by interrelations with others.

She saw that people were stronger and more able to deal with adversity if they engaged themselves in the group life and built a net of outward reaching relationships. In her Hull House she promoted practical arts and emphasized creativity in place of rote learning. Nationalism fundamentalists criticised her internationalism, some expelled her, but she received the Nobel Peace Prize in 1931.

To Lester Frank Ward and to his followers, society is an organism, not a simple random group of individuals. Society definitely evolves if it uses its collective intelligence to reach out social goals and achieves them through its collective arms and legs, the government. The welfare of the people must be supported by an enormous combination of public services such as education, regulation of minimum wages and maximum hours, and many other social reforms. There should be a minimum standard of living for every individual; there should be positive liberty - liberty from ignorance and exploitation - instead of mere negative liberty of traditional laissez-faire, which typically says that the government should keep its hands off the economy and society.

New Philosophers of Social Action

The men who inspired people for collective action for social reform were not philosophers, prophets, priests, or scholars, but popular writers. Henry George, a California newspaperman, was shocked to see that rich land and productive factories existed in the middle of starvation and unemployment. He concluded that it was the system, not the nature of humankind that produced this suffering. He wrote a book 'Progress and Poverty' in 1879 stating that when civilization pushed ahead, poverty increased. One fundamental cause for this situation is land monopoly. Smart people possess best and most valuable city lots and farmlands, and then skimmed the cream of society's developing wealth by insisting high rents and prices. In spite of all, landowner did nothing: it was the laborious work of other people that made his land valuable. Businessmen had to pay high rents, so they pressed worker's wages to compensate. Farmers also experienced hardships. The solution he suggested: replace all forms of taxation with a single tax that landowners would have to pay on the increased value of their land, the "unearned increment." Consequently, the weight of taxation will be dramatically lessened, and the economy will grow abundantly.

George's single tax solution was very simple and it never worked though. But his proving demonstration about that the system is responsible for present condition and poverty is avoidable. The book Progress and Poverty was published in a hundred editions and read by at least six million men and women. George was "the prophet for whom the people had been searching for years; he was the Columbus for political economy and social science" in Britain, Australia and New Zealand.

In 1887, Edward Bellamy wrote in his book, 'Looking Backward' that society is like a cart with wealthy tycoons sitting on the box above and whipping the working people below as they struggled to pull the heavy vehicle. The solution was to reorganize society until it looked like a well-arranged army. The belief of individualistic competition should be eradicated because it leads to selfishness. He said industry should be nationalized because no one should have the power of ruling over others irresponsibly; There should be a strong central government to plan everything carefully and to stop wasting; there should be large department stores instead of many small shops; and credit cards in place of money; people should work until the age of forty-five and retire to do their own desires. His suggestions appealed more to Yankees.

Many other such books were published and read by social reformers.

The Churches and Social Action

In Churches also a new kind of awareness appeared. Previously, the general hypothesis was that godliness was in alliance with possessions: the general opinion was the wealthy people acquired their money by hard work, and God lauded them with blessings; the poor people earned their sufferings by their own wrong doings. But in the 1880s, a tiny group of young clergymen working in cities observed and shocked by the suffering they saw started to take social action in the churches. The Salvation Army, a British organization, which came to America in 1880, responded with the invasion of the slums by city missions. Another response was the transformation of churches in the poor areas into 'institutional' churches. Like Jane Addams' 'settlement houses,' the institutional churches were designed to care for the whole person, instead of simply to preach a sermon on Sunday. Here the important idea was that a man crushed down by poverty, unemployment, illiteracy, and lack of skills would be too anxious to listen to sermons or practice a religious faith. The new churches furnished reading rooms and classes to combat illiteracy and ignorance; day care centres to help working women; sewing and manual training instruction to provide skills; social clubs and gymnasiums to bring people together and build physical health; and personal advising outside spiritual matters. These kinds of institutional churches spread throughout metropolitan America.

The Religious Challenge of Darwinism

Because of Darwinism's explanation, the churches were also in confusion with biblical interpretation. They began to think if the theory of evolution is authentic, then what happens to the theory of the Garden of Eden? Are humans simply animals, like monkeys and apes, whose current shape was arranged not by God's hands but by the process of evolution? The Darwinian idea looked like a monstrous attack on everything the church preached about man's status in creation and his relation go God. Why should we pray to God if everything operates according to natural laws? What has happened to the faith of their parents? Common church people could not understand it. It appeared that modern science was a great threat to them. So, they tried to turn back modern science with arguments.

Many priests in urban churches followed Darwinism interpreting that god works in his own way to perform wonders. Evolution is the divine means of achieving divine purposes. Rural churches followed the old faith, but the liberal teaching spread in urban churches. They said, 'science and religion were not enemies, but were complementary sources of divine truth.' It means that the Bible should not be interpreted literally, but according to its spirit.

The Growth of the Social Scripture

Consequently, the platform was prepared for the development of the social gospel. A clergyman named Washington Gladden published a book 'Applied Christianity' in 1886. He believed Christianity as a fellowship of love, and the church as having a social mission. He emphasized that people must reach out to one another, assist one another, and not stand back in emotionless personalities while the supposed principle of survival of the fittest functioned. Because the centre was conducting war against working people, employees should have the right to organize. He insisted that there should be a profit-sharing system so that workers would receive a portion of the profit that their hard work produced. His other social reforms endorsement: public control of money; regulation of corporations; the right of black people to equal educational and economic opportunities; and all the reforms of the Progressive age.

Saddened by the horrific life of slum dwellers, Walter Rauschenbusch, a Baptist churchman published a book 'For the Right' in the 1880s advocating Christian socialism. He said, "It is possible to build the Kingdom of God here on earth in this new age of progress." He condemned capitalism as un-Christian; it destroyed people's moral growth and made them corrupt.

William James: Robert Kelly writes that the reformers needed a new image of humanity and its potential in the Progressive age. From the 1890s, Harvard psychologist and philosopher William James was a prominent personality in American thought. An alert, shrewd, amazingly tolerant James' writings and lectures reached out wider circles of Americans and made him a sort of national sage. Intellectuals in the United States and in Europe were deeply influenced by him. Thousands of ordinary people in the educated middle class also bought and read his more popular works. After Benjamin Franklin, no American intellectual was so multicultural and so widely known and read in the transatlantic community.

At first, James struggled hard to understand the true nature of Darwinism. He was horrified about the conclusion that everything is caused by physical influences, that the laws of biology and not the free human spirit determine what we are and what we think. Alternatively, he chose humanity's free will. Summing up his audacious concept of human nature, he published a book "Principles of Psychology," which became a leading work in the field of psychology.

James discarded vigorously the idea that people are like little machines, shaped entirely by their environment. He claimed that there is a self at the centre of each human being and that self has a will or mind of its own. 'Clearly influenced by the external environment, the conscious self at the same time acts upon that environment. People live in continuous interaction with their surroundings, not inactive creatures pushed this way and that way by external forces.'

In his another book "Pragmatism" (1907), he famously distinguished two notions, "Tender-minded" and "Tough-minded." He said,

> "The tender-minded people are unable to face the fact that reality is enormously complicated, often confusing, and perhaps lacking any encompassing structure that one can see. Therefore, they put their faith in abstract, logical theories. Determined to fit themselves and their world into some kind of intellectual structure that they can hang onto, the tender-minded people form an exaggerated faith in the ability of the mind to know all things by the use of reason and logic. By contrast, Tough-minded people are comfortable with the indeterminacy of life, content to work away in the midst of booming confusion and interested most of all in coming to grips with how things really are in some limited area of examination. Skeptical, rather materialistic, they go by facts (observation) and not by theories (rationalism). The Tough-minded people think that the Tender-minded people as sentimentalists and soft-heads. The Tender-minded people feel the Tough to be unrefined, insensitive, or brutal."

He further observed that most people are mixtures of both, but the tough-minded people are growing larger in number. The tough-minded person considers facts, puts together an idea as a possible explanation for the facts, tests it, and tosses it aside willingly if it does not work. James said if a theory works satisfactory, then it is true. In his opinion, experience is the proper test, not logic.

In summary, the message received by Progressive Age thinkers: 'Examine reality directly, be quick to toss aside theories, and test everything by results. Take a kind of joyous delight in the complexity and indeterminacy of life: ride the waves, laugh at the tumbling, and avoid the closed-in clams. Gather huge amounts of facts, think carefully, and then be ready to risk. Pragmatism was taken up eagerly by an age that was confident, hopeful, breaking barriers, and ready to run over people and traditions if results could be achieved.'

Realisms

As a result, scholarships on realism in economics, history, political science, law, literature and journalism began in American universities. In Progressive Age everything appeared open to fresh examination: industrial methods, banking systems, railway franchises, use of political power, nature of education, social relations, and even human life. The gap between formerly separated people of theory and practice appeared to be bridged.

History: One of the scholarships of the new universities was creating the field of modern history inspired by a German historian Leopold von Ranke. His followers began abandoning revered old books of the ancient past and went directly to the sources to trace original documents like tablets to uncover the truth. Range said: discover what things are really like; do not be content with what the old historians said; doing so, the researcher will find a fresh story that tells him unknown things; be sceptical, analytical, take nothing for granted; build from facts, not from theories.

The outcome was a total rewriting of ancient history in the nineteenth century. Scholars unearthed the forgotten history of their own nations. An American historian wrote a vivid explanation of American history and concluded: 'History was a story that concentrated on lively, eruptive, conflicting forces.' Earlier historians presented uplifting stories of Washington and Jefferson that were idealistic and unifying. Progressive historians concentrated on change and social conflict leading towards democracy.

Literature: A new kind of literature emerged that was strikingly realistic. Previously, the Victorian novel had been blatantly escapist, narrating easy fictions that struggled with simple problems and ended happily ever after. But now the new breed of writers started to expose the nasty, false, and shocking stories. Mark Twain's novels concerned too much death, meanness, selfishness, and crudity. It was a cunning, scornful world of little men who blew false stories and ran around looking for success.

Another contemporary of Mark Twain, William Dean Howells' novels dealt with greedy capitalism, the confused life of great cities, the suffering caused by industrialism, and the collapse of morality under the pressures of modern life.

Jack Norris was another realistic writer. In his novels, he combatted 'false views of life, false characters, false sentiment, false morality, false history, false philosophy, false emotions, false heroism.'

Many other realistic writers wrote on the themes: power exploiting weakness; life was nothing except dark forces moving aimlessly; powerful men learn that life is a struggle for survival and push their way to the top of some social pyramid; spend their lives exploiting those below by any corrupt means they can find; have no consciousness of what is known as sin; never gave a thought to the vast uproar concerning evil which was constantly going on; there were just faces to the defence of life - strength and weakness, and so on.

Journalism: In journalism also, a revolution was going on. To reach the huge new readers in the cities, the number of newspapers increased spectacularly. In 1870 there were 600 daily newspapers; in 1909 there were more than 2,500. In 1870, 3 million newspapers were sold every day, but in 1909, the number reached 24 million. The new journalism launched astonishing projects to spread their messages campaigning against vice, sniffing or beating out corruption in city hall, or clean-up-the-city drives. Newspaper publishers realized that readers were concerned about the stories of sufferers in the slums, whether they were young girls or unfortunate families. Sob-sister paper published hidden humanitarian sentiments that the urban life usually stayed out of touch. Consequently, the middle-class developed interest in the conditions of unfortunate lives in Progressive Age. Numerous other newspapers and magazines had large circulations and broadcasted the stories that pitilessly exposed corruption and malpractice.

A great demand emerged for bright writers in the press. Those who were bold could move easily in the chaotic and disorganized human world of the city, write vibrantly, and could draw a good salary. College graduates entered this new profession and brought sophistication to thriving social sciences. Journalism advanced further from these new journalist's high ideals, their sense of responsibility to the public welfare, and their real story behind the closed doors. Developing their relations, they disclosed false politicians, disloyalty of public trust, and bribery. The writers had no great plan for how American life should be organized; they just concentrated on exposure. They enthusiastically described all types of systems of corruption and insisted genuine people to revitalize the nation. One leading journalist Lincoln Steffens wrote about political corruption:

"And it is all a moral weakness; a weakness right where we think we are strongest. Oh, we are good — on Sunday, and we are "fearfully patriotic" on the Fourth of July. But the bribe we pay to the janitor to prefer our interests to the landlord's is the little brother of the bribe passed to the alderman to sell a city street, and the father of the air-brake stock assigned to the president of a railroad to have this life-saving invention adopted on his road. And as for graft, railroad passes, saloon and bawdy-house blackmail, and watered stock, all these belong to the same family. We are… a free and sovereign people, we govern ourselves and the government is ours. But what is the point? We are responsible, not our leaders, since we follow them. We let them divert our loyalty from the United States to some "party"; we let them boss the party and turn our municipal democracies into autocracies and our republican nation into a plutocracy. We cheat our government and we let our leaders loot it, and we let them wheedle and bribe our sovereignty from us. True, they pass for us strict laws, but we are content to let them pass bad laws, giving away public property in exchange, and our good, and often impossible, laws we allow to be used for oppression and blackmail. And what can we say? We break our own laws and rob our own government, the lady at the customhouse, the lyncher with his rope, and the captain of industry with his bribe and rebate. The spirit of graft and lawlessness is the American spirit… (The Shame of the Cities [1904])

The journalists presented detailed studies to the American public with a fresh social perspective. They wrote an intimate, anecdotal, behind-the-scenes history of their own times. They discovered the complex relationship of the police, the underworld, and the local political bosses, the secret connections between the new corporations… and the legislatures and the courts …..

The message of social decay was declared in books, magazines, and newspapers; in university extension courses; testimony before congressional committees and public lectures; in the gatherings of professional, business, and farm association — wherever public attention could be captured. "With this picture of American life before them in the first part of the twentieth century, people of the United States were ready, in unprecedented numbers, to vote for men who called themselves Progressives."

Progressive Age

The new style of progressive thinking about America emerged and transformed politics, remaking new national life that had never seen before.

Previously, the traditional leaders were the advocates of unrestrained capitalistic power, elitism in government, and ruled by the wealthy and privileged few. Shifted against this old type were the progressives of both political parties because progressivism was not the monopoly of either Republicans or Democrats.

Theodore Roosevelt

Among these reformers, President Theodore Roosevelt' contribution is immense. The nation needed to face problems like the railroad system, the power of great corporations, the banking system, the protective tariff, and the problem of natural resources. When progressives were looking for a dynamic national spokesman, they found that person in Theodore Roosevelt.

Robert Kelly writes, "There is no way to summarize Roosevelt's character. A diplomat observed that his temperament was that of a small boy, always excitable, enthusiastic, and impulsive. Certainly, he loved the outdoors and glorified what he called the strenuous life. He could be an impossible joker as one of his friends remarked, 'The gift of the gods to Theodore Roosevelt was joy, joy in life.' A cultivated man - he wrote many books still-valuable in history - he was eager and able to learn quickly. As an official in New York City, he had been horrified at slum conditions and had begun to listen to social reformers.... He never liked people whose only concern was making money, and he habitually spoke of them in terms of contempt and derision. His door was open to intellectuals, poets, prize-fighters, cowboys, artists, and aggressive young reporters."

Republican ideology was not anxious only with elitism and aristocracy, but also agreed with its emphasis on hard work, getting ahead, and living moral and respectable lives. Republicans emphasised that they were the real individualists providing opportunities for ordinary men of talent to become rich or at least live comfortable lives and be independent through industrialization. Roosevelt gave voice to these ideas. He thought big businessmen had gone too far with their greediness and surely believed the poor had a right to honest wages and good living conditions. Like Alexander Hamilton he wanted to build a vigorous America by installing a strong and active central government to lead the nation assertively. He continuously spoke about the need to solve the country's ills by making it Efficient. The only way to do this, he believed, is to give the power to strong people of good character. In his view state legislatures and Congress were always wrong because they were leaderless, confused, and narrow-minded. He advised his subordinates: Always make sure that men of good character are appointed to the administration.

When Theodore Roosevelt became the president in 1901, the congress was dominated by conservatives, and the Republican administration was in orthodox hands. Still he was restless to take bold decisions. He took several campaigns of national reforms in which his favourite cause, conservatism, is one among them. It was an elite movement, operated by scientists, civil servants, engineers, and far-sighted politicians, usually from the eastern states. They discussed the planned use of resources and condemned uncontrolled exploitation. Gifford Pinchot became a leader in this project.

Progressivism: National Parks - Gifford Pinchot

Gifford Pinchot was a New Englander of French Protestant. He studied forestry in Europe and returned to America and found that there was not a single acre of forest land that was under any form of management. What is remarkable is when he died at the age of eighty-one, there were hundreds of millions of acres of public land protected and their use was regulated. This achievement credit belongs to Pinchot because he was a major voice in shaping the country's forestry policy. He said that the greedy lumbering and unrestricted grazing would completely destroy the declining forest lands. He urged that they must be put under the control of national forests, administered by a service of trained professionals, and especially, they should be protected from forest fires. In 1898, he was appointed as the first Forester in the department of Agriculture.

As an efficient public relation officer, Pinchot started to deliver his doctrines through public speaking, and sending reams of information on profitable forest management. President Theodore Roosevelt made him a close adviser for the cause of conservation of forests and rivers in the country. Upon advice from Pinchot, Roosevelt increased the national forests from 46 million to 150 million acres, and finally forests were placed in the hands of regulatory agencies accompanied by a vigorous administrator.

Some people disliked this aristocratic, foreign-trained person as a symbol of illogicalness, and it is un-American of government interference. His passion for high administrative efficiency and his part as chief priest of conservation (not preservation) earned him many enemies. Investors, lumbermen, and miners wanted to destroy his plans and the time was approaching. In January 1910, the new President Taft discharged Pinchot due to great national controversy. 'The Chief Forest Officer was gone from the federal office, but the monument he had created, the huge edifice of national forests, remains his permanent heritage to the nation.'

Progressivism: Educated Motherhood and the Child

Progressivism was not only concerned with corrupt government and capitalism, but it was also a cultural revolution to create a new way of life in America. The periodicals and all kinds of publications were filled with exciting discussions on the New Literature, the New Art, the New Woman, and the New School. All of them attacked the older pretentious and exaggerated culture. The drive to transform the life of the child captured the mind of people enormously. Working-class children in the cities, particularly the children of immigrant families, paid a heavy price for industrialization. The children worked in the mills and factories and were blocked from the care of their mothers. They lived in cheerless slum streets, given no practical value of education, and exposed to bad diet, crime, and disease.

In this circumstance emerged a concept of educated motherhood among progressive's mind. They said the society is too complex and it is not appropriate to simply depend on the instincts of ordinary women, who come from village atmospheres to ugly harmful cities. In reality, even urban middle-class women needed new training in childbearing due to demanding lives that faced young adults. This situation needed new types of schools, new laws relating to children, and new social institutions.

Kindergarten, a German idea of preschool program, spread rapidly in the nation. In 1880 there were only 350 kindergartens, but in 1910 their number increased to more than 5000. The very young children no longer left in the streets without supervision. Instead, they were to be civilized monitoring day and night by teaching good manners, good habits, and self-discipline.

Beyond kindergarten, progressivists also reached mothers to help them to plan a better environment in the home. Mothers Clubs were organized (gradually it became the Parents and the Teachers Association); hygiene and proper habits were taught. One educator expressed about the broad "Americanizing" objectives of school:

> "Our task is to break up their groups or settlements, to assimilate and amalgamate these people as a part of our American race, to implant in their children the Anglo-Saxon conception of righteousness, law and order, and popular government, and to awaken in them reverence for democratic institutions and for those things in our natural life which we as a people hold to be of abiding worth."

Women's Colleges

A new generation of women reformers concentrated not only on simple issues of moral degradation, but also on problems aroused by industrialization, urbanization, and immigration. They taught for women, just moralism is not enough, but they needed to be shrewd investigators and socially conscious activists who worked with labour unions and the working class. Hull Houses provided college graduated women the exciting experiences of living in the slums, college-dormitory fashion, and participating in a circle of lectures, discussion, good talk, and hearty fellowship. They were learning their new social science courses and were supposed to teach the principles of healthy, civilized living to the poor. Contrast to previous generation women who visited the poor with a basketful of food and then returned back to their comfortable homes, the new reform women lived among them offering classes in child development, hygiene, citizenship, American history, English literature, arts and crafts, and highlighting the importance of physical exercise, regular habits, fresh milk, regular medical examinations for children, and clean homes and streets. 'Cooperative loan funds were established to teach the values of saving and responsibility. Settlement houses also established direct aids for mothers; kindergartens, supervised playgrounds, medical clinics, legal advice, and information centres in dealing with city offices.

The Progressive Schools revolutionized the new age. The inspiration was that the school should not simply teach literacy and numbers, but it should actually prepare the child for life. The teaching must include nutrition and carefully designed exercise. It introduced more practical programs with children learning all the arts of democratic self-government, public-speaking, and voting. Some suggested that there should be a school newspaper and regular elections; training should target teaching skills, good character, imaginative planning, and creative accomplishments. Theodore Roosevelt was deeply interested in the future of American family and provided his strong support to these programs.

Progressivism: Democrats - President Woodrow Wilson, 1913

Historians tell that President Woodrow Wilson was the first intellectual in the White House since Thomas Jefferson and James Madison. He came to Washington from the train accompanied by Princeton students for his inauguration as president in 1913. Southerners felt that ultimately the South had returned to White House and with Wilson it was the hope of force in the cabinet, in the White House, in the circle of advisers, in diplomatic positions abroad, and in Congress where Democrats had a majority first time in twenty years.

Woodrow Wilson was an intellectual elite, a brilliant professor of political science and history at Princeton University in the 1890s and had a reputation as an educational reformer. In 1910 he entered into politics with extraordinary performance as Governor of New Jersey, where he abolished boss rule, created strict controls over utilities. With sweeping victory, he became President and Democrats welcomed their exciting leader with gratefulness and admiration.

Woodrow Wilson had a bleak in appearance: Erect, precise in manner, long-jawed, slim, and neat form. He was a strong man of remarkable intellectual powers, disapproving of stupidity, confident of his moral righteousness, and enthusiastic for power and authority. Wilson's passionate nature released completely when he spoke to a large group of people. His huge intellect would operate eagerly over his topic, words would pour from his mouth with burning passion, and normally dull face would come alive. His students at Princeton used to rupture into spontaneous clapping; mocking politicians were mesmerized when they listened to him; and ordinary citizens were ignited into winds of cheering.

Wilson made British public life as his model. As a supporter of free trade, he regarded Adam Smith as a prophet of political economy; fan of sound money and the gold standard; and a political scientist who believed that strong governments were necessary tools of the rich and powerful. According to Kelly, Wilson was an idealistic and moralist. His imagination captured great models of the human spirit. History captivated him as a story of brave men struggling relentlessly and courageously for magnificent ideals.

Woodrow Wilson believed that basically the economy should be kept open, dynamic, and fair so that ordinary people could also get ahead. Roosevelt's New Nationalism was about that government not only to regulate the trusts, but to give direct assistance to the disadvantaged: to workers, women, children, and the unemployed. In contrast, Wilson did not believe in big governments, so he banned social reform. He said that no one really needed help if opportunities were open to all.

Tariff: As soon as he entered the office in 1913, Wilson took drastic steps and electrified the nation by immediately inviting Congress into a special session to reform the tariff. "The new tariff average was set at 29 percent. All products produced by monopolies were placed on the free list, and the new income tax provision was put into effect, the tax was set at a 7 percent maximum in order to make up for the loss of tariff revenues."

Banking System It was not the intention of Woodrow Wilson to destroy the private banking system, but his aim was to establish some kind of public regulation over the financial world. So, Woodrow Wilson suggested to congress the idea of the creation of a Federal Reserve Board to supervise the banking system. The plan as written by Kelly:

> "Its membership would be appointed by the president and confirmed by the Senate, and bankers would be ineligible for such an appointment. The nation would be divided into twelve Federal Reserve regions, in each of which would be placed a Federal Reserve bank. These institutions would be governed by boards elected primarily by the private banks in the region that had affiliated themselves with the system.
>
> "The Federal Reserve System would provide .....
>
> "An important step in this process was that the Federal Reserve Bank would not issue currency up to the full value of the mortgage. In effect, it would charge some interest by discounting the commercial paper - issuing the money in an amount slightly less than the full value of the indebtedness. By charging the borrowing bank a certain percentage of the transaction, the Federal Reserve Bank could make loans easier or harder to obtain by raising or lowering the discount rate. This gave the system the potential power of controlling the money supply and thereby damping inflations or easing deflations."

This decentralized type of banking system helped to relieve the Wall Street monopoly.

J.P. Morgan: The name Morgan invokes a great admiration in the financial world. Joseph Morgan built a fortune in Andrew Jackson's time; his son Junius Morgan built a major international banking company; and his son John Pierpont Morgan further exceeded his father and grandfather. He was a talented mathematician with interest in numbers and a desire for precision and organized co-ordination. He was a genius and knew how to bring order out of the extremely complicated and confused mess of post-Civil War railroading in America. In the 1880s, Morgan surfaced as the banker: he would meticulously gather people, not only in banking but in coal mining and other activities and raise prices - monopolistic, but not illegal - gained profits and exploited consumers.

Morgan attracted British investors and became a channel for enormous flow of British funds into American industry. He became so powerful that in 1895, he rescued the national Treasury itself in a time of gold-buying panic. By 1900, he controlled most of American railroading by financing and organizing their formation. When the House of Reprehensive Committee examined his business transaction in 1913, his business included 112 corporations with $22 billion, an astounding sum.

Morgan was not at all bothered about it. With his big moustache, abrupt and alarming manner, this tall, powerfully built man was confident: He was confident that a man of good character would use this massive network of power well, and he was convinced of his own goodness of character. To J.P. Morgan big business meant only efficient, rational, well-organized business. Morgan believed that politicians were low, disgraceful men and said let the men of good character run the country; they will save it from itself.

The Women's Suffrage Campaign

In the Wilson's period, one of the great victories for social justice was women's right to vote. The reasons behind the delayed action about women's suffrage were powerful interests such as the liquor industry, textile manufacturers, ethnic groups, traditional ideas of male domination in government, and cultural conservatism as a general temper. Surprisingly, until 1900 most women were uninterested to vote and actively opposed the cause. If women were interested, they would have got it like many other reforms such as women's property rights, legal status in marriage, ability to engage in business, and control over their children. In fact, thousands of women in the Social Purity movement and even many prominent reformers openly opposed the suffrage demand.

They feared that the traditional family might be ended. Women in Massachusetts school had the system to vote about school affairs; only one in twenty women bothered to vote. When it was allowed to vote for or against for women's suffrage, four men voted for as women. Actually, 'the national campaign against women's suffrage was organized, staffed, and run mainly by women.'

Then, what changed the situation? In 1900 there was a well-organized campaign conducted by its advocates; there was the mood of the Progressive Era; there were many thousands of college-educated women; and there was the fact that women were involved in great numbers through work and social reform in public life.

The fear that the voting right would jeopardize women's role in the family disappeared when they saw no such changes occurred in those states that allowed women to vote.

The suffrage movement was conducted by two college-trained women: Carrie Chapman Catt and Anna Howard Shaw. The Women's Political Union was formed with the objective of holding public gatherings and launching active campaigns against male politicians who opposed the vote for women. Hundreds of women came from the countryside; spoke to an audience of men and women where they could find; and brought direct pressure on legislators with the leadership of Catt. Thousands of women marched to Washington on the first inauguration of Woodrow Wilson. They had to fight their way to reach the Capitol building because hostile groups booed and mocked at them, and constantly obstructed their line of demonstration. In reality, the democrats always opposed change. They preferred women's position as in the same old fashion that existed in the villages. The women's movement had always been a Republican idea.

Women organized outstanding national voyages from San Francisco to Washington, D.C. obtaining petitions with hundreds and thousands of signatures. The white House was surrounded, and hunger strikes were launched. When both houses voted, it was defeated narrowly.

Nineteenth Amendment: When Woodrow Wilson appeared to speak at the convention of National American Woman Suffrage Association, Anna Howard Shaw addressed to him, "We have waited so long, Mr. President, for the vote - we had hoped it might come in your administration," at that moment the huge audience of women rose silently and stood quietly looking at the president. Within a year, he appealed Congress to take action. In January 1918, the House of Representatives passed the women's suffrage constitutional amendment, mainly because a large number of Republicans were in favour of Women's suffrage, in 1920 the ratification process was completed, and the Nineteenth Amendment became reality.

Black Issues

Even in the prospering Progressive Era, the South crawled far behind. Life for ordinary people was tiring and difficult. In Georgia two-thirds of people who worked in the countryside were desperately poor, and illiteracy among both whites and blacks was high. Except in Atlanta, Georgia had no manufacturing plants. Usually, Georgian people worked in cotton fields, or in the pine woods and cotton mills.

In southern states, usually violent activities like shooting and stabbing was triggered for someone's honor. It was black against black, and white against white. Nevertheless, it was usually the mobs of whites attacking blacks and ghastly lynching was common. Whites were angry because after slavery was abolished, blacks were becoming stubborn and adopting Yankee values of human dignity. As per historian Numan V. Bartley, in the forty years from 1890 to 1930, 450 lynching were reported in a single state of

Georgia. The common accusation was mostly that a black man had raped a white woman, sometimes with no evidence. The lynching was horrific and gruesome. A black clergyman, Bishop Henry Turner noted sadly, "Without multiplying words, I wish to say that hell is an improvement upon the United States when the Negro is involved."

Blacks in America

It was inconceivable that the national government in Washington, D.C. was reluctant to do anything about it. In fact, after Woodrow Wilson became president, his administration began to practice segregation in government branches. 'Black and white workers were separated to reduce friction..... There was a particular touchiness about black civil servants supervising white women. Wilson, when appealed to, insisted that segregation was actually a humanitarian policy, because it would give black workers job areas of their own in which they need not fear white intrusion.' Ironically, black leaders believed the president was a sincere man.

Blacks in North kept their political and civil rights although they suffered from social and economic discrimination. They studied in separate schools, worked and held only the most menial jobs. The concept of racial equality was generally condemned and if black people tumbled behind, it was their own responsibility, said white Americans.

In the South, racial equality was never considered, but the protective view explained that whites should carry out their responsibility as representatives for blacks carefully and thoughtfully. The Northern states pointed out the southerner whites should work in a responsible and civilized way. Black men continued to vote in large numbers, some held public office, served as juries, judges, sat in city, state, and national legislatures.

Jim Crow

There was an outburst of racist stories, numerous allegations that black men were voraciously raping white women, and vociferous attacks on the behaviour of blacks. As a result, black community had to suffer frequent mass violence. In 1898, 400 white men streamed into a black residential area in Wilmington, North Carolina and burned homes, killed, and wounded the terrified inhabitants, and forced hundreds to abscond. In 1900 the whole city of New Orleans was robbed and killed by the frightened blacks. In 1906, the whole city of Atlanta trembled for days by white supremacy. Worried about losing black votes, the Southern Progressivists brought a series of Jim Crow laws.

Consequently, segregation of blacks formed: The railway cars and waiting stations, streetcars, theatre entrances, boarding-houses, toilets, water fountains, ticket windows, parks, circus shows, halls, auditoriums, ball parks, residential areas, textbooks, schools, even prostitutes were segregated. Atlanta courtrooms had separate Bibles for blacks and for whites; public buildings had separate elevators. After the Jim Crow law passed, all relations were transformed, every black person whether intelligent or stupid, well dressed or in rags, cultivated or ignorant, was legally inferior to white person, no matter how crude or brutish he was.

Booker T. Washington

In this situation, African Americans turned inward and said 'yes' to segregation. Now, black people could demand that they too wanted segregation, and the pride of having their own circles. Self-help messages dominated everywhere among the black world.

In the 1890s, Booker T. Washington became a prophet of self-help. He encouraged black people to accept white people's philosophy of hard work and getting ahead in the community by material advancement. Since most black people worked in farms in the countryside as manual labourers, the majority of them were unskilled. The only hope was to obtain skills and work faithfully and not in agitating for racial equality and demanding positions of leadership. He said, "In all things that are purely social, the white and black races can be as separate as the five fingers, yet one as the hand in all things essential to mutual progress." He urged blacks to cooperate with whites, "Be patient, faithful, law-abiding and unresentful. It is extremely important that all privileges of the law be ours; but it is vastly more important that we be prepared for the exercise of these privileges."

Whites thoroughly approved Washington's philosophy, and he became a prominent figure in white eyes. Although they worried what happens if African Americans get ahead and demand more privileges, it promised to keep away all extremism. Charity institutions came forward to help Washington's programs and to receive opinion for the aid of African Americans. Theodore Roosevelt invited him to White House for consultation. After this meeting, 'White House did not appoint any African American to government without clearing them first with Booker T. Washington.'

Majority of black Americans approved Booker T. Washington's advice. Jobs and a respectable standard of living: These were what they wanted. Rocking the boat was not their wish; they expected that some kind of peaceful and modestly comfortable life. Such principles were taught in black schools, in conventions of black farmers, and at meetings of black businessmen's organisations. Self-sufficiency was emphasized. The standards were all in black where black physicians, lawyers, bankers, merchants, and teachers would meet the needs of black workers and farmers. The black church was the centre place of Afro-American life continuously, and from its platform ministers preached the message of self-help, racial pride, and solidarity. Washington was a staunch Republican and he worked hard to elevate black people's life in Northern states.

1. Booker T. Washington (1856-1915) 2. Du Bois (1868-1963)

Black Extremism

The Southern blacks were surrounded by a tempest of wild racism. The dawn of Jim Crow law fostered the scream of white supremacy in the south, savage attacks conducted on houses of black people; particularly a riot erupted in Atlanta, 1906. 'It was one thing for blacks to talk of hard work and patience; it was another when they actually got ahead.' White attacked the property of blacks who had worked hard to acquire them.

In this circumstance, the black Americans in the South summoned a new philosophy. They were surrounded by Progressive movement, which lectured about high moral values of equity and social justice. The new agitators were mainly college-educated professionals and intellectuals who did not like to be constricted in the world of blackness: It was a dilemma to choose between two identities - being a black and being an American like everyone else. An Atlanta University professor W.E.B. Du Bois explained in 1897:

> "One feels his two-ness - an American, a Negro, two souls, two thoughts, two unreconciled strivings, two warring ideals in one dark body… The history of the American Negro is the history of his strife -

this longing to attain self-conscious manhood, to merge his double self into a better and true self… He would not Africanize America for America has too much to teach the world and Africa. He would not bleach the Negro soul in a flood of white Americanism, for he knows that Negro blood has a message for the world. He simply wishes to make possible for a man to be both a Negro and an American, without being cursed and spit upon…"

They reject the complete segregation in Booker T. Washington's philosophy. They demanded Integration, full acceptance on an equal basis as a human being. Obedience and patience in a caste system were unacceptable. The protesters insisted for their civil rights and demanded that their young blacks' education should be given not only in mechanized skills, but also in the liberal arts and sciences.

W.E.B. Du Bois

Du Bois had a Ph.D. from Harvard University and he started his career as a professor at all-black University of Atlanta. First, he accepted Booker T. Washington's view and he would say, 'a good many of our people are not fit for the responsibility of republican government.' His opinion was Blackman must improve himself morally to become a better and more responsible American, more hard-working, and ambitious. Then white society would open the door.

Slowly he began to change his views. He encouraged blacks to protest against the Jim Crow system. He published an essay on Souls of Black Folk and attacked Booker T. Washington. He wrote, "Washington's policies practically accepted the inferiority of the Negro, ignored cultivating the mind while concentrating only on skills for the hands, and taught blacks to accept prejudiced treatment…. What good did it do to work hard and become prosperous when it was precisely the middle-class black person who suffered the bitterest attacks during rioting? Not separation, but integration and the full rights of citizenship should be the new object. Black men must have the best education available, adopt the most challenging goals, and reject segregation as an insult to their manhood." "Separate schools for whites and blacks are not equal, cannot be made equal, and… are not intended to be equal."

NAACP

Many African Americans refused to follow Du Bois. But, a small group of blacks responded to his cause. A small group of white liberals also attracted to black liberalism and gave support to it; Oswald Garrison Villard was a leading person in the movement. In 1909, a group of white liberals joined with Du Bois and created the National Association for the Advancement of Coloured People (NAACP).

First World War

World War I broke out in August 1914. Americans were completely shocked to know that Europe, the centre of Western civilization, had suddenly jumped into a violent war. Of course, in 1914 every third American was of European origin and so the war put painful strains on everyone. Thousands of American scholars had gone to Germany to study, so it was a country whose life and culture were exceptionally well known in the United States even by non-Germans.

Woodrow Wilson honestly tried to keep away from the war and spent two and a half years searching for the solution. He heard that war-defeated British Isles would soon be forced to submission. Still Wilson hesitated. Then he learned that German government (through Zimmerman telegram) was trying to get Mexico to attack the United States by promising to give the American Southwest to Mexico if America entered the war. This stunning news provoked American opinion to enter into the war. Entire America was mobilized by war spirit. It entered the war at a critical time when the British and French were totally exhausted and near defeat. Entering the war was a big struggle for Wilson's liberalism, so he was forced to justify it by seeing the war as one fought for the highest and most crucial interests of all humankind. 'Therefore, he saw any critic of the war as an enemy of human welfare. An Espionage Act was passed in 1917, and a Sedition Act in 1918... Anyone aiding the enemy, obstructing recruiting, hampering the sale of war bonds, or even daring to "utter, print, write, or publish any disloyal, profane, scurrilous or abusive language' about the government, the Constitution, or the military was to be harshly punished.' Additionally, a nationwide spy system was established to search out heretics.

Many Progressives were excited by the social possibilities that the war effort opened up within the nation.

When war ended, 112,000 Americans died (by comparison, seven years of war in Vietnam produced 56,000 dead), and millions of Russians, Germans, Italians, Rumanians, Austro-Hungarians, Serbians, Belgians, French, and British dead. It is estimated that more than 41 million people died in World War I.

Wilson entered to the war in order to win a different kind of peace, which he was sure his allied leaders would agree with. Therefore, he called this reason as the United States is an "associated" instead of an "allied" power. Wilson wanted to prove to the suffering people of Europe that the West also could create a liberal and human peace settlement. In January 1918, his dramatic address caught the stimulated attention of the whole world and delivered his famous Fourteen Points as a basis for peace:

> "They called for an end to secret diplomacy and secret treaties, so that the world's peoples would know what their rulers were doing; a democratic world order so that the people would have a voice in all things affecting themselves; and a League of Nations to serve as an international parliament. In that body, all countries, large or small, weak or strong, would be treated with equal consideration. Furthermore, the League of Nations would make an international system of collective security possible. Each nation would no longer be forced to protect itself, or to join with several allies to protect themselves, but rather the whole world, through the League, would jointly put down aggression if a particular nation attacked another."

Furthermore, Wilson's Fourteen Points called for massive disarmament, which was the root cause of war; for freedom of the seas; for an end of all economic barriers between nations; and for self-government by the world's oppressed nationalities.

When he entered Europe after the war, millions of people cheered him with almost adoring passion. He was not only a peacemaker, but also a prophet.

Urban America in 1920s - Miracle of Age

Automobiles, automobiles, automobiles!!

"It was a miracle, an almost unbelievable sight, and astonishment to the whole world." Merely 65,000 motors cars and millions of horses pulled Americans to reach from point A to point B in 1908. By the 1920s, in a single year 2 million automobiles rolled off assembly lines. In 1929, 5.5 million yearly, and more than 26 million registered automobile owners were there. In 1929, there were 400,000 people working in the industry, which never existed when they were children.

This kind of sight could not be seen anywhere in the world. Millions of common people were moving easily and quickly from here to there, turning the key, conquering the distance, which was the dream of ancients. Even wealthy people did not have the ability to do that before. How this social revolution, which dramatically changed daily lives of people at home and around the world manifested?

Ford, Ford, Ford!!!

In 1893, the appearance of automobiles on American roads was considered as expensive toys. But in 1903, a 40 years old Michigan genius, Henry Ford, with only a high school education was a restless, quick-moving, slender and strong man made a bold and risky decision. Although he had been making cars since 1896, he made an impossible decision to manufacture a 'car for the great multitude.' How could anyone produce cars cheaply for millions of people?

Ford said, "First, you make one automobile like another automobile... make them all alike ... just like one pin is like another pin when it comes from a pin factory. Then you design not a cheap car, but a car that will be durable, easy to operate, simple to repair, with a big enough engine to make it really go — and then figure out how to make it at low cost." By 1908, he literally made it possible and offered it to the public: The Ford Model T., the most famous motor vehicle ever built. It had a strong 20-horsepower engine and a smooth and sturdy transmission, it was made not of wood but of tough vanadium steel, and it came only in black. Ford stopped all other models but Model T.

Nevertheless, the car was priced $950. It was too expensive for common people in the year 1909. Kelly writes, "And it still took over 12 hours simply to put together a single chassis. Ford could get out only about 12,000 of them a year from his Detroit plant. His network of Ford dealers, another innovation, was selling the Model T with evangelical spirit. Still they could not sell to the masses because of its cost."

Ford adopted innovative engineer Frederick W. Taylor's teachings 'scientific management': breaking down, analytically, the actual tasks a workman did, and making detailed time and motion studies and cost analysis. This repetitive motion of Taylorization greatly quickened the production and lowered costs, dehumanizing the worker.

However still more work had to be done to reach the market. After trying many different approaches,

> "he decided to put the several parts of the automobile magneto (it produced the spark which fired the gasoline) on a conveyor belt passing in front of workers, who would each put certain parts together, producing a completed article at the end of the line. The process was successful, and soon they were pulling the chassis through the plant with a rope and windlass, a simple measure that cut the 12-hour chassis assembly time in half. Shortly the whole assembly line had been put into steady, unbroken motion, so that by early 1914, a Ford Chassis

was being produced in an hour and a half. True mass production had been achieved. The revolution began seriously."

In the 1916, every three minutes one car came out of his production lines!! Then what about the price? Ford sold his car for an unbelievable price $360. Why did he choose such a low price? Kelly writes, "Not simply to encourage sales — he had absolutely no competition in the mass market yet, and the demand was so voracious he could certainly have charged more - but because, Ford said, society as a whole should be able to benefit from improved production techniques in American industry."

Henry Ford: Car Revolution

Stunning the entire American business class, he raised the wages to $5 a day, doubling the wages in Detroit at that time. Why? Because, if the goal is to reach the mass market, the masses should have enough income to buy the things produced. Consequently, Detroit had to bring fire hoses to break the crowd of job applicants' uproar outside the Henry Ford building gates.

Henry Ford was a genuine American hero. He was a poor but imaginative boy who grew up with hard work taking bold risks. He was America's most admired man, the miracle worker.

Margaret Sanger - Social Reformer

At the centre of this prospering economy, there was a mode of family life in America. Still Women's life continued as before producing more children. Even sending contraceptive information through the mails was also considered as a criminal offence because it was obscene and interfering with nature's (or god's) plan for human reproduction and regarded as immoral and disrespectful. They considered that a woman's duty was to get married, ready to have babies, and continue having them until menopause. If she had to face suffering and death during child delivery, it was her destiny. Large families were thought as a blessing and women should produce them.

During the Progressive Age, new ideas about human possibility and definitely about women were emerging. In the modernizing process, the ancient self-denying, stoical ethics were no longer enough. There was a nationwide demand for a more humane and more enjoyable life. 1900 onward non-Catholic middle-class women saw the possibilities of contraceptives and started using them. Their families began to shrink, down to one or two children, faster than the families of labourers.

But, this possibility of using contraceptives was not available to working women and farming women. Not surprisingly, a single woman finally shook the shyness of public discussion of sexual matters and demanded Americans boldly and wonderfully to change their ancient ideas and bring new possibilities for women.

Margaret Sanger was a high-spirited radical Irish woman. She had seen woman after woman destroyed by bearing babies, one after another, despite poverty, disease, and physical disability, until they died during childbirth or because of infection after an abortion. She wrote large families are not as blessing, but as related to poverty, toil, unemployment, drunkenness, cruelty, fighting, jails; and the small ones of the middle-class with cleanliness, leisure, freedom, light, space, and sunshine. In New York she observed lines of anxious women standing outside the slum abortionist's operating rooms. She also heard women asking 'what is the secret middle-class women have? How can they keep their families small?'

What is a more pathetic discovery was that even the male activists who fought against inhumane working conditions and revolted against the exploitations of capitalism were indifferent to the sufferings of women. What Margaret Sanger wanted to establish was that women as human beings should have complete control over their own bodies. Her immediate goal was to make contraceptive information and devices available to the poor as they were available to the middle-class. This required changing the public mind about moral rightness, cleanliness and to speak about the subject of Birth Control, the word Sanger itself created in American language.

Sanger founded a magazine, 'Woman Rebel' in 1914, to discuss her purpose. Suddenly it was closed under the Comstock Act. To avoid prosecution, she escaped to England and there in a more sophisticated and liberal society she collected extra information about the contraceptives.

In 1916, she returned to America and opened the nation's first birth control clinic in Brooklyn and started to give advice and contraceptives. Again, she was arrested and sentenced to a month in jail. These irritations redoubled her determination. She became a spectacular public figure and captured people's attention, and regularly she was in the newspapers. Wealthy liberal women who approved her sentiments were eager to support her. The frustrating reality for birth control promoters was the working class women who were dreadfully ignorant about the subject and simply puzzled by the topic. They did not understand what birth control is and ashamed of learning more about it.

Margaret Sanger organized the American Birth Control League. Historians observe that again and again, she argued in her national campaign for "the small family system prevalent among the middle classes, equality for women in the family and in society, and the pursuit of personal satisfaction as a right." Her opponents argued, "That the married woman's place was in the home, her duty was to bear many children, and social duty should always overrule the hedonistic impulses of the individual." She had a long fight in the 1920s to reach her first goal: creating birth control clinics where police would not interfere and leave alone. Finally, Sanger's ideas won within the framework of "Family Planning".

Sanger's accomplishment was a milestone incident in women's history, and in the history of marriage and the family.

Immigration

The Statue of Liberty represents a Roman liberty goddess Libertas. She holds a torch with her right hand, and in her left hand carries a tablet inscribed in Roman numerals with "JULY IV MDCCLXXVI" (July 4, 1776), which is the date of the U.S. Declaration of Independence. The statue became an icon of freedom in the United States and a greeting sight to immigrant refugees from abroad.

> "Give me your tired, your poor,
> Your huddled masses yearning to breathe free,
> The wretched refuse of your teeming shore.
> Send these, the homeless, tempest-tossed to me,
> I lift my lamp beside the golden door!"

Full poem written by Emma Lazarus:

Not like the brazen giant of Greek fame,
With conquering limbs astride from land to land;
Here at our sea-washed, sunset gates shall stand
A mighty woman with a torch, whose flame
Is the imprisoned lightning, and her name
Mother of Exiles. From her beacon-hand
Glows world-wide welcome; her mild eyes command
The air-bridged harbour that twin cities frame.

"Keep, ancient lands, your storied pomp!" cries she
With silent lips. "Give me your tired, your poor,
Your huddled masses yearning to breathe free,
The wretched refuse of your teeming shore.
Send these, the homeless, tempest-toss to me,
I lift my lamp beside the golden door!"

In 1920s, the rural Americans living on the farms and in small towns noticed the new way of life mushrooming in urban America with great distress: its sexual behaviour, its women and youth, its black people, and above all its presence of many strange new peoples from abroad, with their bizarre ideas and styles of life. In reality, even though America had always been a land of immigrants, it never had such a perplexing variety of people entering the United States.

Italians: The new wave of Italians was so numerous, and they received frank bombardment of insults. They were from the poverty-infected south of Italy and from Sicily, where illiteracy and narrowness dominated life, and a darker skin. Sometimes Italian children had to attend black schools. Since the Italians had created the highest rate of murders in Europe and the US, they were pointed out as violent people. One senator referred to southern Italians as 'only half-civilized.'

Jews: The arrival of an enormous flood of eastern European orthodox Jews whose diet, dress, and styles of hair as well as speech were thought strange and untidy, even to Native Americans. Now discrimination increased. Help wanted ads specified "Christians only" in newspapers; Universities established quotas; city neighbourhoods became crowded Jewish ghettos. In spite of all these roadblocks, Jews constantly demonstrated their hard work and their passion for education and willingness to reach high levels among all American ethnic groups. They were attempting to prove that they are Americans by discarding their cultural identity and heritage. They followed American ways of dress, worship, and family life. But Jews were excluded from social contact with Americans. John Higham, a cultural historian, suggests that this happened because people usually believed that Jews were more intelligent and more capable than other peoples, and so they felt more threatened by Jews.

Mexicans: A historic Immigration Act was passed to stop the arrival of these strange people from European countries, in 1924. By discontinuing the European labourers who usually worked on the lowest paid and unwanted jobs, the door was open to the non-WASP[27] Catholic population in the United States. This law did not exclude Mexican workers. Now, immigration from Mexico increased sharply.

Very small number of Mexicans became American citizens. Probably this was because their homeland was next door, and the minority group was sharply different in its attitudes. For so many reasons, Mexican's ability to improve their condition was practically non-existent - particularly when American labour unions refused to admit them.

One interesting article, "The Labyrinth of Solitude: Life and Thought in Mexico [1961].

> "Millions of peoples entering America from many cultures had an often bewildering experience. America was so different from southern Italy, from the Orient, or from the ancient Mexican way of living that for many centuries had cantered in and radiated outward from the high valleys of central Mexico. One of Mexico's great poets, Octavio Paz, has reflected upon his two years in America in the 1940s. In Los Angeles he observed his country's "Mexicanism—delight in decorations, carelessness and pomp, negligence, passion and reserve" - existing beside but never mixing with "the North American world based on precision and efficiency." The Mexican, he wrote, "succumbs very easily to sentimental effusions," and therefore adopts a stern reserve, shown in the "scowling expression" of young Mexicans living in southern California. They hide, Paz suggests, a "sense of inferiority - real or imagined" — induced in part by the Mexican's "dazzled impression of [America's] grandeur...When I arrived in the United States I was surprised above all by the self-assurance and confidence of the [American] people, by their apparent happiness and apparent adjustment to the world around them. [They are critical of their society, but]...it is a criticism that respects the existing systems and never touches the roots... [The] United States is a society that wants to realize its ideals, has no wish to exchange them for others, and is confident of

surviving, no matter how dark the future may appear." By contrast, Paz goes on, in the Mexican's character, derived from Mexico's long history of bloody exploitation by dictators, is a "willingness to contemplate horror: he is even familiar and complacent in his dealings with it. The bloody Christs in our village churches, the macabre humour in some of our newspaper headlines, our wakes, the custom of eating skull-shaped cakes and candies on the Day of Dead, are habits inherited from the Indians and Spaniards and are now an inseparable part of our being. Our cult of death is also a cult of life, in the same way that love is a hunger for life and a longing for death…The North Americans are credulous, and we are believers; they love fairy tales and detective stories and we love myths and legends…We are suspicious and they are trusting. We are sorrowful and sarcastic, and they are happy and full of jokes. North Americans want to understand and we want to contemplate. They are activists and we are quietists; we enjoy our wounds and they enjoy their inventions. They believe in hygiene, health, work and contentment, but perhaps they have never experienced true joy, which is intoxication, a whirlwind. In the hubbub of a fiesta night our voices explode into brilliant lights, and life and death mingle together, while their vitality becomes a fixed smile that denies old age and death but that changes life to motionless stone…North Americans consider the world to be something that can be perfected, and… we consider it to be something that can be redeemed."

It seems this poem is over exaggeration. After the 1940s, Mexicans dramatically improved their status and wealth, and began to demand American dream.

The Ku Klux Klan (KKK)

Every city in America was populated by different types of new babbling of tongues, languages, styles of life, cultures, and religious congregations, which traditional Americans saw with bewilderment. As a result, the traditional WASP community in the countryside decided to impose uniformity on the United States and save the country. The Ku Klux Klan (KKK) appeared as the most violent tool on the new peoples and the new cultures attacking American life. Initially, it was a Democratic activity in the South, and strongly Republican in other areas. The Protestant origin KKK organized boycotts on Catholics, physically assaulted Catholic churches and priests, burned crosses, hymns, and kneeling prayers. Almost five million of people registered in KKK in the middle of 1920s. But many law enforcement rules curbed the KKK growth.

A Rush of Confidence

In 1920, most of the people in United States enjoyed the miracles of the new technology that became the part of their daily lives - unlike ever seen before their generations: electric lights, the car in the driveway, airplane rides when they landed on the nearby airfields, smooth hard-surfaced roads, the magical floating and exciting scenes in the movie theatres, and touch of a switch could bring music in the homes. Obviously, the machine age had arrived with full blessings. As an historian Merle Curti wrote: "The machine actually increased the power of ordinary Americans. The movie in effect gave him a magically far-seeing eye, the talkie and the radio multiplied the powers of his ears and thereby opened up worlds hitherto unknown… No wonder that the machine became celebrated as the eighth wonder of the world, destined to set man free!"

In 1927, people in America watched with a positive feeling that Charles Lindbergh was flying the first nonstop airplane flight over the Atlantic. Charles' amazing achievement opened up a new and fruitful future for humankind. In fact, the progress appeared unavoidable because the American system signified producing more and more marvels. Urban business companies experienced a proud responsibility and declared the arrival of the New Era. Technology had opened many opportunities with many doors and opportunities looked endless. America reached the peak in popularity, never achieved before and may be never again. One businessman worshipped business and equally hated the government. He said, "The man who builds a factory builds a temple. The man who works there worships there."

The Adoration of Success

In the meanwhile, the trend of prosperity and personal success induced popular literature. It declared that the spending was the greatest of the economic advantages, not thrift or savings. A writer quoted, "The reason for America's prosperity is that we have committed ourselves to a standard of living far beyond our wildest pre-war dreams. …. It is impossible to call Americans back to a petty thrift, and I personally am glad of it." Personal success stories appeared in newspapers, magazines. One editor said that instead of stories of misery, hardship, and struggle, now the stories of success and happiness are pouring in. "You, Business Executives, sitting at your desks, thinking ever in terms of factories and output and financial setup, you have been making a fairy tale come true!"

Powerful industrial leaders and financiers received plentiful admiration from the public. 'Without these leaders and dreamers, the mass would eat their heads off, and as we have seen in the history, it would decline into barbarism. ... The masses are the recipients of this success, and very few are investors.' Henry Ford was a most admired and influential person because he had proved extraordinary success and had a positive vision of a new life for all humankind. Ford said,

> "Modern mass production has opened unlimited possibilities. Abundance: that was the new economic fact. High output, low prices, and high wages: This was the secret. These fundamentals are all summed up in the single word SERVICE. Serving The Public, Not Grabbing The Highest Possible Profits: This Was The Road To Success."

1 & 2. First Flight from New York to Paris in 1927, 3. 1850s: Railroad expansion. People had the confidence and convinced that "If They Jumped Forward, The Future Will Catch Them." 4. Moon Landing 1969.

Confidence among Intellectuals

To new intellectual practical psychology became a popular trend. Books explained everything from the psychology of golf to selling of life insurance.

Psychologists conducted intelligence tests and used medical devices to confidently forecast personal success and to advise businessmen. The behaviourist J.B. Watson said that by proper training anyone could be transformed into anything he or she wishes to be. If appropriate scientific training were given, there are no limits to human potentialities.

Sociologists were also developing national importance on the grounds of scientific technique 'Survey', in which quantitative studies of all sides of social aspects were made. Kelly writes, "Sociologists were confident that a point would soon be reached when trained minds, ruminating over these growing mountains of accurate social information, would distil from the social laws that govern human life. These, in turn, would allow sociologists to provide guidance to politicians, who would enact appropriate legislation."

John Dewey was certain that 'people could mould the future in any way they wished if they depended on the proficient intelligence of experts and used central planning. He believed at the heart of everything should be a new educational system that would train young people to test all hypotheses by experience and scientific data. Ignorance and bad thinking were the only obstacles of social progress. Everything constricting in what was old and traditional be bumped under the term cultural halt, an annoying stumbling block to be swept away. In the end, reason would wash out human and political tensions.'

In big-city churches and seminaries the Social Gospel was victorious. It saw humanity not as incurably perverted by its nature, but as damaged only by ignorance of how to live a truly righteous life. They envisioned the future could be more perfect. The priests of god should work confidently in social reform to generate "a growing perfection in the collective life of humanity, in our laws, in the customs of society, in the institutions of education for the administration of mercy."

The US-USSR Relation

One event of historic importance happened in American history in 1917. So far, American vista had been Great Britain and Western Europe only. Germany had fascinated American reformers and intellectuals. Then the war with Germany changed everything and ended that country's role as an example. But British did not disappear from American's view. Several American intellectual elites - writers, philosophers, economists, jurists, journalists, historians, and social reformers sustained their relationship with them. Americans never gave any attention to Russia before the 1917 revolution, except condemning its tyrannical czar's rule and its anti-Semitism. After the Russian Revolution, American reformers and intellectuals started to travel to the Soviet Union to study what was going on there and started to judge America from the world's first communist revolution.

It is fascinating to understand that Russian leaders also paid close attention to America to what was going on. One historian mentioned that Americans who visited the USSR in 1920s were surprised to see the degree of Russian interest, fascination, respect, and fondness of their hosts displaying appreciation towards American visitors. Why? It was because Russians liked the words of industrialization and Fordization more than communism. A historian Hans Rogger observed and described an image of America in Russian mind:

> "America implied competence, responsibility, punctuality, accuracy, and diligence. America meant to work steadily and efficiently, with an economy of materials and of energy, but also with daring inventiveness and a readiness to depart from routine and bureaucratism. America signified youth and invincibility, the triumph of the machine and the possibility of freeing humanity from the burdens of poverty and toil; it stood for mass production, the assembly line, and Fordizatsia - one of the words of power... with which Soviet orators spellbound their audience."

A completely new international relationship emerged, and it was one of the historical events for some time.

The Great Strong Economic Growth

The 1920s was a New Era of Efficiency. In Herbert Hoover's Commerce Department, the catchword was "efficiency" aiming to eliminate industrial waste and duplication, and to introduce scientific management, planning and rationalization. The continuous success story of the 1920s in America was solid, deep, astonishing economic growth.

The Republican view of the outside world was an impossible mix of nationalist and internationalist. The force of events unavoidably changed American involvement in international politics requiring a major role. The League of Nations was shunned; membership in the World Court was discussed, which in fact rejected eventually; and many other drastic steps were taken to establish foreign relationships.

The Great Depression - Economic Crash

In 1929, there were many economic danger signals. For the last six years, money was pouring into the stock market from millions of investors in the United States and Europe. Profit looked endless. The Federal Reserve Board made loans easily available. Author Robert Kelly writes,

> "With no public supervision, the stock markets could make purchases ridiculously easy. Investors could put down no more than 10 percent on a stock and the stockbrokers themselves made up the balance by issuing loans. As the speculative craze mounted, buyers competed so eagerly for loans that interest rates soared from about 5 percent to 20

percent. Money poured in from abroad in order to be lent out at high interest rates. Where normally the price of a stock might stand at eight or ten times its earnings, prices now soared to as much as twenty times earnings. This mania spread everywhere. Following the stock market and making speculative plunges became as common as following the baseball scores."

The vital element to this whole speculative spring was the confidence. Soon it began to diminish and the consequence was predictable. On Wednesday, October 23, 1929, a rush of "sell" orders flooded Wall Street, and since there were not many buyers, stock prices began to tumble. Then the disaster began. Bankers, such as House of Morgan with huge resources tried to make huge purchases to stop the fall. White house, the Treasury Department, and Economists were giving statements not to panic. But the fear was enormous.

Some scholars explained the reason as "the Great Depression that actually developed was caused by underconsumption. That is, in the 1920s businessmen kept too much of their profits to themselves instead of paying them out in higher wages, so that ordinary Americans could not buy the huge output of the factories. Income, it has long been said, was so highly unbalanced—most of it being placed in the hands of the wealthy, who then misspent it in disastrous speculation— that fewer and fewer could buy what business wished to sell. Farmers in particular were a depressed class, because farm prices had been slumping so long, and this made the economy even more likely to tumble into complete collapse when a triggering event like the stock market crisis occurred."

The economy plunged lower and lower, year after year, the hope of the 1920s disappeared, and hopelessness began to zoom in the country by late 1930. Unemployment devastated people's life. Millions of people were unemployed throughout the industrialized nations of the world. One person looking for the job lamented, "... and I walked out into depression ... I would get up at five in the morning in San Francisco and head for a Sugar Refinery factory, outside the gates there would be a thousand men. You know damn well that there are only three of our jobs. The guy would come out with two little Pinkerton cops and say 'I need two guys for the bull gang/unskilled workers. Two guys to go into the hole.' A thousand men would fight like a pack of Alaskan dogs to get through there ..."

The tragic effect of continued unemployment was eventually deep humiliation, loss of self-respect, and hopelessness. In the beginning they waited patiently looking for the job; then started an intense search for a job; then became discouraged and emotionally disorganized; and finally, they dropped into lifelessness. An English worker said, "Whenever I am out of work, I feel like a bloody dog." The unemployed became bitter, gloomy, and leaned to drinking habits and wild rage.

In America, where it was taught that each person was responsible for his or her own success, and where there were no social systems for taking care of the jobless, the pain of unemployment was more penetrating and unavoidable than in any other country.

In the year 1932 alone, in cities, towns, out in the farms, 273,000 American families had been expelled from their homes. Twenty five percent of Americans had no jobs, urban welfare systems were out of money, and panic was widespread. William Manchester writes,

> "Millions stayed alive by living like animals. In the Pennsylvania countryside they were eating wild weed-roots and dandelions; in Kentucky they chewed violet tops, forget-me-nots, wild lettuce, and weeds which heretofore had been left to grazing cattle. City mothers hung around cocks, waiting for spoiled produce to be discarded and then fighting homeless dogs for possession of it.... Whole families were seen plunging into refuse dumps, gnawing at bones and watermelon rinds; a Chicago widow always removed her glasses so she wouldn't see the maggots."

To Americans the depression was more than simply the failure of business; it was like an earthquake that uprooted and destroyed their dreams; their old expectations and beliefs were completely meaningless. Their whole world was falling apart.

Miracle Man: President Franklin Delano Roosevelt (FDR)

In this kind of national situation, Franklin Delano Roosevelt (FDR), a tall man with large shoulders, reached inaugural platform in front of the Capitol building with his crutches. He placed one hand on an old Bible, raised the other hand recited the presidential oath in a strong, clear voice standing in front of Chief Justice Charles Evans Hughes:

> "I, Franklin Delano Roosevelt, do solemnly swear that I will faithfully execute the office of President of the United States and will, to the best of my ability, preserve, protect and defend the Constitution of the United States. So help me God!"

Then he turned to the multitude of people and to the radio microphones, which for the first time in America carried the president's words to millions of people throughout the nation and across the Atlantic to Europe. He said, "this great nation will endure as it has endured, will revive and will prosper. So, first of all, let me assert my firm belief that the only thing we have to fear is fear itself…. ."

FDR was a progressive democrat, a kind man who understood personal suffering. At the age of thirty-nine the infantile paralysis caused him permanently crippled, but not poverty. As an only child, he was nurtured by a loving family in his father's Hudson Valley estate. He was dynamic and quick to learn, entered politics as a senator in 1910. Woodrow Wilson appointed young Roosevelt as assistant secretary to the navy. In 1921, paralysis struck him down, but he refused to quit and went to a year-long physical therapy program. Soon he returned back to politics.

The Banking Crisis: After entering the White House, Roosevelt's first challenge was to reopen the banks. He did not insist on nationalizing the banks, but he advised to dissolve the weak ones, and to help the good ones. Within a few days the president had bills before Congress authorizing him to investigate the banks, permit perfect banks to reopen, give loans from the Reconstruction Finance Corporation to those who needed help, and dissolve any banks that were hopelessly bankrupt.

In his first famous Hundred Days, fifteen major laws were reached on the books; they dealt with banking, the gold standard, relief, mortgages, hydroelectric power and regional planning, the stock market, and national planning in industry and agriculture. FDR's policy was the government must intervene as a manager: it must regulate, compensate, and control; and all with the goal of safeguarding the public interest and maintaining stability together with progress.

Agricultural Crisis: The basic problem for farmers was enormous overproduction, which was causing a catastrophic depression. Plantation income remained at one-third what it had been in 1929; prices had dropped more than 50 percent. Soon after the inauguration, Roosevelt proposed Congress to plan a strong federal control of agriculture. The producers of seven basic crops, wheat, cotton, corn, hogs, rice, tobacco, milk and dairy products, would receive federal payments if they reduced production. The mission was to raise farm income to 100 percent of uniformity by restricting production.

Relief Programs: The most important program that Roosevelt took was helping 15 million people who were out of work. It was the opportunity to achieve his favourite cause - the conservation of national resources. A vast number of young adults were roaming aimlessly in the streets. He engaged them with healthful and socially productive work in the forests.

Within days of the inauguration, as a response to the president, Congress established the Civilian Conservation Corps (CCC) and by June 1933 more than 300,000 young men started working in more than a thousand forest camps. They planted trees, built reservoirs, erected flood control works, constructed bridges and fire towers, cleared out plant diseases, cleaned beaches, and rebuilt campgrounds. He also established a Federal Emergency Relief Administration, which would grant $500 million to the states for relief programs. Some shouted, "It is socialism." But the immediate problem was very urgent, and the bill passed without any obstruction.

Hundreds of thousands of projects were instigated: building or improving village side roads, employing teachers in deprived schools, founding schoolhouses, developing playgrounds, and constructing hundreds of airports, parks, waterways, and swimming pools.

A Prosperous Economy

According to research in economics, it was astonishing point to realize that the American economy rebounded dramatically from the 1933 depth of the Depression.

Eleanor Roosevelt

Franklin Roosevelt's wife Eleanor Roosevelt provided an exceptional quality of vigour to the White House that was never seen before. She was a teacher for ten years before arriving to White House; a publicist and a business executive; had a radio contract; she was a contributor to a newspaper column "My Day"; and she was an editor of a magazine, "Babies - Just Babies." She was eyes and ears to a wheelchair stuck husband FDR, and she travelled endlessly throughout America, visiting, talking, inspecting, and returning home to report to her husband what she had seen. 'She insisted on speaking to women reporters, who were excluded by the male reporters from their meetings with the president.'

Eleanor was a sympathetic woman; she criticized labour sweatshops, advised women to buy only from merchants who gave their employees decent working conditions; advocated the end of child labour; and appealed for open-minded foreign policy to help a grievously distressed world. Though she had a warm graciousness as a tall First Lady, she thought herself an unattractive woman. Many people, both men and women, mocked her saying she neglected her husband and family and rebuked her reformism activities.

She constantly spoke to women encouraging them to take a reforming role and help to raise the nation from Depression. A 40,000 words book,

"It is Up to the Women," which included her articles and speeches appeared after she entered the White House. Along with the advice on menus and household budgets, it appealed to women to lead the fight for social justice, support labour unions, create consumer's groups to scrutinize prices, and get into politics. She said, the understanding heart of women and their special momentum must mould the new order of things; force to end the war; help youth; toil to abolish poverty and to improve the rights of minorities. Eleanor said, selfishness, greed, unchecked hunger for profit have brought the United States to its present calamity. She urged Americans to learn the lesson and embrace "interdependence" of the community to face and solve the national crisis. Actually, Eleanor Roosevelt was more radical than her husband in reform ideals.

Her earnestness of appeals for progressive education, battle against illiteracy, speeches at women's jails, lecture tours throughout the country were endless. Wherever she went, her refined language and remarkable clarity of speech, her high-pitched voice, and her genuine dignity captured the public's attention and affection. Undoubtedly, Eleanor Roosevelt remarkably extended and elevated the ideal of the woman in public office.

Social Security Act

One of the most important projects FDR launched in his Second Hundred Days was the Social Security Act. Frances Perkins, the first woman secretary of labour was demanding to make a wide attack on the problem of personal security, particularly among the helpless: the old, the physically handicapped, and the mothers of children with no father to support. For a long time, American reformers were learning that the unemployment and old-age insurance assistance existed in Great Britain and Germany. It was clear that in the United States such social humanitarian programs were absent. Perkins said, "I see no reason why every child, from the day he is born, should not be a member of the social security system… cradle to the grave…" She suggested that there should be an insurance system, solidly based on regular contributions by both employees and employers, so that no future politician could take the program's funds away for some other purpose. Thus, it was to be self-supporting, by means of its own special taxes.

In 1935, when the social security bill was produced before the Congress, a big turbulence erupted from conservatives:

1. "It will destroy initiative, thrift, and individual responsibility"
2. "No one will work; no one will save to provide for old age or widowhood.

3. "There will be moral decay, financial bankruptcy, and the collapse of the United States government.
4. "It would sooner or later bring about the inevitable abandonment of private capitalism."
5. "The downfall of Rome began with such measures."
6. Never in the history of the world has any measure been brought in here so insidiously designed as to prevent business recovery, to enslave workers, and to prevent any possibility of the employers providing jobs for the American people.
7. .....

Nevertheless, Roosevelt altered some parts and managed to pass the bill with a large majority from both sides of the house. Its final document of the bill solved the arguments that had angered over social security:

> "It assigned to the states the responsibility of implementing the system. Washington would only collect and redistribute the money to the states, on a matching basis.....
>
> "It was county-level officials who established the welfare departments, staffed them, supervised them, and paid their employees. The result was a crazy-quilt unemployment-compensation and welfare system with widely varying benefits, often warped in strange ways by segregation and other forms of racism. However, by this means state and county governments were brought directly in touch with millions of Americans never seen before — a helping, supportive way — and this initiated a long learning process that has had an immense impact on American life. The old, the jobless, the sick, the needy, the blind, the mothers who had children to care for and no husbands, the children themselves: all were now aided by the Social Security Board, through local agencies."

Artists and Intellectuals in Depression America

During the period of Depression, the mentality of art for art's sake abandoned, and there emerged a new type of creative energy in the form of plays, novels, articles, and paintings awakening a new concept of Community. Ruth Benedict, an anthropologist, in her "Patterns of Culture", described the numerous ways in which the mental life is shaped by the surrounding culture in which people live. Writers discovered traditional America: its farms, villages, common folk, farm implements, square dances, harvest celebrations; its sweating labourers in the steel mills, in the mines, in the automobile factories. John Steinbeck's "Grapes of Wrath" was about social protest as well as a loving representation of common folk in close relation to the land. A new kind of poetry celebrated the traditional, rural beauty of America. The development of technology, efficiency, science, which was the success symbol, became the enemy, and culture of values, speech, life, became the new hope. The outburst of writings, films, recordings, and paintings portrayed every aspect of American life; common people were treated with a warmth and sensitivity unlike the disregard attitude of the 1920s.

There was a new understanding towards the group consciousness and cooperation that made intellectuals extremely exciting. The CCC, which sent boys to forests; the Tennessee Valley Authority, erecting dams throughout the wilderness to control floods and bringing confidence to deprived farmers; and many other programs brought hope to American community. There was despair in the Depression, but there was excitement also.

Breakdown between USA and Russia

In the middle of 1930s, Joseph Stalin's decision to centralize Soviet agriculture system by taking away all land from the peasants and forcing them into huge shared farms caused tragic sufferings and millions of deaths in Russia. Simultaneously, he resumed organized terror with great brutality erasing all internal opponents to his rule and instituting absolute dictatorship. People of great honor standing in the movement were put through public 'show trials,' compelled to confess to unbelievable anti-Soviet crimes, and put to death. Thousands of people were killed or sent to labor in the notorious Siberian camps.

In America, the Communist Party members and writers rationalized all of this as compulsory to remove the corruption from the world's first Communist experiment. But to most liberals who were friendly towards the Soviet experiments assuming its goals were humanitarian, the purging, removing, and killing ordeals were a horror. In the end, some liberals concluded that the Soviet system and democracy and human rights are incompatible, so they turned away from it. Formerly pro-Soviet writers like Louis Fischer learned to treasure freedom above all else. They claimed, 'Without civil rights there is no economic security even when unemployment has disappeared. The dictatorship in Germany, Italy, Japan, and the USSR have taught us to love democracy more.'

World War II and America

The Great Depression terminated the shaky and uncertain peace of the

1920s. Eventually, the collapsing economy, widespread misery and disappointment, and short-tempered forces triggered World War II. The Western democracies reacted to the hardships of the Depression by creating programs for internal reform; Germany, Italy, and Japan reacted by initiating crusades of external aggression. Americans wanted to be free of foreign wars, and to ensure non-involvement in the war, Congress passed a number of neutrality acts. But the terror and panic executed by Adolf Hitler, gradually declined isolationism. Finally, it became inevitable to both Americans and to the President to get involved in the war to survive as a nation if Hitler gained control over Europe. In the meanwhile, he pursued Japan's aggression also. But, on December 7, 1941, Japan attacked Pearl Harbour; Germany and Italy obeyed their treaty commitments to Japan by declaring war on the United States; and America was thrown into war.

The West Coast was literally hysterical fearing that any moment the Japanese military would appear on the coast and attack the coastline. When Japan attacked Pearl Harbour on December 7, 1941, America responded by using an atomic bomb on Hiroshima and Nagasaki.

Shortly after the Hiroshima bombing, President Truman issued a statement:

> "Sixteen hours ago, an American airplane dropped a bomb on Hiroshima, an important Army base... It is an atomic bomb. It is a harnessing of the basic power of the universe. The force from which the sun draws its power has been loosed against those who brought war to the Far East. It was developed in a race against the Germans involving over a hundred thousand workers, scientists, and engineers.
>
> "What has been done is the greatest achievement of organized science in history...We are no prepared to obliterate more rapidly and completely every productive enterprise the Japanese have above ground in any city...If they do not now accept our terms they may expect a rain of ruin from the air, the like of which has never been seen on this earth. Behind this air attack will follow sea and land forces in such numbers and power as they have not yet seen and with the fighting skill of which they are already well aware.
>
> "The fact that we release atomic energy ushers in a new era in man's understanding of nature's forces. Atomic energy may in the future supplement the power that now comes from coal, oil, and falling water........."

Finally, Japan surrendered.

Robert Oppenheimer

Born in 1904 in New York to a wealthy family, Robert Oppenheimer was a remarkable man, undeniably genius, a gifted scientist who also wrote poetry, and mastered many languages. He read Plato in the original Greek language and Hindu Bhagavad-Gita in Sanskrit and created the first centre of theoretical physics at the University of California, Berkley. He liked to wander on high mountains and hills of New Mexico on horseback. In 1942 during World War II, he invited physicists from all over the nation to Los Alamos. There within a guarded fence, he formed a community of scientists and engineers whose responsibility was how to make and build atomic bombs from fissionable uranium. As a result, he remained spellbound before the enormous fireball of testing the atomic bomb in the New Mexico desert, horrified by its power. As he watched, Oppenheimer immediately remembered the words from the Hindu book Bhagavad-Gita:

> If the radiance of a thousand suns
> Were to burst into the sky
> That would be like
> The splendour of the Mighty One —
> I am become Death, the Destroyer of worlds.

Later he realized that he was wrong. Although he thought that America should have the bomb before Hitler got it, he was always haunted by the ethical question of being an armaments maker. After Hiroshima and Nagasaki vaporized on August 6 and 9, 1945, he became so popular and his picture appeared in the national press making him a charismatic hero of the new age.

Soon the guilt at the thought of thousands of dead replaced the former excitement of success. Now, almost all scientists talked of nothing but how to stop the atomic race, how to keep the world from burning itself, how to put the sinister genie back in the bottle. Oppenheimer said to Harry Truman, "Mr. President, I feel I have blood on my hands." He tried consistently to make atomic energy denationalized and placed under international control, and to stop making even greater horror, the hydrogen bomb. But, because his wife and close relatives were Communist activists, he had been under suspicion. It is said that from his laboratory, Soviet spy-scientists had sent crucial atomic information to the Russians. They alleged that Oppenheimer is opposing the hydrogen bombs because Russia is opposing. Therefore, he was removed from the atomic program from the Eisenhower administration's order in 1954. But in 1960, the Atomic Energy Commission awarded him the Enrico Fermi Award.

Douglas MacArthur

Douglas MacArthur was an unbelievably bossy, publicity-monger, and a person thirsting for glorification. At the same time, he was one of the great generals of history, a brilliant commander who guided the army to sweeping victory with remarkably low casualties. His greatest influence on the world came in peacetime. MacArthur was posted as a Supreme Commander in Japan after the war and he significantly reorganized Japanese life. Unlike other Westerners, he knew Japanese culture, folklore, politics, and economy for a long time. After the enormous air attacks and the atomic bombs, the Japanese were crushed and shocked people. Immediately, his compassionate and courteous actions to rebuild Japan made him a national hero.

MacArthur considered his great obligation was to introduce *demokrashi* to Japan. He ended the *zaibatsu*, old Japanese financial system of outdated authoritarianism; decisively stopped Shinto and emperor worship and made them no longer the state religion; freed labor urging it to unionize; and dissolved both the former industrial monopolies and the great landholdings, distributing land to those who tilled it. As soon as Japanese troops were demobilized, he ended all former Japanese restrictions on political, civil, and religious freedom. Political prisoners were released, and newspapers were told they could publish anything they liked, because the Supreme Commander wanted an informed electorate. American republicanism had come to Japan.

A new philosophy was taught in the public schools: that the government is the servant, not the master of the people. MacArthur wrote a democratic constitution in Japan that rejected war forever 'as a sovereign right.' Even today the same constitution is in use in Japan, which was the single most important accomplishment by him, and some people point that his land reforms were also significant. MacArthur's involvement to liberate women was genuine. In 1946, fourteen million Japanese women joined men to go to the polls. After giving women the right to vote, he opened high schools and universities, removed contract marriage and concubinage.

Now, Japan is so westernized beyond recognition even though traditional Japanese values still make that country greatly different from the West. This responsibility and esteem goes to a dominating American general where a few men in history have left such a great and lasting impact.

Deming is also best known for his work with the leaders of Japanese industry in Japan after WWII. In August 1950, Deming delivered a speech in the Convention Center in Tokyo, on what he called "Statistical Product Quality Administration." Many in Japan credit Deming as one of the inspirations for the Japanese post-war economic miracle of 1950 to 1960. Japan rose from the ashes of war to become the second-largest economy in the world through processes partially influenced by the ideas Deming taught:

1. Better design of products to improve service
2. Higher level of uniform product quality
3. Improvement of product testing in the workplace and in research centers
4. Greater sales through global markets

United Nations

After World War II, all world leaders assembled at Yalta to make the world war-free zone. The Soviet Union suggested a policy of 'balance of power' to safeguard the USSR. In this policy, 'the great powers come to agreement on the regions of the world they will individually dominate, and by their own strength they impose order and peace in those regions. In this system, peace in the world at large is kept by periodic negotiations between the great powers.'

Franklin Roosevelt and his secretary of State Cordell Hull differed with this policy because this policy had caused the two world wars. Alternatively, they suggested a one-world, in which all nations are considered to be equal; no nation is dominated by any other, and an international body, the United Nations, keeps the order. Roosevelt believed only such a world order protects world peace and alleviates the fear of aggression by great powers. Roosevelt worked hard to convince Russian leaders and to establish a good relationship with it, yielding gracefully to their demands wherever possible, and laying the foundation for a peaceful post-war world in which all nations would work together on a mutual understanding.

Russia was an ancient country with no protection from geographic boundaries. So, Russia was afraid that Germany may once again start a new invasion and they wanted to punish Germany. Roosevelt also wanted to punish Germany, but British remembered that after World War I, the economically poor Germany pulled all Europe into depression.

Finally, "The Americans won approval for the project they considered crucial — formation of the United Nations. At first the Russians argued closely on the matter of voting: they were openly scornful of small nations and recoiled from the prospect of being outvoted by them. When they learned that the great powers — to include France, China, the USSR, Britain, and the United States — would have the right of veto over any actions by the United Nations Security Council, they dropped their objections."

The United Nations was established in April 1945 and everyone returned home happily.

Unfortunately, just after two months good relationships between Russia and the West broke down when Russia refused to install a democratically based government in Poland that ended in the Cold War later.

The Sputnik Shock

In October 1957, Russia launched the first globe-circling satellite Sputnik I, which electrified the world with spectacular incidents. Around the world, hundreds of thousands of people watched the tiny, shining satellite that appeared over the sky and then followed its calm, unyielding path across the sky, conveying the successful message of Russian brilliant technological achievement. Khrushchev claimed happily that this spectacular event demonstrated the superiority of the Communist system, and he began an intensive publicity to encourage uncertain neutralist nations to join the Soviet side.

This Sputnik launch created a national crisis in the United States. President Eisenhower increased defence spending, particularly for missiles and nuclear submarines. He strongly pushed through a centralization of the Defence Department giving the secretary of defence vast new powers to join the efforts of the military services. When the army successfully stationed a small satellite in orbit in January 1958, the tension was relieved.

Cold War

How did the Cold War start? Historian Kelly writes, "In May 1960 the president Eisenhower left for Paris, where he met with the British, the French, and Khrushchev. At this moment occurred one of those events, relatively minor in themselves, that deflect world history. An American U-2 reconnaissance plane, flying higher over Russian territory and deep within its borders, was shot down. Eisenhower refused to take refuge in the customary denial of responsibility. The Soviet premier exploded, gave a frightening tirade, broke up the conference, and returned to Moscow, where he soon revived the Cold War by threatening talk and gestures. Much of the free world blamed Eisenhower for the timing of the flight. During the rest of his administration, the bitterly disappointed president stayed home in the White House, watching a political storm build-up in which conduct of the presidency came under unending attack."

John F. Kennedy

It is evident that American public life fluctuates between the periods of crisis politics and cultural politics. In the past thirty crisis years America encompassed the Great Depression, World War II, and the Cold War. The need to restore the economy was a common goal of the nation. After 1960, when prosperity and fair security returned, cultural politics began.

There were no Roman Catholic presidents for more than 100 years in American politics. In 1950, a significant change happened, and Church leaders and religious thinkers of all faiths emphasized the unity of all faiths, Jewish and Christians. Now the country was ready to accept a non-Protestant president. A young Irish Catholic Democratic senator from Massachusetts, a millionaire's son John Fitzgerald Kennedy, was a Harvard educated, a historian, sharp, intelligent, and wealthy and sophisticated, with his extremely good looks and his extraordinarily beautiful wife, Jacqueline had luminary quality. To many people, Kennedy was an exciting, charismatic dignitary. Those who saw him and heard his speech could never forget his driving voice. He was a cool hero, but caring person.

As he travelled through the country, he condemned immobility and laziness, shouted for renewed national vigour. His Boston accent attracted millions and asserted that he could get the country moving again. One columnist Walter Lippmann wrote, "Truly impressive to see the precision of Mr. Kennedy's mind, his immense command of facts, and his instinct for the crucial point .... his coolness and courage. He was a natural leader, organizer and ruler of men." He was a most spectacular national figure to the young generation. This new generation filled the national stage with urgency and new dreams: in drama, literature, scholarship, politics, and in the leadership of minority groups.

Kennedy, in his inaugural address, instructed Americans to take up a long, self-sacrificial struggle to revitalize the nation's power, its spirit, and its economy. His famous quote still reverberates in the minds of Americans, "Ask not what your country can do for you; ask what you can do for your country." Kennedy was a Master of Television for the first time, and he held regular press conferences that mesmerized millions of people. He staffed his new administration with multi-ethnic group bringing people from Catholics, Jews, intellectuals, veterans of urban politics, liberal internationalists, southerners, and blacks. 'The famous Democratic political style, confident, self-consciously brainy and boldness permeated Washington social life.'

Kennedy's National Reforms

Kennedy presented thirty-nine messages and letters to Congress calling for legislation to revive the economy, and to change the quality of life for seriously ill society. There were letters on health and hospital care, education, natural resources, highways, housing and community development, farm needs, the reforming of independent commissions, civil rights, Interstate Commerce Commission (ICC), transportation, consumer protection, aid for the mentally ill, the poor, and the elderly.

Farmer's problems were very critical: massive overproduction due to increased mechanization; swelling government warehouses; low farm income; yet millions of starving poor here and abroad. According to the advice of scholarly experts instead of agricultural businessmen, Kennedy's Secretary of Agriculture Orville Freeman, organized a new national framework for agriculture. 'The Food for Peace program sent food surplus abroad; the Food Stamp plan enabled the poverty-stricken people to join in the benefits of high food production, at the same time helping farmers. Basically, the government purchased excess farm crops and distributed them to those whose income was below the government's poverty income level. Receivers bought the food stamps, paying $46 for $100 worth of food that could be exchanged for that much foodstuff." To farmers who kept strict control on production, the government made direct payments to replace their sacrificed profits. Not used land was kept in a national soil bank. At the same time, consumers benefited from the action that food prices were kept relatively low. As a result, farm income rose a billion dollars each year, and surpluses came down to a reasonable national storage level.

Kennedy was immensely concerned about education. He would spin listening to horrifying statistics of young people in the country: 'Only six children of every ten in the fifth grade would finish high school; only nine of every sixteen high-school graduates would go on to college; a million young people were out of school and out of work; and school dropouts were a constant drain on public resources.' Kennedy introduced a scheme of specialized aid to the elementary and secondary schools, obtaining grants for occupational education, providing literacy training to the unemployed, instigating efforts to halt the dropout and misbehaviour problems, and building libraries. Meanwhile, educational televisions also received assistance. "The Office of Education, surveying the record, described the Kennedy years as the most significant for education in its hundred-year history."

Recommendation for Medical Reforms

In 1945 President Harry Truman had suggested a plan to Congress to establish a Medical Insurance for all Americans. Medical Association groups got enraged at the suggestion and Truman's plan had been turned down. Increasing medical costs and the low incomes of the elderly people created numerous social distresses. It was a tragedy that older people could not get or retain medical insurance when they needed most. The entire savings of lifetime could be wiped out by one illness. When that really happened, the respectable people who spent their life independently with dignity had to accept the disgrace of being charity patients.

President Kennedy also proposed a plan that would have provided medical assistance to those over sixty-five through the process of the social security system. Again, the American Medical Association denounced the idea and kept the bill locked up. It had to wait for Lyndon Johnson to unlock in July 1965.

Another plan he suggested was to train unemployed young men and women, who were roaming on the streets, also failed. But he established professional schools and initiated the Area Redevelopment Act of 1961 concentrating on the most depressed communities. Its objectives were to deliver job retraining and encourage the building of new industry. When he read a book written by Michael Harrington, 'The Other America' where he described the suffering of millions of forgotten and poverty-stricken citizens, he ordered to prepare separate plans to wage a 'war on poverty.'

Energizing the Economy

Kennedy seriously contemplated on boosting the lagging economy so that many national problems would be solved. City people, farmers, black people, the unemployed, poorly schooled and unsuccessfully policed, those badly housed would get benefit by restored prosperity.

Peace Corps

President Kennedy transformed foreign relationships dramatically towards the Third World countries - Latin America, Asia, and Africa. The most dramatic example of his view towards these countries was his creation of the Peace Corps to put young people to work. The response of young people was very enthusiastic, and the program became the shining lights of the new administration. 'By 1964 around 10,000 young Americans were at work in forty-six countries, labouring to bring such assistance as they could to the impoverished of the world.'

The Space Competition

Simultaneously fighting against the disaster, the Kennedy administration was researching for the nation's space program. The president was determined that acquiring supremacy in space technology was essential to both for national security and for psychological importance in rebuilding American confidence. He found that space endeavour was understaffed, underfunded, and uncoordinated, he concluded to select one lofty objective that would inspire the whole nation and enable everyone, scientist and technologist alike to pull together. What is that objective? Placing a man on the moon! The author writes, "In the year 1961 this seemed an impossible visionary conception, but the very grandness of it caught his imagination." Therefore, he called Congress and addressed: "Now it is time to take longer strides, time for a great new American enterprise, time for this nation to take a clearly leading role in space achievement, which in many ways may hold the key to our future on earth." What a foresight! Congress responded enthusiastically and poured billions of dollars to finance space technology and space science.

Cuban Missile Crisis

Cuban missile crisis is one of the major events in Kennedy's administration, which he handled very intelligently. In 1962, American airplanes flying over Cuba noticed a horrifying sight that Soviets were stationing their missiles on the island of Cuba, 90 miles away from Florida's coast. Kennedy saw this as a test of his administration and for ten days White House conducted secret meetings, discussed, argued, and decided over alternative actions. On October 22, 1962, Kennedy went on television and addressed the nation, "This sudden clandestine decision to station strategic weapons for the first time outside of Soviet soil is a deliberately provocative and unjustified change in the status quo which cannot be accepted by this country, if our courage and our commitments are ever to be trusted again by either friend or foe." He declared a blockade around Cuba that allowed everything but missile carrying ships. After an excruciating wait, the Soviet ships headed back to their ports.

This action was harshly criticized by those who believed that the president was completely unjustified by taking the world to the verge of nuclear war. Now the situation was suitable to reach an agreement between the USSR and the United States. In June 1963, President indicated his readiness to work toward that agreement. In a speech at American University at Washington, D.C., he advised Americans to stop believing Russian conspiratorial theory and Russians also to stop believing terrible things about the United States. He said, "There must be increased understanding between the Soviets and ourselves .... increased contact and communication." Khrushchev also responded favourably and signed the Test Ban Treaty in Moscow. The president was happy and felt it was an important gift to the world and it was his greatest achievement thinking that the world has escaped from the darkening prospects of mass destruction. He gave a brilliant speech at American University:

> "It is discouraging to think that their leaders may actually believe that their propagandists write...But it is also a warning - a warning to the American people not to fail into the same trap as the Soviets, not to see only a distorted and desperate view of the other side, not to see conflict as inevitable, accommodation as impossible, and communication as nothing more than an exchange of threats.
>
> "No government or social system is so evil that its people must be considered as lacking in virtue. As Americans, we find communism profoundly repugnant as a negation of personal freedom and dignity. But we can still hail the Russian people for their many achievements - in science and space, in economic and industrial growth, in culture and in acts of courage....
>
> "Let us re-examine our attitude toward the cold war, remembering that we are not engaged in a debate, seeking to pile up debating points. We are not here distributing blame or pointing the finger of judgment. We must deal with the world as it is, and not as it might have been had the history of last 18 years been different.... Above all, while defending our own vital interests, nuclear powers must avert those confrontations which bring an adversary to a choice of either a humiliating retreat or a nuclear war. To adopt that kind of course in the nuclear age would be evidence only of the bankruptcy of our policy - or of a collective death wish for the world.... We are unwilling to impose our system on any unwilling people - but we are willing and able to engage in peaceful completion with any people on earth.....(Public Papers of the Presidents of United States: John F. Kennedy [1964])

The Blacks Revolution

The revolution of black America dramatically transformed national life, which was caused by one incident. On a December Day in 1955, a black woman Rosa Parks boarded a bus in Montgomery, Alabama. She was a middle aged, tailor and tired on that day, after boarding the bus, she sat down on a seat in front portion of the bus usually reserved for whites. The bus driver instructed her to move to the back side of the bus. As she was very tired, she could not obey the order of the driver. Thus, Rosa Parks inspired a revolution which insisted that the equal protection of the laws be made in all American life.

Martin Luther King, Jr

Martin Luther King was a greatly philosophic and learned man; he closely studied Socrates, Plato, Kant, Hegel, Marx Henry David Thoreau, Reinhold Niebuhr, the Social Gospel leader Walter Rauschenbusch and other great thinkers in the University of New England. He strongly believed in Rauschenbusch's philosophy in a loving and improving humanity; in Niebuhr's warning that we must be content with fragmentary advance, given our obvious selfishness as human beings; and above all in Mahatma Gandhi's message that to win freedom from a powerful superior people, oppressed people must non-violently absorb all punishment, return it with love, and stimulate the conscience and morality of the oppressors.

Mass teaching of nonviolence began in black southern states. The instructions were taught in black churches through lectures, films showed the techniques and methods of nonviolence: If cursed, do not curse back. If struck, do not strike back, but demonstrate love and goodwill at all times. If another person is being ill-treated, do not arise to go to his defence, but pray for the oppressor.

Martin Luther King led a year-long boycott of the bus system in Montgomery, which resulted in the end the Supreme Court ruled that segregation on buses was unconstitutional. King preached Mahatma Gandhi's philosophy of non-violence. He said that oppressed people attain their goals most successfully by invoking the conscience of their oppressors. He anticipated an integrated, interracial America, and that beloved community in which blacks and whites would recognize their common bonds of humanity.

In 1960, a group of young black college students in North Carolina occupied the lunch centres reserved for whites and refused to leave their seats. They sat resolutely in their seats, calmly faced verbal and physical abuse providing an inspiring example of nonviolence response. The same type of protests went on in movie theatres, restaurants, hotels, and bowling alleys tolerating tear gas, fire hoses, and mass arrests.

In late 1959, Martin Luther King changed his nonviolent views:

> "Token integration is the developing pattern.... There is reason to believe that the Negro of 1959 will not accept supinely any such compromises.... It is axiomatic in social life that the imposition of frustration leads to two kinds of reactions. One is the development of a wholesome social organization to resist with effective, firm measures any efforts to impede progress. The other is a confused, anger-motivated drive to strike back violently to inflict damage. Primarily, it seeks to

cause injury to retaliate for wrongful suffering. Secondly, it seeks real progress. It is punitive — not radical or constructive....

"There are incalculable perils in this approach.... The greatest danger is that it will fail to attract Negroes to a real collective struggle, and will confuse the large uncommitted middle group, which as yet has not supported either side. Further, it will mislead Negroes into the belief that this is the only path and place them as a minority in a position where they confront a far larger adversary than it is possible to defeat in this form of combat.... It is unfortunately true that however the Negro acts, his struggle will not be free of violence initiated by his enemies, and he will need ample courage and willingness to sacrifice to defeat this manifestation of violence. But if he seeks it and organizes it, he cannot win....

"In the history of the movement for racial advancement, many creative forms have been developed - the mass boycott, sit-down protests and strikes, sit-ins refusal to pay fines and bait for unjust arrests - mass marches - mass meetings - prayer pilgrimages, etc...There is more power in socially organized masses on the march than there is in guns in the hands of a few desperate men. (Liberation [October 1959])

The Kennedy administration played a major role in enforcing civil rights in the South. President promoted an extensive survey of black employment and found a miserable record, and then pushed hard to hire a large number of black professionals. He realized that simple executive action is not enough to ensure equal rights, so he reached the third branch legislation to appeal for passing of new civil rights. 'He then asked Congress to pass a law that assure equal access to all public accommodations; empower the attorney general to sue for enforcement of the Fourteenth and Fifteenth Amendments; and forbid discrimination in any state program—such as schools, welfare, and highway construction-receiving federal aid. In essential, he asked Congress to outlaw discrimination in employment and voting.'

In Birmingham, Alabama, some 150,000 black citizens marched to city hall protesting segregation in public facilities and in job hiring. When police used the brutal force, they tumbled to their knees and prayed. Thousands of young and old blacks chanted, "Freedom! Freedom! Freedom!" Malcom X, a leader of the Black Muslims, and a nationalist denounced King and addressed a black audience: "You need somebody who is going to fight. You don't need any kneeling in or crawling in."

In August 1963, Martin Luther King conducted a huge march to Washington, which reached Lincoln Memorial. There he electrified the audience with a speech in which he roared again and again, "I have a dream!" He emphasized that I have a dream of America in which there would be freedom and equality for all, in which black and white would be united. Southern congressmen avoided Kennedy's Civil Rights bill. Unfortunately, Kennedy was assassinated, and later Lyndon Johnson continued his mission, and finally blacks obtained the right to vote.

American Indians

In 1968, Lyndon Johnson appealed to Congress to give Indian Americans an opportunity to remain in their homeland without surrendering their dignity, if they choose; an opportunity to move to the towns and cities of America trained with skills to live in equality and dignity, if they choose. Eventually, he ordered to provide large funds to improve community, the training of workers, youth activities, and health service of American Indians.

The Immigration Revolution

John F. Kennedy succeeded to toss the policy of immigration that restricted only to northern European countries and to give opportunities to all nationalities equally. He believed that America should admit immigrants not on the racial basis, but simply on the grounds of possessed skills of individuals. He said, "our country needs and on the humanitarian ground of reuniting families. The special discrimination against people in the Asia-Pacific region, who were limited to 100 immigrants a year per nation, should be ended as well. With such a policy we can turn to the world, and to our own past, with clean hands and a clear conscience." Gradually, immigrants absorbed into the dominant American population, and took on its ways of living. At the same time, there was a largely shared culture in American life: the stress upon individualism, values as getting ahead, efficiency, hard work, orderliness, and material improvement. There was also mixed and shared culture, a pluralism of subcultures: different ways of living, believing, and speaking.

To take advantage of the new immigration law, the flow of immigrants that poured into the United States after 1965 was immense. The arrival of Europeans dropped and by the mid-1970s immigrants from seven countries increased: Taiwan, Philippines, Korea, India, Cuba, Mexico, and the Dominican Republic. The new immigrants were different from previous immigrants. Many of them were professionally or technically skilled, and they progressed right into the grades of middle-class America, or even higher. As a result, the countries losing these well-trained people grumbled bitterly of a "brain-drain" to America.

Medicare

President Lyndon Johnson who favoured Kennedy's Medicare program won a landslide victory in 1964. He made health care one of his top-priority items. Again, the American Medical Association continued to fight frantically against it. Finally, in July 1965 the Medicare bill passed providing millions of Americans over the age of sixty-five with a type of security they had never known before. The plan was, 'Under the Social Security System, funds were set aside to provide payment of doctor and hospital bills, nursing-home fees, and the cost of necessary drugs. Medicare, so violently condemned, soon became one of the pillars of American society that no one, any longer, would propose taking away.'

It is important to know that even though America did not end racial inequality, eliminate poverty, equalize income, or establish full employment (achievements beyond the reach of any human government in any reasonable time span), it did make considerable improvements in the national standard of living by elevating the poor to a minimum standard of living, and by opening new doors to a better life for many previously ignored.

Moon Landing

One of the biggest American milestone achievements in human history was the moon landing. The space program achieved its most breath-taking success when astronaut Neil Armstrong descended on the moon from his Apollo II spacecraft, saying "That is one small step for a man, one giant step for humankind." This world's first message astonished the multitude and victorious President Nixon called Armstrong on the moon by telephone to exchange his congratulations. Later on, space travel became common.

Vietnam War

President Eisenhower was worried about Southeast Asia's situation. South Vietnam was on the edge of being invaded by a Communist revolt. And in the faraway Laos, the left and right divisions were at war in the conflict between democracy and communism. Eisenhower thought if it went to the Communists, the other south-eastern countries would become communist countries one after another like a string of dominoes. So, he thought that the United States might have to fight. From 1946 to 1954, America had poured billions of dollars assisting French efforts to suppress Ho Chi Minh's Communist rule in North Vietnam. The Geneva Convention separated Vietnam and gave the northern half to the Communists. Considering this settlement as a disaster, the United States nudged France in South Vietnam and took over it, strengthening non-communist government in Saigon. Regrettably, that government was failing.

Vietnam is a country of 1200 miles and Americans thought that since it is a small country, it could easily be covered by American military power. It was a tragic decision that continued years together culminating in the death of millions of people on both sides.

After taking office, President Kennedy obtained the neutralization of Laos, but felt the necessity to spend major resources on South Vietnam in order to avoid Communist takeover. In this way started the tragic American involvement in the Vietnam War and finally ending in 1973 with defeat and disappointment.

Anti-War Protests

Soon after American troops began fighting in Vietnam, anti-war protests started in America. In fact, most Americans undoubtedly disliked Communism, uncritically patriotic, and tenderly supported the fighting. But, critics of war said that the attack against the South Vietnamese government was a civil war. They said that the domino theory was wrong; all Southeast Asia would not automatically collapse in case South Vietnam became a Communist country; and there was no inherent threat to America's security. Also, the protestors argued that the cause itself was criminally wrong. They reiterated that the South Vietnamese government was a hopelessly corrupt system, which cruelly mistreated its own people; besides, the well-deserved revolt against it had already begun in 1957. Johnson's critics complained that the idea that America intervening in an ancient domestic conflict in a faraway country and imposing its desire was ridiculous.

Anti-war protesters argued that the reason why America was in Vietnam was not for noble purposes, but because America's military and industrial organizations wanted it. Radical accusations claimed that the US had sent a huge army, navy, and air force to wage war in Vietnam because of a corruption deep within American society itself. They said "It was a corruption produced by the domination of powerful corporations whose aim was to exploit the whole world. To get their way, to ensure their profit-making control of the Third World, they even use the lives of young Americans in foreign wars. It was the Establishment that had brought on and was directing this war. What was the Establishment? It was the national network of bankers, industrialist, multinational corporations, politicians hungry for power, the military, the great federal agencies — the CIA, the Department of Defence, the FBI, and the like - and the elite universities."

Henry Kissinger was a German Jew whose family escaped from Hitler. He was a brilliant Harvard professor and a Republican intellectual of high standard. He was advising President Nixon to be flexible in the manner of American involvement in foreign relations. He respected Otto von Bismarck who helped to keep Europe at peace for many years skilfully transferring Germany's alignments in order to keep a balance of power in the world. He had no faith that the United Nations, a kind of international government, does not have the ability to provide a stable world order, but he believed in a balance of power diplomacy. Because the international tensions never disappear, the correct task for a big power was to stay well-armed and keep itself free to move quickly and easily in case of political conflicts - in other words, carry a big stick. In such a system, the enemy will soon likely become a friend.

Kissinger was certain that the war in Vietnam was really a Civil War and not a part of worldwide Communist attack. His suggestion was that the United States should slowly withdraw its military and supply huge funds to the South Vietnamese army to prepare it to fight its own war. The president announced the Vietnamization policy in 1969; fighting stopped; and American draft demands were greatly reduced. American and Vietnamese battle deaths began dropping. Nixon stated in his Guam Doctrine as "Asian solutions to Asian problems. The free Asian countries would need henceforth to take care of themselves more than they had in the past."

Comparisons - People and Nation

In 1867, Mark Twain, who was a newspaper reporter travelling through the countryside of France in a railway carriage, suddenly realized that he found a highly civilized country France. He began comparing it with 1867 America's situation at that time that looked like a village.

> "What a bewitching land it is! Surely the leagues of bright green lawns are swept and brushed and watered every day and their grasses trimmed by the barber. Surely the straight, smooth, pure white turnpikes are jack-planed and sand-papered every day. How else are these marvels of symmetry, cleanliness, and order attained? It is wonderful. There are no unsightly stone walls. No dirt, no decay, and no rubbish anywhere-nothing that even hints at untidiness. All is orderly and beautiful.

He compares America with France and notices the absence of village like American atmosphere in France:

> "hog-wallows, broken fences, cow lots, unpainted houses, mud, absence of cleanliness, potholes and inequality of surface...."

It does not mean that America was so hopelessly bad. It had already produced many intellectuals and writers like Mark Twain by 1867. Mark Twain's comparison about the appearance of things in France is the same as people from underdeveloped countries see when they visit America.

Twenty-First Century America

How American people from the year 1870s would react if they were somehow transported to 21st century America? What kind of comparisons would they make? They would be wonderstruck by the cleanliness, by the neat and meticulous arrangements of the public sight. The average American people of the 1870s would scream about the lack of dirt and dust; the absence of stinking outhouses set behind homes, standing in multi-storey columns beside tenement houses, or arranged in great lines outside hotels. 'They would be surprised at the odorless rest rooms amply provided; the garbage-cans placed everywhere to drop litter from the streets; the pure water, clean food, hygienic packaging, and detailed public inspection of restaurant kitchens; the gleaming heaps of washed fruits and vegetables in the stores; the lack of wrinkled clothing, tobacco split, cigar butts, stains, and patches.' Probably Abraham Lincoln and his cabinet members would look like refugees sitting next to the neatly dressed modern time President and senators.

They also would wonderstruck by the absence of thousands of animals used for transportation and labour, and thus the lack of manure and humming clouds of flies on the streets; neat roads, painted lines, smoothly riding automobiles, discreet curbs and gutters; cars and people waiting quietly at traffic lights, orderly lines in stores and theatres; the water supplies, heating systems, food markets, flood-control systems, communication networks, and vast departmentalized stores, all logically arranged, measured, and centrally regulated.

The 1870s visitors would continue their journey to see their wonder world America and observe the flood of colours - kaleidoscopic, rich, and bright - radiating from buildings at night and are displaying in everyday clothes, buildings and advertisements; the America of the 1870s with its dull black leather, its dirt and stains has been replaced by a world of astonishing oranges, yellows, blues, and reds; light is everywhere, blurring daytime and evening — light in rooms, streets, buildings, constantly glowing across the countryside, dotting the whole earth with vast blankets of various colours, zipping, flashing, steadily burning; the stations of communications system dumping torrents of information, music, TV, video, email, internet, etc.

Lifestyles

Our visitor from 1870s America would note that enormous variety in most people's life style: the distances they travel for business or enjoyment; the vast range of occupations, most of them unheard of a century ago; many ways of entertainment; they would be surprised by the strange cosmopolitanism of taste in books, music, art, and most importantly their land of America is no longer dependent on slaves for labour, and on Europe for its cultural life because America itself has become a source of cultural example and standards and its influence gushing out to all the world.

In 1870s, the common people had not much concern about aesthetics, but in the 2000s they would see a widespread concern about beauty, styling, and urban beautification. Other wonders: music is everywhere, in automobiles, offices, supermarkets, and homes; thousands of symphonies play- companies and art programs have jumped to life; strangely aesthetics is a new attitude toward wilderness, which had considered as savage type which needed to be tamed and cut down.

1870s Americans would be surprised to know the personalization of literature, the uniqueness of every writer's vision expressed in many changing forms; the personalization of dance, people expressing their own feelings in their own patterns; the disappearance of clear social instructions on dressing, eating, and behaving. Today's society would appear absurd to them because in some areas it has become orderly and standardized and in others chaotic and individualized.

Naturally, 1870s visitors would be astonished to see America's wealth, enormous social power of government and business corporations. The speed of travelling would be an endless wonder to them not because traveling to long distance, which railways had provided to them too. But because it is a short distance; the ease of going ten miles in one direction, five miles in another direction, and ten miles in still another, all in one sequence of a morning commute!

Pollution

This remarkable affluence and power produced polluted skies, lakes, and rivers in modern day America. Would 1870s Americans be surprised by this also? Probably not. Definitely the cities of their time were massively polluted with human excrement, foul smells, disease, filthy water, rotten food, choking coal smoke, and the sound of traffic. Urban people lived by crowding together because transportation facilities were insufficient, and jobs had to be nearby. In London, men and women stumbled together in the late nineteenth century because of blinding fog from particles of coal ash. Same thing happened in Pittsburgh, Chicago, Boston, Philadelphia, and New York due to widespread coal-fired industries and coal stoves in homes. 'Humanity has probably never lived in such a polluted environment as those of the great cities of Europe and America a century ago.' Then steelworkers of Pittsburgh loved coal smoke because it meant jobs for them.

Robert Kelly writes, "Environmental concern is a sophisticated state of mind. Its development depends on mass education, an instantaneous communication system, the ability to look at the world at arm's length and become conscious of a polluted planet." What a statement!

Wealth and Masses

To 1870s average Americans, it could be amazing to see safer working conditions and shorter hours of work week. In the 1870s, the average working hours per week were 70 hours, that has been reduced to 40 hours or less in the 2000s. This reduction enabled people to enjoy more time in leisure and entertainment. In a nutshell, the standard of living escalated unbelievably high from the 1870s to the 2000s.

Innovative technologies transformed American homes in the last decades: every home has television sets, air conditioners and heaters, dishwashers, vacuum cleaners, computers, telephones, and all kinds of electronics that was unthinkable in 1870s.

The 1870s visitors would be shocked to see that the poor people they knew in their time are no longer in that condition. In their time Yankees monopolized the highest income. But modern study indicates that the family incomes of Jews and European Catholics actually excelled those of protestant Yankees although they still have a higher rate of occupational dynamism, securing higher-prestige positions in bigger numbers than other groups.

The Diversity of Cultures

Visitors from 1870s would be astonished to see the huge population of the United States of America; enormous size of the cities, some metropolis contain more than eight million people, among them are thousands of American Indians going to work like everyone else; equally astonishing sight would be black Americans flocked in cities, not in the villages.

Life Expectancy

1870s visitors would be mesmerized to see the physical appearance of

Americans: not the rich and colourful clothing worn by common people in more comfortable places, but the ABSENCE of disfigured and mutilated people - before they used to see individuals with open sores, bruises of limbs, damaged faces, swelling, filmed eyes, gap-toothed and deformed mouths - the human rubbish of a premedical society as America had been a century ago.

The other side of the story is as the life expectancy is growing and at the same time problems also are growing. Hence, Americans in 2000s have not only the gift of long and healthy life, they have new problems related with that fact: the support and care of millions of elderly people by a fairly smaller population of working adults, and the pervasive impact of diseases related with age - cancer, heart disease, and strokes (surprisingly decreased after 1970). Death also, like birth, changed its location to hospitals furnished with tremendously sophisticated technology. The wiping away of pain - in most chronic disease, in surgical operations, in the trauma of physical injuries, dental care - would be seen by 1870s visitors as a marvellous, even miraculous blessing.

Manners and Social Justice

William Gladstone, a British political leader observed one of the major changes: kind manners, decrease in social arrogance by the wealthy, and increasing sensitivity to the sufferings of the unfortunate. Shameless pride of class, arrogance of manners toward the poor has been greatly reduced.

They will come to know that twentieth century's ordinary Americans are always ready to care about others in need. In the 1870s the unemployed, the blind and the crippled, the old, the children without fathers, and the extremely poor were ignored by the taxpayer and by the government. "There were no schools for the mentally retarded; no public medical care for the needy or the elderly; no old-age pensions; no public fundraising drives continually in motion to aid victims of various rare diseases, help minority young people get college educations, or pay for the legal costs of people whose rights had been unjustly violated by some local or federal agency in a far distant state."

The author writes, "In the history we have seen how in traditional societies the people of each village were hostile to strangers, uninterested in helping people beyond their own community; public executions used to be popular. The idea of caring for strangers, of being concerned about suffering and cruel death outside the circle of one's family, is an aspect of modernizing societies."

In inefficiently organized America in 1870s, people believed passively thinking that it is all common that trains running unpredictably and uncomfortably; drinking water would smell and look impure; streets would be filled with heaps of garbage; politicians would take bribe; government would be massively ineffective; and epidemic diseases would arrive annually to sweep off thousands to an early death. They thought it was all common.

Now that level of passivism does not exist. Americans expect everything to work well. They expected the life of risk-free in all circumstances and they crowded the courts to sue each other in case of injuries or harmed lives for the modest payment. Americans expected surgeons to perform open-heart surgery successfully; automobiles and jet airliners always to work; food and water to be pure; government to be financially honest and relatively effective; and the streets to be not only well paved and lighted but also orderly. "Social efficiency is a self-feeding mechanism: the more of it there is, the more of it is expected. It is a benign process that generates continual criticism and reform."

The Information Revolution

Even though 1870s Americans were aware of Telegraph, they were not ready for the extraordinarily instant and omnipresence of information from other sources. The husband calls his wife, friends and family keeping in touch over long distances, the enormous humming network of communication lines and radio signals that links business houses and directs government — all these far more complex and wider webs of communication that any individual in the 1870s ever imagined.

Today more average people understand than a wisest scholar did in the 1870s about the body and the universe, about psychology, society, politics, world affairs, and economics. The knowledge revolution has created an incredible number of intellectuals; there are a record number of learned professions and skilled occupations that did not even exist in their time. In the 1870s, the average American was illiterate or had only three or four years of schooling, now almost everyone is educated, at least high school and higher education is becoming common. 'The level of technological knowledge alone required to read and understand a modern newspaper is extraordinary when compared to earlier times.'

Internet

Mother of all Inventions is the Internet. The concept of the Internet started early in the 1960s to share information on research and development in scientific and military fields. J.C.R. Lickliter of MIT joined the Defense

Advanced Research Projects Agency (DARPA) and began developmental work. Leonard Kleinrock, a professor of UCLA developed the theory of packet switching, which became the foundation of Internet connections. An American scientist Lawrence Roberts and his team created the ARPANET using packet switching techniques invented by British computer scientist Donald Davies. The ARPANET was a predecessor to the modern Internet and connected a Massachusetts computer with a California computer in 1965 over dial-up telephone lines.

In 1969, the Internet connected four major computers at universities: University of California Los Angeles, Stanford Research Institute, University of California Santa Barbara, and the University of Utah. Then MIT, Harvard, Stanford, Carnegie-Mellon were added. Then NASA MITRE, Burroughs, RAND, and the U of Illinois plugged in. Afterward, all universities in the US connected the Internet for the use of faculty, staff and students for research purposes.

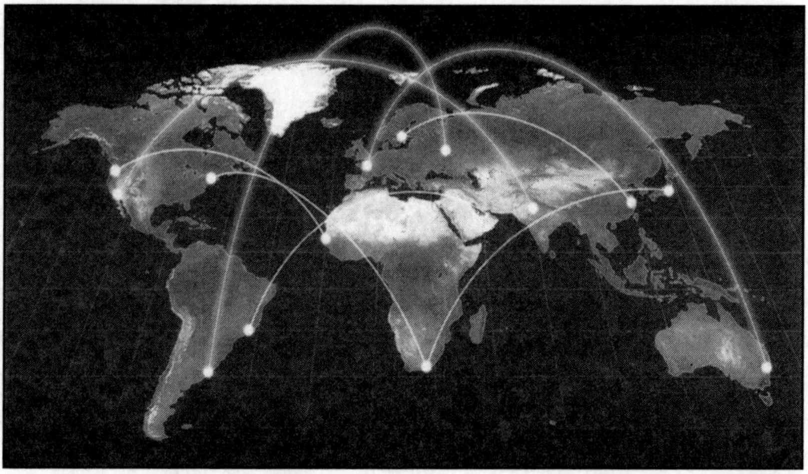

INTERNET exploded like anything ever seen before.

Libraries began automating and networking their catalogues in the late 1960s.

The Internet was designed to provide communications networks that would work even if some of the major sites were down. If the direct route is not available, routers would direct information traffic via alternate routes around the network.

First the Internet was used by only computer experts, engineers, scientists, and librarians. Until 1994, there were no home or office personal computers. Because the Internet was initially funded by the government, it was limited to research, education, and government uses only. Commercial use was prohibited unless they directly served the goals of research and education. This policy continued until the early 90's, until independent commercial networks began to grow.

Delphi was the first national commercial online service to offer Internet access. As a result, AOL, Prodigy, and CompuServe came online. Microsoft developed full scale internet with the browser, server, and Internet Service Provider over to a commercially based Internet.

E-MAIL was customized for ARPANET by Ray Tomlinson of BBN in 1972. He chose @ symbol from the existing symbols on his teletype to link the username and address.

Telnet was introduced in 1972. The telnet protocol, which enables to log on to a remote computer, was named as a Request for Comments (RFC).

FTP (File Transfer Protocol) was introduced in 1973. The ftp protocol enabled file transfers between Internet sites. And so on....

As the Internet has become global, it is enabling people to communicate and share information in many ways. Sites like Facebook, Twitter, Linked-In, YouTube, Instagram, and blogs are everywhere. Protecting privacy is a big challenge in this environment and requires a regulation. Here is a short list of major American inventions. Apart from this list, there are millions of products, which cannot be listed. Counting is lost.

Important American Inventions from 1801 to 1999

- 1801 - Modern Suspension Bridge
- 1815 - Dental Floss
- 1831 - Dry Cleaning
- 1851 - Washing Machine
- 1853 - Potato Chips
- 1856 - Condensed Milk
- 1879 - Electric Light Bulb
- 1883 - Shoemaker Machine
- 1885 - Eastman Photographic Film
- 1887 - Disc Record
- 1887 - Phonograph
- 1861 - Machine Gun
- 1885 - Skyscraper
- 1893 - Zippers

- 1897 - Cotton Candy
- 1894 - Mousetrap
- 1901 - Assembly Line
- 1902 - Hearing Aid
- 1903 - Airplane
- 1905 - Ice Pop
- 1912 - Electric Traffic Light
- 1913 - Modern Day Zippers
- 1926 - Liquid Fuel Rocket
- 1929 - Sunglasses
- 1929 - Frozen Food
- 1930 - Chocolate Chip Cookies
- 1937 - Polarized Sunglasses
- 1937 - Digital Computer
- 1938 - Nylon
- 1939 - Fully Automatic Transmission for Automobiles
- 1940 - Duct Tape
- 1940 - Chemotherapy Equipment
- 1945 - Microwave
- 1945 - Nuclear Bomb
- 1947 - Defibrillator Paddles
- 1948 - Video Games
- 1949 - Radiocarbon Dating.
- 1949 - Crash Test Dummy
- 1950 - Credit Card
- 1950- The Disposable Diaper
- 1954 - Nuclear Submarine
- 1956 - Pantyhose
- 1958 - Integrated Circuit
- 1960 - Forrest Parry Invented the Magnetic Stripe Card
- 1960 - First Laser
- 1962 - LED Lighting (Light Emitting Diodes)
- 1965 - Compact Disk
- 1965 - Kevlar
- 1968 - Lunar Module

- 1969 - Laser Printer
- 1970 - Fiber Optic Cable
- 1971 - Personal Computer
- 1971 - First Email on Arpanet
- 1973 - Mobile Phone
- 1981 - Space Shuttle
- 1982 - Internet Protocol Suite
- 1994 - GPS
- 1994 - DNA Computing
- 1994 - CMOS Image Sensor
- 1995 - Computer Mouse
- 1995 - JavaScript
- 1997 - Mars Rovers
- 1999 - The Torino Scale

This is a short list of major American inventions. Apart from this list, there are millions of products, which cannot be listed. Counting is lost. Thanks America!!

Not-So-Bright Side of America

Some sections of America are plagued by many social problems, such as divorce, drugs, and guns, and psychological disorders. Divorce putting children's life into confusion and drug addiction of modern youth are heart-breaking. An adult growing up in America is a challenge, difficult and dangerous process.

America in 2000s

The USA has achieved innumerable number of its dreams that it has lost count. Things that had seemed fantasies in the 1870s are common in 2000s. For most Americans, life is much easier, more bountiful, and potentially more interesting than it was in earlier times. It is richer in its forms, more open, less problematic by the limitations of ignorance, poverty, and social weakness.

The opportunity of experiencing the bliss of healthy life itself is excellently beautiful. The chances of a lifetime of labour in brutalized conditions, injury and death in factories built without concern for human safety, oppressive work for long hours and meagre wages, having individual's dignity violated by the arrogance and exploitations of superiors, all have been tremendously reduced.

America is still soured and twisted by social prejudice and unequal treatment. Millions live in wretched poverty, subsisting on welfare checks, frightened by inner-city crime, and surrounded by the wasting social disease of drug addiction. Until the end of 2000s, the solution had not been discovered. Hopefully, America achieves this dream also in the near future.

As mentioned before, it is important to know that even though America did not end racial inequality, eliminate poverty, equalize income, or establish full employment (achievements beyond the reach of any human government in any reasonable time span), it did make considerable improvements in the national standard of living by elevating the poor to a minimum standard of living, and by opening new doors to a better life for many previously ignored.

A Note

History is not only a tale of kings and queens, emperors and rulers, palaces and forts, swords and shields, or presidents and secretaries, it is also a story of farmers and merchants, artisans and artists, philosophers, and scientists. Hopefully, with a better knowledge of history, a clearer understanding of the world will occur.

> *"Let noble thoughts come to us from all directions."*
>
> – *Rig Veda 1.89.1*

Research shows that the more educated and well informed a person or a nation is, the less violence and civil unrest among its people will prevail. In today's hyperlinked world, solving problems anywhere, solves problems everywhere. It is worth knowing as much as we could about our world because everything is connected. It instils the importance of all these places and subjects in people's mind and helps to reduce hate.

Some thoughts are impossible to understand without a sense of the historical context. As a matter of fact, geography and history are connected directly or indirectly. The deeper we go in any direction, the sooner we find how it was entangled with another, apparently in unrelated subjects. It also gives the opportunity to understand how far we have come from hunting and gathering stage to more civilized human beings.

Notes

1. The Andronovo culture is a collection of similar local Bronze Age cultures that thrived during 2300–1000 BCE in western Siberia and the west Asiatic grassland.
2. Megasthenes (350–290 BCE) was a Greek ethnographer in the Hellenistic period and author of the book Indica. He was born in Asia Minor (modern day Turkey) and became an ambassador of Seleucus I of Syria to the court of Sandrocottus (Chandragupta Maurya) in Pataliputra, India.
3. The name of Chandragupta is written by the Greeks Sandrokottos, Sandrakottas, Sandrakottos, Androkottos, and Sandrokuptos.
4. Pataliputra (Patna)
5. This is the akasha, or all-pervading element, of ancient Indian philosophy.
6. Greek military writer of the 2nd century, who lived in Rome.
7. The mountain range which runs from northwest to southeast between the (Black Sea) and the Caspian Sea;
8. Upper most of a column, a horizontal part in classical architecture that rests on the columns.
9. Sushrata was an ancient Indian surgeon and the author of the book Sushruta Samhita, in which he explains over 300 surgical procedures, 120 surgical instruments, and classifies human surgery in 8 categories.
10. Megasthenes (350–290 BCE) was a Greek ethnographer in the Hellenistic period and author of the book Indica. He was born in Asia Minor (modern day Turkey) and became an ambassador of Seleucus I of Syria to the court of Sandrocottus (Chandragupta Maurya) in Pataliputra, India.
11. The Periplus of the Erythraean Sea is a Greek periplus, which, describes navigation and trading routes from Roman-Egyptian ports through the coasts of Arabian Gulf, Indian Ocean, Northeast Africa, and India. Periplus means 'Sailing around'.
12. Fabric made of camel hair.
13. Rom = range of motion.

14. Tumbrils = A two-wheeled cart.
15. Potassium nitrate or the mineral niter, the important oxidizing component of gunpowder and also food preservative.
16. *Zīj* is the generic name applied to Islamic astronomical books that tabulate parameters used for astronomical calculations of the positions of the Sun, Moon, stars, and planets. The name is derived from the Middle Persian term *zih* or *zīg*, meaning cord. The term is known to refer to the arrangement of threads in weaving as the arrangement of rows and columns in tabulated data.
17. Hellenistic Age is a period from Alexander's death in 323 BCE to Cleopatra, 30 BCE.
18. The terms Near East and Middle East denote the same territories comprising the countries of the Arabian Peninsula, Cyprus, Egypt, Iraq, Iran, Israel, Jordan, Lebanon, Palestinian, Syria, and Turkey.
19. Shamanism is a custom that contains a specialist reaching altered states of consciousness in order to see and interact with a spirit world and direct these transcendental energies into this world.
20. Earliest name of the citizens of Ancient Rome.
21. iugera = 5/8 acre or 2,530 square meters. Approximately 3000 square yards. This was roughly the area of land a pair of oxen could plough in a day)
22. Allowance, a kind of social security.
23. Sumptuary means regulating or controlling expenditure; discouraging construction of large houses on small plots, restricting spending behaviour
24. A disease caused by vitamin C deficiency with swollen bleeding gums and the opening of previously healed wounds that affected poorly nourished early sailors.
25. Parchment is a writing material prepared by raw skins of animals usually sheep, calves, and goats. It has been used as a writing material for thousands of years. Vellum is a refined quality parchment made from the skins of young animals like lambs and calves.
26. White Anglo-Saxon Protestant.

Further Readings

One of the greatest joy of writing this book was the opportunity to research and visit many places to understand the reality of the facts, to read innumerable books and dozens of academic papers on topics ranging from moral philosophy to political economy, from ancient to modern world histories. The book's list of references will help the reader to go through the massive amount of scholarly networking on the topics addressed in this book. Since there is so much material to know about the world, I suggest reader it is useful to read the books mentioned in the reference section to broaden their knowledge.

Bibliography: Books Quoted and Recommended

1. A. Jayaram. Karnataka's Illustrious Rajput Connection, The Hindu, May 31, 2004.
2. A. Leo Oppenheim, 1964. Ancient Mesopotamia: Portrait of Dead Civilization, The University of Chicago Press, Chicago.
3. A.K. Sharma, 2004. The Prehistoric Narmada Man, Prehistoric Cultures of North East India and South East Asia, A Comparative Study, Proceedings of Robert Bruce Foote on Indian Prehistory and Protohistory,
4. A.L. Basham, 1959. The Wonder that was India, The Macmillan Co., New York.
5. A.L. Basham, 1967. Hinduism: The Concise Encyclopaedia of Living Faiths, Beacon Press, Boston.
6. A.T. Olmstead, 1948. History of the Persian Empire, The University of Chicago Press, Chicago.
7. Adrienne Koch & William Peden Ed., 1944. The Life and Selected Writings of Thomas Jefferson, The Modern Library, New York.
8. Amartya Sen, 2005. Argumentative Indian, Penguin Books Ltd. USA
9. Amaury de Reincourt, 1960. The Soul of India, Harper & Bros; 1st Edition.
10. A. Leo Oppenheim, 1977. Ancient Mesopotamia: Portrait of a Dead Civilization, University of Chicago Press; Revised Edition.
11. Ancient Greece. Marshall Cavendish Corporations, 2011. An Illustrated History, New York.
12. Ancient History Encyclopaedia
13. B. Pattabhi Sitaramayya, 1935, The History of the Indian National Congress, Working Committee of the Congres.
14. Bannanje Govindacharya (Kannada Original). 1997. Madhvacharya**.** Electronic version published by English version translated by Dr.K.Krishnamurthy & Dr. U.P.Upadhyaya.

15. Barbara D. Metcalf and Thomas R. Metcalf, 2006. A Concise History of Modern India, 2nd Ed. Cambridge University Press.
16. Benjamin Jowett, 2000. Plato: The Republic, Dover Publications, Inc. USA
17. Bernard Grun, 1946. The Timetables of History, 3rd Edition, Simon & Schuster, New York.
18. C. Rajagopalachari, 1954. Mahabharata, Bharatiya Vidya Bhavan.
19. Charles Phillips, 2004. The Lost History of Aztec & Maya, Herms House, London
20. Charles River, 2017. The Empires of Ancient Persia: The History and Legacy of the Achaemenids, Parthians, and Sassanids in Antiquity.
21. Clifford J. Jolly, Fred Plog, 1987. Physical Anthropology and Archeology, 4th Edition, Alfred A Knopf, Inc.
22. D. Devakunjarim, 2010. Madurai Through the Ages, Society for Archaeological, Historical and Epigraphical Research, Madras,
23. D. P. Sharma, 2004. Prehistoric Cultures of North East India and South East Asia, A Comparative Study, Proceedings of Robert Bruce Foote on Indian Prehistory and Protohistory.
24. David M. Knipe, 1991. Hinduism. HarperCollins Publishers, N.Y.
25. Dr. D. Devakunjari, 2010. Madurai Through the Ages, Arulmigu Meenakshi Sundareswaran Thirukkoil, Madurai.
26. E.A. Wallis Budge, 1973. OSIRIS & the Egyptian Resurrection, Dover Publications, Inc., New York
27. E.J. Rapson, Ed. 1922. The Cambridge History of India, Vol. I, The University Press.
28. Edith Hall, 2014. "Introducing the Ancient Greeks". W.W. Norton & Company, New York.
29. Edmund Morris, 2001. The Rise of Theodore Roosevelt, Modern Library a division of Random House, Inc., New York.
30. Edward C. Sachau, 1845–1930. (Translator and Editor) 2 vols. 1910, Kegan Paul, Trench, Trubner & Co. Ltd., London.
31. Edward C. Sachau, 1910. Alberuni's India, An account of the religion, philosophy, literature, geography, chronology, astronomy, customs, laws, and astrology of India about A.D. 1030. (Edited with Notes and Indices by Edward.)
32. Edward James Rapson, 1922. The Cambridge History of India, CUP Archive, India.
33. Encyclopaedia Britannica.
34. Gregory L. Possehl, Mehrgarh, Period I, Period II, Period III, Craft Production in Early Periods, Periods IV–VII, Hordeum vulgare, vulgare.
35. Harbans, Mukhia, 2004. The Mughals of India, Blackwell Publishing.
36. Harold M. Tanner, 2010. "China: A history" Hackett Publishing Company, Inc., Indiana, USA
37. Howard Zinn, 2015. A People's History of the United States, Harper Perennial Modern Classics
38. I.B. Horner, 1967. Buddhism: Mahayana. Concise Encyclopedia of Living Faiths, Beacon Press, Boston,

39. I.B. Horner, 1967. Buddhism: Theravada. Concise Encyclopedia of Living Faiths, Beacon Press, Boston,
40. Ismail ragi al Faruqi (Ed) & David E. Sopher (Ed), 1974. Historical Atlas of the Religions of the World, Macmillan Publishing Co., Ind. New York.
41. J.W. McCRINDLE, 1877. "Ancient India as described by Megasthenes and Arrian", Brubner & Co, London,
42. Jason Thompson, 2008. A History of Egypt: From Earliest Times to the Present. American University in Cairo Press.
43. Jeanne Bendick, 1997. Archimedes and the Door of Science, Bethlehem Books/ Ignatius Press, ND, USA
44. John Hirst, 2012. The Shortest History of Europe, Black Inc., Australia
45. John Keay, 1981. India Discovered, HarperCollins Publishers, London.
46. John Keay, 200. India A History, Grove Press, New York.
47. John Keay, 2009. China A History, Harper Collins Publishers, New York
48. John Whitney Hall, Editor, 1988. History of the World, World Publication Group, Inc.
49. Joshua J. Mark, Ancient History Encyclopedia
50. Kalyan Ray, Craftsmen Lived in South India 1.5 mn years ago: Deccan Herald. 26 March 11.
51. Leonard W. King, 1910. A History of Sumer and Akkad, Frederick A. Stokes Company, New York.
52. Muhammad Ahli Shirazi. A Thousand Years of the Persian Book. Library of Congress
53. Norman Davis, 1998. Europe: A History, Harper Perennial.
54. Paul A Zoch, 2013. Ancient Rome: An Introductory History. University of Oklahoma Press, 2000
55. Paul Kriwaczek, 2010. Babylon: Mesopotamia and the Birth of Civilization, Atlantic Books. Great Britain.
56. Peter Mansfield, 2013. A History of the Middle East, Penguin Books, 2013
57. R. Shamasastry 1915. Kautilya's Arthashastra. Translated into English, Bangalore Government Press.
58. Raghunath S. Pappu, Contribution of R.B. Foote to the Indian Paleolithic Studies. Prehistoric Cultures of North East India and South East Asia, A Comparative Study, Proceedings of Robert Bruce Foote on Indian Prehistory and Protohistory, 2004.
59. Ramachandra Guha, 2007. India After Gandhi, Harper Collins Publishers, New York.
60. Richard N. Frye, Wolfram Th. von Soden, Dietz O. Edzard, An overview of Mesopotamia. The Editors of Encyclopædia Britannica
61. Robert C. Lester, 1987. Buddhism, Harper & Row, Publishers, San Francisco.
62. Robert Kelley, 1975. Shaping of the American Past, Prentice-Hall, Inc., N.J.
63. Robert Sewell, Fernão Nunes, Domingos Paes, 2004. A forgotten Empire: Vijayanagar. Kessinger Publishing.

64. Robin Waterfield, 1998, Herodotus, Oxford University Press, Oxford.
65. Romalia Thaper, 1978. Ancient Indian Social History: Some Interpretations, Orient Blackswan.
66. Romila Thaper, 1997. Early India: From the origins to 1300 AD. University of California Press, Los Angeles
67. S. Radhakrishnan, 1923. Indian Philosophy, Vol.I, George Allen & Unwin Ltd.
68. S. Radhakrishnan, 1923. Indian Philosophy, Vol.II, George Allen & Unwin Ltd.
69. S.R. Sarma, S.M.R. Ansar, A.G. Kulkarni, 1992. Two Mughal Celestial Globes. Indian Journal of History of Science.
70. Sailendra Nath Sen, 1999. Ancient Indian History and Civilization. New Age International.
71. Samuel Noah Kramer, 1956. History Begins at Sumer, University of Pennsylvania Press, Philadelphia.
72. Samuel Noah Kramer, 1963. The Sumerians: Their History, Culture, and Character, The University of Chicago Press, Chicago.
73. Stacy Schiff, 2010. Cleopatra A Life, Hachette Book Group, New York
74. Subodh Kapoor. The Indian Encyclopedia, Volume 1.
75. Thapar, Romila (1978). Ancient Indian Social History: Some Interpretations, New Delhi: Orient Longman.
76. The Autobiography of Thomas Jefferson, 2005. Library of Congress Catalogue77. Thomas R. Martin, 2013. Ancient Greece, Yale University Press; Second Edition.
78. Toby Wilkinson, 2010. The Rise and Fall of Ancient Egypt, Random House, New York.
79. Tony Joseph, Early Indians: The story of our ancestors and where we came from, Juggernaut Books, New Delhi
80. Vincent Arthur Smith. Akbar the Great Mogul, Oxford University Press, London.
81. Vivekananda, 1992. Lectures from Colombo to Almora, Advaita Ashrama, Calcutta, 13th Edition.
82. Walter Isaacson, 2003. Benjamin Franklin, Simon & Schuster, New York.
83. Whitefield Foy, 1988. The Religious Quest, Rutledge, London.
84. Wolfram Th. von Soden, Dietz O. Edzard, Richard N. Frye History of Mesopotamia

Index

O

P

Q

R

S

T

U

V